Don't Shoot

Part III

Until You See The Whites of Their Eyes

OR

Don't shoot until you are sure you can hit them or I will put the end of my musket up your arse!

Supposedly said by General Israel Putnam at Bunker Hill

by AJ Berry & James F. Morrison

Order this book online at www.trafford.com
or email orders@trafford.com

Most Trafford titles are also available at major online book retailers.

Printed in the United States of America.

ISBN: 978-1-4269-4118-4 (sc)

Our mission is to efficiently provide the world's finest, most comprehensive book publishing service, enabling every author to experience success. To find out how to publish your book, your way, and have it available worldwide, visit us online at www.trafford.com

Trafford rev. 08/02/2010

www.trafford.com

North America & international
toll-free: 1 888 232 4444 (USA & Canada)
phone: 250 383 6864 • fax: 812 355 4082

Non-Fiction

Books by James F. Morriosn

A History of Fulton County in the Revolution (1978)

Colonel James Livingston: The Forgotten Livingston Patriot of the War of Independence (1988)

Books by James F. Morrison & Gavin K. Watt

The British Campaign of 1777 (2001)

Burning of the Valleys

Books by AJ Berry

Non-Fiction

Times Past

The Terror Series

A Time of Terror

So It Was Written

Brothers in Arms

Fiction

Out of Time Series

Out of Time

In Her Time

Time for Healing

The Time Traveler's Children

The Time Traveler's Husband

Into The Time Slip

Stuck In Time

Non-Fiction

Revolutionary War Pension Series

By James F. Morrison & AJ Berry

Don't Shoot, Part 1

Don't Shoot, Part 2

From the Department of Veterans Affairs
Various Pension Laws

In 1776 the Continental Congress sought to encourage enlistments and curtail desertions with the nation's first pension law. It granted half pay for life in cases of loss of limb or other serious disability. But because the Continental Congress did not have the authority or the money to make pension payments, the actual payments were left to the individual states.

This obligation was carried out in varying degrees by different states. At most, only 3,000 Revolutionary War veterans ever drew any pension. Later, grants of public land were made to those who served to the end of the war.

In 1789, with the ratification of the U.S. Constitution, the first Congress assumed the burden of paying veterans benefits. The first federal pension legislation was passed in 1789. It continued the pension law passed by the Continental Congress.

By 1808 all veterans programs were administered by the Bureau of Pensions under the Secretary of War. Subsequent laws included veterans and dependents of the War of 1812, and extended benefits to dependents and survivors.

There were 2,200 pensioners by 1816. In that year the growing cost of living and a surplus in the Treasury led Congress to raise allowances for all disabled veterans and to grant half-pay pensions for five years to widows and orphans of soldiers of the War of 1812. This term later was lengthened.

A new principle for veterans' benefits, providing pensions on the basis of need, was introduced in the 1818 Service Pension Law. The law provided that every person who had served in the War for Independence and was in need of assistance would receive a fixed pension for life. The rate was $20 a month for officers and $8 a month for enlisted men. Prior to this legislation, pensions were granted only to disabled veterans.

The result of the new law was an immediate increase in pensioners. From 1816 to 1820, the number of pensioners increased from 2,200 to 17,730, and the cost of pensions rose from $120,000 to $1.4 million.

·When Congress authorized the establishment of the Bureau of Pensions in 1833, it was the first administrative unit dedicated solely to the assistance of veterans.

The new Bureau of Pensions was administered from 1833 to 1840 as part of the Department of War, and from 1840 to 1849 as the Office of Pensions under the Navy Secretary. The office then was assigned to the new Department of the Interior, and renamed the Bureau of Pensions. In 1858 Congress authorized half-pay pensions to veterans' widows and to their orphan children until they reached the age of 16.

Regulations Under the Act of June 7, 1832.

(Or why some men were rejected; what qualifications had to be met in order to qualify for a pension
and the format required to apply for a pension.)

The following Regulations have been adopted:

This law has been construed to extend, as well to the line, as to every branch of the Staff of the Army, and to include under the terms "Continental Line," "State troops," "militia," and "Volunteers," all person enlisted, drafter, or who volunteered and who were bound to military service, but not tose who were occasionally employed with the army upon civil contracts, such as Clerks to Commissaries and to Store Keepers, &c. Teamsters, Boatmen, &c. Persons who served on board of Private Armed Vessels are also excluded form the benefits of the law, as well as persons who turned out as patrols, or were engaged in guarding particular places at night, and were not recognized as being in actual military service.

Four general classes of cases are embraced in this law:

1. The Regular Troops.
2. The State Troops, Militia, and Volunteers.
3. Persons employed in the Naval Service.
4. Indian Spies.

As rolls of the regular troops in the Revolutionary War exist in this department, al persons, claiming the benefit of this law as officers, non-commissioned officers, musicians or privates, will in the first instance, make application by transmitting the following declaration, which will be made before a Court of Record of the County where such applicant resides. And every Court having by law a seal and Clerk is considered a Court of Record.

Declaration,

In order to obtain the benefit of the Act of Congress of the 7th of June, 1832.

State, Territory, or District of }
County of } *SS.*

On this [ ] day of [ ] personally appeared (a) before [ ] A.B. resident (b) of [ ] in the county of [ ] and State, Territory or District of [ ] aged (c) [ ] years, who being first duly sworn, according to law, doth on his oath make the following declaration, in order to obtain the benefit of the provion (sic) made by the act of Congress, passed June 7th 1832. That he enlisted in the Army of the United States in the year (d) [ ], with [ ] and served in the [ ](e) regiment of the [ ], under the following named officers:

[Here set forth the names and rank of the Field and Company Officers; the time he left the service; (and if he served under more than one term of enlistment, he must specify the particular period, and rank and names of his officers;) the town or county and State in which he resided when he enered [sic] the service; the battles, if any, in which he was engaged and the country through which he marched. This form is to be varied so as to apply to the cases of officers and persons who belonged to the militia, volunteers, navy, &c.]

He hereby relinquishes every claim (f) whatever to a pension or annuity, except the present, and he declares that his name is not on the Pension Roll of any Agency in any State, or (if any) only on that of the Agency in the State of [ ] A.B._______

And the said Court do hereby declare their opinion (g) that the above named applicant was a revolutionary Soldier, and served as he states.

I [ ] of the Court of [ ]do hereby certify (h) that the foregoing contains the original proceedings of the said Court in the matter of the application of [ ] for a pension.

In testimony whereof I have hereunto set my hand and seal of office (i) this [ ] day of [ ] &c.

If, on examination of the proper record the names of applicants, making such declaration, cannot be found, they will produce such proof as the rule given in note (j) points out.

Every applicant who claims a pension by virtue of service in the State Troops, Volunteers or Militia, except those who belonged to the New Hampshire Militia in State Troops of Virginia, will make and subscribe a declaration similar to the foregoing, with the following additions, viz:

(k) We, A.B., a Clergyman, residing in the [ ] and C.D. residing in (the same) hereby certify, that we are well acquainted with the [ ], who has subscribed and sworn to the above declaration; that we believe him to be [ ] years of age; that he is reputed and believed, in the neighborhood where he resides, to have been a soldier of the Revolution, and that we concur in that opinion.

Sworn and subscribed the day and yea aforesaid.

[And then will follow the certificate of the Court.]

And the said Court do hereby declare their opinion, after the investigation of the matter, and after putting the interrogatories prescribed by the War Department, that the above named applicant was a Revolutionary Soldier, and served as he states. And the Court further certifies, that ti appears to them that A.B. and that C.D., who has also signed the same is a resident in the [ ] and is a credible person, and that their statement is entitled to credit.

I, [ ] Clerk of the Court of [ ] do hereby certify that the foregoing contains the original proceedings of the said Court, in the matter of the application of [ ] for a pension.

In testimony whereof, I have hereunto set my hand and seal [ ] of office, this [ ] day of [ ] &c.

Every applicant will produce the best proof in his power. This is the original discharge or commission; but if neither of these can be obtained, the party will so state under oath, and will then procure, if possible, the testimony of at least one credible witness, stating in detail his personal knowledge of the services of the applicant, and such circumstances connected herewith, as may have a tendency to throw light upon the transaction.

If such surviving witness cannot be found, the applicant will so state in his declaration (l) and he will also, whether he produce such evidence or not, proceed to relate all the material facts, which can be useful in the investigation of his claim, and in the comparison of his narrative with the events of the period of his alleged service, as they are known at the Department. A very full account of the services of each person will be indispensable to a favorable action upon his case. The facts stated will afford one of the principal means of corroborating the declaration of the applicant, if true, or of detecting the imposition, if one can be attempted; and unless, therefore, these are amply and clearly set forth, no favorable decision can be expected. All applicants will appear before some Court of Record in the County, in which they reside, and there subscribe and be sworn to, one of the declarations above provided, according to the nature of his case.

The Court will propound the following (m) interrogatories to all applicants for a pension, on account of service in the Militia, State troops, or Volunteers, except the Militia of New Hampshire and the State troops of Virginia.

1. Where and in what year were you born?
2. Have you any record of your age, and if so, where is it?
3. Where were you living when called into service; where have you lived since the Revolutionary war, and where do you now live?
4. How were you called into service; were you drafted, did you volunteer, or were you a substitute? And if a substitute, for whom"
5. State the names of some of the Regular Officers, who were with the troops, where you served; such Continental and Militia Regiments as you can recollect, and the general circumstances of your services.
6. {To a soldier.} Did you ever receive a discharge from service, and if so, by whom was it given and what has become of it? {To an Officer} Did you ever receive a

commission, and if so, by whom as it signed, and what has become of it?

7. State the names of persons to whom you are known in your present neighborhood, and who can testify as to your character for veracity, and their belief of your services as s soldier of the Revolution.

The Court will see that the answers to these questions are embodied in the declaration, and they are requested to annex their opinions of the truth of the statement of the applicant.

The applicant will further produce in Court, if the same can be done, in the opinion of the Court, without too much expense and inconvenience to him, two respectable persons—one of whom should be the nearest clergyman, if one lived in the immediate vicinity of such applicant, who can testify, from their acquaintance with him, that they believe he is of the age he represents, and that he is reputed and believed in the neighborhood to have been a Revolutionary Soldier, and that they concur in that opinion. If one of these persons is a Clergyman, the Court will so certify, and they will also certify, to the character and standing of other persons, giving such certificates.

The traditionary evidence of service is deemed very important, in the absence of any direct proof, except the declaration of the party. And the Court are requested to be very particular in the enquiry whether the belief is general, and whether any doubts have ever existed upon the subject.

Applicants unable to appear in Court by reason of bodily infirmity, may make the declaration before required, and submit to the examination, before a Judge or Justice of a Court of Record of the proper county, and the Judge or Justice will execute the duties, which the Court is herein requested to perform, and will also certify that the applicant cannot, from bodily infirmity, attend the Court.

Whenever any official act is required to be done by a Judge or Justice of a Court of Record, or by a Justice of the peace, the certificate of the Secretary of State or Territory, or of the proper Clerk of the Court or County, under his seal of office, will be annexed, stating that such person is a Judge or Justice of a Court of Record, or a Justice of the Peace, and that the signature annexed is his genuine signature.

No payment can be made on account of the services of any person, who may have died before the taking effect of the act of June 7, 1832; and in case of death subsequent thereto, and before the declaration herein required is made, the parties interested will transmit such evidence as they can procure, taken and authenticated before a Court of Record, showing the services of the deceased, the period of his death, the opinion of the neighborhood respecting such services, the title of the claimant, and the opinion of the Court upon the whole matter.

[a] The declarant must appear in open Court, unless prevented from doing so by reason of bodily infirmity; in which case the declarant will follow the rule laid down for his guidance.

[b] The declarant must make his declaration in the county where he resides. If he should fail to do so, he must assign a sufficient reason for not conforming to the rule.

[c] The age of the claimant must invariably be mentioned.

[d] The declarant must mention the period or periods of the war when he served.

[e] Every continental officer or soldier must give the name of the Colonel under whom he served; otherwise a satisfactory examination of the claim cannot be had. Every claimant must state, with precision, the lengths of his service, and the different grades in which he served, in language so definite as to enable the Department to determine to what amount of pension he is entitled. In a case where the applicant cannot, by reason of the loss of memory, state precisely, how long he served, he should amend his declaration by making an affidavit in the following words:

"Personally appeared before me, the undersigned, a Justice of the Peace, &c. A.B. who, being duly sworn, deposeth and saith, that, by reason of old age, and the consequent loss of memory, he cannot swear positively as to the precise length of his service; but, according to the best of his recollection, he served not less than the periods mentioned below, and in the following grades: -- For_______year_____months, and_____days, I served as a ______. For _____months and _____days, I served as a _____; and for such service I claim a pension."

It is important, in all cases, to determine with precision the period for which each applicant served, and the particular rank he held, as the law is too indefinite, and all such qualifying expressions are objectionable. Some persons who apply for pensions merely state that they served two years in the militia, &c without specifying the tours, the names of the officers, and other particulars respecting their service. This form of a declaration is highly objectionable. It must, in every case, be clearly shown under what officers the applicant served; the duration of each term of engagement; the particular place or places where the service was performed; that the applicant served with and embodied corps called into service by competent authority; that he was either in the field or in garrison; and for the time during which the service was performed, he was no employed in any civil pursuit.

[f] The law makes the relinquishment indispensable.

[g] The opinion of the Court is always required.

[h] The clerk must give his certificate in every case.

[i] The Clerk must affix his seal, and if it has no device or inscription by which it can be distinguished from any other seal, or if he has no public seal of office, the certificate of a Member of Congress, proving the official character and signature of the certifying officer, should accompany the papers.

Mode of Authenticating Papers.

In every instance where the certificate of the certifying officer who authenticates the papers is not written on the same sheet of paper which contains the affidavit, or other papers authenticated, the certificate must be attached thereto by a piece of tape or narrow ribbon, the ends of which must pass under the seal of office of the certifying officer, so as to prevent any paper from being improperly attached to the certificate.

Proof of Service.

[j] In a case where the name of the applicant is not found on the records of the Department, he must prove his service by two credible witnesses, who are required to set forth in their affidavits the time of the claimant's entering the service, and the time and manner of his leaving the same, as well as the regiment, company, and line to which he belonged. The magistrate who may administer the oaths must certify to the credibility of the witnesses, and the official character and signature of the magistrate must be certified by the proper officer, under his seal of office.

The notes from [a] to [j] are all equally applicable to the cases of Militia men, Volunteers and State Troops. The proof required by rule in note [j] applies to continental troops only.

[k] This traditionary evidence is indispensable in militia cases.

[l] If a witness cannot be found, the declarant must state the fact.

[m] The answers to the interrogatories must all be written, and sent to the War Department, with the declaration.

And now a word about the word Esquire or abbreviated, Esq.

Periodically you will see this word used in the text and it does mean something. Esquire is a term of British origin, originally used to denote social status. Ultimately the word was derived from the medieval word squires indicating those who assisted knights. The term came to be used automatically by men of what was called, "gently born".

The social rank of Esquire is that above gentleman. More specifically, though, a distinction was made between men of the upper and lower gentry, who were "esquires" and "gentlemen" respectively (between, for example, "Thomas Smith, Esq." and "William Jones, Gent."). A late example of this distinction is in the list of subscribers to *The History of Elton*, by the Rev. Rose Fuller Whistler, published in 1882, which clearly distinguishes between subscribers designated "Mr." (another way of indicating gentlemen) and those allowed "Esquire."

Today, however, the term may be appended to the name of any man not possessing a higher title (such as that of knighthood or peerage) or a clerical one. In the United States, however, "esquire" is most commonly assumed by lawyers in a professional capacity and has come to be associated by many Americans solely with the legal profession.

Prisoners of War, During The Revolutionary War

There were thousands of American prisoners held by the British during the war. Many prisoners taken in Tryon County went to Niagara or to Quebec or Montreal. Some were sold as slaves to the British officers and some endured captivity among the Indians.

New York City was the main place where prisoners taken along the Hudson and the southern part of the state were held.

By the end of 1776, there were over 5,000 prisoners held in New York City. More than half of the prisoners came from the soldiers captured at the battle of Fort Washington and Fort Lee. With a total population of New York City around 25,000, this meant that 1 out of every 5 people in the city were prisoners. This was a big expense to support for the British, and they were a long distance from their home shores.

During the war, more military men on the British prison ships died than were killed in battle. A Prisoner Exchange

Program was used between the British and American forces during the American Revolutionary War.

You will note that in the pensions, some men mentioned they were a prisoner but on parole. This was part of the prisoner exchange program. The premise of the exchange was to be able to exchange a sailor for a sailor, a soldier for a soldier, with the prisoners being of equal rank. Later on in the war, the exchange program was stopped by the British.

Most of the men who were on parole ignored the promise not to take arms against the British and promptly enlisted again. Another reason for stopping the exchange program was the American forces were smaller than the British forces; the British didn't want to let the Americans get back more of their men by using the rate of attrition being that the Americans didn't have nearly as many military personnel as the British.

After the major British defeat at the battle of Yorktown in 1781, the British wanted to restart the program due to the severe shortage of soldiers and sailors in the British military. It was not easy for the British to wage war far from their shores and they suffered from a manpower shortage. Gen. George Washington realized this, and he figured the war would soon end, and he didn't want to participate in an exchange program.

Prisoners onboard the British prison ships could win their release if they signed an oath to serve as sailors with the British Royal Navy. When a man is starving, this didn't sound like a bad option. Often the prisoners in Canada were offered freedom if they would join the fight on the British side.

By the end of the war, almost 25% of the sailors serving aboard ships in the British Royal Navy were former American prisoners who signed the oath. Some men who were not soldiers or sailors were simply seized and pressed into service in addition to the former prisoners. But still the British had problems obtaining manpower for their navy.

The British were having trouble with finding enough places to house these captured Americans as the war went on. There was only one prison building in New York City at this time, it was the Sugar House. There was no choice, the British took over most of the empty buildings in the city for use as prisons and storehouses, and there still wasn't enough room for the need Since it would be too expensive to build enough prisons to facilitate the number of prisoners on hand, plus the estimated number of future prisoners, the British had to come up with a solution.

The prison ship was the solution. There were about a dozen Royal Navy ships in the New York City area not being used because the ships weren't seaworthy. It was decided to use these ships as prisons for the captured Americans and the ships were put in at Wallabaugh Bay, which is near Brooklyn. The Wallabaugh Bay was really nothing more than mud flats because of the shallow water depth not being deep enough for a regular ship to navigate in.

Another idea to use these ships and prisoners came about. Some of the derelict ships used the prisoners to print paper money, money to flood the American market and to devalue the continental money. This was very successful and the money became known as "Shin Plasters" because that was about all it was worth.

The most infamous British prison ship was the H.M.S. Jersey. It was a decrepit, former hospital navy ship that was dilapidated and in serious need of repair to become seaworthy again. Normally, the ship would have a crew of about 350 sailors. When it became a prison ship, it held over 1,000 prisoners. Most never made it off the ship alive and had to suffer winter without blankets or adequate clothing along with little food. In addition, the prison ships made a good breeding place for illness. Smallpox and yellow fever outbreaks were at an epidemic proportion among the prisoners.

The dead were thrown in ditches which were dug by American soldiers as part of the entrenchments during Washington's occupation of Manhattan in the spring of 1776. In many cases the young men were digging a grave for themselves.

Letters were permitted, and sometimes even encouraged because prisoners could receive food and clothing from home or their government. Some of the items were simply seized by the guards and never reached the men.

Prisoners were encouraged to enlist in the army of the other side in exchange for escape from the prison ships. It is estimated that over the course of the war, as much as a quarter of each army had actually seen service on the other side.

As for the British and Hessian prisoners, many were paroled to American farmers. Their labor made up for shortages caused by the number of men serving in the American army. Usually their return was room and board, supplied by the farmer. Many Hessians stayed in America and fought on the side of the Americans, and you will find their depositions in the pension records also.

If you are interested in downloading the book American Prisoners of The Revolution by Danske Dandridge, 1910, the book is out of copyright and in the Google scanned books to be downloaded free.

http://books.google.com/advanced_book_search.

Type in the name of the book and then download the book to read on your computer.

It is not a fun book to read, but it is well done and gives an accurate picture of the prison ships, mostly the Jersey. Letters were allowed and the book contains many of the letters written by these desperate men. In the Appendix there is a list of 8,000 men who were prisoners on board the Old Jersey.

Authors' Notes

The pension books are a collaboration between AJ Berry and James F. Morrison. Whose name is first? We switch back and forth, every other book, this seems perfectly logical to us. AJ transcribes the documents; Jim corrects the transcriptions and adds the end notes. We will try to bring 10 of these books to publication.

And finally, a bit of a red-faced apology from AJ. Spelling of many words differ from those of today and the spell checker in MS Word is handy but sometimes it is not. I finally succumbed to letting some words be corrected so that I didn't have to go back and change it several times. For instance the word untill, the spell checker corrects it to until, and I finally succumbed.

Many words differ from today's spelling and some are beginning to look correct, such as the word staid [stayed] and the word him [hymn] and so forth. Then there are those that in my clever fingers end up being spelled very differently. For those I apologize! Jim can't possibly find all my mistakes, but he patiently tries.

As a further note: brackets appearing **[ ]** are used to indicate something not in the original document, and the usage of the brackets are confined to the pensions themselves. AJ Berry

Table of Contents

Pension Applications with End Notes by James F. Morrison

Pension Application for Albert Acker or Acher

R.15 (Wife: Sarah)

Albert Acher (62 years) Groveland in the State of N. York, was a private in the Regiment commanded by Colonel Gansvoort of the N. York [piece missing] for the term of 3 yrs (or the war) 1776. Entered on the Roll of N. York at the rate of 8 Dollars per month, to commence on the 24th of May 1819. Certificate of Pension issued the 22d of June 1822 and sent to O. Seymour Esqr. Canandaigua, NY. Arrears to the 4th of March 1822 267.09. Semi anl. All'ce ending 4 Sept. 1822 48.00. [piece missing] yrs. 9 mos. 12/31$315.09. Revolutionary Claim Act 18th March, 1818 & May 1820. Livingston Co.

Case of Albert Acker. Albert Acker Prv. Col. Gansvoort Regt 1776. 3 yrs or for the war. Not found on N. York rolls. 3 N.Y. Regiment Co2? May 1819 mustered March 1779. Deserted March 1, 1781. Admitted. Groveland Livingston Co'y.

State of New York

Ontario County SS.

On this 24th day of May 1819 before me the subscriber a Judge of Ontario's Commonpleas personally appeared Albert Acker aged fifty nine years, resident in the Town of Groveland in the County aforesaid who being by me first duly sworn according to law doth on his oath make the following declaration in order to obtain the Provision made by the late Act of Congress entitled an act to provide for certain persons engaged in the Land and Navel Service of the United States in the Revolutionary War that he the said Albert Acker Enlisted in the spring of the year 1776 as he then supposed for three years on the Continental Estab't but learned by his officers afterward that he was Returned for during the war that he was enlisted in the Town of Pokupsey [Poughkeepsie] in the State of New York by a Recruiting Officer called Captain Swartwort (1) and mustered to Albany and was then marched and served in the Company commanded by Captain Henry Teabout (2) in the 3d New York Regiment commanded by Colonel Gansvoort and that he continued to serve in said Corps until some time in the year 1782 when he received a furlough to return home and was not again called on again until Peace was ratified and that he sold his right to bounty lands before he left the army to Captain Blaker (3) and has since been informed that the land in his right has been drawn as a during war man, and that he was in the Battles of Bimis Hight, Fort Stanwix (4) and in Sullivan's Expedition (5) against the Indians and that he is in reduced circumstances and unable to labour on account of ill health and in need of the assistance of his country for support and that he has no other evidence now in his power of his said services. (Signed with his mark) Albert Acker

Sworn and Subscribed the day & year aforesaid before me. Stephen Phelps a Judge &c.

Letter responding to a request for information, dated August 12, 1924.

I have to advise you that from the papers in Revolutionary War pension claim, R.15, it appears that Albert Acker or Acher was born in 1760.

He applied for pension May 24, 1819, while living in Groveland, Ontario County, New York, and stated that he enlisted at Poughkeepsie, New York, in the spring of 1776, served in Captain Henry Tiebout's Company, Colonel Gansevoort's Third New York Regiment, was in the battles of Bemis Heights, Fort Stanwix and in General Sullivan's Indian Expedition and served until some time in 1782 when he was furloughed to return home and not again called out.

He was improperly allowed pension as upon an examination of the rolls of the Third New York Regiment, received after the allowance of pension, it was found that he enlisted in March 1779 and deserted March 1, 1781. He died June 10, 1832 in Groveland, New York.

Soldier married at Pepper Cotton, Sussex County, New Jersey, July 17, 1786, Sarah Hart who was born October 17, 1779. Her claim for pension, executed May 26, 1845, while a resident of said Groveland, was not allowed for the reason that her husband was a deserter.

Their children were:

Anna B. born May 10, 1786, married July 18, 1806 to Stephen Banker.

Silas born January 24, 1791, married May 18, 1814 to Elisabeth McClenen.

John born April 20, 1792.

Henry born October 15, 1794, married September 15, 1819 to Mary Holden.

Francis born October 15, 1797, married September 30, 1819 to Permely Pond.

Nathan born October 30, 1799.

Elisabeth born June 25, 1802, married January 11, 1819 to John Neukerk (?)

Samuel born October 21, 1804.

Pemelia (Parmelia) born Febrary 2, 1807.

Albert born January 30, 1811.

Levy (Levi) born May 16, 1813.

Sarah Anna born April 16, 1820.

Note: see NY Archives Vol. 1. P. 207 for this man's record & date of desertion. Did not mention John Acker who died in Oct 1770 as relationship is not stated. Did not give 1767 as date of soldier's birth as too young for service then & he states in 1819 he was 59 & in 1822 he was 62.

End Notes—R.15—Albert Acker

1. Abraham Swartwout was appointed Captain of the Fourth Company on November 21, 1776 in Colonel Peter Gansevoort's Third New York Continental Regiment.
2. Henry Tiebout was appointed Captain of the Seventh Company in November 21, 1776 in Colonel Gansevoort's Regiment. According to Captain Tiebout's Muster Rolls Albert was mustered in March of 1779 for during war. Albert is not listed in Tiebout's Company or the regiment before March of 1779. FROM: Revolutionary War Rolls 1775-

1783, Series M-246, Roll 70, Folder 47, National Archives, Washington, D.C.

3. Albert is probably referring to Captain Leonard Bleecker. On January 1, 1781, the First and Third New York Continental Regiments were consolidated into one regiment. Captains Bleecker, Tiebout and Aaron Aorson were transferred to the First New York along with the enlisted men that still had time left to serve. Albert is still listed as serving in Captain Tiebout's Company. He is listed as deserting on March 1, 1781. According to the muster rolls he never returned to finish his enlistment. FROM: Revolutionary War Rolls 1775-1783, Series M-246, Roll 66, Folder 15, National Archives, Washington, D.C.
4. As Albert did not enlist into the Third New York until 1779, he could not have been at the Battle of Bemis Heights on September 19, 1777 or the Siege of Fort Schuyler (which was Fort Stanwix) in August of 1777. After Major General Benedict Arnold raised the Siege at Fort Schuyler, he left the First New York at the fort to reinforce the garrison at the fort which was the Third New York. If any of the First and Third New York did return to Saratoga with General Arnold it would have been a small detachment unfortunately the muster rolls for both regiments do not show that any men from these regiments had been detached for that service.
5. In 1779 the Third New York with other regiments went with Brigadier General James Clinton and joined forces with Major General John Sullivan. Together they attacked and destroyed the Iroquois Village int he western part of New York.

Pension Application for Jacob Acker

W.2046 (Widow: Mary. This woman pensioned on account of service of former husband; See John Vanderbilt NY W.16803)
Southern District of New York
Westchester County SS.

Jacob Acker of the Town of Greensburgh in the County of Westchester aforesaid being duly sworn on his oath and examination before me on this day saith that he was a private in Captain George Comb's (1) company of Militia in the Regiment commanded by Colonel James Hammond (2) which said Regiment was attached to the Continental Army—and this deponent further saith that he amongst others of the said Captain Combs company was detached from the Continental Army there being a place called Pines-bridge in York Town in the said County on or about the first or second day of March in the year one thousand eight hundred and eighty two and put under the command of Captain Israel Honeywell (3)as a scout or reconnoitering party to examine the line of the British troops then lying at Morrisamia in said County –and the deponent further saith that on their retreat from Morrisina [Morrisania] he the deponent and others then under the command of Ensign Thomas Boyce (4) on the third day of March aforesaid at the Town of New Castle in said County were attacked by a body of dragoons or Light horse and that during the said attack he the deponent received a wound from the sword of a British soldier on the head from the top sloping towards the left side and that he was taken prisoner (5) by the enemy at that time and carried to the Hospital in New York where he was kept for about the space of three months when he was exchanged and the deponent further saith that on his return immediately after his exchange as aforesaid he found the company to which he belonged disbanded and discharged from the Continental service—and was not to the best of this deponent's knowledge and belief called upon again during the war. And the deponent further saith that he hath made several applications to obtain a pension in consequence of his said wound within a few years after the close of the war but did not succeed in obtaining it in consequence of some defect in the papers presented as this deponent was informed and understood. And he further saith that the trouble and vexation that attended those applications and the want of success therein deterred him from making any further effort until his age (the deponent now being of the age of seventy two years) and his frequent total inability to work in consequence of the effect of his wound induced a benevolent friend of his to interest himself in procuring a pension for the deponent and the deponent further saith that he is not on the pension list of any State of the United States and that he never had received any pension from any State or the United States—and the deponent further saith that he hath ever since the war and now doth reside in the Town of Greensburgh aforesaid and that he is a farmer which occupation he hath pursued ever since the war and that immediately after his Exchange as aforesaid he moved on the farm he now occupies and further saith not. (Signed) Jacob Acker

Sworn the 8th day of May 1826 before me. Nathaniel Bayles, Commissioner &c

End Notes—W.2046—Jacob Acker

1. George Combs was the First Lieutenant in Captain Abraham Storm's Company (Tarrytown Company) in Colonel Joseph Drake's First Regiment of Westchester County Militia. On October 23, 1776, Gload (Claude) Requa (Requaw) was elected Captain in place of Captain Storm. Combs was promoted to Captain on June 16, 1778 in place of Captain Requa as he had resigned.
2. James Hammond was the Lieutenant-Colonel in Colonel Drake's Regiment.
3. Israel Honeywell Jr. had served as a First Lieutenant in Captain Isaac Vermilya's Company in Colonel Drake's Regiment. He was appointed Captain on June 16, 1778.
4. Ensign Thomas Boyce in Captain Combs' Company.
5. Jacob was taken prisoner on March 4, 1782 and he was released on June 6, 1782. The following were also taken prisoners. Ensign Thomas Boyce, Ensign Stephen Sherwood of Honeywell's Company, Private Archer Burgess, Private Henry Hornbeck and Private Solomon Purdy.

Pension Application for Peter Acker or Ackert

S.31510
State of New York
Rensselaer County SS.

On the 19th day of July 1833 before me the undersigned first Judge of the Court of Common Pleas for said County personally appeared Peter Acker yet a resident of Schaghticoke in said County, who being duly sworn deposeth & saith that by reason of the age and consequent loss of memory he cannot swear positively to the precise length of his service but according to the best of his recollection he served not less than the periods mentioned below and in the following grades.

That he first entered the service of the United States as a corporal in the month of March 1776 at Schaghticoke then Albany now Rensselaer County in a company of militia commanded by Capt. Walter Grosbeck (1) in the regiment commanded by Col. John Knickerbacker as stated in this deponent's declaration hereunto annexed & about the 1st of April 1776 was detached from said company with others and marched with a company commanded by Captain Hodge (2) to Fort George and was then in actual service cutting timber, building a hospital for the sick & keeping guard for the term of three months at the expiration of which time deponent & the said company commanded by said Hodge marched to Fort Ann & was then engaged in building a picket fort and repairing roads for the further term of three months at the expiration of which time and about the middle of October this deponent was discharged & returned home—that during the time he was at Fort Ann Col. Christopher Yates (3) had the command of the militia there employed & Col. Gansevoort (4) had the command of the militia at Fort George & this deponent was in actual service at the two last mentioned places in the year 1776 for the full term of six months as a corporal.

That in the year 1777 this deponent again entered the service about the latter part of the month of June in a company of militia commanded by Capt. Walter Grosbeck in a regiment commanded by Col. John Knickerbacker, marched from Schaghticoke to Lake George & was in actual service until Gen. Burgoyne's(5) surrender on the 17th Oct 1777—Deponent & the company to which he belonged was ordered to retreat from Lake George by Major VanRensselaer (6) & did retreat to Fort Edward from thence to Stillwater & was in actual service in the battle of the 7th (7) of October & the 17th of October when Burgoyne surrendered—that after the surrender of Burgoyne this deponent was dismissed & returned home & this deponent further says that during the said year 1777 this deponent was in actual service three months and twenty days.

That in 1778 the said company to which this deponent belonged was employed in garrisoning and guarding the different posts & Forts on the Northern frontiers and this deponent was appointed a Sergeant in said company & marched about the 1st of May 1778 to Palmertown from thence to Fort

Edward back to Palmertown where deponent & others were engaged in building a block house & from thence to a place called Jessup's Patent & was in actual service as a Sergeant in the year 1778 for the term of three months & thirteen days during a part of which time Matthew DeGarmo (8) commanded said company as Captain in the absence of said Grossbeck.

That in the year 1779 this deponent was twice or three times called out in an alarm & was in actual service as a sergeant of said company to the best of this deponent's recollection thirty days one time marched to Palmertown about 18 miles from home under Capt. Jacob Yates (9) & once to Saratoga & from thence to Fort Edward under the same Captain, the said Jacob Yates then having been appointed Captain & Peter Yates Col. of the said regiment.

That in the year 1780 this deponent in the month of March again entered the service as a sergeant marched to Ticonderoga under said Captain Yates, Peter Yates Col. was three months in actual service at this time watching the movements of the British shipping, guarding the Fort.

That in 1781 this deponent at different times was called out & from thence to the last of the war but after the year 1781 commenced the deponent was only occasionally in service for short periods of time and this deponent cannot recollect the precise periods of service but verily believes that from the commencement of the year 1781 until the close of the war this deponent was in the actual service of the United States for a term not less than three months and a half during which time this deponent acted all the time as sergeant under the command of Captain Jacob Yates, Peter Yates, Col., (11) and during which time this deponent marched two or three times to Palmertown - a number of times to Saratoga, once to Ticonderoga and once to Crown Point and this deponent further says that he has no documentary evidence of his services—that he verily believes that in this foregoing affidavit he has stated & set forth the periods of his service less or not more than they actually were & further saith not. (Signed with his mark) Peter Acker

Sworn and subscribed this 19th day of July 1833 before me H. Knickerbocker Judge as above stated.

Letter responding to a request for information, dated October 11, 1929.

I advise you from the papers in the Revolutionary War pension claim, S.31510, it appears that Peter Acker or Ackert was born in Esopus, Ulster County, New York, date not given.

While a resident of Schaghticoke, Albany County, New York, he enlisted and served with the New York Troops as follows:

From March, 1776, for six months as a corporal in Captains Walter Groesbeck's and Hodge's Companies in Colonels John Knickerboacker's, Christopher Yates' and Gansevoort's Regiments.

From sometime in June, 1777, three months and twenty days as a corporal in Captain Walter Groesbeck's Company in Colonel John Knickerboacker's Regiment; he was in both battles of Stillwater. (12)

In 1778, for three months and thirteen days as a sergeant in Captain Matthew DeGarmo's Company in Colonel John Knickerbocker's Regiment.

In 1779, he served two or three short tours, amounting to one month in all, as a sergeant in Captain Jacob Yates' Company in Colonel Peter Yates' Regiment.

From March 1780, served three months as a sergeant in Captain Jacob Yates' Company in Colonel Peter Yates' Regiment.

From sometime in 1781 until the close of the Revolution he served at various times, amounting to three and one half months in all, as a sergeant in Captain Jacob Yates' Company in Colonel Peter Yates' Regiment.

He was allowed pension on his application executed August 6, 1832, at which time he was seventy-eight years of age and was a resident of Schaghticoke, New York.

He died March 17, 1845, leaving one child but his name is not given.

There are no further data on file relative to his family.

This is the only soldier by the name of Peter Acker (searched under all spellings of the name) that is found on the Revolutionary War records of this bureau.

End Notes—S.31510—Peter Acker

1. Walter N. Groesbeck was Captain of the Second Company in Colonel John Knickerbocker's Fourteenth Regiment of Albany County Militia.
2. Probably Captain Samuel Hodges of Colonel Lewis VanWoert's Sixteenth Regiment of Albany County Militia.
3. Christopher Yates of Schenectady was the Lieutenant-Colonel of Colonel Abraham Wemple's Second Regiment of Albany County Militia. As Peter was under these two officers from two different regiments means that a draft of men was made from the various Albany County Militia Regiments and sent to Lake George and the surrounding areas for work details.
4. Peter Gansevoort was appointed Lieutenant-Colonel on March 19, 1776 in Colonel Goose VanSchaick's (Unnumbered) New York Continental Regiment. Gansevoort with several companies from VanSchaick's Regiment were stationed at Fort George.
5. Lieutenant General John Burgoyne with about 7,000 British troops and Allies had invaded New York from Canada via the North River (Hudson River) in 1777. General Burgoyne surrendered his army on October 17, 1777 at present day Schuylerville to Major General Horatio Gates.
6. John VanRensselaer was the Second Major in Colonel John Knickerbocker's Regiment.
7. Most of the Albany County Militia present on October 7, 1777 were in Brigadier General Abraham TenBroeck's Brigade. They were not heavily engaged in the battle, under Major General Benedict Arnold although he had been relieved of duty by General Gates, TenBroecks' Brigade along with other troops he had gathered attacked the German Redoubt which helped turn the battle into an American Victory.

8. Matthew DeGarmo was the Second Lieutenant in Captain J. Bleecker's Company (Third Company) in Colonel Knickerbockers Regiment. DeGarmo was appointed Captain on June 22, 1778 in place of Bleecker.
9. Jacob had served as Ensign and Lieutenant under Captain Groesbeck. On March 4, 1780 he was appointed Captain in place of Captain Groesbeck.
10. Peter Yates was appointed Colonel of the Fourteenth Regiment of Albany County Militia on June 22, 1778 in place of Colonel Knickerbocker.
11. Peter also had served in Captain James Hadlock's Company In Colonel Yates' Regiment.
12. Peter in his declaration states he was only in the Battle of October 7, 1777. The first battle was on September 19, 1777.

Pension Application for Aaron Adams

W.9323 (Widow: Sarah)
Green Mt. Boys, Vt.
State of Indiana
Johnson County SS.

On this 6th day of August in the year of our Lord, eight hundred and forty one personally appeared before me James. R. Alexander associate Judge of the Circuit Court of Johnson County, Sarah Adams a resident of said County of Johnson and State of Indiana aged eighty four years, who being first duly sworn according to law doth on her oath make the following declaration in order to obtain the benefit of the provision made by the act of Congress passed July 11, 1836. That she is the widow of Aaron Adams who was a Sergeant in the Militia in the Army of the revolution, that she has always understood from her said husband the said Aaron Adams entered the service as a volunteer somewhere in the State of Vermont in the year seventeen hundred and seventy five that he marched through Castleton from whence under the Command of Colonel Ethan Allen (1) to the fortress of Tyconderoga (2) and that he was present at the capture of it in this expedition it is the impression of the said Sarah Adams from the statements of her said husband the said Aaron Adams he the said Aaron was out and in the service four or five moths again in the spring of the year seventeen hundred and seventy seven the said Sarah says from the statements of her said husband and the other persons who are now deceased she believes her husband entered the service as a Sergeant in the militia was at and engaged in the Battle of Bennington (3) from which time he continued in the service until the latter part of September of the year last aforesaid the company to which he belonged she thinks was commanded by Captain John Spafford of Tinmouth in the State of Vermont. His Colonel was Seth Warner. (4) The said Sarah further states that to her own knowledge the said Aaron her said husband was in the service and on duty as a sergeant in Captain Spafford's (5) company in the fall and winter previous to his intermarriage with her and after that event for something over two years on several occasions was in the service one of which was a tour to Meshaba (now Brandow) against a body of Indians. She also further declares that she was married to the said Aaron Adams on the twenty first day of May AD 1778, that he husband the said Aaron Adams died on the thirteenth day of December in the year AD 1833 and that she has remained a widow ever since that period as will more fully appear by reference to the proof hereto annexed. (Signed Sarah Adams)

Letter of reply to an inquiry, dated September 21, 1937

Reference is made to your request for information relative to the Revolutionary War soldier, Aaron Adams, W.9323.

The data which follow were obtained from papers on file in the pension claim, W.9323, based upon the military service of Aaron Adams.

Aaron Adams was born March 22, 1747. The place of his birth and the names of his parents were not given.

While a resident of Tinmouth, Vermont, he enlisted in 1775 and served at various times, amounting to four or five months in all, with the Green Mountain Boys under Captain Oliver Potter (6) and Colonels Ethan Allen and Seth Warner; he was in the battle of Ticonderoga. He enlisted in the spring of 1777 and served until sometime in the fall or winter of that year as sergeant in Captain John Spafford's Vermont company; he was in the battles of Hubbardton, (7) Bennington and at the capture of Burgoyne. (8) After May, 1778, he served at various times, amounting to at least two years in all, officers not stated.

He married May 21, 1778, Sarah Hard who was born June 11, 1757.

Aaron Adams died December 13, 1833.

His widow, Sarah, was allowed pension on her application executed August 6, 1841, at which time she was a resident of Johnson County, Indiana. In 1841 she was living in Milen, Erie County, Ohio.

Aaron and Sarah Adams had the following children:

Charlotte born August 17, 1780, Married May 6, 1800

Mary born December 21, 1781, married December 28, 1801

Aaron born November 25, 1783, married December 22, 1803 was resident of Franklin County, Indiana in 1841.

Abraham born September 29, 1785, married January 21, 1819 and was a resident of Avon, Livingston County, New York in 1845.

Elisa born September 7, 1787

Sebastian born August 3, 1789

Cylindia born April 7, 1792, married January 31, 1810

Noble born February 3, 1794

Malissia born February 12, 1798

Lysander born May 31, 1799

End Notes—W.9223—Aaron Adams

1. Ethan Allen was the Colonel of the Green Mountain Boys until September 25, 1775 when he was taken prisoner in his failed attack on Montreal.
2. Fort Ticonderoga, NY was captured on May 10, 1775.
3. The Battle of Bennington was fought on August 16, 1777.
4. Seth Warner was appointed Lieutenant-Colonel of the Green Mountain Boys on July 27, 1775. After Colonel Allen was captured Warner commanded the regiment. On July 5, 1776 he was appointed Colonel of one of the Sixteen Additional Continental Regiment.
5. Captain John Spafford's Company belonged to the Vermont Militia not to Warner's Continental Regiment.
6. Oliver Potter served in the Green Mountain Boys from May to December 1775.
7. The Battle of Hubbardton, Vermont was fought on July 7, 1777.

Pension Application for Aaron Allis or Ellis

S.45187
Massachusetts.

Testimony in the case Aaron Allis an applicant to be placed on the Pension List, under the act of Congress of the 18 March 1818.

State of New York
Rensselaer County SS.

Aaron Allis a resident of the City of Troy, in the County of Rensselaer and State of New York being duly sworn, doth depose and say, that he served in the Revolutionary Army of the United States. That in the month of April 1777, he enlisted as a private in a company commanded by William Watson, Col. Weston in the ninth regiment of the Massachusetts line, which regiment was commanded by Col. _____ Weston (1). That this deponent served in the said company and regiment, for the term of three years, (being the term of his enlistment.) and that he was honorably discharged at West Point in the State of New York, on the ninth day of April 1780. And this deponent further says that he again enlisted in the service of the United States in the month of March 1781, in a company Capt---Wade, in the Massachusetts line, in the Third Regiment commanded by Col. Michael Jackson, (2) in which last mentioned company and regiment this deponent served nearly three years, part of the time as a Sergeant, and was honorably discharged, at West Point in the State of New York, on the 23d December 1783. That the evidence of the last mentioned discharge, signed by Major Gen. Knox, (3) at that time commanding the American Forces on the Hudson's River, is now in the possession of this deponent. And this deponent further says that "by reason of his reduced circumstances in life, he is in need of assistance from his country for support." (Signed) Aaron Allis (4)

State of New York
Rensselaer County SS.

On the 30th day of March 1818, the above named Aaron Allis came personally before me, subscribed the foregoing declaration and being duly sworn, declared it to be true according to the best of his recollection and belief. Jas. Malloy, Judge of the Court of Common Pleas in & for the County of Rensselaer State of New York.
State of New York
City of Troy in the County of Rensselaer

In the Court of Common Pleas called the Mayor's Court of the City of Troy.

On this first day of August 1820, personally appeared in open court, (being a court of record in and for the said City according to the solemn adjudications of the Supreme Court of this state, and being a court which proceeds according to the course of common law; with a jurisdiction unlimited in point of amount; keeping a record of its proceedings; and possessing the power of fine and imprisonment) Aaron Allis aged fifty six years, resident in the City of Troy in said County, who being first duly sworn according to law, doth on his oath declare, that he served in the revolutionary war as follows:--Three years in the Third Regiment of Massachusetts line commanded by Michael Jackson, & in a Company Commanded by Capt. Wade and was discharged at West Point by Henry Knox Major Gen'l (Discharge sent to War Department) That the number of my certificate of pension is 427, and the date of my original declaration is the thirtieth day of March 1818.

And I do solemnly swear that that I was a resident citizen of the United States on the 18th day of March, 1818; and that I have not, since that time, by gift, sale, or in any manner, disposed of my property, or any part thereof, with intent thereby so to diminish it, as to bring myself within the provisions of an act of congress entitled "An act to provide for certain persons engaged in the land and naval service of the United States in the revolutionary war," passed on the 18th of March, 1818; and that I have not, nor has any person in trust for me, any property or securities, contracts, or debts, due to me; nor have I any income other than what is contained in the schedule hereto annexed, and by me subscribed. (Signed) Aaron Allis.

Sworn to and declared on the First day of August 1820. Arch'd Bell Deputy Clerk

Schedule of all the property both real and personal (necessary bedding & clothing excepted) of Aaron Allis a pensioner under the Laws of the United States of the 18 March 1818.

Real Estate I have none, Personal Property as follows.

6 chairs, 2 chests, 1 table, 1 stand, 1 set knives & forks, 1 slice & Tongs, 1 pot, 1 kettle, 1 spider $11.25

Tea Kettle & skillet, teapot, sugar bowl, cream cup, 2 platters 4 bowls, 2 decanters 4 small tumblers $2.62 ½

3 [?] glasses, 5 glass bottles, 2 jugs, 2 stone[?] 2 wooden bowls, 2 Barrels, 1 water cask, 2 Wash Tubs, 2 pots $3.62

1 shovel, 1 pick, 1 old axe, 1 handsaw, 1 Jointer, 1 Jack plain, 1 wood saw, 1 pr andirons $4.25 ½.

I Aaron Allis being sworn say that the above list of my property is estimated at its true Value. That I am fifty six years of age and am unable to support myself on account of sickness and the continued indisposition of my wife, I have no other family but my wife named Huldah aged fifty years who has out of health 19 years & unable to work & for nineteen months last past has been confined to her bed—I was bred to the farming business but for many years have been a day laborer—and this deponent says he is indebted to more than 90 Dolls [dollars]. (Signed) Aaron Allis

Sworn to this first day of August 1820 in open court. Arch'd Bell, Deputy Clerk

End Notes—S.45187—Aaron Allis

1. Colonel James Wesson of the Ninth Massachusetts Continental Regiment. He retired from the service on January 1, 1781. Captain William Watson had been appointed First Lieutenant on January 1, 1777 and then to Captain on July 25, 1779.
2. Michael Jackson was Colonel of the Eighth Massachusetts Continental Regiment. He transferred to the Third Massachusetts Continental Regiment on June 12, 1783. The Colonel of the Third Massachusetts was John Greaton from November 1, 1776 to January 7, 1783 when he was appointed Brigadier General.
3. Major General Henry Knox.
4. It is interesting that Aaron does not mention any of the battles that Ninth Massachusetts was engaged in. They fought in the Battles of Saratoga on September 19 and October 7, 1777. They were also in the Battle of Monmouth, N.J. on June 28, 1778 where Colonel Wesson was wounded.

Pension Application for Robert Ayres, Ayrs or Eyrs

W.20648 (Widow: Sarah. Married Robert Ayres on the first day of March 1785, he died the thirtieth day of April 1833.)

Pension awarded Widow $70.88 per annum

New York

Saratoga SS.

On this 25th day of December 1832 personally appeared in open court before the Court of Common Pleas held in and for the county of Saratoga now sitting Robert Ayrs of the Town of Saratoga Springs, County & State aforesaid aged sixty seven years, who being first duly sworn according to Law doth on his oath make the following declaration in order to obtain the benefit of the Act of Congress passed June 7th 1832, that he entered the service of the United States under the following named officers and served as stated.—

On being asked where & in what year were you Born? He answers & says that he was born April 12th 1765 near the present Town of Stillwater in the (then) County of Albany now County of Saratoga—

On being asked have you any record of your age & if so where is it? He answers & says that he has a record of his age in his family Bible at his present residence—

On being asked where were you living when called into service, where have you lived since the revolutionary war & where do you now live? He answers & says that he was living at Stillwater in the County of Saratoga when called into Service, since the Revolutionary War he has lived in the county of Saratoga, part of the time in Stillwater & part in Saratoga Springs where he now resides.—

On being asked how were you called into service; where you drafted, did you volunteer or were you a substitute? And if a substitute for whom? He answers & says he was called into service by Enlisting & served for three years.

On being asked To state the names of some of the Regular Officers who were with the Troops where you Served, such continental & militia regiments as you can recollect & the general circumstances of your service—he answers & says that about the 1st day of April 1782 at Stillwater aforesaid he enlisted in the New York State Troops for the term of three years in the Regiment commanded by Colonel Marinus Willett under Capt. Job Wright (1) who was then recruiting in said town. From which place he was marched to Ballston in said County to protect the Inhabitants & there remained until about the 15th Day of July thereafter—he was then marched to Stone Arabia near Johnstown on the Mohawk River to guard the Inhabitants while they were engaged in harvesting—from thence he marched to Fort Plains, on the Mohawk River & there worked on the fortifications & did garrison duty until the Winter when we went to Fort Herkimer & remained about a month & then went on an expedition against the Enemy at Fort Oswego (2) near the mouth of the Oswego, then returned to Fort Herkimer and said Mohawk River & there remained on garrison duty until the next Fall, was then marched to Schenectady on the Mohawk & was then marched to Schenectady on the Mohawk & was there discharge in consequence after Peace, about the 8th January 1784 (3) The said Regiment being discharged in small parties at Intervals—at the time of his discharge he belonged to the company of Capt. Peter. B. Tearse (4) who granted his discharge according to the best of his recollection—which discharge is lost—That he was discharged in common with the rest of the Regiment as having served the full Term of their Enlistment he enlisted as a private & was when discharged a non commissioned officer—He has no documentary evidence of his service & knows of a person by the name of Samuel Ashman living in Champlain near the Canada line & Albert Baker now living in Queensbury, County of Warren who entered & served in the same company with Deponent, Besides these deponent knows of no one whose testimony he could procure to prove his service—and deponent intents to present the Testimony of the said Albert Baker (whom deponent has long known & who is a person of much Respectability & a credible Person) But deponent is not able to defray the expense of procuring the evidence of the said Ashman—

On being asked Did you receive a discharge from the service & if so by whom was it given & what has become if it? He answers & says he has already answered as hereinbefore stated—

On being asked to state the names of Persons to whom he is known in his present neighborhood & who can testify as to his character, for veracity & their belief of his services as a soldier of the Revolution—he answers & states the names of Hon'l Esch Cowen, Hon'l John H.Steel a Judge of this Court, Hon'l James Thompson, First Judge of this Court. Wm. L F. Warren Esquire, Ransom Cook Esqr, Thomas J. Marvin Esqr & others.

And Deponent further states that he hereby Relinquishes every claim whatever to a pension or annuity except the present & declares that his name is not on the pension roll of the agency of any state—Deponent further says that he is unacquainted with any clergyman whose attendance he can procure without a great expense—

Deponent further says that when he went to Fort Oswego as above mentioned, his regiment was joined by a Rhode Island Regiment (5) at Fort Herkimer, Both Regiments then moved on in the Month of February in Sleighs to Fort Oswego, which it was calculated to take by surprise, but the Troops did not arrived till near day light & in consequence thereof the expedition failed & was extracted, one company & Capt. James Cannon's (6) company went to Herkimer & the rest marched to Fort Plains. Major Benschoten or Van Benschoten, & Adjutant Pliny Moore--& Quarter Master Trotter & Paymaster Ten Eyck (7) accompanied the detachments to Fort Oswego—Ten Eyck was paymaster and thinks he remained at Albany then. (Signed) Robert Ayrs

Sworn & Subscribed the day & year aforesaid in Open Court Wm L. Goodrich Dep. Clerk

Letter of inquiry dated September 11, 1838, included in the pension folder.

The data which follow were obtained from papers on file in pension claim, W.20648, based upon service of Robert Ayrs in the Revolutionary War.

Robert Ayrs was born April 12, 1765, at Stillwater, Albany County (later Saratoga County), New York. Names of his parents are not shown.

While a resident of Stillwater, Saratoga County, New York, Robert Ayrs enlisted April 1, 1782, served in Captains Job Wright's and Peter B. Tearce's companies, Colonel Marinus Willett's New York Regiment, was on guard duty on the Mohawk River and garrison duty at Fort Herkimer and was on an expedition against the enemy at Fort Oswego, and was discharged at the close of the war. His service was rendered as private and non-commissioned officer.

The soldier was allowed pension on his application executed December 25, 1832, then a resident of Saratoga Springs, Saratoga County, New York.

He died April 30, 1833, at Saratoga Springs, New York.

Robert Ayrs married March 1, 1785, at Stillwater, New York, Sarah Ashton, daughter of John Ashton. She was born August 22, 1766. They were both residing in Stillwater, New York at the time of marriage. The name of Sarah's mother is not shown.

The soldier's widow, Sarah Ayrs, was allowed pension on her application executed March 18, 1840 at which time she was residing in Milton, Saratoga County, New York. In August 1843 she was residing in Saratoga Springs, New York, and in 1848 in Milton, New York.

The names of the children of Robert and Sarah Ayrs are shown as follows:

John-Born May 1, 1788
Isaac-Born May 18, 1789
Reuben-Born March 24, 1791, died July 23, 1791
Mary-Born April 27, 1792
Rebecca-Born April 21, 1793, died March 1, 1794
Sarah-Born December 2, 1796
Rachel-Born May 6, 1799

In 1840, their daughter Sarah, the wife of Elisha Rockwell, was residing in Milton, New York.

In 1840, soldier's sister, Mary, aged seventy-nine years, widow of Eleazer Millard, made a statement in Saratoga County, New York in regard to the marriage of Robert and Sarah Ayrs. In the same year one Rebeccah Morey was aged sixty-seven years and a resident of Malta, Saratoga County, New York, and stated that at the time Robert and Sarah married she was residing with the family of Sarah's father, no relationship stated.

Reference was made to one Eleazer Millard who was superintendent of a class in Colonel Van Veghten's New York regiment in 1782, no relationship to the family shown.

End Notes—W.20648—Robert Ayres

1. Captain Job Wright's Company in Colonel Marinus Willett's Regiment of New York State Levies.
2. Fort Oswego is on Lake Ontario, New York. This expedition was in February of 1783.
3. According to the "Extract from the Register of the New York State Battalion" as follows:--Robert Ayers (Discharge) January 6, 1784. FROM: Revolutionary War Rolls 1775-1783, Series M-246, Roll 78, Folder 173, National Archives, Washington, D.C.
4. Robert is listed as a Corporal in Captain Wright's Company. He served as a corporal for 10 months and transferred to Captain Peter B. Tearce's Company of Light Infantry in Colonel Willett's Regiment and served as a corporal for 2 months. FROM: Revolutionary War Rolls 1775—1783, Series M-246, roll 78, folder 173, National Archives, Washington, D.C.
5. The First Rhode Island Continental Regiment.
6. Captain James Cannon was in Colonel Willett's Regiment.
7. Major Elias VanBenschoten, Adjutant Pliney Moor, QuarterMaster Matthew Trotter and PayMaster Abrahan TenEyck were all in Willett's Regiment.

Pension Application for Albert Baker

S.28989. Private under Captain Tearse, served 16 months 18 days.
State of New York
City & County of Albany
Justices Court SS. On this 24th day of November 1845 before said Court it was proved by the adduction of testimony satisfactory to said Court that Albert Baker late of Sandy Hill in the County of Washington and State aforesaid died on the twenty second day of September one thousand eight hundred and forty five. That at the time of his death, left no widow but left him surviving the following named children viz. Kezia Baker, Rachel Clary, Gannetta Brian, Ann Brayman, Isaac Baker, Charles L. Baker, and Walter Baker. That they are his only surviving children and each of them are over twenty on years of age.

In testimony whereof I have hereunto set my hand and hereby direct the official seal of said court to be affixed the day and year first above written. Abraham Morrel, a Justice of the Justices Court the City of Albany County of Albany, NY.

State of New York
City & County of Albany
Justices Court

On this 24th day of November one thousand eight hundred and forty five in open court before the Justices thereof the same being a court of record, personally appeared Kezia Baker aged forth five years a resident of said city and county who from conscientious scruples is averse to making oath and who being first duly affirmed according to law doth on her solemn affirmation make the following declaration in behalf of the children of Albert Baker decease in order to obtain the pension which was due the said Albert Baker under the Act of Congress passed June 7th 1832. And as she has been informed & believes is now due the children from the 4th of March 1831 to the 22d of September 1845 being the day of the death of the said Albert Baker—That she is one of the children of Albert Baker deceased who was a private soldier in the war of the Revolution and served three years under Capt. Peter B. Tearse (1) as she has always understood & believes, and as will fully appear on reference to an original discharge now in possession of declarant dated the 5th of January 1784 & is herewith delivered for the purpose of forwarding to Washington which discharge declarant saith has been in the possession of her said father from her earliest recollection until his death.

Declarant further saith that from conscientious scruples her said father, on being solicited by various persons to make application for a pension has at all times declined and repelled any action upon the subject and further that about the year one thousand eight hundred and thirty five or six Nathaniel Pitcher Esq, who as declarant believes was then a member of Congress, procured some evidence of identity of her said father in the aforesaid service and as declarant has also been informed & believes, caused the same to be filed in the pension office at Washington at which time the said Pitcher procured the said discharge for a few months for the purpose of exhibiting it to the pension Department & there as declarant has been informed & believes recording it for the benefit of those concerned. Declarant further saith that her said father the aforesaid Albert Baker died on the twenty second day of September one thousand eight hundred and forty five. And at the time of his death left no widow but left him surviving the following named children viz. Kezia Baker, this declarant, Rachel Clary, Gannetta Brien, Ann Brayman, Isaac Baker, Charles S. Baker and Walter Baker. That they are his only surviving children and each of them are over twenty one years of age. (Signed) Kezia Baker

Subscribed and affirmed to before me this 24th day of November 1845. Abraham Morrell a Justice of the Justices Court of the City of Albany County of Albany NY.

End Note—S.28989—Albert Baker

Albert enlisted in 1781 as a private in Captain Silas Gray's Company in Lieutenant-Colonel Commandant Marinus Willett's Regiment of New York State Levies.

Captain Gray's Company was sent to Stillwater under Major John McKinstry of Willett's Regiment. They stayed in that area during most of that year.

In 1795 his father Albert Baker Sr. received his owed pay of £ 5..6..8. FROM: Revolutionary War Rolls 1775-1783, Series M-246, Roll 78, folder 173, National Archives, Washington, D.C.

On May 31, 1782, Albert was a class enlistment for 2 years. He was born in New York, New York County, New York. When he enlisted, he lived at Fort Edward. Description at this time: age 17, size 5 ft 5 in., complexion light, eyes light, occupation- labourer. FROM: Manuscripts and Special Collections, New York State Library, Albany, N.Y. Collection Marinus Willett's Regt. Descriptive Book No 4, Doc. No. 11105

In 1783, Albert was listed as a private in Captain Job Wright's Company in Willett's Regiment. He served ten months. He had been paid £ 26..60 and was owed £ 40. FROM: Revolutionary War Rolls 1775-1783, Series M-246, Roll 78, folder 173, National Archives, Washington, D.C.

In 1782, Albert either served in Captain Gray's or Wright's Company. Captain Gray was recruiting a company but he could not fill his company quota and the company was disabled. Those he had recruited were put into other companies.

Pension Application for Cornelius Barnhart

W.8347
B.L.Wt.26580-160-55
State of New York
County of Schenectady SS.

On this nineteenth day of October in the year of our Lord one thousand eight hundred and thirty two personally appeared in open court before the Judges of the Court of Common Pleas in and for said County now sitting Cornelius Barnhart a resident of the town of Niskayuna in said state & County aged seventy eight years who being first duly sworn according to law doth on his oath make the following declaration in order to obtain the benefit of the act of Congress passed June 7th 1832.

He was born at the Wappingers Kill in the County of Dutchess in the said State on the twenty sixth day of July 1755. He has no record of his age.—

When he was called into the service of the United States in the Army of the Revolution he was living in the town of [?] county of Orange NY and since the Revolutionary was he has lived in the State of Massachusetts and he now lives in the town of Niskayuna—aforesaid.

He entered the service of the United States under the following named officers and served as herein stated.

In the spring of the year 1776 he enlisted as a private in Captain Francis Smith's (1) Company in Colonel Marvin's (2) Regiment of State troops and served in said Company of Captain Smith for the term of six months at the following posts: viz Schoharie.

In the spring of the year 1777, he enlisted in Captain John Woolsey's (3) Company of State troops or Militia the names of his company & field officers he cannot recollect.

The place of his enlistment in this last named Company was at New-Nulbury NY the term of his enlistment and service four—months, and the place he marched to and served at in mounting guard was Schoharie at the middle fort of that town.

In the fall of the year 1778, he enlisted & served for the term of one year in Captain Peter Bunschoten's (4) Company of State troops. His other company &b field officers he cannot recollect.

The place of his enlistment in the company last named was at New Hackensack N. York the term of his enlistment one year as aforesaid, and the posts he served at Hackensack aforesaid in mounting guard.

In the Spring of the year 1779 he was enrolled at the Rhinebeck flats in Captain James Kipp's (5) Company of Militia & served therein under one engagement until the end of the said war. The names of his other company & field officers he cannot recollect except Colonel Graham & Major Harman. (6) The places he served at were West Point, Fishkill, Eospus [Kingston] & other places not recollected.

The following are the names of some of the regular officers whom he knew, or who were with the troops where he served, and such continental and militia, regiments or companies with which he served, or as he can recollect, viz: Colonel Cortland, General TenBroeck & others—

He never received any written discharge from the service.

He has no documentary evidence, and knows of no person whose testimony he can procure who can testify to his service, his associates in most he believes are all dead—

The following are the names of persons to whom he is known in his present neighborhood, and who can testify as to his character for veracity, and their belief of his services as a soldier of the revolution, to wit: Lawrence Vrooman & William Burgess—

He hereby relinquishes every claim whatever, to a pension or annuity except the present, and declares that his name is not on the pension roll of the agency of any state. (Signed) Cornelius Barnhart

Subscribed and sworn to the day and year first aforesaid. John S. Vrooman, Clerk.

And the said Cornelius Barnhart being further duly sworn deposeth and saith, that by reason of old age & the consequent loss of memory he cannot call to mind the different terms of his engagement as a private in Captain Kipp's company of Militia aforesaid, yet is certain that the whole period of his services as such private exceeds in the whole two month and this Deponent further saith that he served four months in Captain Woolsey's company of State Troops for one year in Captain Peter Benschoten's Company of State troops partially set forth in the written declaration and for the aforesaid actual and active service of eighteen months this deponent claims a pension - and this deponent further said that serving said eighteen months, he was not engaged in any civil pursuit. (Signed) Cornelius Barnhart

Subscribed and Sworn this 6th day of June 1833 before me. J. D. Harman. Justice of the Peace.

Another deposition on April 18, 1854 was given by his widow Elizabeth. In this deposition she states she was married to Cornelius Barnhart on or about the 20th day of February one thousand eight hundred and nine and that her husband died on the seventh day of March one thousand eight hundred and thirty four in the Town of Niskayuna. She stated they were married by Nathan Bennett Esquire, a Justice of the Peace at the Town of Ballston in the County of Saratoga, at the time stated.

End Notes—W.83447—Cornelius Barnhart

1. Francis Smith was Captain of the Fifth Company in Colonel Jesse Woodhull's First Regiment of Orange County Militia.
2. Elihu Marvin was the Lieutenant-Colonel of Colonel Woodhull's Regiment.
3. So far no record has been found for Captain John Woolsey.
4. The only Peter VanBeuschoten that could be found served as a First Lieutenant in the Fourth New York Continental Regiment. The name of Cornelius Barnhart could not be found on the muster rolls for this regiment.

5. Jacobus or James Kip was the Captain of the Fifth Company in Colonel Morris Graham's First Regiment of Dutchess County Militia.
6. No record of Major Harmon has been found.

Pension Application for Frederick Baum

W15835 (Widow: Margaret Duesler)
State of New York
Montgomery County SS.

On this 21 day of September 1832, personally appeared in open court before the Judges of the Court of Common Pleas in & for the said County , now sitting Frederick Baum a resident of the Town of Oppenheim, County of Montgomery & State of New York aged about seventy two years who being first duly sworn according to law doth on his oath make the following declaration in order to obtain the benefit of the Act of Congress passed June 7, 1832, that he entered the service of the United States in the Revolutionary War in the Militia of the State of New York under the following named officers & served as herein stated viz. That in or about the first day of April 1778 he the said Frederick Baum entered as a volunteer as a private into the militia of the State aforesaid in the Company whereof Robert McKean (1) was Capt, John Smith Lieutenant & he (he thinks) Solomon Woodard Ensign of said company that the regiment & its officers to which said company that he belonged he does not recollect. He volunteered as aforesaid for nine months. He resided in the Town of Palatine then County of Tryon & in the now County of Montgomery in said State where he volunteered his service as aforesaid. He was marched in the said company from the Town of Palatine to the German Flatts to Fort Dayton where the company was stationed for said nine months, but while in said Fort in part of this company, himself was dispatched in pursuit of some British Indians & Tories that broke into the German Flatts settlement & while also said company was stationed in Fort Dayton a part of the said company about 18 men were sent from said Fort under Ensign Woodward into Oneida & as far as to what is now called Stockbridge—were gone three days & when they returned—he does not know the object of their going to Stockbridge—that while said company was stationed in said fort the Indians & Tories broke into Shallsbush in the now County of Herkimer when Captain McKean & this company marched in pursuit of the Indians & Tories about three days in pursuit & return to the Fort & that he & others of the company to the number of six or eight men was sent to guard three men to Albany which they did & returned, again to the Fort & while in said Fort he did other service not of importance & remained with said company until New Year's day following having served said nine months & then returned home—no state troops were during said nine months at said Fort except a few German Flatts militia whose officers names he does not remember. He was repeatedly out on some scouting parties while in Fort Dayton. That he left said last service on Jan 1 1779 having served nine months.

That about 1st April 1779 he again volunteered as a private in the Militia Company of which Garret Putman (2) was Capt—Isaac Paris son of Isaac Paris who was killed in the Oriskany battle was (as he thinks) Lieutenant and Solomon Woodard was his Ensign—but he cannot distinctly recollect—but believes so & the same [blot] served in the company & acted (he thinks) as such & Lieut & Ensign & to what regiment [blot] belonged he cannot say, recollect the company, whole regiment was not commanded by field officers left Major Andrew Finck (3) & Col or Major Charles Newkirk (4) informed [blot] they were living the said company belong to their Regiment—He resided in Town of Palatine & in the now County of Montgomery, when he volunteered in the last mentioned service, that he volunteered for nine months—that the said company was marched to Fort Dayton where it was stationed [blot] he went in the scouting parties several times—about forty men of said company including some German Flatts militia were dispatched, --his Capt. Putman calling for volunteers, the number aforesaid volunteered from the Fort to go after some Indians & Tories that had broken into the surrounding settlements burning & destroying every thing in their way—they marched about five miles from the Fort & then on their return to the Fort within a mile of the Fort they found in their absence the Indians & Tories had broken in & killed some of the citizens & assisted in removing to the Fort the wounded - the tories & Indians retreated & fled on the approach of Capt. Putman's men & that he & some others made several trips from said Fort to guard some provisions to Fort Stanwix (6) where he understood Col. Gansevoort (5) commanded, but he did not know him--& did not see him but saw a number of officers at Fort Stanwix whose names he did not hear & know during said last nine months service that Capt. Putman Company & several other companies, towards the end of said nine months service were at Fort Stanwix about six weeks relieving the troops in the Fort Stanwix [blot] just off to the eastward as he understood & only one officer called a major a tall man remained & commanded the troops who had arrived at the Fort & hand the command of the Fort then—Col. Gansevoort with other forces in the Fort when he [blot] in Capt. Putman company & the other companies arrived moved & went off—that Putman company in which said Fred'k Baum was a private stayed about six weeks at Fort Stanwix when some Continental troops (as he then understood) came to the Fort & then Capt. Putman & his company left, the Fort & [blot] after [blot] was dismissed but rec'd no written discharge. That in March or 1st April or thereabouts in the year 1780 the said Frederick Baum again volunteered as a private in the militia of said state in the company whereof Lawrence Gross (7) was Capt. -One Wynne (8) was Lieutenant according to his recollection & Simon Vrooman (9) he thinks was ensign in the said company in the Regt. of Col. Marinus Willett's that he volunteered for nine months & resided there in the Town of Minden & in the now County of Montgomery & then County of Tryon where he so volunteered in the last mentioned company—that the company of Capt. Gros in which said Baum belonged was marched to Fort Plain where Col. Willett Commanded—that the principal part of said time of nine months & said Baum with the company to which said Baum belonged was stationed in Fort Plain—that Capt. Gros several times while at said Fort sent said Baum with some other men & some friendly Indians on Scouting parties to Springfield a distance of about 10 or 12 miles from said fort—that said Baum was several times selected by Capt. Gros as express from the Fort Plain to Fort Herkimer where there was a major whose name he does not recollect to whom he handed his package of letter & returned to Fort Plain sometimes with letters from Fort Herkimer that said Baum once during said nine months while on express from Fort Plain to Fort Herkimer was pursued by a party of Indians by [blot] he escaped & arrived safe to Fort Herkimer with letters said Baum & was sent on express to Fort Herkimer when Col. Willet had the battle at Turlock (10) which prevented his being engaged in the said battle - that said Baum was while in said last service in Gross Company also engaged in repairing the Fort Plain—that adjutant Fonda (so called) (11) was at Fort Plain & does not remember the other field officers at Fort Plain—that he left the Service in Capt. Gros' Company about 1 Jan 1781 having served nine months in said Capt. Gros' Company. That said Baum when the Battle at Johnstown was had by Col Willett was employed & directed by Capt. Gros to press teams to go after Col. Willett & men to supply them with provisions & that shortly after the Oriskany battle [blot]about 14 Augt 1777, said Baum was called out into service into the Militia company of Henry Diefendorf (12) who had however personally was [blot] on the Oriskany battle - said company of the said Baum entered was commanded by Lieut. Jacob Diefendorf in said Jacob Klock Regt of Militia in that he lived in that new town of Minden in now County of Montgomery & State aforesaid when he entered the company Commanded by Lieut. Jacob Diefendorf—that said Baum was marched about 13 Augt 1777 from Minden in said last mentioned company to Fall Hill near the dwelling house of Genl Herkimer (13) who had been wounded at Oriskany battle of which wounds he died & that he was about six days in said last in said company of which Geo Countryman (14) was the Lieut.—Ensign name not recollected—said Baum having served said six days returned home to Minden being dismissed, but rec'd no discharge—

And said Baum further states that at other times he served in the militia during said war of the revolution under different officers and amounting to [blot] in all, enclosing of aforesaid service but things it unnecessary to give a further or more full statement thereof as he served twenty months besides & before particulars specified & detailed.

That he was born in the Town of Palatine in the then county of Tryon (now said county of Montgomery) & in the year 1760 as he believes but does not exactly know his age—has no record of his age—then where he rendered the services before mentioned he resided in the Town of Palatine & Minden in the County of Montgomery In State of New York as before stated & has since the revolution lived partly in the Town of Minden & partly in the Town of Palatine & now resides in the Town of Oppenheim in said County of Montgomery—that he volunteered into the service for the twenty seven months before mentioned by him, severing nine months at a time & was for the other services called out by his officers—that he cannot further state the general circumstances of his services nor the names of officers & Regts than he has before stated—that he never recd any discharge from service, except one from Capt. Gros when he served in said Capt's Company which is lost—that said Baum is known to his neighbors Marcus Duesler & Henry Flander who can testify to his character for veracity & their belief of his services as a soldier of the revolution—

That he has no documentary evidence of his services—He hereby relinquishes every claim whatever to a pension or annuity except the present & declares that his name is not on the pension roll of the agency of any state—that no clergyman resides in his neighborhood—that he knows of no person whose testimony he can procure who can testify to his services in the company of Capt. Robert McKean first mentioned services of nine months detailed in [blot] his declaration & nor does he know of any person who can testify to his other services except Marcus Duesler and Henry Flander in relation to his other two nine months service before set forth that he has & knows of no other person or persons who can testify to his other services during the revolutionary war that he cannot write his name. (Signed with his mark) Frederick Baum

Sworn & Subscribed the day & year aforesaid before me in open court.

Geo. D. Ferguson, Clerk

State of New York

Montgomery County SS.

Personally appeared before me the undersigned a Justice of the Peace of the Town of Oppenheim in & for said County this 15 day of January A.D. 1833. Frederick Baum of the same town & County & to me personally known & who being duly sworn says in order to amend & correct his declaration made the 21st day of September in the Court of said County for a pension, that by reason of old age & the consequent loss of his memory he has made some mistakes in his said original declaration in this that he therein states "that on or about the first day of April 1778", he entered as a soldier the company whereof Robert McKean was Capt & left said service "on Jan 1, 1779" & also in the time he entered & left the service in Capt. Garret Putman's Company--& that he desires in his said declaration in those particulars to be considered as amended as stated below—that since he made his said original declaration he recollected that while he served in said Capt. McKean's company at Fort Dayton he heard of General Sullivan's expedition against the Indians & that some of the soldiers who went with that expedition came to Fort Dayton & then served in the same company of Capt. McKean. That those circumstances corrected his memory & he believes it was in the year 1779 he served his said company & he further says that by reason of his old age and the consequent loss of memory he cannot swear positively as to the precise length of his services but according to the best of his present recollection he served not less than the periods mentioned below & in the following grades viz: That he served as a private soldier in the company whereof Robert McKean was Capt. John Smith Lieut from the first day of April 1779 to the first day of January 1780 for nine months—that the said company according to his recollection served & were considered as New York State Levies –is positive he served nine months in said company—but he does not remember that any of the field officers accompanied said company, nor does he know the Regt to which said company was attached & cannot be believes ascertain that fact--& knows of no person he can procure to testify to said nine months service.—

2. That he served as a private soldier in the New York State Levies in the company whereof Garret Putman was Capt. Solomon Woodworth Ensign, Isaac Paris Lieutenant in the Regt whereof Lewis Dubois (15) was Col. John Harper Lieut Col. for nine months the year following he served in Capt. McKean's Company that is he served in said Putman's company from first day of April 1780 to the first day of January 1781, as a private for nine months & hereby desires his said original declaration to be amended accordingly & further says that while in said nine months service the said Putman's company he saw Marcus Duesler at or near where Utica City now if according to his recollection or in the previous (near where he served in McKean's company .

3. That he served as a private soldier in the company whereof Lawrence Gros was Capt. in that Regt whereof Marinus Willett was Col & Josiah Throop (16) was the Major from the first day of April A.D. 1781 to the first day of January 1782 for nine months as one of the New York State Levies--

That he served as a private soldier in the Company commanded by Lieut. Jacob Diefendorf from the 14 Augt 1777 to the twenty first day of August 1777 for six days & for aforesaid services. (Signed with his mark) Frederick Baum

Subscribed to & Sworn this 15th day of January A.D. 1833 before me Ashabal Loomis, Justice of the Peace.
State of New York
Fulton County SS.

On this 22 day of April 1854, appeared before me Wm. Spencer a Justice of the Peace in and for said County, the subscriber Margaret Baum, (17) who being duly sworn deposes & says that she is the widow of Frederick Baum deceased that said Frederick received a pension for services rendered in the Revolutionary war with Great Britain said deponent says that she does not recollect the number of said Baum's pension certificate nor has she the means of obtaining as the said Baums agent returned said certificate to the office of the Interior at Washington after the death of said Baum said Baum's certificate entitled him to ninety six dollars per year deponent further says that said Baum departed this life in the fall of 1843—that the undersigned was married to the said Frederick Baum in the spring or summer of 1840 & in proof thereof the affidavit of Henry F. Baum is hereunto attached she therefore claims the benefit of the act of Congress of February 1853 and she requests that her name may be inscribed on the roll of pensioners under the said act. (Signed with her mark) Margaret Baum

Sworn & Subscribed before me this 22 day of April 1854—Wm. Spencer, Justice of the Peace, attest James N. Everest

End Notes—W.15835—Frederick Baum or Boom

1. The service was in 1779, Frederick corrected his errors in his January 15, 1833 application. Robert McKean was appointed Captain in Lieutenant Colonel Commandant Henry K. VanRensselaer's Regiment of New York State Levies in April of 1779. There is no record of a muster roll for this company. John Smith was appointed a lieutenant in this regiment and many of the pensioners mention Smith as one of their lieutenants. Solomon Woodworth's name does not appear on the list of officers appointed for this regiment. Some of the pensioners mentioned Walter J. Vrooman as the other lieutenant for this company. Vrooman is listed on the list of officers that were appointed to this regiment. FROM: Revolutionary War Rolls 1775-1783, Series M-246, Roll 75, folder 134 (listed under Pawling's Regiment as both regiments of Levies were raised at the same time.) National Archives, Washington, D.C
2. This service was in 1780. Garret Putman was appointed on May 11, 1780 in Lieutenant-Colonel Commandant John Harper's Regiment of New York State Levies. Isaac Paris and Solomon Woodworth were lieutenants in this company. FROM: Revolutionary War Rolls 1775-1783, Series M-246, Roll 74, folder 112, National Archives, Washington, D.C.
3. Andrew Finck in 1780 was captain in the First New York Continental Regiment under Colonel Goose VanSchaick. The 1st NY was stationed at Fort Schuyler which was once called Fort Stanwix, until about October 1st when Harper's Regiment replaced the 1st NY.
4. He may be referring to the John Newkirk who was the Major in Colonel Frederick Visscher's Third Regiment of Tryon County Militia. Charles Nukirk or Newkirk served as a Captain in the Second New York Continental Regiment until January 1, 1781.
5. Peter Gansevoort was Colonel of the Third New York Continental Regiment. This regiment was not in the Mohawk Valley in 1780 or Fort Schuyler.
6. Harper's Regiment was replaced by the Fourth New York Continental Regiment on November 22, and Harper's Regiment marched out of the fort on the 23rd. The regiment was discharged on November 30. This service was actually only for seven months.
7. Frederick enlisted as a private on April 29, 1781 in Captain Lawrence Gros' Company in Lieutenant-Colonel Commandant Marinus Willett's Regiment of New York State Levies. FROM: Revolutionary War Rolls 1775-1783, Series M-246, Roll 78, folder 173, National Archives, Washington, D.C.
8. Lieutenant Jacob Winney was in Willett's Regiment but in Captain Peter VanRensselaer's Company.
9. The lieutenants in Captain Gros' Company were Jacob Sammons, Simon J. Vrooman and Timothy Hutton.

10. The Battle of New Dorlach was fought on July 10, 1781.
11. Jellis A. Fonda served as a Lieutenant and Adjutant in Willett's Regiment until November of 1782 when he was promoted to Captain.
12. Henry Dieffendorf was Captain of the Fifth Company in Colonel Ebenezer Cox's First Regiment of Tryon County Militia. Captain Dieffendorf was killed at the Battle of Oriskany on August 6, 1777. Jacob Dieffendorf a brother of Henry, was the First Lieutenant and after the death his brother Jacob was promoted to Captain of the Fifth Company.
13. Nicholas Herkimer, Brigadier General of the Tryon County Militia Brigade.
14. George Countryman was appointed the Ensign in the Fifth Company on August 26, 1775. He was appointed First Lieutenant on March 4, 1780 in the Fifth Company.
15. Lewis DuBois was the Colonel of a different regiment of New York State Levies.
16. Josiah Throop was appointed Major on April 28, 1781 in Willett's Regiment.
17. In Margaret's application James Wilson made out a supporting deposition for proof of her marriage as follows: "On the 9th day of May Frederick Baum of the Town of Oppenheim County of Fulton and Margaret Duesler of the same place were married by me & Henry F. Baum & wife and Joseph Baum were present as witnesses at said marriage", dated February 13, 1855. Wilson was a Justice of the Peace in 1840. She was still alive on May 30, 1871 because she applied for an increase in her pension under the Act of July 27, 1868. She was living at Garoga, Town of Ephratah, Fulton County at the age of 81.

Pension Application for Aaron Baxter

S.12064
Aaron Baxter was granted pension of $60.00 per annum.
State of New York
Steuben County SS.

On the 17th day of October in the year 1832 personally appeared in open court before the Court of Common Pleas now sitting Aaron Baxter a resident of the town of Addison in the County of Steuben and State aforesaid aged sixty-six years in November last, who being first duly sworn according to law doth on his oath make the following declaration in order to obtain the benefit of the act of Congress passed June 7, 1832—That he entered the service of the United States under the following named officers and served as herein stated.

That he first entered the United States service, in the month of March about the first of that month 1782, in the town of Spencer in the County of Columbia & State of New York where he then resided, by enlisting into the New

York State of Troops, as a substitute for a classman, nine months - was mustered and received into service at Kinderhook in said county—joined his company at Albany -Capt. Henry (1) commanded the company, don't recollect the names of his other officers—marched to Schenectady—thence to Fort Hunter up the Mohawk river, --remained for some time—thence to Johnstown—thence sent with a party to a small place called CorryTown (2) where there was a small picket fort returned in about a month to Johnstown - sent from there to White Plains—while on the march to White Plains an express was sent after us and we were ordered back as the Indians and Tories were doing much mischief—marched back to Johnstown—remained some time at Johnstown thence to Canada Creek which empties into the Mohawk river. This applicant was engaged there with a small party as Indian Spies—sent him there to Fort Herkimer—Returned to Fort Plain when we arrived near Fort Plain, an officer came out and met us—said the people at the Fort had the small pox—and there said that we were dismissed—this was on the last day of the year 1782—arrived at home about the 6th of January 1783 at Spencertown, Columbia County. The above service was performed in a Regiment commanded by Col. Willet—remembers the names of the following officers belonging to said corps—Capt. Fondey (3)—Capt. Tearce & Lieutenant Johnson, having served ten months—Did not receive a written discharge.

That early in the Spring about the ninth of May 1783, Samuel Hosford (4), a soldier belonging to Col. Willetts Regiment returned home and this applicant went out as a substitute for him; joined the company at Schenectady and remained there, except that went occasionally on scouts, until we were discharged which was on the sixth day of January 1784 as appears by the annexed discharge, signed by Capt. Peter B. Tearce (5), Capt. Command't & Countersigned by Adjutant P. Moore at Schenectady having served eight months. That he has no other proof of his services, documentary or otherwise.

Was born in Hebron, County of Hartford and State of Connecticut in the [year] 1766. Has no record of his age. Lived at Spencertown in Columbia. When called into service moved from there to Smithfield Chenango County: thence to Addison Steuben County where he now resides—Called into service in the manner already stated & performed service as he has stated in the manner herein before mentioned. The discharge which he received is hereto annexed.

He hereby relinquishes every claim whatever to a pension or annuity except the present and declares that his name is not on the pension roll of the agency of any state. (Signed) Aaron Baxter

Sworn & subscribed the day and year aforesaid. M. L. Rumsey Dep. Clerk, Steuben County

End Notes—Aaron Baxter—S.120641

1. Aaron served as a private in Captain National Henry' Company in Colonel Marinus Willett's Regiment of New York State Levies.
2. Currytown is in the present day Town of Root, Montgomery County. The small picket fort may be Fort Lewis.

3. Captains Jellis A. Fonda, Peter B. Tearce and Lieutenant Witter Johnson [Johnston] were officers in Willett's Levies.
4. Samuel Horsford served as a private in Captain Joseph Harrison's Company in Colonel Willett's Regiment. According to Harrison's company Payroll for 1783, Samuel served 10 months. After Captain Harrison retired, Samuel was transferred to Captain Simeon Newell's Company which company he served another month. Under the causalities column the following was written. "Exchanged for Baxter". This means Aaron actually did not serve until December 1, 1783. FROM: Revolutionary War Rolls 1775-1783, Series M-246, Roll 78, Folder 173, National Archives, Washington D.C.
5. Extract from the Regiment of the New York State Battalion as follows—Name of Men: *Aaron Baxter.* Remarks *In place of Samuel Horsford.* Discharged: *January 6, 1784.* Schenectady January 7th, 1784. Attest P. Moor Adjut. Peter B. Tearce Capt. Commandant State Batt. Colonel Willett land Major Andrew Finck Jr. had retired on November 1, 1783. The command of the regiment then fell to Major Elias VanBenschoten who retired on January 1, 1784 and now Captain Tearce commanded the regiment. FROM: Revolutionary War Rolls, 1775-1783, Series M-246, Roll 78, folder 173, National Archives, Washington, D.C.

Pension Application for Andrew Bearup or Barob or Barrup

W.16188 (Widow: Magdalene)
Bateaumen under Captain William Peters and in a company of Joseph Peek and in a company of Captain Peters.
State of New York SS.
Albany County

On this fifth day of June 1837, personally appeared before me James Haliday one of Judges of the Court of Common Pleas in and for said County Magdalena Barob, or Barup, a resident of the town of New Scotland in the county of Albany and State of New York, aged eighty years, who being first duly sworn according to law, doth on her oath, make the following declaration, in order to obtain the benefit of the provision made by the act of Congress, passed July 4, 1836; that she is the widow of Andrew Barop who was a private soldier in the militia of the State of New York & the Department of the QuarterMaster General of said State as in particularly set forth in the depositions hereto annexed.

She further declares that she was married to the said Andrew Barop on the seventh day of July (1782) in the year seventeen hundred and eighty two; that her husband Andrew Barop died in the month of October 1796 and that she has remained a widow ever since that period, as will more fully appear by reference to the proof hereunto annexed. (Signed with her mark) Magdalone Barrup

Sworn to and subscribed on the day and year above written before me, said Judge Jas Haliday.

This deposition of Christopher Ward of the City of Schenectada in the County of Schenectada and State of New York who being duly sworn and examined testifies and says, that he is now of the age of Eighty years and was a soldier of the revolutionary war and is a pensioner of the United States under the Act of 7th June 1832. This deponent was during the life time of Andrew Bearup the same person referred to in the annexed papers as the husband of the before named declarant was acquainted with said Andrew Bearup. That this deponents acquaintance with the said Andrew or Andries commenced in the year 1765 when he this deponent was a resident of said City then Township of Schenectada. This deponent is well acquainted with Magdalen Bearup the widow of the said Andrew Bearup and also knew her before her intermarriage with the said Andrew Bearup when she was born the name of Magdalena Cramer. The said Magdalen was married to the said Andrew as this deponent thinks in the year 1781. The said Magdalena is still living and remains the widow of the said Andrew Bearup or Bearop having never intermarried since his death according to the best of this deponents knowledge information and belief. This Deponent further saith that his personal knowledge of the military services of said Andrew Bearup [?] to the following particulars to wit. This deponent and said Andrew Bearup were both members of the same company of Militia in the District of Schenectada when the revolutionary war commenced to wit in the company commanded by Capt. John Mynderse (1) of the Regiment of Col. Abraham Wemple at the end of the year 1775 or beginning of the year 1776 when the said Andrew Bearup and this deponent proceeded together in said company & with the militia from said district and from other places to Caughnawaga to capture Sir John Johnson & his tenants & dependents in this aforesaid Andrew Bearup was on the march and Garrison more than 9 or 10 days. The next time this deponent saw Andrew Bearup perform military duty was at Stone Arabia in the fall of the year 1779 he this deponent being at this same time on duty and at the same place for this time of six weeks said Andrew Bearup was on duty at said Fort in that [?] for the like time of six weeks—Andrew Bearup then informed of this deponent his said term on duty ten days before he this deponent arrived and Andrew Bearup also informed this deponent that he [?] served said six weeks and five days, part of this time on [can't make out several lines] part of this time as a substitute for the aforesaid. General TenBroeck had command of Fort Paris at Stone Arabia in this season, Andrew Bearup & this deponent performed duty together in said company of Capt. Mynderse at Fort Hunter in the spring season the month of May in the year 1780, said Andrew for the term of at least eight days. In the year 1779 (3) from January till May when he & this deponent was a [?] blacksmith and on duty as such at Saratoga. He this deponent and said Andrew Bearup serving in the company commanded by Captain William Peters (4) in the Department of the QuarterMaster General and left him there in the month of May 1780 when as this deponent understood said Andrew Bearup was a member of the company of Captain Joseph Peek (5) in the same department and in the fall of this year last mentioned when Ballston was destroyed by the enemy this deponent saw said Bearup on duty in said company of Captain Joseph Peek at Saratoga. (Signed with his mark) Christopher Ward

On this 23d day of August 1837 personally appeared before me the undersigned Christopher Ward above named who made oath that the facts set forth in the foregoing deposition by him signed are true and I certify that said Christopher Ward is a credible witness and I further certify that the said Christopher Ward signed the above affidavit by making his mark or Cross in consequence of weakness or bodily infirmity. [?] Justice of the Peace.

County of Schenectady SS.

Christopher Ward of the City of Schenectada in the said county, aged eighty-one years, a pensioner of the United States, being further duly sworn saith, that in addition to the facts set forth in his affidavit, heretofore made in the matter of the application of the aforenamed Andrew Bearup for a pension, he remembers well that said Andrew served in the company of Batteaumen fatigue men and laborers commanded by Captain William Peters, as well as in the company of Captain Joseph L. Peek as heretofore testified and that he served in said company of Captain Peters in the year 1779, this deponent saw him several times doing duty in said company of Captain Peters from the spring of the year 1779, until the spring of the year 1780, when as this deponent believes he joined the company of said Captain Peek, and this deponent entertains no doubt but that said Andrew Bearup served in said company of Captain Peters for the full term of one year—This deponent also remembers hearing at the time thereof & is assured of the fact, that said Andrew served in the State Troops under Colonel Willett in 1781 or 1782 (6), but this deponent can give no specification of such service. (Signed) Chris Ward

On this 31st day of July 1838 personally appeared before me Christopher Ward above named & made oath that the facts set forth in the above deposition by him signed are true & I certify that said Christopher Ward is a credible witness. John H. Van Eps, J.P.

End Notes—Andrew Bearup (Barope, Barup, Barcup, etc.)- W.16188

1. Andrew served as a private in Captain John Mynderse's Company (Second Company) in Colonel Abraham Wemple's Second Regiment of Albany County Miltia.
2. Brigadier General Abraham TenBroeck.
3. Andrew is listed on Captain Nicholas Veeder's pay roll for a company of Carpenters at Saratoga and Fort George in building barracks, battoes, commencing the seventh day of January and ending the (rest is torn). Andrew is shown as enlisting January 26. The year could be 1779. They were building bateaus for Brigadier General James Clinton in preparation for the 1779 Iroquois Campaign. FROM: Revolutionary

War Rolls 1775-1783, Series M-246, Roll 122, folder 77, National Archives, Washington, DC.

4. So far a muster or pay roll for this company of batteaumen has not been found.

Pension Application for Abraham Becker

S.12,994
Pension granted $80.00 per annum
State of New York
Otsego County SS.

On this 19th day of June AD 1833, personally appeared in open court before the Judges of the Court of Common Pleas in and for the County of Otsego aforesaid now sitting, Abraham Becker a resident of the Town of Worcester in the County of Otsego and State of New York aged Eighty three years who being first duly sworn according to Law doth on his oath, make the following declaration in order to obtain the benefit of the Act of Congress passed June 7th 1832—

That early in the spring of the year 1776 he the said Abraham Becker volunteered and enlisted into a company commanded by Capt. Marcellus (1) of the City of Albany in the State of New York in Col. Gansevorts Regiment (2) for the period of nine months at this time he resided with his father on the Charlotte in the County of Tryon, now Otsego County in the State of New York—he volunteered at Schoharie and immediately went to Albany where he joined in Capt. Marcellus Company and which was as early as the first of April in the year 1776—and he further saith that he remained with said company in the City of Albany about one month and then marched in said company to Fort George and was there stationed and continued in actual service for the full period of nine months and was then discharged and received a discharge in writing signed by Capt. Marcellus—but which has been lost or destroyed for a great number of years past.—

And he further saith that some part of Col. Gansevort's Regiment was stationed at Skeensburgh (3), some part at Ticonderoga and at Fort George—That he was frequently at Ticonderoga during the said nine months service—and was frequently out in scouting parties in different directions—recollects that Col. Dubois (4) of Catskill had command of a regiment at Fort George at the time he the said Abraham Becker was at Fort George several times, recollects well of having marched there—and at Ticonderoga. He was not engaged in any Battle during the said nine months and when he was discharged, he returned home to his father on the Charlotte—

And he further states that in the month of April 1777 he again volunteered into a Company of militia commanded by Capt. Alexander Harper (5) and Lieutenant Bartholomew (6) in a Regiment commanded by Col. John Harper for the period of nine months—That he joined the company on the Charlotte—and within a few days thereafter Capt. Harpers Company took John Dockstader, Daniel Servos & Jacob Servos prisoners - who were all Tories then residing on the Charlotte, and who were harbouring and had joined with the Indians in opposition to the Revolution. That Capt. Harpers company took said Tories as far as Cherry Valley and there delivered them over to the Committee of Safety to be conveyed to Johnstown Jail and Capt Harpers company return back to Charlotte and remained there stationed at Lieut. Bartholomews for a considerable time how long cannot precisely recollect from the Charlotte was marched to Brakebeens on the Schoharie Kill and was there stationed for some time, cannot exactly recollect—and was stationed at Turlough now Sharon in Schoharie County—and at Harpersfield Delaware County during that nine months service and in the fall of the year he and the soldiers under Capt. Harper assisted in building the Forts in Schoharie which were erected this season and he the said Abraham Becker was stationed at the upper Fort for some time cannot say how long, but well recollects of marching to Harpersfield and was then discharged by Col. Harper at the expiration of the said nine months service—and at this time the snow was about six inches deep—and he further saith that during this nine months service his father and family removed from the Charlotte to Schoharie near the upper fort—and on receiving his discharge he went to his fathers house and continued there through the winter.

And the said Abraham Becker further declares that in the Spring of the year 1778 he volunteered at Schoharie into a company of Militia commanded by Capt. Jacob Hager (7) in Col. Peter Vrooman's Regiment—He went into the service at the time as early as the first of May and continued in actual service in said company until between Christmas and New Year—during this season Col. Harper went to Albany to obtain assistance to repel the Indians and Tories who were destroying every thing that came in their way—Col. Harper obtained a company of light horses at Albany and came back to Schoharie and the enemy [?] was well acquainted with Col. Vroomans and Col. Hager—during this year he was frequently our in Scouting parties in CoblesKill and the country in the region of the forts and he further states that he was in the service this year at least seven months. And the said Abraham Becker further declares that he entered into a company of Militia Commanded by Capt. Gray (8) in Col. Van Schaick (9) Regiment the first of April 1782 for the period of nine months and was stationed with said company in said Regiment at the Middle Fort on the Schoharie Kill and continued then in actual service for the full period of nine months and was then marched to Schenectady and discharged from the service—was frequently out in Scouting parties during this nine months service—well recollects that Col. Dubois (10) was stationed at Schoharie at this same time—recollects that Storm Becker (11) was a Lieutenant in Capt. Grays Company.

And that when he was discharged from this nine months service he received a written discharge but cannot recollect by whom it was signed and the same has been lost or destroyed for a great number of years—

And he further declares that he was Born in New Jersey nigh Hackensack in the year 1750—

That he has no record of his age to his knowledge or believe.

That he was living when first called into service on the Charlotte as above stated—and also the second time he went into the service as above stated and during the remainder of his service and until the close of the war he resided at Schoharie in the State of New York—The manner of his being called into service is as above stated—and that he never served as a substitute for any person.

The names of the officers who were with the troops where he served are as fully set forth as the same can now be recollected—

That since the Revolution has resided in Coeymans in Albany - also in Upper Canada—from which place he removed to Worcester in the County of Otsego New York where he now resides—

That he received written discharges from the service at the times and in the manner above stated—and which have been lost or destroyed—

And he further declares that he is known to John Flansburgh, Abraham Fisher Esq., Jacob P. Becker who reside in his present neighborhood and who can testify as to his character for veracity and their belief of his services as a soldier of the Revolution—

And he further declares that he has no documentary evidence and that he knows of no person whose testimony he can procure who can testify to his services except the testimony of Jacob France and Catharine Flansburg which is hereunto annexed—and also that there is not any clergyman residing in his neighborhood, or in the section where he resides, wherefore he cannot procure the testimony of a clergyman in compliance with the instructions from the War Department.—

And the said Abraham Becker hereby relinquishes every claim whatever to a pension or annuity except the present and declares that his name is not on the pension roll of the agency of any state—and he the said Abraham Becker further saith that by reason of old age and the consequent loss of memory he cannot swear more positive as to the precise length of service than as herein before set forth and further saith not. (Signed with his mark) Abraham Becker

Sworn to and subscribed the day and year aforesaid in open court. Horace Lathrop. Clerk.

And the said Abraham Becker further states and declares in answer to the interrogatories prescribed by the War department in manner following that is to say.

1st I was born in the State of New Jersey nigh Hackensack in the year 1750.

2d I have no record of my age.

3d I was living at Charlotte in the County of Otsego New York and at Schoharie in the County of Schoharie when called into service—That since the revolution I have resided in Coeymans in the County of Albany New York—also in the Province of Upper Canada—and on the Charlotte in the Town of Worcester in the County of Otsego New York where I now reside.

4th I volunteered at each time I was called into service, and never served as a substitute for any person.

5th I have stated the names of the officers who were with the troops where I served in my original declaration hereto annexed as fully as I recollect the service and also the general circumstances of my service I have therein stated as fully as I now recollect the same.

6th I received a written discharge from the first nine months service performed in the year 1776 signed by Capt. Marcellus in whose company I served. I also received a written discharge from the nine months service performed in the year 1782 but by whom it was signed I cannot recollect both of which said discharges have been lost for many years.

7th I am acquaintcd with John Flansburgh, Jacob P. Becker, and Abraham Becker of my present neighborhood who can testify to his character for veracity and their belief of my services as a soldier of the Revolution. (Signed with his mark) Abraham Becker

Sworn & subscribed in open court June 19, 1833. Horace Lathrop, Clerk

End Notes—S.12994—Abraham Becker

1. Henry Merselis was a Captain in Colonel Cornelius Van Dyck's Additional New York Continental Regiment.
2. He is mistaken as Peter Gansevoort was appointed Lieutenant-Colonel on March 19, 1776 in Colonel Goose VanSchaick's Continental Regiment. He was appointed Colonel of the Third New York Continental Regiment on November 21, 1776.
3. Skenesborough is present day Whitehall, Washington County, N.Y.
4. Colonel Lewis DuBois was appointed Colonel of a regiment of New York Continentals (not numbered) on June 21, 1776. On November 21, 1776 he was appointed Colonel of the Fifth New York Continental Regiment.
5. Captain Alexander Harper in Colonel John Harper's Fifth Regiment of Tryon County Militia.
6. First Lieutenant Joseph Bartholomew in Captain Lodowick Brakeman's (Breakman, etc.) Company in the Fifth Regiment of Tryon County Militia.
7. Captain Jacob Hager of the Second Company in Colonel Peter Vrooman's Fifteenth Regiment of Albany County Militia.
8. Captain Silas Gray's Company in Colonel Marinus Willett's Regiment of New York State Levies. This company did not reach its enlistment quota and by July of 1782, all of Captain Gray's recruits were transferred to other companies in Willett's Regiment. Abraham was transferred to Captain Joseph Harrison's Company.
9. Several other pensioners also claim to have enlisted in Captain Gray's Company in Colonel Goose VanSchaick's First New York Continental Regiment of New York in 1782 but as the enlistments never reached the quota needed and Willett was not filling his own regiment with

badly needed recruits, it became necessary to discharge several company officers and keep the recruits for his regiment.

10. Abraham is wrong on this tour. Colonel DuBois and the Fifth New York were at the Schoharie Forts from December 1778 to about June of 1779. The regiment then marched under Brigadier General James Clinton to join Major General John Sullivan in an expedition against the Iroquois in the western part of New York. Colonel DuBois resigned from the Fifth New York on December 22, 1779. Colonel DuBois was appointed on July 1, 1780 to command a regiment of New York State Levies but for the most part he was in the Mohawk Valley. He retired from the service after 1780.
11. Storm A. Becker was a Lieutenant in Captain Joseph Harrison's Company in Colonel Willett's Regiment.

Pension Application for Constant Beebe

S.14942
State of New York
Columbia County SS.

On this 3 day of September 1833 personally appeared before Medad Butler a Judge of the Court of Common Pleas in and for the said County of Columbia, Constant Beebe, a resident of the town of Chatham county and State aforesaid aged 68 years who first being duly sworn according to law, doth on his oath make the following declaration in order to obtain the benefit of the provision made by the act of congress passed June 7, 1832.

That he entered the service of the United States under the following named officers and served in the militia or Levy service as herein stated.

On or about the 15 June 1778 he volunteered as a private under Captain Josiah Warner (1), Lieut. Davenport (2), and served as waiter to his Uncle Major Martin Beebe (3) who was an inhabitant of the same neighborhood and town with the applicant. This declarant believes that the manner of service as waiter was understood before his engagement—he was organized at New Concord (4) so called and Albany County (now Columbia) Thence marched through Albany to guard the Western frontier—was stationed at Cherry Valley for some time was frequently on guard, when not otherwise engaged as waiter to his uncle who he thinks commanded the Corps which went or march from this county and district to the north.—he recollects standing on guard in an orchard, whilst at Cherry Valley, the inhabitants of which come within the guard every night for safety, and frequently when the inhabitants were sent to milk their cows, a guard was sent with them. Col. Campbell (5) and Major Dixon (6) were at this place but he does not recollect that they had any command—thence marched to Caughnawaga from thence to Johnstown, he recollects of going into the church at that place and for the first time heard church organs, thence marched to Albany and home where he arrived the first of August, making in this tour of service as he verily believes not less than 1 ½ month

(See Sam. Doty's deposition marked A) On or about the 1 of June 1779 he volunteered as private in the militia service under Captain Gideon King (7) of New Lebanon—Lieut. Deavenport, Colo. Asa Waterman (8) was organized at New Concord in the immediate vicinity and place of residence of this declarant—Thence marched to Albany, thence to Schenectada was there billeted (9) village and was then out on scouts and scoured the then forests in Duanesburgh and other places in pursuit of Indians and Tories thence marched back to Albany there was dismissed and returned home on or about the 15 July—this tour of service as he verily believes was not less than 1 ½ month.

On or about the 1 of October 1779 he volunteered as a private under Captain Ebenezer Cady, Lieut Nathaniel Rowley (10), Colo. Asa Waterman the time for which he engaged was 3 months, was organized at New Concord Albany County, thence marched to Fishkills. Other Regiments at this place were Colo. Platts, Colo. Heathhorn's, Colo Graham's and Colo. Dubois' (11)–was there on guard and performed the usual duties of a camp then was dismissed and returned about the last of Nov. he recollects well that it was cold weather before he was dismissed. They had to and did build fire places of turf—this term of service as he verily believes was not less than 3 months--(Vide Saml Doty's Deposition marked A)

On or about the 1 of May 1780 he volunteered as a private under Captain John Davis of the neighborhood of this declarant—Colo. Asa Waterman, Major Martin Beebe, was organized at New Concord, Albany County – and thence marched by the way of Albany to Schoharie was there billeted out, was on various scouts in different places during his station in that place then marched back to Albany was there dismissed and returned home on or about the 15 June his service in this tour as he verily believes was not less than 1 ½ month (Vide Daniel Darrows deposition marked B).

On or about the 1 July 1780 he hired out as a substitute for one Rowly who was head of a class of militia – he was recruited for 3 months under Captain Elijah Bostwick, Lieut. John Calendar, Orderly Sergt. Samuel Brown (12) was organized at the house of Jonathan Warner in Kings district Albany County the company then went different ways to Fishkills, was at that place joined to Colo. John Graham's Regiment. Lieut Colo. Livingston, Major Woolsey, Adjutant Funday Quartermaster Sergt. Truesdell—the other Regiments which were stationed there were nearly the same as those the preceding year (viz.) Platts, Heathorn's, Debois, (13) and some others, he staid at this place 2 or 3 days, thence marched to West Point here he assisted in drawing cannon from Fort Put (14) to the water side for the grand army to the south as was then said; at this place he was on guard when a man was hung as a spy—staid in this place about 3 weeks dthence marched to Haverstraw, thence to Dobb's ferry—whilst at Dobb's ferry a Row Gally belonging to the army got aground or came into Tappan Bay and some shoes were exchanged, but the Gally made off—thence marched back to West Point at this place this Declarant was detached from Capt. Bostwick's company and put under one Capt. Williams (15), who as he was informed was allowed to raise a company from Colo. Graham's Regiment by detaching—from West Point this Declarant with others embarked in Sloops and sailed to Albany—thence the company to which he belonged evacuated by the way of General Schuyler's to Fort Edward to Fort George remained a few days, thence marched to Fort Ann, remained a few days, thence marched back to Fort Edward, there were stationed on guard and other duties of a camp till it was marched by the American's after the enemy had destroyed Fort George and Fort Anna, a party of Indians and Tories came to Fort Edward and burned a number of buildings in sight of the Fort but did not approach so as to be reached by small arms from the Fort during their stay this declarant and others lay on their arms all night expecting an attack, they however decamped and disappeared without any serious injury to the small army in the fort—he well recollects that the women and children came into Fort Edward during the enemy's burning in the vicinity of Fort Ann and Fort Edward. This declarant volunteered to stay longer than his first engagement and did stay and did not arrive at home till about the 1 of Nov. making in this tour of service as he verily believes not less than 4 months (Vide Daniel Darrow's deposition marked B and also William Lius marked C.)

And further this Declarant has no documentary evidence to prove his services, and that he knows of none others by whom he can prove his services excepting those whose depositions he has already obtained and are hereunto attached—

He hereby relinquishes every claim whatever to a pension or annuity except the present, and declares that his name is not on any pension roll of the agency of any state.

In answer to the first interrogatory prescribed by the war department his says.

1. He was born in the town of Sharon, Connecticut, April 5, 1765.
2. He has no other record of his age than that transmitted to him by his parents in a family Bible.
3. & 4. He resided in Kings district Albany County colony of New York and has lived in the aforesaid Kings district until Chatham and Canaan were divided into towns from it, since he has resided a part of the time in Canaan, and the remainder of the time he has resided in Chatham where he now resides and not to exceed 3 miles from the place where he was called into service, he volunteered in every instance, but went as a substitute for one Rowley in the last campaign.
4. (Malcomb, Van Horne) and others herein before mentioned.
5. He does not recollect that he ever received a written discharge, but was dismissed and told to return home. (Signed) Constant Beebe

Sworn and Subscribed the day and year aforesaid. Medad Butler.

End Notes—Constant(ine) Beebe (Beebie, Beeby)—S.14942

1. Josiah Warner was appointed Second Lieutenant in Captain Philip Frisby's Company (Third Company) in October of 1775 in Colonel William B. Whiting's Seventeenth Regiment of Albany County Militia. On June 16, 1778, Captain Frisby was commissioned Second Major of the regiment, First Lieutenant Ebenezer Cady was commissioned the Captain of the Third Company and Warner was now commissioned the First Lieutenant. The Second Lieutenant was Ezra Murray and the Ensign was Elijah Cady.
2. Peter Davenport was the First Lieutenant in Captain Walter Groesbeck's Company (Second Company) in Colonel Peter Yates' Fourteenth Regiment of Albany County Militia.
3. Martin Beebe was commissioned the First Major on June 16, 1778 in the Seventeenth Albany. As Constant was serving as a waiter at age 13 to his uncle this usually would not count as military service as he was under age.
4. Present day Canaan, Columbia County, New York.
5. Samuel Campbell of the First Regiment on Tryon County Militia commissioned on June 25, 1778.
6. There was no major Dixon (Dickson, Dickinson, etc.). There were several Dickson's living in and around Cherry Valley at the time. James Dickson was Captain of a Company of Batteaumen in 1778 and his brother Benjamin was serving as a Lieutenant in Captain Garret Putman's Company of Rangers in 1778.
7. Gideon King was commissioned Captain on March 6, 1779 of the Fourth Company as Captain Nehemiah Fitch had resigned. The other officers were First Lieutenant Peter Barker, Second Lieutenant David Darrow and Ensign David Curtice. They were all in the Seventeenth Albany.
8. Asa Waterman was the Lieutenant-Colonel of the Seventeenth Albany.
9. Billeted usually means they were quartered in inhabitant's homes instead of in a fort.
10. Nathaniel Rowley was the First Lieutenant in Captain John Davis' Company (Fifth Company) in the Seventeenth Albany.
11. Colonel Zephaniah Platt of the Dutchess County Regiment of Associated Exempts, Colonel John Hathorn of the Fourth Regiment of Orange County Militia, Colonel Morris Graham of the First Regiment of Dutchess County Militia and Colonel Lewis DuBois of the Fifth New York Continental Regiment.
12. Captain Elijah Bostwick, Lieutenant John Calender and Sergeant Samuel Brown were all from the Seventeenth Albany. Morris Graham (not John) was appointed as a colonel in 1780 to command a regiment of New York State Levies and Bostwick was appointed Captain in the regiment on July 1, 1780. Henry Livingston was the Lieutenant-Colonel, Major Melancton Woolsey, Adjutant Jellis A. Fonda, and Quartermaster Sergeant William Trusdall all of Graham's Levies.

13. Colonel DuBois had resigned from the Fifth New York on December 22, 1779 and on July 1, 1780 was appointed colonel of a regiment of New York State Levies.
14. Fort Putnam was built as part of West Point's fortifications. It's still part of West Point, New York, and is open to the public for tours.
15. On May 11, 1780, Daniel Williams was appointed Captain in Lieutenant-Colonel Albert Pawlings' Regiment of New York State Levies. Captain Williams and his company had been sent to garrison Fort Edward. In July or August Captain Williams was transferred to Colonel Graham's Regiment. Constant is shown on Captain Williams Muster Roll as enlisting as a private on July 26, 1780. He is not listed on Captain Bostwick's Muster Roll. Many times officers are ordered to collect men and attach them to their companies until they can join their proper company. FROM: Revolutionary War Rolls 1775-1783, Series M-246, Roll 72, Folder 75, National Archives, Washington, DC.
16. Fort Ann was destroyed on October 10, 1780 and Fort George was destroyed on October 11, 1780 by British forces under Major Christopher Carleton. Constantine's father was John Beebe, Jr., who had held several civil offices at New Concord and had kept a diary which included the time period of the War of Independence. A few excerpts relating to Constant are included here: October 1779, 21. Thursday. Col. Waterman (17) with part of the militia march'd for fishKill with whom Constantine went. Mr. Hide Return'd to preach with us again. May 1780. 26. Friday. A small rain some few of the militia turn out and march to Day with whom went Brother Martain (18) and Constant. Col. Whiting called here on his way to the assembly.

    July 1780. 22. Satterday. Cap. Bostwick with part of the militia set out for New York Constant went in the Company. Sep. 1780. 11. Monday. Philo (19) came from Albany where he had been to see Constantine who was about to march to guard the frontiers. Came home came by a fall from his horse. October 1780. 18 Wednesday. News that Ballstown (20) is burnt by the enemy this day married Henry Mott and Lydia Ray, also Joseph Brown and Margaret Mott. Constantine came home from Fort Edward broght new that Fort George and Fort Ann was taken and burnt by the enemy with all the soldiers therein towards 200. FROM:Excerpts from a Diary of John Beebe, Jr., covering the Revolutionary War years 1779 and 1780 in New Concord (Canaan), Columbia County, NY. Transcribed by Richard C. Perry, 1983. MS. No. 13329, New York State Library, Special Collections and Manuscripts, Albany, NY.
17. Asa Waterman had married Lucy Beebe, a sister of John Beebe, Jr., and Aunt of Constant. Also refer to end note no. 8.
18. Martin Beebe, a brother of John Beebe, Jr. Refer to end note no. 3.
19. Philo son of John Beebe, Jr. and Constant's brother.

20. BallsTown was destroyed on October 17, 1780 by British forces under Captain John Munro. BallsTown is present day Ballston Spa, Saratoga County, NY. Constant served under his relatives in the militia of the Seventeenth Albany including Captain John Davis who had married his Aunt Sarah Beebe. Captain Ebenezer Cady had also married his Aunt Chloe Beebe. Eleazer Cady, a private in Captain Cady's Company married Constant's Aunt Tryphena Beebe.

Pension Application for Hopson Beebe

S.4262
Conn., Mass., New York
State of Ohio
Athens County SS.

On this 13th day of October 1832 personally appeared in open Court before the Court of Common Pleas now sitting Hopson Bebee [sic] aged 83 years, who, being first duly sworn, according to law, doth on his oath make the following declaration, in order to obtain the benefit of the Act of Congress passed June 7, 1832. That he entered the service of the United States under the following named officers and served as herein stated viz. That the said Hopson Beebe at Salisbury in the State of Connecticut, in the month of May 1776, as he verily believes, but he knows that it was but a few weeks after the burning of Danbury (1) inlisted into the Service of the United States for the term of nine months in the Company of Abel Catlin (2) in the Regiment then under the charge of Captain Prentiss, (3) the oldest Captain of the same, afterwards commanded as the Deponent believes by Col. Meigs. (4) That after inlistment the Deponent immediately repaired to Fairfield, with the other recruits inlisted at Salisbury; that the regiment was assembled at Fairflied. Here we tarried 3 or 4 weeks, when the said regiment was ordered to White Plains in the State of New York, when we arrived at Danbury, all the men who were inlisted for 9 months, among whom was the deponent, were stationed at said Danbury, under the command of Beriah Bills (5)to guard the said Town, that there the deponent remained in service until the expiration of the 9 months for which he inlisted, where when not on guard, during his leisure time he was employed in making cartridges for the use of the army, under the direction of Doctor Wood (6) of Danbury. That the deponent being discharged at the end of his term went immediately to Salisbury aforesaid, where he arrived as he verily believes in the month of February 1777.

That afterward the Deponent, with his family, removed from Salisbury aforesaid to Nine Partners in the State of New York, where in February 1779, the time he cannot exactly remember, he was drafted and put under the care and command of Lieutenant Wood (6) to guard the Prison at Nine Partners, which was called the Hemlock Jail, where many Tories and British officers were confined. That there the Deponent served on month at the expiration of which time a new guard arrived, and the deponent was discharged.

That afterward the deponent removed to Lanesborough, State of Massachusetts, where he remained until the close of the war, and while there received a Lieutenant's Commission and afterward a Captain's Commission in the Militia of Massachusetts, which are now in the deponent's possession.

That sometime in 1806 the Deponent removed to the State of Ohio in the year following to Athens County, Rome Township, where he resided, following the occupation of a farmer, until 1826 when he removed to the Town of Athens, where he now resides.

That he was born as he believes on the 28 day of February of this however he has not any evidence except the copy of his father's family record transcribed many years ago.

That he never had any written discharge, nor has he any other documentary evidence nor does he know of any person who can give evidence of his said service.

And he hereby relinquishes every claim whatever to a pension or annuity except the present, and declares that his name is not on the pension roll of the agency of any state. (Signed) Hopson Beebe

Sworn to and subscribed, the day and year aforesaid, Henry Barttelt, Clerk

End Notes—S.4262, Hopson Beebe

1. The Danbury, Connecticut Raid took place from April 25 to 27, 1777. His enlistment was in 1777 not 1776.
2. The Abel Catlin found was a Surgeon in the Fourth Connecticut Continental Regiment in 1775 and after that a Surgeon in the Connecticut Militia.
3. Jonas Prentice was a Captain in the Sixth Connecticut Continental Regiment from January 1, 1777 until he resigned on March 31, 1779.
4. Return Jonathan Meig's Colonel of the Sixth Connecticut Continental Regiment on September 10, 1777 to rank from May 12, 1777. He retired January 1, 1781.
5. Beriah Bills was appointed First Lieutenant on January 1, 1777 in the Fourth Connecticut Continental Regiment. He was appointed Captain in the same regiment on November 24, 1777.
6. There are several Doctor Woods but it cannot be determined which one his is referring to.
7. Robert Wood was appointed, First Lieutenant of a Company in the Reg't formed from Detachments of Militia for the defence of the State, under Col. Morris Graham, First Regiment of Dutchess County Militia. There is at least one "Pay roll of Eight Hired men as a Guard 13 The Goals in Amenia Precinct". They were employed by Lieutenant Robert Wood from January 5 to January 24, 1779. The Pay Roll was found in the Revolutionary War Rolls 1775-1783, Series M-246, Roll 78, folder 178, National Archives, Washington, D.C. Four more pay rolls for Lieutenant Wood's Guards are found in the same Series M-246, Roll

74, folder 106, (Col. Morris Graham's Militia 1778-1779). Unfortunately Beebe's name does not appeared in any of them.

Pension Application for Matthew Bell

W.21658 (Widow Esther)
State of New York
County of Fulton SS.

On this seventh day of October 1844, personally appeared in open Court before the Judges of the Court of Common Pleas in and for said County now sitting, Esther Bell, a resident of the town of Ephratah in said County, aged eighty-four years, and who being first duly sworn according to law, doth on her oath make the following declaration in order to obtain the benefit of the provision made by the act of Congress passed passed [sic]7 July 1836. That she is the widow of Matthew Bell who served in manner and for the terms & under the officers herein after set forth, and as detailed in the documents to accompany this Declaration.

She further declares that she was married to said Matthew Bell in the spring of the year one thousand seven hundred and eighty four (1784).

That she was married at the time aforesaid, at Cambridge in the County of Washington in said State by the Reverend Thomas L. Beveridge of the Presbyterian Church who resided in [blot] of Cambridge & that her maiden name was Clyde". The said Matthew Bell died on the thirteenth day of September in the year one thousand eight hundred & thirteen and since his decease, she this declarant has remained single and unmarried and is still his widow.

This Declarant further saith, that she resided with her said husband Matthew Bell in said town of Cambridge from the year 1784 or from the day of her marriage as aforesaid until the year 1792, or there abouts, when she moved to Johnstown in said County of Fulton. She continued to reside in said town of Johnstown until about two years ago, when she took up her residence in said town of Ephratah, where she now resides.

This Declarant has no personal Knowledge of the revolutionary services of said Matthew Bell. (1) She has heard him give an account of his services in the war of the revolution, but she cannot remember all the particulars of said accounts that remembers that he stated a service of six & nine months in two single tours—that he was a prisoner for several months to gather with his father and oldest brother. She thinks the following were the names of some of his officers—David Allen Ensign (2) Col. Harper Lieut Sherwood (3)
& others. Note "1792" written on razure. (Signed with her mark) Esther Bell

Subscribed and sworn the day & year first aforesaid before me, Oct. 7th, 1844.

S. Wait, Clerk

End Notes—W.21658—Matthew Bell

1. Matthew Bell served as a private in Captain John Chipman's Company in Lieutenant-Colonel Commandant John Harper's Second Regiment of New York State Levies in 1780. Captain Chipman was promoted to Major and Chipman commanded the Company until it was transferred from Fort Edward to the Mohawk Valley. On September 26, 1780, Captain Joshua Drake transferred from Colonel William Malcom's Regiment of New York State Levies to Lieutenant Colonel Harper's Regiment. Drake was now put in command of the former Captain Chipman's company. Harper's Regiment was sent to Fort Schuyler to replace the First New York Continental Regiment by October 1st. Harper's Regiment was discharged on November 30th.
2. Ensign David Allen is unknown at this time.
3. Lieutenant Seth Sherwood served in Captain Chipman's Company and then under Captain Drake.

Pension Application for Adam Bellinger

W.23583

Declaration. In order to obtain the benefit of the act of Congress of the 7th July 1838 entitled "an act granting half pay and pensions to certain widows"-

State of New York

County of Orleans

On this 9th day of July 1844 personally appeared before the subscriber, a judge of the court in and for said county, Lena G. Bellinger, a resident of Shelby and said county, aged seventy seven years, who being first duly sworn according to law doth on her oath make the following declaration in order to obtain the benefit of the pension made by the act of Congress, passed July 7, 1838, entitled "an act granting half pay and pensions to certain widows"--

That she is the widow of Adam Bellinger who was a soldier in the war of the revolution; that her husband the aforesaid Adam Bellinger served at Stone Arabia on the Mohawk River at the time of the war of the revolution; and was a long time in the boating service, (1) for this army on the Mohawk River; and he was in the army as a private in the war of the revolution under various officers from 1778 or 1779 to the close of its disturbance; Capt Jacob Dievendorf (2), Capt Peter Suits (3), Capt House, Col. Clyde, Col. Waggoner, and perhaps Col. Willett (4), but as to officers, she cannot be sure, but she believes the above named were at least some of those mentioned by her husband, and under whom he must have served, he was in the Battle of Johnstown. (5)

She further declares that she was married to the said Adam Bellinger near Little Falls on the Mohawk River, she believes by Rev. Mr. Rosencrantz in the fall of 1786 seven hundred and eighty six, that her husband the aforesaid Adam Bellinger, died in September 1822 eighteen hundred and twenty two. That she was not married to him prior to his leaving the service, but the marriage took place previous to the first of January seventeen hundred and ninety four. Viz, prior to the time above stated that she has no family record. Lena Bellinger (her mark)

Sworn to and subscribed on the day and year above written before James Gilson one of the Judges of Orleans County Courts.

State of New York
County of Orleans

Personally appeared before the subscriber a Justice of the Peace in and for said county Anna Eve Garter of Shelby in said county, aged forty six years, being born in 1798 seven hundred and ninety eight, after being duly sworn according to law, deposeth and saith that widow Lena G. Bellinger who is applying for a pension as the widow of Adam Bellinger, late a soldier in the war of the revolution was this deponents father and that this deponent is the fifth child of her said father and mother that she has no doubt of her age, being as stated, that she was of sufficient age at the time of the "Great Eclipse" in 1806 to recollect it distinctly; that she can recollect that she was at that time eight years of gage, that she has from a child always understood and believed that her said father resided near the Mohawk river serving the war of the revolution and that he served in that war as a soldier; that her said father died in September 1822, eighteen hundred and twenty two, leaving as his widow the said Lena G Bellinger, who still remains his widow.

Subscribed and sworn before me this 9 day of July 1844, James Gilson, J.P.
Ann Eve Bellinger (her mark)

State of New York
County of Orleans

Personally appeared before the subscriber a Justice of the Peace in and for said county, Jacob Bellinger, of Shelby in Said county, aged thirty nine years after being duly sworn according to law, deposeth and saith that widow Lena G. Bellinger, who is applying for a pension as the widow of Adam Bellinger is this deponents father and that this deponent is the eighth child of his said father and mother, that he has from a child been informed and believed that his said father had been engaged in the service in the war of the revolution this deponent can well recollect that his eldest sister was a young woman grown when he was a little child; that his said father died in the fall of 1822, eighteen hundred and twenty two leaving as his widow the said widow Lena G. Bellinger, who still remains a widow.

Subscribed and sworn before me. This 9th day of July 1844. James Gilson J.P. Jacob Bellinger

I certify that the above named Jacob Bellinger is a respectable person.

State of New York
County of Orleans

Personally appeared before the subscriber a Justice of the Peace in and for said county, Nicholas Smith of Shelby in said county, aged sixty one years, after being duly sworn according to law, deposeth and saith, that he has for forty seven years been acquainted with widow Lena G. Bellinger and her late husband Adam Bellinger late a soldier in the war of the revolution on whose account she is applying for a pension, that she is the identical person who was the wife of the late Adam Bellinger at the first acquaintance of this deponent that this deponent resided for several months in the family of the said parties when he was fourteen years of age, that the said parties had a legal fruit of their marriage at that time then children that this deponent while recollecting their children at and from that time, and can judge from his own age and from his age at the time he resided in the family that the said parties and from a comparison of his age and the oldest child of the said parties, that the eldest child [ends]

State of New York
County of Orleans

Judge and surrogate of the said county and state at a Surrogate Court holden in my office in the said county on the 8th day of December 1851, I hereby certify that satisfactory evidence was thus exhibited to said court that Lena G. Bellinger (widow of Adam Bellinger deceased) who had made application for a pension from the state of New York, died a widow in the first day of April 1848 eighteen hundred and forty eight, leaving at her death the following named children her surviving and who still survive, being her only children her surviving and that each of them is over the age of twenty one years, to wit—Ann Garter, Elizabeth Hall, Christiana Wetherwax, Catherine Wetherwax. I further certify that Robert Garter of Shelby, Orleans County in the right of his wife Ann Garter above named as one of the children has been appointed administrator of the whole of the said Lena G. Bellinger and that he is duly qualified to act as such, and further that he has appointed Arad Joy of Ovid New York his agent and attorney to manage his claims.

In testimony whereof I have here unto set my hand and affixed by official seal, this 8th day of December 1851.
H. R. Curtis, County Judge of Orleans County, NY acting as Surrogate.

State of New York
County of Herkimer
February 20th 1845

I Augustus Beardsles one of the acting judges of the county courts of said county, do hereby certify that I have examined an old book of the record of marriages and baptisms said to have been kept by Rev. Abraham Rosencrantz, Grandfather of Abraham G. Rosencrantz of Little Falls in said county and said book is now in my presence. Said book is a manuscript book bound in parchment and I certify that I am fully satisfied of the fact of the penmanship of the said book as being what it purports to be, a record of marriages he ??? the old book which as kept by the Rev. Abraham Rosencrantz that in said book is the record of the following marriage viz "1786, 31st October, Adam Bellinger and Lena G. Timmerman" and that said record has every appearance of having been made and entered at the time of the date of said marriages as ?? entered.

Augustus Beardsles one of the judges of the County Courts of Herkimer County.

Letter in file dated December 19, 1935, written in response to an inquiry.

Reference is made to your letter in which you request the Revolutionary War record of Adam Bellinger, pension claim W. 23583.

The data furnished herein were obtained from the papers on file in pension claim, W. 23538, based upon the service of Adam Bellinger in the Revolutionary War.

The date and place of birth of this solider are not given, nor are the names of his parents stated.

While a resident of Herkimer County, New York, on the Mohawk River, Adam Bellinger was in the boating service, no dates of this service given. He served from sometime in 1778 or 1779 as private at various time in the New York Troops under Captain Jacob Diffendorf, Peter Suits, Joseph House, Colonels Samuel Clyde and Peter Waggoner, was in the Battle of Johnstown and on the "Mohawk Frontier" to protect the inhabitants, continued in the service until the close of the war.

Adam Bellinger married, October 31, 1786 near Little Falls on the Mohawk River, Lena G. Zimmerman. They were married at her father's house (names of her parents not given), by the Reverend Abraham Rosencrantz of the Reformed Protestant Dutch Church.

Adam Bellinger died in September, 1822 or 1823 in Shelby, Orleans County, New York.

His widow, Lena G. Bellinger was allowed pension on her application executed July 9, 1844, at which time she was seventy-seven years of age and living in Shelby, New York. She died April 1, 1848 in Orleans County, New York.

Their eldest child, Betsey, was born about the year 1790; their fifth child, Ann Eve, was born about the year 1798, she in 1844 was living in Shelby, New York, then signed "Ann Eve Garter; their eighth child, Jacob was thirty-nine years of age in 1844, then a resident of Shelby, New York.

The following children survived their mother: Ann Garter, Elizabeth Hall, Christiana Wetherwax, and Catharine Wetherwax.

Robert Garter of Shelby, New York, husband of the above named Ann Garter, was in 1851 appointed administrator of the estate of the widow, Lena G. Bellinger.

There are no further data in this claim concerning their children.

Margaret Reid or Reed, sister of the widow, Lena G. Bellinger, was eighty years of age in 1844 and living in Wales, Erie County, New York. Nancy

Eve Petrie, the soldier's sister was eighty years old in 1848, then living in Herkimer County, New York.

End Notes—W.23583—Adam Bellinger

1. Adam is on Captain Samuel Gray's Company of Bateaumen Muster Roll for 1780. FROM: Revolutionary War Rolls 1775-1783, series M-246, Roll 122, folder 78, National Archives, Washington, D.C.
2. There was more than one Adam Bellinger who served in the Tryon County Militia so it is hard to prove which one served under whom. Captains Jacob Diefendorf and Jost (Joseph) House would have been in Colonel Samuel Campbell's First Regiment of Tryon County Militia (Canajoharie District). This regiment was formed on the south side of the Mohawk River. Samuel Clyde was the Lieutenant-Colonel of this regiment.
3. Captain Peter Suts was in Colonel Jacob Klock's Second Regiment of Tryon County Militia (Palatine District). There was an Adam Bellinger who served in Captain Severinus Klock's Company in the same regiment. This regiment was formed on the north side of the Mohawk River unless Adam moved from one side to the other side, he could not have served in both regiments. Lieutenant-Colonel Peter Waggoner served in Colonel Klock's Regiment.
4. Marinus Willett was appointed Lieutenant-Colonel Commandant on April 27, 1781 of a regiment of New York States Levies which was stationed in the Mohawk Valley. Willett also had command of the Tryon County Militia so Adam would have at times been under Willett.
5. The Battle of Johnstown was fought on October 25, 1781. Willett was the commander of the Americans in this battle.

Pension Application for Catharine Bellinger (Petrie, Richard Marcus or Hondedrick M. former widow)

R729
State of New York
County of Onondaga SS.

Be it know that before me a Justice of the Peace in and for the county aforesaid, duly authorized by law to administer oaths personally appeared Catharine Bellinger a resident of the Town of Lysander in the County of Onondaga in the State aforesaid, who being first duly sworn according to law States that she is the Daughter of Marks Dedrick Petrie—the name Dedrick sometimes called Richard who was killed in the Oriskany Battle during the Revolutionary War and also the Daughter of the late Catharine Bellinger who was the widow of said Marks Dedrick Petrie and an applicant for a Pension previous to her death for Services rendered the United States by her first husband said Marks Dedrick Petrie in the Revolutionary War and that she believes the United States are still indebted under existing laws for the Pension that was due under the application heretofore made and that she is directly interested as a claimant in the pension for which application was heretofore made as aforesaid. And constitutes appoints George C. Ames of Washington DC her true and lawful attorney with power to examine into investigate and establish the claim for said pension and do all acts necessary thereto.

In witness whereof Catharine Bellinger has on this twenty fourth day of February 1853 hereunto signed her name and affixed her seal. (Signed with her mark) Catharine Bellinger
Witness Alanson Dunham, James Campbell

State of New York
County of Herkimer SS.

On this sixth day of June 1838 personally appeared before the Court of Common Pleas of said county in open court Catharine Bellinger a resident of Danube in the County of Herkimer and State of New York aged Eighty six years, who being first duly sworn according to law doth on her oath make the following declaration in order to obtain the benefit of the provision made by the act of Congress passed July 4, 1836 and the act explanatory of said act passed March 3, 1837.

That she was married to Richard M. Petrie, called in the German Hondedrick M. Petrie, who was an Ensign in the company commanded by Captain Small (1) in the Regiment Commanded by Col. Peter Bellinger, who was the father of the deponent that as such ensign her said husband was in the Service of the United States that he left home at different times and went in the service, that he was in service much of the time but that she cannot recollect the particular service. That he went to Oriskany and was in the Oriskany (2) battle and was killed in the battle as she was told immediately after his brother and other friends afterwards went to the battle ground to inter him and informed her that they did inter his body. That she recollects that her said husband Richard M. Petrie was stationed at Fort Dayton some time but cannot state the time as she was not there. She further declares that she was married to the said Richard M. Petrie called in German Hondedrick Petrie, in the month of June in the year seventeen hundred and seventy one the day and month she cannot recollect but recollects the month & year and that the nuptials were celebrated by the Reverend Abraham Rosecrants at the house of her father. That Peter P. Bellinger was present. That her said husband died as before stated in the month of August in the year 1777 being killed at Oriskany before mentioned. That she was afterwards married to John Bellinger who died in the month of February in the year 1820—and that she was a widow, as will more fully appear by reference to the proof hereto annexed on the 4th of July 1836 and still remains a widow.
(Signed with her mark) Catharine Bellinger

Sworn to and subscribed in open court the day and year above written. In witness thereof I as the Clerk of this Court have hereunto subscribed my name & affixed the seal of said Court which is a court of record. J. Dygert Clerk.

State of New York
Herkimer County SS.

Marks Crants of the Town of Columbia in the said County of Herkimer and State of New York being duly sworn deposeth and saith that he was seventy seven years of age on the 12th day of February last past and that he is now on the Pension Roll under the act of 1828, as he thinks, for Eighty dollars a year that the deponent was born on the Mohawk River about four and a half miles below the village of Herkimer on the north side of the River, that the place of his birth at the time of his birth was called Germanflatts but was afterwards called Herkimer and is not included in the Town of Little Falls in said County—that this deponent continued to live at the said place where he was born from the time of his birth until the year 1779 when he enlisted into the service and left home—that Richard M. Petrie, who was the husband of Catharine Bellinger who as this deponent is informed is an applicant for a Pension under the act of Congress July 4th 1836 was at the time of the birth of this deponent and from that time forward until the year 1779 when this deponent enlisted and left the place as here before stated a resident also of the same place where this deponent there resided, and lived within one half a mile of the residence of this deponent, that this deponent from; his earliest recollection was well acquainted with the said Richard M. Petrie and also with the said Richard M. Petrie and also with the said Catharine Bellinger who at the time of the war and until the death of the said Richard M. Petrie in the year 1777 and intermarried with the said Richard—that according to that Deponents present recollection and which this deponent believes true the said Richard M. Petrie and the said Catharine Bellinger were married together before the commencement of the Revolutionary War—That the said Richard M. Petrie at the commencement of the war was an Ensign in the Militia in the district in which he and this deponent then resided—That the said Richard M. Petrie was an Ensign in a company of Militia commanded by Jacob Small as Captain, George Helmer 1st Lieutenant (3) and John Davy 2d Lieutenant—

That the said Richard M. Petrie continued to act in the said company in the capacity of Ensign from the commencement of the said war until the 7th [6th] day of August 1777 when he was killed in the Oriskany Battle near Fort Stanwix that in the year 1775 commencing early in the summer or spring the said company on occasions of alarms and inroads repeatedly made by the enemy into the district and neighborhood in which the members of the said company resided, the said company was repeatedly called together at the house of the said Jacob Small in the commandant of the said company who also resided until he was afterwards killed by the enemy in the immediate neighborhood and within one half a mile of the residence of this deponent—that although this deponent was not at the time of sufficient age & subject him to military duty—yet he repeatedly saw the time and under arms in different terms in periods varying from three to eight days, that this deponent during said season repeatedly saw portions of said company on duty at the house of said Capt. Small where they were stationed and on duty and that the occasions of these assemblies were the approaching of the enemy and that the duties performed by the said company on those occasions were the usual garrison duties and scouts and at times pursuing the enemy—that the said Richard M. Petrie attended the said company on those occasions as the Ensign of the said company and at times had the command of the said company and at times the command of portions of the said company—that although this deponent cannot state precisely how long the said Richard M. Petrie as such Ensign as aforesaid in the summer of 1775 - That this deponent believes and has no doubt that he served at least for the period of two months.

That late in the fall in December in the year 1775, the said Richard M. Petrie went to Johnstown now in the County of Montgomery on a military expedition that the occasion of this expedition was to take Sir John Johnson (4) who with a party of Indians and Tories were about to attack as it was represented the inhabitants on the Mohawk—That the company to which the said Richard M. belonged was attached to a Regiment of Militia commanded by Col. Peter Bellinger and that the whole regiment was called out on this occasion and proceeded to Johnstown—that the said Richard M. Petrie was out on this service for the period of one month as this deponent believes—that this service was performed when there was snow on the ground and sleighing and this deponent does not know but this service may have been performed in January or the winter of 1776.—

That in the summer of the year 1776 the month this deponent cannot now state the said Richard Petrie but thinks it was in July, went out also as such Ensign with a part only of his said company on an Excursion to Mount Edmunston, a place now in the Southern part of Otsego County in pursuit of Tories who it was reported were in the neighborhood of Edmunston where a Mr. Carr and Mr. Edmundston who were reported to be Tories also resided—That this deponent remembers the going away and return home of the said Richard M. on this occasion and believes and therefore states that he was absent on this excursion one month.—

That the said Richard M. Petrie on other occasions during the said season of 1776 was absent occasionally with part of said company in pursuit of the enemy and at times stationed for short periods at the house of said Capt. Small and also at one time at the house of the said Richard M. Petrie that this additional service was rendered on occasions of alarms and approaches of the enemy and amounted to at least one half a month's service in addition to the said one month rendered in the same year as aforesaid—

That in the spring of the year 1777 the said Richard M. Petrie and the whole of his company went out on an expedition to the south to the Unadilla River (5) in pursuit of Brant and the Indians & Tories and that on this occasion he was out for the period of at least one month—that shortly after his return home from the [cut off] the said Richard M. Petrie and the company [cut off] was ordered to Fort Stanwix (6) and remained stationed there and on duty falling trees and blocking up wood creek and the road to prevent the approach of St. Leger and his army who was about to invest the Mohawk Country and who afterwards besieged Fort Stanwix. That this service continued for at least three weeks.

That immediately after his return home from Fort Stanwix the whole militia of the district under the command of General Herkimer including the company of the said Richard M. Petrie together with the said Richard M. were again ordered out and after being on duty in the vicinity of Herkimer at Fort Dayton (7) were marched towards Fort Stanwix for the relief of the garrison then in Fort Stanwix under the command of Col. Willett & Gansvoort and when the said Militia was attacked at Oriskany by the enemy and which brought on the Oriskany battle wherein the said Richard M. Petrie fell, that this deponent cannot state how long this last service continued but should say and is quite certain that it continued over five weeks and no doubt that the two last services the chopping at Fort Stanwix and the service in which he afterwards fell while this deponent considers a continued service was together at least two months actual service. That this deponent was not in any service with the said Richard M. Petrie but having lived in the immediate neighborhood of the said Petrie this deponent generally knew of his going off and frequently saw him when he went -away on the occasions of his said service and would also generally know of his return home that the said Richard M. Petrie was a true Patriot and had the reputation of being among the foremost and most prompt in opposing the enemy and in promoting the American cause during his life—that the knowledge of this deponent that the said Richard M. Petrie was killed in said Oriskany battle is the positive knowledge of this deponent that the said Richard left his home to go with the militia to said Fort Stanwix that he never returned and that it was immediately after said battle and forever since that time reported and believe that the said Richard was killed in the Oriskany Battle.—That the said Richard M. Petrie was the son of Marks Petrie and had an uncle by the name of Richard and that the said Richard M. Petrie was called by the German while in his neighbourhood and by the family Hondedrick Petrie. That the maiden name of the said Catharine the wife of the said Richard M. Petrie was Bellinger she being a daughter of Col. Peter Bellinger the commandant of the said Militia Regiment aforesaid that after the death of the said Richard M. Petrie the said Catharine intermarried with John Bellinger and the said John Bellinger the second husband of the said Catharine has been dead for more than ten years last that the said Catharine is yet living and is yet remaining a widow and unmarried. That the said Richard M. [cut off] said Catharine at the time of the death of the said Richard Petrie had two children which survived the said Richard M. Petrie—and further saith not—(Signed with his mark) Marks Crants

Subscribed and sworn this 1st day of June 1838 before me. Chas Gray Judge of Herk. Co. Courts.

State of New York
Herkimer County SS.

Peter P. Bellinger (8) of Danube in the said county & State aforesaid being duly sworn saith that he was seventy eight years of age on the 24th day of April last past—that Catharine Bellinger now is an applicant for a pension under the act of Congress of July 4, 1836 is a sister of this Deponent—that the said Catharine was married to Richard Marcus Petrie sometime about the year 1770 this deponent cannot state the precise time of their marriage but having been present and having witnessed the ceremony of the marriage he can state positively the fact of the marriage that the nuptials were celebrated by the Revd Abraham Rosecrants as this deponent believes in the house of Peter Bellinger the father of this deponent and the said Catharine who at the time of the said marriage lived on the Mohawk River at a place now called Little Falls in the said County of Herkimer—that the said Richard M. Petrie the husband of the said Catharine was killed in the Oriskany Battle under General Nicholas Herkimer on the 7th [6th] day of August 1777—That this deponent was not present in said Battle, but knows that the said Richard left home to go to Fort Stanwix that this deponent accompanied said Richard up the River as far as Fort Dayton where Herkimer Village is now built. That he there parted with him that immediately after the said battle news was brought to this deponent and the family by those persons who were in said battle with said Richard. That he the said Richard was killed in the said battle—that this deponent had never since seen the said Richard or heard in contradicted in any way that he was so killed in the said Battle and this deponent believes & has no doubt that he was killed in said Oriskany Battle, that at the time of his death he and the said Catharine had two children—that after the death of the said Petrie and sometime after the close of the war she intermarried with John Bellinger—

That she continued to be the wife of the said John Bellinger until about sixteen years ago when the said John Bellinger also died—that the said Catharine has not since the death of the said John Bellinger been married and that she is now living and still is a widow that this deponent was acquainted with the said Richard M. Petrie ever since this deponent had any recollection of events and up to the time of the death of the said Richard—that the said Richard at the commencement of the Revolutionary War war an Ensign in the Militia and that this deponent is informed and believes that he held the commission of Ensign under the provincial government—that he at the commencement of the war espoused the cause of liberty and the Americans and received the appointment of the Ensign in a Company of Militia commanded by Capt. Jacob Small who was also killed by the enemy in the Revolutionary War—that the said was attached to a Regiment commanded by Col. Peter Bellinger who was the father of this deponent in the Brigade of General Nicholas Herkimer—that the said Richard Petrie with the Regiment of Militia of the said Col. Peter Bellinger in the winter of 1775 in the month of January as this deponent believes were ordered and went on an expedition to Johnstown now in the County of Montgomery in the State of New York—That Col. .Peter Bellinger who was the father of this deponent & who commanded the said regiment with the said Regiment went on the said Expedition—but how long the said expedition continued from the time the same left home until they again returned this deponent cannot now recollect nor can he state—that this deponent has no personal knowledge that the said Richard performed any military service except the time when this deponent accompanied him to Herkimer on his way to the Oriskany battle here before mentioned—that this deponent in the war lived on the South side of the Mohawk and belonged to a company of Militia on the south side of the Mohawk River commanded by Capt. Michael Ittig (9) and that the said Richard M. Petrie belonged to a company on the north side of the Mohawk River commanded by Capt. Jacob Small which is the reason that this deponent did not accompany the said Richard M. Petrie in any Military service—That the said Richard from common report did service in the Militia as such Ensign from the commencement of the War until his death—that before the Oriskany Battle whether said Richard was killed, the said Richard as was reputed at the time and which this deponent believes true performed service also in the neighbourhood of Fort Stanwix falling trees & into Wood Creek to impede the approach of St. Leger & his Army but how long he was engaged in said service this deponent does not now remember that he ever understood.

Letter in the Pension folder dated October 3, 1939, written in response to an inquiry.

The data which follow were obtained from papers on file in pension claim R.729, based upon the military service of Richard (in German Hondedrick) Marcus Petrie, in the War of the Revolution.

The date and place of birth of Richard Marcus Petrie are not given. He was the son of Marck Petrie, and the nephew of Richard Petrie, name of his mother not shown.

Richard Marcus Petrie married in 1770 or in June, 1771, Catharine, the daughter of Colonel Peter Bellinger. They were married at her father's home in Little Falls on the Mohawk River, Herkimer County, New York, by the Reverend Abraham Rosencrantz. The date and place of birth of Catharine, and the name of her mother were not stated. Richard Marcus Petrie was killed in the battle of Oriskany. His widow, Catharine Petrie, married, date not given, John Bellinger, who died in the month of February, 1820. No relationship between said John Bellinger and Catharine was given.

Catharine Bellinger, June 6, 1838, then aged eighty-six years, and a resident of Danube, Herkimer County, New York, applied for the pension that might have been due on account of the services of her former husband, Richard Marcus Petrie, and stated that before the commencement of the Revolution, and while residing in German Flats, which was later called Little Falls, New York, Richard Marcus Petrie was an ensign in Captain Bells company, engaged in protecting the frontier along the Mohawk River from the depredations of the Indians and Tories; that from the beginning of the Revolution, he served at various times on tours as ensign in Captain Jacob Small's company, Colonel Peter Bellinger's (Catharine's father) New York regiment, under General

Nicholas Herkimer; that he assisted in the construction of Forts Stanwix and Dayton, went on expeditions to Johnstown, to Unadilla and to Ticonderoga, was out on scouting parties against the Indians, which scouting parties were generally under his command; he was promoted lieutenant, and was in the battle of Oriskany, where he was killed. It was stated that after the battle his body was found by a party of friends and neighbors and interred. No dates of service were given.

The claim for pension of Catharine Bellinger was not allowed as she failed to furnish proof of service, as required by the pension laws.

Richard Marcus Petrie and his wife, Catharine, had two children when Richard died. The only name of a child of this marriage that is shown is a daughter, Catharine Bellinger, who was living in Lysander, Onondaga County, New York, in 1853. One James Bellinger made affidavit in Lysander, New York, in 1853, but it is not shown that said James was the husband of Catharine.

David Bellinger, a son of Catharine by her second husband, John Bellinger, was living in Danube, New York in 1854. His age was not given, and no names of any other children of John and Catharine Bellinger are designated. In 1840, one George Bellinger lived in Little Falls, New York; his relationship to the family was not stated. Peter P. Bellinger, son of Colonel Peter Bellinger and brother of the widow, Catharine Bellinger, born April 24, 1760, and was living in 1838, in Danube, New York; he served in the War of the Revolution. The widow, Catharine Bellinger, was deceased in 1853, exact date not given.

Very truly yours, A.D. Hiller, Executive Assistant to the Administrator.

End Notes - R.729—Richard Marcus Petry

1. Capt. Jacob Small was not appointed captain until sometime in 1776. Peter Bellinger was not appointed colonel until about February of 1776 of the Fourth Regiment of Tryon County Militia. There are no muster rolls known for Captain Small's Company from 1776-1778.
2. The Battle of Oriskany was fought on August 6, 1777.
3. George F. Helmer was commissioned the Second Lieutenant in Captain Small's Company on June 28, 1778. Jacob Petry was commissioned ensign on the same date and for the same company. On the muster rolls for 1779 and 1780 there is not a Lieutenant John Davy listed. So far a muster roll for 1781 has not been found. Captain Small was killed on October 15, 1781. Muster rolls are in Box 14—Tryon County Militia, Special Collections and Manuscripts, New york State Library, Albany, New York. They were transcribed in October 1896 by the R.&P. Office, War Department. They are found under Bellinger's Regiment, Revolutionary War Rolls, 1775-1783, Series M-246, Roll 72, folder 78, National Archives, Washington, D.C.
4. This happened in January of 1776.
5. Mark Crants is probably referring to the conference of June 27, 1777, held at Unadilla between Captain Joseph Brant and Brigadier General Nicholas Herkimer.

6. Detachments from the Tryon County Militia were sent in July 1777 to Fort Schuyler or Fort Stanwix to cut and fall trees into Wood Creek in hopes of at least slowing down the progress of Brigadier General Barry St. Leger's advancing British Army and Allies.
7. Fort Dayton was built during June, July, and August of 1776 in the present day Village of Herkimer, Herkimer County. It was named in honor of Colonel Elias Dayton of the Third New Jersey Continental Regiment.
8. Peter P. Bellinger also applied for a pension, P.A. R.731 and R.732.
9. Captain Michael Ittig or Edick, Ihic, Edegh, etc., served in Colonel Bellinger's Regiment.

State of New York Dr to Catherine Petri widow of Richard Petri late a Lieutenant in Col. Peter Bellinger's Regt of Montgomery County Militia. To seven years half pay which I am entitled to by the death of my husband Richard Petri who was slain in the Field on the 6th August 1777 as [per] Col. Bellinger's Certificate.

1st yr pension due	6th Aug	1778...64..____..___
2d do	do	1779 & 1 yr Int. 3..... 64..____..___
3d do	do	1780 2 yr 6..8..___64..____..___
4th do	do	1781 3 yr do 9..12..___ 64..____..___
5th do	do	1782 4 yr do 12..16___64.____..___
6th do	do	1783 5 do 16..___64.____..___
7th do	do	1784 6 19..4.. ...___64.____..___
		67..4 448..____..___
		Amount of Interest 64.____..___
		515..4___

Audited 3d May 1785
FROM: Audited Accounts Vol. A., Page 228, Special Collections and Manuscripts, New York State Library, Albany.

Pension Application for Frederick Bellinger

S.12991
State of New York
County of Herkimer SS

I John Dygert Clerk of the Court of Common Pleas Holden at Herkimer in and for the County of Herkimer do Certify that satisfactory evidence has been this day, established to said court before the Judges thereof in Open Court that Frederick Bellinger was Entitled to a Pension under the laws of the United States according to the letter of JL Edwards commissioner of Pensions bearing date May 29, 1839 for eleven months and one day services in the war of the Revolution.—That he was a resident of the County of Herkimer in the State of New York and died in the County of Herkimer in the State of New York in the year one thousand eight hundred and thirty three on the fourteenth day of July that he left no widow but that he left six children whose names are Frederick Bellinger, Junr., Peter F. Bellinger, Elizabeth Piper, Nancy Bell, Catharine Reese & Lainy Spoon—and that all of the said children are over twenty one years of age.

In testimony whereof I have hereunto set my hand and affixed my seal of office this fourth day of June 1839. John Dygert Clerk.

State of New York
Herkimer County

On this Twelfth day of October one thousand eight hundred and thirty two personally appeared in open court before the Judges of the Court of Common Pleas now sitting Frederick Bellinger a resident of the Town of German Flatts in the said County of Herkimer and State of New York aged Seventy nine years in November last who being first duly sworn according to law doth on his oath make the following declaration in order to obtain the benefit of the act of Congress passed June 7, 1832—

That he entered the service of the United States under the following Officers and served as herein Stated—that he in the year 1779 as he believes although he is not certain as to the year enlisted into the service of the United States for the term of nine months as he now believes, as a Boatman—that at the time of his enlistment he resided at Germanflatts then in the County of Tryon now in the County of Herkimer in the State of New York—that he enlisted into the said Boat service in a company commanded by Captain Samuel Gray (1) of Palatine then also in said County of Tryon that he so enlisted either on the 7th or 17th day of April of that year and whether it was on the 7th or the 17th he cannot now determine but is certain it was on one of those days—that under said Enlistment he served with said Gray except occasionally when said Gray was absent on other service when he was under the command of Captain Lefler (2) who was also a Boat Captain and whose Company and the company of said Gray into which he was enlisted were employed together during that season until about Christmas of that year when he was discharged at Schenectady—that at Schenectady in the spring of the year, shortly after his enlistment he was mustered and put on the Augusta Bull and drew clothing—From John Glen or Henry Glen (3) Commissary a pair of Pantalones (4) A vest and coat and a shirt and Blanket—that at Albany he was furnished with a pair of shoes—that although his term of service had not yet fully expired yet owing to the peace & severity of the season they were then discharged and returned home about Christmas of that year—that said Captain Gray and Lefler were under the command of Colonel Christopher Yates (5) who resides at Schenectady—as he believes—that said Yates was a Colonel but whether he belonged to the militia or state or continental service he cannot say—that he recollects distinctly—that he saw said Yates and heard him give orders and directions to the said Boat Captains aforesaid in relation to their duties and service—that the principal part of the said Boat service was rendered on the Mohawk River—from Schenectady to Fort Stanwix at the head of the navigation of said River—that they were employed in the transportation of supplies of the Garrison at Fort Stanwix—that they made several trips also during said service on the Hudson River from Stilwater in Saratoga to Fishkill a short distance above West Point that in the fall and early part of the winter after the close of the navigation he and the rest of the company and the company of said Lefler were employed at Schodack and at Niskayuna in the vicinity of Albany in getting fire wood for the Soldiers in Barracks at Albany and was discharged at Schenectady and proceed home to Germanflatts about Christmas—

And the said Frederick further states that he served in the Militia prior to the Revolutionary War under Captain George Herkimer (5) who was a Captain under the King of Great Britain—that at the commencement of the Revolution as he now believes the said George was superseded in his Command and Michael Ittig in(7) Germanflatts in Tryon County was appointed Captain—Jacob Basehorn Lieutenant and Frederick Frank Ensign—that in obedience to the orders which were then issued to the Militia of that District he provided himself with a Gun and the usual equipage and kept himself in readiness to march at a minutes warning—

That said company of said Ittig to which he belonged was under the command of Gen. Nicholas Herkimer and Colonel Peter Bellinger Lieut Col. Frederick Bellinger & Major Denis Clapsattle (9) who were officers in the Militia—that whilst he was so enrolled in said company under said Ittig he was drafted and under the command of Captain Henry Harter Lieutenant Richard Petrie and Ensign John Myers (10) marched to Fort Stanwix (11) and was there employed in opening and making roads and bridges and some of the out works of said Fort Stanwix—that he was employed at said Fort one Fortnight—when he went home to Germanflatts where he then resided—that at another time whilst under said Ittig he and some others went out as a Scouting party to Schuyler Lake and other Lakes in its vicinity now in Otsego County. That when Fort Herkimer was building he under the Command of said Captain Ittig was employed in the building of said Fort.—

That when Fort Dayton (12) on the north side of the Mohawk River where Herkimer Village now stands was building, he under the command of Sergeant John Campbell both belonging to the company of said Ittig was ordered to Fort Dayton and was stationed there as a guard for about a week—That he also served repeatedly as a guard at Fort Herkimer—that when some of his guard duty at Fort Herkimer was performed he thinks Frederick Frank who was his Ensign under Capt Ittig promoted to a Captain and some of said service was done by him under Captain Frank—

That he continued to serve in the Militia at Germanflatts under the said Officers or some of the Officers aforesaid until the year 1779 when he enlisted into the Boat Service as aforesaid that he cannot now say in what years his service at Fort Stanwix and at Fort Herkimer and Fort Dayton and his other Militia service was rendered but that the same was rendered in the several years from the commencement of the war to the year 1779 in the spring—that he has no doubt that some of said service and much other military service not mentioned nor particularly remembered was rendered by him in each of said years.

That he remembers also that during said period the year he cannot now remember when Andrustown (13) was burnt he was marched from Fort Herkimer to that place in pursuit of the enemy—that when the British and Indians besieged Fort Stanwix he was again ordered out and under Colonel Benedict Arnold (14) who was then marching up the River to relieve the American Garrison at said Fort marched to within about four or five miles below where Utica is now built on the Mohawk River when an express arrived bringing the news that the British and Indians had abandoned the siege when he and the rest of the Militia were discharged and sent home—that in the winter after his term of boat service he removed from Germanflatts where he was born and was living until then to Fort Plain—then also in Tryon County now in the County of Montgomery in the State of New York—that at Fort Plain he was immediately enrolled in a company then commanded by Captain Adam Lipe (15), Lieutenant Robert Crouse (16) as he thinks and Ensign William Seeber—that Lawrence Gross (17) was a Captain also part of the time that he remained at Fort Plain in the three and four moths men - That said company of said Lipe in which he served was under the command of Colonel Seeber (18) of Colonel Marinus Willett as he thinks—that from the year 1780 he continued to reside at Fort Plain until the close of the war and was continually in the Militia service until the close of the war—

That he was not continually on active duty but was at all times in readiness to march at a minutes warning and was for the greater part of the time in actual service—that during said period from the year 1780 to the close of the war the particular year he cannot say nor can—he state the precise time he was on duty repeatedly at Fort Plain.

That he was on duty at Fort Plain—that he was on duty at Fort Windecker—all of which Forts were on the Mohawk River in the county of Tryon—that the duties rendered at said Forts were to guard and defend said Forts and the Inhabitants collected and living at each of said Forts, against the enemy—that during said period he went out in pursuit of the enemy repeatedly—that one time he and a party went to Cherry Valley (19)—that the occasion of their going to Cherry Valley was to pursue the enemy when Cherry Valley was burnt and many of the Inhabitants of that place were murdered by the enemy - that at another time he was marched to Bowman's Creek in pursuit of the enemy—that on another occasion he was sent out with some others from said Fort Plain where he was stationed during the whole period of the last mentioned services to Otsquago Creek and from there to Fort Herkimer and from Fort Herkimer back again to Fort Plain on a scouting party—that at another time he was marched with the rest of the Militia of that district under General Henry Van Rensselaer (20) up the Mohawk River in pursuit of the Enemy who had engaged and defeated Colonel Brown (21) at Stonearabia—that they proceeded to the upper part of Germanflatts when General VanRennselaer gave up the pursuit and returned home—that in the year 1781 as he believes although he is not certain as to the year he was in the Battle of Johnstown (22) now in the County of Montgomery—that he was under the command of Captain Adam Lipe in said Battle—that the Militia were then ordered by Colonel Marinus Willett who commanded at said Battle—that he remained in the Militia service being almost constantly employed in some public service or other until the close of the Revolutionary War when he was marched back again from Fort Plain to German flatts where he has resided ever since—that he has no documentary evidence of any of his services—

That he was born in Germanflatts then in the County of Tryon in the year 1752 November 12th.

That there was a record of his age in the church records of Germanflatts but that the same was burnt during the Revolutionary War.

That he was living at Germanflatts where he was born when he first entered the service—that part of the time during the War of the Revolution he lived at Fort Plain in the Town of Canajoharie, now Minden, then County of Tryon now Montgomery County—that at the close of the war he moved back again to Germanflatts where he was born and where he has continued to live ever since.

That his service was by enlistment or a draft and volunteer service and by ordered issued in accordance of a Resolution of Congress passed in May 1775 as he is informed. That he served under Colonel Marinus Willett when at Fort Plain and was commanded by Col. Willett in the Johnstown Battle—that his militia service at Germanflatts was under Col. Peter Bellinger.

That he never received any written discharge that he now knows of for any of his services—

That he is known to George Fox, Michael Ittig, Cornelius VanDusen Who reside in his neighbourhood and who can testify as to his character for truth—

That he hereby relinquishes every claim whatever to a pension or annuity except the present and declares that he is not on the pension Roll of the agency of any state. (Signed with his mark) Frederick Bellinger

Sworn to and subscribed the day and year aforesaid in Open Court. Julius C. Nelson, Clerk

Letter in Pension Folder dated April 1, 1930, written in reply to an inquiry.

I advise you from the papers in the Revolutionary War pension claim S. 12991, it appears that Frederick Bellinger was born November 12, 1752 in German Flats, New York.

While a resident of German Flats, Tryon County, New York troops as follows:

From sometime in 1776 until sometime in 1779 at various times, amounting to six months in all, as private and corporal under Captain Michael Ittig (23), Frederick Frank and Henry Harter, in Colonel Peter Bellinger's Regiment. Having moved to Fort Plain, Tryon County, New York, he enlisted April 7 or 17, 1779 and served nine months in the boat service and was a private under Captains Samuel Gray and Lefler in Colonel Christopher Yates' Regiment; and from the spring of 1780 served at various times until the close of the Revolution, amounting to one year and six months in all, as a private under Captains Adam Lipe (24) and Lawrence Gross in Colonel in Colonel Marinus Willett's Regiment, and was in the battle of Johnstown.

Prior to the Revolution he served in the Militia under George Herkimer a captain under the "King of Great Britain".

Pension was allowed on his application executed October 12, 1832, at which time he was a resident of German Flats, Herkimer County, New York. He had moved there soon after the Revolution.

The soldier died June 18 or July 14, 1833 in Herkimer County, New York. He left no widow.

He was survived by the following children: Frederick, Peter F., Elizabeth Piper, Nancy Bell, Catharine Reese and Lainy Spoon.

Very truly yours, D. W. Morgan, Acting Commissioner.

End Notes—S.12991—Frederick Bellinger

1. Captain Samuel Gray's Company of Bateaumen muster roll for 1779 shows Frederick as enlisting on March 17 and still serving on May 24th. He was owed £ 19 . . 18 . . 0. On another musterroll fragment is Frederick Bellinger undercast (underpaid) 33 d 12/ £ 21 . . 0. . 0. FROM: Revolutionary War Rolls 1775-1783, Series M-246, Roll 122, folder 78, (Quartermaster General's Dept), National Archives, Washington, D.C.
2. John Leffler is known to have had a Company of Bateaumen in 1778.
3. Henry Glen of Schenectady served as Assistant Deputy Quartermaster in the Northern Department.
4. Pantaloons are a type of overalls which were a full length type of pants as compared to breeches which only went about two inches below the knee.
5. A Christopher Yates served as the Lieutenant-Colonel in Colonel Abraham Wemple's Second Regiment of Albany County Militia. In 1779 he was appointed Deputy Quartermaster General.
6. George Herkimer was also appointed Captain of the Eighth Company on August 26, 1775 in Colonel Hanyost Herkimer's Fourth Regiment of Tryon County Militia. Captain Herkimer was later removed as Captain of this company for striking an enlisted man. Colonel Hanyost Herkimer had declined to accept his appointment and by February of 1776, Lieutenant-Colonel Peter Bellinger was appointed as the Colonel of the Fourth Tryon.
7. In 1776 Captain Michael Ittig's (or Edick, Ittick, etc.) Company officers were as follows: First Lieutenant Jacob Basehorn, Second Lieutenant Frederick Frank and Ensign Patrick Campbell. In 1778 his company officers were First Lieutenant Frederick Frank, Second Lieutenant Jacob Moyer and Ensign Adam A. Staring.

8. Nicholas Herkimer was appointed as Colonel of the First Regiment of Tryon County Militia on August 26, 1775 and was the Chief Colonel (or Senior Colonel). On September 5, 1776 he was appointed Brigadier General of the Tryon County Militia Brigade.
9. Augustinus Clapsaddle was the Second Major in Colonel Bellinger's Regiment. He was killed at the Battle of Oriskany on August 6, 1777.
10. All were officers in Colonel Bellinger's Regiment. Lieutenant Petry or Petrie, Petri, etc., was killed at the Battle of Oriskany on August 6, 1777.
11. Fort Stanwix was being rebuilt in 1776 and 1777. It was renamed Fort Schuyler in honor of Major General Philip Schuyler.
12. Fort Dayton was built in 1776 and named after Colonel Elias Dayton of the Third New Jersey Continental Regiment. This regiment with others were employed in building this fort and then went to Fort Schuyler to assist in its rebuilding.
13. Andrustown, also called Hendersontown, was destroyed on July 18, 1778. This settlement is now near Jordanville, Otsego County, New York.
14. Major General Benedict Arnold. This was in August of 1777.
15. Adam Leipe was commissioned Captain on March 4, 1780. He was appointed in February of 1779. The following were the officers that served under him: First Lieutenant Jacob Mathias, Second Lieutenant William Seeber and Ensign John Countryman.
16. Robert Crouse had been Captain of this Company from April of 1776 until he was killed at the Battle of Oriskany on August 6, 1777. Leipe had been a second Lieutenant in this company.
17. Lawrence Gros was a Captain in 1781 in Lieutenant-Colonel Commandant Marinus Willett's Regiment of New York State Levies.
18. William Seeber was the Lieutenant-Colonel of the First Regiment of Tryon County Militia. He died September 1, 1777 from wounds he received at the Battle of Oriskany on August 6, 1777.
19. Frederick is possibly referring to the April 1781 destruction of the remaining part of the Cherry Valley settlement. The main settlement of Cherry Valley was destroyed on November 11, 1778 by Captains Walter Butler and Joseph Brant.
20. Brigadier General Robert VanRensselaer of the Second Brigade of the Albany County Militia.
21. Colonel John Brown was killed in the Battle of Stone Arabia on October 19, 1890.
22. The Battle of Johnstown was fought on October 25, 1781.
23. On Captain Ittig's muster roll for 1776 and 1777 the following places and dates are listed: Johnstown on February 7, 1776—6 days, Mount Edminston on June 5, 1776—2 days, on scout June 15, 1776—1 day, on guard at Frederick Fox October 17, 1776—5 days, and at the time of the Battle of Oriskany occurred on August 6, 1777, he was not in

the battle. On Captain Ittig's Company muster and payroll Frederick is listed as sergeant from February 28 to November 30, 1778. He served 14 days in June, 6 days in July, 26 days in August, 21 days in September and 14 days in October for a total of 81 days. He was paid £ 8 . . 12. . 9 ½. FROM: Revolutionary War Rolls 1775-1783, Series M-246, Roll 72, folder 78, National Archives, Washington, D.C.

24. On Captain Leipe's company muster and payroll for June 15, 1779 to July 5, 1780 Frederick had served 30 days as a private. He was owed £ 2. . 13. . 4. On Captain Leipe's receipt roll of September 28, 1784, certificate number 11358 he was paid £ 2. . 13. . 4. On Captain Leipe's Company Muster and pay roll for July 6, 1780 to July 20, 1782, he had served 31 days. He was owed £ 2. . 15. . 1.

Pension Application for William Bellinger

S.28641
State of New York
Montgomery County SS.

On this 20th day of Sept'r one thousand eight hundred and thirty two, personally appeared in open court at Johnstown, the Court of Common Pleas in and for the County of Montgomery, Town of Root in the County of Montgomery and State of New York aged Seventy three years 11 months. Who being first duly Sworn, according to Law, doth make the following Declaration in order to obtain the Benefit of the Act of Congress Passed June 7th 1832; That he Entered the Service of the United States under the following named officers and served as herein stated. Vizt. That this applicant declares that Emediately after the commencement of the Revolutionary War he hath been Enroled in the Company of Militia Commanded by Capt. Henry Ekler (1) in the Regt Commanded by Col. Peter Bellinger—

Then Residing in the Town of German Flats;

That this applicant although well sattisifed that he hath been ordered out in performing Militia duty in the year 1775, but that he this claimant does not recollect, but this applicant [?] That the first Campaign he was Ordered Out, he went to Cachnawgo (2) Situate in the Town of Johns Town, There Mett in Joining the Militia from Albany and Schenectady under the Command of Genl Phillip Schuyler(3), there remained for Several days, than marching or going to Johnstown (4) Under the Command of the Aforesaid Genl then Causing Sr John Johnson (5) with about three or four hundred men to surrender up to them, the particular object not ascertained, of Sr John proposing at the time That he Calculating to go with his men to Canada, or to Exercising Cruelties and Barbarities on those attached in atchieveing [sic] their Liberties and Independence of the Americans; this applicant then residing in German Flats That this applicant further declares that in the forepart of summer in the year 1777 Under the Command of General Nicholas Herkimer (6), went to Unindela [Unadilla] down the Susquehannie river, when this claimant was drafted, there mett Capt Brandt (7), who had a large party of Wariors, encamped but about a quarter of a mile distance from their Encampment, from that Genl Herkimer, their situate for some several days when Capt. Brandt with two of his warriors came into the Gen'l Encampment where treaty concluded, avoiding in taking Battle.

Next this Applicant declares that on the Sixth day of August same year 1777 again in Battle Under the Command of Genl Herkimer at Oriskany (8) at distance about four Miles below For Stanwix down the Mohawk River which Terminated a Sorous [serious] Conflict and attended with the loss of a large Number of the Militia, than from Tryon County who were Slain at Battle and a great Number wounded and many taken Prisoner.

That this applicant further declares that in the year 1780 he was ordered to remain at Fort Plain with 14 of the Militia to watch and Guard the Fort and Inhabitants contained In the Fort, While all the Militia in mass were ordered out to march to Fort Schuyler, to relief Capt. Gray (9) who was Obstructed with his company of Boatmen & Bateau, loaded with Provisions and supplies, Calculated for the supply of the Garrison at Fort Stanwix, then when the Enemy hat been laying in wait watching the boats at Last, disappointed when under the command of Genl VanRensselaer, guarding the boats and all safe to Fort Stanwix, when the Enemy passing down the Mohawk River to Fort Plain then part of Canajoharie, now Town of Minden, there making an attack on Fort Plain but not succeeded although but 13 abled bodied were besides this claimant in the Fort, and the meeting house next to the Fort reduced to Ashes, Murdering & taken prisoners, and consuming the most of the buildings throughout the whole, now, Town of Minden.

And that the enemy drove away all his cattle and when the Enemy drove away all his horse creatures and when the enemy left the Burning and Consuming all around and Emiediently near the Fort, this claimant decalres that himself with his thirteen associates leaving the Fort & followed in persuing them at a distance of about four miles, [whole paragraph crossed out]

And That this applicant further declares, that in the year 1778 then under the Command of Capt. Adam Lype (10) Continually watching and guarding against the Incursions of the Common Enemy, drafted to Fort Snell in Stonearabia, twice, frequently drafted to Fort Clyde, Twice drafted to Cherry Valle (11), for two weeks each time frequently ordered and by draft to Fort Blank times he does not recollect, when residing in the Town then German Flats, County of Tryon now Town of Warren, twice in the written drafted to go to German Flats, then on duty of Militia services under the Command of Capt. Eackler, he thinks in the year 76. [another paragraph crossed out.]

That this claimant further declares that on the 23 day of Oct. 1781 Majr Ross (12) with his Incendiary Crew Vizt Tories and Indians and some regular troops unsupported. Early in the morning Aprized the the [sic] Inhabitants some distance off the Mohawk River with their merciless Tomahawk, Scalping knife, and Combustibles to set fire to buildings [sentence crossed out] and down along the River was destroyed, some killed and some taken prisoner, and forced along to Canada with chiefly all the buildings consumed to ashes, when at the same time the father of this Claiment was taken prisoner and one of his brothers killed, this applicant declares that on being ordered out to march to in pursuit of the Enemy when mett Col. Willett on the way to Johnstown, Col. Willett intimately acquainted with the claimant allowing and ordered him to return in consequence of the Situation with his father and brother and his [part written looks like 'and his cattle destroyed and after this they were taken prisoner', but not sure] the consequences escaped the battle in Johnstown But he thinks the next day again went in pursuit of Majr Ross with his incendiary Crew, under the command of Col. Willett at a distance of about fifty miles when overtaking some part of Majr Ross men (13), some killed and several wounded and their pursuing along to the West Canada Creek where Col. Butler was shot dead across the Creek and Ross with his Indendiaries put to flight.

And this applicant further declares that it is altogether impractible for any one Militia Soldier to describe the number of tours and trips, days nor months as not one among thousands this claimant feels assured, can tell as to various duties and services performed from the commencement to the close of the War—Only this claimant declares, that in compliance with the orders and requisitions of his superior officers as well than in conformity to a Resolution passed by the Old Congress May 27th 1775, as also in obedience to the laws and Resolutions passed by the state of new York—That this Applicant declares that from and after the year 1775 always has kept himself well armed and acquipped and always in readiness at a moments warning, and always did perform Militia duty on each and every occurrence or Emergency when called upon hereby relinquishes every claim whatever to a Pension or annuity except the present and declares that his name is not on the pension roll of the agency of any state. Only this applicant further declares that the last of July 1781 then ordered out under Col. Willett at the time when the Indenderiaries had consitituted a Cruel Conflagation around about Fort Timmerman murdering, burning and taken prisoners, when this Claiment in pursuit of the Incendiaries under Col. willet as aforesaid at a distance of about thirty miles in pursuit but in vain—

This Applicant further declares, that in the year 1780 (15) he believes, when a place called Springfield, then Tryon County now Otsego County marching out in mass, under Capt. Lype and under the Emedient Command of Col. Willett after a general Conflagration caused by a large body of Incendairies from Canada and further this applicant saith not—(Signed) William Bellinger

Sworn to and Subscribed the day and year aforesaid. Geo. D. Ferguson, Clerk

End Notes—S.28641—William Bellinger

1. Henry Eckler was appointed captain May 1776 and was commissioned as captain June 25, 1778 in Colonel Peter Bellinger's Fourth Regiment of Tryon County Militia. Eckler's company was raised from the Kyle Settlement (Chyle) area nowt the Town of Warren, Herkimer County. This settlement was destroyed in 1778 and most of the inhabitants

including Captain Eckler abandoned the settlement. Many settled around Forts Plank and Plain.

2. Caughnawaga is nowt the Village of Fonda and the Town of Mohawk, Montgomery County, NY.
3. Major General Philip Schuyler of the Continental Army, lived in Albany. He had a summer home, mills etc., in Saratoga, which is now Schuylerville, Saratoga Co.
4. John's Town is supposed to be two words. Sir William Johnson built the settlement and named it after his son John.
5. Sir William Johnson died on July 11, 1774 and his son John inherited the largest share of his father's estate. Sir John was a Royalist or Loyalist, meaning he was loyal to King George III of England and was arming his tenants and fortifying Johnson Hall. General Schuyler was sent to either arrest him or have him sign a type of parole that stated he would remain neutral. May 1776, Sir John fled to Canada with about 150 of his tenants. In June of 1776, Sir John was granted a warrant to raise a regiment to fight for England. The regiment was named the King's Royal Regiment of New York.
6. Nicholas Herkimer was appointed Colonel on August 26, 1775 of the First Regiment of Tryon County Militia. On September 5, 1776 he was appointed Brigadier General of the Tryon County Militia.
7. On June 27, 1777, Captain Joseph Brant met with General Herkimer at Unadilla for a conference; Herkimer tried to get Brant to either join the American cause or at least to remain neutral. It almost turned into a battle instead of a conference, but it was averted at this time. Captain Brant and his Mohawks remained loyal to the King of England and fought against the Americans.
8. The Battle of Oriskany was fought on August 6, 1777. Sir John's Regiment of Yorkers (men from New York were not called New Yorkers but Yorkers. This applied to the Loyalist regiment as well as the Five New York Continental Regiments in most period writings) and Captain Brant played an important part in the ambush of General Herkimer and the Tryon County Militia.
9. Captain Samuel Gray and his company of Batteaumen. They were warned by a friendly Oneida warrior that Captain Brant lay ready to ambush them on the river. Captain Gray ordered the bateaus to shore and prepared for a fight. He also sent one of his men to get help. Robert VanRensselaer, who had been appointed Brigadier General on June 16, 1780 of the Second Brigade of the Albany County Militia, marched with what Albany County Militia he could gather to the Mohawk Valley. He had also ordered Lieutenant-Colonel Samuel Clyde of the First Regiment of Tryon County Militia to march west along the south shore of the Mohawk River and Colonel Jacob Klock of the Second Regiment of the Second Regiment of Tryon County Militia to march west along the north shore of the Mohawk River. Brant on

learning that at least 500 or more militia were coming in his direction decided to burn the Oneida Village and their Fort named Fort VanDyck. He then circled around the advancing militia and arrived at the Canajoharie District and destroyed the settlements there on August 2, 1780. After completing the destruction of present day Village of Fort Plain and the Town of Minden, he broke his raiding party into three groups. Brant took his party to Vrooman's Land in the Schoharie Valley. He destroyed that settlement on August 9, 1780.

10. In 1778, William was in Captain Francis Utt's Company in Colonel Samuel Campbell's First Regiment of Tryon County Militia. On Captain Utt's payroll for May 27—December 31, 1778, William had served 1 month and 25 days. Pay due to him was £ 4. . 17 . . 9 1/3. FROM: Revolutionary War Rolls 1775-1783, Series M-246, Roll 72, folder 89. February 1779, First Lieutenant Adam Leipe replaced Captain Utt. On Captain Leipe's payroll for June 15, 1779 to July 5, 1780, William had served 96 days as a corporal. He was owed £ 9. . 4. . 0. In February of 1779 he had served 18 days. On the payroll for July 6, 1780 to July 20, 1782 he had served 6 days. He was owed £ 0 . .10. . 8, as a private. In 1784 he produced a certificate number 11319 for £9 . . 7 . . 9. He made his mark for his pay. FROM: Revolutionary War Rolls 1775-1783, Series M-246, Roll 72, folder 89, National Archives, Washington, DC.
11. One of his tours to Cherry Valley was when it was destroyed on November 11, 1778. He made a supplemental application on June 12, 1833.
12. John Ross, a Major in the King's Royal Regiment of New York. Second in command of the raiding party was Captain Walter Butler. They destroyed several settlements from Currytown which is now the Town of Root, Montgomery County, east to Warren's Bush, now Town of Florida, Montgomery County. On October 25, 1781 Lieutenant Colonel Commandant Marinus Willett and his American forces caught up with Ross at John's Town and a battle soon raged until darkness and Ross retreated from John's Town.
13. This was the rear guard under Lieutenant John Ryckman (Rykeman). Ryckman was one of those captured.
14. Captain Butler's party now become the rear guard. His father John was the Lieutenant-Colonel. Captain Butler was killed on October 30, 1781 at the West Canada Creek.
15. Springfield was destroyed in 1778. William corrects this in his supplemental application.

Pension Application for James Benedict

R.742 (Widow: Sarah)

This woman was pensioned as the former widow of her first husband Christopher Hall Conn. and New York W.27521.

Declaration in order to obtain the benefit of the act of Congress passed June 7, 1832.
State of New York
Montgomery County Ss.

On this twentieth day of September in the year of our Lord one thousand eight hundred and thirty two personally appeared in open court before the Judges of the Court of Common Pleas in and for the County of Montgomery in the State of New York now sitting James Benedict a resident of Broadalbin in the County and State aforesaid aged seventy years who being first duly sworn according to law doth on his oath make the following declaration in order to obtain the benefit of the act of Congress passed June 7, 1832. That he entered the service of the United States under the following named officers and served as herein stated—

He enlisted about the middle of May in the year seventeen hundred and seventy eight in Capt. Noble's Company of Infantry in Colonel Wood's regiment of Massachusetts State troops.—That at this time he resided in Lenox in the County of Berkshire in Massachusetts—After enlisting as aforesaid Capt. Noble's company was ordered to Fishkill in Dutchess County in New York and from thence to Peekskill, from whence a detachment, of whom the said Benedict was one, was sent to Haverstraw and thence to White Plains where they joined the Continental Army under Gen. Washington (1) and were attached to Gen. Nixon's (2) Brigade—About the first of September in the year last aforesaid the said Benedict went with the army from White Plains northward to Fredericksborough, Woodberry and Newtown in Connecticut and thence again to Peekskill where they went into winter quarters, and in the month of December of the same year as the said Benedict believes, he left the army, after having procured a substitute who served out the time of his enlistment—And the said Benedict further says that in the year seventeen hundred and seventy nine he resided in Pittstown now in Rensselaer County in the State of New York and was enrolled as one of the Militia of that state for about one year during which time he was called out into actual service at several different times, twice for half a month under Capt. Yates (3) and Col. John Van Rensselaer (4) by order of Governor George Clinton. And the said Benedict further says that on or about the first of July in the year seventeen hundred and eighty he went to the town of Adams in Massachusetts and enlisted a second time in the Massachusetts State troops, for six months—that he then proceeded to West Point, reported himself and joined the Continental Army then lying at Robinson's farms and was enrolled in a company then commanded by Lieutenant Simons or Simonds (5) in Col. Bigelow's (6) Regiment, Gen. Glover's (7) Brigade and Maj. Gen. Howe's (8) Division—that he was with the army in all its movements during that season—was at Orange-town when Major Andre was taken and mounted guard on the day he was executed—returned with the army to West Point and went into winter quarters where he remained till the first of January in the year seventeen hundred and eighty one, when he received his discharge, which he soon after sent to Boston in order to receive his wages and which was never returned to him. And the said James Benedict further says that he is the identical James Benedict mentioned in the affidavit of Isaac Benedict here to annexed, which is the only evidence of his services now in his possession.

He hereby relinquishes every claim whatever to a pension or annuity except the present and declares that his name is not on the pension roll of the agency of any state.

Sworn to and subscribed the day and year aforesaid. (Signed) James Benedict

Sworn to and subscribed the day and year aforesaid. Aaron Seamans, Fones Cole

End Notes—James Benedict—R.742

1. General and Commander in Chief George Washington.
2. Brigadier General John Nixon of the Continental Army. He was appointed on August 9, 1776.
3. Captain Jacob Yates in Colonel Peter Yates' Fourteenth Regiment of Albany County Militia.
4. Lieutenant Colonel John VanRensselaer of Colonel Yates' Regiment.
5. Lieutenant Daniel Simonds of the Fifteenth Massachusetts Continental Regiment.
6. Colonel Timothy Bigelow of the Fifteenth Massachusetts Continental Regiment.
7. Brigadier John Glover of the Continental Army.
8. Major General Robert Howe of the Continental Army.

Pension Application for Ebenezer Benjamin

S.12151
State of New York
Oneida County SS.

On this seventh day of August 1832 personally appeared before the subscriber Judge of the Court of Common Pleas of said County, Ebenezer Benjamin, a resident of said County and State, Aged Sixty six years, who being first duly sworn according to law, doth on his oath make the following declaration, in order to obtain the benefit of the act of Congress, passed June 7, 1832.

That he entered the service of the United States under the following named officers, and served as herein stated: That he was born at Preston Con. April 4th 1766—That there is no record of his age to his knowledge. That he lived at Canaan Col Co. NY when called into service—Since war a company called the Silver Greys and served about four months at & about FishKill. That in April 1781 he enlisted in Canaan in Capt. Silas Gray's in a regiment under the command of as he thinks Col. John McKinstry--at the time of enlistment but afterwards he thinks Col. Willet had command for nine months—and was stationed at Saratoga & about there. On the 6th day of April 1782 this deponent again enlisted at Canaan for nine months in Capt. Joseph Harrisons Co, Col.

Willett's Regiment—and went to Schoharie—and from thence the deponent went to Cattskill & stationed abt two months & then to Schoharie—and the dept was taken sick as stated in written affidavit. This deponent rec'd a written discharge first Service but not the second—and the same has been kept. This deponent is now blind—and he refers to the annexed affidavits said papers as proof of his service and veracity.

He hereby relinquishes every claim whatever to a pension or annuity except the present, and declares that his name is not on the pension roll of the agency of any state. (Signed with his mark) Ebenezer Benjamin.

Sworn to and subscribed the day and year aforesaid. J. Hathaway, Judge of Oneida comm. Pleas.

And the said Judge do hereby declare his opinion, after the investigation of matter, and after putting the interrogatories prescribed by the War Department, that the above named applicant was a Revolutionary Soldier and served as he states: And the Judge further certifies, that it appears to him that Benjamin P. Johnston who has signed the last certificate is a resident in Rome and is a Commissioner and is a credible person, and that his statement is entitled to credit. And that the said Ebenezer Benjamin from bodily infirmity is not in a situation to attend court being entirely blind. J. Hathaway, The Judge of Oneida Comm Pleas.

State of New York
Oneida County SS.

On this 18th day of Nov 1832 before me a Judge of Oneida Com. Pleas personally appeared Ebenezer Benjamin, within named, and makes the following additional declaration or affidavits That as to his service—

In 1779, (he can't state the day of the month or the month) he volunteered in the Militia in a company called the Silver Greys, Commanded by Moses Jones (1) Lt. commandant acting as Captain and Lieutenant Jaques (2), these officers resided in what was called New Lebanon now Columbia Co. NY—This deponent acted as a waiter (3) to Lieut. [J]aques—marched form New Concord in said Col. Co. and marched through Claverack, Livingston Manor, Rhinebeck, Red Hook, Poughkeepsie, to FishKill and was stationed on the hill about half a mile from the Yellow Church in Fishkill, and served about Four Months—This deponent cannot by reason of his age & loss of memory swear positively as to the precise length of his service but according to his best recollection he served not less than four months—that he recollects was the time for which the company was called out.

That in April 1781, he enlisted in Canaan Columbia County NY for nine months in Capt. Silas Grey's (4) company in a regiment commanded as he thinks by Col. John McKinstry (5) when he enlisted but afterwards he thinks Col. Willett had command. Lieut. Fonda (6) belonged to the company—Sergeant Seth Rowley (7) whose affidavit is annexed, marched several of the soldiers of which deponent was one from Canaan through Kinderhook Schodack and Greenbush to Albany - and remained there at the barracks two or three weeks under the command of Lieut Fonda and from there marched under him up the river to Saratoga—and there were placed under the command of Capt. Silas Grey and remained at Saratoga until cold weather and until the term of service of service had expired being about the commencement of the year 1782. When the company were discharged—this deponent received a written discharge—He served his tour his full term of nine months. Recollects Col. VanSchaaick(8)—who was at Saratoga part of the time we were there.—The discharge which deponent received was signed as he believes by a Capt. Darrow (9) who was with the troops—but the same has long been lost—or else signed by Col. McKinstry and he's not certain which.

On the 6th day of April 1782 again enlisted at Canaan Col. Co. for nine months, in Capt. Joseph Harrison's (10) Company Col. Marinus Willet's Regiment and marched to Albany and were there mustered by Col. Willet from there marched to Schoharie Middle Fort and Capt. Harrison had command at the Fort—and remained there at the fort about five months. The deponent went with a Lieutenants grade com'd, by Lieut Loop (11) from Schoharie & Cattskill Greene Co. NY on the North River and remained there about two months when we were sent for and returned again to Schoharie Middle Fort—where this deponent continued to serve until a short time before this deponents time expired (in November as he thinks) when he was taken sick and given over by the surgeon and was taken home by deponents father—in the fall or beginning of winter—The time this deponent served before he was taken sick was seven months certainly and perhaps more—and during rest of term of enlistment this deponent was so sick as to be unable to do duty as a soldier. There was no other company in the fort, but the one to which this deponent belonged.

This deponent refers to the annexed affidavits as to his character and reputation-- he also would state that the last paper annexed, directed to whom it may concern was sent with the other papers not as positive proof, but to show what was the opinion of his neighbors in New Canaan where he lived formerly as to his reputation as an old soldier—It could not be regularly authenticated as many of the Signed have already gone to the grave—the affidavits of "Benj. Benjmain, Seth Rowley and Isaac Richardson" prove this deponents services they are all regularly sworn. (Signed with his mark) Ebenezer Benjamin

Sworn before me. J. Hathaway, Judge &c.

End Notes—S.12151—Ebenezer Benjamin (Benjamius)

1. Moses Jones was the Second Lieutenant in Captain Thadeus Noble's Company of Associated Exempts of Albany County Militia. (King's District)
2. So far a Lieutenant Jaques (Jacques, etc.) has not been located in the militia.
3. As Ebenezer was only 13 in 1779 his service as a waiter would not count as military service.

4. Silas Gray was appointed Captain on April 27, 1781 in Lieutenant Colonel Commandant Marinus Willett's Regiment of New York State Levies.
5. John McKinstry was appointed Major on April 27, 1781 in Lieutenant-Colonel Willett's Regiment. McKinstry was appointed on April 28, 1781 as Lieutenant-Colonel Commandant but because he never completed his regiment with 2 or 3 years men he may never have been commissioned as Lieutenant-Colonel. He is listed as a Major on Willett's Regimental Pay Roll until December 31, 1781.
6. Lieutenant Abraham Fonda was in Captain Gray's Company. Fonda was later appointed Captain to command the former Captain Holtham Dunham's Company in Willett's Regiment.
7. Sergeant Seth Rowley served in Willett's Regiment but not in the same company.
8. Goose VanSchaick was the Colonel of the First New York Continental Regiment.
9. George Darrow was appointed Captain on April 28, 1781 in Colonel McKinstry's Regiment but the company did not complete its enlistment quota.
10. Joseph Harrison served as a Captain in Lieutenant-Colonel Willett's Regiment from 1781 to the end of 1783.
11. Peter Loop served in Willett's Regiment in 1781 and 1782.

Pension Application for Bethuel Bond

W.21,686 (Widow Lydia. Bethuel died 15th Aug 1841. Pension granted to Lydia at the rate of $37.42 per annum.)

State of New York

Chautauqua County SS.

On this twelfth day of October in the year of our Lord one thousand eight hundred & thirty two personally came before the court of Common Pleas of the County of Chautauqua being a court of Record & having a seal & Clerk Bethuel Bond a resident of the town of Chautauqua in said County aged sixty nine years on the twentieth day of May last who being first duly sworn according to law doth on his oath make the following declaration in order to obtain the benefit of the act of Congress passed June 7th 1832. That he entered the service of the United States & served under the following named officers and served as herein stated. That about the first of July in the year one thousand seven hundred and seventy eight the year after Burgoine (1) was [?] at Stockbridge in Berkshire County in the State of Massachusetts, he voluntarily enlisted in Captain Enos Parkers Company of Massachusetts Militia for the term of six months. Captain Parker Resided in Pittsfield, the other officers I do not recollect. We marched from Stockbridge about the first of July 1778 through the towns of Tyringham, Glasco, West Springfield. Crossed Connecticut [next?] & were stationed at East Springfield to guard the magazines & Burgoines Brass Artillery and to transport powder & Cartridges (3) to such places as ordered by

General Washington. (2) When General Washington was stationed at White Plains & after a severe action with the enemy he went to Springfield for Powder Ball & Cartridges. His orders were quickly obeyed thirteen covered waggons were soon loaded & sent to White Plains. My Captain called on me to take with me seven men & go as a guard with the powder to Genl Washington. We crossed the River - went through Suffield, Weathersfield, Hartford, New Haven saw the British fleet in the Sound went on to Genl Washington & delivered said thirteen waggon loads without sustaining the least damage. Returned again to Springfield soon after Genl Washington sent for a number of waggon loads to be forwarded to Peekskill on the North River. My Captain called on me to guard the same & took seven men & went from Springfield through Suffield & Litchfield to Peekksill, near the North river. Delivered the loading safe [sic] & returned to Springfield soon after—Genl Washington sent for a number of waggon loads of the same load as before named to be sent to Providence in Rodesland [Rhode Island]. The Captain called on me the third time to go with the seven men & guard them [?] we went from Springfield to Providence & delivered the loadering in good order returned to Springfield & remained there on duty until the first day of January in the year 1779 & was then honourably discharged by my Captain after a faithful service of six months. About the first day of August in the year 1779. I voluntarily enlisted in Captain Hialls company of Massachusetts Militia at the town of Stockbridge where I then resided the other officers I cannot now recollect. We marched from Stockbridge through Barrington, Sheffield, Canaan, Goshen & Litchfield & from thence to New Haven as Continentals on the seaboard arrived there soon after in battle. Were stationed at New Haven as a guard one month & returned again to Stockbridge. In the year 1780 I went to Weststockbridge where my parents then resided. At this time the Indians & Tories made such havock & inroads on our frontiers at Cherry Valley & Schoharie with Brant (4) & Butler & some British officers that I voluntarily enlisted in Captain Ford's (5) company in which Harrison Richmond (6) was Lieutenant in Col. Browns regiment. I enlisted the latter part of the month of July at Weststockbridge aforesaid & marched from thence through Albany to Schoharrie & was stationed at the upper Fort enlistment was for three months. I enlisted about the time that Butler & Brant (7) went to Schoharrie with several hundred Indians & tories & laid the town in ashes, fought at the middle & lower Fort most of the day. The enemy were defeated & drove through the woods crossed the Mohawk river engaged in battle with Col. Brown (8) at Stonyraba [Stone Arabia] near Johnstown killed and scalped him & a large number of his men. We who were stationed at the Upper Fort followed the enemy up the river to Fort Plain near the German Flatts where they took to the woods & returned from whence they came. The latter part of October or beginning of November I returned to Weststockbridge after having served faithfully three months. And this deponent says that in all he was in the service of the United States during the revolutionary war as least ten months nine months of which he has shown by three affidavits of Zenas Higgins & Warren Hull hereto annexed that as to the other month he has no documentary evidence & knows of no person living by whom he can prove the same. He hereby relinquishes every claim whatever to a pension or annuity except the present and declares that his name is not on the pensions of the agency of any state. (Signed) Bethuel Bond.

Sworn in open Court the 12th day of October 1832 before F. B. Campbell, a judge of Chau. Com. Pleas

Letter in reply to inquiry in the pension file, dated January 25, 1924.

I have to advise you that from the papers in the Revolutionary War pension claim, W.21696, it appears that Bethuel Bond was born May 20, 1762 or 1763, in Dover, Dutchess County, New York.

While a resident of Stockbridge, Berkshire County, Massachusetts, he enlisted July 7, 1778 and served until January 1, 1779 as private in Captain Enos Parker's Company, Colonel Jacob Gerrish's Massachusetts Regiment.

He enlisted July 18, 1779 and served until August 22, 1779 in Captain Ambrose Hill's Company, Colonel Miles Powell's Massachusetts Regiment.

He enlisted July 21, 1780, and served until October 27, 1780 as Corporal in Captain Foord's Company, Colonel John Brown's Massachusetts Regiment.

He was allowed pension on his application executed October 12, 1832, while a resident of Chautauqua, Chautauqua County, New York. He died August 15, 1841, in Chautauqua, New York.

He married in 1791 in Westfield, Washington County, New York, Lydia Dolph. She died August 9, 1845, and was buried in Chautauqua, New York.

Their children were—

Polly, born April 3, 1792, died November 4, 1797
Laura, born November 16, 1793
Olive, born August 7, 1795
William D., born April 26, 1797
Phebe, born April 14, 1799
Ira, born January 24, 1801
Bethuel Jr., born March 10, 1803, died July 8, 1808
Maley or Gamaliel, born May 14, 1805
Minor T. born March 2, 1809
Polly M., born October 18, 1813

End Notes—Bethuel Bond—W.21686

1. British General John Burgoyne surrendered his army at Saratoga (present day Schuylerville, NY) on October 17, 1777.
2. General George Washington, Commander-In-Chief of the American Army.
3. Cartridges are fixed ammunition i/e. for artillery usually, powder and ball or grapeshot in a canvas sack to fit a particular size of cannon. For muskets cartridges were powder and a musket ball wrapped in paper.

4. Captain Joseph Brant, Lieutenant-Colonel John Butler and/or Captain Walter Butler.
5. It appears he is listed as Bartholomew as no Bethuel is listed. Bartholomew is listed as enlisting as a corporal on July 21, 1780 in Captain William Foord's company in Colonel John Brown's Regiment of Massachusetts State Levies. Bartholomew was discharged on October 27, 1780. A Seth Bond served as a private in the same company.
6. The lieutenants in Captain Foord's Company were Alpheus Spencer and Abel Pearson. No Harrison Richmond of any rank has been found serving in Colonel Brown's Regiment.
7. Sir John Johnson with his British forces laid waste to the Schoharie Valley on October 17, 1780.
8. Colonel Brown was killed with about 30 men from his regiment in the Battle of Stone Arabia in the morning of October 19, 1780.

Pension Application for Adam Bouman, Bowman, Bomen, Beauman, Bawman, or Bauman

S.10379
State of New York
Herkimer County

On the Twelfth day of October in the year One thousand Eight hundred and thirty two personally appeared in Open Court before the Court of Common Pleas in and for the said County of Herkimer now sitting Adam Bowman a resident of the Town of Herkimer in said County of Herkimer and State of New York aged Seventy three years in December last, who being first duly sworn according to law doth on his oath make the following declaration in order to obtain the benefit of the Act of Congress passed June 7th 1832.

That he entered the service of the United States under the following named officers and served as herein stated—That in the year of the Oriskany Battle (1) which was in the year 1777 in the Spring of the year he was drafted into the service of the United States and served under Captain Bigbread (2) for the term of five weeks and three days—that the service rendered at said time under said Bigbread was at and in the vicinity of Fort Stanwix (3) in guarding the men employed getting out Timber for said Fort which was then building and for pickets for said Fort and for buildings for Barracks which were then constructing—that he was not himself employed in laboring upon said works but acted as a guard and was daily stationed out side of the works to guard and defend the men employed upon said works—that he does not remember who were the Subaltern Officers under Captain Bigbread—that he at the time resided at Herkimer in Tryon County now Herkimer County and that Captain Bigbread resided at Palatine then also in Tryon County now Montgomery—that when he was drafted he was marched from Herkimer where he resided to Fort Stanwix and at the end of said tour of five weeks and three days service he was discharged and returned home to Herkimer—that no written discharge was ever given him for said five weeks and three weeks service. That afterwards in the same year he was again drafted and went to Fort Stanwix and was there three or four weeks opening a road, He don't remember who was his officer at that time. - That in the year 1778 (4) being the year after his said aforesaid Term of service he enlisted and served for the Term of nine months. That he enlisted for said Tour of nine months into a company of Rangers under the command of Captain Marks Demuth.

That he does not recollect who were the Subaltern Officers in the Company of Captain Demuth except Lieutenant John Damouth and David Gorden—(5)

That said Company was under the command of Colonel Peter Bellinger (6) as he believes who was a Colonel of the Militia at Herkimer. That his said Term of Nine months service was performed chiefly at Fort Dayton at Herkimer when he and the company of Captain Demuth were most of the time stationed to guard said Fort—that he was occasionally during said nine months employed and sent out with others of said company as scouts—that was often as four or five times he served as a guard to guard Boats on the Mohawk River from Herkimer to Fort Stanwix during his said enlistment for nine months—that at the expiration of nine months he was discharged at Herkimer and has no knowledge or recollection that any written discharge was ever given him for said term of nine months service—

The during his said two different periods of enlistment aforesaid he was in no battle but in Skirmishes and does not know the names of any of the officers in the regular service although there were some Regulars at Fort Dayton when he was Stationed there during his enlistment for nine months Was along with the troops when Butler was killed, see him after he was shot—it was up the West Canady Creek. (7)

And the said Adam Bowman further states that he was enrolled in a company of Militia at the beginning of the Revolutionary War under the command of Henry Harter (8) Lieutenant John Demuth and Lieutenant Peter Weber [Weaver], Ensign John Bellinger—That said company was in a Regiment commanded by Colonel Peter Bellinger, Lieutenant Colonel Frederick Bellinger and Major Denis Clapsattle—(9) that the orders were then they must keep themselves in readiness at all times to march at a minutes warning and he during the whole of the war except when at Fort Stanwix under Captain Bigbread and when he was enlisted under Captain Demuth served in the company of Captain Harter and kept himself ready at all times to march at a minutes warning—that he was during the whole of the war Stationed at Fort Dayton and almost continually engaged on duty at said Fort Except when absent on duty—He sometimes worked on a farm and hoeing corn. - That the inhabitants in the vicinity of Fort Dayton were collected At Fort Dayton during most of the War That he and the rest of the Militia of that neighborhood were kept at said Fort to guard said Fort and the inhabitants living at the Fort—That there were times when the Militia were not on duty at the Fort—That sometimes some Continental troops were stationed at said Fort to guard the Fort but that the Militia and he among them were almost continually engaged upon duty at said Fort—That he was sometimes with the rest of the militia ordered out in pursuit of the enemy—that he was in the Battle on the West Canada Creek when Butler was killed that he has no documentary evidence of any of his services.

That he was born at Canajoharie now in the County of Montgomery & State of New York on the [blank] day of December 1758.

Will be 74 years old Dec. 14th next.

That there is a record of his age.

That he has a transcript of said Record with him.

That he lived at Germanflatts now Herkimer in the County of Herkimer then Tryon County when he entered the service—that he has lived at Herkimer ever since the Revolutionary War.—

That his first service was in the Militia—He was next drafted under Capt. Bigbread. He was next enlisted for nine months under Captain Demuth—and he then again served in the Militia under the officers hereinbefore named to the close of the war. That he never received a written discharge for any of his service.

That he is known to Christopher Bellinger, John Dockstader and Philip Harter (10) who can testify to his character for his services as a soldier of the Revolution.

And he hereby relinquishes every claim whatever to a pension or annuity except the present and declares that his name is not on the pension roll of the agency of any state. (Signed Adam Bowman)

Sworn to and Subscribed the day and year aforesaid—in Open Court. Julius C. Nelson, Clerk

Notation on another paper, There is no date relative to wife of children. He died Oct. 4, 1834, date of death taken from Agency Book.

End Notes—S.10379—Adam Bouman

1. The Battle of Oriskany was fought on August 6, 1777.
2. John Breadbake, Captain of the Fifth company in Colonel Jacob Klock's Second Regiment of Tryon County Militia. For many of these work details, detachments were sent from the various regiments of the Tryon County Militia and placed under various officers of the different regiments.
3. In 1776 Fort Stanwix was renamed Fort Schuyler in honor of Major General Philip Schuyler. Most of this work that Adam speaks of was done in 1776 as Fort Schuyler was garrisoned by the Third New York Continental Regiment by March of 1777.
4. Adam is wrong about the year for this service. Captain Hans Marcus or Marks Demuth's Company of Tryon County Rangers was formed on August 1, 1776 and they were discharged on March 27, 1777.
5. There are no muster rolls for this company but one of the lieutenants is John Adam Frederick Helmer, commonly called Adam Helmer. Many

of the pensioners that claim to have been in Captain Demuth's Company mention a Robert Gordon as being the other lieutenant.

6. Peter Bellinger was the colonel of the Fourth Battalion of Tryon County Militia. Adam served in this regiment for most of his service except when he was in Captain Demuth's Company. Most of the men in Demuth's Company had enlisted from Bellinger's Regiment.
7. Captain Walter Butler was killed at the West Canada Creek on October 30, 1781.
8. Captain Henry Harter, First Lieutenant John Demuth, Second Lieutenant Peter James Weaver and Ensign John T. Bellinger were in Colonel Bellinger's Regiment. According to Captain Harter's payroll for 1779 Adam served as follows: June 6 days, July 8 days, August 14 days, September 1 day, October 5 days and November for 3 days. In 1780 he served as follows: March 1 day, April 6 days, May 7 days, June 6 days, July 7 days, August 3 days, September and October 0 days, November 7 days and December 1 day. FROM: Revolutionary War Rolls, 1775-1783, Series M-246, Roll 72, folder 78, National Archives, Washington, D.C.
9. Frederick Bellinger was the Lieutenant Colonel and Augustinus Clapsaddle was the Second Major in Bellinger's Regiment. Bellinger was taken prisoner and Clapsaddle was killed at Oriskany.
10. John Dockstader and Philip Harter served in Captain Harter's Company.

Pension Application for Nicholas R. Bovie

S.12275
Nicholas was granted pension of $80 per annum.
State of New York
Chautauqua County

On this 17th day of August 1832, personally appeared before the Honorable Benjamin Walworth one of the Judges of the Court of Common Pleas in & for the County of Chautauqua in said State, at the town of Villenova in said County Nicholas R. Bovee, a native of Brunswick in the State of New Jersey, now of Villenova aforesaid, aged Seventy one years, who being first duly sworn, according to law, doth on his oath, make the following Declaration in order to obtain the benefit of the act of Congress passed June 7th 1832.

That about the first day of February 1777, he enlisted at Schenectady in the State of New York, for ten months, into the company of Capt. Reuben Symonds (1), as a private in the war of the Revolution, & that he was under Gen. Schuyler (2)—That he was mustered & sworn at Albany and was then marched to Saratoga, where he remained under Capt. Symonds, & in the Regiment commanded by Col. Schuyler for sometime, in cutting, loading & unloading logs for public works—he was then sent to Stillwater, and was engaged in carrying provisions and ammunition for the Army at Fort Edward—He was afterwards marched back to Schenectady, where on the first of January,

1778, he was discharged by Capt. Symonds, having then served Eleven Months—

That on the 1st March 1778, he again enlisted at Schenectady for ten months, under Capt. Cornelius Barhead (3) in the regiment of Col. Yates (4) under Genl Schuyler (5)—was mustered at Albany & marched to saratoga--& from thence to Coeyman's; thence to Fishkill, where he was discharged on the 25th December, 1778, by Capt. Barhead.

That afterwards, & he does not recollect the particular times, he served in the militia under Ensign Beverly (6) of Florida N.Y. Ensign Van Vechten (7) of Florida & Capt. McMasters of Florida, between five & six months, being classed & performing the service at different times.—

Militia, under Ensign Beverly, I was mainly engaged in garrison.

That in the whole he served about twenty five months—He was present & in the battle when Col. Brown (8) was killed, fighting against Sir William Johnson [Sir John Johnson, Sir William was dead before the war began] & the Indians—Col. Dubois then commanded the Regiment in which he served.

That he has no Documentary evidence of his service, and that he knows of no person, whose testimony he can procure, who can testify at his service—

He hereby relinquishes every claim whatever to an annuity or pension, except the present, and declares that his name is not on the pension roll of the agency of any state. (Signed with his mark) Nicholas R. Bovee.

Sworn to & subscribed the day & year first aforesaid before me.

Walworth, Judge B.Com. Pleas. Chau[tauqa]

State of New York
Chautauqua County SS.

I, Nicholas R. Bovee before named do herby, on oath testify & say, in addition to what was herein before stated by me, on the 17th August 1832, that I cannot be more particular as to my services under Captains Symonds & Barhead.—When I was out in the Militia, under Ensign Beverly, I was mainly engaged in Garrison at Johnstown, N.Y. and when under Ensign Van Vechten I was also principally engaged in Garrison duty at the same place—and when under Capt. McMasters, (Col. Vischer commanding the Regiment), I was part of the time doing Garrison duty at Canajoharie & part of the time doing like duty at Fort Hunter, & at the Block houses not far from Johnstown. I was under Capt. McMasters & Col Dubois commanded the Regiment in the Battle with Sir William Johnson [Sir John Johnson] as stated by me in my affidavit or Declaration annexed—After Col. Brown was killed as mentioned in my affidavit annexed, Genl. Van Rensselaer arrived and took command of the American forces & pursued Sir William Johnson and Sir William then went to Canada as I was informed—I was afterwards one of the Guard & pilot in a Boat, which took a number of our wounded men to Schenectady; after which I was discharged. And I do testify and say that I cannot make a more particular statement of my services, or a more minute detail of tours. (Signed with his mark) Nicholas R. Bovee

Sworn before me Jany 10th, 1833. B. Walworth

End Notes—Nicholas R.Bovie—S.12275

1. Captain Reuben Simonds commanded a company of Bateaumen.
2. There were several Colonel Schuyler's in the Albany County Militia.
3. Cornelius Barhydt was Captain of a Company of Bateaumen.
4. Colonel Christopher Yates of the Quartermaster Department.
5. Major General Philip Schuyler of the Continental Army.
6. Ensign David Beverly of Captain David McMaster's Company in the Third Regiment of Tryon County Militia under Colonel Frederick Visscher (Fisher).
7. Ensign Derick VanVechten (VanVeghten) in Captain Emanuel DeGraff's Company in Colonel Visscher's Regiment.
8. Nicholas was not at the Battle of Stone Arabia where Colonel John Brown was killed on October 19, 1780 in the morning. He was in the afternoon Battle of Klocksfield under Brigadier General Robert VanRensselaer. A detachment of the Third Tryon under Lieutenant-Colonel Volkert Veeder were at Klocksfield.

Pension Application for Valentine Boyer (Boyea, Buyer)

Declaration under Act of 7th July 1838

R.1100

State of New York

Oneida County

On this day of April, personally appeared before the Hon. Ralph McIntosh, Justice of a Court of Record and Special Surrogate in and for the County of Oneida and state aforesaid. Elizabeth Boyer of the Town of Lenox, County of Madison and State of New York to me made known, aged eighty seven years who being first duly sworn according to law, doth on her oath make the following declaration in order to obtain the benefits of the provisions made by act of Congress passed July 7th 1838, entitled "An Act Granting Half Pay and Pensions to Certain Widows."

That she is the widow of Valentine Boyer deceased, who was a private in the company commanded by Captain John Keyser (1)in a regiment commanded by Jacob Klock in the War of the Revolution.

That he entered the service aforesaid in about the month of [blank] A.D. 1776, and continued in active service in said War until the third day of December 1782, as this declarant was informed by her said husband Valentine Boyer deceased and which she truly believes to be true. That she well remembers when said Valentine entered the service or left his home for that, purpose which was, to wit, at the time above set forth and that she was informed afterwards by said Valentine as well as others who went with him from the same place to wit, Manheim in the County of Montgomery and State of New York, that being the place of his residence and when he was drafted or enlisted, that on or about the third day of May A. D. 1781, her husband Valentine Boyer was taken prisoner by the British officers and remained so imprisoned at Bucks Island in Canada for a period of 19 months, and who suffered greatly by the abuses practiced upon him by the British authorities. When on the third day of December A. D. 1782, (2) he was released and honorably discharged as will more fully appear by the proof hereunto annexed. That the number of his certificate of discharge as filed by the proper officer of the United States was No. 38052.

She further declares that she was married to said Valentine Boyer on the 20th day of March in the year of seventeen hundred and eighty. That her husband the aforesaid Valentine Boyer died on the 20th day of August A. D. 1832; that she was married to said Valentine Boyer prior to his leaving the service to wit, at the time above stated as will more fully appear by proof hereunto annexed where reference is made for greater certainty.

And she doth further declare that she is physically disabled to appear in open court is the reason why she appears before the Hon. Ralph McIntosh, Justice of a Court of Record and special surrogate in and for said County of Oneida in his office in the Village of Vernon in said county and she makes this application for a pension & arrears of pension which has accrued to her since the death of her husband in virtue of said act. (Signed with her mark) Elizabeth Boyer

Signed and sealed in the presence of W. Brown, Abraham Buyer

End Notes—R.1100—Valentine Boyer

1. Valentine served as a private and was later promoted to Corporal in Captain John Keyser's Company in Colonel Jacob Klock's Second Regiment of Tryon County Militia. He also at some time during the war served as a private under Captain Peter Waggoner (Wagner, etc.) in Colonel Klock's Regiment.
2. Valentine put a claim in for his back pay after the war while a prisoner from May 3, 1781 to December 3, 1782. It is in the Audited Accounts, Volume A., Page 225. Special Collections and Manuscripts, New York State Library, Albany, N.Y.

Pension Application for John Burgess

S.42639

Continental (New York)

The State of Ohio

Champaigne County

Before me the subscriber Samuel Hitt one of the associate Judges of the Court of Common Please [sic] in the County aforesaid personally came John Burgess who being duly sworn deposeth & saith that he this deponent some time in May 1782 enlisted in Capt. Machim Company of Artillery in Colonel Lamb Regiment of the State of New York for three years and was discharged some time in June 1784 and further saith that he is in circumstances which require assistance from his country for support and further saith not. (Signed with his mark) John Burgess

Sworn and subscribed to before me the second day of May 1818. Samuel Hitt; Asso. Judge.

Personally appeared in open court being the Court of Common Pleas of the County of Logan and State of Ohio on the 30th day of August 1820 John Burgess a resident of said County aged 64 years who being first duly sworn according to law doth on his oath declare that he enlisted in the year 1781 or 2 in March in the State of New York under Captain Malchom [Machin] (1) the regiment commanded by Col. Lamb of the artillery on Continental establishment entered for during the war and served out the full period of his Enlistment and was honorably discharged by Major Douty (2) at West Point—he further saith that he has received a pension under the law of the 18th March 1818 date of certificate 13 October 1818 and Number 3600.

And I do solemnly swear that I was a resident of the United States on the 18th of March 1818 and that I have not since that time by gift sale or in any other manner disposed of my property or any part thereof with intent hereby to diminish it so as to bring my self within the provisions of an act of Congress intitled an act to provide for certain persons engaged in the land and naval service of the United States in the revolutionary war passed on the 18th of March 1818 and that I have not nor any person for me any property or securities contracts or debts due to me nor have I any income other than what is contained on the schedule hereto annexed and by me subscribed—viz. two head of horses one calf eight head of hogs and some pigs—I have a debt coming to me of twenty one dollars twenty five cents but place little hope of ever collecting it and I am indebted one hundred and fifty dollars—I am 64 years of age by trade a cooper but for several years past unable to work. I have been under the doctors care for four years I have a wife that 62 years of age and one son named Hampton Burgess aged twenty years he is a cripple and unable to perform any labour. (Signed with his mark) John Burgess.

Sworn to and Subscribed in open Court on the 30th day of August 1820 before us. James McGlain, Levi Garwood & John Shelby; special judges of Logan County

End Notes—S.42639—John Burgess

1. Thomas Machin was a Captain in Colonel John Lamb's Second Continental Regiment of Artillery. John may have served under him in detachment service but he was not in his company.
2. John enlisted as a matross (Private) in Captain John Doughty's Company in the Second Artillery on April 10, 1783. FROM: Revolutionary War Rolls 1775-1783, Series M-246, Roll 118, Folder 41, National Archives, Washington, D.C. On June 17, 1783, Captain Doughty transferred to the Corps of Artillery. Captain Doughty was brevetted Major on September 30, 1783. He was commissioned Major of the Artillery Battalion on August 7, 1784. John Burgess may have served under Doughty in the Corps of Artillery to complete his

enlistment term as the Continental Army was discharged or disbanded on June 17, 1783.

Note: In the U.S. military, brevet referred to a warrant authorizing a commissioned officer to hold a higher rank temporarily, but usually without receiving the pay of that higher rank. An officer so promoted may be referred to as being brevetted and the promotion would be noted in the officer's title.

Pension Application for Michael Burgess

W.18674 (Widow: Hannah)
State of New York
Cayuga County SS.

On this 9th day of November 1850 personally appeared before me a Justice of the Peace in & for said County Jacob Burgess a resident of the County of Tompkins & State aforesaid who being duly sworn according to law doth on his oath make the following declaration in order to obtain the benefits of the Act or Join Resolution of Congress of 1st July 1848.

That he is the administrator of Hannah Burgess deceased who was the widow of Michael Burgess who was a Revolutionary Pensioner of the United States under the Act of March 18th 1818 at the rate of ninety six dollars per annum. That the said Hannah Burgess at the time of her death had not intermarried but continued the widow of the above mentioned Michael Burgess & was at the time of her death a Revolutionary Pensioner of the United States at the rate of $80.00 per Annum & died on the 21st day of May 1849 & that at her death she left the following named children her surviving who are her only children surviving to wit. Jacob Burgess of Ithaca NY & Austin Burgess of Ypsilanti in the State of Michigan.

This claim is made in order to obtain the benefit of the Joint Resolution of Congress of 1st July 1848 granting an increase of the pension of the said Hannah Burgess to the same rate per annum that was allowed her husband to wit ninety six dollars per annum the pension certificate of the said Hannah Burgess was as this deponent believed returned. (Signed) Jacob Burgess

Subscribed & sworn to the day & year first above written before me & I certify that the above named Jacob Burgess is a credible person. Harvey Heath Justice Peace.

Putnam County
State of New York SS.

In Putman County Court of Common Pleas June 1820—On this 7 day of June 1820 personally appeared in open court being a court of record by virtue of the Statute, Michael Burgess aged fifty seven years seven months and twenty seven days resident in the Town of Carmel County aforesaid who being first duly sworn according to law doth on his oath declare that he served in the Revolutionary War as follows. To wit. That he entered under Lieutenant Bowen (1) in Capt. Lenard Blakers [Bleecker] (2) Company in the 3d New York Regm, Commanded by Colo Peter Gansevoort of the New York Line, that after a new

arrangement he was transferred to Capt. Cornelius J. Johnston's Company in Colo Van Schaicks Regm.(3) That he is inscribed on the pension list roll of the New York Agency and his certificate is dated at Washington the War Office of the United States the 29th day of September 1818b and that his pension commenced the 21st day of March 1818 and I do solemly swear that I was a resident citizen of the United States ont eh 18th of March 1818 and that I have not since that time by gift sale or in any manner disposed of my property or any part thereof with intent thereby so to diminish it as to being myself with the provisions of an act of Congress entitled " an Act to provide for certain persons engaged in the land and naval services of the United States in the Revolutionary War passed on the 18th day of March 1818 and that I have not nor has any person in trust for me any property or securities contracts or debts due to me nor have I any income other than what is contained in the schedule hereunto annexed and by me subscribed and that I the same Michael Burgess am a common Labourer not having my [?] That from inability and age am unable to labour steadily that my family consists of the following persons. Viz, Michael Burgess aged as above.
Hannah Burgess aged 58 years unable to labour.
James Burgess aged 15 years unable to support himself.

(Signed) Michael Burgess (4)

Schedule. One cow two swine six chairs 2 pails 2 cots and both broke one frying pan one griddle one churn six plates 2 broken dishes 6 spoons 6 cups 8 saucers 6 knives & forks 1 chest one table one stand one pair of shove & tongs 1 pr handirons 1 smoothing iron two milk pans 1 earthen pot 1 ax one wash tub and barrel. (Signed) Michael Burgess.

Sworn to and subscribed in open court before the Judges of the same this seventh day of June 1820. Attest Rowland Bailey, Clerk

End Notes—W.18674—Michael Burgess

1. 1. Prentice Bowen, Second Lieutenant in Captain Leonard Bleecker's Company (Eighth Company) in Colonel Peter Gansevoort's Third New York Continental Regiment.
2. Michael enlisted as a private in Captain Bleecker's Company on May 22, 1777 for "during war".
3. On January 1, 1781 the First and Third New York Continental Regiments were consolidated into one regiment. Colonel Goose VanSchaick remained the Colonel of the First New York until the end of the war. Captain Cornelius T. Jansen was transferred to the Frst New York from the Third New York on January 1, 1781.
4. It is always interesting that when a soldier applies for a pension that he didn't mention any of the battles or campaigns that he was in to help support his pension application. Michael as part of the Third New York would have been in the siege of Fort Schuyler (Fort Stanwix) in August of 1777. As part of the Third New York he would have been in the Sullivan-Clinton Campaign in 1779 against the Iroquois in the western part of New York. In 1781 while in the First New York,

Michael served in the Yorktown, Virginia Campaign from September 28 to October 19, 1781. These are some of the major campaigns that Michael served in besides other battles that he might have been in.

Pension Application for Peter Warren Cain or Kane

W.16525 (Widow: Angelica)
State of New York
County of Schenectady SS.

On this twelfth day of October in the year of our Lord one thousand eight hundred and thirty two personally appeared in open Court, before the Judges of the Court of Common Pleas in and for said county now sitting Peter Warren Cain, a resident of the town of Glenville in said county & State aged upwards of eighty three years who being first duly sworn according to law, doth on his oath make the following declaration in order to obtain the benefit of the act of Congress passed June 7th 1832.

He was born in the village of Warrensbush in the then County of Tryon now Montgomery in the state of New York on the second or third day of March 1750. He has no record of his age except that contained in his family Bible.

When he was called into the service of the United States in the army of the revolution he was living in a place called Westina included within said town of Glenville, and since the Revolutionary War he has lived in the same place.

He now lives in the town of Glenville aforesaid.

He entered the service of the United States under the following named officers and served as herein stated.

In the spring of the year 1775, he was enrolled in Captain John Van Patten's (1) company of militia & served therein about one month when (he thinks in the month of may) he enlisted in Captain (afterwards Colonel) Cornelius VanDyck's (2) Company of the line of New York on the Continental establishment. His other Company and Field officers whom he recollects were Cornelius Van Slyck first Lieutenant--Guy Young Second Lieutenant—Goosen VanSchaick Colonel. He enlisted for, and served out the full term of nine months in said Company—while in this engagement he marched to Ticonderoga and Crown Point, and mounted guard at those posts. He also marched to the Isle de Aux Nox and his company formed part of the detachment that reduced Chamblee, fought at the siege of St. John's and aided in its reduction. The place of rendezvous of the troops to which he belonged was at St. John's Point.

In the beginning of the year 1776, he volunteered with the detachment of Militia from Schenectady in said Captain Van Patten's Company and proceeded to Johnstown on which occasion Sir John Johnson surrendered himself a prisoner of war & his tenants & dependants were disarmed. On his return he kept guard at Tunis Swart's (3) picket fort in Westina aforesaid—went out with several scouting parties. In which service and in mounting guard at said fort, and in said expedition to Johnstown, he performed military duty during the year 1776 for a term in the whole exceeding two months.

In the year 1777 in the fall thereof he was on duty with the northern army in the retreat of General Schuyler (4) in said Company of Captain Van Patten whose beat extended to that part of the township of Schenectady called Westina aforesaid in which he resided as aforesaid. He was in this expedition for the term of twenty-five days & longer—Previous to this expedition and subsequent thereto - during the year last named, he volunteered in the bateaux service under Myndert Wemple, he served under Myndert Wemple aforesaid for the term of nine months during said year, and was employed in transporting provisions and military stores for the use of the American troops in the Hudson & Mohawk rivers.—

In the year 1776, he served under (Col.) Peter Gaansevoort (5) at Sacondaga for a term exceeding ten days and aided the militia there in erecting works of defence. He was in the battle of Johnstown (6) in October 1781, and marched with the American forces in pursuit of the enemy as far as West Canada Creek (7) where & when Walter Butler was killed by an Indian. In this last expedition he was on duty more than fourteen days.

The inhabitants of Tryon and Albany Counties being threatened with incursions from the enemy at every point, the militia were called out on numerous occasions, and received scarcely any aid from the regular forces to defend their frontiers. He the claimant was out with the scouts of the Militia & Indians on very many occasions, the particular periods of which it is impossible for him to specify. Westina had a fort Called Tunis Swart's fort where the claimant mounted guard almost every day, when not called away to aid in the defence of some post in more immediate danger of attack, or in some expedition for the benefit of his country.

He was three times at Fort Hunter—He made several tours to Ballston, Palmertown, and round Saratoga Lake in search of tories who carried intelligence to the enemy—also to Norman's Kill, Heldebergh & to Bennington under Major Scott & Colonel Lynde (8)—in Captain John Price's (9) Company he thinks in February 1777 & also in 1778. He was at Tappan in the year 1778 and (he believes in the year 1780) assisted the American troops in making a road from Kingsberry to Pompton. In these different tours of service in the revolution he was engaged for a term in the whole exceeding seven months and in addition hereto (every season) for about six months every year in succession after the year 1777, he engaged in the business of boating provisions & Military stores in the Hudson & Mohawk rivers.

Besides the battle above stated he was in no other battles or skirmishes except during the period he served in the aforesaid Company of Captain Van Patten; he discharged the duties of orderly sergeant therein.

From the foregoing statement it will appear that the claimant hereby declares that the period he was engaged in actual duty during said war, exclusive of more than thirty-two months service as a Batteauman exceeds twenty months.

The following are the names of some of the regular officers whom he knew, or who were with the troops, where he served, and such continental and militia regiments or companies with which he served, or as he can recollect, viz:--Mc Tepen [or Mc Tessen], General Arnold, Gen'l St. Clair, General Wooster, General Montgomery, (10) General Schuyler.

He never received any written discharge from the service.

He has no documentary evidence and knows of no person whose testimony he can procure who can testify to his service except those whose depositions are hereto annexed.

The following are the names of persons to whom he is known in his present neighborhood, and who can testify to his character for veracity, and their belief of his services as a soldier of the revolution, to wit: John Sanders and John Van Eps.

He hereby relinquishes every claim whatever, to a pension or annuity except the present and declares that his name is not on the pension roll of the agency of any State. (Signed with his mark) Peter Warren Cain

Subscribed and sworn to the day and year first aforesaid. John S. Vrooman, Clerk

Reply to a letter requesting information dated July 21, 1931.

Your are advised that it appears from the papers in the Revolutionary War pension claim, W.16525, that Peter Warren Cain or Kane was born March 1, 2 or 3, 1750 in WarrenBush, Tryon (later Montgomery) County, New York.

While residing at Westina (later Glenville), Schenectady County, New York, he served with the New York troops, as follows:

In the spring of 1775, one month in Captain John Van Petten's Company, Colonel Abraham Wemple's regiment; from May, 1775,nine months as private in captain Cornelius Van Dyck's company, Colonel Goose Van Schaick's regiment, and was at the siege of St. John's' in 1776, about two months in Captain John Van Petten's company, Colonel Abraham Wemple's regiment and marched to Johnstown, at which time Sir John Johnson surrendered himself a prisoner of war, was afterwards in several scouting parties, a part of the time under Colonel Peter Gansevoort; in 1777,nine months in the bateau service under Captain Myndert R. Wemple, transporting provisions and military stores on the Hudson and Mohawk Rivers; in the fall of 1777, twenty-five days in captain John VanPetten's Company, Colonel Abraham Wemple's regiment; in 1780, four months under Captain William James and assisted in making a road from Kingston to Pompton; in October 1781 he was in the battle of Johnstown. He was out many times against the Indians in protecting the frontiers under Captains Joseph Peck or Peek, John Price and Colonels Lynde and Beekman (11) and he served until the close of the war.

He stated that he served twenty months in the military service, a part of the time as orderly sergeant, and thirty-two months in the bateau service.

He was allowed pension on his application executed January 28, 1832, at which time he was living in Glenville, Schenectady County, New York.

He died July 10, 1833.

The soldier married January 22, 1777 in Schenectady, New York, Angelica, her maiden name not given.

She was allowed pension on her applications executed October 24, 1836, at which time she was living in Glenville, New York, and was aged ninety-four years.

Their son Peter was baptized June 14, 1878 (sic—1778) in the Reformed Dutch Church at Schenectady, New York. There is no further reference to children.

The above noted Peter Cain (all spellings of that name were searched) is the only soldier of that name found on the Revolutionary War records of this bureau.

End Notes—W.16525—Peter Warren Cain

1. John VanPatten was Captain of the Third Company in Colonel Abraham Wemple's Second Regiment of Albany County Militia.
2. Cornelius VanDyck was commissioned Captain of the Second Company in Colonel Goose VanSchaick's Second New York Continental Regiment on June 28, 1775. So far only one muster roll has been found for the company and Peter's name is not on it. It was published in the New York Genealogical & Biographical Record, Vol 48, pp 156-157, April 1917. Peter has the names of the lieutenants correct and what the Second New York's part was in the Canadian Campaign.
3. Teunis Swart was the First Lieutenant in Captain VanPatten's Company.
4. Major General Philip Schuyler of the Continental Army.
5. This happened in April and May of 1779. Peter Gansevoort was the Colonel of the Third New York Continental Regiment.
6. The Battle of Johnstown was fought on October 25, 1781.
7. Captain Walter Butter was killed at West Canada Creek on October 30, 1781.
8. Major Scott and Colonel Lynde are unknown at this time.
9. John Price served as a Lieutenant, Captain and Major in Colonel Jacob Lansing, Jr's First Regiment of Albany County Militia.
10. Major General Benedict Arnold, Major General Arthur St. Clair, Brigadier General David Wooster and Major General Richard Montgomery.
11. Lieutenant Colonel John H. Beekman of Colonel Kilian VanRensselaer's Fourth Regiment of Albany County Militia.

Pension Application for Nicholas Camp

S.12446
Mass. & New York
Otsego Com. Pleas of October Term 1832.
Declaration in order to obtain the benefit of the act of Congress passed June 7, 1832.
State of New York

Otsego County.

On this 17th day of October 1832 personally appeared in open court before the Judges of the Court of Common Pleas, in & for the County of Otsego being a court of record & now sitting Nicholas Camp a resident of the Town of Herkimer, county & state aforesaid who being duly sworn according to law doth on his oath make the following declaration in order to obtain the benefit of the act of Congress passed June 7, 1832. That he entered the service of the United States & served under the following named officers as herein stated.

To wit, that he was seventy seven years of age on the first day of June last & in the year 1776, he was a resident of the Town of Pittsfield in the County of Rensselaer, N. York & in the month of January of that year he enlisted into the service at Pittstown aforesaid for the term of one year in a company commanded by Captain Benjamin Hicks (1) & Lieuts Guy Youngs & Nennon Vanderhyden, Ensign Jonathan Brown in Colo VanSchaick's Regt & Lieut Col Ganesvoorts (2) & in Genl Schuyler's (3) Brigade. He marched from Pittstown to Albany from thence to Saratoga then to Fort Miller & Fort Edward, Lake George & Fort Ticonderoga. Here a part of his regt remained a short time with Col. Wynkoop's (4) Regt & from thence to Lake George where we remained most part of the summer. He thinks it was late in the fall when they were marched back to Albany under Col. VanSchaick in this month they were obliged to ford the Mohawk River & in consequence many of them were taken sick one of whom was this deponent about the last of December being still sick he received a furlough from either Col. VanSchaick or Col. Gansevoort he cannot tell which for fourteen days to return home. His sickness still continuing he remained at home & was there when his time expired & therefore never returned to the Army.

In June 1777 he had moved to Adams Mass. with his father & was called out in the militia under Capt. Shubael Wilmot as a substitute for Samuel Salisbury then of the Town of Adams & this deponent thinks it was in Col. Simon's Regt or in Col. Powell's Regt & he cannot recollect which. He was marched to Saratoga N.Y. on an alarm, where he remained for the term of four weeks when he was discharged & returned home—In the summer of 1778 he was called out under Lieut. Joseph Powers in Adams aforesaid to assist in guarding prisoners to Stillwater N.Y. Their prisoners were men who refused to serve in the American Army after having been drafted. He was in this service twelve or fifteen days & returned home. In the month of May 1780 he went in the place of Sergeant Alger for which he received $5.00 extra. He volunteered in the Militia at Pittstown NY for four months under Capt. Cornelius Wilsey (5) & Lieut Abner VanAma as he thinks & in Col. Peter Yates Regt, Croesbeck (6) was the Major of the Regt. He marched to Saratoga & a place called Palmer Town where they were stationed this place was about 7 miles, west of Ballstown Springs he was stationed there most of the time when he was discharged & returned home. In the month of May as he recollects in the year 1781. He again volunteered under Capt. Thomas Brown (7) in a regt commanded by Col. VanRensselaer (8) & Col. Peter Yates. He was stationed north of Fort Edward,

Fort Ann, Fort Miller, Jessups Patent, PalmerTown & at the Scotch Patent & his employment was north in Scouting parties & in garrison duty. He served this service six months when he was discharged & returned home. He never received a written discharge from the regular service in consequence of being at home on furlough when his time expired as aforesaid nor at any other times. He has no documentary evidence by which to prove his services but he refers the department to the affidavits of Timothy Price & John Price (9) herewith enclosed for further information. He can procure no other testimony to his knowledge.

He hereby relinquishes all claim whatever to a pension or annuity except the present & declares that his name is not on the pension roll of the agency of any state. He never served as a substitute except as before noted. He was born on the 11th day of June 1755 in the Town of [Ritobette?]in the state of Massachusetts where he lived until about 17 years of age when he removed to the Town of Adams with his parents from thence to Pittstown N. York until about 28 years since when he removed to Hartwick aforesaid where he has ever since resided. He has no record of his age but taken from his parents. (Signed with his mark) Nicholas Camp.

Sworn & subscribed the day & year aforesaid in open court. Horace Lathrop, Clerk.

End Notes—S.12446—Nicholas Camp

1. Unfortunately there are no known muster rolls for Captain Hicks' Company (Fifth Company) in 1776. The other company officers were Guy Young as the First Lieutenant, Nanning VanDerhiden (DerHeyden, etc.) as the Second Lieutenant and Jonathan Brown as the Ensign. This company belonged to the un-numbered New York Continental Regiment commanded by Colonel Goose VanSchaick.
2. Peter Gansevoort Jr. was appointed Lieutenant-Colonel on March 19, 1776 in Colonel VanSchaick's Regiment.
3. Major General Philip Schuyler of the Continental Army.
4. Cornelius D. Wynkoop was the Colonel of the Fourth New York Continental Regiment in 1776.
5. Cornelius Witzie's (Wilsey, Wiltsy, etc.) was appointed captain on June 22, 1778 in Colonel Peter Yates' Fourteenth Regiment of Albany County Militia. The following served as officers in Captain Wiltzi's Company. Abney VanAmy as First Lieutenant, Ezekiel Halstead as Second Lieutenant, and John Harvey as Ensign. They were all appointed on the same day as Captain Wiltze.
6. John W. Groesbeck was appointed First Major on June 22, 1778 in Colonel Yates' Regiment.
7. Thomas Brown was appointed captain on June 22, 1778 in Colonel Yates' Regiment. The following were appointed as officers on the same date in Captain Brown's Company: Jacob VanNess as First Lieutenant, Eldert Fonda as Second Lieutenant and Gamaliel Waldo as Ensign.

8. John VanRensselaer was appointed in 1775 as Second Major in Colonel John Kickerbocker's Fourteenth Regiment of Albany County Militia. On June 22, 1778, John was appointed Lieutenant-Colonel in Colonel Yates' Regiment who had been appointed Colonel on June 22, 1778 in place of Colonel Knickerbocker.
9. Timothy and John Price has served as privates in Colonel Yates' Regiment.

Pension Application for John Campbell

S.12667
State of Ohio
Cuyahoga County SS.

On this 4th day of August 1832, personally appeared in open court before the Supreme Court of said state now sitting in said county John Campbell a resident of Chagrin township in the County of Cuyahuga and State of Ohio aged seventy years on the 11th day of May 1832 who being duly sworn according to law doth on his oath make the following declaration in order to obtain the benefit of the act of Congress passed June 7th 1832.

That he entered the service under the following named officers and served as herein stated. In the year 1778 in the month of August he was drafted as a militia man (he was then living in Nobletown Albany County now called Hillsdale and attached to Columbia County) and was put into a company commanded by Capt. VanAlstine (1), Lieut Fonda and was marched to Johnstown and served one month the company was attached to a Regiment commanded by Col. John Harper (2). In the month of September in the year 1779 he entered as a volunteer in a company commanded by Capt. McGonegal, Lieut. Vaughan in Col. Beebees (3) Regiment (New York Militia) for a term of three months, said Regiment & also one or two other Regiments lay at Fishkill two or three miles east of Hudson River. That he was discharged after a service of about six weeks. That Gov. Clinton was there when the troops were discharged.

That in the year 1780 in the month of March he enlisted for a term of nine months in Capt. Walter Vroom [Vrooman's] Company (4), Lieut Bateman (5) in Col. John Harpers Regiment in May in the same year the Regiment marched to Herkimer there in the same month. He enlisted into the continental line under Capt. Titus (6), Lieut. Tuttle to serve the remainder of the nine months and fifteen days in addition was marched to Albany and from there went by water to West Point and from there marched to Orange Town, and was then attached to Col. Wisenfelt's Regiment. That the Regiment lay there & in the neighbourhood during the summer that Genl Washington (7) kept his Head Quarters near there during the time. That he thinks that the American Army was about forty thousand strong then. That Genl Clinton (8) Commanded a Brigade then, that he saw Maj. Andre (9) when he was brought in a prisoner. That he was at work on a Block House at Dobb's Ferry Haverstraw Bay when Andre was executed. That in the month of November in the same year Col.

Wisenfielt's Regiment was marched to West Point and went from there by water to Albany and from there marched to Fort Stanwix that they drove up some cattle & some of the soldiers took up some provisions by water (10), that the regiment went to Fort Stanwix to relieve Col. Vanscank's [VanSchaick] Regiment.

That he returned to Albany in December of the same year with Col. VanSchank's Regiment & was then discharged that he received a written discharge signed by Major Van Scowter (11) but that he lost said discharge a number of years since. That in the year 1781 in the month of March he went to Saratoga and enlisted for a term of nine months into Capt. Dunham's (12) Company, Col. McKinstry's (13) Regiment of New York State troops and in May in the same year agreed to extend the term of his enlistment to the term of three years. That during that season he served a part of the time as a Baker. That in the month of December following he went home to NobleTown aforesaid on a furlough and joined the troops in January following at Albany and was marched to Ballstown and was put into Capt. Wright's (14) Company Col. Marinus Willet's Regiment. That on the last of May or first of June following the regiment was marched Stone Arabia & from there to Fort Herkimer—That in the year 1782 in the latter part of the season he was sick and permitted to return home, and did not regain his health so as to be able to join his regiment until it was discharged—That about the year 1792 he removed to Bainbridge in the County of Chenango County, State of New York, from whence he removed in 1808 to Manillus in Onondaga County same state from which last place he removed in 1823 to Cuyahoga County State of Ohio where he now resides—That he is known to William Wait, John M. Henderson, Daniel Christy, Nehemiah Allen who reside in my neighbourhood & who I think can testify to my veracity & their belief of my being a Revolutionary War Soldier and that he knows of no person who can testify to his service.

That he hereby relinquishes every claim whatever to a pension or annuity except the present and declares that his name is not on the pension roll of any state. That he was born in Blanford Hampshire County State of Massachusetts in the year 1762. (Signed) John Campbell

Sworn to in Open Court Aug. 4, 1832. H. Perry, Clk.

Reply to letter of inquiry dated November 27, 1933.

The record of John Campbell is furnished below as found in the papers on file in pension claim S.12667, based upon his service in the Revolutionary War.

John Campbell was born May 11, 1762 in Blanford, Hampshire County, Massachusetts; the names of his parents are not shown.

While a resident of Nobletown, Albany County (later Hillsdale, Columbia County), New York, he enlisted and served as private in the New York troops as follows: from August 1776, one month in Captain VanAlstyne's company, Colonel John Harper's regiment; from September, 1779, six weeks in Captain McGonegal's company, Colonel Beebe's regiment; from March 1780, in

Captain Walter Vrooman's company, Colonel John Harper's regiment, was transferred in May 1780, to Captain Titus' company, Colonel Weisenfel's regiment, this service amounting to nine months and fifteen days; from March 1781, nine months in Captain Holt Dunham's company, Colonel McKinstry's regiment; from January 1782 until the latter part of the year in Captain Job Wright's company, Colonel Marinus Willett's Regiment.

In 1792, he moved to Bainbridge, Chenqango County, New York; in 1808, he moved to Marcellus, Onondaga County, New York, and in 1823, went to Cuyahoga County, Ohio.

He was allowed pension on his application executed August 4, 1832, at which time he resided in Chagrin Township, Cuyahoga county, Ohio.

In December 1845, John Campbell was residing in Orangeville, Wyoming County, New York; he stated then that he had returned lately from Ohio to live with one of his sons, but did not give the name of said son. The name of soldier's wife is not shown.

In December, 1845, one Lebanah Winchester, of Orangeville, New York, stated that he had been acquainted with the soldier, John Campbell, for more than thirty years.

The name "Winchester" is stated in correspondence as the name of daughter of soldier, at whose home in Orangeville, NY the soldier died (Oct 18, 1846) & is buried there.

End Notes—S.12661—John Campbell (Cammal, Camble, etc.)

1. There are two VanAlstyne's (VanAlstine) that served as Captains in the Seventh Regiment of Albany County Militia—Philip commanded the Third Company and Abraham commanded the Fifth Company. The regiment was commanded by Colonel Andries Witbeck. On April 2, 1778, Abraham VanAlstyne was appointed Colonel and Philip was appointed the Lieutenant-Colonel both of the Seventh Albany. Therefore he would have to have served in one of the companies before 1778 at which time he would have only been 15 years of age. There was no Lieutenant Fonda in this regiment.
2. John is in error as to the year or that Colonel John Harper was in Johnstown in September of 1779. Harper had joined Brigadier General James Clinton's Army as a volunteer and was appointed Captain of the Volunteers. Colonel Harper served in that capacity during the entire Sullivan and Clinton Campaign of 1779.
3. There appears to be no Colonel Beebee in the New York Militia. Also Captain McGonegal could not be found. There was a Second Lieutenant Obadiah Vaughan but by April 1, 1778 Ensign Oliver Bentley was commissioned the Second Lieutenant of the Fourth Company. The Regiment was commanded by Colonel Kilian VanRensselaer. (Fourth Regiment of Albany County Militia).
4. Lieutenant-Colonel John Harper's Regiment of New York State Levies was not organized until May 11, 1780. The regiment was raised only

for seven months. John did enlist as a private in Captain Walter Vrooman's Company.

5. John Bateman served as a Lieutenant in Captain Vrooman's Company. Bateman also served as the Adjutant for Harper's Regiment.
6. Again John has some of this right and some is wrong. Captain Jonathan Titus and Lieutenant Azariah Tuthill (Tuttle) served in the Fourth New York Continental Regiment under Lieutenant-Colonel Commandant Frederick Weisenfels in 1780. According to the muster rolls of the Fourth New York John did not serve in this regiment. Men from the various Levie Regiments were allowed to join the Continental Regiments to fill the under strength companies. Most of these men that joined the Fourth New York enlisted on July 5, 1780. Most of these men did not join the regiment until August of 1780. The regiment eventually returned to West Point, New York and did relieve the garrison at Fort Schuyler (Fort Stanwix). The Fourth New York replaced Colonel Harper's Regiment on November 22 because their enlistments were up on November 30th. Colonel Harper's Regiment had replaced the First New York Continental Regiment under Colonel Goose VanSchaick in late September.
7. Commander in Chief General George Washington.
8. Brigadier General James Clinton.
9. Major John Andre was captured in September of 1780 and Major General Benedict Arnold's treasonable acts were exposed. This was the major reason for the New York Continental Regiments and Levies were marched to West Point to defend it against a British attack. Andre was hanged on October 2, 1780.
10. Captain Samuel Gray's Company of Bateaumen did bring provisions to the fort at this time.
11. Major Elias VanBenschouten of Colonel William Malcom's New York State Regiment of Levies of 1780.
12. Lieutenant-Colonel Commandant Marinus Willett's Regiment of New York State Levies was organized with the officers being appointed April 27, 1781. Captain Holtham Dunham commanded his company until about July of 1781 when he was arrested for treasonable acts with the enemy. Abraham Fonda was serving as a Lieutenant in Captain Silas Gray's company in Willett's Regiment when he was appointed Captain of Dunham's Company.
13. John McKinstry was appointed Major on April 27, 1781 in Colonel Willett's Regiment. According to the pay abstract for Willett's Regiment, Major McKinstry served in that capacity from April 27 to December 31, 1781. FROM: Revolutionary War Rolls 1775-1783, Series M-246, Roll 78, Folder 173, National Archives, Washington, D.C.
14. There is no record so far that shows John as enlisting for the three years service. He is listed as a private in Captain Job Wright's Company for 1782 in Colonel Willett's Regiment.

Pension Application for Kenneth Campbell

S.44726
State of New York
Montgomery County SS.

For the purpose of obtaining the benefits of the act entitled an act for the relief of certain surviving officers and soldiers of the army of the revolution approved on the 15th day of May 1828, I Kenneth Campbell of the Town of Broadalbin the County and State aforesaid do hereby declare that I enlisted in the Continental Line of the Army of the Revolution for and during the war and continued in its service seven years and two months until its termination at which period I was a private in Captain Tiebouts (1) company in Colonel Willet's (2) Regiment the number of which he has forgotten in the New York Line, and I also declare that I received afterwards some certificate for some purpose but whether for his back pay rations or lands from the State of New York, he is unable to state at this period.

I further declare that I was not on the fifteenth day of May 1828, on the Pension list of the United States, New York agency in pursuance of this last mentioned act and the act in 1820. He was stricken off in consequence of said last mentioned act and that since the last mentioned act he has not received or drawn any pension or money from the United States or any of its agents. And I further declare that I received a regular discharge from the Army of the Revolution under the hand of George Washington the then commander in chief and that I forwarded that discharge to the War Department in the year 1818 as a part of the evidence of my services, identity and claim.

Witness my hand this 26th day of June 1828. (Signed with his mark) Kenneth Campbell

Subscribed & sworn to this 26th day of June 1828. Before me, Aaron Haring First Judge of Montgomery County Courts, New York State.

44726, Rev. Invalid, Kenneth Campbell, Rev. War. Act 18th March 1818, Index:--Vol. 3, page 74. [No indication as to disability.]

State of New York
County of Schenectady SS.

On this twelfth day of May 1818, before me Simon A. Groot the Subscriber, one of the Judges of the Court of Common Pleas of said County, personally appears, Kenneth Campbell, resident, late in Montgomery County, and is now in Schenectady, aged seventy five years or there abouts, who being by me first duly sworn according to law, doth on his oath make the following declaration in order to obtain the provision made by the late act of Congress, entitled an act to provide for certain persons engaged in the land and naval service of the United States, in the Revolutionary War, that the said Kenneth Campbell enlisted in Captain Tiebouts (3) Company the Third New York Regiment commanded by Col. Gansevoort in the year 1777 and was afterwards transferred to Col. Sytez' (4) Company in the First New York Regiment commanded by Colonel Van Schaick, and that he continued to serve to the close of the war in said company until the company was disbanded. That he was in Fort Stanwix when besieged by the enemy, at the Battles of the White Plains (5), Manmouth (6) and taking of Cornwallis (7)- And that he is reduced circumstances & stands in need of the assistance of his country for support and that he has no other evidence now but what is annexed. (Signed with his mark) Kenneth Campbell

Sworn before me this 12 day of May 1818. Simon A. Groot, one of the Judges of the Court of Common Pleas in and for the County of Schenectady.

End Notes—Kenneth Campbell (Camble, Cammel, etc.)—S.44726

1. Kenneth enlisted as a private on January 23, 1777 for during the war in Captain Thomas DeWitt's Second Company in Colonel Peter Gansevoort's Third New York Continental Regiment.
2. Marinus Willett was the Lieutenant-Colonel of the Third New York from November 21, 1776 to July 1, 1780.
3. Henry Tiebout was the Captain of the Seventh Company in the Third New York. Kenneth at some point most likely served under Captain Tiebout but it appears that he was not assigned to this company.
4. Actually Captain DeWitt had resigned on January 7, 1780. On July 1, 1780, Captain-Lieutenant George Sytez was commissioned full Captain of Captain DeWitt's Company. When the five New York Regiments were consolidated on January 1, 1781, Captain Sytez was transferred to the First New York.
5. The Battle of White Plains NY was fought on October 28, 1776. The Third New York under Colonel Gansevoort did not exist until November 21, 1776. If Kenneth was in that battle he was a soldier in another regiment.
6. The Battle of Monmouth, N.J. was fought on June 28, 1778. The Third New York was not in that battle. It was still stationed at Fort Schuyler (Fort Stanwix), N.Y. Lieutenant-Colonel Marinus Willett was in the Battle as he had been sent to find General George Washington to get the Third New York relieved from garrison duty at Fort Schuyler. It is not known if any of the Third New York accompanied Colonel Willett. The First New York was at the Battle of Monmouth and later in 1778 they were sent to Fort Schuyler to relieve the Third New York.
7. The Yorktown, Virginia Campaign was from September 28 to October 19, 1781.

Pension Application for Jeremiah Carpenter

R.1713
State of New York
County of Erie SS.

On this second day of August in the year one thousand eight hundred and thirty nine personally appeared before me Jonathan Hoyt a Judge of the Court of Common Pleas and General Sessions of the said County of Erie being a

Court of record, Jeremiah Carpenter a resident of the Town of Wales in the County of Erie and State of New York aged seventy nine years on the twenty eighth day of August instant—who being first by me duly sworn according to law doth on his oath make the following declaration in order to obtain the benefit of the Act of Congress passed June 7, 1832; that he entered the service of the United States under the following named officers and served as herein stated. That he was born in the County of Dutchess in the State of New York in the year 1760. That he has no record of his age—That when he first went into service he lived in the Town of Pittstown then in the County of Albany now Rensselaer County of the State of New York—That he lived for a number of years after the Revolutionary War in the said Town of Pittstown, afterwards in the Town of Pompcy in thc county of Onondaga, and for the last twenty one years he had resided in the said Town of Wales in Erie County in which he now resides—That he served in the Militia of the State of New York and volunteered as herein after stated & excepting once when he was draughted—

That the first time he was out, he was 17 years old, it was in the month of August in the year 1777, he then served as a volunteer under Major Groesbeck (1)—the name of the captain was Thomas Brown (2) of the Ensign Ezekiel Holsted—(3)

That deponent by reason of old age and loss of memory can not remember precisely the name of Major Grosbeck but he thinks his given name was Peter.

That he served as a private at that time under such officers—That he went with the same to Palmer Town (then called) in the said county of Albany and threw up a breast work; that two other companies were at the same place at the same time under Major Groesbeck. That the country was then alarmed by the excursions of the Indians and Tories and that was the reason of the troops going to PalmerTown. That he was then engaged in such service at that time one month before he was discharged.

That afterwards in the same year 1777 he performed two months duty as a volunteer & in the garrison at Fort Edward on the North River in October and November 1777, under Col. Stephen VanRensselaer (4) Captain Richard Woolsey, Lieutenant Joseph Gifford, & Ensign Ezekiel Holsted. That he performed at that time two months garrison duty and was then discharged. That in the summer of 1778 he performed three months service under the same officers in garrison and out of it at Fort Edward—then at Fort George, Crown Point and Ticonderoga as a volunteer in the militia. That Gov. George Clinton then had the command and the object of the expedition was to take the Tories and Indians under Sir John Johnson, that during that period of three months he together with about one hundred men was stationed on the East Side of the North River at one Winney. That in their last tour of service for three months he acted as corporal.

That the next year 1779, he was draughted for a nine months campaign and served nine months as a private in garrison at Whitehall. That the troops occupied a Barracks for the said nine months a stone house belonging to one Skeens (5) a Tory. That the name of the captain was John Stockham (6) and Lieutenant Curtis Hodge. The name of the Ensign he cannot recollect. That he served faithfully nine months under said officers and was discharged. That said service comm'd in May 1779. That during said period no superior officers as he recollects had the command.

That in the next year 1780, he was out as a volunteer one month under Col. Stephen VanRensselaer Captain Vanderhoff, (7) his given name he cannot recollect and Ensign Ezekiel Holsted. That he was also engaged in said last month as a private in garrison duty at Whitehall. That he did never receive any written discharge at any of the periods of his performing the above services. That all the while he was there in the service he was not engaged in any civil pursuit. That he does not know of but one man living who knows any thing personally of his services. To wit. Daniel Hicks (8) of the City of Buffalo in said county. That he was out with him once or twice and probably more times—That he lived in the same town two or three miles apart from the declarant—That excepting him he does not know of any person living who would furnish any direct proof of his services. That he has no papers or documentary proof of any kind to sustain his claim. That the following persons have been acquainted with this declarant for a great number of years and can testify as to the character of this declarant for truth and veracity and also as to their belief as to his services as a soldier of the Revolution to wit. Alvin Burt, Benjamin Earl, Ethan Allen, Hon Jonathan Hoyt, Henry B. Stevens, Silas Cole, Elias Harmon a clergyman of the Baptist Church and many others residing in the Town of Aurora and Wales in said county of Erie in the State of New York.

He hereby relinquishes every claim whatever to a pension or annuity except the present; and declares that his name is not on the pension roll of the agency of any state. (Signed with his mark) Jeremiah Carpenter

Sworn to and subscribed the day and year aforesaid before me. Jonathan Hoyt, a Judge of Erie Co. Courts.

End Notes—R.1713—Jeremiah Carpenter

1. John W. Groesbeck was commissioned First Major on June 22, 1778 in Colonel Peter Yates' Fourteenth Regiment of Albany County Militia.
2. Thomas Brown was commissioned Captain on June 22, 1778 in the Fourteenth Albany.
3. Ezekiel Halstead was commissioned Second Lieutenant in Captain Cornelius Wiltze's Company on June 22, 1778 in the Fourteenth Albany.
4. John VanRensselaer was the Second Major of the Fourteenth Albany. John was commissioned the Lieutenant-Colonel on June 22, 1778 in the same regiment. There was no Stephen VanRensselaer serving in this regiment.
5. Philip Skene, a loyalist helped General John Burgoyne with intelligence etc., in the campaign of 1777.
6. John Stockham and Curtis Hodge are unknown.

Pension Application for Samuel Carpenter

W.641 (Widow: Anna)
B.L.Wt.26087-160-55
B.L.Wt.34509-160-55
State of Ohio
Delaware County SS.

On this sixth day of June eighteen hundred and fifty three personally appeared before me D. F. Fullen Judge of the probate Court in and for the County and State aforesaid Anna Carpenter a resident of Trenton Township in Delaware County in the State of Ohio aged Seventy Nine years who being first duly sworn according to Law doth on her oath make the following Declaration in order to obtain the benefit of the provision made by the act of Congress past on the third of February Eighteen Hundred and fifty three that she is the widdow [sic] of Samuel Carpenter who was a soldier in the War of the Revolution the particulars of service performed by said Carpenter this declarant is at this time unable to get but the said Samuel Carpenter applied for and obtained a pention [sic] of thirty four dollars per annum under the act of Congress past the seventh day of June eighteen hundred and thirty two that he resided in Licking County in the State of Ohio when the said pention was granted that said pention she thinks was paid in the Agency of Cincinnati. She further declares that she was married to the said Samuel Carpenter on the twenty ninth day of March eighteen hundred and thirteen by C. Spangler a Justice of the Peace in Zanesville in the State of Ohio and that then husband died on the twenty fourth day of March eighteen hundred and thirty four that she was not married to him prior to the Second day of January eighteen hundred but at the time above stated she further declares that she is now a widow. (Signed) Anna Carpenter.

Witness my hand and the seal of said Count[y] this 6th day of June A.D. 1853. D. T. Fuller Prob. Judge.

Letter dated August 19, 1925, written in reply to inquiry for information.

I have to advise you from the papers in the Revolutionary War pension claim, W.641, it appears that Samuel Carpenter was born September 4, 1754 in Orange County, New York.

He enlisted in Orange County, New York and served as a private in the New York Troops as follows—

July 1, 1775, six months in Captain Denton's (1) Company, Colonel Clinton's Regiment and was at the siege of St. Johns.

From in November 1777, three months in Captain Samuel Jones' Company, Colonel William Allison's Regiment. (2)

From in April 1778, three weeks under Captains Halstead and Sweasy, and in the fall of the same year, two weeks under Captain Harding. (3)

He also served eighteen months as Rifleman in the vicinity of Northumberland and Fort Borseley, officers not stated.

He was allowed pension on his application executed September 27, 1832, while a resident of Licking County, Ohio.

He died March 24, 1834 at Alexandria, Licking County, Ohio.

Soldier married March 29, 1813 in Zanesville, Ohio, Anna Hilliar. She was allowed pension on her application executed June 6, 1853, while a resident of Trenton Township, Delaware County, Ohio, aged seventy-nine years.

No names of children are mentioned in said claim.

End Notes—W.641—Samuel Carpenter

1. A Muster Roll of the Men raised and passed Muster in Goshen in the County of Orange for Captain Daniel Denton's Company to be employed in the Continental Army In the Third Regiment Raised in the Province of New York whereof James Clinton Esquire is appointed Colonel July 22d, 1775. The following is extracted from the muster roll: Samuel Carpenter enlisted July 9, 1775, age 21, born Goshen, Trade—Labourer, officers who enlisted, Lt (Belthazar) DeHart, Stature 5 ft, 7 ½ in., Black Hair, Gray eyes. FROM: pp 166-167, Documents Relating to the Colonial History of the State of New York, ed. Berthold Fernow, Vol. XV, State Archives, Vol. I, Weed, Parsons and Company, Printers, Albany, N.Y. 1887. There are two other muster rolls and payrolls for Captain Denton's Company in Revolutionary War Rolls 1775-1783, Series M-246, Roll 69, folder 38, National Archives, Washington, D.C. Both of these give his enlistment date as July 9, 1775.
2. Samuel Jones was the Captain of the Third Company (commissioned February 28, 1776) in Colonel William Allison's Regiment of Orange County Militia (this may have been originally the Fourth Regiment but two regiments were consolidated into one on May 28, 1778. It is unknown if they changed their numbers.)
3. All of these officers served in Colonel Allison's Regiment as follows: Captain Daniel S. Sweasy commissioned on February 26, 1778, Benjamin Halstead as Second Lieutenant in Captain John Jackson's Company and Abraham Harding as a Second Lieutenant in Captain John Little's Company. Both were commissioned on February 26, 1778. Harding was commissioned Captain on March 12, 1783 since Captain Little had been killed at the Battle of Minisink on July 22, 1779.

Pension Application for Thomas Carpenter

W.18877 (Widow: Martha)
B.L.Wt.28585-160-55
State of New York
Montgomery County SS.

On this 29th day of June 1839 personally appeared before the Subscriber one of the Judges of the County Courts in and for the County aforesaid Martha Carpenter a resident of the Town of Florida and County aforesaid—aged seventy two years, who being first duly sworn according to law doth on her oath make the following declaration in order to obtain the benefit of the provision made by the Act of Congress passed July 7, 1838 entitled an Act granting half pay and pensions to certain widows; That she is the widow of Thomas Carpenter who was a Private Soldier in the War of the Revolution my said husband enlisted for 9 mo. In the year 1778 or 1779 and served out his full term of 9 months officers names not recollected, in the year 1780 he enlisted in a company of Militia commanded by Captain Drake (1) and Col. John Harper's Regiment – that some time in the fall of 1780 my said Husband was taken a prisoner and remained a Prisoner more than two years (2)—she further declares that she was married to the said Thomas Carpenter on the 25th day of December 1782 in the Town of Stamford Dutchess County and State aforesaid by the Rev'd Conner Bullock and that her husband the aforesaid Thomas Carpenter died on the 9th day of September 1805; that she was not married to him prior to his leaving the service, but the marriage took place previous to the first of January 1794 A.D. at the time above stated. (Signed with her mark) Martha Carpenter

The within declaration was sworn to and subscribed on the day and year aforesaid (in said declaration) before me and she made her mark in subscribing her name to said declaration for the reason that she never learned to write. To all of which I certify. John Hand a Judge of the County Courts of the County of Montgomery.

Reply to letter of inquiry dated April 24, 1930.

I advise you from the papers in the Revolutionary War pension claim W.18877 it appears that Thomas Carpenter was born March 29, 1760.

He enlisted in 1778 or 1779 and served nine months as a private, officers not stated.

He enlisted in 1780 in Saratoga Co., NY in Captain Drake's Company, Colonel John Harper's New York Regiment, and on October 23, 1780, was taken prisoner and held captive until October 26, 1782. He was in several battles during above services, names of battles not given.

He died September 9, 1805.

He married December 25, 1782, at Stamford, Dutchess County, New York, Marther (or Martha) Avery, born May 17, 1767.

Soldier's widow was allowed pension on her application executed June 29, 1839, while a resident of Florida, Montgomery County, New York. She was residing in said Florida in May 1855 with her daughter, which one not designated.

She died April 10, 1856.

It is stated that soldier and his wife had ten children, eight of whom grew to maturity. The following names are given:

Ruth born May 26, 1785

Mary (the fourth child) born March 8, 1790, married, Servoss or Swoop (not plainly written) & was living in Florida, NY in 1839.

William born April 21, 1792.

David born August 1, 1794.

Thomas born September 30, 1796.

Barnard born July 22, 1799.

Marther born October 20, 1801.

Sarah born September 12, 1804.

The following children were alive in 1855, Ruth, Mary, William, Thomas, Martha, and Sarah.

The following also appears of record:

Almira Williams born August 18, 1811.

Almira Williams died September 28, 1812.

David Carpenter departed this life March 31, 1841.

Hannah Carpenter departed this life March 31, 1831.

Thomas Carpenter was born April 1832.

Barnet Carpenter departed this life January 23, 1836 was born the 16 of March 1835.

Thomas Carpenter was born April 6, 1832.

End Notes—W.18877—Thomas Carpenter

1. Joshua Drake was appointed captain on July 1, 1780 in Colonel William Malcom's Regiment of New York State Levies. Originally John Chipman was appointed captain on May 11, 1780 in Lieutenant-Colonel Commandant John Harper's Regiment of New York State Levies. Captain Chipman was promoted to major on June 16, 1780 in Harper's Regiment. The First Lieutenant then commanded the company until Captain Drake was transferred from Malcom's to Harper's on September 25, 1780.
2. On September 26, 1780 Colonel Malcom started marching Harper's Regiment from Fort Rensselaer to Fort Schuyler (Fort Stanwix) to relieve the First New York Continental Regiment, which had been garrisoning this fort since late November 1778. Thomas was taken prisoner on October 23, 1780 and was held captive until October 26, 1782.

Pension Application for Nicholas Casler

S.12424
State of New York
County of Montgomery

On the 19th day of September in the year of our Lord one thousand eight hundred & thirty-two personally appeared in open court before the Judges of Court of Common Pleas of the said county now sitting Nicholas Casler, a resident of the Town of Minden in the County & State aforesaid aged sixty-eight on the fifth day of March last. When being first duly sworn according to law doth on his oath make the following declaration in order to obtain the benefit of the Act of Congress passed June7th 1832.

That he entered the service of the United States under the following named officers served as hereafter stated.

That he enlisted in the City of Schenectady in the County of Schenectady under Captain Guy Young, Lieutenant Christopher Peake. The latter part of March 1782 for nine months that after the company was raised it was mustered and marched up the Mohawk River where they joined a regiment commanded by Colo. Marinus Willett (1) where they were kept on duty and sent out to guard the inhabitants at Fort Clyde, Fort Keysor, Fort Windecker and Fort Plank. And in the fall marched to Fort Dayton in the County of Herkimer where they remained on duty until the latter part of December when they were marched to Fort Plain when they were discharged on the last day of December of that year and that he has no documentary evidence of his services.

That he was born in the [County] of Herkimer & State aforesaid in the year 1765. That he has no record of his age.

That he has lived in the City of Schenectady & County of Schenectady & State aforesaid when he enlisted & entered the service as above mentioned.

That he resided in Schenectady until about two years after the war when he moved to Minden in the County of Montgomery and State aforesaid where he has since continued to live and now lives.

That he entered the service by enlistment as above stated.

That he cannot state the names of officers with troops Continental & Militia Regiments or the general circumstances of his services other than as he has above stated the same.

And that he never received a written discharge from the service.

He hereby relinquishes every claim whatever to a pension or annuity except the present and declares that his name is not on the pension roll of the agency of any state. (his mark) Nicholas Casler

Sworn and subscribed the day and year aforesaid. Geo. D. Ferguson, Clerk.

Letter in pension folder dated September 24, 1930

You are advised that it appears from the papers in the Revolutionary War pension claim S.12424, that Nicholas Casler was born March 5, 1765 in Herkimer, New York.

While a resident of Schenectady, Schenectady County, New York, he enlisted the latter part of March, 1782, and served as a private in Captain Guy Young's Company, Colonel Marinus Willett's New York Regiment until the last day of December, 1782.

He was allowed pension on his application executed September 19, 1832, while a resident of Minden, Montgomery County, New York, where he had moved two years after the war.

He died February 25, 1843.

There are no family data.

Very truly yours, N. W. Morgan

Acting Commissioner

End Note—Nicholas Casler—S.12424

1. Nicholas enlisted in Captain Guy Young's Company in Colonel Marinus Willett's Regiment of New York State Levies on November 7, 1782, Captain Young had retired and Joel Gillet was appointed Captain of the company. Christopher Peak or Peake, was a lieutenant in the company.

Pension Application for Heman Chapman

S.16076
State of Ohio
Washington County SS.

On this 25th day of July 1832, personally appeared in open court before the Judges of the court of Common Pleas now sitting Heman Chapman a resident of Barlow in said county of Washington aged sixty seven years who being first duly sworn according to law doth on his oath make the following declaration in order to obtain the benefit of the act of Congress, passed June 7th 1832.

That he entered the service of the United States under the following named officers, and served as herein stated.

1st he served in the militia as a substitute for a class of Militia (1) in a place called New Concord in the State of New York, went to Albany from thence to Fort Edward from thence to Palmerstown occupied a blockhouse at Palmertown the remainder of the term of three months went to Schenectady and was there discharged he returned home to his father then living in New Concord he cannot recollect any of the officers in this service.

2d He served as a substitute a second time for another class of company of militia there being another draught for the term of nine months went to Albany and there inlisted for the term of two years in a regiment of New York State troops (2) that had served one year of their term of three years went to Schoharie from there to Fort Plain Johnstown Fort Herkimer. They went with a Regiment of Rhode Island Troops from Fort Herkimer to Old Oswego in order to take the Fort but did not succeed.

The names of the officers in this service were in the militia. Captain Tierce (3) and Lieutenant Calander. (4) In the State Troops Colonel Willet, Captain Cannon, Lieut. Cole (5), Adjutant Funday. (6) He has no documentary evidence of service having left his discharge at his father's in New Concord shortly after the war. He knows of no person that is knowing to his service.

He hereby relinquishes every claim whatever to a pension or annuity except the present and declares that his name is not on the pension roll of the agency of any state. (Signed with his mark) Heman Chapman

Witness D.H. Buell.

Sworn to and subscribed the day and year aforesaid. Attest. Geo. Dunlevy Clerk.

In a later deposition, here is a summary of what he said.

Heman Chapman applied on 9th February 1848, 12 years later than the first deposition at age Eighty three "last August". He states he was born in the State of Connecticut in the year 1764 and served in the Continental service; his home was in New Concord New York. His first term was three months and afterwards he "engaged to serve nine months as a substitute and went to Albany" under Capt. James Cannon. He received a land bounty which he sold before he left Albany and he served his enlistment until the close of the war. For the past thirty nine years past, he has been a resident of Washington County, that he never could read or write, he says that when he was in the Revolutionary service that he was sometimes called Herman Chapman which name he answered to, but calls his name Heman Chapman and that he never knew any other Chapman in the service by the name of Chapman except his brother Amos Chapman. (7)

End Notes—S.16076—Heman Chapman

1. A company and or regiment were divided into classes so that when a draft was called for men to serve as levies, each class had to supply a man or pay a man to serve. If they did not furnish a man the man who was the head of the class either paid for someone to serve or he did.
   Heman is listed as enlisting on July 27, 1780 in Captain Elijah Bostwick's company as a private in Colonel Morris Graham's Regiment of New York State Levies. FROM: Revolutionary War Rolls 1775-1783, series M-246, Roll 72, Folder 75, National Archives, Washington D.C.
   Heman served in Colonel William B. Whiting's Seventeenth Regiment of Albany County Militia. He had served under Captain Ebenezer Cady (Third Company) and Captain John Davis (Fifth Company).
2. The following is extracted from the Descriptive Book No. 4, Colonel Marinus Willett's Regiment Doc. No. 11105, Special Collections and Manuscripts, New York State Library, Albany, N.Y.
   Born in Sharon, Litchfield County, Conn. enlisted by Captain James Cannon for 3 years on December 17, 1781. Residence—New Concord, Albany County, New York. Age—17. Size 5 ft 8 in. Complexion—Dark. Hair—Brown. Eyes—Blue. Occupation—Labourer.
   On Captain Cannon's Muster Roll—Pay Roll for 1783, Heman is listed as Henry. Under the casualties column he is listed "from desertion 6 February".
   He is also shown as being paid £18..0..60 and was owed £53..0..30. Total service for 1783 was 10 months and 24 days. FROM: Revolutionary War Rolls 1775-1783, Series M-246, Roll 78, folder 173, National Archives, Washington, D.C.
3. Peter B. Tierce (Tearse, Tearce) commissioned First Lieutenant on November 21, 1776 in the First New York Continental Regiment. He resigned on April 23, 1781. Served as Brigade Major of the Albany County Militia in 1781 for Brigadier General Peter Gansevoort's Brigade

(First Brigade). He served as a captain in Colonel Willett's Regiment in 1782 and 1783.

4. John Calender (Kalender, etc.) served as a Second Lieutenant in Captain John Salisbury's Company in the Seventeenth Albany. In 1780, he was a lieutenant in Captain Bostwick's Company in Colonel Graham's Regiment of Levies.
5. Lieutenant Gideon Cowles of Captain Cannon's Company in Colonel Willett's Regiment.
6. Adjutant and Lieutenant Jellis A Fonda of Colonel Willett's Regiment. Fonda was appointed Captain in the regiment in November of 1782.
7. Amos served as a private in Captain Salisbury's Company in the Seventeenth Regiment as a corporal in Captain Bostwick's Company in Colonel Graham's Regiment of 1780 and in 1781 as a private in Captain Aaron Hale's Company in Colonel Willett's Regiment.

Pension Application for Jonas Churchill

S.15037
State of New York
Herkimer County

Personally appeared before me the undersigned a Justice of the Peace of the town of Little Falls in & for the County of Herkimer Jonas Churchill, who being duly sworn deposeth & saith, that by reason of old age and the consequent loss of memory, he cannot swear particularly as to the precise length of his service; but according to the best of his recollection he served not less than the periods mentioned below and in the following grades. Deponent was drafted into the State levies of the State of New York in the month of April, but the day of the month deponent cannot state in the year 1779 for nine months. (1) It was stated in his first declaration that he entered the service in the month of June but deponent was mistaken in that statement & never intended to have been so understood & begs leave to correct said mistakes.

It is stated in his former declaration that deponent could not recollect the name of the captain under whom he served during his first time, but on the mature reflection deponent can fully state that John Townsend who was mentioned in his former Statement as being his captain during his second term of service, whas [sic] his captain during this first time of nine months. John McBride was Lieutenant deponents company was attached to a regiment commanded by Col. Dubois—the Majors name was Cornelius Benscouten (2) & the Adjutants name was John Ellsworth—The Regiment was collected at Poughkeepsie and marched to overtake & join General Sullivan's & the place appointed for that purpose was called the Cookhouse. The regiment crossed the North River at Esopus & marched for the Delaware to overtake & join Genl Sullivan as above stated—when the regiment arrived at the place appointed—the General had left the day before—The advance guard found a letter in the crotch of a tree, written by Genl Sullivan, directed to the Col. of the Regiment, requesting him to follow if when he arrived at that place to have provisions sufficient to last the troops a day & a half or two days in which time it was supposed he might overtake Genl. Sullivan but if he had not that quantity of provisions, then to return to Luckawack a small fort built on a Creek of that name, but the officers after consultation concluded not to follow Genl Sullivan & returned to Said Fort as directed—It was also understood by Deponent to be the order of General Sullivan, that the Regiment should be divided & small parties sent to different places as their services were required in the surrounding County in the region of the Delaware to guard the inhabitants—The company to which deponent belonged moved around in small parties during the summer till fall, when a greater part of the regiment was collected at Stoney Point, having for that purpose returned to Esopus & the North River & was carried down to Stoney Point in open boats—called Batteau's & remained there doing duty erecting houses & until near new years when they marched up the River to Fishkill & on New Year's day deponent was discharged. During this nine months deponent was on duty & in actual service all the time as above stated—Deponent was once during this time sent with others down towards New York after some deserters & succeeded in taking them & they were tried and punished.

In the fall of the year 1780 deponent believes it was in the month of October he was again drafted at Fishkill where he resided & joined the company at that place. It was stated in his former declaration that John Townsend (3) was Captain of the company at this time, which was a mistake & deponent begs leave to correct the same. Townsend was Captain of the company to which deponent belonged during his first service as above stated—That Captain (whose name deponent cannot recollect) who was appointed to command the company was a stranger to deponent & at the time he was appointed to command the company, deponent understood he was unwell & was expected soon to recover & would then join the company, which was given for this reason into the command of John McBride, (4) who acted as Capt & Lieutenant—and deponent cannot recollect the names of the other officers of the company—The company to which deponent belonged came up the North River in boats to Albany, where they remained about a week, & then marched up the Mohawk River to Fort Plain in the now County of Montgomery & joined the Regiment under Col. Willet (5) of the New York State levies of Militia—The company to which deponent belonged was directed to remain at Fort Plain with Col. Willet while a part of the Regiment was sent up the river to Fort Herkimer & Fort Dayton—Cornelius Benscouten (6) was Major under Col. Willet, the other officers deponent cannot recollect; the troops under Col. Willet were employed as guards to the inhabitants, spies & scouts & they were some part of the time at Fort Plain, Fort Herkimer & Dayton—the two latter about 22 or 23 miles farther up the Mohawk River; While deponent was at Fort Plain as above stated Genl. VanRensselaer (7) came up the Mohawk River from Albany with the Militia to attack the Indians & Tories who were encamped at a short distance from the Fort. At this time a battle was fought between the enemy & Col. Brown who commanded the militia, at Stone Arabia, deponent recollects that Col. Brown

(8) was killed in this battle—the news of the battle was brought to the Fort & the men were called to arms, but did not know how large was the enemies force, & waited till morning expecting General VanRensselaer would come to the support of Col. Brown—Deponent recollects that Genl VanRensselaer was much blamed by the People at that time because he did not come on sooner to the support of Col. Brown at Stone Arabia, and the opinion prevailed that had he come to the support of Col. Brown the enemy might have been defeated, that deponent served at Fort Plain & its vicinity as above stated, till the three months for which he was drafted expired & then he & his company were all dismissed & returned to Albany—deponent recollects that at the request of Col. Willet his company remained three days at Fort Plain after their three months had expired waiting for new levies to take their place--& then were dismissed & returned to Albany as aforesaid, & deponent returned to Fishkill in a boat—deponent further saith that during the aforesaid three months service—the captain before mentioned, came to Fort Plain to take command of the company, but was taken sick immediately& returned home & the command [?] on said McBride who acted during said term as Capt. & Lieutenant.

In the month of March after Brown's battle at Stone Arabia, in which he was killed as above stated—this deponent enlisted at the town of Fishkill where he resided & was to rendezvous, at the Village of Fishkill about three miles from his residence on the first day of April at which time deponent went to said village & joined his company which consisted of 15 individuals besides himself—their Captain's name was William Williams—who was the only officer with the company & deponent does not know that there were any others—The Village of Fishkill was a general depot for the Army where large quantities of provisions clothing & Munitions of war were collected & from there distributed to the troops as necessity required, there was a Gentleman there—who had the command & Superintendence of the whole whose name was Hays (9) as deponent believes & was Some times called General but more frequently Col. Who was sometimes assisted by one Major Keyes who was there part the time. The business of deponent & his company was to labor at loading & unloading the provisions &c. above mentioned & taking care of the same in the stone houses—deponent enlisted for one year as a fatigue man as it was [called] & commenced his term of service on the first day of April as above stated and continued & served at Fishkill at the afore mentioned business to the full end & expiration of the year for which he enlisted—deponent further states, during the year he was sent as an express to carry letters several times twice deponent was sent to Albany on this business once deponent went to a place near White Plains & more than a dozen times to Peekskill—and when he was not engaged in this business—deponent was laboring at Fishkill as above stated—during this year deponent was not engaged in any battles but served as above stated. Deponent & his company drew their regular rations & was promised at the time they enlisted that they would be entitled to draw eight dollars per month, but deponent never drew his pay as was promised & whether his brother soldiers did, deponent cannot say, but understood at the time they did not—deponent was discharged on the last day of March or the first day of April & deponent will not swear positively which but thinks the last day of March the year having expired for which he enlisted. This was deponents last service in the Revolutionary War & he never received a written discharge from the service at any time and further this deponent saith not. (Signed) Jonas Churchill.

Sworn & Subscribed this 23d day of November A.D. 1833 before me. John Dygert, Just. Peace

Herkimer County SS. On this 23d day of November A.D. 1833 before me the undersigned a Justice of the Peace in & for the County aforesaid Jonas Churchill whose name is Subscribed to the foregoing affidavit & made oath to the matters therein contained--& I do certify that I am well acquainted with the said Jonas Churchill--& that he sustains a fair character for truth & veracity & his statement is entitled to full credit & belief. John Dygert JP

End Notes—S.15037—Jonas Churchill

1. Jonas is mistaken as to the company and regiment for his 1779 service. In 1779, Jonas enlisted as a private in Captain William Faulkner's Company in Lieutenant-Colonel Commandant Albert Pawling's Regiment of New York State Levies. The other officers of Faulkner's Company were Lieutenant's Levi DeWitt and Thomas Ostrander. FROM: Revolutionary War Rolls 1775-1783, Series M-246, Roll 75, Folder 134, National Archives, Washington, D.C. In 1779 Colonel Lewis DuBois was still the Colonel of the Fifth New York Continental Regiment until he resigned on December 22, 1779. The Fifth New York was stationed in the Schoharie and Mohawk Valleys and went with Brigadier General James Clinton's Army and joined Major General John Sullivan's Army. Together they marched against the Indians in the western part of New York State.
2. Elias VanBenschoten was appointed Major on May 3, 1779, and John Elsworth, Jr., was appointed Adjutant on May 3, 1779 in Pawling's Levies.
3. So far Captain John Townsend is unknown. There were several Captain Townsend's but not with the first name of John.
4. John McFoght (McFaught, etc.) was appointed Lieutenant in Captain Daniel Gano's Company on July 1, 1780 in Colonel Lewis DuBois' Regiment of New York State Levies. Lieutenant McFoght was promoted Captain after Captain Gano left the regiment. John McBride served as Lieutenant in McFoght's Company. Jonas is listed as James.
5. The regiment was commanded by Colonel DuBois not Marinus Willett. He was not in the Mohawk Valley in 1780. Willett at this time was the Lieutenant-Colonel Commandant of the Fifth New York Continental Regiment.
6. Elias VanBenschoten was appointed Major on July 1, 1780 in Colonel DuBois Levies.
7. Brigadier General Robert VanRensselaer of the Second Brigade of Albany County Militia.

8. John Brown was the colonel of a regiment of Massachusetts's Levies in 1780. Colonel Brown was killed on his 36th birthday at the Battle of Stone Arabia on October 19, 1780.
9. Udney Hays was the Assistant Deputy Quartermaster General with the rank of Lieutenant-Colonel.

Pension Application for Garret Derrick or Derrick Clute

W.23813 (Widow: Margaret {Shibley, maiden name, daughter of John Shibley of Schodac}) Garret D. Clute died April 20, 1843, in the County of Prince Edward in Canada West.

Declaration in order to obtain the benefit of the act of Congress of the 7th of June 1832.

State of New York
Jefferson County SS.

On this 10th day of February 1834, personally appeared before me George Brown Esq., one of the Judges of the Court of Common Pleas in the then County of Jefferson in the State of New York, Garret D. Clute who declares himself to be a resident of the township of Milford late Hanorvill the County of Lenox in the Province of Upper Canada aged seventy two years & eleven months, who being first duly sworn doth on his oath make the following declaration, in order to obtain the benefit of the act passed by Congress passed June 7th, 1832.

That I volunteered as a Militia man about the last of March or first of April & I am of the belief it was the first of April in the year 1778 (I am sure it was the year after the surrender of Burgoyne) (1) for the term of three months; under Capt. Joseph Elliot (2), of Rhinebeck; Lieut. Nicholas VanVrankan of Niskayuna & Lieut. Nicholas VanderCarr of Half Moon. The Regiment was commanded by Col. John Bateman or Beekman (3). The second day of my service Capt. Elliot asked me if I could write? I told him I could; & he there upon appointed me an Orderly Sergeant (4), in which capacity I continued to serve until I was dismissed from the service. At the time I volunteered I resided at Niskayuna about ten miles from the City of Albany in the State of New York & the day after I volunteered I joined my company & went to Albany where I remained until my dismission. My duty consisted principally to call the roll in the morning & at evening & in writing & keeping accounts. While in Albany I was billeted at a home & in the family of one Garret Lansing a Silver Smith in Albany with two other soldiers one of the name of James Jourdan the other of Simon Frazur. Jourdan & Frazier (5) were about this time sent with some prisoners to New Haven, I think where they both enlisted as Continental Soldiers, as I understood. The greatest part of the time while I remained at Albany I performed the duty of Quarter Master Sergeant together with my other duties. About two weeks before the term expired for which I volunteered, our company was ordered to be called out onto Parade, Capt. Elliot appeared in front of the company, took off his hat, made a short speech thanken the soldiers for their good behavior & told us we were dismissed until further orders, & that we might return home. I immediately turned around, took off my hat, pulled out my Cockade, took off my sword, returned to my quarters, packed up my things & returned home to Niskayuna.

In the summer of the year 1778, I volunteered in the militia under a Lieut. Ezekiel Taylor (6) & served over five weeks & during this time I went up to Cherry Valley.

In the fall of 1778 or 1779, I cannot remember exactly, but I know if was the year Cherry Valley (7) was burnt by the Indians, I went as a volunteer in the Militia to Cherry Valley & was in the service over one month. I served at this time under a Capt. Vanderburgh of Halfmoon. I think the Militia was under the general command of a Col. Clock.(8) During a part of this time we lay at Fort Plank.

At another time but I cannot say at what time, but I am pretty certain it was in the year 1779. I served two weeks under Capt. White (9) of Ballston & Lieut. Cook (10) of Newtown. At this time we lay at a fort at Johnstown. The Fort was picketed around the Jail at Johnstown & we were billeted among the Inhabitants. I served two weeks at Stone Arabia and two weeks at Palmerstown in a Picket Fort but I am unable to name my officers.

In the year 1780 about the first of February & now on reflection I am quite certain it was a few days after the New Year in January while I resided at Niskayuna, I enlisted for the term of one year in a company commanded by Capt. Teunis Fisher of Albany & Lieut. William Sowles a soldier in a regiment commanded by Col. Morgan Lewis. (11) I went to Albany where I remained the principal part of the time during the year. I quartered with one Garret Van Vranken in Albany. I then went to Philadelphia with Mr. Edward Chinn (12) who was a paymaster & kept a Bank as I understood in Albany. I was gone to Philadelphia seven weeks. While I was in Albany, I was put by Col. Lewis on board of a Sloop lying in the North River, called the "Magazine" where I remained over three weeks. I received from Col. Morgan Lewis a regular & an honorable discharge for my years service. My discharge I gave to my mother who is dead, & my discharge I suppose is lost as I have not seen it in 54 years.

About the first of April in the year 1781 I enlisted for the term of Nine months in a company commanded by a Capt. Aylesworth.(13) I never saw my Capt. as it was said he was killed by an Indian while he was fishing in a small lake called Schuyler's Lake before I found my company. My first Lieut's name was Hendricks (14) my 2d Lieut's name was John Shaw of Albany. The Regiment was commanded by Col. Willett. I joined my Regiment at Fort Plain, from whence I marched to Fort House, where we remained until Major Ross (15) & his Indians came to Johnstown—Col. Willett then marched down across the Mohawk River at Caughnawaga, towards Johnstown, us met Major Ross & his party in a field in sight of Sir William Johnsons' house at Johnstown; us fought & defeated Ross who retreated across the East Canada Creek—We pursued him & Ross continued to retreat & crossed the West Canada Creek, when he made a stand until Col. Willett came up & then we had another hard fight (16) & Ross was compelled to retreat with considerable loss. The celebrated (17) Butler was killed in this action. We had a field piece (18) which was taken & lost there several times during the battle. After this battle we returned to Fort Herkimer & from Fort Herkimer to Fort Plain. Col. Willett's Regiment was dismissed a few days after Christmas 1781. I never received any discharge. Lieut. Hendricks continued to command our company until I was dismissed.

I have now stated as near as I can, the services I performed during the Revolutionary War, but one remark I wish to make that during the year 1778 & 1779 I served nearly all the time by short turns, but it is utterly impossible for me to state particulars. But putting my services all together I actually served my country faithfully more than three years.

I have no documentary evidence in my possession or within my knowledge of my services as a soldier.

I know of no record of my age; but I expect a record might be found in the City of Schenectady but am not certain. There are several persons living at or near Albany who I expect could testify to my services.

I reside in Canada about 77 miles from Jefferson County & I cannot procure the attendance of my neighbors who know me to certify to my character; but I have brought a written certificate with me which is hereunto annexed. I make this declaration before George Brown Esqr, out of Court, because I am informed & believe that the Court does not set in this county until the last Monday in February this present month.

I hereby relinquish any claim whatever to a pension or annuity except the present & I declare that my name is not on the pension roll of any agency in any state. (Signed) Garret D. Clute.

Sworn before me this 10th day of February 1834. G. Brown Judge Jefferson County Court.

End Notes—W.23813—Garret Derrick Clute

1. General John Burgoyne surrendered his British Army on October 17, 1777.
2. This enlistment appears to be a draft of the Albany County Militia to form a detachment from several regiments. Joseph Elliot was Captain of the Second Company in Colonel Peter R. Livingston's Tenth Regiment of Albany County Militia, Nicholas VanVranken was the Second Lieutenant of the Second Company (Captain Nanning N. Visscher), in Colonel Jacobus VanSchoonhoven's Twelfth Regiment of Albany County Militia. Nicholas VanDerkar was the Second Lieutenant in Captain John VanDenburgh's Company in the Twelfth Albany.
3. Lieutenant Colonel John Beekman of Colonel Kilian VanRensselaer's Fourth Regiment of Albany County Militia.
4. On the existing muster rolls Garret is listed as a private. He does describe some of the duties correctly for the Orderly Sergeant. He had to write and keep records. On some 1775 and 1776 muster rolls, sometimes the word "Clerk" would be written by a man's name.

5. This is interesting that he was able to remember this kind of information. Simon Fraser and James Jourdon did enlist in Captain Thomas Seymour's Second Troop in the Second Continental Light Dragoons commanded by Colonel Elisha Sheldon. Their enlistment date is listed as March of 1778.
6. Garrett is likely to be mistaken because Ezekiel Taylor was the First Major of the Twelfth Albany. There was a Joshua Taylor who was the First Lieutenant in Captain Elias Steenbergh's Company in the Twelfth Albany.
7. Cherry Valley was destroyed on November 11, 1778.
8. Jacob Klock was the Colonel of the Second Regiment of Tryon County Militia.
9. Captain Stephen White (Sixth Company) in the Twelfth Albany.
10. Joseph Coke (Cook, Cooke) was the Second Lieutenant in Captain Elias Steenburgh's Company in the Twelfth Albany.
11. Colonel Morgan Lewis was the Deputy QuarterMaster General of the Northern Department from September 12, 1776 and served in that capacity until the end of the war. Visscher and Sowles (Soles, Soules, etc.) would have been in this department.
12. Edward Chinn was the Paymaster of the Second Canadian Continental Regiment commanded by Colonel Moses Hazen.
13. Peter Elsworth was a captain on April 27, 1781 in Lieutenant-Colonel Commandant Marinus Willett's Regiment of New York State Levies. Captain Elsworth with part of his company was ambushed on July 6, 1781 near Steele's Creek and Elsworth was killed.
14. Bartel Hendricks, John Shaw and William Bloodgood served as lieutenants in Elsworth's Company.
15. Major John Ross of the King's Royal Regiment of New York commanded the raiding force. The Battle of Johnstown was fought on October 25, 1781.
16. The skirmish at West Canada Creek was fought on October 30, 1781.
17. Captain Walter Butler of Lieutenant-Colonel John Butler's Rangers.
18. The 3 pounder brass field piece was captured and retaken at the Battle of Johnstown.

Pension Application for William Cooper

S.12567
Pension awarded $32.86 per annum
State of New York
County of Schenectady SS.

On this twelfth day of October in the year of our Lord one thousand eight hundred and thirty two personally appeared in open court before the Judges of the Court of Common Pleas in and for said county now sitting William Cooper a resident of the Town of Glenville in said County & State aged upwards of seventy years who being first duly sworn according to law, doth on his oath make the following declaration in order to obtain the benefit of the act of Congress passed June 7th 1832.

He was born in the township of Schoharie in the county of Albany now of Schoharie in the State of New York on the thirteenth day of July 1762. He has no record of his age except that contained in the Register kept by the High Dutch Reformed Church of Schoharie.

When he was called into the service of the United States in the army of the revolution he was living in Greenbush in said County of Albany—and since the revolutionary war he has lived in Greenbush aforesaid from thence about six years ago he moved to Schaghticoke & from thence to Glenville & he now lives in the said town of Glenville & has lived in the aforesaid town of Glenville for the last two years—

He entered the service of the United States under the following named officers and served as herein stated.

On the first day of July 1777 he enlisted in Captain Jacob Defreest's (1) Company of Militia in the Regiment commanded by Colonel Henry Van Rensselaer.(2) His other company & Field officers whom he recollects were John Fonda (3), Lieutenant, ______Fonda Major (4) and Jacob Van Alstine (5) Quarter Master. From said first day of July until after the surrender of Burgoyne and his army, he was out in said Company with the northern American Army at Fort Edward, Saratoga & the other posts in that quarter occupied by the American troops during the northern campaign of that year being for the term of more than three months. Colonel Van Rensselaer (6) being wounded he thinks in said month of July Colonel Stephen Schuyler succeeded him & continued to have the command of said Regiment until the surrender of Burgoyne.

In the fall of the year 1778, he was drafted to go out in Captain George Sharp's (7) Company of Militia or State troops under a Colonel whose name he does not recollect and served in said engagement for the term of three months at Fort Paris in Stone Arabia. In the year last named he performed garrison duty at Saratoga for the term of two weeks but cannot now recollect the names of the officers under whom he then served, nor yet the particular period of the year. He also mounted guard at Schenectady for the term of two months and a half he thinks in the year 178_. In the fall of the year 1779, he served again in said Company of Captain George Sharp in an expedition to Schoharie and remained about two weeks in garrison at the lower fort of that place and for the like term of two weeks in the Schoharie Middle Fort.

A few months thereafter he served under the same Captain in an expedition to Beaver Dam in pursuit of about 150 Tories who rendezvoused at that place. He was from home in this expedition between three and four weeks—and thus the whole period of this services in said war was twelve months, not including several short tours, the particular periods, of which he cannot call distinctly to mind, and of which he makes no account.

He never during said service engaged in any battle except an encounter with a part of tories when he the claimant was in a scouting party at Spirghtown (Now Lansingburgh), in New York State.

The following are the names of some of the regular officers whom he knew, or who were with the troops where he served, and such continental and militia regiment or companies with which he served, or as he can recollect, viz: Major Leonard Van Buren (8), General Gansvoort (9), Colonel Van Schaick (10), General Ten Broeck (11)& others.

He never received any written discharge from the service.

He has no _____documentary evidence, and knows of no person whose testimony he can procure who can testify to his services except those whose depositions are hereto annexed.

The following are the names of persons to whom he is known in his present neighborhood, and who can testify as to his character for veracity, and their belief of his services as a soldier of the revolution, to wit: Daniel, C. Groot and Henry Baninger.

He hereby relinquishes every claim whatever, to a pension or annuity except the present and declares that his name is not on the pension roll of the agency of any State. (Signed with his mark) Wm. Cooper.

Subscribed and sworn to the day and year first aforesaid. John S. Vrooman Clerk.

County of Schenectady SS.

William Cooper the applicant before named being duly sworn saith that by reason of old age & the consequent loss of memory he cannot recollect all the tours in which he engaged, nor the number of days he served in each other than those enumerated in the preceding declaration & herein again specified—tours as a private soldier for three months in the northern expedition against Burgoyne, and at least ten days at Stone Arabia, three months at Saratoga two weeks at Schenectady two months and a half under command of his Captain George Sharp at Schoharie two weeks, viz at the lower fort, and two weeks in the middle fort of Schoharie—at Beaver Dam four weeks—This Deponent served in a great many other expeditions the particular of which this Deponent cannot recollect and therefore he makes no account thereof but for the aforesaid terms amounting in all to ten months and a half this Deponent claims a pension. (Signed with his mark) William Cooper

Subscribed and Sworn this 21st June 1833 before Wm. Strong, Justice of the Peace.

End Notes—S.12567—William Cooper

1. Jacob DeFreest (DeFriest, DeForrest) was the Captain of the Sixth Company in Colonel Stephen J. Schuyler's Sixth Regiment of Albany County Militia.
2. Henry K. VanRensselaer was the Lieutenant-Colonel of Schuyler's Regiment.

3. John Fonda was the First Lieutenant in Captain George Sharp's Company in Colonel Schuyler's Regiment.
4. John J. Fonda was the Second Major in 1775 in Colonel Schuyler's Regiment. He was Commissioned First Major on February 20, 1776 in Schuyler's Regiment.
5. Jacob VanAlstine was the QuarterMaster in Colonel Schuyler's Regiment in 1777. On May 28, 1778 he was commissioned Adjutant in Colonel Schuyler's Regiment.
6. Lieutenant-Colonel Henry K. VanRensselaer was wounded on July 7, 1777.
7. George Sharp was commissioned captain on May 28, 1778 in Colonel Schuyler's Regiment.
8. So far only a Private Leonard VanBuren has been found. He served in Captain Sharp's Company. The Major title could be an after the war rank.
9. Peter Gansevoort Jr., was appointed Brigadier General on March 26, 1781 of the First Brigade of the Albany County Militia. He had previously served as the Colonel of the Third New York Continental Regiment.
10. Goose VanSchaick was the Colonel of the First New York Continental Regiment.
11. Abraham TenBroeck had served as the Brigadier General of the Albany County Militia.

Pension Application for Dennis Cronk

S.15061
Pension awarded $23.33 per annum.
Declaration in order to obtain the benefits of the Act of Congress passed June 7th 1832
State of New York
County of WestChester

On this twenty second day of August in the year of our Lord one thousand eight hundred and thirty two personally appeared in open court before the Surrogate of the Surrogate Court of the County of WestChester and State of New York now sitting, Dennis Cronk, a resident of the town of Cortlandt, County and State aforesaid, aged seventy one years who being first duly sworn according to law doth on his oath make the following declaration in order to obtain the benefit of the Act of Congress passed June 7th 1832.

That he entered the service of the United States under the following named officers and served as herein stated: that is to say, he enlisted on or about the first of May 1780 into a company of Levies Commanded by Captain Daniel Williams (1) in the regiment commanded by Col. Morris Graham in the line of the State of New York: that he enlisted at the town of Cortlandt in the said County and for the term of six months, that he served the said six months at German Flats in the State of New York and at the expiration of said term was honorably discharged but that his discharge is lost or destroyed—

That immediately after the expiration of the said term of six months to wit: on or about the first of November 1780 he again enlisted for the term of one month in the regiment of levies commanded by Colonel Wisenfels in the line of the State of New York and was honorably discharged at Albany in the State of N. York the first of December in the year 1780 but he has lost his discharge—that he does not now recollect the name of the commandant of the company in which he served for the last mentioned month.—

And the declarant further states that he was born in the said County of WestChester in the year 1761, that he has no record of his age that he lived in the County of WestChester aforesaid and has lived in the said County every since the Revolution and now lives there.

That the names of the persons to whom he is known in his present neighborhood and who can testify as to his character for veracity and their belief of his services as a soldier of the revolution are Samuel Youngs and Jacob Foshey.—

That he hereby relinquishes every claim whatever to a pension or annuity except the present and declares that his name is not on the pension roll of the agency of any State. (Signed) Dennis Cronk

Sworn to and Subscribed this 22nd day of August 1832 before me. T. Wand Surrogate

Reply to a letter of inquiry.

The record of Dennis Cronk, a soldier of the Revolutionary Was is furnished herein, the data for which were obtained from the papers on file in his claim for pension S.15061, based upon his military service in that war.

Dennis Cronk was born in 1761, in Westchester County, New York, the names of his parents are not shown.

Dennis Cronk enlisted at Cortland, Westchester County, New York, May 1, 1780, served as a private in Captain Daniel Williams' Company, Colonel Morris Graham's New York Regiment. [Written in the margin of letter—"Could not find soldier in NY books but Capt. Daniel Williams was in Col. Morris Graham's Regt."]

He was allowed pension on his application executed August 22, 1832, while residing in Greenburg, Westchester County, New York.

In 1830, soldier stated that he had a wife and six children and that one of his children, a son, Stephen W. Cronk, with his wife and two children resided with him. He did not give any further data in regard to his wife nor is her name of the names of the other five children or the name of the wife and children or son, Stephen W. Cronk shown.

End Notes—S.15061—Dennis Cronk

1. Captain Daniel Williams was originally appointed Captain on May 11, 1780 in Lieutenant-Colonel Commandant Albert Pawling's Regiment of New York State Levies.

2. The company was sent to Fort Edward and was there still on June 8, 1780. A Court martial was held on that day at Fort Edward. This is an extract: *"The Court being met an[d] duly sworn Proseed to the Trial of James Cambel [Campbell] a Sargent in Capt. Daniel Williams company Collo Powlans [Pawlings] Regiment NY State Levies Confined for Plundering the house of Pardon Dayley--"* FROM: Historical Magazine, New Series, Vol. II, Number VII, December 1867, Page 375. This extract is taken from Captain John Chipman's Orderly Book which was for 1779 and 1780. *"Sometime after June 8th Captain Williams Company was transferred to Colonel Morris Graham's Regiment of New York State Levies."* Dennis' name does not appear on Williams' Muster Roll for that regiment. Colonel Graham's Regiment wasn't raised until July 1, 1780. On searching all the muster rolls known for this regiment Cronk's name did not appear on them. There was only one muster roll for Captain Williams' Company. It was for the months of July and August 1780. It was dated Camp Albany September 9, 1780. FROM: Revolutionary War Rolls, 1775-1783, Series M-246, Roll 72, folder 75, National Archives, Washington, D.C.

Pension Application for John Cronk (Cronkhite)

W20926
State of New York
Rensselaer County SS.

On this first day of February in the year of our Lord one thousand eight hundred and thirty eight personally appeared before the Judges of the Court of Common Pleas of the Court of Rensselaer in open court Lois Cronkhite a resident of Pittstown in said County aged seventy years who being first duly sworn according to law, doth on her oath make the following declaration in order to obtain the benefit of the provision made by the act of Congress passed July 4th 1836.

That she is the widow of John Cronkhite who was a Sergeant in the Revolutionary war in a company commanded by Capt. Hicks (1) in a Regiment commanded by Col. Van Schaick that he entered the service as she was informed and believes in 1776 but when he enlisted on in what company She does not know, She was informed and believes truly that he was in the Battles of Monmouth, Eutaw Springs and at the taking of Cornwallis (2) and was present at the Execution of Andre. (3)

That a portion of his service was performed in Capt. Finks (4) Company—but in what Regiment she does not know.

That she was informed by her said husband that he Enlisted for during the war and continued there in till its close in the winter of 1783.

That she was knowing to his having Bounty Lands for his services during the Revolutionary War and that he sold the same for a trifle some thirty five or forty years since.

That she has been informed and believes that there is evidence of the services of her said husband in the office of the war department at Washington to which she begs leave to refer—That she married the said John Cronkhite on the 28th day of March 1782 that she was married by a Squire Van Volkenburgh then residing in Hoosick that he was on a Furlough - that he remained at home about one fortnight after he said marriage and then returned to his company and Regiment which were stationed some where on the North River

That he continued frequently to visit her until he was finally discharged at or near Newburgh in the winter or Spring of 1783—that she has no Documentary Evidence of his Services or of her marriage with the said John Cronkhite.

That the said John Cronkhite died in the month of September 1816 and that she has remained a widow ever since that period as will more fully appear by reference to the proof hereunto annexed.

(Signed with her mark) Lois Cronkhite

Sworn in open court this 1st day of February 1838. Henry R. Smith, Clerk

W.20.926 (Widow: 5818 Albany N. York. Lois Cronk, alias Cronkhite widow of John Cronk, alias Cronkhite N.Y. who was a Corporal in the Revolution. Inscribed on the Roll at the rate of $88 per annum, to commence on the 4th day of March, 1843. Certificate of Pension issued the 9th day of July 1844 and sent to Hon. D. L. Seymour, Troy, N. York. Act of March 3, 1843.)

28th Congress, 1st Session. Rep. No. 158. Ho. of Rep.

Lois Cronk, Alias Cronkhite (To accompany Bill H.R. No. 147)

February 15, 1844.

Mr. J. A. Wright, from the Committee on Revolutionary Pensions, submitted the following.

REPORT

The Committee on Revolutionary Pensions, to whom was referred the petition of Lois Cronk, alias Cronkhite made the following report.

This is an application by the widow of John Cronk, alias Cronkhite, for a pension; and the only questions presented for consideration is, the time of the marriage. The marriage being proved beyond all controversy, the only question raised is, was the marriage prior to 1794?

Matilda Dillingham swears, in 1841, that she is 60 years of age, knew husband and widow for 54 years; that she was well acquainted with the family raised by them; that they were always regarded and reputed as man and wife; and that, from the ages of the children, she has no doubt of the marriage being prior to 1794.

Joseph Lewis married sister of husband and according to the family Bible that came into his possession Hannah Cronk, daughter of widow, died in March, 1816.

Benjamin Gifford, brother of widow, swears that he knows the time of his sister's marriage well, because there were some objections to the match; and one was, that the deceased was a *soldier* at the time.

John Cronk, son of widow, is 45 years of age; his father and mother had 11 children; the eldest was Hannah, she was married and died in 1816; there was a record of the marriage of his parents and of the birth of the children, which fell into the hands of Patsey, his sister, who married Joel Wilson, which record, he is informed, is destroyed; he has a recollection of that said record showed the birth of Hannah to be in the latter part of 1786; that he was born according to this record, in 1794, and there were three children older than he; that there were about two and a half years between the ages of the children; has no doubt of the marriage of his parents prior to the year 1783, and thinks that the record he saw shows the marriage to be in 1782. This was sworn to in August 1839.

Ira Cronk was 45 years of age in 1838; there were 11 children—three older than he alive; his father and mother lived together as man and wife from the first of his recollection.

Then follow a number of old papers connected with services in the Revolution, dated as early as 1780—all of which go to show, from their appearance, the age and connexion [sic] that the deceased sustained to the county; and which papers were found among the papers of the widow.

Hiram Hunt knew the widow and her husband for many years, traded with them for more than 20 years past; has no doubt of the fact of their being man and wife, and of their raising a legitimate family of children. He is 70 years of age.

N. McMasters said that he was 48 years of age in 1838, has no doubt of the marriage of the parents, went to school with the children prior to 1810; always reputed to be children of said widow and deceased.

Manford Smith, a merchant, corroborates the above statement in the way of selling goods and trading with widow and husband.

Joseph Collins swears to services of deceased in the Revolution and to the marriage, and speaks of the difficulty that was made to the marriage; the marriage was in 1782.

Mr. Gilbert swears to the death of his father in the fall of 1816, and that his mother has ever since remained a widow.

The widow's own statement shows she was married in 1782, she gives the name of the justice of the peace who married her.

The good character of all the witnesses is proven.

Taking the whole case into consideration, the committee think the proof shown the marriage was prior to 1794, and, therefore, they report a bill.

An Act for the relief of Lois Cronk, alias Cronkhit.

Be it enacted by the Senate and House of Representiv [es] of the United States of America in Congress assembled, That the Secretary of War be and he is hereby, directed to place the name of Lois Cronk, alias Cronkhite, widow of John Cronk, alias Cronkhite, late a corporal in the New York line of the army of the revolution, on the pension roll under the act of the seventh of July, one thousand eight hundred and thirty-eight, entitled" An act granting half pay and pensions to certain widows," and also under the act of the third of March, one thousand eight hundred and forty-three, entitled "An act granting a pension to the widows of certain revolutionary soldiers, (misprinted in the law, "An act granting a pension to certain revolutionary soldiers,") at the rate of eighty-eight dollars per annum.

Sec. 2 *An be it further enacted,* That the said Lois shall be entitled to the full benefit of all laws and resolves which shall hereafter be passed, continuing in force the said acts, or either of them. Approved My 31, 1844.

End Notes—W.20926—John Cronk

1. John enlisted as a private on November 13, 1776 in Captain Benjamin Hick's Company, Fourth Company, in Colonel Goose VanSchaick's First New York Continental Regiment for during the war. He was promoted to corporal on January 4, 1780
2. The Battle of Monmouth, N.J. was fought on June 28, 1778, the Battle of Eutaw Springs, South Carolina was fought on September 8, 1781. The First New York was not there in that battle and the Yorktown, Virginia Campaign was from September 28 to October 19, 1781.
3. Major John Andre was hung on October 2, 1780.
4. Andrew Fink was the Captain of the Third Company in Colonel VanSchaick's Regiment.

Pension Application for Hannes Dachsteter or John Dockstader

S.29121
State of New York
County of Herkimer

On this Eleventh day of October one thousand Eight hundred and thirty two personally appeared in open Court before the Judges of the Court of Common Pleas now sitting John Dockstader, a resident of Herkimer in the County of Herkimer & State of New York aged Seventy two years who being first duly sworn according to law, doth on his oath make the following declaration in order to obtain the benefit of the Act of Congress passed June 7th, 1832.

That he entered the service of the United States under the following named officers and served as herein stated. That when he attained the age of sixteen years which was the latter part of the year 1777, as he now believes he was enrolled in a company of Militia commanded by Captain Henry Harter (1), Lieut John Damuth, in the Regiment Commanded by Col. Peter Bellinger & Lieut Col. Frederick Bellinger (2), Nicholas Herkimer (3) was their General. That by the orders of his commanding officers he provided himself with a gun and the usual equipage (4) and at all times kept himself in readiness to march at a minutes warning from the time of his enrollment until the close of the Revolutionary war. That he was called into service in the fore part of the year,

1777 in the company aforesaid, in Herkimer, then Tryon County & now in the County of Herkimer & State of New York where he then resided and was ordered to Fort Stanwix in the present town of Rome, Oneida County having been drawn out of the company in which he was. Does not recollect that any officers attended the march after he with deponent arrived at Fort Stanwix he was placed under the Command of Lieut. John George Weaver (5) and was employed constructing roads and bridges near said Fort, some length of time and while thus engaged, he with the company in which he then was, fell in contact with a party of hostile Indians & Tories who after a short but spirited resistance, yielded to the company in which he this deponent was, on examination letters were found with said Indians & Tories written from Canada as this deponent thinks and addressed to several Inhabitants along the Mohawk River who were in favour of the British cause.

The finding of their letters afterwards proved to considerable advantage to the Militia, as many who severally assisted in the British cause were discovered. He was out in this service about a month. And further said that he was afterwards ordered back to Fort Dayton at Herkimer when he was placed on guard and ordered or volunteered on Scouts by turns till sometime in the summer. He was then ordered to proceed to Fort Stanwix, commanded by Capt. Henry Harter and Lieut. John Damuth aforesaid in the Regiment under Col. Peter Bellinger's command as aforesaid and under the Command of General Herkimer when an engagement took place in which Genl. Herkimer was shot near Fort Stanwix commonly called the Oriskany battle (6) in which he this deponent was, Lieut. Col. F. Bellinger was taken prisoner in the said battle and further says he was afterwards marched back to Fort Dayton at Herkimer & was then on guard and building & repairing Fort Dayton some length of time until ordered to Ticonderoga does not recollect his officers attending the march towards that place, but he well recollects that he did proceed on this march with the company almost to Schenectady when the news came that Burgoyne (7) had surrendered to the United States forces and his company was ordered back to Herkimer where he served on Scouts and on guard and also further says that he afterwards volunteered under Ensign Bellinger on a tour south from Herkimer about fifty or sixty miles near & across the Unadilla River where a party of hostile Indians & Tories had killed some of the inhabitants. There took one prisoner, the Indians had a camp or castle there near the Carr place as it was then called, this last mentioned. This last mentioned tour was as this deponent thinks late in the fall of the year but is certain it was in the fall of the year, from the last part of their potatoes out of the ground which were not then gathered and shortly after the Oriskany Battle and also at another time he volunteered under Captain Damuth (8) who commanded a company of Rangers to Oneida & Brothertown to check the progress of the hostile Indians and Tories. That they passed along the Brothertown, Indians the last named Indians he believes were neutral was accompanied in this expedition by a company commanded by Capt. McGee (9) which he believes were nine months men. At another time volunteered to and at Frankfort on a Scout when an engagement took place between us and the enemy and a soldier of ours was killed, one of our party, and killed an Indian. And at another time he volunteered on a tour north some distance to the Mount Place (10) so called where two persons had been killed, there by Indians. Volunteered on a tour East, served sometime does not recollect how long nor does he recollect the officers if any that attended. That he often volunteered & was called out on Scouts when no officers went along. That he was in service as above stated and guarding Fort Dayton until in the fall of the year 1780. He believed he removed from Herkimer to Schenectady where he resided during the winter & in the spring of 1781. He removed to Greenbush when he was immediately called into service under Col. Henry K. VanRensselaer (11) does not recollect the company officers, but refers to Mr. Cornelius Van Deusen, affidavit annexed by whom he can prove the service in part and officers names. That he was then ordered to Tours at Half Moon he and a party were sent to take a party of Tories in the neighborhood proceeded in said [?] in the night time and two of the party were shot by the Tories, proceeded to Half Moon and on his march passed through Lansingbergh to Half Moon where he stayed some length of time about a fortnight as he now believes then marched to Niskayuna & to Schenectady where he also served some time about a month, then marched to Albany & from there he returned to GreenBush and says that he then served on Scouts several times was ordered out by the officers and also says that he served on guard by times at night during the times that he resided there which was nearly one year or thereabouts as near as he can recollect. And he then returned to Fort Dayton at Herkimer, which he thinks was in the latter part of the winter or first part of Spring in 1782. Recollects there was snow on the ground. And days after he arrived at Fort Dayton Herkimer he was in service at fort Dayton on guard and other service most of the time till the close of the Revolutionary war. That he volunteered in pursuit of the Indians and Tories after the engagement between them and Mr. Shull (12) & his family at that time two of Mr. Shull's sons were taken prisoner by the Enemy and further says that he escorted a prisoner to Canajoharrie on his way to Johnstown, and was also ordered to carry officers and soldiers to Johnstown as was engaged a number of days.

Thinks Fort Dayton not occupied till after Oriskany Battle. (13)

And further says that during the whole of the war from the time of his Engagement in the service aforesaid after this Fort Dayton he resided at [?] was occupied Fort Dayton except when he resided at Schenectady and Greenbush as aforesaid and that at Fort Dayton in Herkimer he was much engaged guarding Fort Dayton or on volunteered service or called out by his commanding officers and further says that he was wounded (14) near Fort Dayton by a shot received from a hostile Indian in the Revolutionary War the ball went through his shoulder. And also says that he volunteered to Andrewstown (15) when the Indians had killed four people & I went to bury them. And further says he is certain that he did much service in the Revolutionary War that he has not stated but positively believes that this service which he recollects would amount to about or near three years actual service exclusive of the time he worked on the farm.

And further says that after the Lieutenant Col. Frederick Bellinger was taken prisoner in the battle at Fort Stanwix, Col. Peter Bellinger was left in command of the militia at Fort Dayton, as he believes and that he was at another time ordered out to guard boats with provisions to Fort Stanwix does not recollect the officers under whom he then served but thinks he can prove the service by John Frank for boat. That he was born at Canajoharrie in Montgomery County ninth March 1760. Has no record of his age, resided at Herkimer as before stated when called into service. Has resided at Herkimer since the Revolutionary War and now resides at that place.

Was called into service by his commanding officers & was frequently drafted out of said company or ordered out by the officers on expeditions. Each company giving so many men. Volunteered many times on Expeditions and on scouts as before stated in the declaration that he has no documentary evidence or writing of any kind that he can refer to for particular dates, but knows that from the time of his commencement in 1776 or first part of 1777 until the close of the Revolutionary war he was always kept in readiness at a minutes warning as before stated and was continually in service during said war that he hereby relinquishes every claim whatever to a pension or annuity except the present and declares that his name is not on the Pension Roll of the agency of any State. (Signed) Hannes Dachsteter

Sworn to and Subscribed the day and year aforesaid in open court. Julius C. Nelson, Clerk

End Notes—S.29121—Hannes Dockstader

1. Hannes served in Captain Henry Harter's (Herder, Herter, etc.) Company in Colonel Peter Bellinger's Fourth Regiment of Tryon County Militia. The other company officers were: John Demuth as First Lieutenant, Peter James Weaver as Second Lieutenant and John T. Bellinger as Ensign. Hannes (John, Johannes, etc.) is listed as a corporal on June 1st, 1779 at Fort Dayton and listed as serving 3 days in June, 11 in July, 14 in August, 1 in September, 6 in October and none in November. Hannes is again listed as a corporal in 1780 and served the following: 1 day in March, 5 in April, 8 in May 16 in June, 6 in July, 4 in August, 1 in September and for October, November and December 0. FROM: Revolutionary War Rolls 1775-1783, Series M-246, Roll 72, folder 78, National Archives, Washington, D.C.
2. Frederick Bellinger served as the Lieutenant Colonel under his brother Colonel Peter Bellinger.
3. Nicholas Herkimer was appointed Brigadier General of the Tryon County Militia on September 5, 1776.
4. In Provincial Congress, Militia Law, New York, Aug 22d, 1775. "*6th that every man between the ages of 16 and 50 do with all convenient speed furnish himself with a good Musket or firelock & Bayonet Sword or Tomahawk, a Steel Ramrod, Worm, Priming Wire and Brush fitted*

thereto, a cartouch Box to Contain 23 rounds of Cartridges, 12 flints and a Knapsack agreeable to the directons of the Continental Congress" FROM: Documents Relating to the Colonial History of the State of New York ed. Bertold Fernow, Vol XV, State Archives, Vol .I, Weed Parsons and Company, Printers, 1887, Page 31.

5. George Weaver served as a Second Lieutenant under Captain Henry Staring in Colonel Bellinger's Regiment.
6. The Battle of Oriskany was fought on August 6, 1777. Lieutenant-Colonel Bellinger was taken prisoner and he was exchanged in 1778 for a British soldier.
7. Hundreds of militia were on their way to join the American Army at Stillwater under Major General Horatio Gates. Lieutenant General John Burgoyne surrendered his British forces on October 17, 1777. At that time there could have been 18,000 American Militia and another 4,000 to 5,000 Continental troops there.
8. Captain Marcus Demuth's Company of Tryon County Rangers were raised on August 1, 1776 and they were discharged on March 27, 1777.
9. Hannes is probably referring to Robert McKean who had a company of levies in 1779 that served in the area. This company was in Colonel Henry K. VanRensselaer's Regiment of New York State Levies in 1779.
10. According to The Frontiersmen of New York by Jeptha R. Simms, pages 555-556 Vol. II, Geo. C. Riggs, Publisher, 1883, the Mount homestead was attacked in October of 1777 and two of his three sons were killed. Mr. and Mrs. Mount had gone to the mill at the Little Falls before the raid had taken place. The Mount family abandoned the settlement in what is now the Town of Salisbury, Herkimer County.
11. Hannes enlisted as a private in Captain Jacob DeFreest's (DeForrest, etc.) Company in Colonel Stephen J. Schuyler's Sixth Regiment of Albany County Militia. Henry K. VanRensselaer was the Lieutenant-Colonel of this regiment.
12. Captain Donald McDonald with a raiding party attacked the home of Christian Schell on August 6, 1780, at Schell's Bush. Christian had built a blockhouse near his home for protection. All but the two sons that were captured made the blockhouse and fought off the attackers. In Simm's The Frontiersmen of New York Vol. II, pages 480-484, contain information on this raid and the one on June 24, 1781. Christian was wounded in this attack and he died of his wounds on July 8, 1781. Simm's source for the Schell family story was from *"The account of the Schell family were obtained at interviews with Lodowick Moyer and John Dockstader, corroborated by other old people of Herkimer County. They were mainly from Dockstader. He was a son of George Dockstader's and at our interview was living a mile above Herkimer Village. He was in the Oriskany battle under Capt. Henry Harter, and was near Gen. Herkimer when he fell. He said that at New*

Germantown, opposite Frankfort, Herkimer proposed to wait for tidings from Fort Stanwix, where some of his officers told him that his family was nearly all in Canada and taunted him beyond endurance. This staunch old patriot died within two years of our interview. I was surprised to learn that Gen. Herkimer's wife, at the beginning of the difficulties, went to Canada and remained there. This fact should increase our veneration for the old hero's memory."

13. Fort Dayton was usually garrisoned by the local militia. During the winter it was often hard to get the militia to man the fort. At other times Continental troops and or levies guarded the fort.
14. According to Doctor William Petry's account of those he treated for wounds etc., printed on page 283, Vol. II of The Frontiersmen of New York by Simms states the following. *1780 Aug 8 John Dachstader and Conrad Vols, both wounded with buckshot."*
15. AndrusTown and Henderson Town. These are near present day Jordanville, Otsego County, and were destroyed on July 18, 1778.

Pension Application for Henry Deck

S.8314 (Widow: Hannah)
Declaration in order to obtain the benefit of the act of Congress passed June 7, 1832.
State of New York
Herkimer County SS.

On this Eleventh day of October one thousand eight hundred and thirty two personally appeared in open court before the Judges of the Court of Common Pleas of the County of Herkimer, now sitting Hannah Deck the widow and relict of Henry Deck dec'd late of the town of Stark in the County of Herkimer, and State of New York—aged fifty nine years, who being first duly sworn according to Law, doth on her oath, make the following declaration in order to obtain the benefit of the act of Congress passed June 7, 1832.

That this deponent married the said Henry Deck dec'd on the twenty ninth day of July 1792 at the town of Canajoharrie in the present County of Montgomery in the State of New York, that she continued to live and reside with the said Henry Deck dec'd from the time of her marriage aforesaid, until the twentieth day of September 1832, when he departed this life at the town of Stark in the County of Herkimer aforesaid—leaving the deponent his widow, and leaving also nine children.

And this deponent further says, that she was informed by the said Henry Deck dec'd in his life time, and this deponent has frequently heard him talk of the same, that he was a soldier in the revolutionary war, that he enlisted in the Regiment commanded by Col. Marinus Willett (1) that he served about two years and three months—and that he was also a minute man and in the militia service and that she believes the said Henry Deck never drew a pension in his life time and that he was not on the pension list roll of the agency of any state—that the said Henry Deck also informed her that he was out with Genl.

Sullivan when he went through the western part of the State of New York. (Signed with her mark) Hannah Dick

Sworn in open court Oct 11th 1832. Julius C. Nelson, Clerk

State of New York
Herkimer County SS.

On the eleventh day of October 1832, personally appeared in open court before the Judges of the Court of Common Pleas in and for the County of Herkimer now sitting John Lepper of the Town of Minden Montgomery County State of New York who being duly sworn deposes and saith that he has been personally acquainted with Henry Deck in the war of the Revolution and ever since that and this deponent & Henry Deck enlisted at Fort Plank then Tryon County now County of Montgomery Town of Minden under Capt. Davis (2) in the service of the United States in the war of the revolution some time early in the spring of the year 1779 this deponent and said Henry Deck enlisted into the aforesaid service for the term of nine months by the aforesaid Capt. Davis and was put in the regiment commanded by Colonel Frederick Wisenfeldt he this deponent further saith that he and said Henry Deck left Fort Plank early in the spring and proceeded on our march under the command of Capt. Davis and Colonel Wisenfeldt in the western parts of the State of New York we proceeded on till we arrived at Otsego at a place now called Cooperstown there was holden about three weeks was imployed in throwing a dam across the crick at the foot of the lake in order the dam said lake to procure water to assist us in carring our boats down the Susquehannah river we proceeded down the river with a great number of boats or more three days after we let the water go we then consisted of several regiments and was commanded by General Clinton (3) this deponent further saith that after arriving at Tioga Point where we were joined by General Sullivan thence we proceeded to Newtown (4) thence thru the western parts of the State of New York thence back to Wioming, Eastown in Pennsylvania thence to New Jersey place called Morristown there this deponent and said Henry Deck received our discharge said Deck was discharged by Colonel Wisenfeldt as this deponent thinks, but further saith that he this deponent and said Henry Deck left Fort Plank early in the spring of 1779 together and remained together in one mess thru the western parts of the State of New York, Pennsylvania and New Jersey and was present when he received his discharge in Morristown some time in the winter of 1780 this ended his term of enlistment of Nine months thence he proceeded home and further saith not. (Signed with his mark) John Lepper

Sworn to in open court Oct 11th 1832. Julius C. Nelson Clerk

End Notes—S.58314—Henry Deck

1. Henry enlisted May 22, 1781 in Captain Lawrence Gros' company in Lieutenant-Colonel Commandant Marinus Willett's Regiment of New York State Levies. He was discharged on December 31, 1781. FROM: Revolutionary War Rolls 1775-1783, Series N-246, Roll 78, Folder 173, National Archives, Washington, D.C. In April of 1782, Henry enlisted

in Captain Abner French's Company in Colonel Willett's Regiment. In November, Captain French retired from the service and Lieutenant Jellis A. Fonda was appointed captain in his place. Henry was discharged on December 31, 1782.

2. Henry enlisted as a private in Captain John Davis' Company which was the Second Company in Lieutenant-Colonel Commandant Frederick Weisenfel's Fourth New York Continental Regiment. He was discharged on January 1, 1780. FROM: Revolutionary War Rolls 1775-1783, Series M-246, Roll 70, Folder 49, National Archives, Washington, D.C.
3. Brigadier General James Clinton joined forces with Major General John Sullivan and together they destroyed Iroquois Villages in the western part of New York.
4. Newtown now present day Elmira, New York was the only battle of this campaign was fought the battle took place on August 29, 1779.

Pension Application for David Demaray (Demoray, Demoree)

R.2,859

Declaration: In order to obtain the benefit of the Act of Congress passed June 7th 1832

State of New York

Orleans County SS.

Personally appeared in open court, the Honourable the Judges of the Court of Common Pleas of said County now sitting David Demaray aged seventy three years, a resident of the Town of Shelby in said County of Orleans and State of New York, who being first duly sworn according to law doth on his oath, make the following Declaration in order to obtain the benefit of the Act of Congress passed June 7th 1832.

That he entered the service of the United States under the following named officers and served as herein stated.

That he entered the service in the month of April 1778 on the 25th of April 1778. That he volunteered to service his County for the period of one month and a half of a month. That he joined a company of troops under the command of Captain Henry Vanderhoof (1) of old Albany County in the State of New York (now Rensselaer County), or in that part now in Rensselaer Co.

That he joined said company in Pittstown in said County of Albany and was ordered to march up to StillWater in said state where this applicant and his fellow soldiers were encamped for a few days to recruit and reconnoiter. It was reported that the hostile Indians were committing murders and depredations on the Frontier settlements and this applicant with the corps to which he was attached were ordered to their relief. That he marched from thence to Fort Edward and from thence to White Hall on Lake Champlain at that time called Skeensborough, where he was encamped and took his turn in standing sentry days and nights. That the British Indians were as he was informed afterwards apprised of his approach and pursuit of them and they fled. The Frontier inhabitants had principally left their habitations for places of Safety. That this applicant at the expiration of his tour of one month and one half of month was ordered home to Pittstown this period of service as a volunteer commenced on the 25th of April and ended 12 of June 1778, making out a tour of one month and one half of a month as a soldier of the Albany County Militia.

And the said applicant again volunteered into the service. That he joined a detachment of drafted militia of said Albany Co., commanded by Capt. Vanderhoof on the 20 of June and served as a volunteer soldier until the 21 of September 1778. That he was marched from Pittstown aforesaid to Fort Edward on the Hudson River—another report was brought by Express for the militia to turn out and drive off the enemy. The Lieutenant of the company was Vandercook (2). Nathan Ford was the Ensign. The Drummer's name was John Ford son of the Esign [Ensign]. This applicant's mess soldiers were John Ford, Michael Francisco, Wm. Golden, and Conrad Bush. That the said applicant with his companions in arms were ordered on to Fort Edward and there stationed to watch and protect the people from massacre. That at said Fort he performed duty as a sentry and other garrison duties—that he served in this tour a part of June, all July, August and part of September 1778, making a term of three months.

That he was marched back to Albany Co. aforesaid and verbally discharged from the service by his commanding officer, Capt. Vanderhoof.

And again the said applicant turned out as volunteer and joined a body of militia under the Command of Lieut. Vandercook and Ensign Ford for a tour of two months. That he commenced this 3rd tour on the 4th October 1778 and served as a volunteer soldier during the remainder of October, all November and until the 6th of December following 1778.

That he was ordered to repair to Fort Ann, & Fort Edward where he performed Garrison duty for two months as above and was then discharged from the service by the officer who commanded at Fort Edward (not recollected) making a tour of two months service as a volunteer in the Malitia [militia] from Albany Co. NY.

And this applicant afterwards volunteered to serve in a Regiment of Albany Col. Militia that he fell in and joined a company of Militia under the command of Captain Vanderhoof in an expedition against the Indians. That this term of duty began on the 3rd of May 1779 and ended on the 4th of June following 1779 making a period of one months duty. That he was ordered on an expedition against the Indians who were collecting as it was reported at Crown Point. That the forces sent against them were some hundreds strong and were principally under the command of General George Clinton then Governor of the State of New York. It was called the Governor's alarm. That he was ordered on to Fort George at the south part of Lake George where this applicant with a detachment embarked in boats for Crown Point—first stopping at the garrison at Ticonderoga and from thence he went over to Crown Point. That the enemy had left Crown Point about three hours as he was informed before this applicant arrived there and thus the expedition failed. That this applicant was then ordered back on home where he was verbally released from his military engagement of one month as above by his commanding officer.

And this applicant was out again to serve his country as a volunteer against the savage foes. That he joined a corps of drafted men of his regiment under the command of Peter Yates. That he commenced this tour as near as his memory served on the 19th of June 1779 and served for two months and one half a month. Served from 19th June to 4th of September 1779.

That this applicant was marched from Albany Co. on to the Forts along the Hudson River above Saratoga and performed duty as occasion required at said Forts as a guard.

That he was at the end of his tour discharged from the service verbally. That he was so often called out on sudden alarms that he cannot tell now how much longer he did serve than the periods above stated. But he is sure of having served in the ensuing year 1780. 3 three months of different tours against the enemy making in all his revolutionary services a full period of thirteen months. The Major of the regiment in which this applicant served was Major VanVechten (3) who was killed by the Indians nearly at the close of the Revolutionary War. The three months service in 1780 was served during Jun, July & August under Capt. Vandercook of the Albany Co. Militia under Col. Yates at Albany. And the said applicant further says that no living witness can be procured by whom he can prove the above services of thirteen months or any part thereof and that he was not engaged at any time during his revolutionary services in any civil employment—but was faithfully and cheerfully devoted to the Army. (Signed with his mark) David Demaray.(4)

Sworn before me in open court June 15th 1835. A.B. Mills Clerk of Orleans County

Interrogatories

1st When and in what year were you born?

Ans. I was born in the year 1762 on the 29th of April of said year.

2nd Have you any record of your age and if so where is it?

Ans. I have a record of may age recorded in my family Bible at home from which I know my age to be seventy three years & rising—

3rd Where were you living when you were called into the service. Where have you lived since the Revolutionary War and where do you now live?

Ans. When I was called into the service I lived in PittsTown in Old Albany Co. now it is in Renssaellaer Co. NY. and since the Revolutionary War I have lived in the County of Rensselaer in the said State of N. York and in the County of Schenectady in said State and in the County of Orleans in the state of New York where I now live and have lived for the space of twenty four years.

4th How were you called into the service & were you drafted? Did you volunteer or were you a substitute and if a substitute for whom?

Answ. I was not drafted neither was I a substitute but I volunteered to service the United States for the periods above mentioned of thirteen months.

5th State the names of some of the regular officers who were with the Troops when you served, such Continental and Militia Regiments as you can recollect and the general circumstances of your services.

Ans. General George Clinton (5), Capt. Vanderhoof,Ensign Ford, Lieut.Vandercook, Genl Schuyler (6), Major Van Vechten, Col. Peter Yates.

6th Did you ever receive a written discharge from the service and if so by whom was it given and what has become of it.

Answer. I never did receive a written discharge from the services above specified, but I was always verbally discharged by my commanding officer.

7th Did you ever receive a commission?

Answ. I never did receive a commission but served as a private soldier for the different tour of Thirteen Months. (7)

8th State the names of persons in your present neighborhood to whom you are a known and who can testify as to your character for truth and veracity and their belief of your services as a soldier of the Revolution.

Ansr. I will name the following: viz, David Wetherwax, Jacob Wetherwax, Henry Wetherwax, Col. Ellicott, S.A.G.B. Grant, Samuel Bidleman, L. J. Griswold.

End Notes—R.2859—David Demaray

1. Henry Vanderhoof, Captain of the First Company in Colonel John Knickerbocker's Fourteenth Regiment of Albany County Militia. On June 22, 1778, Peter Yates was commissioned Colonel and John VanRensselaer was commissioned Lieutenant-Colonel both in the Fourteenth Regiment.
2. On June 22, 1778 the following were commissioned officers in Captain Vanderhoof's Company. Nathaniel Ford (Fort) as the First Lieutenant, Jacob Hallenbeck as the Second Lieutenant and Simon VanderCrook as the Ensign.
3. Major Dirck VanVeghten of the Fourteenth Albany was killed on August 8, 1777.
4. On April 6, 1855 another application was made on David's behalf at which time he was ninety three years of age. It was also stated his father actually spelled the name Demarest and he (David) answered to both names.
5. Governor of New York and General George Clinton.
6. Major General Philip Schuyler of the Continental Army.
7. It also appears that David had served at least one tour under Captain James Hadlock in the Fourteenth Albany.

Pension Application for Anthony Devoe

S.10,562

Declaration to obtain the benefit of the Act of Congress passed June 7, 1832.

State of New York

County of Herkimer SS.

On this tenth day of October 1832, personally appeared in open court before the Court of Common Pleas in & for the County of Herkimer and State of New York now sitting Anthony Devoe, a resident of the Town of Warren, County & State aforesaid, aged sixty nine years & upwards, who being first duly sworn according to law, doth on his oath make the following declaration, in order to obtain the benefit of the act of Congress passed, June 7, 1832.

That he entered the service of the United States under the following officers, and served as herein stated.

That he was enlisted by his father, and within his county, in the company of Captain Isaac Bogert (1), whose Colonel this deponent believes was Colonel Van Schaick (2), and that he cannot state the names of any other of the company or Field officers; that he entered the service about in the month of July 1779 and left it late in the months of January in the cold winter of 1780 but on what day he cannot recollect. That he was in no engagement—that during all the time he was in service he was stationed at a fort in the City of Albany. That at the time of his enlistment he resided in the Town of Half-Moon, now in the County of Saratoga & State of New York. That while he was stationed at the fort, some regular troops were sometimes in the same, but this deponent did not know the names of any of their officers—That he has no documentary evidence of his services, but received no written discharge and that he does not know of any person whose testimony he can procure who can testify to his service.

And this deponent further saith that while he was stationed at the fort in Albany, where he served from the time of his enlistment until he was discharged, he use to hear that the British were making attempts to come up to Albany but that they were prevented by a large chain stretched across the Hudson River. That he served two years after the Battle of Bemis Heights (3) and the surrender of Burgoyne—and also two years after the battle of Bennington in which General Stark (4) was victorious.

And this deponent further declares, that he was born in the Town of Newtown in the present County of Saratoga, in the year 1763, as he is informed and believes.

That he has no record of his age, except one which he made himself 14 or 15 years ago, in his family Bible.

That when called into service he lived at Half-moon point, so called in the Town of Half-moon aforesaid.

That since the Revolutionary War, he has lived at Schaghitcoke in Rensselaer County State of New York about ten years, when he removed to the town of Warren, Herkimer County where he has resided ever since, and now resides. That he was always a Volunteer, that he never received any written discharge.

That this deponent is known to James [?] Esq, John Overaker, Rufus Gram, esq, Daniel Talcott, Nicholas Shoemaker, George Yule, Henry Crim & the Rev'd W. Balla, who can testify to this deponents character for veracity and to their belief of his services as a soldier of the revolution. That he was not in service with any of the regular troops excepted a few who were sometimes in the Fort aforesaid, but he cannot state the names of any of the Regular Officers, nor can he state any Continental or Militia Regiments except that in which he served as aforesaid while on duty in the said fort.

He hereby relinquishes every claim whatever to a pension or annuity except the present, and declares that his name is not on the pension roll of the agency of any state.

Sworn to and subscribed the day and year aforesaid. (Signed with his mark) Anthony Devoe

Sworn and Subscribed in open court this 10th day of October 1832. F. E. Spinner Dept Clerk.

End Notes—S.10562—Anthony Devoe

1. Captain Isaac Bogart was appointed as captain in April of 1779 in Lieutenant-Colonel Commandant Henry K. VanRensselaer's Regiment of New York State Levies, unfortunately no muster rolls have been found for the regiment.
2. Goose VanSchaick was the Colonel of the First New York Continental Regiment.
3. The Battle of Bemus Heights was fought on September 19, 1777. Lieutenant General John Burgoyne, surrendered his British Army on October 17, 1777.
4. Brigadier General John Stark commanded the American forces at the Battle of Bennington on August 16, 1777.

Pension Application for Benjamin Dickson (Dickinson, Dixon)

S.22210

Declaration in order to obtain the benefit of the act of Congress passed June 7, 1832 by Benjamin Dickson

State of Pennsylvania

County of Crawford

On this [blank] day of August one thousand eight hundred and thirty two personally appeared in open court before Henry Shippen, President and Stephen Barlow and John H. Marks Esqr. Judges of the Court of Common Pleas of Crawford County now sitting - Benjamin Dickson a resident of Vernon township in the county and state aforesaid who being first duly sworn according to law doth, on his oath, make the following declaration in order to obtain the benefit of the act of Congress passed June 7, 1832.

That he entered the service of the United States under the following named officers and served as herein stated viz—

That in the month of February 1776 he went as a militia man in the company of Captain Samuel Clyde (1) of Cherry Valley Montgomery County, (2) New York to Johnstown distant about 30 miles, to suppress some Tories, who, it was said, had collected there at the time under Sir John Johnston [Johnson] and were threatening the peace and safety of the inhabitants and after accomplishing this object of their march, the company returned after an absence of one week.

That about ten days after he went with a detachment of men under the command of Ensign James Cannon (3), of Capt. S. Clyde's Company to Butternut (4) and Otego Creek between 30 & 40 miles from Cherry Valley to bring in a number of Tories who were harboring some hostile Indians and which they accordingly did; one of the Tories, John Hicks died on the way of a fit of apoplexy. The detachment was out about 7 or 8 days.

That in January or February 1777 he was drafted as a militia man into Capt. Dievendorf's (5) company attached to Colonel Ebenezer Cox's regiment of New York & marched with the regiment to reinforce Gen'l Anthony Wayne (6) at Ticonderoga who was threatened with an attack by the British forces after being absent two months & thereabouts the regiment was discharged and the men returned home.

That a few days after his return, in April he went with a detachment of some 25 or 30 men under Ensign James Cannon to a place near the Delaware River, 30 miles from Cherry Valley to quell a number of Scotch Tories living in the neighborhood of the place, and after dispersing them, and taking two of them as hostages, who were sent to prison at Albany, the detachment returned after an absence of about 7 days.

That in May following he went several times in the company of Captain T. Whitaker (7), successor to Captain Clyde, with most of the Militia of Cherry Valley to the German Flats in the Mohawk River, to protect the inhabitants from the ravages of the enemy.

That in June following Capt. Whitaker's company marched with the regiment of Colo. Cox, with some other men commanded by Brig. Genl Herkimer to the mouth of the Unadilla (8) on the Susquehanna River distant 70 miles from Cherry Valley to make battle or treat, with one Brandt (9) an Indian educated by Sir William Johnston [Johnson] who had collected about 200 Indians and Tories 28 miles lower down the river and from where dangers were apprehended—A treaty therein was made and in about 20 days the men returned home—

That in the latter part of July, same year he again met in Capt. Whitakers company with a body of men under Genl Herkimer to the German Flatts and thence to within 4 miles of Fort Stanwix at that time besieged by the British forces under Genl St. Leger. (10) The engagement took place between the two armies in which the Americans lost 346 men killed and prisoners, Capt. Whitaker's company however did not reach the ground until after the engagement when his men assisted in taking care of the wounded &c the time of absence was about 15 days.

That in September following he was drafted for a tour of one month and marched under Major Sam'l Clyde to reinforce Genl Gates (11) at Saratoga. He was in several skirmishes with Genl Burgoyne's (12) men, not at the time of his surrender to Genl Gates, the time of month served had expired and he returned home.

That in the month of March or beginning of April 1778 he was appointed a first Lieutenant in Captain Garret Putman's Company, New York Militia, and was drafted into what was called the "Rangers Service" for a tour of nine months active duty, which time of service he fully completed, and for the greater part of the time acted as and did the duties of captain of the Company. Capt. Putman being sick, and unfit for duty. The company during the time was stationed at Fort Herkimer by the Mohawk River and as he recollects & believes was the only company regularly stationed there at the time, several skirmishes, took place between the men of the fort and the Indians about & at some distance from the fort in two of which he received slight flesh wounds, but not sizable, one the right leg by a buck shot, and the other on the left leg by an Indians spear, at the expiration of the nine months service he with the rest of the company was regularly discharged and returned home. He recollects of Major Copeman (15) of the New York Militia being at the fort several times while he was stationed there, but he has no recollection of his having any particular command of the station.

That he [?] no actual service of any account until the spring of 1780 when he with the militia of Montgomery County were called out to repel the British forces under Sir J. Johnston (14) who at that time was committing much injury to the settlements in the Cochnawaga [Caughnawaga] 20 miles above Schenectady N. York.

That he was acquainted with Genl Gates, Wayne & Herkimer and Colo. Ebenezer Cox of the New York Militia, Colo. Samuel Campbell who was an uncle of his (applicant), Major Isenlord (16) of Colo. Cox's Regiment & Major Copeman, all these persons he knew well—

That he has no documentary evidence whereby to establish the foregoing facts. That what he might have had he has lost, particulary a small journal in which he had noted several incidents which if recollected at present might be satisfactory. In Nov 1777, while stationed at Fort Herkimer he had house with its contents burnt by the Indians as he was afterwards informed & verily believes & what papers he had prior to that time of his service must have then destroyed.

He states that he was born the 26th December 1753 at Cherry Valley N. York where he resided until 1789 when he moved to Owego N. York, thence to Ontario County N.Y. then to North East Erie County Penn in 1815 and thence to Vernon Township Crawford County Penn about 5 years since where he has and continues to reside with his son James M. Dickson. The record of his age is contained in the family bible of his father of whose sons he is the eldest and that the bible is in his possession and produces in court.

He has procured the testimony of his brother James Dickson of Erie County taken the 5th of August inst. before the Hon. Henry Shippen aforesaid and which is hereto annexed, to prove many or all of the foregoing facts.

He is acquainted with David Brackenridge Esqr and John H. Work, Judge of this Court (that the clergyman of the neighborhood are not acquainted with his reputation as a soldier of the Revolution) who can testify as to his character for veracity and their belief of his services as a soldier of the revolution.

He hereby relinquishes every claim whatever to a pension or annuity except the present, and declares that his name is not on the pension roll of the agency of any state.

Says he had a warrant or commission from a committee in New York which has been lost for several years. (Signed) Benjamin Dickson

Sworn & subscribed the day and year aforesaid, August 16, 1832. Henry Shippen.

Letter replying to inquiry dated January 15, 1935.

Reference is made to your request for data in regard to Benjamin Dickson, soldier of the War of the Revolution, served in the New York militia and died in Crawford County, Pennsylvania.

The Revolutionary War record of Benjamin Dickson which follows was obtained from the papers on file in pension claim, S. 22210, based upon his service in that war.

Benjamin Dickson was born December 26, 1753 in Cherry Valley, Montgomery County, New York; he was the son of William Dickson, and was the eldest of six sons, the name of his mother not given.

While a resident of Cherry Valley, New York he served in the New York troops on various tours as follows: in February, 1776, one week as private in Captain Samuel Clyde's company, and about ten days later, seven or eight days in same company; from sometime in February, 1777, two months in Captain Diefendorf's company, Colonel Ebenezer Cox's regiment; in April 1777, seven days under Ensign James Cannon; in May 1777, several alarms in Captain Thomas Whitaker's company, and in June 1777, twenty days in same company; in July 1777 fifteen says as sergeant in Captain Thomas Whitaker's company; from; sometime in September, 1777, one month under Major Samuel Clyde, during which he was in several skirmishes; in November 1777, sometime at Fort Herkimer, officers not named. Subsequently, he was appointed 1st Lieutenant and from April 1, 1778, served nine months in Captain Garret Putnam's company, during which period he was in several skirmishes, and received a flesh wound by a buckshot in his right leg and a flesh wound in his left leg by an Indian's spear. He was called out in September, 1780 (17) to protect the settlements about twenty miles above Schenectady.

Benjamin Dickson resided in Cherry Valley, New York, until 1789, then moved to Oswego, New York; then to Ontario County, New York, and from there in 1815 to Erie County, Pennsylvania.

He was allowed pension on his application executed August 16, 1832, at which time he was residing with his son, James M. Dickson, in Vernon Township, Crawford County, Pennsylvania, where he had lived about five years. The name of the soldier's wife is not shown.

James Dickson, soldier's brother, was born February 3, 1756, was living in 1832 in Erie County, Pennsylvania.

End Notes - S.22210—Benjamin Dickson

1. Samuel Clyde was the Captain of the First Company, appointed on August 26, 1775, in Colonel Nicholas Herkimer's First Regiment of Tryon County Militia.
2. This county was known as Tryon County from 1772 to 1784. This part of Montgomery County became Otsego County in 1791.
3. James Cannon was the Second Lieutenant in Captain Clyde's Company.
4. The Butternuts and Unadilla were loyalists settlements and frequently aided raiding parties.
5. Captain Henry Diefendorf of the Fifth Company in Colonel Ebenezer Cox's First Regiment of Tryon County Militia. Herkimer was promoted to Brigadier General on September 5, 1776.
6. Colonel Anthony Wayne of the Fourth Pennsylvania Continental Regiment. Wayne was appointed Brigadier General on February 21, 1777. A draft of the Tryon County Militia was made in January and February 1777 and the detachment under Colonel Cox went to Ticonderoga and Mount Independence. They helped build and repair fortifications and build the floating bridge across Lake Champlain from Fort Ticonderoga on the New York side and Mount Independence on the Vermont side.
7. Thomas Whitaker was appointed captain as Samuel Clyde had been promoted to Second Major. At this time James Cannon was appointed Adjutant of Cox's Regiment. The other officers under Whitaker were as follows: First Lieutenant John Campbell, Second Lieutenant Samuel Campbell and Ensign Samuel Whorfield.
8. This meeting took place on June 27, 1777.
9. Captain Joseph Brant. He did have a regiment called Brant's Volunteers which was a mix of Natives and Loyalists.
10. Barry St. Leger was a Lieutenant-Colonel in the 34th Regiment but for this expedition he was appointed a Brigadier General to stop any problems arising from the seniority of rank. The Battle of Oriskany was fought on August 6, 1777.
11. Major General Horatio Gates of the Continental Northern Army.
12. Lieutenant General John Burgoyne surrendered his British forces on October 17, 1777.
13. Two companies of Rangers of sixty men each were to be raised by the order of Marquis Marie Jean de Lafayette in March of 1778 after holding a conference with the native tribes at Johnstown. On April 6th a meeting of the field officers, also known as Regimental Officers, submitted the following names to be approved: Captain John Bradpick or Breadbake, Lieutenants Adam Helmer and John Smith, Captain Garret Putman and Lieutenants Victor Putman and Benjamin Dickson. FROM: Public Papers of George Clinton, First Governor of the State of New York, Vol. 3, pp 251-252.

14. He is referring to the raid of May 22, 1780. Johnson's forces burned Tribes or Tripes Hill and Caughnawaga which is the present day Village of Fonda and the Town of Mohawk now called Montgomery County.
15. Abraham Copeman, Captain of the Sixth Company in Colonel Samuel Campbell's First Regiment of Tryon County Militia. Colonel Cox was killed at the Battle of Oriskany on August 6, 1777.
16. John Eisenlord was the Second Major in Colonel Peter Bellinger's Fourth Regiment of Tryon County Militia.
17. Benjamin's application says the spring of 1780 as well as his brother James' supporting testimony.

Pension Application for John Dill

S.10569
State of New York
Cayuga County SS.

On this eighteenth day of June AD 1832 before me the subscriber first Judge of the Court of Common Pleas in and for the County of Cayuga and state aforesaid personally appears John Dill aged seventy four years resident in the town of Camillus in the County of Onondaga and state aforesaid who being by me first duly sworn according to law, doth on his oath make the following declaration in order to obtain the provisions made by a late act of Congress entitled "An act supplementary to the act for the relief of the surviving officers and soldier of the Revolution."

That he the said John Dill enlisted in the town of New Windsor in the County of - - - in the State of New York in the company of artificiers commanded by Captain James Young in the Regiment commanded by Col. Baldwin (1) about the month of December AD 1777 or the month of January AD 1778. That he continued to serve in said company or in the service of the United States until the expiration of three years from the time of said enlistment when he was discharged at the town of Fish Kill in the County of Dutchess in the State aforesaid, that the said company was commanded by Capt. --- Purdy (2) after the command thereof was relinquished by Capt. James Young (3), that subsequently said company was commanded by Captain John Shepherd (4) who continued in command of said company when he said Dill was discharged—that he has no other proof of his said services except the following affidavit of Caleb W. Adams. (Signed) John Dill

Sworn to & declared before me the day & year first aforesaid. J.L. Richard as first Judge of Cayuga.

End Notes—S.10569—John Dill

1. Jeduthan Baldwin served as a Colonel of Artillery Artificer Regiment from September 3, 1776 to March 29, 1781.
2. Monmouth Purdy was appointed Captain in Colonel Baldwin's regiment on April 12, 1778 and he retired in March of 1781.
3. James Young was appointed Captain in Colonel Baldwin's Regiment on August 1, 1777 and he served until 1780.

4. John Shephard was appointed Captain in Colonel Baldwin's Regiment on November 24, 1779 and he served until he retired in March 1781.

Pension Application for John Dockstader (Docksteter, Dockstater, Docksteater)

S.31654
State of New York
Montgomery County SS

On the 19th day of September 1832 personally appeared in Open Court, John Dackstader, aged Eighty one years and 1 month the 19th born this day of Augt 1751 In the Town of Johnstown then County of Tryon now County of Montgomery and State of New York, aforesaid, who being first sworn according to Law doth on his Oath make the following declaration in order to obtain the benefit of the act of Congress passed the 7th day of June 1832.

This applicant declares under oath that Emediately after the Commencement of the Revolutionary War, that he this claimant was enrolled in the Company of Militia Commanded by John Davis, Capt.(1) In the Regiment of Militia Commanded by Col. Frederick Fisher in the then County of Tryon in the Brigade of Gen'l Nicholas Herkimer—That after Oriskany Battle where Capt. Davis was Slain therewith under the Command of Capt. Abr'm Veeder (2)in the same beat.

This applicant declares that Emediately after the Commencement of the Revolutionary War, Conformable and in Compliance of A Resolution, passed by the Old Congress on the 27the day of May 1775 that the Militia of New York be armed and trained and in constant readiness to Act, at a Moments Warning.-----

That in compliance of Which this Applicant did furnish himself with sufficient arms and aquipment [equipment], and always kept himself in readiness at a Moments Warning to the close of the War, and that he had performed Service under the forgoing named Officers.

In the Militia—That he this claimant declares, that he was called out to go to Cachnawaga, [Caughnawaga] there joined Genl Schuyler (3) with his Militia in the winter 1776 there remained for several days. Once General Parade on the Ice, after went to Johnstown causing surrender of Sir John Johnson with about four hundred men, all armed, his object not Particularly known, but supposing that he either hath Calculated to go to Canada, to Join the British or to Commit depredation on those friendly to the Cause of liberty and Independence before they went to Canada, again previous same year 1776 in summer with the Militia to Sacondaga in pursuing the Enemy.—

This claimant also declares, that in the year 1777 on the Sixth day of Augt under the command of General Herkimer engaged in Oriskany Battle which was a serious conflict &c.

This claimant further declares that he hath been in the contested Battle at Johnstown then under the Emediant Command of Col. Marinus Willett, against Maj'r Ross

(4) and a large party of Indians, Tories and some British Troops from Canaday, on the 25th day of October 1781.

And this Applicant further declares that he has been drafted on many and Frequent Occasions, and Also Guarding and Watching at the blockhouses at Cachnawaga and Fort at Johnstown, and often directed to March at a distance to watch Guard and repel the Incursions of the Common Enemy and finally this Applicant declares that from the time he was armed and aquipped [equipped]and in constant readiness at a moments warning, and always did March out on Every Emergency when called on, That this claimant views the Services performed as only one term that for and during the war from the commencement to the Close of the War, that this claimant, has resided in the Town of Johnstown during the war, and for a number of years, past a resident of the Town of Palatine, and now a resident of the said Town of Palatine, County of Montgomery aforesaid.

And that this Claiment hereby relinquishes every claim whatever to a Pension or Annuity except the present, and declares that his name Is not on the Pension Roll of the Agency of any State, according to the Claiments knowledge. And further this Claiment saith not. (Signed) John Dackstater

Sworn and Subscribed the day and year aforesaid. Geo. D. Ferguson, Clerk

End Notes—S.31654—John Dockstader

1. John Davis was appointed Captain of the Second Company on August 26, 1775 in Colonel Frederick Visscher's Third Regiment of Tryon County Militia.
2. Abraham Veeder was the First Lieutenant in Captain Davis' Company. Veeder was commissioned captain on March 8, 1781.
3. Major General Philip Schuyler of the Continental Army.
4. Major John Ross of the King's Royal Regiment of New York commanded the British forces.

Pension Application for William Doney

S.15102
State of New York
Schoharie County SS.

On this second Day of October 1832, personally appeared in open court before the Judges of the court of common Pleas in the County of Schoharie now sitting William Doney a resident of the town of Middleburgh in Said county of Schoharie aged 68 years who being first duly Sworn according to law, doth on his oath make the following declaration in order to obtain the benefit of the act of Congress passed June 7th 1832 that he entered the Service of the United States under the following named officers and Served as herein Stated.

That he the Said William Doney Inlisted in Middle fort in Schoharie, for the term of nine months on the first of April 1782 in the company commanded by Captain Gray (1) in the regiment commanded by Colonel Van Schaick (2) in the Line of the State of New York on the Continental Establishment, that he Served in Middle fort in Schoharie and in that vicinity, that he continued to serve in said corps, that he Served faithfully out his term of Inlistment until the first of January 1783, that he was honorably discharged by his officers in the city of Schenectady in the State of New York, that he hereby relinquishes every claim whatever to a Pension or annuity except the present; and Declares that his name is not on the Pension Roll of the Agency of any State of the United States that he has been mustered in Middle fort in Schoharie, that he has been informed and believes the Same to be true, that the muster Roll has been Last or absent this must be the reason that his name is not on the register in the State of New York.

That he the said William Doney answered in court, that he was born the 10th day of October in the year 1764 that the record of his age is in his possession, that he lived in Schoharie ever Since the American revolution that he was Discharged by captain Gray in the city of Schenectady, as he has stated in his declaration.

(Signed with his mark) William Doney

Sworn and Subscribed the day and Year aforesaid in open court. John Gebhard Jr. Clk.

We Martinus Mattice residing in the Town of Middleburgh in the County of Schoharie and State of New York, and Joseph Bouck residing in the same place hereby certify that we are well acquainted with William Doney who has Subscribed and Sworn to the above declaration, that we believe him to be Sixty eight years of age that he is respected and believed in the neighborhood where he resides to have been a Soldier in the revolution and that we concur in that Opinion, (Signed) Martinus Mattice, Joseph Bouck

Sworn and Subscribed the third day of October 1832 in open court—John Gebhard Jr. Clk.

State of New York
Schoharie County SS.

Peter Bouck of the town of CobelsKill in the County of Schoharie, a United States Pensioner, being duly Sworn doth depose and Say: the he has been acquainted with William Doney of the town of Middleburgh in said county ever since the American Revolution that he the said William Inlisted for the term of nine months, on the first of April 1782, in the State of New York in the company commanded by Captain Gray, in the Regiment commanded by Colonel Van Schaick, in the Line of the State of New York, on the Continental Establishment, that he Served his term out faithfully; until the first of January 1783 when he the sd William Doney was hononuably discharged from the Service in the city of Schenectady in the State of New York; this deponent further deposed and Say that he and the Said William Doney, Jacob France, John Schoolcraft and Johannes Koenig; Served together in the company and Regiment aforesaid until they was honourably discharged in the city of Schenectady aforesaid.

(Signed) Peter Bouck

Submitted and Sworn before me Henry Shafer a Judge of Schoharie Common Pleas this 14th day of July 1832.

Henry Shafer a Judge of the Court of Common Pleas in and for the Said County of Schoharie do certify that Peter Bouck who took the foregoing oath is a man of credibility and to be believed on oath. Henry Shafer.

State of New York
Schoharie County SS.

Johannes Koenig of the Town of CobelsKill in said county ["auditing Pension" is in the margin] being duly sworn doth depose and Say that he has been well acquainted with William Doney of the to9wn of Middleburgh in said county ever since the American Revolution, that he the said William Doney Enlisted for the term of nine months, on the first of April 1782 in the State of New York in the company commanded by Captain Gray, in the regiment by Colonel Van Schaick in the Line of the State of New York, on the continental Establishment; that he served his term out faithfully until the first of January 1783, when he was honorably Discharged from the Service in the City of Schenectady in the State of New York.

This deponent further deposed and Says that he and the said William Doney and Jacob France, Heinrich Shafer Junior, John Schoolcraft and Peter Bouck a Revolutioner Pensioner, Served together in the company and regiment aforesaid and was discharged together in the city of Schenectady it the State of New York as aforesaid. (Signed) Johannes Koenig

Subscribed and Sworn the 14th day of July 1832 before me Henry Shafer a Judge of Schoharie Common Pleas.

I Henry Shafer a Judge of the Court of Common Pleas in and for the County of Schoharie; do certify that Johannes Koenig who took the foregoing oath is a man of credibility and believed on oath. Henry Shafer

End Notes—William Doney-- S.15102

1. William enlisted as a private in Captain Silas Gray's Company in Colonel Marinus Willett's Regiment of New York State Levies for 1782. Captain Gray was unable to enlist his quota of men and he was discharged by July 1st and his men were put into other companies. William was placed in Captain Joseph Harrison's Company until he completed his enlistment term.
2. Colonel Willett was supposed to raise Levies to serve in Colonel Goose VanSchaick's First New York Continental Regiment but he was having difficulties in completing his own regiment.

Pension Application for Gerrit (Garret) Dubois

W.20995 (Widow: Sarah)
State of New York
County of Ulster SS.

On this tenth day of September one thousand eight hundred and thirty two personally appeared in open court before the Judges of the Court of

Common Pleas for said county now sitting being a court of record having by law a clerk and a seal, Garret Dubois a resident of the town of Marbletown in the County of Ulster and State of New York aged 69 years who being first duly sworn according to law doth on his oath make the following declaration in order to obtain the benefit of the act of Congress passed June 7, 1832, that he entered the service of the United States under the following named officers, and served as herein stated.

That said applicant volunteered and entered the service in April 1781, at a place called Ashocan [Ashokan or Shokan] in the town of Marbletown in said County of Ulster in a company of Militia commanded by Capt. Henry Pawling (1)—Henry Van Hovenburgh first and John Van Deusen second Lieut & belonging to a regiment commanded by Col. Albert Pawling--one Benschoten (2) was Major was - was stationed at Ashocan aforesaid which was on the frontier and continually harassed by the Indians and Tories—was on frequent scouts along said frontiers up as far as Paghkatachkan in Delaware County - and said company was exposed to great danger, and were very frequently alarmed by the incursions of the said tories and Indians—that he enlisted for the term of nine months and served till between Christmas and New Year in the said year 1781 and was then discharged at Ashocan in Marbletown afore said - received no written discharge.

And in answer to the interrogatories put to him by the Court as required by the War Department said applicant on his oath states that he was born on the 13th day of July 1763 at Marbletown in Said County of Ulster and State of New York, that he lived there when he entered the service, and has lived in said town ever since the Revolution and still resides in said town—that his age is on record in the Records of the Reformed Dutch Church in Marbletown—that he volunteered in the aforesaid service—that there were no regular officers nor continental troops where he laid—that he received no written discharge, and that he can state the names of Peter A. Cantine Esq. & Abraham E. Hardenburgh—in his present neighborhood who can testify to his character for veracity and their belief of his services as a soldier of the Revolution.—

And said Applicant would farther state that the clergyman of his neighborhood is a young man who lately settled in the congregation, and he has therefore produced in court as witnesses two, respectable inhabitants of his town viz. Peter A. Cantine and Abraham E. Hardenburgh who are well acquainted with said applicant—and also that he has as documentary proof the affidavit of Henry Van Hovenburgh his Lieut. whom he served under, and also the affidavit of Solomon Crispell who lived at the place where we laid—which are both hereto annexed.

He heerby relinquishes every claim whatever to a pension or annuity except the present and declares that his name is not on the pension roll of the agency of any state. (Signed) Gerrit Dubois

Sworn to and subscribed the day and year aforesaid. A. Draper, first judge, John Jansen, Abm A. Deyo, Judges.

State of New York
Ulster County SS.

On this twenty first day of January in the year one thousand eight hundred and forty three before me Jacob Snyder one of the Judges of the County Courts in and for the County of Ulster aforesaid personally appeared Sarah Dubois a resident of the town of Marbletown County of Ulster and State of New York aged seventy six years who being first duly sworn according to law, doth on her oath make the following declaration in order to obtain the benefit of the provision made by the act of Congress passed July 7th 1838, entitled an act granting half pay and pensions to certain widows:--

That she is the widow of Garret Dubois who in the revolutionary [war] resided in the said town of Marbletown where he continued to reside until the day of his death.

That during said war he the said Garret Dubois was a private soldier in defence of his country for which he received a pension at the rate of twenty six dollars and sixty six cents per annum which he continued to receive until the day of his death.

She further declare[s] that she was married to the said Garret Dubois the seventeenth day of February in the year one thousand seven hundred and eighty six—

That the ceremony was performed by the Reverend Mr. Goethes Clergyman of the Protestant Dutch Reformed Church in the town of Marbletown.

That her maiden name previous to her marriage was Sarah Roosa and that her husband the aforesaid Garret Dubois died the sixth day of April in the year one thousand eight hundred and forty two:--

That she was not married to him prior to his leaving the service but the marriage took place previous to the first day of January in the year on thousand seven hundred and ninety four viz at the time above stated.

She further declares the annexed proof of her marriage and the certificate of pension of her dec'd husband is the only evidence she has procured to prove the same.

For proof of the services of her said husband she would respectfully refer to his declaration and proxy on file [at] the War Department under the act of the 7th of June 1832.

She further declares that ever since the death of her husband she has not intermarried but remains the widow of the said Garret Dubois as will more fully appear by reference to the proof hereto annexed. (Signed with her mark) Sarah Dubois

Sworn to and subscribed on the day and year first above written before me and I certify that I am personally acquainted with said Sarah Dubois and believe her deposition entitled to credit and I further certify that said applicant from bodily infirmity is unable to attend court. Jacob Snyder one of the Judges of the County Court of Ulster County.

End Notes—W.20995—Garrit Dubois

1. Captain Henry Pawling, Lieutenants Henry VanHovenburgh and John J. VanDeusen were appointed April 27, 1781 in Lieutenant - Colonel Commandant Albert Pawling's Regiment of New York State Levies.
2. Elias Van Bunschoten and Thomas DeWitt were appointed Majors on April 27, 1781 in Pawling's Regiment.

Pension Application for Samuel Dubois

R.3100

Declaration in order to obtain the benefit of the act of Congress the 7th June 1832.

State of New York

Ulster County SS.

On the twenty fourth day of April in the year one thousand eight hundred and thirty four personally appeared before me Henry Wynkoop one of the Judges of the County Court of the County of Ulster aforesaid Samuel Dubois a resident of the town of Woodstock of Ulster County aged ninety six years who being first duly sworn according to law doth on his oath make the following declaration in order to obtain the benefit of the act of Congress passed the 7th of June 1832.—

That he entered the service of the United States under the following named officers and served as herein after stated.

That in the month of July in the year 1777 in the revolutionary war this deponent volunteered in the Military Service of the State of New York in Captain Philip Swart's (1) Company in a detachment commanded by Major John Cantine (2) that he with the said company rendezvoused in the village of Kingston and went from there by water to Albany and from there marched to Stillwater and Beames Height [Bemus Heights] and Joined the army under the command Genl Gates (3) and was there during the battle was not in any battle and continued in that vicinity until after the surrender of the Army of Genl Burgoyne and was discharged after a full term of three months for which they were originally engaged received no written discharge.

That in the summer of 1778 deponent was drafted in a company commanded by Captain Moses Cantine (4), Major John Wynkoops (5) Regiment rendezvoused at Kingston and marched from there to the County of Schoharrie in the said state of New York and continued in the said company and regiment about two weeks then went to a place called Harpersfield remained there a few days, then returned Schoharrie and remained there a few days and was discharged after a service of six weeks or more.

And this deponent further says that in the same year deponent volunteered as a substitute for whom he does not know for the term of one month under the command of Lt. Tobias Myer (6) and was stationed in the town of Woodstock until discharged.

Also one month under the command of Lt. Martin Hommel (7) and was stationed along the frontier in the town of Shandaken until discharged.

And this [deponent] further says that he was engaged for one month under the command of Lt. Peter Post (8) in the year 1779 and was stationed in the town of Saugerties at the house of one Tobias Wynkoop. Also one month under Lt. Peter Brink (9) and was stationed at the house of one Longyear in the town of Shandaken.

And this deponent further says that in the fall of the year of 1779 deponent again volunteered in Capt. Evert Bogardus (10) Company for three months, the company met at Kingston and went from there by water to the town of Fishkill in the County of Dutchess & State of New York and there joined Genl Clinton's (11) Brigade and continued there until at the end of two months and was discharged by Captain Borgardus in person.

And this deponent further says that late in the fall of 1779 or 80 deponent again volunteered in Captain Philip Swarts Company for three months and was stationed at the house of one Longyear in the town of Shandaken for the protection of the inhabitants on the frontier of the County of Ulster and was discharged at the end of the said term of three months received no written discharge.

And this deponent further says that in the year 1781 he served as a substitute for one month in Capt. Moses Yeoman's (12) Company and was stationed at the house of one Major Houghtaling (13) in the town of Kingston.

Also one month in Captain Jeremiah Snyder Company and was stationed at the house of on Tobias Wynkoop in the town of Saugerties at the foot of the Catskill mountains.

Also one month in Captain Livingston's (14) Company and was stationed at the house of Evert Wynkoop in the town of Saugerties all in the County of Ulster to protect the inhabitants of said County against the Indians and Tories.

And this deponent further says that all the forementioned services deponent has actually served in person as a private soldier and either called out or was drafted or was a substitute or volunteered which particular deponent cannot recollect but were called out by the authority of Colonel Johannis Snyder of Kingston yet deponent does not recollect the names of any officers except those already stated nor does remember any other companies stationed at the time and places—deponent was out on the frontiers of Ulster County as aforesaid to protect the inhabitants on the frontier against the invasion of the Indians, Tories who frequently made depredations on the inhabitants in those districts.

That deponent has actually served the above term of fourteen months & a half in the revolutionary was as a private soldier but owing to his extreme old age and the consequent loss of memory may not be correct as to the dates of said services that he has no documentary evidence of and in consequence of his retired habit of and his living in a remote part of the town he does not know of any living witness to prove the same that he has had no written discharge during the revolutionary war.

To the interrogatories, prescribed by the war department, he answers viz.

1st That he was born in the town of Woodstock County of Ulster & State of New York in the year 1735.

2nd That he has no record of his age.

3rd That he lived during the revolutionary war that he lived since and that he always lived and now lives in the said town of Woodstock.

4th That he was drafted was a volunteer and a substitute.

5th That he remember no officers except those stated.

6th That he never had a written discharge.

7th That he knows Samuel Culver member of Assembly, Alexander Hunt Esquire Justice of the Peace, and William Deforest all respectable inhabitants of the neighborhood in which he resides, who can testify as to his character for truth and veracity and their belief of his services as a soldier the revolution.

He hereby relinquishes every claim whatever to a pension or annuity except the present and declares that his name is not on the pension roll of the agency in any state. (Signed with his mark) Samuel Dubois

Sworn to and subscribed the day and year aforesaid before me Henry Wynkoop one of the Judges of the County Courts of the County of Ulster.

End Notes—R.3100—Samuel Dubois

1. Captain Philip Swart in Colonel Abraham Hasbrouck's First Regiment of Ulster County Militia. On February 19, 1778, Johannes Snyder was commissioned Colonel of the First Ulster.
2. The Battle of Bemus Heights was fought on September 19 and the Battle of Stillwater was fought on October 7, 1777. Lieutenant General John Burgoyne surrendered his British Army on October 17, 1777.
3. Horatio Gates was a Major General of the Continental Army and was the commander of the American Army at Stillwater.
4. Captain Moses Cantine of the Second Company in Colonel Snyder's Regiment.
5. First Major Adrian Wynkoop of Colonel Snyder's Regiment.
6. Second Lieutenant Tobias Myer in Captain John L. Dewitt's Fourth Company in Colonel Snyder's Regiment.
7. Second Lieutenant Martines Humble or Hommel, etc., in Captain Jeremiah Snyder's Company in Colonel Snyder's Regiment.
8. First Lieutenant Petrus Post in Captain Matthew Dedrick's Third Company in Colonel Snyder's Regiment.
9. Ensign Petrus Brink in Captain DeWitt's Company in Colonel Snyder's Regiment.
10. Evert Bogardus Captain of the First company in Colonel Snyder's Regiment.
11. Brigadier General James Clinton.
12. Lieutenant Moses Yeoman's Ranger Company ordered out by Governor George Clinton on June 8, 1781 and were to be attached to Colonel

Albert Pawling's Regiment of New York State Levies. Lieutenant Yeoman's Rangers were discharged on December 8, 1781. FROM: Audited Accounts Vol. A, Page 158, Special Collections and Manuscripts New York State Library, Albany, NY.

13. Second Major Philip Hooghteling of Colonel Snyder's Regiment.
14. Probably Captain Gilbert Livingston of Colonel Albert Pawling's Regiment.

Pension Application for Martin Dubois

S.29129
BL Reg 140536-1850
Declaration. In order to obtain the benefit of the Act of Congress passed June 7th 1832.
Territory of Michigan
County of Washtenaw

On this 5th day of November A.D. 1832 personally appeared in open court before the Court of Probate in and for the said County now sitting Martin Dubois a resident of the Township of Saline in the county and Territory aforesaid aged sixty eight years who being first duly sworn according to law doth on his oath make the following declaration in obtain the benefit of the act of Congress passed June 7th 1832.

That he entered the service of the United States under the following named officers and served as herein stated—He entered the service on or about the first day of April 1782 in the Company Commanded by Capt. Gilbert Livingston & Lieutenant Cornelius Dubois (1) and attached to the Regiment commanded by Colonel Wisingvelt [Weisenfels] in which he remained for nine months was verbally discharged between Christmas and New York by Capt. Livingston. The Colonel being obliged to secure his personal safety by leaving his regiment before they were discharged having rendered himself obnoxious to many of his officers and men during the service who were determined to be revenged upon him after their discharge. He resided at the time he entered the service at Marbletown in the county of Ulster and State of New York where he remained with most of the regiment during the nine months except when sent out on short scouts into the agacent [adjacent] county Marbletown was at that time on the frontier and constantly exposed to the attack of the Indians and Tories. He was not in a battle during the time. In a skirmish with a small scout of the enemy near Pockotocka were [where] we took a prisoner by the name of Sheffer. The Militia of the County of Ulster was at that time all classed into classes of fifteen each of which was bound to furnish one man. The deponent was then enrolled as a militia man in the company of Captain Shoemaker (2) of Ulster County as aforesaid which was classed as afore said that the class to which this deponent belonged hired this deponent to serve the term for which they were bound to furnish. That Mathew Contine was at the head of the class that this deponent did serve the nine months as aforesaid as a substitute for the class aforesaid. That he has no documentary evidence and knows of no person whose testimony he can procure who can testify to his service. That John D. Speer, Catharine Jacobs, Orin Howe, Stephen Goodman & Smith Lapham are acquainted with this deponent and reside in the same township and neighbourhood. He hereby relinquishes every claim whatever to a pension or annuity except the present and declares that his name is not on the pension roll of the agency of Michigan or any state in the US. (Signed) Martin Dubois (3)

Sworn to and subscribed the day and year aforesaid. James Kingsly, Judge of Probate Court for Washtenau County.

End Notes—S.29129—Martin Dubois

1. Captain Gilbert Livingston and Lieutenant Cornelius DuBois were commissioned July 10, 1782 in Lieutenant-Colonel Commandant Frederick Weissenfels Regiment of New York State Levies.
2. Captain Frederick Schoonmaker served in Colonel John Cantine's Third Regiment of Ulster County Militia.
3. In other papers in his file he stated he was born on October 21, 1764 at Marbletown, Ulster County, N.Y. He died August 14, 1850.

Pension Application for Francis Dunkle or Dunckle (Dunckel, Dunkill, Dunghill

R.3130
State of New York
County of Montgomery SS

On the 19th day of September in the year of our Lord one thousand eight hundred & thirty two personally appeared in open court before the Judges of the Court of Common Pleas of said County now sitting Francis Dunkle a resident of the town of Canajoharie in the county & State aforesaid aged sixty six year in April last who being first duly sworn according to law doth on his oath make the following declaration in order to obtain the benefit of the Act of Congress passed June 7th 1832. That he entered the service of the United States under the following named officers and served as herein after mentioned.

That in the month of June 1780 (1) he was called upon & volunteered in the service of his country in a company of militia men commanded by Capt. Adam Lipe, Lieut. Jacob Matthise (2) thinks Ensign William Seber in Colo. Clyde's Regiment, that he was kept under arms on duty & at work for the government in the building of Fort Clyde until about the last of November following when hostilities in that season ceased and they were dismissed for the winter. And that during that season he did as he believes five months duty as above mentioned in the service of his country.

That about the first of May 1781 he was again called out & entered the service under the command of his said officers above mentioned was stationed at Fort Clyde, there kept on duty & out in scouting parties at different times & in various directions to check the Indians and Tories who were doing great mischief in that place and its vicinity until about the last of November following when hostilities in that season again ceased, and that during that season he did as he believes at least six months actual duty in the service of his country.

That about first of May 1782 he was again called upon & entered the service under command of his said officers above mentioned was again at Fort Clyde, there kept on duty & out in Scouting parties at different times & in different directions as above mentioned until some time in the month of November following when hostilities in that season again ceased and that during that season he did as he verily believes as many as six months duty in the service of his country.

That in the month of May 1783 (3) he was again called in to service by his said officers stationed again at Fort Clyde where he was kept on duty as above mentioned until some time in October following when hostilities again ceased, and that he did in that season as he believes five months actual duty - and that he has no documentary evidence of his services—and never received a written discharge.

That he knows of no person whose testimony he can procure who can testify to all his service.

That he was born in Germany in April 1766 and the same season came to America as he has been informed & believed.

That he has no record of his age.

That he was living in the town, County & State aforesaid when called into service as aforesaid where he has continued to live since the revolution and now lives.—

That he was called into service at the different times & in the manner above mentioned—

That at Fort Clyde during the time he was there on duty as aforesaid Lieut. Putman, (4) with some regular Troops as he now thinks were stationed at different times Lieut. Peake (5) & Lieut. Baker (6) with nine months troops as they were called were stationed there also at different times and that he cannot state the names of any other officers or troops where he served nor the circumstances of his service other than as he as above stated.—

That the Rev'd Jonas Diefendorf & John Yordon are the names of persons to whom he is known in his present neighborhood who can testify as to his character for veracity & their belief of his services as a soldier of the revolution.

Her hereby relinquishes every claim whatever to a pension or annuity except the present and declares that his name is not on the pension roll of the agency of any state. (Signed with his mark) Francis Dunkle

Sworn to & Subscribed the day & year aforesaid. Geo. D. Ferguson, Clerk

End Notes—R.3130—Francis Dunkle

1. Francis or Frank is listed on Captain Adam Leipe's muster and pay roll for July 6, 1780 to July 20, 1782. He served 9 days during that time period and his pay was £ 0. . 16. . 0. On Captain Adam Leipe's Roll of Certificates that were paid by September 28, 1784, certificates that

were paid by September 28, 1784, certificate number 11382 he was paid £ 0. . 16. . 0. Captain Leipe's Company was in Colonel Samuel Campbell's First Regiment of Tryon County Militia. FROM: Revolutionary War Rolls 1775-1783, Series M-246, Roll 72, folder 89, National Archives, Washington, D.C.

2. The other company officers of Captain Leipe's Company were as follows: First Lieutenant Jacob Mathias, Second Lieutenant William Seeber and Ensign John Countryman.
3. Francis was not 16 years of age until 1782 which means his prior service did not count. He corrected this statement in his January 2, 1834 declaration in which he stated the following: "That in 1782 & 1783 I was of the age which enjoined me to bear arms and in those years I was called out & put on duty by my said Captain,". His pension probably was rejected because he could not prove six months of service.
4. Victor Putman had served as a lieutenant in Colonel Frederick Visscher's Third Regiment of Tryon County Militia, in 1780 in Lieutenant-Colonel Commandant John Harper's Regiment of New York State Levies and in 1781 in Lieutenant-Colonel Commandant Marinus Willett's Regiment of New York State Levies.
5. Lieutenant Christopher Peak or Peake of Colonel Willett's Regiment.
6. He is referring to Lieutenant Albertus Becker in 1780 in Colonel Harper's Regiment or to Lieutenant Storm Becker in Colonel Willett's Regiment.

Pension Application for George Dunkle or Johann George

Name also appears as Dunckle, Dunkil, Dunkel, Dunghill, etc.

W.24086 (Widow: Elizabeth)
State of New York
County of Montgomery

On this twenty first day of August 1845, personally appeared, before John Darrow, Judge of the County Courts in and for said County, Elizabeth Dunkle, a resident of the town of Palatine in said county, aged seventy six years and upwards, and she being first duly sworn according to law, doth on her oath make the following declaration in order to obtain the benefit of the provision made by the act of Congress passed 7th July 1838, and the several acts subsequently passed, amendatory of, and additional to the same. That she is the widow of George Dunkle, who served for the terms, and under the officers, and in manner particularly set forth in forth in the passing of her husband the said George Dunkle in the matter of his application under the Act of Congress passed 7th June 1838.

She further declares that her maiden name was "Countryman", that she was married to the said Dunkle by the Rev. Philip Jacob Groz a minister of the Gospel of the Lutheran persuasion, in the town of Palatine in the said county on the twenty seventh day of January in the year of our Lord, one thousand seven hundred and eighty nine.

She further declares that her said husband George Dunkle departed this life on the twenty second day of February, one thousand eight hundred and forty five, leaving her this declarant him surviving as his widow—That since his decease she has remained single and unmarried, and that she is still his widow.

And She further declareth and saith that she had by her said husband the following named children viz. George G. Dunkle, Peter G. Dunkle, John Dunkle, Jr., Daniel Dunkle, Elizabeth Dunkle, Catharine Dunkle, and Jonas Dunkle.

That her first child "George G." was born on the twenty second day of July 1791, and her second child named "Peter G." was born on the fourth day of April 1794. That "John" her third child was born on the twenty fourth day of May 1797, and Daniel her fourth child, on the third day of December 1800 & that Elizabeth her daughter was born on the sixth day of April 1805, and Catharine her second daughter, on the twenty first day of April 1807, and that the last child named "Jonas" was born on the twenty eighth day of March 1811.

That she has been informed and believes, that there is no record now extant of the date of her said marriage, on the register or records of the church, by the pastor of which she was married as aforesaid—That there is a record of her marriage in her family Bible which is now in the possession of her son John Dunkle, Junr. That the entry in her family Bible containing the record of her said marriage is true and correct, and declarant thinks it is in the handwriting of Uriah Potter, but is not certain. The same was copied from a leaf or leaves of an old German book was in the handwriting of the said declarant's father—The said entries in her said family bible were made at least fourteen years ago—That among the persons present at her marriage was Catharine Goertner now living who was her bridesmaid.

And this declarant further saith that her said husband George Dunkle received a pension of fifty three dollars, and ninety nine cents per annum, under the Act of 7th June, 1832. (Signed with her mark) Elizabeth Dunkle

Witness Peter G. Dunckel

Subscribed & sworn before me the said Judge the day and year first aforesaid, and I certify that said Elizabeth Dunkle is unable to attend court by reason of bodily infirmity. John Darrow, Judge of Montgomery County Courts.

State of New York
Montgomery County SS.

On the thirteenth day of June 1834 personally appeared before Abraham Morrell, David Spraker, Samuel A. Gilbert, Henry J. Devendorff and John Hand Judges of the Court of Common Pleas of said County now sitting John Yordon (1) and Adam Garlough (2) both of the town of Canajoharie County of Montgomery and State aforesaid, who having been duly sworn according to law do on their oaths depose and say viz, the said John Yordon says that he is aged seventy five years past and the said Adam Garlough for himself says that he is aged seventy nine years past and they jointly and separately say that they have been personally acquainted with George Dunckle previous to and during the "Revolutionary War and ever since a Revolutionary Soldier who claims a pension. And said deponents further say that the aforesaid applicant proved a true and faithful soldier during the revolutionary war from the year 1775, to the time when he received a wound, vizt forepart of July 1781. And the said deponent further say that the said applicant received a wound in the head from a musket ball injuring severely the head and destroying the right eye while under the command of Col. Willett and during the Turlough Battle, thereby disabling him entirely for more than a year.

And the said deponents further say that they have heard the Claimants declaration read, both original and supplemental and that they have been eyewitnesses to the most of the services rendered and contained in the supplemental declaration and do believe that the whole length of service contained in the said supplemental declaration was rendered as stated therein and that deponents further say positively that claimant did and hath rendered services to the United States for at least two years and more during said revolutionary war. And that we and each of us jointly and separately declare and state that claimant is a person of irreproachable character as to truth and veracity and entitled to full credit. (Signed with his mark) John Yordon, (Signed with his mark) Adam Garlough

Sworn to in Open Court this 13th day of Aug 1834 Geo. D. Ferguson, Clerk

State of New York
Montgomery County SS.

George Dunkle of the town of Canajoharie and County aforesaid being duly sworn deposeth and saith that he is the identical person mentioned and described in the original certificate hereunto annexed Examination by Abm. Ten Broock and Ph. Schuyler bearing date the twenty second day of September in the year of our Lord 1786. (Signed with his mark) George Dunkle

Sworn and subscribed this 5th day of May 1824 before Nathan Soule one of the common plea judges in & for said County of Montgomery.

Letter replying to an inquiry dated Aug. 10, 1906.

In reply to your letter dated the 16th ultimo, received the 18th you are herewith furnished statements of the military histories of the only three soldiers (brothers) named Dunkle, Dunckle, Dunkel, or Dunkill found on the Revolutionary War records of this Bureau.

It appears from the papers in claim, Widow's File 24,086 that George Dunkle, (Johann George Dunkle) was born in July, 1756, and resided at Canajoharie, Tryon County, New York when he enlisted in 1775 and served in the New York troops at various times until 1782, as a Private under Captains Peter S. Lygart, (3) Robert Crouse, Copeman, Adam Lipe, Samuel Gray (4), and Dieffendorf (5), Colonels Ebenezer Cox (6), Gansevoort (7), Willett (8), Clyde

(9), Harper and Wagoner; he was in the battles of Oriskany, Johnstown (10) and New Dorlach (11), in which last engagement he sustained a gunshot would resulting in loss of one of his eyes, for which he was allowed an invalid pensions from September 22, 1786. Soldier had a brother Peter who died prior to 1834.

He married at Palatine, New York, January 27, 1789, Elizabeth Countryman, and died February 22, 1845.

His widow was allowed pension on an application executed August 1, 1845 at which time she was a resident of Palatine, New York and seventy-six years of age.

Their children were:

Johann George (or George G.) born July 22, 1791
Petrus (or Peter G.) born Apr. 4, 1794
John born May 24, 1797
Daniel born Dec. 3, 1800
Elizabeth born Apr. 6, 1805
Catharine born Apr. 21, 1807
Jonas born Mch. 28, 1811

Medical Statement:

We the subscribers, Abraham Ten Broeck and Philip Schuyler Do certify that upon an Examination, in pursuance of the Law, entitled, "An Act making Provision for Officers, Soldiers, and Seamen, who have been disabled in the Service of the United States, "Passed the 22nd of April, 1786, We do find that George Dunkil, residing in the State of New York—Aged twenty seven years, late a private in Capt" Adam Liep's Comp'y in the Regiment of Militia commanded by Colo. Clyde and Claiming Relief under the Act of Congress, recited in the said Law, as an Invalid in Fact; and that he became disabled in the Service of the United States, in Consequence of a shot in the right eye (which he has lost) on the 10th July 1781.

And Do further certify, that upon the principles of the said Act of Congress the said George Dunkil is entitled to the Pay of five dollars per month,

Given under our Hands, in the City of Albany, on the twenty second day of September in the year of our Lord one thousand seven hundred and eighty six. Abm. Ten Broeck, Ph. Schuyler

End Notes—W.24086—George Dunkle

1. John Yordon served in Captain Adam Leipe's Company in Colonel Samuel Campbell's First Regiment of Tryon County Militia and was wounded in the left hip at the Battle of Johnstown on October 25, 1781.
2. Adam Garlough does not appear on any of Captain Leipe's Company muster or pay rolls. There were at least 2 Adam Garlock's (Gerlach, Kerlach, Garlough, etc.) that served in the First Tryon.
3. Captains Peter S. Dygart, Robert Crouse and Abraham Copeman all served in the First Tryon. Unfortunately no payrolls or muster rolls have been found for these companies.

4. George's name does not appear on Captain Samuel Gray's Company of Batteaumen.
5. Henry Dieffendorf was the Captain of the Fifth Company in the First Tryon. Henry was killed at the Battle of Oriskany on August 6, 1777. Afterwards his brother First Lieutenant Jacob Dieffendorf was promoted Captain of this company. There is no muster roll for Henry's Company and George does not appear on Jacob's muster roll.
6. Ebenezer Cox was the Colonel of the First Regiment of Tryon County Militia until he was killed at the Battle of Oriskany.
7. Peter Gansevoort was the Colonel of the Third New York Continental Regiment.
8. Marinus Willett had served as Lieutenant-Colonel of the Third New York, then the Fifth New York and then of a regiment of New York State Levies from 1781-1783.
9. Lieutenant-Colonel Samuel Clyde of the First Tryon.
10. John Harper was the Colonel of the Fifth Regiment of Tryon County Militia. In 1780 he commanded a regiment of New York State Levies.
11. Lieutenant-Colonel Peter Wagner of Colonel Jacob Klock's Second Regiment of Tryon County Militia.
12. The Battle of Johnstown was fought on October 25, 1781. Willett commanded the American forces in this battle.
13. The Battle of New Dorlach (Turlock, Terlow, Turlough, etc.) was fought on July 10, 1781. Willett commanded the American forces in this battle.

Pension Application for John Featherly, [Junior] also [Fetherly, Federly, Vatterly, Vetherly]

S.10658
State of New York
County of Seneca SS.

On this third day of October 1832 personally appeared in open court before the Judges of the Court of Common Pleas of the County of Seneca State of New York, now sitting John Featherly resident in the town of Junius, in said County & State who being duly sworn according to law doth on his oath make the following declaration in order to obtain the benefit of the Act of Congress passed June 7th 1832.

1st that he is of the age of seventy two years and upwards.

That he entered the service of the United States under the following named officers and served as herein stated.

First he entered the service as a volunteer in the company of militia commanded by Capt. Robert Crouse, (1) of the Regiment commanded by Col. Ebenezer Coxe, in the month of January 1777, & continued in such service for one year—that when he volunteered he resided in Canajoharie, Montgomery County, NY that during such service he marched to Ticonderoga (2) thereof to

Fort Standish [Stanwix] (3) (now Rome) thence down the Susquehanna river to the Big Bend, thence to Rome, thence to Stillwater (4) under Captain Lipe. (5)

Second, in January 1778 he joined the militia under Capt. Lipe in the Regiment now commanded by Col. Samuel Campbell with whom he continued in service as a volunteer one year—during that time he was ordered to various places in that part of the State of New York, some of which are Springfield, Cherry Valley, Herkimer, & Rome.

Third in March 1779 he enlisted as a private in the company commanded by Capt. Peter Ehle (6) Regiment of New York State Troops commanded by Col. Christopher Yates, that he continued with them in service for the period of ten months, during which time he marched to Fort Edward, Schenectady, Fort Standish, down the Susquehanna to Oneida Lake &c that at the expiration of said ten months he was honourably discharged.

Fourth—That soon after such discharge & as he believes in the month of January 1780 he again enlisted as a private soldier in the New York line State troops—Company commanded by Capt. John Dana, (7) in the Regiment under command of Col. Hay, whose first name he does not recollect—that he continued in the service with them until January 1781 nearly one year, during most of the time he was stationed at FishKill, Dutchess County NY Where he was honourably discharged—Neither of which discharges are in his possession, several names having been included in the same discharge.

That in the fall of the year 1824, as this deponent believes, this deponent by his agent Graham H. Chapin, of Lyons, Wayne County New York, made application to the War department to be placed on the pension list, that he then made proof of most of the services so rendered as such soldier, by the testimony of Andrew Failing & George Ratnower, as this deponent believes, whose testimony this deponent cannot now obtain in consequence of the death of said Failing & not knowing the residence of said Ratnower but this deponent believes that the testimony by them, at that time, given is now on file in the office of the War department, as said Chapin has informed this deponent that he received a letter from that department, expressing an intention to place the papers, relating to that application, on file & informing also that that application was rejected on the ground that this deponent served in the New York line of State troops—at the time of the application in 1824 this deponent resided in Galen Wayne County NY and this deponent further saith that he knows of no witness by whom the services of this deponent can be proved.

This deponent further saith that he was born in the year 1760 at Canajoharie, County of Montgomery, State of New York—that he has no record of his age—that when he first entered the service he resided at said Canajoharie—that after the Revolutionary War he removed to Springfield in said county—that he removed to Phelps in the County of Ontario in said State about the year 1790; from thence to Sodus, Wayne County NY, thence to Galen in said county & lastly to Junius, Seneca County NY where he now resides.—That the manner of his going into service & the names of his officers under whom he served are as stated in this declaration to the best of his recollection.

That he received discharges at the times herein stated, but that he cannot obtain the same, several names having been included in one discharge & none having ever been delivered to him.

That this deponent is well known to James Otto & John Cuger, two of his present neighbours, residing near him, who can testify as to his character for veracity & their belief as to his services as a soldier of the Revolution.

This deponent hereby relinquishes every claim whatever to a pension or annuity, except the present & declares that his name is not on the pension roll of the agency of any state or territory. (Signed with his mark) John Featherly.

Subscribed & sworn in open Court the day & year aforesaid. Seba Murphy, clk.

Letter of inquiry included in the pension folder, dated September 28, 1923.

I have to advise you that from the papers in the Revolutionary War pension claim, S.10658, it appears that John Featherly was born 1760 in Canajoharie, Montgomery County, New York, and while residing there reenlisted January 1777 and served as a private one year in Captain Roberts Crouse's company, Colonel Ebenezer Cox's New Your regiment. He enlisted January 1778 and served one year under Captain Lipe in Colonel Samuel Campbell's regiment.

April 1, 1779, he enlisted and served ten months in Captain Peter Ehle's company, Colonel Christopher Yate's regiment, and on March 1, 1780, he enlisted and served eleven months in Captain John Dana's company, Colonel Hay's regiment.

In 1823, soldier resided in Galen, Wayne County, New York and had a wife and five children, names and ages not stated.

He was allowed pension on his application executed October 3, 1832, while living in Junius, Seneca County, New York.

End Notes—S.10658—John Featherly (Junior)

1. Captain Robert Crouse was appointed Captain in 1776 in place of Jacob W. Seeber who had received a commission as Captain in the Fourth New York Continental Regiment under Colonel Cornelius D. Wynkoop. The First Regiment of Tryon County Militia was first commanded by Colonel Nicholas Herkimer from August 26, 1775 to September 5, 1776 when he was appointed Brigadier General of the Tryon County Militia. The regiment was commanded then by Ebenezer Cox who had been the Lieutenant-Colonel. Colonel Cox and Captain Crouse both were killed at the Battle of Oriskany on August 6, 1777. On June 25, 1778, First Major Samuel Campbell was commissioned Colonel of the First Tryon.
2. A detachment was raised from the Tryon County Militia Brigade under Colonel Cox and went to Fort Ticonderoga. Detachments went from January to about April performing various tasks such as building fortifications and the floating bridge from Fort Ticonderoga NY across Lake Champlain to Mount Independence, Vermont.

3. Detachments of the Tryon County Militia were sent to Fort Schuyler to work on the fort garrison duty, work on the road & bridges and to cut trees down to fall into Wood Creek which would impede the progress of a British invasion which would come by bateaus. He does not mention anything about the Battle of Oriskany so his service is probably in one of the work details.
4. After the Battle of Oriskany detachments of the Tryon County Militia went to Stillwater and served as wagoneers and building fortifications under Major General Horatio Gates who was expecting to meet Lieutenant General John Burgoyne at or near Stillwater with his invading British Army and stop is advance towards Albany.
5. Adam Leipe (Lipe, Lype, Leib, etc.) was appointed on August 26, 1775 as Second Lieutenant in Captain Jacob W. Seeber's Company, Fourth Company. When Captain Crouse took command of the company the lieutenant remained the Second Lieutenant. He received his commission in 1778, dated June 25, 1778. In 1778, Francis Utt who had been the First Lieutenant under both captains was appointed captain of the company and Leipe was appointed the first lieutenant. In 1779, Captain Utt moved out of the company beat and Leipe was appointed captain. Leipe was commissioned Captain on March 4, 1780. FROM: Revolutionary War Rolls 1775-1783, Series M-246, Roll 72, Folders 84 and 89, National Archives, Washington, D.C.
6. There is no known muster roll for Captain Peter H. Ehle's Company of Bateaumen in 1779. These men were part of the Quartermaster General's Department.
7. Captain John Dana (also given as Denny) was also in the Quartermaster General's Department. Lieutenant-Colonel Udney Hays was the Assistant Deputy Quartermaster General.

Pension Application for Alexander Fergeson (Ferguson)

R.3499
Declaration: In order to obtain the benefit of the act of Congress passed June 7th 1832.
State of New York
Tompkins County SS.

On this ninth day of October in the year of our Lord one thousand eight hundred and thirty two, personally appeared before me, Nicoll Halsey, a Judge of the Court of Common pleas in and for the county of Tompkins, at the dwelling house of the petitioner who by reason of bodily infirmity is unable to attend Court, Alexander Fergeson resident of the Town of Dryden in the County of Tompkins, and State of New York aged Seventy years, who first being duly sworn according to law, doth on his oath make the following declaration in order to obtain the benefit of the act of Congress passed June 7th 1832.

That he entered the Service of the United States under the following named officers, and served as herein stated—In the year 1780 in the month of

April at the Town of Montgomery in the County of Orange and State of New York, he entered the service as a volunteer in the Militia under the command of Capt. Cross (1) and marched to a place called Nipingaugh, In the county and state aforesaid, served there four days then he was dismissed and returned to Montgomery aforesaid, and in two days then after he was called out by an alarm to go to Nipingaugh, aforesaid from thence to Mamakating under the command of Capt. Cross—from thence he marched to Warsink in the county of Ulster and State of New York (at the provision store was kept under the care of Col. Hornbeck) (2) from that time during the season in the last of December he served as a volunteer private soldier at the place called Nipingaugh, Mamakating, Warsink and [blot]ambacey in guarding the frontiers from the ravages of the Indians (who was then under their commander Brant) at the last of December he was dismissed and returned home to Montgomery from aforesaid.

The year 1781 the last of May he substituted for John Comfort and served two weeks under the command of Captain Fevers Johnson (3), Marched from the Town of Montgomery aforesaid to Nipingaugh then he was dismissed and returned to Montgomery the [blot] About the first of June he substituted for Samuel Ferguson (4) at the Town of Montgomery aforesaid, under the Command of Capt. Conklin (5), Marched from thence to the Town of Mamakating, [?] County near the Blue Mountains, thence to MarbleTown thence to Shandakin and Served at that place two weeks. Then he was dismissed and returned to Montgomery. In the month of August next following an alarm was made and the Militia was called out he then volunteered and went to the Town of Mamakating, under the Command of Capt. Conklin.

He served one week and was dismissed and returned to Montomery (6) aforesaid. In the month of September next following at the Town of Montgomery he Substituted for William Foresyth and marched to Shandakin in Ulster County under the command of Captain Robertson (7) and served there two weeks, and returned to Montgomery aforesaid.

In the month of October the same year he volunteered to go to Nipingaugh he marched to that place and served two weeks, he then was dismissed and returned to Montgomery, the first of November next following at the Town of Montgomery aforesaid he substituted for Matthias Millspaw (8) to go to a place called Hunk, under the command of Captain Gautt (9), he marched to Mamakating thence to Nipingaugh, thence to the place called Hunk (at which place he had a skirmish with the Indians and Lieut. John Gayshams(10) was killed and also Sergeant Adam [Epsiles?] Was killed.) (11) Served there three weeks, and then was dismissed, and returned to Montgomery Town; In the month of December next following he volunteered and marched to Warsink, he has forgotten who commanded at this time, (at Warsink the Indians and Tories attempted to drive off Cattle and also to burn the meeting house at that place but was prevented by the Militia at this time the Indians Met John Kettle (12) and killed him) He served at this place about [blot] weeks, then was dismissed and returned to Montgomery town.

The first of April in the year 1782 he volunteered at Montgomery Town aforesaid to go to Mamakating from thence marched to Nipingaugh and served from the first of April aforesaid, until the last of December next following, at Nipingaugh, Mamakating, Shandakin and Mamloius, under the command of the aforementioned officers, who command in their turn, the last of December aforesaid he was dismissed and returned to Montgomery Town aforesaid, That he served several times there, and four days at a time which he the said applicant can not particularize all the times aforementioned to guard as a private soldier (that about the time he first commenced his service, the regular Army lay at Marble Town, who were commanded by Col. Philip Van Cortland (13) they marched from the frontiers at or near MarbleTown to Join Genl Sullivan & Genl James Clinton (14), which occasioned a call for volunteers and militia at the aforementioned place.

That he has no documentary evidence and that he knows of no person whose testimony he can procure who can testify to his services. (Signed) Alex'r Fergeson

Sworn & Subscribed the 8th day of October 1832 before me Nicoll Halsey.

That he was born in the Town of Little Brittian near the North River [Hudson] in the County of Ulster and State of New York in the year 1762. That the record of his age is lost.

That he resided in Montgomery Town in the County of Ulster then, now Orange and State of New York when he entered the Service of the United States as a soldier, and entered his service at Montgomery Town aforesaid at the different periods of his service. That since the Revolutionary War he has resided as follows-viz that in the Town of Rochester in the county of Ulster and state aforesaid he resided two years from thence he moved to the Town of Dryden in the County of Cayuga, now Tompkins and State aforesaid which two last mentioned places he has resided ever since Revolutionary War and now resides in the Town of Dryden in the County of Tompkins and State aforesaid.

That he was called into the service by drafts, and calls for the Militia as he has above stated. The foregoing declaration at the different periods of his service, in the year 1780 he served as a volunteer & Draft 1781 substituted for John Comfort, Saml Ferguson, William Forsyth and Matthis Millspaw. That the names of some of the officers where he served were as follows to wit, Captain Wm. Cross, Lieut Robert Thompson (15), Joseph Crawford had no field officers there remaining to guard the frontiers and they acting by Companies only and were not committed with the Continental Troops—

That he never received any discharge during his services in the Revolution, were merely dismissed from the Service—

That he is known in his present neighborhood by James McElhiny, John Ellis, Esqr., Parly Whitmon, Abram Farmer, Esqr, Price Weed, Esqr, Gilbert Sutpin, William Sutpin, Elder Amos, Daniels, the Reverend William Clark the Honb'l Samuel Critendin, who can testify as to his character for veracity and their belief of his services as a soldier of the Revolution.

He hereby relinquishes every claim whatever to a pension or annuity except the present and declares that his name is not on the pension roll of the agency of any state. (Signed) Alex'r Ferguson

Sworn to and Subscribed the day and year aforesaid before me Nicholl Halsey, a Judge of Tompkins County.

En Notes—R.3499—Alexander Fergeson

1. William Cross was a captain in Colonel Jonathan Hasbrouck's Fourth Regiment of Ulster County Militia.
2. Jacob Hornbeck was the Lieutenant-Colonel in Colonel Levi Pawling's Third Regiment of Ulster County Militia.
3. Captain Matthew Jansen served in Colonel Hasbrouck's Regiment. He replaced Thomas Jansen Jr. as Captain on March 9, 1778.
4. Private Samuel Ferguson served in Captain Jansen's Company.
5. Jacob Conklin served as a captain in Colonel Hasbrouck's Regiment.
6. William Foresyth or Forsyth, etc., served as a private in Captain Jansen's Company.
7. A Johannes Roberson served as an Ensign in Captain Jansen's Company.
8. Mathias or Mattias, etc., served as a private and sergeant in Captain Cross' Company.
9. So far a Captain Gault cannot be found.
10. Lieutenant John Graham of Colonel James McClaughrey's Second Regiment of Ulster County Militia was killed on September 6, 1778.
11. On pages 16-19 <u>The Clinton Papers of George Clinton, First Governor of New York, Vol IV</u> you will find the report of Lieutenant Graham's fight. In the letter dated Marbletown 9th Sept. 1778 from Colonel John Cantine of the Third Regiment of Ulster County Militia, to Governor George Clinton, Colonel Cantine states the following were killed in the fight; Lieutenant Graham, Robert Temple, and Adam Ambler.
12. John Kettle or Kittle served as Colonel Cantine's Regiment. He was killed August 12, 1781.
13. Philip VanCortlandt was the Colonel of the Second New York Continental Regiment.
14. Major General John Sullivan and Brigadier General James Clinton each raised armies in 1779 and joined together to destroy the Iroquois Villages in western New York.
15. John Crawford was the First Lieutenant and Robert was the Second Lieutenant and Robert Thompson was the Second Lieutenant in Captain Cross' company

---

Pension Application for Isaac Ferguson

R.3503
State of New York
County of Dutchess SS.

On this ninth day of December in the year one thousand eight hundred and thirty three—personally appeared before Robert S. Livingston one of the Judges of the Court of Common Pleas of the County of Dutchess aforesaid—Isaac Ferguson a resident of the Town of Red Hook in the County of Dutchess and State of New York aged Eighty two years, who being first duly sworn according to law, doth on his oath, make the following declaration in order to obtain the benefit of the Act of Congress passed June 7, 1832.

That he entered the service of the United States under the following named officers and served as herein stated. He first entered the service at Frederickstown in the County of Dutchess aforesaid, now Carmel in the County of Putnam, in the month of October in the year 1775, in the militia company to which he belonged, commanded by Captain John Crane (1) in the Regiment of Colonel Henry Luttenton. The militia were called out for the purpose of assisting at the battle of White Plains and this applicant went under the officers aforesaid. They marched as far as Northcastle church where Colonel Luttenton on account of sickness in his family left them in charge of Comfort Luttenton (2), and returned home. They then proceeded under command of the said comfort Luttenton to near White Plains (3) where they received intelligence that the battle was over and then pursuant to orders they returned to Northcastle church taking with them the stores and wounded—at this place they remained to guard the stores, <u>three weeks</u>, when they were discharged and this applicant returned home to Frederickstown aforesaid at which place he resided previous to and during the Revolutionary war.

In the month of December in the year 1776, all the militia in that part of the country where this applicant resided and he among the rest were ordered out for the purpose of attempting to take fort Independence near Kingsbridge—The company met on the 28th day of December 1776. They ordered to take twelve days provisions and to march on the 1st day of January 1777, and on that day they accordingly met, and proceeded under the command of Captain Nathaniel Schribner (4) in the regiment of Colonel Henry Luttenton aforesaid to Northcastle church were they joined the regiment—Here they remained three or four days and drew ammunition and then marched on to near White Plains where they joined the brigade of General Scott (5) from here they marched on to Stephen Wards fourteen or fifteen miles farther south, where they met the brigade of General Peter TenBroeck—(6) They proceeded thence south through Yonkers to Valentine's near Fort Independence where they encamped—Here they remained a few days skirmishing with the enemy in the Fort when the British receiving a reinforcement, sallied out of immediately with the intention of surrounding them—Upon this they moved on to Valentine's Hill and drove the enemy back to the Fort (7)—On this hill they remained encamped a short time and then the brigade returned to White Plains and were stationed there for some time—They then marched up to Northcastle church where they arrived about the 1st of [blot] 1777 and here they remained until April 1st 1777 when they were discharged and returned home. This applicant having been engaged in this tour of service <u>three months</u>—

In the year 1777 and as he thinks in the month of April he was called out on an alarm and went under Captain Comfort Luttenton to Ridgefield in Connecticut. Here they met a party of the British returning from the burning of stores at Danbury.(8) They attacked them and pursued them to their shipping and then returned to Ridgefield and remained there sometime for the purposes of guarding. In this service he was engaged, at least three weeks when he was discharged and returned home.

In the month of January in the year 1778 he was called out under the orders of General Washington (9) and was engaged in foraging under the command of John Doty (10) acting as captain in Frederickstown aforesaid and in the vicinity six weeks, when he was discharged and returned home—He received a written discharge from this service, which is lost—

In the year 1778 and as near as he can recollect in the spring he was called out to go with a flag of truce to Valentine's near Kingsbridge and went accordingly under command of Captain John Berry. (11) In this service he was engaged at least one week when he was discharged and returned home.

In the fall of the year 1778 he was again called out and went with a flag of truce under command of Captain Nathaniel Scribner to the place last above mentioned and was engaged in this service at least one week when he was discharged and returned home.

In the forepart of the month of November in the year 1778 as near as he can recollect, he was called out and went under Captain John Crane in pursuit of disaffected persons who were on their way to Joining the enemy—They succeeded in taking seventeen of them in the Highlands and brought them before the Committee of Safety. He was engaged in this service in arresting and guarding the prisoners and conveying them to prison after trial at least three weeks when he was discharged and returned home.

In the month of April in the year 1779 he was called out and went with a flag of truce under Captain Comfort Luttenton to the City of New York and was engaged in this service at least two weeks when he was discharged and returned home—In addition to the several services above set forth this applicant was very frequently called out and went on alarms in the militia company to which he belonged, commanded by Captain John Crane in the year 1777, 1778, 1779 and 1780 to different places; mostly along the Hudson River and was kept in service sometimes two or three days sometimes a week and sometimes ten days and was thus engaged in actual service at least three months during which he was not engaged in any civil occupation or pursuit.

This applicant was born in Frederickstown in the County of Dutchess and State of New York now Carmel in the County of Putnam on the second day of February in the year 1750. He has no record of his age. He was living in Frederickstown aforesaid when called into service. He lived in the same place since the revolutionary war until in April 1806 when he removed to the Town of Red Hook in the County of Dutchess aforesaid where he has lived ever since, and where he now lives—The names of some of the regular officers who were with the troops where he served are Colonel Henry Luttenton, Captain John

Crane, Captain Nathaniel Schribner, General Peter Ten Broeck, General Scott, Captain Comfort Luttenton.

He never received but one written discharge which was at the expiration of the six weeks service above mentioned and which is lost—He has no documentary testimony of his services and knows of no surviving witness whose testimony he can procure. He believes one person, Benjamin Caprenter, who knows of part of his services is still alive, but where he resides, this applicant does not know—The following persons to whom he is known in his present neighborhood can testify to his character for veracity and their belief of his services as a soldier of the revolution—Philip N. Bontsteel, Henry Staats, Jacob C. Elmendorf, Nathanial Rowe, Frederick Barringers, Philip Pitcher, John W. Pitcher, Nathan Beckwith. There is no clergyman residing near this applicant. The one whose church he formerly attended and with whom he was well acquainted has left the United States.

He hereby relinquishes every claim whatever to a pension or annuity except the present pension roll of the agency of any State. (Signed with his mark) Isaac Ferguson

Sworn to and subscribed the day & year aforesaid. Robt. L. Livingston.

End Notes—R.3503—Isaac Ferguson

1. John Crane was the Captain of the Fourth Company in Colonel Henry Luddington's Seventh Regiment of Dutchess County Militia.
2. Comfort Luddington was appointed Captain on February 26, 1776 in Colonel Jacobus Swartwout's Second Regiment of Dutchess County Minute Men.
3. The Battle of White Plains was fought on October 28, 1776.
4. Nathaniel Scribner was a Captain in Colonel Luddington's Regiment.
5. Brigadier General John Morin Scott.
6. Petrus Ten Broeck was the Brigadier General of the Dutchess County Militia.
7. There was a Battle at Ward's House on March 16, 1777, but it could have been a different engagement; there were several battles and skirmishes at that time.
8. The Danbury, Connecticut raid was from April 25-27, 1777 with the Battle of Ridgefield taking place on the 27th.
9. General and Commander in Chief, George Washington.
10. John Doty would have served in the Quartermaster General's Department.
11. John Berry was appointed Second Lieutenant on May 28, 1778 in Captain Crane's Company in Colonel Luddington's Regiment.

Pension Application for James Fitzgibbons

R.3587
B.L. No. 1591-100
Schoharie County SS.

George Shafer being duly sworn saith that he was well acquainted with James Fitzgibbons at Fort Montgomery, that said Fitzgibbons was in the battle of that place and was killed as this deponent understood and verily believes to be true, this deponent resides in the town of Blenheim in Schoharie County and that said Fitzgibbons belonged to Stewart's Company and the Dubois Regiment and that said Fitzgibbons was a standing troop in the service of the United States. (Signed with his mark) George Shafer

Sworn the 6th day of Febry 1821 before me Elias Halliday Justice of the Peace.

State of New York, Schoharie County SS.

Mary Teabout being duly sworn deposeth and saith that she was well acquainted with James Fitzgibbons, that she was present at his marriage with Anna Swart, which was in the Spring of the year 1774, in May some time according to the best recollection and belief of this deponent, that they were married by the Reverend Mr. Sommers at the old parsonage house in the Town of Schoharie, that in that summer or fall after his marriage he enlisted into the service of the United States as she understood and verily believes and that she has never seen him since and this deponent further saith that the said James Fitzgibbons had one child by his wife named Eleanor, that the said Anna wife of the said James Fitzgibbons has since died and further this deponent saith [rest was not microfilmed.]

War Department, Revolutionary Claim
State of New York
Schoharie County SS.

I, Eleanor Feeck (late Fitzgibbons) daughter and only heir at law of James Fitzgibbons deceased do upon oath declare, & testify to the best of my knowledge & belief that James Fitzgibbons did enlist January 1777 for the term of during the war, and served in Regiment number Five under the command of Colonel Lewis Dubois of the New York line; and that he continued in the Service until he was killed at Fort Montgomery in the month of October in the year 1777.

I do further declare that I have never received a warrant for the Bounty Land promised to James Fitzgibbons on the part of the United States; nor do I believe he ever received it nor do I believe he ever received it or transferred his claim to it in any manner whatsoever; therefore,

Know all men by these presents that I Eleanor Feeck aforesaid do hereby constitute and appoint John Ogden Deyo of the City of Albany to be my true and lawful Attorney for me and in my name to demand and receive from the Secretary at War of the United States a Warrant for the quantity of land due to me as aforesaid; and my said attorney hereby fully authorized and empowered to constitute and appoint one or more substitutes or attorneys under him for the special purposes above expressed. Dated this 26th day of December 1829. (Signed) Eleanor Feeck

Witness -- H. Manning

Auburn Cayuga Co. NY
May 31st 1853
Hon'd J.E. Heath, Commissioner of Pensions.
Sir,

James Fitzgibbons private enlisted in the United States service Jany 1st 1777 for the term of the war in Capt. Stewarts company in the NY Regiment commanded by Col. Dubois and continued in the service until he was killed in battle at Fort Montgomery at the time of the evacuation of that Fort.

His only child and legal heir Eleanor Feak received from the State of New York 100 acres of Bounty Land, and 100 acres from the United States. She is now nearly 90 years of age, infirm, and very poor. Is there no law or provision by which she is entitled to benefits of pension, and equal quantity of Bounty Land with those who survived & served until the close of the war providedthe facts above stated can be clearly shown. Yours truly H.H. Bostwick

End Notes—R.3587—James Fitzgibbons

1. George enlisted in Captain Thomas Lee's Company, the eighth company, as a private on January 25, 1777 in Colonel Lewis DuBois' Fifth New York Continental Regiment. Captain Lee resigned on May 19, 1778. George was eventually transferred to Captain Philip DeBevier's Company, which was the fourth company, by May of 1779. When the second, fourth, and fifth New York Regiments were consolidated on January 1,1781, George was transferred to Captain Henry DuBois Company in Colonel Philip VanCortlandt's Second New York Continental Regiment. FROM: Revolutionary War Rolls 1775-1783, Series M-246, Roll 72, folder 68 (5th NYCR, and Roll 67, folder 23 (2 NYCR, National Archives, Washington, D.C. George claims to have understood that Fitzgibbons was killed on October 6, 1777 at Fort Montgomery. He did not see him killed or captured.
2. James enlisted as a private on January 1, 1777 for during the war in Captain James Stewart's Company, the third company in Colonel Lewis DuBois' Fifth New York Continental Regiment. FROM: Revolutionary War Rolls 1775-1783, Series, M-246, Roll 72, folder 71, National Archives, Washington, D.C.
3. James is listed as deserting on October 6, 1777, and not killed in the Battle of Fort Montgomery which was fought on that date. He was owed £ 2. . 19. . 0. List of Deserters, Dead, and Prisoners of the Fifth New York Regt of Foot in the Service of the United States of America, Commanded by Coll. Lewis Duboys from 1st June 1777 to the 1st August 1778, with the wages due to each in the Pay Master's Hands. FROM: Revolutionary War Rolls 1775-1783, Series M-246, Roll 71, folder 62, National Archives, Washington D.C.

Pension Application for Peter Flagg, Flack, Flock, etc.

W.12099 (Widow: Lee, Roxy or Roxana, former widow.)
B.L. WT.6025-160-55

Pension Awarded $32.53
Declaration in order to obtain the benefit of the Act of Congress passed June 7th 1832.
State of New York
Herkimer County SS.

On this 10th day of October in the year of our Lord one thousand eight hundred and thirty two. personally appeared in open Court before the Judges of the Court of Comm. Pleas of the County of Herkimer now sitting. Peter Flagg a resident of the town of German Flatts in the County of Herkimer and the State of New York, aged eighty two years on the fifteenth day of November next, Who being first duly sworn according to Law doth on his oath make the following declaration in order to obtain the benefit of the act of Congress passed June 7, 1832. That he entered into the service of the United States under the following named officers.

The first service this Deponent performed was in the year in the beginning of the war at which time he was a private in Capt. Michael Ittig's (1) Company in Col Peter Bellinger's Regiment that Jacob Bishorn (2) was Lieutenant and Frederick Frank was ensign in Genl Nicholas Herkimer's Brigade of Infantry of the Militia of the State of New York.

That the Regiment was ordered down to Caughnawaga a distance of about forty miles for the purpose as deponent was informed to capture Sir John Johnson and the Indians under his Command that the regiment was paraded on the ice and was there three or four days and was absent about eight days when the regiment returned.

And this deponent further says, that in the month of May or June 1776 the deponent enlisted in Capt Demuth's Company (3) of rangers not connected with any regiment as this deponent believes for the term of nine months, Adam Helmer (4) was Lieut. in said company, that he enlisted in the Town of Herkimer in the then County of Tryon, in the State of New York. That the first service they performed the company was marched up to fort Stanwix and brought down a number of boats from Wood Creek to the Fort, that the boats belonged to some Bob Ellice an Indian trader that they got away with several of them that the boats were left by deponents company at Fort Stanwix when they came back to Fort Herkimer that he was employed as a Scout in marching in several places in the neighbourhood until the fall of the year and before. And winter set in they were disbanded. And the deponent further days that he was again in Michael Edick's Company and that in the month of July and as Deponent believes in the next year the regiment was again called out and marched down to Cherry Valley, the whole regiment having assembled at Fort Herkimer that Genl Herkimer (5) had Command of the detachment, that after remaining at Cherry Valley a short time proceeded to the foot of Otsego Lake, the whole country then being a wilderness, and from there they went by an Indian footpath down to the Unadilla river. One Col. Cox (6) was with them, down there to see the Indians, where they lay four or five days until a dispatch was sent for Brandt (7) the Indian Chief who came up within a mile of the

Militia, and were said to be several hundred strong, that an attempt to form a treaty was made but the Indians set up a great shout and were off, and then discharged their fire arms, the Militia then returned again to fort Herkimer being absent about fifteen or sixteen days. That the battle of Oriskany was fought on the fourth of August (8) following but deponent on account of ill health was unable to go out with his company.

That this deponent after the battle of Oriskany in the month of August 1777, continued doing military duty as a militia man in Capt. Michael Ittig's Company of Infantry aforesaid, and continued to do duty as long as he was Captain and when removed down to Schenectady, Frederick Frank became Captain of the Company and John Campbell was ensign (9), that deponent did duty in said Company and turned out whenever there was an alarm, that in the Summer Season deponent was most of his time doing duty in Fort Herkimer, taking his regular turn standing guard until the year 1781.

And this Deponent further says, in the month of May or June 1781, he enlisted at Fort Plain in the then County of Tryon, now County of Montgomery in the State of New York under one Capt. McKee (10) in Col. Marinus Willett's regiment for the term of nine month and was discharged in the month of November or December thereafter.

That during said term the Company to which this Deponent belonged and one or two other Companies in the said regiment and some militia from the neighbourhood were engaged in the fall of the year with the English Tories & Indians at a place called Turlock (11) in the County of Tryon now in the county of Schoharie about ten miles South East of Fort Plain aforesaid then all woods.

That afterwards this Deponent under the command of Col. Willett with about four hundred men of his Regiment and some militia fought the enemy at Johnstown in the present County of Montgomery the British and Indians were about seven hundred in number under the Command of Maj. Ross (12), were defeated by Col. Willett who took one brass field piece which had been lost in the early part of the action by a company of Artillery attached to the regiment commanded by Capt. Moody (13), that the field piece when taken was spiked by having a large nail drove in the touch hole.

There were fourteen English prisoners taken in the engagement, The Company then returned to fort plain, at which place, in the fall of the year, the news was received that Lord Cornwallis (14) had surrendered to the American and French Armies on which occasion Col. Willett procured and had roasted whole a large ox for the regiment and such of the militia as were with them and fired a twelve pounder and their small arms in rejoicing at the Victory and this deponent remained at Ft Plain until late in the season, when he was discharged as aforesaid.

And this Deponent further Says he was born in the town of Ambell as he believes in the State of New Jersey and when young his parents removed to the town of German Flatts, in the County of Herkimer and the State of New York, where he last resided since the Revolutionary War and still continued to reside there and this Deponent was born in the year 1750 on the fifteenth day of November.

That Deponent has a record of his age at home on a piece of paper Copied from the family Bible.

That he resided at German Flatts in the County of Herkimer when he was first called into the service that he has lived there since the War and still resides there.

That Deponent was part of the time a drafted man, volunteered twice and acted also by Command of his Militia officers when Commanded.

That Deponent was acquainted with Col Willett has seen Col Gansevort (15) and said Genl Washington, Gov. Clinton (16) & when they came up the Mohawk River after the end of the war.

That Deponent served with several militia regiments Col Waggoners (17) Regiment or Corp's & Col Clyde's (18) regt both militia regiments.

That Deponent never rec'd a written discharge

That Frederick Bellinger and Frederick Bellinger Jun., John Mahon and several other persons who can testify to deponents character under their belief.

He hereby relinquishes every claim whatever to a pension or annuity except the present and declares that his name is not on the pension roll of the agency of any state. (Signed with his mark) Peter "PF" Flagg. (19)

Sworn to and subscribed the day and year aforesaid in Open Court. F. E. Spinner Dept. Clerk.

State of New York
Herkimer County SS.

On this the 15th Day of March One Thousand Eight hundred & Fifty five personally appeared before me a Justice of the Peace within & for the County & State foresaid, Roxana Lee who resides in Frankfort Herkimer County & State of New York who being by me duly sworn according to law declares that she is now seventy three years old. That she was married in the year 1825 to Peter Flagg a soldier of the Revolution who received for his service a Pension from the Government of the United States. She further declares that he [sic, her] said husband, Peter Flagg died on the 20th day of June AD 1841—She further declares that after the death of her said husband Peter Flagg & on about the 15th day of August 1844 she was married to Elisha Lee who died in the year 1850. She further declares that since the death of the said Elisha Lee she has never married & now continues his widow. She makes this declaration for the purpose of obtaining the Bounty land granted by the act passed March 8, 1855 & she hereby declares that she has not applied for or received & she believes she is not entitled to bounty land except as above stated & she hereby appoints John H. McCutchur esquire of Washington City her attorney to prosecute her said claim for Bounty land & to receive her warrant when issued. She further hereby Empowers & appoints the said John H. McCutchur as her lawful attorney for her & in her behalf to prosecute, her claim for pension & she hereby revokes all other power of Attorney. Given by her to any person whatsoever. (Signed with her mark) Roxana Lee

Sworn to & Subscribed before me on the day & year above written & I hereby certify that I have no interest as the result of this case & am not consumed in its prosecution & that Roxanna Lee is well known to me. William Schooley, Justice of the Peace.

Letter of inquiry dated November 10, 1927 in the pension folder.

I have to advise you that from the papers in the Revolutionary War pension claim W.12099 it appears that Peter Flagg (German, "Flock") was born November 15, 1760? In Ambell, New Jersey and when young moved with his parents (names not given) to German Flatts, Tryon County, (later Herkimer County), New York.

While a resident of German Flatts, New York, he enlisted in 1775 and served at various times until late in the fall of 1781, over two and one half years in all, as a private under Captains Michael Ittig, Frederick Frank, Robert McKean and Marks Demuth, and Colonels Peter Bellinger and Marinus Willett in the New York Troops and was in the battles of Turlock and Johnstown.

He was allowed pension on his application executed October 1, 1832 while living in German Flatts, New York.

Soldier married October 23, 1825 in German Flatts, New York, Roxana, or Roxy, whose maiden name was Mixture. He died June 21, or 22, 1841 in German Flatts, New York. She married August 15, 1844, Elisha Lee who died September 13, 1847 or in 1850 in Frankfort, Herkimer County, New York.

His widow Roxy Lee was allowed pension on account of the services of her former husband Peter Flagg, on her application executed March 30, 1853 at which time she was living in German Flatts, New York aged about seventy-one years. She died November 6 or7, 1860 in Frankfort, new York. She left no children of her own.

Said peter Flagg's son, Jacob Flagg, was living in Frankfort, New York in 1853 aged seventy-two years. The name of his mother is not stated, nor the date of that marriage.

End Notes—W.12099—Peter Flagg

1. Captain Michael Ittig was in Colonel Peter Bellinger's Fourth Regiment of Tryon County Militia.
2. The following were officers in Captain Ittig's Company: Jacob Baschauer or Baselhorn or Basehorn, etc., was the First Lieutenant, Frederick Frank was the Second Lieutenant and Patrick Campbell was the Ensign.
3. Captain Hans Marcus or Marks Demuth's Company of Tryon County Rangers was formed on August 1, 1776 and they were discharged on March 27, 1777. So far a payroll or muster roll has not been found for this company.
4. His full name is John Adam Frederick Helmer.

5. Nicholas Herkimer was the Brigadier General of the Tryon County Militia Brigade.
6. Colonel Ebenezer Cox was the Colonel of the First Regiment of Tryon County Militia. He was killed at the Battle of Oriskany on August 6, 1777.
7. General Herkimer met with Captain Joseph Brant at Unadilla on June 27, 1777. The purpose of the meeting was an attempt to get Brant and if possible the Mohawks to side with the Americans against England or at least for them to remain neutral.
8. The Battle of Oriskany was fought on August 6, 1777.
9. John Campbell was sergeant. The officers in Captain Frederick Frank's Company were as follows: Timothy Frank was the First Lieutenant, Patrick Campbell was the Second Lieutenant and Adam Staring was the Ensign.
10. Robert McKean's role in Lieutenant-Colonel Commandant's Marinus Willett's Regiment of New York State Levies in 1781 is confusing at best. His name does not appear on the April 27 or 28, 1781 officers' list appointed to Willett's Regiment. There is no muster roll for this company but Willett does mention the following in his Letter and Orderly Book:--"*Capt. Marshall's Comp. is to be formed of the troops already assembled at Johnstown under the charge of Capt. McKain".* FROM: Colonel Marinus Willett's Letter and Orderly Book, Fort Rensselaer 1781, Doc. No. 15705, Special Collections and Manuscripts, New York State Library, Albany, New York. Peter's name does not appear on Captain Marshall's Company payroll for 1781. FROM: Revolutionary War Rolls 1775-1783, Series M-246, Roll 78, folder 173, National Archives, Washington, DC.
11. The Battle of New Dorlach which is present day Sharon Springs, Schoharie County was fought on July 10, 1781.
12. The Battle of Johnstown was fought on October 25, 1781. Major John Ross commanded the British forces.
13. Captain Andrew Moody of the Second Regiment of Continental Artillery.
14. Lord Cornwallis surrendered his British Army at Yorktown, Virginia, on October 19, 1781. Colonel Willett received the news of General George Washington's victory at Yorktown about November 1.
15. Peter Gansevoort of the Third New York Continental Regiment.
16. Governor George Clinton, the First Governor of the State of New York.
17. Peter Waggoner was the Lieutenant-Colonel of the Second Regiment of the Tryon County Militia.
18. Samuel Clyde was the Lieutenant-Colonel of the First Regiment of Tryon County Militia.
19. According to Captain Ittig's Muster Roll Peter served in John'sTown Feb ye 7 1776 for 6 days, for Albany Octob'r 10th 1776 for 2 days and on guard at ye house of Fred Fox October 17 1776 for 5 days. He is listed

as 0 for Oriskany. On Captain Ittig's Muster Roll for 1778 Peter is listed as serving 6 days in June and 13 days for July. Total days served for 1778 was 19 days. FROM: Revolutionary War Rolls 1775-1783, Series M-246, Roll 72, folder 78, National Archives, Washington, DC. Peter is listed as a Corporal in Captain Frederick Frank's Company. He served 23 days in 1779 and 32 days in 1780. Colonel Peter Bellinger, Doc No. 00203, Box 14, No. 4, Special Collections and Manuscripts, New York State Library, Albany, New York. Peter's name does appear on Captain Adam Leipe's Muster Roll in Colonel Samuel Campbell's First Regiment of Tryon County Militia. The date of the roll is 6 of July 1780 till the 20 of July 1782 for a total of 8 days and was owed £0. . 14. . 2. According to another roll dated 28th day of Sept'r 1784, Peter Floyg [sic] had been paid the £0. . 14. . 2 that was owed to him and the certificate number was 11489. FROM: Revolutionary War Rolls 1775-1783, Series M-246, Roll 72, folder 89, National Archives, Washington, D.C.

Pension Application for Thomas Folger

S.10697
State of New York
County of Saratoga

On the fourth day of September one thousand eight hundred and thirty two, personally appeared in open court before the Judges of the Court of Common Please in and for said county now sitting, Thomas Folger of the Town of Charlton in said County aged seventy four years and upwards, who being first duly sworn according to law, doth on his oath make the following declaration in order to obtain the benefit of the Act of Congress passed June 7th 1832.

He was born in the Town of Illington in the County of Norfolk, England on the twenty-sixth day of April one thousand seven hundred and fifty six. He has a certificate of his age signed by the Rector of the Parish in which he was born. He came over to America with his parents in the year one thousand seven hundred and seventy-four and settled in Curriesbush in the then County of Albany, now town of Princetown in the County of Schenectady. After the Revolutionary War he removed to said Town of Charlton and has resided there ever since.

He entered the service of the United States under the following named officers, and served as herein stated.

In the spring of the year one thousand seven hundred and seventy five, he volunteered his services in the Army of the Revolution as aforesaid. He procured his name to be enrolled in the militia company in his beat, to wit, the Company of Captain Thomas Wasson (1) in Colonel Abraham Wemple's Regiment. The name of the other company and field officers whom he recollects were as follows, Abraham Swits and Myndert Wemple (2) Majors,

John Thornton (3) Lieutenant, William Moore Ensign, John Swertin (4) Orderly Sergeant.

He performed military service with the detachments of militia from said regiment and were from time to time ordered out, sometimes to cooperate with the regular troops and at other times to defend the inhabitants of different settlements on our frontiers from the depredations of the British, Indians and Tories. In these services he was employed for a longer or shorter period every year from the time he entered into the service as aforesaid until the termination of the war.

How often he was out every year and how long in each expedition, it is impossible for him to remember yet he conscientiously believed that the time he served his country in the Revolutionary War exceeds two years.

He has performed garrison duty at sundry times at the following military posts and forts, at the upper, middle and lower forts of Schoharie on three different occasions, was on several occasions at Schenectady, Fort Hunter, and Fort Paris (Stone Arabia). He was at Fort Edward in the fall of the year, 1776, also when General Burgoyne (5) and his army were in that vicinity in the fall of the year, 1777, was at Fort George when it was destroyed by the American troops & was in General Schuyler's retreat to Bemis's Heights.

The next day after General Gates arrived at Bemis's Heights he was discharged. The term of his tour of duty on that occasion having expired. He then went home, and had remained there only two days when he was again ordered out to the west. He was several times at the German Flatts, performing garrison duty there, also several times at Johnstown and at Boman's [Bowman's] Creek. After the last named place was destroyed by the British and Indians, he went out as a scout in company with Red Jacket, (6) two other Indians and Lieutenant Thornton aforesaid. He was out as a scout also on several other occasions.

There was a noted Tory named Joseph Bettis in the neighborhood of Ballston, who was continually communicating intelligence to the enemy. It therefore became a matter of some importance to have said Bettis, and he associates, apprehended. Small parties of militia men were from time to time ordered out for this purpose, but for a great while with little success. He was at length however, taken prisoner and executed at Albany as a spy. He (the claimant) was several times in pursuit of said Joseph Bettis.

He was at the middle fort of Schoharie in the fall of the year 1780, when Sir John Johnson arrived there with a large party of British and Tories to destroy the settlements in the valley of Schoharie Creek. He saw the celebrated Murphy of Morgan's Rifle Corps, (7) fire upon the British flag as it approached said fort with a demand to surrender.

In the summer of 1781, he was with the troops under Colonel Willett in their engagement with the British and Indians under Major Ross. (8)

He was with the troops that pursued Major Ross in his retreat on this occasion, and in company with the party of Oneida Indians who followed Walter Butler, saw said Walter at West Canada Creek, shot at by an Oneida Indian, (9) who then swam across said creek, (said Walter being on the opposite side) and tomahawked and scalped his fallen foe.

He went from thence with Colonel Willett's Regiment to Mayfield (10) and encamped there. He assisted in taking a British soldier prisoner, who was by order of Colonel Willett given up to the Oneidas, who tomahawked him in revenge for the loss of one of their number, that had been stabbed by one of the enemy, and as their prisoner was found with a bloody knife in his hand, he was suspected to have been the murderer.

The following are some of the regular officers whom he knew: to wit, General Arnold, General Van Rensselaer, Adjutant Jellis A. Fonda, Colonels Gansevoort, VanDyck and Van Schaick. (11)

He never received any written discharge from the service, and believes it was not customary to give written discharges to those who served in the militia.

The following are the names of persons to whom he is knows in his present neighborhood, and who can testify as to his character for veracity, and their belief of his services as a soldier of the revolution, viz: Ahusuerus Wendell, Benjamin Marvin, Kenneth Gordon, Eleazer Dows.

He knows of no witnesses now living who can state in detail their personal knowledge of his services as aforesaid, and can produce no witnesses to prove any part of said services other than those whose affidavits are herewith procured and hereto annexed, viz the affidavits of John J. Schermerhorn, Bartholomew Schermerhorn and John I Vrooman of the County of Schenectady.

Here hereby relinquishes every claim whatever to a pension or annuity except the present and declares that his name is not on the pension roll of the agency of any state. (Signed) Thomas Folger

Sworn and subscribed the day and year aforesaid in open court, Thomas Palmer, Clerk

We, Benjamin Marvin, residing in the Town of Charlton in the County of Saratoga aforesaid, and Kenneth Gordon residing in the said town of Charlton, do hereby certify that we are well acquainted with Thomas Folger, who has subscribed and sworn to the forgoing declaration, that we believe him to be seventy-four years of age, that he is reputed and believed in the neighborhood where he resides, to have been a soldier of the revolution, and that we concur in that opinion. (Signed) Benj. Marvin, Kenneth Gordon

Sworn and subscribed the day and year first aforesaid. Thomas Palmer, Clerk

End Notes—S.10697—Thomas Folger

1. Thomas Wasson was commissioned captain on June 20, 1778 in Colonel Abraham Wemple's Second Regiment of Albany County Militia (Schenectady District).
2. Abraham Swits was the First Major and Myndert M. Wemple was the Second Major in Colonel Wemple's Regiment. Nicholas Veeder was

originally appointed the Second Major and Wemple was commissioned on June 20, 1778 in place of Veeder.

3. On June 20, 1778 the following officers were also commissioned in Captain Wasson's Company: John Little as First Lieutenant, John Thornton as Second Lieutenant and Jacob Solivan (Sullivan) as the Ensign. On February 25, 1780 John Thornton was commissioned First Lieutenant as John Little had moved to Johnstown, Tryon County, William Moore as Second Lieutenant as Thornton was promoted and Alexander Crawford as Ensign and Solivan had died.
4. On examining the muster rolls of Captain Wasson's Company this name or any name close to this was not found. FROM: Revolutionary War Rolls, 1775-1783, Series M-246, Roll 77, Folder 170, National Archives, Washington, D.C.
5. Lieutenant General John Burgoyne with a British Army and Allies were invading New York from Canada. They were using the North River (Hudson River) as their mode of travel heading to Albany. The American Army under Major General Philip Schuyler and later (August) Major General Horatio Gates replaced Schuyler retreated before Burgoyne's Army until Stillwater. Here after two large battles and on trying to escape back to Canada with his army, Burgoyne surrendered his army on October 7, 1777.
6. This Red Jacket is unknown. The most noted Red Jacket was a Seneca and served with the British against the Americans.
7. On October 17, 1780 Sir John Johnson with about 700 British, Loyalists, and Indians, attacked the settlements in the Schoharie Valley. Timothy Murphy in 1780 actually was a private in Captain Isaac Bogart in Lieutenant-Colonel Commandant John Harper's Regiment of New York State Levies. In 1779 when Murphy's enlistment was up in Colonel Daniel Morgan's Corps of Riflemen (The Seventh Virginia Regiment) he remained at Schoharie. Murphy did fire on the flag of truce.
8. The Battle of Johnstown was fought on October 25, 1781. The American forces were commanded by Lieutenant-Colonel Commandant Marinus Willett and the British forces were commanded by Major John Ross. On October 30th, the advance guard of Willett's troops on reaching the West Canada Creek were opposed by enemy troops under Captain Walter Butler and after a brief skirmish, Butler and several of his man were killed or wounded.
9. The Oneida Indian usually credited with shooting Butler and scalping was Anthony.
10. This appears to be a faulty memory on this incident. After Willett left the West Canada Creek on the 30th he returned to Fort Rensselaer in the present day Village of Fort Plain. Thomas has the incident mixed up with where it happened, year, and the officer in charge.

Unfortunately at this time it is unknown when this incident may have taken place or where.

11. Major General Benedict Arnold, Brigadier General Robert VanRensselaer, Adjutant Jellis A. Fonda served in several regiments including Willett's in 1781, Colonel Peter Gansevoort of the Third New York Continental Regiment, Lieutenant-Colonel Cornelius VanDyck and Colonel Goose VanSchaick both of the First New York Continental Regiment.

Pension Application for Jacob Fonda

S.10687
State of New York
Montgomery County SS.

On this nineteenth day of September 1832 personally appeared in open court before the judges of the Court of Common Pleas of said county now sitting Jacob Fonda a resident of Mayfield in the County of Montgomery and State of New York aged seventy one years & up, who being first duly sworn according to law doth on his oath make the following declaration in order to obtain the benefit of the act of Congress passed June 7th 1832.

That he entered the service of the United States under the following named officers and served as herein stated. That he enlisted in the town of Hoosick in the State of New York during the revolutionary war. That on the twelfth day of August in the year 1778 he turned out or volunteered to go in the service of the United States for two months. That he went to fort Edward was discharged at the end of two months which was in October on the 12th day as he thinks. Thomas Brown (1), was Captain. Jacob Van Ness, J, Eldred Fonda, were first and second Lieutenants, J. Gamaliel Waldo was ensign, Col Peter Yates, Lieut Col. John Van Rensselaer & Major John W. Grosbeck commanded regiment in which he was in. In the year 1779 in the fore part of summer in June he thinks volunteered and or turned out so long as he should be wanted out & would be necessary to repel the incursions of the British & Indians. That he continued in service till October was at Fort Edward. In the year 1780 volunteered in the month of June marched to Lake George was at Fort Edward, was in service this year till the month of October. In the year 1781 in the month of July turned out and volunteered & went to Fort George, Fort Edward & Granville and turned out and served there some time in the fall as near as can be recollected in the month of November. In the year 1782 was out about two months in the summer of said year went to fort Edward and served two months. That he resided within a day march of the places and forts where he served & marched and remained. That the British and Indians was in the almost constant habit of plundering the country and killing the inhabitants from the spring of the year till fall or as long as the lakes and waters at the north were free from ice so that they could come down Lake Champlain from Canada—That in the year 1779 when he was in said service he was stationed at Fort Edward. That during all his services he was under the same company and regimental officers mentioned at the time. He was first in June in the year 1778—That he has no documentary evidence of his service. That he was born in Watervliet in the County of Albany & State of New York in the year 1761 on the 14th day of March. That he has no record of his age—But John Dillenbake has a family bible in which his age is recorded. Lived in the said town of Hoosick when called into service. Has lived there since the revolutionary war till the year 1794 since which time he has lived in the said town of Mayfield in Montgomery County & said State of New York & where he now lives. That he was told by his officers that he was turned out and that he did volunteer when it was necessary to defend the country as aforesaid - supposed that he must go and stay as long as he was ordered—and upon that he volunteered as aforesaid--General Schuyler (2) recollects though he was not with the troops with which he served recollects Lewis Van Woert (3) a colonel who commanded a regiment with which he was a part of time does not recollect any others more than recollected except Col. Webster (4) who was at Lake George, Col. Warner (5) he thinks commanded at Fort George when he was there. Never received any discharge from service. That he is known in this present neighborhood to the Reverend Jeremiah Wood and John Dillenbake who can testify to his character for veracity and their belief of his services as a soldier of the revolution. That he hereby relinquishes every claim whatever for a pension or annuity except the present an declares that his name is not on the pension roll of the agency of any state. (Signed) Jacob Fonda

Sworn to & Subscribed in open court, 19th September 1832. Geo. D. Ferguson, Clerk.

Letter in the Pension Folder, dated March 12, 1936, written in response to an inquiry.

Reference is made to your letter in which you request the records of Jacob and John Dowe Fonda, of New York, soldiers of the Revolutionary War.

Because of the great demand for Revolutionary War data and the limited trained clerical force available for furnishing such information, it is not possible to comply in full with each request for Revolutionary War data. The record of Jacob Fonda is furnished herein as found in pension claim, S.10687, based upon the military service in the Revolutionary War of that soldier.

Jacob Fonda was born March 13, 1761, in Watervliet, Albany County, New York. The names of his parents are not shown.

While residing in Hoosick, New York, Jacob Fonda enlisted and served at the forts and on scouting parties on short tours as a private in Captain Thomas Brown's Company, Colonel Peter Yates' New York Regiment, also, under Colonels Lewis Van Woert, Webster and Warner in the New York Troops, as follows: from August 12, 1778 to October 12, 1778; from June, 1779 to October, 1779: from June, 1780 to October, 1780; from July, 1781 to November 1781; and from June, 1782, two months.

In 1794, he moved to Mayfield, in Montgomery County, New York, where he was residing when he was allowed pension on his application executed September 19, 1832.

It is not stated that soldier ever married.

In 1832, one Abraham Fonda made affidavit in Montgomery County, New York, and in 1833, one Eldred Fonda made affidavit in same county: no relationship of either to the soldier was shown.

End Notes—S.10687—Jacob Fonda

1. On June 22, 1778, the following were commissioned as officers in the Fourteenth Regiment of Albany County Militia: Peter Yates, Colonel; John VanRensselaer, Lieutenant-Colonel; John W.Groesbeck, First Major; Thomas Brown, Captain; Jacob Van Ness, First Lieutenant; Eldert or Eldred Fonda, Second Lieutenant, and Gamaliel Waldo as Ensign.
2. Major General Philip Schuyler of the Continental Army.
3. Lewis VanWoert was the Colonel of the Sixteenth Regiment of Albany County Militia.

Alexander Webster was commissioned Lieutenant-Colonel on April 4, 1778,

Pension Application for Peter Fox (or Peter W.)

W.7294 (Maria) Pension granted $42.32 per annum commencing the 4th day of March 1848

B.L.Wt.9468-160-55 (Bounty Land)

State of New York

Montgomery County

On this fifteenth day of February one thousand eight hundred and fifty one personally came before me a justice of the peace within and for the county and State aforesaid. David L. Shull who being duly sworn according to law deposes and says that he resides at Stone Arabia in said county and he is a member of the Dutch Reformed Church of Stone Arabia that he had the records of said church in his possession and upon examination of said records he finds that Peter Fox was married to Maria Richter on the 17th of January A.D. 1796 by the rev. D. C. Pick, who was for several years the regular pastor of said church and was authorized by law to solemnize marriages. The record of the marriage is in the words and figures following viz:

Married on the 17th Jan 1796 Peter Fox

Married to Maria Richter by D.C. Pick

And that the above is a true copy of said record.

D.L. Shull

Subscribed and sworn to before on this 15th day of February 1851. And I certify that deponent is entitled to full credit

James W. Hamilton, Justice of the Peace

State of New York

Montgomery County

On this 19th day of Sept in the year 1832 Personally appeared in open court before the now sitting, Peter Fox a resident of the town of Palatine County of Montgomery aged seventy three years, 3d Sept this Inst. Month past has been first duly sworn according to law doth on his oath make the following declarations in order to obtain the benefit of the act passed June 7th 1832 that he entered the service of the United States under the following officers and served as herein stated vitz:--

That this claimant declares that he belonged to the Regt of Militia commanded by Col. Jacob Klock and Peter Waggoner Lieut Col in the company commanded by Christopher W. Fox (1) that he was born in the month of Sept in the year one thousand seven hundred fifty nine as appears by family record that he this applicant was inrolled [enrolled] and kept himself in readiness armed and acquipt [equipped] in compliance with the requisitions of his superior officers and the laws of this country from the year 1776 to the conclusion of the war, that he been satisfied that he was called out on duty and that he hath performed services but the particulars doth not recollect.

That the applicant declares that he hat performed some duties which he knows, it to be impractible to describe, and those he is satisfied and yet doth recollect he cannot describe neither date nor years with some exceptions only.

That this applicant declares that early in the war he was ordered to march under Capt Fox with his Company to George Saltsman in Palatine. They remained for about eight days, Scouting and guarding against the incursions of the common enemy and at another time for about two weeks at George Gettmans, the same alike the preceding, also stationed at Fort Snell and like service under Capt Fox and his company, also at Fort Blank the three weeks in about same. Also at Frederick Empies - the like time, does not recollect under Capt Fox—also under command of Capt Henry Miller (2) for about two weeks, stationed at a place now called St. Johns Ville now Town of Oppenheim according to his belief about two weeks the like services latter part Febry & in fore part in March 1779.

That he went & marched to now county of Herkimer then Tryon to Fort Dayton there remained for about three weeks and performed the like duties and services to the best of his knowledge in the year l779. That this applicant further declares that he was ordered out to march to German Flatts, now County of Herkimer in Mass with his Capt under Col. Klock. There stationed for a number of days. From thence marching to Andrustown southwest from German Flatts to the lakes but did meet no enemy at that time having been out for about two weeks.

Also ordered out to March to Young's Lake where the enemy generally would have recourse to harbour at the house of Adam Young but not discovering nor Mett [met] any Tories or Indians from Canada. There he believes in the year 1778.

That the applicant further declares that in the latter part of July men ordered out under Captain Christopher W. Fox to march to Fort Stanwix and on this march from Herkimer under the command of General Nicholas Herkimer, which on our way at about four miles this side of the Fort those engaged in that memorable Battle at Oriskany (3) when claimant sustained his ground until that part of Genl St. Leger's (4) army retreated and left them.

That previous to Oriskany Battle same Summer Under the command of Genl Herkimer after he hath been drafted out of Capt Fox's company, marching down the Susquehanna River to Unadilla those with Capt Brandt who had a large number of warriors at his command with him and after several days, Genl Herkimer & Capt Brandt (5) held a conference at Genl Herkimer's encampment, escaped. In coming to an engagement that having, he had been out for at least three weeks. That is to say the latter tour [?] In June and July 1777 and the former when the battle was fought at Oriskany happened the 6th of August 1777 same year.

That this applicant further declares that in October 19th in the year 1780 after the battle generally called Col. Brown's battle in the Town of Palatine after Sir John Johnson with his Incendiaries which caused a general conflagration of all or nearly the whole old settlement of Stone Arabia and up along the Mohawk River, applicant declares that he went in pursuit of the enemy and there in battle at Klocks and Failings Flats.(6) Then continued in battle until the enemy took flight retreating.

This claimant further states that he volunteered in what is called Landmans Battle against a Large Party of Indians and Tories from Canada the Indian chief killed & several wounded which occurrence happened July 29th 1781.(7)

That this applicant further declared that in October 25th 1781 same year again in battle then under the Emmediate [immediate] command of Col. Marinus Willett against Major Ross and Capt Butler (8) and supposed about 500 of their incendiery crew from the enemy retreating which Battle terminated when with the loss of many killed on both sides and many taken Prisoner on both sides.

This applicant further declares that himself and eight others engaged for three months service by Col. Jacob Klock and Major Christopher W. Fox in the year 1780 for running scout on snow shoes during the winter enlisted to guard against the incursions of the enemy that this applicant states that he hath served faithfully under Capt Christian Gettman (9) for and during the term of three months, which company was divided into three classes. When out, in rotation continually, also in July 1781 when murder and depredation [?] committed at and round about fort Timmerman under the command of Col. Willett in pursuit of the enemy for about thirty miles. (10)

That this applicant further declares that he was ordered out Emmediately after the cruel merciless butchering and inhuman murder at Cherry Valley (11) to march there all in mass. He believes under the command of Col. Klock but he feels satisfied that Col. Klock's Regt was ordered out previous not knowing at which place the enemy would approach situate & stationed at now Town of Canajohary for several days from there marched to Cherry Valley.

That this claimant further and last declares that often and very frequently hath been under the necessity to watch and to guard against the invasions of the daily expected Enemy at their Principal Fort vizt: Fort Paris with the Militia soldiers were so trained and instructed when Ascertaining and hearing the report of the alarming cannon generally each one not waiting for his corporal to be warned but would without any hesitation or equivocation shoulder his arms in hastening to the fort and prepared to march out on any occurrence or emergency which formed or thought expedient by their Superior officers.

That this claimant declares that after lapses of time for exceeding halfe a centrey [half a century] has rendered it impracticable to describe or remember all the duties and services performed during the Revolution but sufficient for his honor the secretary of the war department to be satisfied that he this claimant was always in compliance in the orders of his superior officers and also conformable to the resolution passed May 27 1775 hereupon it is resolved that the Militia of New York armed and trained man in constant readiness to act at a moments warning.

And that in conformity to the preceding resolution passed by the old congress as early then the year and date above mentioned. That this applicant not only in obedience to the orders and directions of his superiors, officers and the court of his country, but also, did consider it a duty incumbent on him to have kept himself always well-armed and acquipt [equipped] and in constant readiness so when called upon always willing on a minute's warning to march out on each and every emergency in defending the rights and liberties of his country.

And further this applicant saith not--

That he hereby relinquishes every claim whatever to a pension or annuity except the present and declares that his name is not on the pension roll of the agency of any state. (Signed) Peter Fox. (12)

Sworn to and subscribed the day and year aforesaid. Geo. D. Ferguson, Clerk

End Notes—W.7294—Peter Fox

1. Peter enlisted in Captain Christopher W. Fox's Company, the Third Company, in Colonel Jacob Klock's Second Regiment of Tryon County Militia. Peter Waggoner or Wagner, etc., served as the lieutenant-colonel from August 26, 1775 till the end of the war in Colonel Klock's Regiment. FROM: Revolutionary War Rolls 1775-1783, Series M-246, Roll 75, Folder 121, National Archives, Washington, D.C.
2. On September 29, 1780, Captain Fox was commissioned as major in Colonel Klock's Regiment and First Lieutenant Henry Miller was commissioned captain in his place.
3. The Battle of Oriskany was fought on August 6, 1777. Brigadier General Nicholas Herkimer commanded the Tryon County Militia in the battle.

4. Brigadier General Barry St. Leger commanded the British forces that besieged Fort Schuyler. Lieutenant-Colonel Sir John Johnson commanded the British forces that attacked General Herkimer's forces at Oriskany.
5. General Herkimer met with Captain Joseph Brant at Unadilla on June 27, 1777. He could not persuade Brant to side with the Americans or to remain neutral. Captain Brant was at Oriskany with Sir John.
6. The Battle of Stone Arabia was fought in the morning and the Battle of Klocksfield was fought in the afternoon of October 19, 1780. Colonel John Brown commanded the Americans at Stone Arabia and Brigadier General Robert VanRensselaer commanded the Americans at Klocksfield. Colonel Brown was killed at Stone Arabia and General VanRensselaer was ridiculed for not being aggressive at Klocksfield which allowed Johnson and his troops to escape. It is a common misconception of the 19th century writers that VanRensselaer was Court Martialed, he was brought before a Court of Inquiry to see if he should be Court Martialed.
7. The Battle of Lampman was fought on July 29, 1781 near Mother's Creek.
8. Major John Ross of the King's Royal Regiment of New York and Captain Walter Butler of Butler's Rangers.
9. Christian Getman served as a Captain of the Second Company of the Tryon County Rangers from August 1, 1776 to March 27, 1777. Peter's name does not appear on the muster roll or payroll. This is the only time Getman served as a captain. FROM: Revolutionary War Rolls 1775-1783, Series M-246, Roll 74, folder 103, National Archives, Washington, D.C.
10. The raid on Fort Zimmerman or Timmerman took place in August of 1781. The exact day is unknown but it ranges from August 5 to the 22.
11. The Cherry Valley Massacre took place on November 11, 1778. Colonel Klock was criticized for not arriving at Cherry Valley a day or two before Captains Walter Butler and Joseph Brant attacked Cherry Valley. If he had arrived on the ninth or tenth as expected to reinforce the garrison at Fort Alden, many believe that the massacre would not have happened.
12. Maria Richter Fox widow of Peter applied for the widow's pension on April 8, 1851 at the age of 81 in the Town of Palatine, Montgomery County, New York. She stated Peter died May 10, 1847 in Palatine. Peter and Maria Richter were married January 17, 1796 according to the Marriage Book of The Stone Arabia Dutch Reformed Church, Page 203.

Pension Application for Valentine Freligh (Fraligh)

W.16995
State of New York
County of Fulton

On this fifth day of April, One thousand eight hundred and forty-one, personally appeared before the Judges of the Court of Common Pleas in and for said County now sitting, John Freligh, a resident of the town of Glen NY who being first duly sworn according to law, doth on his oath, make the following declaration, in his own behalf and in behalf of his sister Margaret Van Etten children of Maria Freligh, widow of Valentine Freligh (or Felter Fraligh) in order to obtain the benefit of the provision made by the act of Congress passed July 4th 1836. That the mother of this Declarant the aforesaid Maria Freligh was the lawful widow of said Valentine Freligh who served in the war of the revolution as herein after and with annexed affidavits is set forth.

This declarant well recollects, that when he, this declarant, was about ten years of age, his father the said Valentine in company with several active soldiers, of whom he recollects, Richard Coppernol, George Herkimer and Nicholas Coppernol (1) engaged in a scouting party to Saratoga and were away from home in this expedition, a number of days. This declarant being too young at the time to understand and more recollect, if it had been at the time explained. To him the particulars of the different tours of military duty performed by said Valentine Freligh (2) in said war, yet he well recollects having been informed many years ago and long before the decease of his father, by his said father as well as others who knew the fact that his said father served with the militia of the Tryon County in the expeditions against the British when the Battle of Oriskana (3) took place, that he was in said battle and also the battle of Oswegatchie (4), Oriskany and Johnstown (5) that he said Valentine Freligh was enrolled in the Regiment of Colonel Jacob Clock and served under the different officers of said regiment from time to time, serving every year of said war that he was almost constantly engaged in performing garrison duty at the Stone Arabia fort in the neighborhood of which he resided. This declarant has also heard his own father often declare that he served during these years at least in the company of Rangers commanded by Captain Getman or Kitman. (6)

He also remembers the names of Dillenback (7) or Dygert (8) and as officers under whom he served, and this declarant further saith that he is now seventy years and about six months old. That his sister the said Margaret Van Etten widow of the late Peter Van Etten, deceased is seventy three years of age and that he the declarant and said Margaret Van Etten are the only surviving children of said Valentine Freligh and Maria Freligh. That his mother's maiden name was Maria Hanlenbech and that they the said Valentine and Maria had other children born previous to the birth of his said sister Margaret Van Etten vizt, one son not married having died at his birth who was born about two years and a few months before Margaret Van Etten his sister.

That said Valentine Freligh and said Maria Freligh, the father and mother of this declarant were lawfully married at Lunenburgh NY by the Lutheran clergyman of that place on about the _______ day of _________ on thousand seven hundred and sixty four, that the said Valentine Freligh departed this life on the tenth day of March one thousand eight hundred and ten and that said Maria Freligh remained a widow ever since that day until the day of her death as will appear from the proof hereto annexed and said widow Maria Freligh died on the twelfth day of December one thousand eight hundred and thirty six. (Signed with his mark) John Fraleigh

Subscribed and Sworn to in open Court, before the Judges aforesaid, the day & year first above written. Witness the seal of said court and the signature of the Clerk Thereof. T. A. Stoutenburgh, Clerk

State of New York
Montgomery County.

Personally appeared before the undersigned a Justice of the Peace in and for said county on the 8th day of August 1839, John L. Nellis of the Town of Palatine in said county, who being duly sworn saith that during the war of the revolution he was well acquainted with Valentine Freligh, that same person referred to in the accompanying papers, in behalf of whose widow not long since deceased, application is now being made for a pension.

That this deponent will recollects that said Valentine and Maria were a married couple during the war of the revolution and deponent understood at the time and believe the same to be true that they had been married several years before the commencement of said war of the revolution.

That said Valentine and Maria lived together as husband and wife and were universally esteemed and respected to be such until the death of said Valentine which occurred about thirty years ago that said Maria remained or continued to be the widow of said Valentine Freligh until the day of her death.

That said Maria Freligh departed this life between two and three years ago.

And said deponent John L. Nellis further deposeth and saith that he served during said war in the company of Militia commanded by Captain Henry Miller from the year 1778 until the close of said war which company was attached to the Regiment of Colonel Jacob Clock in the then County of Tryon in said state.

That said Valentine also belonged to and served in said Regiment of Colonel Jacob Clock, but by reason of said Valentine Freligh serving in a different company in said regiment, this deponent is unable to say in how many expeditions or in what tours of duty said Valentine Freligh served during said service but this deponent often saw him under arms at Stone Arabia, Fort Plain, and at other posts and forts in said war.

This deponent also recollects hearing at the time thereof that said Valentine Freligh served in a company of Rangers raised in said county commanded by one Captain Kitman or Getman. (Signed) John L. Nellis

Sworn before me.........

Letter included in the Pension Application, written in repose to an inquiry.
February 26, 1927

I have to advise you that from the papers in the Revolutionary War pension claim, W.16995, it appears that Valentine Freligh, Felter, Freligh or Velten Frelighen, while a resident of Tryon (which was later Montgomery) County, New York, served at various times from 1776 until sometime in 1782 as a private in the New York troops under Captains Christian Getman, John Hess, Severinus Klock, Peter Suts and Colonel Jacob Klock; he was in the battles of Oriskany, Oswegatchie and Johnstown.

He Married March 27, 1764, in Lunenburgh at Athens, Greene County, New York, Maria Hallenbeck.

He died March 10, 1810.

His widow, Maria, died December 12, 1836, in Glen, Montgomery County, New York.

On an application executed April 5, 1841, by John Freligh, the pension that was due the soldier and his widow, Maria, was allowed the two surviving children, said John Freligh (9) of Glen, New York, and Margaret Van Etten, widow of Peter Van Etten and at that time they were aged seventy years and about six months and seventy-three years respectively. There were other children but their names were not stated.

This is the only soldier by the name of Valentine Freligh, searched under all spellings of the name, that is found in the Revolutionary War records of this bureau. Respectfully, Winfield Scott, Commissioner

End Notes—W.16995—Valentine Freligh

1. All three men had served in Colonel Jacob Klock's Second Regiment of Tryon County Militia.
2. Valentine's name is on the rolls of Captains John Hess, Severinus Klock, and Peter Suts Companies in Colonel Klock's Regiment. A certificate for pay in Captain Sut's Company No. 17001 dated December 31, 1782 gives his pay as £ 2..13..4. It was extracted from Book No. IV. Also "from the same book that the said Valentine Frelick served his term above named under Captain Peter Suts & on the 31st Decr 1782, Marinus Willett was Col. Comd't." This book was in the New York State Comptroller's office in Albany, N.Y. on January 31, 1840. This bit of information was included in the pension application. The book along with many of the records in the comptroller's office were destroyed in the capitol fire of 1911. (Albany is the capitol of New York State).
3. The Battle of Oriskany was fought on August 6, 1777.
4. The Battle of Stone Arabia was fought on October 19, 1780. This battle has several nicknames. It was the battle as some pensioners claim was at or near the road to Oswegatchie.
5. The Battle of Johnstown was fought on October 25, 1781.

6. Valentine enlisted as a private on August 9, 1776 in Captain Christian Getman's Company (Second Company) of Tryon County Rangers. He was discharged on March 27, 1777. On the payroll , (no date given), he was paid £ 9..6..0. The muster roll and payroll was submitted by John Bacchus and were in his pension application. FROM: Revolutionary War Rolls 1775-1783, Series M-246, Roll 74, folder 103, National Archives, Washington, D.C.
7. Captain Andrew Dillenbach of the Fourth Company and Colonel Klock's Regiment. Dillenbach was killed at the Battle of Oriskany
8. He is probably referring to Captain John Dygert. He served in Klock's Regiment. He was also killed at Oriskany.

Additional Information

Margreth or Margaret was baptized February 21, 1768. FROM: Book of Baptism, page 83, Dutch Reformed Church of Stone Arabia.
Johannes (John) born October 6, 1770. FROM: Book of Baptisms, page 33, Lutheran Church of Stone Arabia.
Jacob born September 30, 1778, baptized October 9, 1778. FROM: Book of Baptisms, page 54 same Lutheran Church.
George born December 4, 1781. FROM: Book of Baptisms, page 51, Dutch Reformed Church of the German Flatts.

Pension Application for Abraham Gardinier

S.29.171
State of New York
Montgomery County SS.

On this 19th day of September in the year of our Lord one thousand eight hundred and thirty two, personally appeared in open court before the court of Common Pleas of the County of Montgomery, now sitting, Abraham Gardinier of the Town of Root, County of Montgomery and State of New York aged 76 years who being first duly sworn according to law doth on his oath make the following declaration in order to obtain the benefit of the Act of Congress passed June 7, 1832. That he entered the service of the United States under the following named officers and served as herein stated: Your applicant says that he drafted or enlisted in the State troops of New York, in the year 1777 on the first day of March and entered upon duty on that day and went from Johnstown Tryon County, then called, now Montgomery to the City of Albany and from thence to Fort Miller, from thence to Fort Edward, and was at Saratoga at the time of the Surrender of Burgoyne, that he was under Captain John Clute (1) the other officers names belonging to the company he does not recollect, that this company belonged to Colonel Christopher Yates,(2) Regiment & Major Christopher P. Yates (3) was the major as he believes, the then Regimental officers names he does not recollect, That he was annexed to the Brigade of Gen. Schuyler,(4) and was under his command during this term: That he enlisted for nine months and served the full term of nine months and was verbally discharged on the first of January 1778 at which time his nine months expired: Your applicant says that he again in March following in the year 1778, he enlisted in the same company and in the State Troops, for nine months and went from the same place aforesaid to Albany and from thence to West Point, under Captain Simon DeGraff,(5) Lieutenant Nicholas Schmerhorn, the other officers of the company he does not recollect, belonging to the same regiment and Brigade above mentioned and served the full term of nine months and was discharged on the first of January when his time was out, and has no written discharge. Your applicant says that he was out frequently on scouts, and alarms during the Revolution in the militia (6) at different places and was out in this manner at least five or six months: And he says that he was born in the Town of Johnstown, Tryon County, State of New York in the year 1756 on the 8th of March And has no other record of his age, except his father's Family Bible. That he resided at Johnstown, when called into the Service and went as a draft. That he was acquainted with the following regular officers, with whom he served, to wit Gen. Schuyler, his aid[e] a man by the name of Lansing,(7) Colonel Lewis: (8) He has resided in the County of Montgomery since the revolution.

Your applicant says that he is acquainted with the following persons residing in his neighborhood, who can testify as to his character for truth and veracity and their belief of his services as a soldier of the revolution to wit, Rev. Abraham Van Horne and Robert Lenardson.

Her hereby relinquishes every claim whatever to a pension or annuity except the present and declares that his name is not on the pension roll of the agency of any state. (Signed) Abraham Gardinier

Sworn and subscribed the day and year aforesaid in open court. Geo. D. Ferguson, Clerk.

Michigan Territory
County of Monroe

On this 6th day of October A.D. 1835 before me the subscriber a Justice of the Peace for the said County of Monroe personally appeared Abraham Gardinier who on his oath declares that he is the same person who formerly belonged to the company commanded by Captain Simon DeGraff in the regiment commanded by Colonel Christopher Yates in the service of the United States that his name was placed on the pension roll of the State of New York from whence he has lately removed. That he now resides in the Territory of Michigan where he intends to remain and wishes his pension to be there payable in the future. The following are his reasons to the Territory of Michigan that his children resided in said Territory of Michigan and that there is great inconvenience in Drawing his money from the State of New York. (Signed) Abraham Gardinier

Subscribed and Sworn before me the Day & year first above written. Norman D. Curtis, Justice of the Peace.

End Notes—S.29171—Abraham Gardinier

1. Captain John Clute's Company of Bateaumen were not considered State Troops but were considered civilians working for the military and

this type of service usually was not allowed as military service for a pension application.

2. This Christopher Yates was from Schenectady.
3. Christopher P. Yates was from the Palatine District in Tryon County. At this time he was a Captain in the First New York Continental Regiment under Colonel Goose VanSchaick. Companies from this regiment were stationed at various forts from Fort George on Lake George to Schenectady until about July of 1777.
4. Major General Philip Schuyler.
5. Captain Simon DeGraff's Company of Bateaumen. On the muster roll Abraham is listed as enlisting on April 9, 1778. FROM: Revolutionary War Rolls 1775-1783, Series M-246, Roll 122 (Quartermaster General's Dept.), Folder 78, National Archives, Washington, D.C.
6. Abraham served as a private in Captain Robert A. Yates' Company, which was the Third Company, in Colonel Frederick Visscher's Third Regiment of Tryon County Militia.
7. Possibly Jacob Jno. Lansing. He served in many capacities during the war including a Deputy Muster Master in 1777, Commissioner of Musters, State of New York in September 1781 and as Judge Advocate for Brigadier General Peter Gansevoort's First Brigade of Albany County Militia.
8. Colonel Morgan Lewis was appointed Deputy Quartermaster General in the Northern Department on September 12, 1776.

Pension Application for John Gardineer
(Gardner, Gartnere, Gardinier, etc.)

R.3900
State of New York
Montgomery County SS.

I do certify that on the 16th day of November 1839, personally appeared before me, David F. Sacia one of the Judges of the County Courts of said County, & being a Court of Record, John Gardineer of the Town of Root in the County & State aforesaid and makes the following declaration to entitle him to a pension under the act of the 7th June 1832.

That he was seventy eight years of age in October 1839. That this applicant was called into the service of the United States in the Revolutionary War early in the month of April of the year 1777, as a private soldier to a place called Caughnawaga in the then County of Tryon now Montgomery and was then and there enrolled in a Company of Militia commanded by Capt. Abraham Veeder, (1) Lieut Col. Volkert Veeder, Col. Frederick Fisher. That this applicant and his said company under the aforesaid officers remained at Caughnawaga aforesaid, guarding Fort at that place, protecting the Inhabitants and their property going out on scouting parties & in being disciplined in Military tactics from the early part of April of said year 1777 until in the beginning of the month of June of that year when this applicant & his said company under the command of said Capt. Veeder & Col. Fisher were ordered out to a place called Johnstown in the then County of Tryon now (Fulton) where this applicant as a private & his said company commanded as aforesaid & other companies of soldiers numbering in all about three hundred men performed duty and service in encountering conquering & driving off about the like number of Indians & Tories collected in and about a building called Sir William Johnson's Hall (2) from whence the Indians and Tories were there and about that time spring forth into the county destroying life & property. That this applicant & his said company commenced as aforesaid remained at Johnstown aforesaid sometime after said Battle (3) performing duty in guarding the inhabitants & their property & in going out on Scouting Parties, pursuing & destroying the Indians & Tories and then returned again to Caughnawaga aforesaid distance about four miles from Johnstown aforesaid.

That this applicant & his said company were gone on this last tour one month & were subsisted & paid by the Government that this applicant & his said company commanded by said Capt. Veeder Lieut Col Veeder & Col. Fisher after their return as aforesaid from Johnstown aforesaid remained at Caughnawaga guarding said Fort at Caughnawaga in protecting the Inhabitants & their property [? [?] for six days and then were called out to go and did go to a place called Sacondaga in the then County of Tryon now (Saratoga) distant from Caughnawaga aforesaid about 30 miles. That at this last mentioned place called Sacondaga this applicant as a private & his said company commanded by said Capt Veeder & Col. Fisher performed duty & service in going out on scouting parties in guarding Fort at that place & in protecting the Inhabitants & their property & in being disciplined as aforesaid, that there was at this time at Sacondaga about 200 men including this applicants said company which numbered about 60 men, all provisioned & paid by the government.

That sometime in October of said year 1777 this applicant & his said company commanded as aforesaid left Sacondaga aforesaid having been absent on said tour to that place over two months & returned to Caughnawaga aforesaid when this applicant & his said company commanded by said Capt Veeder, Col Fisher & Lieut Col. Veeder remained doing duty & service in guarding Fort at that place in protecting the inhabitants & their property & in going out on scouting parties until in November of said year 1777 a period of 15 or 20 days or more & then this applicant & his said company were discharged & went to their respective homes (this applicant then residing near Caughnawaga).

That in the spring of the year 1778 and in the month of April or May of that year according to this applicants best recollection at this time. This applicant & his said company under the command of said Capt. Abm Veeder Lieut. Col. Veeder & Col. Fisher were called out to the said Fort at Caughnawaga aforesaid where they remained performing duty and service in standing sentry at said Fort at Caughnawaga a night & day in protecting the Inhabitants & their property, in going out on scouting parties & in being disciplined until the month of July of said year 1778 according to this deponent's best recollection at this time. That during this last period of service this applicant was a private in his said company and was paid & subsisted by the government. That in the said month of July & towards the middle of that month. This applicant as a private & his said company under the command of the said Capt. Abm. Veeder & Col. Fisher were called out to a place called Sandflats in the then County of Tryon, now Montgomery.

That when arrived at Sandflats this applicant's said company was divided and one division to which this applicant was attached as a private commanded by the said Capt. Veeder & Col. Fisher proceeded to a place called Fort Stanwix (4) in the then County of Tryon now Oneida. That the applicant performed service during this last tour in going to Fort Stanwix in carrying & conveying baggage & provisions for his said company with his own team and that when this applicant & his said company arrived at Fort Stanwix on this last tour they performed duty & service at said Fort Stanwix, in guarding & standing sentry thereat in protecting the Inhabitants & their property & in going out on scouting parties and then this applicant & his said company returned to Caughnawaga aforesaid distant about 60 miles from said Fort Stanwix.

That on this last tour there was stationed at Fort Stanwix about 250 soldiers including this applicants said company which numbered about 40 men provisions & paid by the government. That on returning as aforesaid from Fort Stanwix to Caughnawaga which took place in the beginning of the month of October 1778, this applicant as a private & his said company now numbering about 70 men commanded by the said Capt. Veeder, Lieut Col. Veeder & Col. Fisher remained at the said Fort at Caughnawaga, protecting the inhabitants & their property, going out on scouting parties & guarding Fort night and day for the period of at least one month & were then discharged & went to their respective homes, that during the last service at Caughnawaga this applicant & his said company were paid & subsisted by the Government—

That in the month of May in the beginning of that month of the year 1779 this applicant (5) again called out to said Fort at Caughnawaga under the command of said Capt. Veeder one Lieut. Nich. Dockstader & said Lieut Col. Veeder & Col. Fisher. That at this last mentioned time & place this applicant was promoted to the rank of Corporal in his said company and that this applicant as such Corporal & his said company commanded by the said Capt. Veeder, Lieut. Nicholas Dockstader, Lieut. Col. Veeder, & Col. Fisher remained at said Fort at Caughnawaga from the beginning of the month of May in said year 1779 until the last of July of said Year 1779 a period of at least one month & one half of a month performing duty & service in guarding said Fort at Caughnawaga, protecting the inhabitants & their property & going out on scouting parties & being disciplined as aforesaid & were provisioned during this last period of service & paid by the government.

That in the month of July or first of August of said year 1779 this applicant as such Corporal as aforesaid & his said company commanded by the said Capt. Abraham Veeder, Lieut Col. Vedder & Col. Fisher were ordered to go & did go to a place called Stone Arabia (6) in the then County of Tryon now

Montgomery distant about 14 miles from Caughnawaga aforesaid when this applicant as such corporal as aforesaid & his said company commanded as aforesaid performed duty & service at Stone Arabia aforesaid in guarding a fort at Stone Arabia aforesaid in protecting the inhabitants and their property & in going out on scouting parties & driving off the Indians & Tories who were then infecting the County & vicinity of Stone Arabia & then returned again in August of said year 1779 & towards the middle of this month to Caughnawaga aforesaid.

That this applicant & his said company on this last tour were about at least 8 or 9 days & were paid & provisioned by the Government. That on returning as aforesaid from Stone Arabia aforesaid to Caughnawaga aforesaid this applicant as such Corporal as aforesaid or a private and which this applicant does not now recollect and his said company commanded by said Capt. Veeder, Lieut. Col. Veeder & Col Fisher were immediately or very soon thereafter were ordered out & did go again to said place called Fort Stanwix in the then County of Tryon now Oneida and then & there this applicant at such private or corporal & his said company commanded as aforesaid & other companies of soldiers numbering in all about two hundred men performed duty and service in guarding the said Fort Stanwix in protecting the inhabitants and their property in repelling and driving off the Indians & Tories and then again returned to Caughnawaga aforesaid in the month & towards the last of September of said year 1779.

That on this last tour this applicant & his said company performed duty & service as aforesaid for the period of at least 20 days & were paid and provisioned by the Government. That this applicant and his said company on returning as last aforesaid from Fort Stanwix to Caughnawaga which took place towards the last of September or first of October of said year 1779, performed that & served under the command of said Capt. Veeder, Lieut Col. Veeder, Col. Fisher at Caughnawaga aforesaid in guarding the fort at said Caughnawaga in protecting the inhabitants and their property & in going out on scouting parties until sometimes in November of said year 1779 & for the period of at least one month. That this applicant performed this last mentioned service at Caughnawaga as Corporal in his said company.

That this applicant & his said company during this last period of service were provisioned & paid by the Government. That generally during said year 1779 this applicant acted as corporal in his said company & performed the duties of that rank. That in the month of November of said year this applicant & his said company were discharged and went to their respective homes. That in the month of April of that year 1780 this applicant & his said company were again called out to said Fort at Caughnawaga when this applicant a corporal in his said company & his said company commanded by the last mentioned officers again performed duty and service in guarding said Fort at Caughnawaga in protecting the inhabitants & their property in going out on scouting parties & in being disciplined until in the month of May in said year 1780 a period of one month at least & during that time were paid & provisioned by the Government and that in the said month of May 1780 this applicant as such corporal & his said company commanded by said Capt Veeder & Col. Fisher were ordered out and did go to a place called Fort Plank in the then county of Tryon now Montgomery, distant about 15 miles from Caughnawaga aforesaid when this applicant as such Corporal & his said company & other companies in all about 150 men performed duty & service in guarding Fort at said Fort Plank in protecting the inhabitants & their property & in going out on scouting parties, scouring the country & driving off the Indians & Tories who were numerous & destructive about this time. That one Major Fink & one Col. Willis. (7)

This applicant recollects were also in command at this last time at Fort Plank. That this applicant as such Corporal & his said company were gone on this last tour to Fort Plank performing duty & service as before stated at least two months & the half of one month & was paid & provisioned and paid by the government. That this applicant & the said company commanded by said Capt. Veeder & Col. Fisher returned from Fort Plank aforesaid to Caughnawaga as aforesaid in the latter part of July or first of August of said year 1780 when this applicant as a private or Corporal & which this applicant does not recollect & his said company commanded by said Capt. Under Lieut. Col. Veeder & Col. Fisher performed duty & service until sometime in November of said year 1780 a period of at least 3 months, in guarding said Fort (8) at Caughnawaga aforesaid in protecting the inhabitants & their property & in going out on scouting parties & in having disciplined & & then were discharged & sent to their respective homes, that during this past period of service this applicant this said company were paid & provisioned by the government and this applicant further says he is the same individual mentioned & named in a certificate of the comptroller of this state attached to this declaration. And that there was no other Gardeneer in the said company in which this applicant served as above stated, who has the same Christian name with this deponent & applicant and this applicant further states that he served as corporal & private at the times & places before stated at least one year & one half of one year, and this applicant says he has no documentary evidence whatever of his said services except said certificate hereto annexed and that he relies upon the affidavit & certificates (9) hereto annexed as evidence of his said services in said war & that this applicant had never been on any pension list of the United States. Whatever and further this applicant says not. (Signed) John Gardineer

Subscribed and sworn to the day & year above written before me. D. T. Sacia, Judge of Montgomery County Court.

End Notes—R.3900—John Gardineer

1. Abraham Veeder was appointed First Lieutenant in Captain John Davis' Second Company on August 26, 1775 in Colonel Frederick Visscher's (Fisher) Third Regiment of Tryon County Militia. Any service prior to 1778 would have been in Captain Davis' Company. Captain Davis was killed at the Battle of Oriskany on August 6, 1777. Lieutenant Veeder

then assumed command of the company and was in 1778 appointed captain. His commission is dated March 8, 1781.

2. The former home of Sir William Johnson. Sir William died on July 11, 1774 and his son John inherited the Hall. Sir John , being a staunch loyalist fled his home in May of 1776 to Canada and raised a regiment of loyalists called the King's Royal Regiment of New York.
3. It is hard to pinpoint this "Battle" at Johnson Hall as he gives the month of June 1777 which is wrong on several accounts. A raid took place in October 1778 to Johnson Hall to retrieve Johnson's papers that had been buried which were virtually ruined. There was a small skirmish but the British force may have been no longer than 100 Royal Yorkers and Indians. The closest to the month of June was when Sir John Johnson raided the Mohawk Valley on May 22, 1780. He went to Johnson Hall to retrieve the silver still buried in the cellar in flour barrels in the Hall. Lieutenant-Colonel Commandant John Harper with his regiment of New York State Levies and men from the Third Regiment of Tryon County Militia met up with Johnson at the Hall and started on attack. Johnson quickly sent a messenger under a flag of truce to Harper. *If you persist in attacking the Indians who had over 30 persons including women and children would kill them.* Harper disengaged his troops and pulled back and allowed Johnson to retreat from Johnson Hall. Colonel Visscher had been tomahawked and scalped in this raid. He was taken to Schenectady where he recovered from his wounds. Visscher would not return to the Mohawk Valley until after the war. From this time forward Lieutenant-Colonel Volkert Veeder commanded the regiment. The next battle was on October 25, 1781 at the Hall. Major John Ross and Captain Walter Butler with about 600 British Troops and allies were resting at the Hall after burning and destroying settlements in the Mohawk Valley on the 24th and into the morning of the 25th. Lieutenant-Colonel Commandant Marinus Willett with a mixed force of his regiment of New York State Levies, Tryon County Militia, Massachusetts State Levies and a company of the Second Continental Artillery caught up with Major Ross at the Hall and commenced to attack the enemy. After several hours of fighting, Major Ross with his forces retreated under the cover of darkness heading back towards Canada thru the north country.
4. Fort Schuyler (Fort Stanwix) stood in present day City of Rome, Oneida Co., N.Y.
5. Nicholas Dockstader was appointed Second Lieutenant in Captain Davis' Company and was commissioned as such on June 25, 1778. When Captain Veeder was commissioned Captain on March 8, 1781, Dockstader was commissioned First Lieutenant.
6. Fort Paris was built in 1776 at Stone Arabia and named after Isaac Paris.

7. This would be in the year 1781. He is referring to Lt.-Col. Comd't Willett and Brigade Major Andrew Fink of Willett's Regiment. Willett and Fink were in Continental Regiments in 1780. Major Fink was a Captain in the First New York Continental Regiment and was stationed at Fort Schuyler until September when they were relieved and marched to West Point, N.Y. area.
8. It is not clear during this application what "Fort at Caughnawaga" refers to. There was a blockhouse built to protect the mills of John Veeder which may have been stockaded but there is no real proof to suggest that it was stockaded. The Dutch Reformed Church was of stone and troops and civilians used this church for protection during raids. The closest fort was at Johnstown, other than the homes which were picketed in the area. He never mentions the fort as such but Captain Veeder's Company may have been the blockhouse at the mills he was referring to. Caughnawaga during the War of Independence took in what is now the Village of Fonda and a big part of the Town of Mohawk. It was part of what was called the Mohawk District. After the war, the name of Tryon County was changed to Montgomery County. The Caughnawaga District was formed and went north to include the Village and Town of Johnstown and Mayfield.
9. On a Receipt Roll dated February 16, 1786, sworn to by Lieutenant-Colonel Volkert Veeder that the following certificates of money were paid on May 24, 1785 to John Gardineer.

No.	Amt.
30949	£3..13..0
32067	0..19..6
32260	0..11..8
32297	0..11..8
31909	0..8..10
32342	0..16..0
32156	0..19..6
31888	0..8..10
32849	0..19..6

FROM: Revolutionary War Rolls 1775-1783, Series M-246, Roll 74, Folder 100, National Archives, Washington, D.C.

Pension Application for John Garnett (Or Garnet)

Continental (N.Y.)
W.19484 (Widow: Elizabeth)
Garnet, John. His name appears on a list of applicants for invalid pension returned by the District Court for the District of New York, submitted to the House of Representatives by the Secretary of War on April 25, 1794, and printed in the American State Papers, class 9, page 93
Rank: Private
Regt: Artillery (1)

Disability Wounded, and lost two fingers at the taking of Fort Montgomery.
When disabled: October 6, 1777
Residence: Goshen
Remarks: This man continued to the end of the war.
Evidence transmitted by the District Court incomplete viz: No evidence of his quitting the service, no examination of surgeons.
State of New York
Orange County SS.

Be it known that before me the subscriber one of the Justices of the Peace in and for the county aforesaid, personally appeared John Garnet and made oath that he is the identical John Garnet to whom a pension of five dollars per month was heretofore granted as an Invalid of the United States and that by virtue of a late law of the Congress of the United States he is now entitled to and for about two years pay did actually draw and receive a pension of eight dollars per month on account of wounds and disabilities received and incurred in the service of the United States during the Revolutionary War. That he had never to his recollection received or had in his possession a certificate on account of said pension—it not having been heretofore necessary in order to draw his pay—that lately as he has been informed his friends have taken measures to procure such certificate—but for reasons to him unknown have not as yet obtained it—That he served in Captain Andrew Moody's company in Lieutenant Colonel Lambs regiment of Artillery at the time he was disabled—that he now resides in the town of Goshen County aforesaid and has resided there for about then years last. (Signed with his mark) John Garnett. (2)

Subscribed and sworn to this 25th day of March 1820 before me. Nathan Stock, Justice of aforesaid.

End Notes—W.19484—John Garnet

1. John enlisted as a matross (private) for during the war in Captain Andrew Moody's Company in Colonel John Lamb's Second Regiment of, Continental Regiment, on August 21, 1777. He was wounded and taken prisoner on October 6, 1777 at Fort Montgomery, NY. He returned to the regiment in August of 1778. FROM: Revolutionary War Rolls 1775-1783, Series M-246, Roll 119, folder 45, National Archives, Washington, D.C.
2. His wife Elizabeth Dye Garnet made a declaration on November 1, 1838, age 77 years, living at Goshen in Orange County, New York. A Joshua Conkling on October 4, 1845 made an affidavit stating he was acquainted with John and Elizabeth and lists the following Children: Elizabeth, John, Priscella, Clarissa, Jonathan, Sally, Joshua and Fanny. Joshua Conkling was the Poor Overseers and John had bound out several of his children. In the pension application there is an Indenture made on October 27, 1813 for Fanny Garnet. The Poor Overseers Joshua Conkling and Samuel Durland with the consent of the Justices Stephen Jackson and Edward Ely, "presents, placed and bound Fanny Garnet a poor Girl of Said Town of the age of six years

the sixth day of May past to be an apprentice with them the said Asa W. Jackson & Elizabeth his wife." In the indenture it states she is bound to them until she is 18 years of age. They were to teach her to read and write. Also they were to give her "sufficient Meat Drink Apparel Washing Lodging and all other things needful." At the expiration of Fanny's term they were to get her "a new Bible and a good ful [1] suit of Sunday Clothes besides her everyday wearing Apparel."

Pension Application for John Geesler

R.4394
State of New York
Montgomery County SS.

On this 26th day of September in the year of our Lord one thousand eight hundred and forty two personally appeared before me Phinas Randall a Judge of the Court of Common Pleas of the County of Montgomery, John Geesler a resident of the Town of Canajoharie in the County of Montgomery & State of New York of the age of eighty four years who being first duly sworn according to law doth on his oath make the following declaration in order to obtain the benefit of the act of Congress passed June 7th 1832. That he entered the service of the United States under the following named officers and served as herein stated to wit. He volunteered and enlisted for the term of nine months about the first of June in the year 1781, in the county of Montgomery & State of New York in the company commanded by Captain Frederick K. Getman (1) in the Regiment commanded by Colonel Andrew Gray (2) in the State of New York and that he continued to serve in said Corpse [sic, Corps] until about the first day of March 1782 when the term for which he had enlisted expired.

And further says, that in the year 1783, in the month of May he again enlisted for the term of three months in the State of New York in the company commanded by Capt. Nicholas Coppernoll (3) in the regiment commanded by Colonel Andrew Gray in the Line of the State of New York that he continued to serve in said Coprse until about the first of August 1783 at which time the term of his enlistment terminated when he was discharged from the service in Stone Arabia in the State of New York, that at the time he volunteered & enlisted last above mentioned he resided in the town of Palatine County of Montgomery and State of New York, that at neither time he received no written discharges. And that he has no documentary evidence of the service he performed in the Revolutionary War. And that he knows of no person living whose testimony he can procure who can testify to his said services. And that during said terms of nine months & three months he was engaged in no civil employment.

And that he marched from Stone Arabia to Fort Plain and thence up the Mohawk River to Fort Herkimer & through the Counties of Montgomery, Herkimer, and Schoharie along the valley of the Mohawk River; that since that time he has resided in the State of New York, that he hereby relinquishes every claim whatsoever to a pention [pension] except the present and declares that his name is not on the pention roll of the agency of any state. (Signed with his mark) John Geesler

Subscribed and sworn before me the day and year first above mentioned. P. Randall the first Judge of the Montgomery County Courts.

Montgomery County SS

We John Warner and Peter Plets residing in the town of Canajoharie and County aforesaid hereby certify that we are well acquainted with John Geesler who has subscribed and sworn to the above declaration, that we believe him to be eighty four years of age that he is reputed & believed in the neighborhood where he resides to have been a soldier of the revolution, and that we concur in that opinion. John Warner, Peter Plets.

Sworn before me this 26th day of September AD 1842.

Questions proposed to said John Geesler

Q1. Where and in what year were you born?

Ans. I was born in Hesse Castle in Germany—in the year seventeen hundred and fifty eight.

Q2nd. Have you any record of your age and if so where is it?

Ans. I had a record—which in Germany but lef [left] it there—or have lost the same since I came to this country.

Q3d. Where were you living when called into service; where have you lived since the Revolutionary War; and where do you now live?

Ans. I was living when first enrolled in Stone Arabia—then in Tryon County now Montgomery County—N. York—and also at the second enrollment—I have lived since the Revolutionary War—for the first year when enlisted—then about eleven years in Canajoharie same county—Then about thirteen years in the town of Sullivan Madison County—N. York—Then in the town of Clay & Canton in Onondaga County N. York—for many years & now lives in Canajoharie Montgomery County N. York.

Q4th. How were you called into service; were you drafted; did you volunteer; or where you a substitute and if a substitute for whom?

Ans. There was a requisition for a draft of militia—And on both occasions I volunteered to serve a draft—on my own account and not as a substitute for another.

Q5th. State the names of some of the regular officers who were with the troops when you served; such Continental and Militia Regiments as you can recollect, and the general circumstances of your services.

Ans. Andrew Gray was the Col. of his Regiment—One Newkirk (4) was the oldest Col. My Capts. name was Frederick Getman—I was a stranger to the Country & the Language & do not recollect names I remember the name of Col. Willett (5) Col. VanRensselaer (6) & Gen. Schuyler (7) but was not personally acquainted with them—I deserted from Burgoyne's (8) Army near the Highlands—and was wounded in the act of desertion—And my horse shot from under me—

Q6th. Did you ever receive a discharge from the service and if so by whom was it given? And what has become of it?
Ans. I received a written discharge from Capt. Frederick Getman & from Capt. Coppernoll—I have long since lost them—I do not know where they are.
Q7th. State the names of persons to whom you are known in your present neighborhood and who can testify as to your character for veracity & their belief of your services as a soldier of the Revolution.
Ans. Peter Pletts—John Warner, Lawrence Gros—Jonas Diefendorf & Andrew Roof.

I Phinehas Randall a Judge of the Court of Common Pleas of the County of Montgomery do certify that I proposed the above interrogatories to said John Geesler, and that I wrote his answers to said Interrogatories as above; and I also certify that said John Geesler (9) on account of old age and bodily infirmity, in my opinion is unable to attend in open court for the purpose of submitting to the above examination. Dated this 26th day of September AD 1842. P. Randall first Judge of the Montgomery Courts.

End Notes—R.4394—John Geesler

1. Frederick Getman was a Captain in Colonel Peter Bellinger's Fourth Regiment of Tryon County Militia. Captain Getman was taken prisoner on June 21, 1782. There is only a muster roll for 1779 and 1780 for this company but no one living at Stone Arabia would have served in this company.
2. Andrew Gray served as a sergeant in Colonel Jacob Klock's Second Regiment of Tryon County Militia. A check of officers for the Montgomery County Militia to 1800 do not show Gray as a Colonel. On October 2, 1786, in Lieutenant-Colonel Commandant Peter Schuyler's Regiment of Montgomery County Militia appointed Captain of the Second Company was Samuel Gray; Frederick Getman, lieutenant; Jacob G. Snell as Ensign. FROM: Military Minutes of the Council of Appointment of the State of New York, 1783-1821, ed. Hugh Hastings, James B. Lyon, State Printer, Albany, 1901, Vol. I, P. 102.
3. Nicholas Coppernoll was commissioned Ensign on September 29, 1780 in Captain Henry Miller's Company in Colonel Klock's Regiment. Nicholas was appointed Captain of the Ninth Company of Light Infantry on October 2, 1786 in Schuyler's Montgomery County Militia. Same source as end note 2, page 103. It appears that the service John refers to is after the War of Independence, which is one of the reasons that his pension application was rejected.
4. He is probably referring to Lieutenant-Colonel Commandant John Newkirk of the Montgomery County Militia.
5. Marinus Willett, Colonel of New York State Regiment of Levies in 1782 and 1783 in the Mohawk Valley.
6. There are several Colonel and Lieutenant-Colonel VanRensselaer's.
7. Major General Philip Schuyler

8. Apparently John was in one of Lieutenant General John Burgoyne's German Regiments attached to his campaign army of 1777. John does not state if he was taken prisoner before or after General Burgoyne surrendered his army on October 17, 1777.
9. John amended his pension application on November 21, 1842 and also the testimony of Henry Murphy and Peter House. Murphy and House had served in the First Regiment of Tryon County Militia during the War of Independence. John Geesler, son of the applicant applied for his father's pension on September 16, 1852. He stated his father died about 1845 leaving no widow surviving. This John was living in the Town of Minden, Montgomery County in 1852.

Pension Application for Daniel Gilbert

S.13111
State of New York
County of Orange SS.

On this twenty seventh day of Aug't 1832 personally appeared in open court before me Samuel S. Seward first Judge of the Court of Common Pleas in and for the County of Orange, at my office, Daniel Gilbert a resident of the Town of Warwick in the County and State aforesaid aged seventy five years who being first duly sworn according to law doth on his oath make the following declaration in order to obtain the benefit of the act of Congress passed June 7th 1832.

That the said Daniel Gilbert was born in Orange County in the State of New York and still resides in the Town of Warwick in said County. That about the commencement of the Revolutionary War he became liable to do military duty. That he entered the service of the United States under the following named officers and served as herein stated. That the first service he recollects to have rendered was an expedition to Ramepo under Capt. John Sayre (1) Maj. John Poppino (2) and Col. John Hathorn was absent from Florida where he resided about three weeks. That the same kind of service to the same place and the neighborhood of Judge Sufferen's and the mountain pass he repeated five or six times some times under the same Cap. sometimes under Cap. Minthorn (3) and sometimes under Cap. Blain (4). Went on an expedition to keep guard at Tappan thinks he was under the command of Capt. Peter Bartholf but not positive was several times under his command. He was also stationed at Harverstraw does not recollect his Captain but thinks it was one of the Captains of Hathorn's regiment. Afterwards was sent on an expedition to Niar. Served there as one of the guard. Was on another to the English neighborhood the New Bridge and Closter and along the lines in New Jersey under different officers under Col. Hathorn's command. Was several different times at Fort Montgomery under different officers was once sent as one of a guard with prisoners to Kingston under the command of Cap. Henry Wisner. (6) Was once sent as one of a guard to escort ammunition wagons from Goshen in Orange County to Easton in Pennsylvania does not recollect his commanding officer.

Went as a militiaman from Florida to New Windsor and after laying there sometime was marched to Morristown after laying there some days was marched by the way of Bascon ridge and Burdentown, to Red Bank was there when Fort Miflin (7) was evacuated was under the command of Cap. Cole (8) and Col. Seward (9) and part of the time under Gen. Wayne. (10) Was several times stationed at different parts along the Delaware then the Indians frontier under different Captains but he thinks always under Col. Hathorn's command. Was frequently called out on alarms to short tours to short tours of duty both along the Jersey Mountains and at Miniskink, (11) was on the march in consequence of one when the Indian Battle at Minisink was fought and met the defeated a short distance on their retreat. This deponent recollects distinctly of being on duty on the west side of the Hudson river during the Battle of White Plains (12) and heard distinctly the firing in that battle and was afterwards marched by way of the three Pidgeons to near Polous [Paulus] hook and was encamped between that and Hackensack. He was also called from the militia service to press Hay for the Continental Army under the direction of a Mr. Ervine who had some distinction in the forage department, about two or three weeks. This deponent cannot fix the time of his different services, with precision on each of the different tours of duty but the verily believes that his time spent in the service put it all together during the revolutionary war cannot be less than five years and perhaps more. He further states that he does not know of an officer under whom he served that is now living and that he has no documentary evidence of any of his services. Has a record of his age in his family Bible.

He hereby relinquishes every claim whatever to a pension or annuity except the present and declares that his name is not on the pension roll of the agency of any state whatsoever nor ever has been. (Signed with his mark) Daniel Gilbert

Sworn to and subscribed the day and year aforesaid on the 27th day of Aug't 1832 before me. Samuel S. Seward, first Judge of the Courts of said county.

End Notes—S.13111—Daniel Gilbert

1. John Sayres was a captain of the Florida Company in Colonel John Hathorn's Fifth Regiment of Orange County Militia. On May 28, 1778, the Second and Third Regiments of Orange County Militia were consolidated into one. Hathorn's would therefore change from 5th to the 4th Regiment.
2. John Popino was appointed Second Major in 1775 and he was promoted to First Major on February 19, 1778 in Colonel Hathorn's Regiment,
3. John Minthorn was commissioned captain on February 19, 1778 in Colonel Hathorn's Company.
4. Captain William Blain of the Wawayanda Company in Colonel Hathorn's Regiment. Blain was appointed to Second Major in February 19. 1778.

5. Peter Bertolf was commissioned captain on February 19, 1778 in Colonel Hathorn's Regiment.
6. Henry Wisner, Jr. was Captain of the Pond Company of Colonel Hathorn's Regiment. Peter Bertolf succeeded him as captain.
7. Fort Mifflin, Pennsylvania.
8. Captain Cole possibly of the New Jersey militia.
9. Possibly Colonel John Seward of the New Jersey Militia.
10. Brigadier General Anthony Wayne of the Continental Army.
11. Battle of Minisink, NY was fought on July 22, 1779.
12. The Battle of White Plains, NY was fought on October 28, 1776.

Pension Application for Philip Graff

W.23154 (Widow: Deborah)
State of New York
Montgomery County SS.

On this 19th day of September in the year of our Lord one thousand eight hundred and thirty two personally appeared in open court before the Court of Common Pleas of the County of Montgomery & State of New York, now sitting, Philip Graff a resident of the Town of Johnstown in the County & State aforesaid aged sixty four years on the sixteenth day of November last past, who being first duly sworn according to law doth on his oath make the following declaration in order to obtain the benefit of the act of Congress passed June 7, 1832. That he entered the service of the United States and served as herein stated: Your applicant says that he went as a substitute for one Conradt Steen in Militia service in the year 1779 under Captain Pattingales, (1) that he does not recollect the names of any of the other officers that he resided at this time in Johnstown Tryon County now Montgomery and went from the latter place to Mayfield in same county of Tryon, about ten miles distant, and remained there two weeks and was after that time discharged verbally. Your applicant says that he again in the year 1780 went as a substitute in the place of one William White, for two weeks and remained for that time as such substitute at the Johnstown Fort until said White returned from visiting his family and that this was in the month of June in that year.

Your applicant further says that on the return of said White he your applicant went from Johnstown down to Noble Town then Albany county now Columbia County & State of New York for the purpose of going to his father's (2) family who had removed from Johnstown to Noble Town, while he lay and remained at the Johnstown Fort, that when he arrived there he again went out as a substitute for one Johnathan Reece, in the militia service under Captain Christopher Miller (3), Lieutenant John Ostrander, Ensign Jeremiah Miller, a company belonging to Colonel Grahams Regiment, that he went from that place to wit, Noble Town to Claverack, Albany County, Now Columbia, and from thence he proceeded under the above named officers, to Livingstons Manor, and from thence again to Poughkeepsie & from thence to Fish Kill where his said company joined the said Regiment three other Regiments commanded by

Colonels Malcom, (4) Livingston & Paine, Malcom being the oldest of the four Colonels, acted as Brigadier General & took the Command of the four Regiments.

Your applicant went from Fish Kill under the before named officers to West Point, where the army remained for two weeks and from thence proceeded to Stony Point, and from thence to Haverstraw and from thence to Tappan and from thence they proceeded back again to Albany County.

Your applicant says that he went out as such substitute for three months and served the full term of three months, that he went out sometime in the month of July in this year, but is unable to state the day of the month and was discharged sometime in the latter part of October, but cannot state the day.

Your applicant, further says, that in the year 1781, he again went out as a substitute, in the place of Peter Groat in the Militia service for four months, under Captain Peter Van Ransalaer (5), Lieutenant Spencer (6), commanded by Colonel Marinus Willett, that he at this time lived at Claverack Albany County now Columbia & State aforesaid, went from there went up to a place now called Herkimer then Fort Herkimer in Tryon County and that he went there under those officers to guard the frontiers of New York State and prevent the Indians from destroying the Whigs of the place and different other places in Tryon County and served for the full term of four months, at this time.

Your applicant says that he went out in the month of August of this year and was discharged sometime in the latter part of November or then December. Your applicant says that he was born in the Town of Johnstown County of Tryon & State of New York in the year 1767. He has a memorandum of his age in his family Bible, your applicant says that he is acquainted with the following persons in the neighborhood who can testify to his character as to truth and veracity and their belief of his services as a soldier of the revolution to wit.

Your applicant says that he knows of no person or persons with whom he can prove the two terms of two weeks and the other term of three months who he went out for Jonathan Reece but is only able to prove the last four months and has no documentary evidence of his services. He hereby relinquishes every claim whatever to a pension or annuity, except the present and declares that his name is not on the Pension Roll of the agency of any State. (Signed Philip Graff)

Sworn and Subscribed the day & year aforesaid in open court. Geo. D. Ferguson, Clerk
State of New York
County of Montgomery SS.

On this 15th day of December 1838 personally appeared before me Samuel A. Gilbert one of the Judges of Montgomery county Court Deborah Graff, a resident of Johnstown, State and County aforesaid aged 66 years, who being first duly sworn according to law, doth on her oath, make the following declaration in order to obtain the benefit of the provision made by the Act of

Congress passed July 7th 1838, entitled "An Act granting half pay and pensions to certain widows". That she is the widow of Philip Graff, who was a private Soldier in the enlisted troops, in the war of the Revolution, and was a Pensioner of the United States under the Act of Congress of June 7th 1832—She further declares that she was married to the said Philip Graff at Caughnawaga by the Rev'd Thomas Romeyn on the fifteenth day of April in the year seventeen hundred and ninety one and that her name prior to being married was Deborah Wemple, daughter of Barent Wemple and that her husband the aforesaid Philip Graff died on the nineteenth day of August in the year eighteen hundred and thirty seven at Glen State and County aforesaid; that she was not married prior to his leaving the service, but the marriage took place previous to the first of January seventeen hundred and ninety four, viz, at the time above stated. She further declares that her husband the aforesaid Philip Graff after serving in the troops in the said County of Montgomery for which he was pensioned as above stated, removed to the County of Columbia and there was enrolled in the militia and served there in General Van Rensselaer's division a tour of one month for which he, the said Philip Graff stands accredited on old books of credit at the Pension office, and that for said service she now claims that her pension certificate shall be increased beyond what it formerly it was to her husband the said Philip Graff, and that her pay certificate was surrendered up at the time of drawing the arrearages of her said husband. (Signed with her mark) Deborah Graff

Sworn to and subscribed on the day and year above written below me. Sam'l A. Gilbert a Judge of said County.

End Notes—W.23154—Philip Graff or Graft

1. Philip is in error as to the Captain of this tour of service. Samuel Pettingell was the Captain of the Fifth Company in Colonel Frederick Visscher's Third Regiment of Tryon County Militia. Captain Pettingell was killed at the Battle of Oriskany on August 6, 1777. Philip would have been only ten years old in 1777. William Snook was the First Lieutenant of this company and after the death of Captain Pettingell, Snook was appointed Captain of the Fifth Company. Philip probably served under Captain Snook in 1779 and Philip would have been 12 years old. Philip was too young to legally serve in the militia but according to Daniel, Philip's younger brother in his July 30, 1833 deposition which he made in support of Philip's pension application states the following: "And this deponent says that Philip was quite young when he went out but was very large and active for his age."
2. Philip's father and mother might be Jacob and Sarah Putman Graff as a Daniel Graff was born on June 10, 1769 according to the Stone Arabia Lutheran Church baptism book, page 29. Daniel in his deposition stated he was born in 1769. Jacob and Margaret had the following children: Margaret born April 12, 1772 and baptized June 6, 1772, Dutch Reformed Church of Caughnawaga Baptism Book page 22, and

Maria born June 19, 1777 and baptized July 13, 1777, Dutch Reformed Church of Caughnawaga Baptism Book, page 22.

3. Captain Christopher Muller and Lieutenants John Ostrander and Jeremiah Muller served in Colonel Morris Graham's Third Regiment of New York State Levies in 1780. Philip served as a private for 3 months and was discharged about October 27, 1780. FROM: Revolutionary War Rolls 1775-1783, M-246, Roll 72, folder 75, National Archives, Washington, D.C.
4. William Malcolm was the Colonel of the First Regiment of New York State Levies, Henry Livingston was the Lieutenant-Colonel in Colonel Graham's Regiment, and Brinton Paine was the Lieutenant-Colonel in Colonel Lewis DuBois' Regiment of New York State Levies.
5. Philip enlisted as a private on August 23, 1781 in Captain Peter VanRensselaer's Company in Lieutenant-Colonel Commandant Marinus Willett's Regiment of New York State Levies. He was discharged on December 1, 1781. FROM: Revolutionary War Rolls 1775-1783, Series M-246, Roll 78, Folder 173, National Archives, Washington, D.C.
6. John Spencer was appointed July 24th as a lieutenant and Jacob Winney was appointed on July 31, as a lieutenant. Both of them were arranged or assigned to Captain VanRensselaer's Company. Lieutenant Spencer signed the muster roll on October 7, 1781 at Fort Herkimer. Philip was still there on October 7, 1781.

Pension Application for Jehiel Green

W.7556 (Widow: Esther)
State of New York
Steuben County SS.

On this sixteenth day of October AD 1832, personally appeared in open court before the Court of Common Pleas of the said county of Steuben new sitting Jehiel Green, as resident of the Town of Howard in the said County of Steuben, and State of New York aged seventy one years and upwards who being first duly sworn according to law doth on his oath make the following declaration in order to obtain the benefit of the Act of Congress passed June 7, 1832. That he entered the service of the United States under the following named officers and served as herein stated—

That he was first drafted into the Militia of the State of New York some time in the Spring of the year 1779 at the town of Bedford in the County of Westchester in a company commanded by Captain Daniel Bouton (1) belonging to the regiment commanded by Colonel Nathan Delavan (2)—That at the time he was so drafted as aforesaid the said Regiment was divided into what were called classes which said classes alternately did duty for a regular period of times. That he belonged to said company during the years 1779, 1780, and 1781. That he was employed while in active service during that time in guarding the County from the attacks of small parties of British troops and Tories along the North River from Westchester County down the river to the

British lines—That during that time he was engaged in actual service only part of the time—That whenever there was an alarm given a part or all of the Militia were called out to repel an attack or to punish depredations committed within the said county and were then permitted to return home until it became necessary to call them out again—That the part of the county into which he lived was very much exposed by its situation to the attacks of the marauding parties of the enemy and was very frequently attacked—That he was out in this quarter during the years aforesaid very frequently and was sometimes out for three and four weeks at a time—That he was unable to state what particular length of time altogether he was engaged in this service under arms during the said years but from his best recollection he thinks he was so engaged at various times during the said time in the whole to make from twelve to fifteen months.—

That about the first of April 1782 he enlisted at Bedford aforesaid where he then resided for the term of nine months in a company commanded by a Captain Thomas Hunt (3) With a Lieutenant Tuttle—That said company belonged to the Fourth New York Regiment commanded by a Colonel Wisenfelt. That company to which he belonged did not remain with the said regiment during the said term of nine months but was stationed in the said County of Westchester for the purpose of guarding it from the attacks of parties of British and Tories—that during said time while he was with said company he was employed in a skirmish in the town of Salem with a party of Tories in which he was wounded by the thrust of a bayonet through his arm. That he continued in the said company engaged in the said County of Westchester until the expiration of the said term of nine months when he was discharged there from.—That he has no recollection of ever having received a written discharge and if he did so receive one he has lost it, that the only evidence of his said services which he has been able to procure is contained in the affidavits he this declaration annexed—

That he was born at Bedford in the County of Westchester in the State of New York on the 27 November 1761—that he has no record of his age and knows the same only from his recollection of the information given to him by his parents—

That after the close of the war he resided at Bedford aforesaid about one year then removed to Balltown Saratoga County where he resided about seventeen years, then removed to Ulyssus now Tompkins County where lived four or five years and from thence removed to Howard in the said County of Steuben where he has since continued to reside.

That in his present neighborhood he is known to Rev'd Toule, William Goff, Simeon Bacon, Charles Graves, Daniel N. Bennett, Rev'd Joseph Jacobs, Hubbard W. Rathbun who can testify as to his character for veracity and their belief of his services as a soldier of the revolution—

He hereby relinquishes every claim whatever to a pension or annuity except the present and declares that his name is not on the pension roll of the agency of any state. (Signed) Jehiel Green

Sworn to and subscribed this day and year aforesaid, M. S. L. Rumsey, Dep. Clk. Steuben County.

Reply to a letter of inquiry dated May 3, 1936:

Reference is made to your letter in which you request the Revolutionary War records of Jehiel Green of Westchester County, New York, and of Luther Kerry, Cary, Karry of Washington County, Pennsylvania.

The Revolutionary War records of this office have been searched and no claim for pension found based on the service of a Luther Kerry, who served from the State of Pennsylvania. The surname was searched under similar spellings.

The data which follow were obtained from papers on file in pension claim, W. 7556, based on the military service of Jehiel Green in the War of the Revolution.

Jehiel Green was born November 27, 1761 in Bedford, Westchester County, New York. The names o his parents were not stated.

While residing in Bedford, New York, Jehiel Green enlisted in the spring of 1779, served as a private at various times, until sometime in 1781, guarding the country along the North River, under Capatin Daniel Bouton, and Colonel N. Delavan in the New York troops, length of entire service about fifteen months. He enlisted about April 1, 1782, served nine months as private in Captain Thomas Hunt's company in Colonel Weissenfels' New York regiment, and in a skirmish at Salem, was wounded by a bayonet thrust through his arm.

Jehiel Green lived after the Revolution in Bedford, New York, about one year, then moved to Ballston, Saratoga County, lived seventeen years, moved to Ulysses, Tompkins County, lived about sixteen years, moved to Reading, Steuben County there four or five years, thence to Howard, Steuben County, New York.

He was allowed pension on his application executed October 16, 1832, then living in Howard New York.

He was living in Medina County, Ohio, in 1834, where he stated most of his children were living, he did not name the children then living in Ohio.

Jehiel Green died September 27 or 28, in 1845.

Jehiel Green married in Bedford, New York, in the month of January, "soon after Proclamation of Peace", Esther Armstrong of said Bedford. She was born October 2, 1763, place not stated, nor were the names of her parents given.

The widow, Esther Green, was allowed pension on her application executed August 21, 1846, at which time she was living in Chatham, Medina County, Ohio.

She was living in 1853, in Michigan, with her son, who had lately moved from Ohio to Michigan, name of son not designated.

The following are the names of the children of Jehiel Green, and his wife, Esther, as shown in the claim:

Daniel born September 25, 1782
William born December 29, 1784

Ezra born April 20, 1787
Caleb born January 20, 1789
James born January 21, 1791
Sarah born February 6, 1793
Jehaunah (?) born February 28, 1795
Thomas born March 11, 1798
---ahel born September 7, 1800
Joseph born April 15, 1803
Else(?) born February 13, 1805.

Their son, Caleb Green, was living in 1846 in Chatham, Ohio, and son Joseph Green, was living in 1863 in Lenawee, County, Michigan.

The following data are shown, also relationship to the family of the soldier, Jehial Green, not designated:

Catharine Green born July 9, 1793
Salley Green born September 30, 1828
Everey (?) Green born September 14, 1830
William Green born April 21, 1833
Mary Jane Green born February 8, 1837
Rachal Green born April 4, 1839
Jehiel Green born May 24, 1841
Orrin V. or W. Green born December 30, 1842

Daniel Green born September 10, 1811
William Green born January 4, 1813
Betsey Green born December 15, 1814
Sally Green born October 11, 1816
Aaron Green born October 24, 1818
Hiram Green born July 10, 1820
Jane Green born July 1, 1822
Benjamin J. Green born April 13, 1824
Rachiel Green born June 11, 1826
Caleb Green born April 4, 1826
Deborah Green born August 10, 182-
Alvira Green born March 2, 1832
Catharine Green born October 11, 1833

Thomas Armstrong of Tompkins County, New York in 1832 stated that he was born in Bedford, New York, that he would be sixty-eight years of age in January, 1833, and was well acquainted with the soldier, Jehiel Green, and served with him in the nine months tour, during the Revolutionary War. It was not shown that he was a relative of the widow, Esther Green.

End Notes—W.75556—Jehiel Green

1. Captain Daniel Bouton of Lieutenant-Colonel Thaddeus Crane's Fourth Regiment of Westchester County Militia. Several companies were taken from Colonels Thomas Thomas' and Samuel Drake's Regiment of Westchester County Militia in 1779 to form this new regiment.

2. Nathan Delevan had served under Colonel Drake as Major and he was transferred to Crane's Regiment and served under him as a Major.
3. Thomas Hunt served as a captain in Lieutenant-Colonel Commandant Frederick Weisenfel's Regiment of New York State Levies in 1782. The Fourth New York Continental Regiment had been consolidated with the Second New York Continental Regiment on January 1, 1781.

Pension Application for James Gregg

W.17025 (Widow: Mary, granted pension of $480 per annum.)
B.L. Wt.826-300. Capt. Issued July 3, 1790 to Nathan Brewster administrator on the estate of J.G.
State of New York
Cayuga County SS.

On this 12th day of December in the year 1836, personally appeared before the undersigned, Augustus F. Ferris, one of the Judges of Cayuga County in & for the county aforesaid it being a Court of Record, Mary Gregg of the town of Victory in said County aged seventy four years who being by me duly sworn according to law doth on her oath made the following declaration in order to obtain the benefit of the provision made by the Act of Congress passed July 4, 1832. That she is the widow of James Gregg (who as this deponent has often been informed and now believes, a Captain in the Continental Army (1) during the war of the Revolution that he entered the service of the United States on or about the first of the war, as this deponent has been informed by her husband, James Gregg and verily believes the same was true, and has also been informed that he joined the New York Regiment commanded by Col. Peter Gansvoort, (2) that he the said James Gregg continued in the service as Captain to the end of the war as she has always understood and now believes, and also that he was wounded at or near Fort Stanwix (3) & scalped by an Indian and this deponent further declares that she was born in the year 1762, and was married to said James Gregg in Bloomingrove Orange County about the year 1782 by the Rev'd Constant, that she kept no record of her age or marriage either in the Bible or otherwise, that her said husband James Gregg died on the 22d day of September 1785 and that she has remained his widow ever since as will more fully appear by reference to the evidence hereunto annexed. (Signed with her mark) Mary Gregg

Sworn to and subscribed this 12th day of December 1836, before me. Augustus F. Ferris One of the Judges of Cayuga County courts.
State of New York
Wayne County SS.

Matthew Brewster of Sterling in the County of Cayuga being duly sworn, desposes and says that he was acquainted with Captain James Gregg who was an officer in the revolutionary army, that he had seen the scar on Captain Gregg's head which was caused (as said Captain Greg informed deponent, and which said appearance –verily believes to be true) by being scalped by an Indian that said Captain James Gregg after he had received said wound married Mary Brewster, now Mary Gregg, whereas sister to said deponent, that said Captain Gregg died some years ago, and that Mary Gregg now of the town of Victory is the widow of said James Gregg. And further saith not. (Signed) Matthew Brewster.

Subscribed and sworn before me this 10th day of Nov 1836. Amos Snyder, Justice of the Peace.

Reply to letter of inquiry dated July 9, 1925.

I have to advise you that from the papers in the Revolutionary War pension claim, W.17025 it appears that James Gregg served from an early period of the Revolution as a Captain in Colonel Peter Gansevoort's Third Regiment of the New York Line, and whilc at Fort Stanwix in 1777 was wounded by a ball shot through his body, and at the same time was tomahawked and scalped by an Indian. He served until the army was disbanded in 1783. He was a member of the Cincinnati. He died September 22, 1785 in Albany, New York. The date and place of his birth are not given.

Soldier married in 1782 in Bloomingrove, Orange County, New York, Mary Brewster who was born in June 1762. She was allowed pension on her application executed December 12, 1836 while a resident of Victory, Cayuga County, New York. She died June 24, 1844. It is not stated whether they had children.

End Notes—W.17025—James Gregg

1. James was appointed Second Lieutenant on June 28, 1775 in Captain John Nicholson's Second Company in Colonel James Clinton's Third New York Continental Regiment. James was appointed First Lieutenant on June 26, 1776 in Colonel Lewis DuBois' unnumbered New York Continental Regiment.
2. James was appointed captain of the Sixth Company on November 21, 1776 in Colonel Peter Gansevoort's Third New York Continental Regiment.
3. Captain Gregg and Corporal Samuel Mattison were attacked on June 25, 1777 near Fort Schuyler (Fort Stanwix). Corporal Mattison was killed and Captain Gregg was left dying but he recovered from his wounds and continued to serve until the end of the war. In 1779, Captain Gregg with the Third New York served in the Sullivan-Clinton Expedition. On January 1, 1781, the First and Third New York Continental Regiments were consolidated and Captain Gregg was transferred to the First New York under Colonel Goose VanSchaick. Captain Gregg served in the Yorktown, Va. Campaign with the First New York from September 28 to October 19, 1781. Captain Gregg remained with the regiment until he was discharged in June 1783 at the New Windsor Cantonment near Newburgh, N.Y.

Pension Application for Asa Hall

S.6945
State of Virginia
Montgomery County SS.

On this 30th day of April A.D. 1833, personally appeared in open court, before the Judge of the Circuit Superior Court of Law and chancery for the county of Montgomery aforesaid, now sitting, Asa Hall a resident of the said county and state, aged seventy four years, last June who being first sworn according to law doth, on his oath, make the following declaration in order to obtain the benefit of the Act of Congress passed June 7th 1839 [1838].

That he entered the service of the United States under the following named officers and served as herein stated.—That he, on the 2nd of March 1776, in the County of Dutchess & State of New York, enlisted in the service of the United States, to continue in such service during the pleasure of Congress, and was enlisted and commanded by Captain Nathan Pierce (1), who having shortly retired from service this applicant was put under the command of Captain Balding (2) in the regiment commanded by Colonel Richmon. In consequence of the loss of many of our men at Long Island (3), & White Plains (4), in which actions applicant participated, he served but nine months and five days, up to the 8th of December following the time of his enlistment, at which latter period he was discharged, at the encampment near the Peakskiln Mountain—That he afterwards, on the 1st of July 1777 in the County of Albany and State of New York, enlisted under Captain John Salisberry (5) for three months in the regiment commanded by Colonel Fariness (6) (he thinks)

He was at the taking of Burgoyne, under General Gates, and was continued in the service, not three but four & a half months, up to the 15th December, according to his best recollection.

That he has lost his discharges & has no documentary evidence of his service, and has been able to procure no other evidence of his service, except what accompanies this declaration.

He hereby relinquishes every claim whatever to a pension or annuity except the present and declares that his name is not on the pension roll of the agency of any state. (Signed with his mark) Asa Hall

Reply to a letter of inquiry dated May 24, 1928.

I advise you that from the papers in the Revolutionary War pension claim,S.6945, it appears that Asa Hall was born in June, 1758, place not stated.

He enlisted in Dutchess County, New York, March 2 or 3, and served until December 8, 1776, as a private in Captains Nathan Pierce's and Palding's or Balding's Companies in Colonel Richmore's or Richmon's and Wisenfelt's New York Regiments; he was in the battles of Long Island and White Plains. He enlisted July 1, 1777 and served until December 15, 1777, as a private in Captain John Salisbury's Company in Colonel Fornass' New York Regiment; he was at the capture of Burgoyne.

He was allowed pension on his application executed April 30, 1833, at which time he was a resident of Montgomery County, Virginia.

There are no data on file relative to his wife and children.

Montgomery County To Wit

This day Asa Hall of lawful age came personally before me Joseph King a Justice of the peace of the county aforesaid, and made oath that Asa Hall of said county is now seventy two years of age and has been a resident of the aforesaid county of thirty five years, and that he the said Asa Hall entered for and during the pleasure of Congress on the 3d day of March 1776 in the County of Dutchess & State of New York and was commanded by Capt. Nathan Pearce who having shortly retired from service he was put under the command of Capt. Balding in the Regiment commanded by Capt. Richmore finally under the command of Capt. Wisinfelt (7) and that he continued under that enlistment nine months & five days till 8th day of December following when he was discharged.

Given under my hand & seal this 28th day of December 1828. Joseph King JP. Crt.

End Notes—S.6945—Asa Hall

1. Captain Nathan Pearce, Jr. was in Colonel Rudolphus Ritzema's Third New York Continental Regiment of 1776.
2. On the September 20, 1776, Harlem, NY, weekly return of Colonel Ritzema's Regiment it has on the bottom the following: Captain Pearce Dismist. From the service by order of the General. Lieutenant Baldwin Appointed to the Command of Pearce's Company. Baldwin's first name is not given. FROM: Revolutionary War Rolls 1775-1783, Series M.-246, Roll 69, folder 39, National Archives, Washington, DC.
3. The Battle of Long Island NY was fought on August 27, 1776.
4. The Battle of White Plains, NY was fought on October 28, 1776.
5. A Captain John Salisbury served in Colonel William B. Whiting's Seventeenth Regiment of Albany County Militia.
6. Colonel Fariness, Faornas etc. is unknown.
7. Frederick Weisenfels was appointed Lieutenant - Colonel on March 8, 1776, in Colonel Ritzema's 3rd NY.

Pension Application for Jesse Hall

S.8666

State of Virginia, Montgomery County SS.

On this 30th day of September 1833 personally appeared before the Judge of the Circuit Superior Court of law and chancery for the county aforesaid. The same being a court of record, Jesse Hall a resident of said County and state, aged seventy three years last march, who being first duly sworn according to law, doth on his oath, make the following declaration, in order to obtain the benefit of the provision made by the act of Congress passed June 7th 1832.—

That he enlisted in the Army of the United States, in February 1776, for nine months, under Captain Nathan Pierce (1), in Dutchess county, State of N. York, and was attached to and served in the regiment commanded by Colonel Richmon which regiment belonged to the Brigade of Genl. M'Dougal. He was in the battle of the White Plains (3), and was discharged near Fort Montgomery in the State of New York some time in the month of December following his enlistment—Afterwards, in the said County of Dutchess and State of N. York, on the first day of May 1777, being drafted, he again entered as a militia man into the service of the U. States under Colonel Morehouse (4), in the company of William Pierce. He was marched to a point about fifteen miles above the City of N. York, on the Hudson, at this time the British were in possession of the city of N. York. At this station he remained three months in the regiment commanded by the said Colo. Morehouse & company of Capt. Wm. Pierce.—Afterward, early in August (there being no interruption of his service) he was connected with a division of the army under command of Genl. Putnam, (Morehouse still being his Colonel & Pierce his Captain) and marched near to Fort Montgomery, with a view to its relief but the forces to which he belonged was unable to give any assistance and the Fort was taken. He then fell back to the place from whence he had started—the point fifteen miles above the city of N. York, having been absent one month, according to his best recollection. He continued at this latter point after his said return, in the service, three months until the first of December or the early part of that month, when, and where he was discharged. He was, at the time of his discharge, in the regiment of Colo. Morehouse & company of Capt. William Pierce. Afterwards, in the month of March 1778, in the same state & county, he enlisted under a Captain Johnston, as a regular, for the term of nine months and joined the regiment commanded by Colonel Gonsay (the name is spelt to give the sound.) This applicant was stationed for the greater part of this tour of service at Fort Plank or Blank on the Mohawk River. Colo. Gonsay during the time had his station some twenty miles higher up the river at Fort Stanwock. There was but a captain's command at Fort Plank, and that command, as this applicant understood, was part of Gonsey's regiment. The soldiers at Fort Plank, believed the name of the Colonel to whose regiment they belonged to he Gonsay or Ganzier. The applicant had no personal acquaintance with him. A part of this tour of service was spent in an expedition to a place called Cherry valley, for the purpose of surprising some Tories and Indians who had done considerable mischief to that neighborhood while on this expedition he and his company were attached to a militia regiment commanded by one Colonel Clock. He returned again to Fort Plank, and his nine month tour being expired, he was discharged in December 1778—Afterward in the month of August 1779, in the same county and State he went as a draft, in the service of the U. States under the command of Colo. Burcham in the company of Captain Israel Veal and was stationed during the three months for which he was drafted, at West Point on the Hudson, where he was discharged in the month of November 1779, having served three months, from some period in the preceding August. His discharges have long since been lost. This applicant was born in the State of Rhode Island on the 22nd March 1760. He has a record of his age at his own house where he resides.

He came, an infant from Rhode Island to Dutchess County in the State of New York, which latter place was his residence when called into service. His residence for the last forty four years has been in the county of Montgomery, State of Virginia.

He received discharges but whether he received one of each tour of service or not he cannot now recollect. He cannot now recollect whether his discharges were signed by a Captain, Colonel or an officer of some other grade. He well remembers, however, to have received several of them which he thought would be of no value in future & permitted them to be lost or were cast away. He has no other evidence of his said services, but that accompanying this declaration.

He hereby relinquishes every claim whatever to a pension or annuity, except the present, and he declares that his name is not on the pension roll of any agency in any state. (Signed with his mark) Jesse Hall

Sworn to & subscribed the day & year aforesaid.

Reply dated September 8, 1936 to a letter of inquiry.

Reference is made to your request for the Revolutionary War record of Jesse Hall who applied for pension while residing in Montgomery County, Virginia.

The data furnished herein were obtained from papers on file in the pension claim, S.8666, based upon the military service of Jesse Hall.

He was born March 22, 1760 in Rhode Island. The names of his parents were not given.

While living in Dutchess County, New York, where he had moved from Rhode Island when an infant, he enlisted in February 1776, served nine months as private in Captain Nathan Pierce's company in Colonel Richmore's New York regiment and was in the battle of White Plains. He enlisted May 1, 1777, in Captain William Piece's (5) company in Colonel Morehouse's New York Regiment and was discharged in December 1777. He enlisted in March, 1778, in Captain Johnston's (6) company in Colonel Genzie's (Gonsies, Gonseys) Company New York regiment and was discharged in December 1778. He enlisted in August , 1779, in Captain Israel Veal's (7) company in Colonel Burchan's (8) York regiment and was discharged in November 1779.

He was allowed pension on his application executed January 7, 1833, at which time he was a resident of Montgomery County, Virginia, and he then stated he had lived there for the last forty-four years.

In 1832 one Asa Hall of Montgomery County, Virginia, stated that he had served in the Revolution with Jesse Hall but he did not state that they were related. There are no further data relative to the family of Jesse Hall.

End Notes—S.8666—Jesse Hall

1. Captain Nathan Pearce, Jr. raised a company from Dutchess County which was attached to the Third New York Continental Regiment commanded by Colonel Rudolphus Ritzema in 1776.
2. Alexander McDougall, Colonel of the First New York Continental Regiment was appointed brigadier general on August 9, 1776. He was appointed major general on October 20, 1777.
3. The Battle of White Plains, NY was fought on October 28, 1776.
4. Lieutenant-Colonel Andrew Morehouse in the Third Regiment of Dutchess County Militia Commanded by Colonel John Field.
5. Captain William Pierce was in the Third Dutchess County. Jesse also had served in Captain Joseph Dyckman's Company in the same regiment.
6. Jesse is mistaken about the officers' names. He may be referring to Captain Cornelius T. Jansen in Colonel Peter Gansevoort's Third Continental New Your Regiment. Jansen is often referred to as Johnson or Johnston. Gansevoort is misspelled as well. Most of the Third New York was stationed at Fort Schuyler (For Stanwix) in 1778. The other New York Continental Regiments were at or near Valley Forge, Pennsylvania and eventually marched to New Jersey and several of the regiments were in the Battle of Monmouth, New Jersey on June 28, 1778. From the muster rolls of the Third New York there were no levies attached to the Third New York in 1778.
7. Israel Vail (Veal) was a captain in Colonel James VanDenburgh's Fifth Regiment of Dutchess County Militia.
8. Benjamin Birsdall was the Lieutenant-Colonel of the Fifth Dutchess. From October 10, 1779 to November 23, 1779 a detachment of the Dutchess County Militia Regiments were out under Colonel Morris Graham of the First Dutchess.

Pension Application for Philip Herter, Harter, Herder, etc.

S.28760

Declaration in order to obtain the benefits of the act of Congress passed June 7, 1832

State of New York

Herkimer County SS

On this twelfth day of February in the year of our Lord, one thousand eight hundred and thirty four, personally appeared in open court, before the Judges of the Court of Common Pleas, now sitting Philip Harter a resident of the town of Herkimer In the County of Herkimer and State of New York, aged seventy two years on the twenty sixth days of January last past, who being first duly sworn according to law, doth on his oath make the following declaration in order to obtain the benefit of the act of Congress passed June 7, 1832.

That he entered the service of the United States under the following named officers and served as herein stated, but he this deponent belonged to a company of Militia commanded by Henry Harter (1), John Damuth was first lieutenant and Peter Weber was second Lieutenant and John Bellinger was Ensign in Col. Peter Bellingers Regiment and Genl Nicholas Herkimer's Brigade (2) –that deponent resided in the then town of German Flatts—Tryon County now Herkimer in the County of Herkimer, that the first duty deponent did was in the Spring of the year 1778. The Company was stationed at Fort Dayton in the said town of German Flatts on the Mohawk River. That the company was employed doing garrison duty in said Fort during the Summer, that deponent acted in a Military Capacity and was employed in said Fort the whole time except four days when he was sant [sent] with the rest of the company and with other troops & about five hundred under the Command of Genl Van Rensselaer (3) to guard boats loaded with provisions on their way to Fort Stanwix a distance of about thirty miles from Fort Dayton up the Mohawk River, that said duty was performed in a military capacity and under the direction of his officers, whom he understood had authority to compel said service & also to compel this deponent to do duty in said Fort, that deponent was compelled to do duty until very cold weather in the fall or winter, that he did not do duty the whole of said Spring and Summer as he was allowed to go out occasionally and did go out part of the time—that he was once compelled to go to Germantown (4) in the night a distance of five or six miles to bring in the bodies of several persons that had been killed and wounded of the Indians and tories, that the whole time that he was actually employed and above duty in said Fort as a soldier in said company and under said officers in the year 1778 was three months.

And this deponent further says, that the next year, being the year 1779, this deponent with other members of the company were again called out to do duty in said Fort. That the same officers still had charge of the company, that this deponent done duty in several garrisons as a soldier during said year four months, that he was out but very little that year, and then on scouts, or excursions against the enemy on many civil pursuits, that he done military duty for that length of time, by the command of his officers.

And this deponent further says, that he was a private during said time in said duty in said company that in the Spring of the year 1780 deponent's father and family and this deponent removed to the County of Columbia on the North River [Hudson] at a place called Germantown and remained there until the end of the war—that the above seven months service was the only military service (5) that this Deponent rendered, that this deponent did not make application before because he understood that he could not obtain pay for so short a period of service and that he has lately heard that others had obtained pay who did not perform service for any greater length of time.

And this deponent further says, that he was born in the present town of Herkimer in the County of Herkimer on the 26th day of January 1762. That a record of his age is in the family bible of his grandfather now in the possession of Thomas Shoemaker of the present town of German Flatts in the County of Herkimer, that this deponent resided at German Flatts now Herkimer when he entered the service, that he has resided in the present town of Herkimer, ever since the Revolutionary War and still resides there—that he entered the service under the supposition that he was compelled to do duty, that he was not enlisted or a substitute for any person, and may be called a volunteer--that there was a regiment of soldiers at said Fort part of the time, called the Jersey blues commanded by Col. Dayton after whom said Fort was named, but this was before deponent was compelled to do duty, then other officers at said Fort at different times, Col. Willett (7), Genl Van Rensselaer, Col. Gansvoort and other—that this Deponent was not engaged in any battle, and never received any written discharge from any person—that he does not know certainly of any person that is now alive by whom he can prove the above service—that he expects to prove his general character for truth and his reputation as a Revolutionary Soldier , by the Rev'd John P. Spinner and by Christopher Bellinger—and John Doxtater and others old habitants of said town.

Here hereby relinquishes every claim whatever to a pension or an annuity except for the present and he declares that his name is not on the Pension roll of any agency of any state.

(Signed) Philip Herter

Sworn to & Subscribed the day and year aforesaid in open court. H. Nelson, Clerk

The John P. Spinner a clergyman residing in the town of Herkimer in the Church of Herkimer, and Christopher Bellinger residing in the town of German Flatts in said County; hereby certify; that we are well acquainted with Philip Harter who has subscribed and sworn to the above declaration; that we believe him to be seventy two years of age; that he is reputed and believed, in the neighborhood where he resides, to have been a soldier of the Revolution (8) and we concur in that opinion.

(Signed) John P. Spinner V.D.M, Christopher Bellinger

Sworn & Subscribed the day and year aforesaid in open court. J.C. Nelson, Clerk.

End Notes—S.328760—Philip Herter

1. Henry Harter was appointed captain in 1776 in place of Captain Frederick Bellinger of the Fourth Company in Colonel Peter Bellinger's Fourth Regiment of Tryon County Militia who had been promoted to Lieutenant-Colonel of the regiment. Harter was commissioned on June 25, 1778 as captain as were the following officers. John Demuth as First Lieutenant (Second Lieutenant in Captain Bellinger's), Peter J. Weaver as Second Lieutenant (Ensign under Captain Bellinger) and John T. Bellinger as Ensign.
2. Nicholas Herkimer, Colonel of the First Regiment of Tryon County Militia was appointed Brigadier General of the Tryon County Militia Brigade on September 5, 1776. General Herkimer was wounded at the Battle of Oriskany on August 6, 1777 and later died from complications of the amputation of his leg.

3. Robert VanRensselaer was appointed Brigadier General of the Second Brigade of Albany County Militia on June 16, 1780. General VanRensselaer did guard the bateaus in July of 1780 not in 1778.
4. This German Town was in the Town of Schuyler, Herkimer County, New York.
5. Philip apparently did serve again as his name is listed as serving in Captain Hendrick Pulver's Company in Colonel Peter R. Livingston's Tenth Regiment of Albany County Militia.
6. Colonel Elias Dayton of the Third New Jersey Continental Regiment. Colonel Dayton's Regiment were the main builders of the fort before they were sent to Fort Schuyler (Fort Stanwix) to help in repairing this fort in 1776.
7. Lieutenant-Colonel Marinus Willett and Colonel Peter Gansevoort belonged to the Third New York Continental Regiment.
8. On Captain Harter's Muster Roll for 1779 Philip is listed as serving the following: June 6 days, July 8 days, August 14 days, September 2 days, October 5 days and November 3 days. FROM: Revolutionary War Rolls 1775-1783, Series M-246, Roll 72, folder 78, National Archives, Washington, D.C.

Pension Application for Reuben Hill

S.22831
B.L.Wt.30,625-160-55

[The copy is so poor for this pension that it can't be transcribed so only the letter written November 25, 1924 in response for information about this soldier will be put on this website. Ajberry]

I have to advise you that from the papers in the Revolutionary War pension claim, S.22831, it appears that Reuben Hill was born in 1765 at Goshen, Litchfield County, Connecticut.

While a resident of Little Hoosick, Rensselaer County, New York, he enlisted in the fall of 1780 and served six weeks as private in Captain Samuel Shaw's Company (1), Colonel VanRensalaer's (2)New York Regiment.

He enlisted August 1, 1781, as private in Captain Abraham Livingston's (3) Company, Colonel Marinus Willett's New York Regiment, was in a battle with the Indians at West Canada Creek (4), and was discharged December 1, 1781.

He enlisted November 1, 1782, a private in Captain Leonard's New York Company, and was discharged January 1, 1783.

He served six weeks in 1814 as wagon Master, was engaged in conveying baggage from Utica to Fort Niagara.

He was allowed pension on his application executed March 5, 1834, at which time he resided at Catlin, Tioga County, New York.

In May, 1855, he was a resident of Wauonda, Lake County, Illinois, and then stated that he was ninety years and five months of age.

There is no data on file relative to his family.

In another letter dated March 6, 1912, another piece of information was given.

The enlistment under Captain Leonard in 1782, he was stationed at Schenectady, two months.

End Notes—S.22831—Reuben Hill

1. Captain Samuel Shaw of Colonel Stephen J. Schuyler's Sixth Regiment of Albany County Militia.
2. Henry K. VanRensselaer was the Lieutenant-Colonel of Colonel Schuyler's Regiment.
3. Reuben served as a private in Captain Abraham Livingston's Company in Lieutenant-Colonel Commandant Marinus Willett's Regiment of New York State Levies. In 1785 he was paid the balance of his back pay -- £ 9..10..3. FROM: Revolutionary War Rolls 1775-1783, Series M-246, Roll 78, folder 173, National Archives, Washington, D.C.
4. The skirmish at West Canada Creek was fought on October 30, 1781.

Pension Application for Ezekiel Hubbard

R. 5315
Wife: Mary
Declaration under act July 4, 1836
State of New York
County of Clinton SS.

On this Fifth Day of February 1839 personally appeared before William Hedding one of the Judges of Clinton County Courts Mary Hubbard a resident of Chazy in said County aged Eighty two years who being first duly sworn according to law doth on her oath make the following declaration, in order to obtain the benefit of the provision made by the act of Congress passed July 4, 1836. That she is the widow of Ezekiel Hubbard who was a private in the army of the revolution and served as follows—

She believes he enlisted for one year or eighteen months after September 30, 1777, at Huntington Long Island N. York & was taken a prisoner during the period of his service and detained three months in the New York prison, when he was paroled & after remaining at Huntingon a short time he joined his regiment & was not at home for nearly one year. She thinks her husband served in the same company & Reg't with Henry Ostrander who was a private in Col. Dubois and Holmes (1) New York Regt & who was a pensioner under the act of 1818.—That her husband served five months & ten months with said Ostrander previous to her marriage in Capt. Rosecrantz Co.—Col. Holmes or Dubois' (2) NY Regt on examination of Ostrander's pension papers, she thinks her husband's affidavit will be found which will throw light on his services. She is confident her husband served in the New York Militia (3) & Levies previous to her marriage & that after the marriage he enlisted & joined the army & soon after he came to Huntington with a flag of truce & she went with him to New England—She is unable to give the names of his officers or to state the lengths of his service. She thinks he may have belonged to the companies raised in Huntington NY (Militia or Levies interlined)—

She further declares that her maiden name was Mary Guildersleeve & she was married to the said Ezekiel Hubbard at Huntington N.York by the Rev. Mr. Prime on the thirtieth day of September 1777.—She has no record of their marriage but one of the birth of her children which accompanies this declaration.

Her husband the aforesaid died on the twenty second day of February 1829 and she has remained a widow ever since that period, as will more fully appear by reference to the proof hereto annexed. (Signed with her mark) Mary Hubbard.

Sworn & subscribed to on the day a[nd] year first above written & I certify that deponent cannot write her name owing to infirmity. She cannot by reason of bodily infirmity attend court. She is quite feeble and confined to her house most of the time, this declaration was taken at her dwelling which is some twelve miles from the Court House. William Hedding—Judge of Clinton County courts.

Family Record (torn from Bible)
Births
Ezekiel Hubbard - Born June 24th 1755
Mary Hubbard - Born December 14, 1757
Olley Hubbard, Born July 30th, 1778
Charity Hubbard, Born August 14th, 1783
Elizabeth, Born September 2th, [sic] 1785
John, Born November 27, 1787
Eben, Born November 1789
Ebenezar, Born February 3th, 1792
Henry, Born September 20th, 1796
Joel S., Born October 1th, 1798

The age of Henry's Children
Jeremiah Born October 31th, 1819
Henry Born Feby 9, 1822
Isaac Born July 25, 1825
John Born Jany 15, 1829

The witnesses state that below the horizontal line the ages of Henry Hubbard's Children and the date of birth was written by another person (except the first Jeremiah, Isaac Aldridge, Justice.

Deaths
Elizabeth Deceased August 2, 1817
Eben Deceased September 1791
Ezekiel Hubbard died February 22nd 1827, aged 71 years 2 months and 28 days.

I do hereby certify that I saw Betsey Hubbard tear out this sheet out the family Bible of Ezekiel Hubbard and did annex it to the affidavits of Betsey Hubbards and Charity Domming this 22 Jany 1839. Isaac Aldridge [Agnt?]

Marriages

Page included but nothing recorded on the page.

Declaration of the children of Mary Hubbard to obtain a pension.
State of New York, County of Clinton SS.

On this fifteenth day of May 1846, before the Court of Common Pleas in & for said County held at the Court House in Plattsburg present William Hedding, Josiah T. Everest and Isaac H. Patcher Judges thereof, the same being a Court of Record, personally appeared in open Court Henry Hubbard and resident of Chazy in said County aged forty nine years who being first duly sworn according to law, doth on his oath make the following declaration in order to obtain the benefit of the provisions made by the acts of Congress passed July 4, 1836 & July 7, 1838, and other acts of Congress relative to pensions to the widows & children. That his Father Ezekiel Hubbard was as he has been informed and believes a private in the army of the revolution and enlisted at Huntington Long Island & served and was imprisoned about eighteen months. (4) His service commenced in 1775 and he was a prisoner three months in the New York prison in 1777 and after his release he joined his regiment and served a year. Declarant believes his father served a tour of five and one of ten months in the New York Militia, and has heard him say that he served with Henry Ostrander (5) and mention the names of Col. Holmes & Dubois & Capt. Rosekrans, and declarant supposes his said father served under those officers. He further declares that his said Father was as he has been informed and believes married to Mary Guildersleeve at Huntington aforesaid, by the Rev. Mr. Prime on the thirtieth day of September 1777 and that there is no record of said marriage but one of the birth of the children of said marriage. He further states that the said Ezekiel Hubbard died at Beekmantown aforesaid on the twenty second day of February 1827, leaving a widow whose name was Mary Hubbard who in the year 1839 applied for a pension, but failed to procure sufficient evidence of her said husband's services. He further declares that the said Mary Hubbard died at Beekmantown aforesaid on the eighteenth day of September eighteen hundred and forty three leaving the following children her surviving viz.

1. John Hubbard born Nov. 27 1787, residence Elizabethtown NY
2. Ebenezer Hubbard born Feby 3, 1792, residence Port Kent NY
3. Joel S. Hubbard born Oct 1, 1798, residence Chazy NY
4. Henry Hubbard. Born Sept. 20, 1796, residence Chazy NY
5. Olly Hubbard born July 30, 1778 residence Plattsburg NY wife of Jacob Green same place.
6. Charity Hubbard born August 14, 1783, resident Beekmantown widow of Henry Sominy deceased—

And that said children are the only surviving children and heirs at law of the said Mary Hubbard and are all of the age of twenty one years & upwards. (Signed) Henry Hubbard.

Sworn and subscribed to in open court on the day and year first above written and I certify that Deponent is a credible person. Charles H. Jones, Clerk

End Notes—R.5315—Ezekiel Hubbard

1. Ezekiel enlisted as a private on August 9, 1775 in Captain James Rosekrans' Company (recruited from Dutchess County, North Company) in Colonel James Homes' Fourth Continental Regiment. The muster roll was dated Still Water Oct 17, 1775. FROM: Revolutionary War Rolls, 1775-1783, Series M-246, Roll 70, folder 50, National Archives, Washington, D.C.
2. On June 21, 1776, Lewis Dubois was appointed Colonel of a Continental Regiment which was un-numbered. So far muster rolls for this regiment have not been found. On November 21, 1776, Colonel DuBois was appointed Colonel of the Fifth New York Continental Regiment. James Rosekrans was appointed a captain of this regiment on November 21, 1776. On examining the muster rolls for this company and regiment—Hubbard's name was not found on them.
3. There is an enlistment for an Ezekiel Hubbard as a private in Captain Noah Wheeler's Company in Colonel Rosewell Hopkin's Sixth Regiment of Dutchess County Militia.
4. Nothing has been found about his imprisonment. There were several battles and skirmishes in and around New York City in 1776 and 1777 and casualty lists, especially for enlisted men, are few at best.
5. Henry Ostrander served in Captain Rosekran's Company in Colonel Holmes Regiment in 1775.

Pension Application for Henry Hubbard

S.22848
State of New York
Suffolk County SS.

On this Twenty seventh day of May in the year 1834, personally appeared in open Court, before the Judges of the Court of common Pleas in and for the County of Suffolk aforesaid, now sitting, Henry Hubbard, a resident of the Town of Southampton, in said County and State, aged Eighty one years, who being first duly sworn according to law, doth, on his oath, make the following declaration, in order to obtain the benefit of the act of Congress passed June 7, 1832. That he entered the service of the United States under the following named officers, and served as herein stated: Joshua Rogers, (1) Captain—William Clark, First Lieutenant, ______ Drake, (2) Colonel.

That he entered the service on or about the first day of April in the year 1776 in the company commanded by Captain Joshua Rogers, for the Term of six months, and was duly discharged from the same on or about the first day of October then next ensuing—That at the time he entered the said service he was residing at Middle Island, so called, in the Town of Brookhaven, in said County of Suffolk—That he enlisted there as a volunteer soldier—That soon after his enlistment he marched with said Company on foot to Huntington in said County, a distance of upwards of twenty miles, and thence embarked on board a Sloop for the City of New York—That until the battle upon Long Island, near Brooklyn; he was engaged on duty in and near the City at Greenwich in making fortifications or Forts—That he was engaged in the battle upon Long Island, near Brooklyn, in the month of August 1776—Saw General Washington (3) and Sullivan (4) there—assisted in collecting the wood for the fires made on the evening of the defeat of the Army—and was one of the soldiers that retreated by order of General Washington off the Island to the City of New York and thence into the State of New Jersey, across the Hudson or North River—

That after they landed in New Jersey they marched up the Hudson several miles and the company to which he was attached again crossed the river into the State of New York—That after regularly serving out the term of his enlistment in said Company he was duly discharged by Captain Rogers in West Chester, in the State of New York aforesaid. That on his return home he passed through the western part of the State of Connecticut to New Haven—thence across the Long Island Sound aforesaid to Brook Haven, his home—That it was late in the fall of the year 1776, (5) and cold, when he crossed the sound.—

That he was born in Satanket Town, Suffolk County, New York in the year 1753. The record of his age is not in his possession and believes it to be destroyed. Since the Revolution he has lived in Satanket and in the Town of Southampton, in Suffolk County aforesaid and that he now resides in Southampton—That he has no documentary evidence in his possession and that he knows of no person living who can testify to the said service.

That he is acquainted with the Reverend Nathaniel Peter Fanning, Deacon Joseph Penny and the Reverend William Benjamin who can testify to my character for veracity, and their belief of my services as a soldier of the Revolution—

I hereby relinquish every claim whatever to a pension or annuity except the present and declare that my name is not on the pension roll of the agency of any state—

Sworn to and subscribed the day and year aforesaid. (Signed) Henry Hubbard

Attest: Joseph R. Huntting, Clk

End Notes—S.22848—Henry Hubbard

1. Joshua Rogers was appointed First Lieutenant on December 12, 1775 in Captain Johannes Titus' Second Company in Colonel William Floyd's First Regiment of Suffolk County Militia. On April 5, 1776 regimental return Rogers is listed as Captain, unfortunately the lieutenants were not mentioned.
2. There were no Drake's serving as Colonel or Lieutenant-Cornel in the First Suffolk. Joseph Drake and Samuel Drake had served as Colonels

in the Westchester County Militia. Gilbert Drake had served as Lieutenant-Colonel in the Third Regiment of Westchester County Militia. These regiments were sent to New York City to reinforce the American troops already there. It is likely that the Suffolk, Orange County, Ulster and Westchester Counties Militia served together from time to time during 1776.

3. George Washington was appointed June 15, 1775 as general and commander-in-chief of all the forces to be raised.
4. John Sullivan was appointed Major General on August 9, 1776. Sullivan was captured on August 27, 1776 in the Battle of Long Island, N.Y. He was exchanged in December of 1776 for a prisoner captured by American troops.
5. New York City and the surrounding area was occupied by British forces until November of 1783. It is interesting on that note that Henry went home after this service to Long Island and gives no further military service after 1776.

Pension Application for John Hubbard

S.45399
Dutchess County
State of New York SS.

On this 30th day of April 1818 came before me the subscriber one of the Judges of the Court of Common Pleas in & for the County of Dutchess in the State of New York, John Hubbard by me well known aged 87 years, resident of the Town of North east in the County aforesaid, who being by me first duly sworn according to law—doth on his oath make the following declaration in order to obtain the provision made by the late act of Congress entitled "an act to provide for certain persons engaged in the land and naval service of the United States, in the revolutionary war." That the said John Hubbard enlisted in this said Town aforesaid in the company commanded by Capt. Piercy (1) of the 4th Regt commanded by Col. Livingston; that he enlisted as aforesaid in the spring season of the same year in which Genl Burgoyne (2) & army were captured—that he was engaged and active against the enemy at that capture—and at the capture of Gen'l Cornwallis & Army at York[town]—also in a variety of other less important engagements and continued to serve in the American Army under different officers from the time of his enlistment until after peace took place between England & America - that he was then in the company of Capt. Dunscomb (3) in the 2nd Regt commanded by Col. Cortland (4)—stationed west of Newburgh, in the State of New Jersey, as he believes—and formed at that time part of the main army under the command of Gen'l Washington—that he received an honourable discharge & drew bounty land which his necessities soon compelled him to sell at which time he also parted with his discharge—that he is now in reduced circumstances, and stands in need of the assistance of his country for support, land that he has no other evidence now in his power of his said services. Tyler Dibblee, one of the Judges of the Court of Common Pleas in & for the County of Dutchess.

At a Court of Common Pleas held at the Court House in the Village of Poughkeepsie on Monday the ninth day of October one thousand eight hundred and twenty.

Present the Hon. James Emett, First Judge

Abraham D. Van Wyck, Thomas Sweet, Enos Hopkins, Esquires, Judges.

Dutchess County SS. Be it remembered that on the ninth day of October in the year one thousand eight hundred and twenty personally appeared in the Court of Common Pleas in open Court the said Court being a Court of record for the county of Dutchess in the State of New York John Hubbard 2nd aged about ninety one years resident in the Town of North East in the said County of Dutchess, who being first duly sworn according to law doth on his oath declare that he served in the revolutionary as follows: That about the year one thousand seven hundred and seventy seven at North East, he enlisted under Lieutenant VanBenschoten's (5) in a company commanded by Captain Pearce in Colonel Henry B. Livingston's Regiment of the New York Line of the Army of the revolution for during the war, that he served therein as a private soldier until the new arrangement of the New York line in 1781, when he was placed in the second regiment commanded by Colonel VanCortlandt, and served in said regiment under several captains until he was discharged on disbanding the Army at the close of the War, and that his original declaration is dated the 20th day of April one thousand eight hundred and eighteen and that his pension certificate is No. 2145—

And I do solemnly swear that I was a resident citizen of the United States on the 10th day of March 1818 and that I have not since that time by gift, sale, or in any manner disposed of my property or any part thereof with intent thereby so to diminish it as to bring myself within the provisions of an act of Congress entitled "An Act to provide for certain persons engaged in the land & naval service of the United States in the Revolutionary War, passed on the 18th day of March one thousand eight hundred and eighteen and that I have not, nor has any person in trust, for me any property or securities, contracts or debts due to me nor have I any income other than what is contained in the schedule hereto annexed and by me subscribed to wit.

Real estate, I have none—Personal estate, wearing apparel and bedding excepted I have none—

The deponents family consists of himself and his wife aged rising eighty years, that he is a shoemaker by trade, but from his age is unable to work—That he & his wife have for many years been supported by the Town of North East aforesaid as paupers thereof. (Signed) John Hubbard.

Sworn in open Court this 9th day of October 1820. John Johnston Clerk

End Notes—S.45399—John Hubbard

1. Captain Jonathan Pearce (Piercy, Pearse, etc.) of the Third Company in Colonel Henry B. Livingston's Fourth New York Continental Regiment. John enlisted as a private for "during War" on May 21, 1777. He deserted on April 1, 1780 and returned tothe regiment by July of 1780. FROM: Revolutionary War Rolls 1775-1783, Series M-246, Rolls 70 and 71, National Archives, Washington, D.C.
2. British General John Burgoyne fought with the American Army under Major General Horatio Gates on September 19 and October 7, 1777. General Burgoyne surrendered his army on October 17, 1777.
3. Edward Dunscomb was appointed a First Lieutenant on November 21, 1776, Captain-Lieutenant on April 23, 1778 and Captain on April 11, 1780 all in the Fourth New York Continental Regiment. When the New York Regiments were consolidated on January 1, 1781 they were not kept in the service. There were too many officers for the number of enlisted men that were still in the service. The term used for this type of downgrade is "deranged". Officers were "arranged" into regiments and companies and were discharged when they became "supernumary" or "degranged".
4. Colonel Philip VanCortlandt of the Second New York Continental Regiment. John served in 1781 in Captain Theodosius Fowler's Company. FROM: Revolutionary War Rolls 1775-1783, Series M-246, Rolls 67 and 24, National Archives, Washington, D.C. John served in this company and regiment during the Yorktown, Virginia, Campaign from September 28 to October 19, 1781.
5. Peter VanBenschoten was appointed Second Lieutenant on November 21, 1776 and was appointed First Lieutenant on November 9, 1777, all in the Fourth New York Continental Regiment.

Pension Application for George Kelly

W.20303 (Widow) Elizabeth was granted $66.00 per annum.
State of New York
Montgomery County SS

On this tenth day of September in the year one thousand eight hundred and thirty eight personally appeared before the undersigned a Judge of Montgomery County Court of Common Pleas, John Kelly who being duly sworn doth depose and swear that he has made diligent search to find a record of the marriage of his father George Kelly (Now deceased,) and his mother Elizabeth Kelly now the widow of the said George Kelly—and that he has been unable to find any record whatever of anything relating to the said marriage—Deponent further swears that in searching the records of the church where such records are usually made he found the records in the church book containing records of marriages for the years 1780 & 1781 missing and that the reason of his being unable to find a family record is because his father being unable ever to write did never make one. That from tradition derived from both his parents he is well satisfied that the marriage of his parents took place on the sixth day of

November seventeen hundred and eighty being always informed that they were married ten months saving eight days before he was born, and that he was born on the fourteenth day of September Seventeen hundred and Eighty one, that his father the said George Kelly died on the ninth day of December eighteen hundred and twenty nine and further this deponent says not. (Signed John Kelly)

Sworn to and subscribed this 10th day of September 1838 before D. F. Sacia, Judge of Montgomery County Courts.

State of New York
Montgomery County SS

On this 11th day of September in the year of our Lord one thousand Eight hundred and thirty eight personally appeared before the undersigned a Judge of the Court of Common Pleas in and for the said County of Montgomery (being a court of record) Elizabeth Kelly a resident of the town of Palatine in the County of Montgomery and State of new York aged seventy eight years who being first duly sworn according to law doth on her oath make the following declaration in order to obtain the benefit of the provision made by the act of Congress passed July 4th 1836. That she is the widow of George Kelly who was a private soldier in the Militia Service, and a Marine or Batteau-man in the Boat Service of the United States during the Revolutionary War. That from the evidence she has been able to procure she has reason to believe that her husband the said George Kelly then a resident of the town of Palatine aforesaid entered the service of the United States as a private soldier in the year 1775 in the company of Captain Andrew Dillenbach (1) in Colonel Jacob Klock's Regiment and General Nicholas Herkimer's Brigade. That he was drafted and served three months at Ticonderoga under Captain Henry Diefendorf (2) in Colonel Ebenezer Cox Regiment. That he served as a Marine in Captain William Peter's (3) Company of Batteau-men in the year 1778 nine months, and that he served nine months in each of the succeeding years viz 1779 and 1780—in the same capacity vis a Batteauman in the Company of Captain Samuel Gray, and in the two succeeding years vis 1781 and 1782 he again did his share of militia duty as a private in Captain Sevrenus Cook's Company and on the evidence herewith accompanying she rests her claim.

She further declares that she was married to the said George Kelly on the sixth day of November in the year seventeen hundred and eighty that her husband the aforesaid George Kelly died on the ninth day of December one thousand eight hundred and twenty nine and that she has remained a widow ever since that period as will more fully appear by reference to the proof hereto annexed. (Signed with her mark) Elizabeth Kelly

Subscribed & Sworn the day & year above written before me. D. F. Sacia, Judge of Montgomery County Court.
Letter of reply to an inquiry.

Reference is made to your letter in which you request information in regard to Elisabeth Kelly, a pensioner in 1840 in Montgomery County, New York, then aged eighty years.

The data which follow were obtained from papers on file in pension claim, W. 20303, based on the service of George Kelly in the War of the Revolution.

The date and place of birth of George Kelly were not given, nor were the names of his parents stated.

While a resident of Palatine, Montgomery County, New York, George Kelly, served from the spring of 1775, as a private at various times in Captains Andrew Dillenbach's Henry Diefendorf's Severines Cook's companies, Colonel Jacob Klock's and Ebenezer Cox's New York Regiments, until the spring of 1778, when he entered the boat service and served nine months as bateau man under Captain William Peters, nine months in 1779 and nine months 1780 under Captain Samuel Gray, during this service, he was transporting provisions and supplies from Schenectady to Fort Stanwix, and in 1781 and 1782, he continued to serve at various times in Captain Severines Cook's company, part of the time was stationed at Fort Keyser in Stone Arabia.

George Kelly married November 22, 1780 in Palatine, New York, Elizabeth, daughter of Francis Reno, Ranno or Renno. The date and place of her birth was not given, nor was the name of her mother stated.

The widow, Elizabeth Kelly, was allowed pension on her application executed September 4, 1838, at which time she was aged seventy-eight years, and living in Palatine New York.

The papers on file in this claim contain no further discernable data in regard to family.

End Notes—George Kelly—W.20303

1. Captain Andrew Dillenbach of Colonel Jacob Klock's Second Regiment of Tryon County Militia. Captain Dillenbach was killed on August 6, 1777 at the Battle of Oriskany and First Lieutenant Severinus Klock was appointed Captain of this Company.
2. Henry Dieffendorf Captain of the Fifth Company in Colonel Ebenezer Cox's First Regiment of Tryon County Militia. A detachment was drafted from the four Tryon County Militia Regiments in January of 1777 and were sent under Colonel Cox to Fort Ticonderoga.
3. Captain William Peters and Samuel Gray commanded companies of Bateaumen in the Quartermaster Department.

Pension Application for Michael J. [or I.] Keyser (Cayser, Kaiser, Syser)

R.5900
State of Michigan
County of Lenawee SS

In the year of our Lord one thousand eight hundred and forty, personally appeared me William H. Horg, [or Haig?] an associate judge of

Circuit Court in and for said County of Lenawee at my office in the Village of Tecumseh in said county Michael Keyser a resident of Tecumseh aforesaid aged seventy-nine years and six months, who being first duly sworn according to law doth on his oath, make the following declaration in order to obtain the benefit of the act of Congress passed June seventh in the year of our Lord one thousand eight hundred and thirty two.

That he entered the service of the United States under the following named officers, and served as herein stated: viz:

That in the years 1776, 1777 and 1778 he served in a company of militia commanded by Captain John Keyser (1) except four months which he served under Captain Michael Moyer, a nine months officer in the year 1776, as a substitute for his brother John Keyser Junior who was at that time in poor health and took his place which was nearer home and also one month in the year 1777 when he was lent to a picket fort under the command of Captain Henry Hoover, (2) all said companies being the Regiment Commanded by Colonel Peter Bellinger, in the County of Tryon (now Herkimer) in the colony (now state) of New York.

That he entered into the service on or about the first day of May 1776 and that he remained in the service until on or about the twentieth day of March 1778, (3) at which time last mentioned he was taken prisoner by the common enemy called the Tories and Indians, and was taken by them to Canada where he was kept a prisoner of war until the close of the Revolutionary War in the fall of the year 1782 quite late.

That while he was in the service he had often times to go on scouting parties, was often out one day and sometimes longer, that he and his companions were often put on duty at different posts, to keep a look out and to give notice when they discovered the enemy. That he was in the employ at different times in the year 1776 & 1777. That he was warned to serve as a militia man that during all the time he served as a private under the command of the said Captains; that he bring Situate on the frontier. The service was on scouting parties, building picket forts, and defending the settlers and their houses and property.

That all the service which he performed was in the said county of Tryon; that he was not engaged in any regular engagement, that embodied corps with which he served was called into service as he understood by Colonel Peter Bellinger, that in the year 1777 he assisted in building two log houses and picket forts at the house of Melchert Ocks (4) in the said County of Tryon for the purpose of defending the soldiers & people and in the year 1778 he assisted in building a picket fort around the house of Henry Remensnyder (5) for a place of retreat and defence.

That several times they were driven from their houses & shelters by the enemy and took shelter in a stone mill at Little Falls on the Mohawk River; that at the time he was taken prisoner the whole town was [?] by the enemy and that many were taken prisoners among whom were Captain John Keyser, John Keyser Junior, Henry Clack, & Henry Shaver, that for the whole time

during which the service was performed by him and during his imprisonment, he was not employed in any civil pursuit [rest of line cut off] said county of Tryon in Stonerobby in December of the year 1760 where he resided with his father until he entered the service. That his Father then had a record of his age which he had kept in the family Bible, that said Bible was burned together with the house of his Father in the time of the war and that since that time he has not had any documentary evidence of his age on day of birth and cannot speak positive as to the day of his birth. That he resided in said County of Tryon after returning from Canada, after the war until in the month of February AD 1813 when he removed to the Town of LeMay in the County of Jefferson in the State of New York, where he resided until the fifth day of July AD 1839 when he removed to the town of Techumseh in the said County of Lenawee where he now resides with his son Henry Keyser: he hereby relinquishes every claim whatever to a pension or annuity except the present and declares that his name is not on the pension roll of the agency of any state.
(Signed) M. Keyser

Sworn and Subscribed before me the day and year aforesaid.
Wm. H. Horg, Associate Judge Lenawee County

Interrogatories to be answered by Michael Keyser, claimant for a pension.

1. Where and in what year were you born? *I was born at Stonerobby* [Stone Arabia] *in the county of Tryon (now Herkimer* [Montgomery]*) in the colony (now state of New York).*
2. Have you any records of your age? *I have not. My father kept a record of my age in the family Bible which was burned in the time of the Revolutionary War And since that time I have not kept any record.*
3. Where were you living when called into service; where have you lived since the revolutionary war? And where do you now live? *I lived at the Stonerobby in the then County of Tryon when I was called into service where resided until February AD 1813 where I removed to the town of LeRoy in the County of Jefferson where resided until the 5th day of July AD 1839 when I removed to this place where Henry resides.*
4. How were you called into service; were you draughted, did you volunteer or were you a substitute and if a substitute form whom? *I was draughted into service and served as a substitute for John Keyser Junior for four months during the time of my service.*
5. State the names of some of the Regular officers who were with & troops where you served such continental & militia regiments as you can recollect, and the general circumstances of your service. *I recollect Colonel Peter Bellinger Colonel of*

the regiment in which I served. John Keyser Captain of the company which I served most of the time, Captain Michael Moyer (6) and Captain Henry Hoover. Do not recollect any other regiments, my services were mostly on scouting parties as a [?] building picket forts and defending the neighbourhood and town.

6. Did you every receive a discharge from the service? *I never did.*
7. State the name of persons to whom you are known in the your present neighbourhood, and who can testify as to your character for veracity and their belief of your services as a soldier of the Revolution. *I recollect and am acquainted with many in Jefferson County & I am here acquainted with Elias Scofield, Elnathan [Scofigld?], Thomas Goodrich & Ansel Winslow & in Jefferson County in the State of New York, there is William Father, Peter Wooliver, Henry Ritter, & Elisha Scofield.*

(Signed) M. Keyser

Sworn & subscribed before me this thirtieth day of June AD 1840. William Hoig [Haig?]

State of Michigan
County of Lenawee SS

Personally appeared before me the undersigned an associate Judge in & for the circuit court in said County. Michael Keyser, who being duly sworn, deposeth & saith that by reason of old age, and the consequent loss of memory he cannot swear positively as to the precise length of his services but that according to the best of his recollection, he served not less than the periods mentioned below and in the following grades. For one year & ten months & twenty days I served as a militia man was on scouting parties and some times as Indian spie: for that I had seven months was a prisoner of war in Canada where I was treated as such, and for such services I claim a pension.

(Signed) M. Keyser

Sworn & subscribed before me this thirtieth day of June AD 1840. Wm. H. Hoeg, Associate Judge Lenawee County

End Notes—R.5900—Michael Keysor

1. On the muster rolls that exist for Captain John Keyser's Company, Michael or John Keyser Jr. are not on them. Michael is listed as a Corporal in Captain Severinus Klock's Company in Colonel Jacob Klock's Second Regiment of Tryon County Militia. He was paid July 25, 1785 for a single certificate number 18838 £ 5..1..8. FROM: Revolutionary War Rolls 1775-1783, Series M-246, Roll 75, folder 121, National Archives, Washington D.C. Captain Klock was not appointed Captain until 1778 as Andrew

Dillenbach had been captain of the company until he was killed at the Battle of Oriskany on August 6, 1777.

2. Henry Huber (Hoever, Hoover) served as a captain in Colonel Peter Bellinger's Fourth Regiment of Tryon County Militia. Captain Huber had been taken prisoner at the Battle of Oriskany and he was exchanged for a British prisoner held by the Americans in 1778. It was probably a detachment from both regiments and Captain Huber commanded the detachment.
3. Michael was taken prisoner on March 15, 1780. Father and sons eventually enlisted into the British service. Michael and John Keyser Jr. enlisted on April 3, 1780 as a private in the First Battalion of the King's Royal Regiment of New York which was commanded by Sir John Johnson. They served in Captain Patrick Daly's Company and served until the regiment was disbanded. In 1784 they were living in Royal Township No. 2, which is Cornwall, Canada. John Keyser, Sr., did not enlist until May 10, 1781 as a private in the Second Battalion of the King's Royal Regiment of New York. John Sr., also served until the regiment was disbanded. Obviously they were not prisoners of war the entire time while in Canada. FROM: MG21: Non-commissioned officers, drummers, & private men 1KRRNY. Since formation, Point Clair 17th May 1781. These are lists of names with enlistments etc. There are many patriot soldiers who had been taken prisoner or deserted on this roll.
   FROM: MG 21: Roll of men enlisted for 2 KRRNY Point Clair 17th May 1781. Both are found in Governor Frederick Haldiman's Papers. (Haldiman was the Governor of Canada.) Theyare on microfilm and are full of information of the Schoharie and Mohawk Valleys during the War of Independence.

Pension Application for John Keader (Cater, Kidder)

W.26,949 (Widow: Elizabeth)
B.L.Wt. 7350-100, issued 1790-no papers
B.L.Wt.127-60-55
Rev. War and War of 1812
[On one of the documents it notes that he was a drummer and died April 12, 1857 and aged 106 years.]
State of New York
County of Saratoga SS.

On this 27th day of August 1860, personally appeared before me a Justice of the Peace within and for the county and state aforesaid Elisabeth Keader or Cater, aged about seventy four years a resident of Saratoga Springs, Saratoga County, N.York, who being duly sworn according to law, declares she is the widow of John Kidder or Cater, deceased, who was a Drummer in the Revolutionary War and also in the company commanded by Captain Nellis, Colonel Simon, Lieut. Hary Wendell, Hugh Little, Sargeant in the Regiment of [blank] in the war with Great Britain declared by the United States on the 18th day of June 1812. The her said husband enlisted at Schenectady, State of New

York in 1812 for the term of the war and continued in actual service for the term of the war and was honorably discharged at Albany was at Albany and Greenbush in the service in 1812.

She further states that she was married to the said John Keador or Cater in Schoharie NY on the 31st day of March AD 1800 by one Martin Seelye a Justice of the Peace and that her name before her said marriage was Elizabeth Garner. The her said husband died at Milton Saratoga Co. NYork on the 12th day of April 1857 and that she is now a widow.

She makes this declaration for the purpose of obtaining the bounty land to which she may be entitled under the "Act approved March 3, 1855", and she further declares that she has not received or applied for bounty land under this or any other Act of Congress, but receives a pension of eight dollars a month as the widow of said John Keader or Cater under Act of 1853. (Signed with her mark) Elizabeth Keader or Cater.

Subscribed & Sworn to before me this 27th day of August 1860. Wm. C. Barrett, Justice of the Peace. Witness Andrew Mc.Iwain.

State of New York
County of Schenectady SS.

On the Twenty first day of April 1818, before me the subscriber, one of the Judges of the Court of Common Pleas in and for the County of Schenectady, personally appears John Cater otherwise called John Keader, aged about Fifty two years resident in the City of Schenectady in the State aforesaid, who being by me first duly sworn, according to law, doth on his oath make the following declaration, in order to obtain the provision made by the late law of Congress entitled "an act to provide for certain persons engaged in the land and naval service of the United States in the revolutionary War".

That he the said John Cater enlisted at Stone Arabia in the State of New York he thinks sometime in the fall of the year 1778, in the company commanded by Captain Sackett (1) in the Regiment of the New York State line commanded by Colonel Weisenfels; that he was a drummer, and continued to serve in the said corps, or in the service of the united States until about the eighth day of June in the year 1783 when he was discharged from service at Newborough Huts in the State of New York, that he was in the siege of Yorktown (2) at the surrender of Cornwallis, that he is in reduced circumstances, & stands in need of assistance from his country for support; and that he has no other evidence now in his power of his said services except that contained in the affidavits herewith. (Signed with his mark) John Cater.

Sworn to & declared before me the day & year aforesaid. John Yates
[On his schedule of property he lists no real estate, no personal property, no income, no occupation. Under family he lists himself age 57, Elizabeth wife William Son apprentice 20, Isaias son Onondaga 18, Andrew son 16, John son 14, Henry son 12, Lucas son 8, James son 5, Jacob son 4.]

State of New York

County of Montgomery SS.

On this 17th day of April 1855 before me the undersigned a Justice of the Peace duly authorized by law to administer oaths within and for the County and State aforesaid personally appeared John Cater alias John Keader, aged 104 years a resident of Amsterdam in said County and State, who made oath in due form of law that he is the identical John Cater alias John Keader to whom under the provisions of the act of March 18th 1818 a pension of ninety six dollars per annum has been allowed for his services as a drummer of the Revolutionary War.

He further states that his pension certificate under the aforesaid act of March 18th 1818 is numbered 1653, and bears date of the 30th day of June 1818, being signed by J.C. Calhoun. That the same is made payable in semi annual instalments of forty eight dollars each due on the 4th of March and 4th of September in each year & that the said instalments are drawn & paid at the United States Pension Office in the City of Albany.

He makes this declaration for the purpose of obtaining the bounty land to which he may be entitled under the act of March 3d 1818 never having received or known himself entitled to receive any Bounty Land & never having made any application for bounty land under any previous act of Congress.

The evidence of his identity & proof of service he respectfully refers to the proofs heretofore adduced now on file in the Pension Office and upon which his annuity was granted as aforesaid and to the accompanying affidavits.

And he appoints as his attorney for the within specified purpose and to procure the warrant to which he may be deemed entitled Gerry W. Hazelton of Amsterdam Montgomery County State of New York.

This deponent further saith he does not sign his name for want of Education but makes his mark instead. (Signed with his mark) John Carter.

Attest. Nathaniel Reese, Caroline Cater.

Sworn to subscribed &acknowledge before me the day and year first above written and I hereby certify that I know the aforesaid John Cater alias John Keader, to be the identical person he alleges himself to be a pensioner of the United States and that I am not interested in his claim as agent attorney or otherwise. Joseph French Justice of the Peace.

End Notes—W.26949—John Keader

1. John is listed as first mustered June of 1779 as a drummer in Captain Samuel Sacket's Company which was the First Company in Lieutenant Colonel Commandant Frederick Weisenfel's Fourth New York Continental Regiment for during war. FROM: Revolutionary War Rolls 1775-1783, Series M-246, roll 71, folder 56, National Archives, Washington, D.C.

   On January 1, 1781 the Second, Fourth, and Fifth New York Continental Regiments were consolidated into one regiment. Colonel Philip VanCortlandt remained the Colonel of the Second New York Continental Regiment. Captain Israel Smith of the old Fourth New York along with others that still had time left on their enlistments were transferred to the Second New York. John went on and served as a drummer in Captain Smith's Company. FROM: Revolutionary War Rolls 1775-1783, Series M-246, Roll 69, folder 32, National Archives, Washington, D.C.

2. The Yorktown, Va. Campaign was from September 28 to October 19, 1781. John doesn't mention it but the Fourth New York served in the Sullivan-Clinton Iroquois Campaign in 1779.

Pension Application for Daniel Kittle

W. 21528 (Widow: Sarah)
State of New York
Albany County SS.

On this eighteenth day of February 1837 personally appeared before Robert J. Hilton one of the Judges of the Court of Common Pleas in and for the County of Albany Sarah Kittle a resident of the City of Albany in the county of Albany and State of New York, aged ninety five years, who being first duly sworn according to law, doth on her oath, make the following declaration, in order to obtain the benefit of the provision made by the act of Congress, passed July 4, 1836; that she is the widow of Daniel Kittle deceased who was a private in the army of the revolution as particularly set forth in the affidavits hereunto annexed.

She further declares that she was married to the said Daniel as will appear by certificate annexed on the ninth day of July (1761), in the year seventeen hundred and sixty one; that her husband, the aforesaid Daniel Kittle died in the month of April 1814 and that she has remained a widow ever since that period, as will more fully appear by reference to the proof hereunto annexed. That she is unable to write her name & that she makes her mark. (Signed with her mark) Sarah Kittle

Sworn to and subscribed on the day and year above written, before me by making her mark she being unable to write. R. J. Hilton. Judge Albany County Courts Counsellor

Supplemental Declaration or affidavit.
County of Albany SS.

The above Declarant Sarah Kittle being further duly sworn and examined, doth depose and say, that her late husband, the said Daniel Kittle served during the war of the revolution according to the best of the recollection, knowledge, and belief of this Declarant as follows to wit: That the said Daniel was, during said War, a private in a company of Militia (1) of the state of New York in a regiment belonging to the County of Schenectady that she does not recollect the names of any of the officers of the company or regiment—That owing to her great age & consequent defect of memory she has forgotten them—This Declarant remembers that her said husband was called into the service & went on an expedition to Oriskany (2), under Genl Herkimer (3) but she does not recollect the year in which he was so called out—She also remembers that her said Husband was called out on several other expeditions or tours of duty, as a private in said company, during the revolutionary War, but is unable to state any particulars respecting his said services. (Signed with her mark) Sarah Kittle

Sworn & subscribed (by making her mark) this 18th day of February 1837 before me. R. Hilton, Albany County Courts Counsellor.

City of Schenectada in said County of Schenectada, being aged seventy nine years and upwards, being duly sworn and examined doth depose and say that he was well acquainted with Daniel Kittle, the same person referred to and described in the annexed documents during the life time of said Daniel, that his acquaintance with said Daniel commenced at least seventy years ago, or as long as this deponent can remember anything—that said Daniel at the commencement of the war of the revolution was enrolled as private in one of the said City [forts?]—at this fort this deponent & said Daniel Kittle performed garrison duty, and engaged in scouting for the term of about ten days, that at the expiration of said ten days, said Daniel and this deponent marched with their detachment to Fort Plain, where they performed the like duty and service for the term of seven or eight days—from thence they marched to Stone Arabia, where they performed garrison & scout duty with the troops there stationed for the term of one month when this deponent & said Daniel Kittle came off together to Schenectada. (Signed) John Corl

Sworn this 20th day of Feby 1837, before me. J.D. Harman. Justice of the Peace.

Schenectada County SS.

Christopher Ward of said city of Schenectada in said county, aged seventy-nine years & upwards, being duly sworn and examined doth depose and say, that he was during the lifetime of the aforesaid Daniel Kittle referred to in the preceding affidavits, well acquainted with said Daniel Kittle, that said Daniel Kittle and this deponent were both members of the regiment of militia commanded by Colonel Abraham Wemple during the war of the revolution but this deponent cannot say to what particular company said Daniel was attached, but thinks it was the one of Captain Jesse VanSlyck. This Deponent himself being a member of the Company of Captain Abraham Oothout in said Regiment—this deponent cannot specify the services performed in said war by said Daniel except those which he performed in connection with this deponent at Stone Arabia & Germantown or German Flatts in this state in the years 1779 & 1781: to wit—this deponent was on duty in the garrison at Stone-Arabia in that state in the month of October 1779, and when he had nearly served out the term for which he was called to serve on this occasion, namely about ten or twelve days before his time expired, he saw said Daniel Kittle on duty in said garrison, but cannot tell (as he then did not enquire) how long said Kittle had been there on duty before he this deponent started for Schenectada at the expiration of his said term over and above or in addition to said ten or twelve days, that this deponent remembers the circumstance of Daniel Kittle's being at said garrison at the time and for the period specified before he this deponent returned home to Schenectada, from having seen him at the same mess with one Harmanus Peters with whom this deponent was familiarly acquainted—that he this deponent on his return home to Schenectada after he performed the tour or served out the term above referred to, was immediately drafted to serve another term at Stone Arabia aforesaid—on his arrival at Stone Arabia in pursuance of this Draft, which was not more than a week from the time or day on which his first term above described, had expired, he found said Daniel Kittle still on duty at said fort of Stone Arabia and that said Daniel Kittle continued on duty as aforesaid until about ten days or more of the second term of service of this deponent had expired.

The detachment of militia from said city with which this deponent served out his first term, was Captain Banker (4), and he served his second term under Lieutenant Roseboom(5) but this deponent cannot tell who the officers were that commanded the detachment to which said Daniel Kittle belonged—but remembers that General Ten Broeck (6) from the City of Albany had command of the garrison at Stone Arabia, when said Daniel Kittle was stationed there—That in the summer of the year 1781, the whole Regiment of Colonel Abraham Wemple aforesaid was ordered to Fort Plank—that this deponent & said Daniel Kittle as members of said Regiment accompanied it to Fort Plank under command of Major Wemple who was attached to said Regiment—That after said Regiment had been on duty at Fort Plank about two weeks, a detachment of said Regiment under command of said Captain Banker was ordered to Germantown to guard the farmers at that place which bringing in their harvest, which they did, and after performing this service returned again to Fort Plank aforesaid that said Daniel Kittle and this deponent served both in said detachment & returned together to said Fort Plank that the time said Detachment thus served, or the time that elapsed for in going to Germantown, remaining there while the farmers brought in their harvest & returning to said fort Plank was not less than two weeks—that when said detachment returned to said Fort Plank they were discharged & returned home—this deponent further saith, that he remembers well to have seen Daniel Kittle on duty at the taking of Burgoyne, but cannot tell how long he served in that expedition. (Signed) Christopher Ward.

Sworn this 20th day of Feby 1837 before me, J.D. Harman, Justice of the Peace

This file has many depositions giving a little service here and a little there.

End Notes—Daniel Kittle W.21528

1. Daniel served as a private in Captain Jesse VanSlyck's Company in Colonel Abraham Wemple's Second Regiment of the Albany County Militia.
2. The Battle of Oriskany, N.Y. was fought on August 6, 1777.
3. Brigadier General Nicholas Herkimer of the Tryon County Militia Brigade.

4. Captain Thomas B. Banker Second Albany.
5. First Lieutenant John Roseboom in Captain Oothout's Company in the Second Albany.
6. Brigadier General Abraham TenBroeck of the First Brigade of the Albany County Militia.

Pension Application for Leonard King

S.42783
State of New York
Schoharie County

On the Sixth Day of October in the year of our Lord one thousand eight hundred and twenty nine, personally appeared in open court being a court of record to wit, a court of common Pleas in and for said county of Schoharie and constituted such court by Law and Statues of the State of New York; Leonard King a resident of the County of Schoharie aforesaid aged seventy six years who being first duly sworn according to law doth on his oath make the following declaration in order to obtain the provision made by the act of Congress of the 18th of March 1818 and the first of May 1823 that he the said Leonard King enlisted on the first of April 1779 in captain Dubois' Company in Col. Dubois' (1) regiment on Continental Establishment New York service for nine months. That he continued to serve in said regiment until the first of January 1780, when he was honourably discharged at Middle Fort at Schoharie in the State of New York, that he is willing to relinquish every claim whatever to a Pension except the Present, that his name is not on the Roll of any State except the State of New York and the following are the reason for not making earlier application for a pension. I could neither read or write in English and was always to poor that I could not git proper counsel to make out my papers, correctly; and I have neglected to make out my claim partly in consequence of being told that the nine months men could not have a pension; and in pursuance of the act o the first of May 1820. I so solemnly swear that I was a resident citizen of the United States on the 18th day of March 1818 and that I have not since that time by gift sale or in any manner disposed of my property or any part thereof with an intent thereby so to diminish it as to bring my self within the provision of an act of Congress entitled an act of provide for certain persons engaged in the land and naval Service of the United States in Revolution War passed on the 18th day of March 1818, and that I have not nor has any person in trust for me any property or Securities contract or debts due to me; not have I any income other than what is contained in the Schedule hereunto and by me subscribed.

I have no real estate either in possession, reversion or remainder either in law or equity. Personal property I have nothing else as my bed, bedding and clothing.

In the year 1778 I was under the command of Captain Patrick (2) I was with him and company in a Battle engaged against the enemy of my country at Cobelskill (3) now in the county of Schoharie that I was wounded in my hand in said battle in consequence of said wound I am ever since lame to this day.

I have a wife sixty six years old five children I have no children that are able to support me. I have no debt due to me there has been no changes on my real or personal property since the 18th of March 1818 as I have had none to dispose of.

(Signed with his mark) Leonard King

Sworn the 6th day of October 1829 before me Henry Shafer, Judge of Schoharie Common Pleas.

State of New York
Schoharie County SS

Henry Shafer Esquire one of the Judges of the Court of Common Pleas of the County of Schoharie being duly sworn deposeth and says that he has been well acquainted with John Borst and John King subscribers of the within Affidavits hereunto annexed during and ever since the Revolutionary war and knows that they served as soldiers, sustaining them as they have ever since respectable and honest characters and know them respectively to be unquestionable credibility.—

And also that he was during the Revolutionary War & ever since has been well acquainted with the Petitioner Leonard King—that he does not recollect the particular days of his enlistment and discharge but does distinctly remember of seeing the said Leonard frequently on duty in the Regiment and company of Colonel and Capt. Dubois and understood that he was enlisted at the time for nine months and verily believes that he served during said time & was honorably discharged—And also that the said Leonard King did then and has ever since sustained a good reputation and is a man of credibility. The said deponent further saith that the said Leonard is a poor man and has been acquainted with him and family since the 18th March 1818 and that he did not at that time nor since own any real or personal property but what is mentioned in his schedule and further saith not—

(Signed) Henry Shafer

Subscribed and sworn the 4th day of November AD 1829 before me Demosthenes Lawyer, a commissioner to take affidavits in and for Schoharie County.

End Notes—S.42783—Leonard King

1. Leonard is mistaken about this service. He served as a private in Captain Benjamin Dubois' Company in Lieutenant-Colonel Commandant Marinus Willett's Regiment of New York State Levies in 1781. Leonard was owed £ 20..16..0 and Alexander Chesnut received the sum. No actual date of Payment is given but payment was sworn to as correct by Colonel Marinus Willett on October 28, 1785, Revolutionary War Rolls 1775-1783, Series M-246, Roll 78, Folder 173 (Willett's Levies).

2. Captain William Patrick of Colonel Ichabod Alden's Sixth Massachusetts Continental Regiment.
3. The Battle of Cobleskill was fought on May 30, 1778. Captain Patrick with several of his men were killed in this battle.
4. Leonard may have served in Captain Christian Brown's Company in Colonel Peter Vrooman's Fifteenth Regiment of Albany County Militia. Captain Brown's Company was from the Cobleskill area and was in the battle. The surname does not appear on the rolls of Vrooman's Regiment. King could be a corruption of Keoning or Konig. A Leonard Koening served in Brown's Company as did John Koning (King?) and John Borst. A John King and John Borst attested to Leonard's service. Leonard was born circa 1753 and would have served in the militia prior to 1781 according to New York's Militia Law when an able bodied male turned 16 he had to serve in the local militia.

Pension Application for Leonard Kretzer

W.21541
State of New York
Montgomery County SS.

On this 11th day of September 1838 personally appeared before the Hon. Abraham Morell, David F. Sacia, Samuel A. Gilbert, John Hand and Stephen Yates Judges of the Court of Common Pleas in and for said County Elizabeth Kretzer a resident of Ephratah in the County of Fulton (associated with the said County of Montgomery for Judicial purpose) and State of New York aged seventy six years who being first duly sworn doth depose and according to law doth on; her oath make the following declaration in order to obtain the benefit of the provision made by the Act of Congress passed July 7, 1838 entitled "an act granting half pay and pensions to certain widows" That she is the widow of Leonard Kretzer who was a corporal Boatman and private in the army navy and militia of the United States during the War of the Revolution. That he entered the service of his country as a corporal in the company of Rangers under the command of Captain Christian Getman (1) on the 8th day of August 1776 and served therein until the 27th day of March 1777 when they were discharged. That in the Spring of 1778 he enlisted in the Boat service under Captain John Lefler (2) and served until the first day of Jany following a period of nine months, that in the campaign of 1780 he served a term of nine months in the company of Volunteers under Captain John Cosselman (3) in Coll. Jacob Klocks Regiment of Militia and in 1782 a tour of nine months in Captain Abner French (4), company of State Troops in Colonel Willetts Regiment that he left the Service on the 1st of January 1783—All of which service she has reason to believe will be found satisfactory by reference to records of the War Department and the proof hereto annexed and on which she rests her claim.

She further declares that she was married to the said Leonard Kretzer on the sixth day of January seventeen hundred and Eighty four. That her husband the aforesaid Leonard Kretzer died on the 12 day of April Eighteen hundred twenty eight, that she was not married to him prior to his leaving the service but the marriage took place previous to the first of January seventeen hundred and ninety four—(Signed with her mark) Elizabeth Kretzer

Sworn to and Subscribed on the day and year above written in open court. A. J. Comrie, Clerk

State of New York

Montgomery County

On this 29th day September 1838 personally appeared before the undersigned a Justice of the peace in and for said County, Henry Kretser who being duly sworn doth depose and swear that he has made diligent search for records in relation to the marriage of Leonard Kretser and Elizabeth Kretser (now his widow) but has not been able to find any of the records of the church where he has reason to believe the entry should have been made show no records of marriage from the year 1782 to 1785 and the said Leonard Kretzer having never learned to write kept no family record. Deponent further swears that he is the son of the said Leonard Kretzer and Elizabeth Kretzer that he is now in the fifty first year of his age and knows of his own knowledge that his father and mother were man and wife previous to the first of January seventeen hundred and ninety four and that Elizabeth Kretzer the present applicant for a pension has remained the widow of the said Leonard Kretzer since the time of this death, which was on the 13th day of April Eighteen hundred and twenty eight and further this deponent says not. (Signed with his mark) Henry Kretser

Subscribed & sworn this 29th day of Sept. 1838 before Henry M. Livingston J.P.

Reply to a letter of inquiry dated April 16, 1929

Reference is made to your request for information relative to Elizabeth Kretcher [sic] who received a pension as the widow of a soldier for the Revolutionary War.

The data which follow were obtained from papers on file in the pension claim, W.21541, based on the military service of Leonard Kretser.

The date and place of birth of Leonard Kretser and the names of his parents are not shown.

He enlisted August 8, 1776, place not stated, and served until March 27, 1777, as corporal in Captain Christian Getman's New York Company. In the spring of 1778 he enlisted under Captain John Lefler in the bateau service and was discharged January 1, 1779, having served nine months. In 1780 he served nine months in Captain John Casselman's company in Colonel Jacob Klock's New York Regiment. In 1782 he served nine months in Captain Abner French's company in Colonel Willett's New York New York regiment and left the service the first of January, 1783. (5)

He married January 6, 1784, Elizabeth Cool, the daughter of Philip Cool.

Leonard Kretzer died April 12 or 13, 1828.

His widow, Elizabeth, was allowed pension on her application executed September 11, 1838, at which time she was seventy-six years of age and was living at Ephratah ,Fulton County, New York, and she was living there in 1843.

It was stated that they reared a large family of children but the only name given was that of a son, Henry, who stated in 1838 that he was in the fifty-first year of his age.

In 1838 one Hannah Cool stated that she was present at the marriage of Leonard Kretzer and Elizabeth Cool but she did not give her relation to Elizabeth.

The papers in this claim contain no further data relative to the soldier's family.

End Notes—W.21541—Leonard Kretzer or Kretser, or Cretser, etc.

1. Christian Getman was the Captain of the Second Company of Tryon County Rangers. Elizabeth is correct as to Leonard's rank and time of enlistment and discharge. FROM: Revolutionary War Rolls, 1775-1783, Series M-246, Roll 74, folder 103, National Archives, Washington, D.C.
2. Leonard enlisted as a private in Captain John Leffler's Company of Bateaumen on April 24, 1778. FROM: Revolutionary War Rolls, 1775-1783, Series M-246, Roll 122, folder 78, National Archives, Washington, D.C.
3. Leonard enlisted as a private in Captain John Casselman's Company of Tryon County Rangers on May 14, 1780. As of August 31, he had served 110 days at £ 3..4..0 per month for a total of £11..14..8. FROM: Revolutionary War Rolls, 1775-1783, Series M-246, Roll 75, folder 121, National Archives, Washington, D.C.
4. Abner French was a captain in Colonel Marinus Willett's Regiment of New York State Levies in 1782. Captain French retired in November and Lieutenant Jellis A. Fonda was promoted to Captain of this company.
5. Leonard also served in the militia in between the other stated services. Leonard served as a private in Captain Christopher W. Fox's Company, the Third Company in Colonel Jacob Klock's Second Regiment of Tryon County Militia. On September 29, 1780, Captain Fox was commissioned a Major in Colonel Klock's Regiment and First Lieutenant Henry Miller was promoted to captain of the company.

Pension Application for George Lambert

R.6098
State of New York
Montgomery county SS.

Personally appeared before me the undersigned a Justice of the Peace in & for the County aforesaid George Lambert who being duly sworn deposeth & saith that by reason of old age & consequent loss of memory he cannot swear, positively as to the precise length of his service—but according to the best of his recollection he served not less than the period mentioned below & in the following grade—to wit for three years & five months he served as a private & for such service he declares a pension.

In further explanation of his original declaration the applicant states under oath that he was put into the commissary department in his last tour of service in the month of November 1780 & was discharged in the fall of 1783—that his Captain was Leipe, (1) George Countryman (2) Lieut [?] all the time in Col. Willett's Regt -- that his services in the last period [?] enlistment with the state troops—as he believes though militia officers were frequently stationed with garrison. That he served in an embodied corps called into service by competent authority.

That he was either in the field or in garrison all the time. And for the time during which the service was performed he was not employed in any civil pursuit. As to the interrogatories put by the subscribing magistrate he answers—

He was born in the City of Philadelphia in 1764. That by the record of his age kept in his father's Bible now in applicant's possession he is 69 years of age. Lived at Minden County of Montgomery the State of New York when called into the service & has since the war lived in Minden & Canajoharie where he now resides—was called into the service he enlisted—volunteered as a substitute for his brother Peter Lambert—never received any written discharge—recollects of his officers Col. Rynier, Col. Weisenfelts, Col. Willett, Gen Washington when he went up the Mohawk—Capt. Fowler, Capt. Davis Capt. Titus (3) & many others. (Signed) George Lambert.

Sworn & subscribed before on July 3, 1833. Wm. Lane J.P.

Letter in folder, written in response to an inquiry.

I have to advise you from the papers in the Revolutionary War pension claim, R.6098, it appears that George Lambert, the son of Peter was born March 18, 1764, in Philadelphia, Pennsylvania.

He alleged that while a resident of Fort Plains (later called Minden), Montgomery County, New York, he enlisted in the fall of 1778 and served with the New York Troops at various times until the close of the Revolution, amounting to one year, two months, and twenty-nine days, in all, as private and spy under Captains Belden, (4) John Breadbig, (5) George Countryman, Adam Leyp, Gross, (6) and Piercy, Colonels Samuel Clyde, (7) Harper, (8) Brown, (9) and Willett.

He stated that his father's property at Otsego, eight miles from Cherry Valley, was destroyed by the Indians and in 1780 his mother, sister, and two younger brothers (their names not given) were taken prisoners by the Indians. His brothers returned home after the war but no mention is made of the fate of his mother and sister.

He applied for pension September 19, 1832, while living at Canajoharie, Montgomery County, New York. He was called upon for further specification in regard to his service, to which he did not reply, and his claim was never completed.

The above noted George Lambert is the only soldier of that name who served with the New York Troops, found on the Revolutionary War records of this Bureau, and he was a brother of the Revolutionary War soldier, Peter Lambert, (10) whose history is herewith furnished you.

End Notes—R.6098—George Lambert

1. Adam Leipe (Lype, Lipe, Libe, Leib, etc.) was a Captain in Colonel Samuel Campbell's First Regiment of Tryon County Militia. George received his pay for certificate no. 11465 £ 0..10..8 on September 28, 1784. FROM: Revolutionary War Rolls 1775-1783, Series M-249, Roll 72, folder 89, National Archives, Washington, D.C.
2. George Countryman served as an ensign in Captain Henry Dieffendorf's (Fifth Company) in Colonel Ebenezer Cox's First Regiment of Tryon County Militia. He was commissioned on June 25, 1778. On March 4, 1780, Ensign Countryman was commissioned First Lieutenant in Captain Jacob Dieffendorf who had replaced his brother who had been killed at the Battle of Oriskany on August 6, 1777.
3. Lieutenant-Colonel Pierre Regnier deRoussi, Lieutenant-Colonel Frederick Wiesenfels both had served in the Fourth New York Continental Regiment, Lieutenant-Colonel Marinus Willett served in several regiments but he served last in command of a New York State Regiment of Levies 1781-1783, Commander in Chief General George Washington, Captain Theodosius Fowler, Captain John Davis and Captain John Titus all served in the Fourth New York.
4. Captain Belden is unknown.
5. John Breadbake (Bedling, Breadbig, etc.) was Captain of the Fifth Company in Colonel Jacob Klock's Second Regiment of Tryon County Militia. He was Captain of a Company of Rangers in 1778 and in 1780 he served as Captain in Colonel Lewis Dubois Regiment of New York State Levies.
6. Lawrence Gross had served as a First Lieutenant in Captain John Winn's Company of Tryon County Rangers from July 1776 to March 27, 1777. He was appointed captain on April 27, 1781 in Lieutenant-Colonel Commandant Marinus Willett's Regiment of New York State Levies.
7. Samuel Clyde commissioned Lieutenant-Colonel on June 25, 1778 of the First Tryon.
8. John Harper had served as Colonel of the Fifth Regiment of Tryon County Militia and was commissioned on March 3, 1780. On May 11, 1780 he was appointed Lieutenant-Colonel Commandant of a regiment of New York State Levies.
9. John Brown was Colonel of a regiment of Massachusetts State Levies in 1780. He was killed in the Battle of Stone Arabia on October 19, 1780 on his 36th birthday.

10. George's father Peter and brother Peter {Jr.} also had served in captain Leipe's Company. George didn't turn 16 until 1780 so any service before that did not count towards his requirements for proof of service.

Pension Application for Abraham Lawyer

S.23296
State of New York
Schoharie County SS.

On this fourth day of June in the year of our Lord one thousand eight hundred & thirty three personally appeared in open court before the Honorable the Court of Common Pleas of the County of Schoharie and State of New York now sitting Abraham Lawyer a resident of the Town of Middleburgh in the said County of Schoharie & State of New York aged seventy five years who being first duly sworn according to law doth on his oath make the following declaration in order to obtain the benefit of the Act of Congress passed June 7th 1832—

That he was born & has always resided in that part of the State of New York now the town of Middleburgh in the County of Schoharie. That he was enrolled as a private in the Militia of the State of New York as early as the first day of August in the year 1775. That the Regiment & Company in which he was enrolled at the time of his enrollment was commanded by the following named officers, Colonel Peter Vrooman, Lieutenant Colonel Peter Zelie, Major Thomas Eckerson and Joseph Becker (1), Captain Jacob Hager (2) & Lieutenant Cornelius Feek. That he does not recollect the name of the ensign. That he belonged to the same Militia Regiment & company until the first day of April in the year 1783. That the said Regiment and company were commanded by the above named officers during that time as near as he can recollect.

That from the said first day of August in the year 1775 untill the first day of April in the year 1783 he was very frequently on duty in the service of the United States for short periods of from one day to one month at a time. That he does not recollect the number of different times he was on duty.

That he was during most of those periods under the immediate command of some officers of the Regiment or Company to which he belonged but which officer had the command each period he cannot tell. That he does not recollect the exact time he entered the service each or any of those periods nor the time when he left the service nor how long he was engaged on duty each time.

That he was not drafted, a volunteer, or substitute any of the above periods to his knowledge. That he was ordered into the service by some officer of his regiment or company and entered the service in obedience to such orders.

That he was in no Battle during the war. That he marched from the middle Fort in Schoharie in the year 1780 under Colonel Vrooman in pursuit of the Indians & Tories under McDonald (3) who had been massacring the inhabitants of Schoharie. Colonel Harper with a party of Light Horse from Albany were with the American party. That he was in the upper Fort in Schoharie when Schoharie was burnt in the year 1780 (4). That he went several times into that part of the State of New York now counties of Delaware, Green[e] & Albany.

That he was frequently in the Fort in the now County of Schoharie on garrison duty. That he does not recollect where he was engaged on duty each period. And the said Lawyer saith he is positive he was engaged on duty in the service of the United States as a private Soldier from the said first day of August in the year 1775 untill the first day of April in the year 1783 at different periods in the whole amounting to at least three years. [End of written declaration.]

Letter in the pension application folder, dated November 9, 1937, written in response to an inquiry.

Reference is made to your letter in which you request the Revolutionary War record of John Bray who died in 1823 in North Carolina, and Abraham Lawyer who was born 1767 and died in 1824 in New Jersey.

The data furnished relative to John Bray are not sufficient to enable this office to identify the record of the John Bray in whom you are particularly interested; as much as possible of the following data in regard to him are essential—approximate date of his birth and places of residence at enlistment and after service.

The record of Abraham Lawyer which follows was obtained from papers on file in pension claim, S.23296, based upon his service in the Revolutionary War. This is the record of the only Abraham Lawyer found on file in the Revolutionary War records of this office.

Abraham Lawyer was born and reared in Schoharie County, New York, near what was later the town of Middleburgh. The date of his birth and names of his parents were not given.

While residing in said Schoharie County, Abraham Lawyer enlisted August 1, 1775, served as private and corporal at various times under Captains Becker (5), Jacob Heager, Miller, Brown, Stubrach, in Colonel Peter Vrooman's New York Regiment, during the service he was out in pursuit of Tories and Indians, and did garrison duty in forts in Schoharie County, and continued in the service until April 1, 1783.

The soldier, Abraham Lawyer, was allowed pension on his application executed June 4, 1833, at which time he was seventy-four years of age and living in Middleburgh, Schoharie County, New York.

It was not stated whether soldier was ever married. One John J. Lawyer was referred to, but it was not shown that he was related to the soldier.

End Notes—S.23296—Abraham Lawyer

1. These officers belonged to the Fifteenth Regiment of Albany County Militia, which were the United Districts of Schoharie and Duanesburgh. Colonel Vrooman was in command of the regiment for the entire war.

Thomas Eckerson was the First Major and Jost or Joseph Becker was the Second Major.

2. Jacob Hager was appointed October 20, 1775 as Captain of the Second Company in Colonel Vrooman's Regiment. The other company officers that were appointed at this time were Martin VanSlyck as the First Lieutenant, Johannes W. Bouck as the Second Lieutenant and Johannes L. Lawyer as the Ensign. On February 20, 1778 the new officers under Captain Hager were as follows: Ephraim Vrooman as the First Lieutenant, Cornelius Feeck as the Second Lieutenant, and Peter Swart as the Ensign.
3. This incident happened in August of 1777. The Loyalists were led by Captain John McDonell. Colonel John Harper of the Fifth Regiment of Tryon County Militia was able to obtain a troop of dragoons commanded by Captain Jean Louis deVernejoux from the Second Connecticut Continental Dragoons of Light Horse or Cavalry to reinforce the militia at Schoharie. There was a battle on August 14, 1777 between the Americans and Loyalists called the Battle of the Flockey.
4. Lieutenant-Colonel Sir John Johnson burnt the Schoharie Valley on October 17, 1780.
5. Captains Storm Becker, Dirk Miller, Christian Brown and Christian Stubrach served in Colonel Vrooman's Regiment.

Pension Application for Johannes J. Lawyer

R.6208
Fultonham April 11, 1859
Schoharie Co. NY

It appears that 6 or 7 years Ago that Susan Lawyer, Sarah Defraigh & Christian Van Wol Applied for a pension for Johannis Lawyer for a pension in Revolution War.

It appears that they have rec'd something or some boddy has Rec'd it unbeknown to Samuel Lawyer the husband of Susan Lawyer Have the goodness to examine the books & send me a line so that I can ascertain what was done & if the money was got who recd it you can tell by Rects. Samuel Lawyer

State o Michigan
County of Washtenaw SS.

On this twenty first day of April A.D. one thousand eight hundred and fifty three personally appeared before me a Justice of the Peace within and for the County and State aforesaid William Maynard resident of Ann Arbor who being duly sworn according to law declares that he is guardian duly appointed by the Judge of Probate of Washtenaw of Gertrude Fletcher one of the heirs of Johannes J. Lawyer (1) who was a Revolutionary Soldier in the State of New York holding the rank of Lieutenant in the 137th Regiment (2) of NY Militia that his commission was dated in 1778 and he served to the end of the war, that he died on the 17th day of July 1818 and that deponents mother named Angelica Lawyer died on the 25 day of April 1836 and that they were married on the 1 day of May 1780 that they were resident of Schoharie County living their respective lives—that this affidavit was made for the purpose of obtaining from the U.S. Government the rights in all and any remainder of claim for arrears of pension or land or commutation money that may be due to her as heir of Johannes J. Lawyer and Angelica his wife, who both died leaving the same undrawn as in right of law she may be entitled.

William Maynard

Sworn to and subscribed before me this 21 day of April 1853. J.J.A Wood, Justice of the Peace

State of New York
County of Schoharie SS

On this Sixteenth day of April A.D. One Thousand eight hundred and fifty three personally appeared before me a Justice of the Peace within and for the County and State aforesaid Christina Van Veghten, Sarah Defrate, Susan Lawyer, residents of Schoharie County in the State of New York, who being duly sworn, according to law, declared that they are children and heirs at Law of Johannes J. Lawyer who was a Revolutionary Soldier in the State of New York, holding the rank of Lieutenant in the 137th Regiment of NY Militia, that his commission was dated in 1778 and he served to the end of the war—that he died on the 18th day of July 1818, and that deponents mother named Angelica Lawyer died on the 25th day of April 1834, that they were married on the 1st day of May 1780 and that they were residents of Schoharie in the State of New York and resided there during their respective lives and that deponents make this affidavit for the purpose of obtaining from the U.S. Government their rights in all and any manner of claim for arrears of pension or claims and land or benefits that may be due to them, as heirs of said Johannes J. Lawyer and Angelica his wife who died leaving the same undrawn; as in right of law they mey be entitled. (Signed) Christiana Van Veghten, Susan Lawyer, Sarah Defrate.

Sworn and subscribed before me this 16th day of April 1853. A. B. [Para]

End Notes—R.6208—Johannes J. Lawyer

1. Johannes J. Lawyer was appointed on October 20, 1775 as the First Lieutenant in Captain George Richtmyer's Company, the Third Company, in Colonel Peter Vrooman's Fifteenth Regiment of Albany County Militia, which consisted of the United Districts of Schoharie and Duanesburgh. He was commissioned First Lieutenant of the same company in the same regiment on February 20, 1778. He also had served in detachment details under Captain Christian Stubrach and Captain Christian Brown in Colonel Vroomans' Regiment.

2. The 137th Regiment is a post 1800 time period militia regiment. American Regiments whether militia, levies or Continental were never numbered higher than in the low twenties.

Pension Application for Frederick Lepper or Lapper, Leppard, etc.

W20447 (Widow: Mary)
Montgomery County SS.

On this third day of June 1837 personally appeared before the undersigned Judge of the Court of Common Pleas in and for the County aforesaid Mary Lepper a resident of the town of Amsterdam in the County aforesaid aged Eighty five years who being first duly sworn according to law doth on her oath make the following declaration in order to obtain the benefit of the provision made by the act of Congress passed July 4th 1836,--That she is the widow of Frederick Lepper who was a private in the Militia of the State of New York in the Revolutionary War—but that the knowledge she has of her said husband's services in said war is derived from traditionary evidence in some or from the facts and circumstances dictated to her by her husband and other persons serving in said War at the time of such service and since which she believes verily which is that he served & done duty at various times & places in said war all of which times and places she does not now recollect—but he was called out in the service under Captain Win (1) and Colonel Willet's (2) Regiment in the year 1777 and served nine months called out in the year 1778 under Capt Gerrit Putman (3) & the same Colonel and served at that time nine months—called out in the year 1780 under Capt. Victor Putman (4) & served nine months & all the above service was done in the regiment commanded by Colonel Willet. She further states & believes that her said husband was inlisted at the periods above stated—She further states that she was taken prisoner (5) by the Indians & carried to Canada & remained a Prisoner thirteen months but owing to old age, cannot recollect the year she was made a prisoner—She further declares that she was married to the said Frederick Lepper on the 10th day of January 1777—that her said husband the aforesaid Frederick Lepper died on the 16th day of April 1820 and that she has remained a widow ever since that period—as will more fully appear [part of document appears to be missing]
(Signed with her mark) Mary Lepper

Sworn to and subscribed on the day and year aforesaid written before me. John Hand, a Judge of the Montgomery County Courts.

State of New York
Montgomery County SS.

On this third day of June AD 1837 personally appeared before me John Hand a Judge of the County Courts of this county aforesaid Jacob Lepper of the Town of Amsterdam in the said County, aged Eighty Six years, who being by me duly sworn—and upon his oath doth depose & says—That he was well acquainted with and is a brother to Frederick Lepper deceased who is named in the annexed declaration of his widow, Mary Lepper—and knows that said

Frederick has done service at various places and at various times in the war of the Revolution—this deponent has se [sic seen] said Frederick—go from his home in said War at several times--& return home and he said at that time he had been in service in said War—nine months under Captain Putman and nine months under Capt. Winn and nine months under Capt Shaver (6)—this deponent was also a private in said war, but deponent served under Capt. Sever (7) & others- and this deponent has examined a declaration made by said Mary Lepper hereto annexed and believes the statements made in said declaration there—and this deponent further says that he was present when the said Mary Lepper was married to the said Frederick Lepper—on or about the 10th day of January A.D. 1777—and that he was present when her husband the said Frederick Lepper died on the 16th day of April 1820 (8)—and that she the said Mary has remained a widow ever since the day of the said Frederick's death. (Signed with his mark) Jacob Lepper

Sworn to and Subscribed on the day and year above written before me John Hand a Judge of the Montgomery County Courts.

Letter dated April 26, 1932, replying to an inquiry.

Reference is made to your letter relative to Frederick and Jacob Lepper, soldiers of the Revolutionary War. Their histories follow. Frederick Lepper W.20447

The data furnished herein are obtained from the papers on file in the Revolutionary War claim for pension, W.20447, based upon the military service of Frederick Lepper in that war.

Frederick Lepper, while a resident of Johnstown (9), Canajoharie District, Tryon County (which was later Montgomery County) New York, enlisted in 1777 and served during the years 1777, 1778, 1780, 1781, and 1782, nine months in each year, as a private under Captains John Winn, Bradbick (or Bradbig) (10), Garrett Putnam, Shaver, Abner French and Jacob Diffendorff (11), and Colonels John Harper and Marinus Willett in the New York Troops.

He died April 16, 1820 His age is not stated.

The soldier married in Herkimer County, New York, that part which was later called Warren, Mary, whose maiden name was not stated. They were married in January, 1775, or January 10, 1777, both dates given by the soldier's widow Mary. The soldier's brother, Jacob Lepper, who was present at their marriage, stated that they were married January 10, 1777. Said Jacob was aged eighty-six years in 1837 and resided in Amsterdam, New York. Statements also appear in the claim that soldier's widow, Mary, was taken prisoner by the Indians during her husband's service, carried to Canada with her second child and held thirteen or fourteen months or three years, a prisoner among the Indians.

Soldier's widow, Mary, was allowed pension on her application executed June 3, 1837, at which time she was aged eighty-five years and resided in Amsterdam, New York. In 1840, it was stated she was aged eighty-six years.

She died March 14 or March 18 (both dates appear in the claim), 1843.

The following children survived her: Jacob Frederick or Jacob F. born May 11, 1777, the oldest child; Hannah, wife of Joseph Lepper; and Mary or Polly, wife of Joshua Stearns, all of Amsterdam, New York; Margaret or Peggy, wife of Lawrence Hoak or Hough, of Springfield, Otsego County, New York; and Catharine, wife of Henry Bolsom or Balsom, of Brutus, Cayuga County, New York. In 1846, Jacob Frederick Lepper was deceased. Frederick Lepper was administrator of the estate of Jacob Frederick Lepper, no relationship of Frederick to Jacob Frederick shown.

End Notes—W.20447—Frederick Lepper

1. Frederick enlisted as a private on August 10, 1776 in Captain John Winn's Company of Tryon County Rangers. The company was discharged on March 27, 1777.
2. Marinus Willett was not associated with the ranger company. Willett was appointed Lieutenant-Colonel of the Third New York Continental Regiment on November 21, 1776. The regiment was stationed at the Highlands area until March and April of 1777 when the regiment was ordered to garrison Fort Schuyler (Fort Stanwix).
3. Garret Putman was appointed Captain on May 11, 1780 in Lieutenant Colonel Commandant John Harper's Regiment of New York State Levies. Frederick's name appears on Captain Putman's pay roll as a private. FROM: Revolutionary War Rolls 1775-1783, Series M-246, Roll 74, folder 112, National Archives, Washington, D.C.
4. Victor Putman served as a Lieutenant in Captain Isaac Bogart's Company in Harper's Regiment in 1780. In 1781, Victor served as a lieutenant in Captain Garret Putman's Company in Lieutenant-Colonel Commandant Marinus Willett's Regiment of New York State Levies. Frederick did not serve in the company or regiment in 1781.
5. Mary was taken prisoner on August 2, 1780 in Captain Joseph Brant's Raid on the Canajoharie District in Tryon County.
6. Lieutenant John C. Shafer of Colonel Willett's Regiment in 1782. Frederick enlisted as a private in Captain Abner French's Company in Willett's in 1782. When Captain French retired in November, Lieutenant Jellis A. Fonda was appointed Captain in his place.
7. Captain Jacob W. Seeber's Company, Fourth Company, in Colonel Ebenezer Cox's First Regiment of Tryon County Militia.
8. Frederick died in the Town of Amsterdam and is buried in the cemetery on Lepper Road.
9. Johnstown was in the Caughnawaga District and Frederick didn't live in Johnstown.
10. Frederick served as private in Captain John Breadbake's Company of Tryon County Rangers in 1778. The company was under the command of Colonel Morris Graham. FROM: Revolutionary War Rolls

1775-1783, Series M-246, Roll 74, folder 106, National Archives, Washington, D.C.

11. Frederick most likely served in Captain Henry Dieffendorf's Company, Fifth Company in Colonel Cox's Regiment. Captain Dieffendorf was killed at the Battle of Oriskany on August 6, 1777. A muster roll for this company has not been found. First Lieutenant Jacob Dieffendorf, Henry's brother, was appointed Captain in place of Henry and was commissioned as captain on March 4, 1780. Frederick's name appears on a pay roll for Jacob's Company. FROM: Revolutionary War Rolls 1775-1783, Series M-246, Roll 72, folder 89, National Archives, Washington, D.C.

Pension Application for Abraham J. Lighthall

W.16631 (Widow: Catharine)

Declaration, in order to obtain the benefit of the act of Congress of the 7th July 1838, entitled "An act granting half pay and pensions to certain widows."

State of New York

Madison County SS.

On this first day of April 1839, personally appeared before the undersigned one of the Supreme Court Commissioners for said County Catharine Lighthall—a resident of Wampsville In the County of Madison aforesaid aged seventy six years, who being first duly sworn according to law, doth on her oath make the following declaration in order to obtain the benefit of the provision made by the act of Congress passed July 7, 1838, entitled "An act granting half pay and pensions to certain widows." That she is the widow of Abraham (or Abraham J.) Lighthall who was a private in the Regiment of Colonel Abraham Wemple (1) in the District of Schenectada & then County of Albany to wit in the company of militia commanded by Captain Jellis J. Fonda (2) and Abraham Van Eps (3) as this declarant has been informed and believes to be true, and that said Abraham Lighthall otherwise served in the war of the revolution as is set forth in the papers hereto annexed but that this declarant has no personal knowledge of his services, yet remembers hearing him relate, that he served in the campaign of 1777 at the taking of Burgoyne (4) & that he was at Fort George (5) making boats in 1779.

And she furthers declares that her maiden name was "Cuyler, that she was married at Stillwater NY at the time herein after set forth by some clergyman whose name she cannot recollect that she has no documentary or record evidence of her marriage, except that contained in her family bible & that the leaf on which the same was written is hereto annexed—

She further declares, that she was married to the said Abraham Lighthall on the ninth day of April in the year seventeen hundred and eighty-seven, that her husband, the aforesaid Abraham Lighthall died on the Eleventh day of March 1831; that she was not married to him prior to his leaving the service, but the marriage took place previous to the first of January seventeen hundred and ninety four viz. at the time above stated. (Signed) Catharine Lighthall.

Sworn to and subscribed on the day and year above written, before me the said commissioner and I certify that said Catharine Lighthall is unable to attend court by reason of bodily infirmity. John T. Spinner, Sup. Court Comm.

Family record from the Bible

Marriages

Abraham Lighthall was married to Catharine Cuyler April the 9 1787.

Nancy Lighthall was married to Peter Bovie in the year 1815 Sep 10

Janehelen Lighthall was married to Joseph Blakesly in 1822 Feb 4

William Lighthall was married to Harriet Jackson July the 1, 1832.

Births

Janehelen Lighthall was born, October the 12 1800

Caty Mariah Lighthall was born February the 11, 1803

William Lighthall was born June the 1 1806

Abraham J Lighthall was born 9 July 1753

Catharine Cuyler was born 11 January 1763

Sarah Lighthall was born 30 April 1788

Nancy Lighthall was born 13 March 1790

James Lighthall was born 24 April 1792

Cornelius Lighthall was born 9 March 1794

John Lighthall was born 7 June 1796

Jacob Wendel Lighthall was born 5 July 1799

JaneHelen Lighthall was born 12 Oct 1800

Caty Mariah Lighthall was born 11 Feb. 1803

William Lighthall was born 1 June 1806

End Notes—W.16631—Abraham J. Lighthall

1. Abraham Wemple was the Colonel of the Second Regiment of Albany County Militia of the Schenectady District.
2. Jellis J. Fonda was the Captain of the First Company in Colonel Wemple's Regiment.
3. Captain Abraham VanEps served in Colonel Wemple's Regiment.
4. The "Burgoyne Campaign" was in 1777. Lieutenant General John Burgoyne surrendered his British Army on October 17, 1777.
5. Bateaus were built to transport supplies and troops for Brigadier General James Clinton in 1779. Clinton joined forces with Major General John Sullivan and the combined army marched against the Iroquois Villages in the western part of New York State. Fort George was located near Lake George. Abraham served in Captain Nicholas Veeder's Company in the Quartermaster General's Department during this service. FROM: Revolutionary War Rolls 1775-1783, Series M-246, Roll 122, National Archives, Washington, D.C.

Pension Application for George Lighthall

S.13341

State of New York
Oneida County SS

On this ninth day of October 1832, personally appeared in Open Court before Nathan Williams Vice Chancellor of the State of New York for the fifth Circuit at a Court of Chancery now sitting in the City of Utica. George Lighthall, a resident of the Town of Columbia in the County of Herkimer and there the said circuit, aged eighty five years, who being first duly sworn according to law in Open Court doth on his oath make the following declaration in order to obtain the benefit of the act of Congress passed June 7th 1832.

That he entered the service of the United States under the following named officers and served as herein stated. Was born in the town of German Flatts now County of Herkimer and State of New York in the year 1747 that he has always during his whole lifetime lived in German Flatts aforesaid at Oriskany in the now County of Oneida and at Columbia & County of Herkimer except the two last year of the war of the Revolution which two years he lived in Schenectady in the State of New York—That in the year 1778 when this applicant resided in German Flatts aforesaid he was drafted and served in the Militia of the State of New York under Captain Robert McKean (1) this term of service lasted nine months and was performed at Fort Dayton now Herkimer—That he was a soldier under Capt. Getman (2) of German Flatts and under Capt. Van Patten (3) of Schenectady during the whole revolutionary War except as aforesaid and stood as a minute man ready to be called into actual service at all times and was frequently called out into actual service during that period and he verily believes that his whole amount of actual service exceeded two years but he cannot now particularize the precise times and places of such services—he recollects that he was with Col. Willett (4) when Butler (5) was taken on Canada Creek where the town of Russia now is situate—That the was on duty for one length of time at Fort Stanwix and was frequently detached a guard to provisions of which were sent to Fort Stanwix and on one occasion he was employed to guard two officers from Fort Stanwix down the Mohawk River to General Herkimers (6) residence—the names of these officers he does not now recollect.

That his property was twice during the war destroyed by the enemy once at Oriskany and once at German Flatts—he has no record of his age—never had a commission never had any written discharge and has no written evidence of his service. Is acquainted with George Michael Weaver and Henry Apple the former of whom lives in Deerfield and County of Oneida the latter in the town of Minden in the County of Herkimer. He knows that this applicant performed some of the terms above mentioned.

He hereby relinquishes every claim whatever to a pension or annuity except the present and declares that his name is not on the Pension Roll of the Agency of any State or Territory whatever.
(Signed with his mark) George Lighthall

Sworn & subscribed this 9th day of October 1832, before me N. Williams, Vice Chancellor.

Letter in the Pension Folder dated October 4, 1929.

I advise you from the papers in the Revolutionary War Pension claim S.13341, it appears that George Lighthall was born in 1747 in German Flats, Herkimer County, New York.

While residing in said German Flats, he enlisted in 1778 and served nine months at Fort Dayton later Herkimer, as a private in Captain Robert McKean's New York Company.

He stated that during the entire war he stood as a minute man and was frequently called out into active service; he served as a private under Captain Gettman of German Flats, and under Captain Van Patten of Schenectady, a part of the time at Fort Stanwix, and that he was with Colonel Willett when Butler was taken on Canada Creek. The entire length of his service was a least two years, no dates are given.

He stated that during the last two years of the Revolution he resided at Schenectady, New York, and with the exception he had always lived in German Flats and Columbia, Herkimer County, New York and in Oriskany, Oneida County, New York.

He was allowed pension on his application executed October 9, 1832, at which time he resided in Columbia, New York.

There are no data concerning his family.

The above noted is the only soldier named George Lighthall under any spelling of the surname, that is found on the Revolutionary War records of this Bureau.

Very truly yours, Earl D. Church, Commissioner

End Notes—S.13341—George Lighthall

1. George is mistaken about the year as Captain Robert McKean's Company in Colonel Henry K. VanRensselaer's Regiment of New York State Levies was organized in April of 1779, unfortunately there is not a muster roll for this company. In 1778, George is listed on Captain Michael Ittig's (or Ittick, Edick, etc.) Company Payroll for February 28—November 30, 1778 in Colonel Peter Bellinger's Fourth Regiment of Tryon County Militia. George is listed as a private and served 13 days in July of 1778. He was owed £1..3..1 ¼ for his service. FROM: Revolutionary War Rolls 1775-1783, Series M-246, Roll 72, folder 78, National Archives, Washington, D.C.
2. George is listed as a private in Captain Frederick Getman's Company in Colonel Bellinger's Regiment. He is listed as serving 10 days in April and 10 days in May of 1780. He is again listed as serving 3 days in October of 1780. FROM: Revolutionary War Rolls 1775-1783, Series M-246, Roll 72, folder 78, National Archives, Washington, D.C.
3. George served as a private in Captain John VanPatten's Company (Third Company) in Colonel Abraham Wemple's Second Regiment of Albany County Militia.

4. In 1781, Marinus Willett was the Lieutenant-Colonel Commandant of a regiment of New York State Levies.
5. Captain Walter Butler was killed at West Canada Creek on October 30, 1781. Colonel Willett was in command of the Americans in this skirmish. Captain Butler was the second in command of the British raiding part that had raided and destroyed several settlements in October.
6. Brigadier General Nicholas Herkimer of the Tryon County Militia Brigade. His home is a New York State Historic Site and is open to the public. http://www.littlefallsny.com/HerkimerHome/Page1.htm

Pension Application for William Lighthall

S.42862
B.L. Wt. 1223-200 Lieut. Issued Aug 8, 1789 to John Doty Assignee no papers.
Continental - New York

Declaration of William Lighthall
State of New York
County of Schenectady SS.

William Lighthall formerly a Lieutenant in the service of the United States now a resident of the City and County of Schenectady in the State of New York, being duly sworn deposeth and saith, That on the Twelfth day of June in the year of our Lord one thousand and seven hundred seventy six he was enlisted by Lieut. Walter Swits and was attached to a company of New York State Rangers commanded by Captain John A. Bradt (1) the seventh day of March 1777 he reenlisted under the said Lieutenant Walter Swits (2) to serve during the war—that he was attached to Captain Giles Woolcotts (3) Company in a Regiment on the Continental establishment commanded by Colonel Seth Warner that he remained attached to said company and regiment as a Sergeant until the Fourteenth day of November 1778—when he was promoted to the rank of Ensign in said Regiment and received his commission as such—That in the year 1779 he was promoted to the rank of Lieutenant in said Regiment and was on active service as such, until sometime in the month of October 1780—when at Fort George (4) in the State of New York he was captured and and [sic] taken to the province of Canada where he remained a prisoner of war until the month of November 1782 (5), when he was paroled and returned home, to remain until he was exchanged or otherwise ordered—That he was not exchanged but remained on Parole until the army of the United States was disbanded in the year 1783 after the close of the war—That his accounts were settled he finally paid by a Mr. John Peirce who was the paymaster of the United States Army—sometime in the month of May in the year 1784—All of which will probably appear by vouchers & which were at that time lodged in the War or other Department of government.

This deponent further says that he served in the War of the Revolution on the Continental establishments, as before stated, that is by reason of his reduced circumstances in life in need of assistance from his country for support and he further says that he has never had any pension allowed him for his services aforesaid by the Laws of the United States. He further says that he is now about sixty two years of age. (Signed) Wm. Lighthall

Sworn before me this 31st Day of March 1818. (signature cut off)

The next document pretty much is the same as the above except he lists his assets. Real Estate—none; Personal Estate, household furniture value $30.00; Income-Occupation - none - unable to work.

Family-William Lighthall, myself aged 64 past; Sarah Lighthall - wife- aged 59 years.

Nicholas Lighthall - son 25 years [?]

Asasuarus Lighthall—apprentice shoemaker, aged 19

Ann Lighthall—daughter 17 years.

This document signed by Jelles A. Fonda, Clerk of the County of Schenectady, 15 May 1820.

End Notes—S.42862—William Lighthall

1. The only muster roll and pay roll for Captain John A. Bradt's Company of Rangers are all dated for October of 1776. FROM: Revolutionary War Rolls, 1775-1783, Series M-246, Roll 72, folder 81, National Archives, Washington, D.C.
2. Walter Swits after serving in Captain Bradt's Company was discharged on March 27, 1777 and was appointed Second Lieutenant on April 1, 1777 in Captain Giles Wolcott's Company in Colonel Seth Warner's Regiment of Additional Continentals.
3. William enlisted as a private on March 5, 1777 for "During War" in Captain Wolcott's company. He was promoted to sergeant and commissioned ensign on November 14, 1778. Then he was promoted to lieutenant in March of 1780.
4. Major Christopher Carleton with a large British force raided and destroyed a large area from Fort Ann to Fort George on Lake George. The forts were destroyed and the American garrisons were either killed or captured. William was taken prisoner on October 11, 1780.
5. If a soldier was paroled while waiting to be exchanged he was not supposed to take up arms and fight until the exchange could be transacted. This practice was used even as late as the Civil War.

Captain John Little

On June 2nd and 3rd, 1778 the inhabitants at Fish House and Mayfield were attacked by a party of Indians and Loyalists under Lieutenant John Ross. Little* at Fort Johnstown, on receiving word of this invasion, gathered a scouting party. Thomas Butler, Isaac De Graff and John Higgins under Little marched to Fish House and found several homes burned and the inhabitants missing and the scouting party returned to Fort Johnstown. Little then went to Caughnawaga for additional troops but the enemy were now too far ahead to catch.

On May 15, 1780 Captain Andrew Wemple deserted to the enemy with several of his Company and Little was appointed Captain in his place. Captain Little with his company were stationed at Fort Johnstown performing garrison and scouting duties.

On October 24th, 1781, Major John Ross and Captain Walter Butler with 607 men were in the Mohawk Valley burning and killing. Colonel Marinus Willett who was in command at Fort Rensselaer on learning of the invasion sent messengers to Forts Clyde, Paris and Plank for additional troops while he would gather what men that could be spared from the fort and go in pursuit of the enemy.

In the morning of October 25th, Colonel Willett and his men left the fort in pursuit of the enemy. Captain Little at Fort Johnstown, on being informed of the invasion, organized a scouting party to go in search of signs of the enemy. Captain Little, Lieutenant Zepheniah Batcheller, Sergeant John Eikler, Sergeant Henry Shew, Corporal Jacob Shew, Privates John Brothers, William Feeter, Peter Yost Jr., David and John Moyer and three others left the fort in search of the enemy.

Shortly after the scouting party left the fort, Major Ross and his men appeared before the fort. Stephen Shew, then on sentry duty, fired at them and the men in the fort turned out to defend the fort. After a few minutes of musket and cannon fire the enemy retreated from the fort. The garrison pursued the enemy through the Village of Johnstown when they were joined by Captain Little and his scouting party. Captain Little ordered the garrison back to the fort while he and his men would follow the enemy.

Shortly after the garrison arrived at the fort, Colonel Willett and his men arrived. The garrison informed Colonel Willett what had happened and that the enemy were encamped near Johnson's Hall. Colonel Willett and his men left the fort and headed for Johnson's Hall. Just as Colonel Willett and his troops arrived on the field, Captain Little and his men fell in with the rear guard of the enemy.

Captain Little was hit in the right shoulder with a musket ball and the scouting party with their wounded captain took to the woods to find cover. Here another brief exchange of musket fire took place and Sergeant Eikler was killed. The scouting party now joined Willett on the battlefield.

The battle raged until the coming of darkness and with the enemy retreating. Captain Little with the rest of the wounded were taken to Fort Johnstown. Captain Little's wound was properly dressed and by the spring of 1782 Little was back on duty at the fort. Captain Little served until the end of 1783 when he was discharged.

John was commissioned Second Major in Lieutenant-Colonel Volkert Veeder's Regiment of Montgomery County Militia in Brigadier General Frederick Visscher's Brigade on October 2, 1786. He resigned his commission on March 23, 1790. John also served as sheriff and as Justice of the Peace and he also served in other positions as well.

John was born in 1745 in Ireland and he died at Johnstown on September 29, 1822. His first wife was Leah Crawford but when she died is not known. John married for a second time Catherine McIntyre. She was born May 12, 1757 and she died on June 15, 1821. John and Catherine are buried in the Johnstown Colonial Cemetery on Green Street in Johnstown.

*It is not known in what capacity he was serving until 1780 when he was appointed Captain. I believe Little was serving in Captain Andrew Wemple's company in Col. Frederick Visscher's Regiment. As of 1991 no Muster Rolls for this company have been found which would clear this matter up.

DIED

In Johnstown, on Sunday last, Major John Little, aged 77. He was one of the remaining patriots, who are fast droping off from life, whose youthful vigor was spent in achieving our independence. Major Little was a brave and active officer during the whole of that ardous struggle, rendered particularly dangerous from the situation in which he was placed. He was appointed to the comand of the fort at Johnstown for the protection of the surrounding country from the hordes of savage Indians and more savage tories, commanded by Sir William Johnson (sic), who resided near there, and whose horrid cruelities will never be forgotten. (Amsterdam Mohawk Herald, Wednesday October 2, 1822, Vol. 1, no. 31, p. 3)

Disability Application for John Little

Dis. No Papers
Little, John

His name appears on a list of applicants for invalid pension returned by the District Court for the District of New York, submitted to the House of Representatives by the Secretary of War on April 25, 1794, and printed in the American State Papers, class 9, page 93.

Rank: Captain

Regt: Col. Fisher's

Disability: wounded in the shoulder in an action with the enemy, under Major Ross.

Where disabled: Johnstown

Residence: Johnstown

Remarks: No disability. There are no militia rolls in this office.

Evidence transmitted by the District Court incomplete, viz: Disability from known wounds not properly proved. No authentic proof of his being in service, and in the actual line of his duty. No examination by surgeons. No testimony of freeholders, or of the continuance of disability.

John Little's Petition.

5th March 1798. Referred to the Committee of Claims.

17th April 1798, report made, and ordered to lie on the table.

15th January 1799, Committed to a committee of the whole House tomorrow.

13th March, 1800. Referred to the Committee of Claims.

3d May, 1800 Committee of Claims discharged from further consideration.

To the Honorable The House of Representatives of the United States in Congress Assembled. (1)

The Petition of John Little of the County of Montgomery and State of New York. Humbly therewith.

That your petitioner was a Captain (2) of Militia in the late war. That in an Engagement between the American and British Forces near Johnstown (3) in the then County of Tryon, your petitioner was wounded in the right shoulder which wound so disables him that he is wholly incapacitated of obtaining a livelihood by labour, owing to his certificates having been informal heretofore he has been as yet neglected, but having obtained new & sufficient certificates, he now prays your honorable Body to take his case into consideration & to make such immediate provision in the premises as to you shall appear just & right.

And your petitioner as In Duty bound & Shall Ever Pray. John Little.

Additional Vouchers for Capt. John Little an Invalid viz.

No 1 & 2—Evidence of being wounded in Service.

3—ditto of three Freeholders, who have known him ever since.

4—Examination by two Physicians.

5—Commission from the District Judge.

6—Letter from ditto to the Secretary of War.

7—ditto from John Little to ditto.

8—John Little's Commission.

NB. This former Evidences are in the office of the Clerk of the House of Repress.

I certify that John Little Esqr, entered as a Volunteer in my Regiment in an Expedition against General St. Ledger (4) in the year 1777, then commanding the British Troops at the Seige [Siege] of Fort Schuyler, that from his knowledge of the Country on our march to the Relief of the Garrison of Fort Schuyler he was peculiarly serviceable to the American Army and distinguished himself upon every occasion during that Campaign as a Zealous Friend to the American Cause—That shortly after the Campaign above mentioned he was appointed a Major (5) in one of the Regiments of Militia commanded by Col. Frederick Visscher of the County of Montgomery and State of New York, and was wounded at the battle near Johns Town and to the best of my knowledge, he has never received any Compensation for the same.

Jas. Livingston late Colo. (6)

Given under my hand this 15th June 1792.

Johnstown Feby 20th 1798

Hornor'd Sir,

I received your letter last fall inclosing the Law respecting Invalid Pensioners I wrote to a Judge Troup who appointed three Commissioners to Examine the Evidences & Physicians which they have done and inclosed the certificates to Judge Troup. I have procured the Bearer Mr. Shurtleff to convey the Letter to Judge Troup who will I suppose forward them on to you. I trust your honor will make a speedy decision on the Business as the Bearer will wait the Issue—You Informed me that the certificate respecting my not applying for a pension previous to 88 was sufficient the others that are required I believe have been obtained, as I have been for these some years expecting some relief in this way. I pray that something may be done immediately to supply my needy family.

I am in due respect, Your Very Hble Servt. John Little
Hon'r J. McHenry Es.

Montgomery County
State of New York

Be it known that on the fifty day of January one thousand seven hundred and ninety eight came before me, James Livingston Richard Dodge and John McArthur, three persons specially authorize by Commission from the honourable Robert Troup Esquire Judge of the United States for the district of New York in virtue of the laws of the United States in that case made and provided. Thomas Read (7) and Caleb Smith two physicians who being duly sworn depose and say—that they were, each of them personally acquainted with John Little in the year one thousand seven hundred and eighty four that the said John Little did then to each of them respectively complain of a wound which he said he had received in an action between the American and British troops near Johnstown in the year one thousand seven hundred and eighty one, and that they did each of them respectively examine the said wound of the said John Little which was in his right shoulder, which appeared to have been given by some blunt instrument that the said John Little did appear to be much injured by the said wound so said to have been received—that they the said deponants have been personally and intimately acquainted with the said John Little from the year one thousand seven hundred and eighty four until the present time and that they do each of them respectively believe that from the said wound so said to have been received the said John Little has been and still is wholly incapacitated from obtaining a living by Labour. Thos. Read, C. Sweet.

The word wholly first interlined.

Sworn before us this 5th day of January one thousand seven hundred and ninety eight. Jas. Livingston, Rich'd Dodge, John McArthur.

The People of the STATE of NEW-YORK,

By the Grace of GOD, FREE and INDEPENDENT;

To John Little Esquire - - - GREETING.

WE reposing especial Trust and Confidence, as well in your Patriotism, Conduct and Loyalty, as in your Valour and Readiness to do us good and faithful Service; HAVE appointed and constituted, and by these Presents, DO appoint and constitute you the said John Little - Captain of a Company in the Regiment of Militia, in the County of Tryon, whereof Frederick Fisher Esquire is Colonel — — — — —

YOU are therefore, to take the said Company — into your Charge and Care, as Captain — — thereof, and duly to exercise the Officers and Soldiers of that Company — in Arms, who are hereby commanded to obey you as their Captain — — and you are also to observe and follow such Orders and Directions, as you shall from Time to Time receive from our General and Commander in Chief of the Militia of our said State, or any other your Superior Officer, according to the Rules and Discipline of War, in Pursuance of the Trust reposed in you; and for so doing, This shall be YOUR COMMISSION, for and during our good Pleasure, to be signified by our Council of Appointment. IN TESTIMONY whereof we have caused our Seal for Military Commissions to be hereunto affixed. WITNESS our trusty and well beloved George Clinton Esquire our Governor of our State of NEW-YORK, General and Commander in Chief of all the Militia, and Admiral of the Navy of the same, by and with the Advice and Consent of our said Council of Appointment, at Albany — — the Eighth — Day of March — in the fifth — — Year of our INDEPENDENCE, and in the Year of our LORD, One Thousand Seven Hundred and Eighty one

Passed the Secretary's Office, April 17th 1781.

By His EXCELLENCY's Command,

Robt Harpur Dy Secretary.

Geo. Clinton

County of Montgomery
State of New York

Be it known that on the fifth day of January one thousand seven hundred & ninety eight came before us Thomas Read & Caleb Sweet two Physicians appointed and authorized specially by Commissions from the honorable Robert Troup Esquire Judge of the United States for the District of New York in virtue of the Laws of the United States in that case made and provided John Little who being duly sworn deposeth and saith, that he was present in a Battle Between Colonel Willett of the continental Troops and a Major Ross of the British, near Johnstown in the now County of Montgomery, on the twenty first or twenty second of October in the year one thousand seven hundred and Eighty one that he there received a wound by the head of a tomahawk, in the right shoulder, and that he has since that time by reason of said wound been incapacitated from obtaining his living by Labour. (Signed) John Little

Sworn before us this 5th day of January 1798. Thos. Read, C. Sweet.

Montgomery County

State of New York

Be it know that on the tenth day of February one thousand seven hundred and ninety eight came before us James Livingston Richard Dodge & John McArthur three persons specially authorized by commission from the Honorable Robert Troup Esquire Judge of the United States in & for the District of New York in Virtue of the Law, of the United States in such case made and provided. Henry Shew, who being duly sworn by us, deposeth and saith that John Little in the commission to this deposition annexed named was in the year 1781 a Captain in Col. Frederick Fishers Regiment of Militia of the County of Montgomery and that on or about the 21st or 22nd of October 1781. That the said John Little was in the Battle called Willett's Battle in the Hall Field in Johnstown in said County in the actual line of his duty in the Service of the United States during the late war that they were there within ten yards of the Indians and that they were obliged to retreat. That on their return the said Little said he was wounded in the shoulder and this deponent deponent [sic] further saith that on their returning from the action the said Little several times told him to go and leave him and that he would give up to the Enemy for that he was unable to go any further. The distance from the American Garrison was about one & a half miles and that this deponent did assist the said Little with his hand in getting along and that he believes that if he had not so assisted him he would have fallen into the hands of the Enemy. (Signed) Henry Shew

Sworn before us this 10th February 1798—Jas. Livingston, Rich'd Dodge, John McArthur.

Montgomery County
State of New York

Be it known that on the tenth day of February one thousand seven hundred & ninety eight came before us James Livingston Richard Dodge & John McArthur three persons specially authorized by Commission from the Honorable Robert Troup Esquire Judge of the United States in and for the District of New York in Virtue of the Law of the United States in such case made and provided William Lard (8) and John Mason (9) who being duly sworn depose and say that John Little in the commission to this deposition annexed named was in the year 1781 a Captain in Col. Frederick Fishers Regiment of Militia of the County of Montgomery was present in an Engagement between the American Troops commanded by Col. Willet and the British and Indians commanded by Major Ross near Johnstown in the now County of Montgomery in the Actual Line of his duty and that he was there wounded in the right shoulder, which wound we saw the Evening after the Engagement which appeared to be a contusion by the head of a tomahawk or some other blunt instrument (this Engagement was on or about the twenty first or twenty second of October 1781—we have lived neighobours to the said John Little sever since the date above mentioned and he has frequently complained of the said wound ever since said action and further these deponents say that since the said action the said John Little has never done a days labour to their knowledge. His mode of Life has for some few years immediately after the aforesaid action been that of a Deputy Sheriff and Goaler, since that a Justice of the Peace and since that a Sheriff of the County but at present has no means of a living but his by hand and further they say that within three weeks from the time aforesaid or thereabouts they were dismissed from duty—and further say not--(Signed) William Lard, John Mason.

Sworn before us this 10th Feby 1798. Jas. W. Livingston, Rich'd Dodge (10), John McArthur.

Petition of John Little, of Montgomery County and State of New York.

23d January 1805, referred to the Committee of Claims.

24th January 1805, Committee of Claims discharged from consideration, and petition referred to the committee of the whole House, to whom was committed, on the 2d instant, the bill in addition to an act to make provision for persons that have been disabled by known wounds received in the actual service of the United States during the revolutionary war.

25th February 1806 Referred to the Committee of Claims.

28th March 1806, Case given to withdraw.

To the Honorable, the Senate, and House of Representative of the United States in Congress Assembled.

The Petition of John Little of the County of Montgomery in the State of New York; Humbly Sheweth:

That your Petitioner was Captain of a Company of Militia in Colonel Fisher's Regiment, in the Revolutionary War—That in an Engagement between the American and British forces, near the Town of Johnstown in said County, he received a wound from an Indians tomahawk, in the right shoulder, which so disabled him, that he has ever since been incapable of obtaining a livelihood, by labour, as will appear by the certificate and depositions, here with presented, taken before Commissioners appointed by Robert Troop Esquire, District Judge, pursuant to a law of Congress, for the relief of Invalids.—

That your Petitioner, had procured this necessary evidence, to establish his claim, to a pension, in the year 1798, when he expected to be placed on the pension list, without any further provision, but on his applying to the Secretary of War, with his voucher, he was told, that the time limited for exhibiting those claims, had expired.

That although, a law passed the Honorable Congress, in the year 1803, for the relief of the disabled officers, soldier, and seamen, wounded during the revolutionary war, and who had not been provided for, your Petitioner, is informed, that it does not embrace his case, because, he was serving in the Militia, and not in the regular Army, at the time, he was wounded.—

Her therefore prays your Honorable body, to take his peculiar case, into consideration, and grant him such relief, as shall be Just—and as in duty bound. He will pray, &c. (Signed) John Little. (11)

End Notes—John Little

1. Records of the House of Representatives, Record Group 233, 6th Congress, Series Title—Petitions, File Number HR 6A—F1.1, National Archives, Washington, D.C.
2. John Little (Little) was commissioned Captain on March 8, 1781, in Colonel Frederick Visscher's (Fisher, etc.) Third Regiment of Tryon County Militia. He was serving as Captain possibly as early as 1779.
3. The Battle of Johnstown was fought on October 25, 1781.
4. Brigadier General Barry St. Leger besieged Fort Schuyler (present day Rome, NY; Fort Stanwix) from August 2, 1777 to August 23, 1777.
5. Little actually served as Major after the War of Independence in the Montgomery County Militia.
6. James Livingston was the Colonel of the First Canadian Continental Regiment. Little served as a volunteer, which means he did not receive pay for this service in the First Canadian Regiment.
7. Thomas Read had served as Surgeon in the First Canadian Regiment.
8. William Laird (Lare, Lard, Lord), had served as a Lieutenant in Colonel Visscher's Regiment. In 1781 he served as a private in Captain Garret Putman's Company in Colonel Willett's Regiment.
9. John Mason had served as a Corporal under Captain Little in Colonel Visscher's Regiment. In 1781, John served also in Captain Putman's Company in Colonel Willett's Regiment. Mason also was wounded in the Johnstown Battle.
10. Richard Dodge, had served as a fifer in the Fifth New York Continental Regiment in Captain James Rosekrans Company. His brother Henry was the First Lieutenant and Samuel Dodge was the Second Lieutenant in the same company.
11. Although he doesn't mention it, he had been commissioned First Lieutenant on June 20, 1778 in Captain Thomas Wasson's Company in Colonel Abraham Wemple's Second Regiment of Albany County Militia. John moved sometime afterwards to Johnstown, New York. He died on September 29, 1822 and is buried in the Colonial Cemetery in Johnstown.

Pension Application for Jacob Lobdell

S.13787
State of New York
West Chester County SS.

On this 11th day of December in the year 1833 appeared before me Ezra Lockwood Esqr. one of the Judges of the Court of Common Pleas of the County of West Chester the same being a Court of Record, Jacob Lobdell a resident of the Town of North Salem in the said County aged Seventy Seven years who being first duly sworn according to Law doth on his oath make the following Declaration in order to obtain the benefit of the Act of Congress passed June 7th 1832.

That he entered the service of the United States under the following named officers and served as herein stated. That in the year 1775 Declarant was enrolled in a Company of Militia commanded by Captain Nathaniel De Lavan (1) in the Regiment of Colonel Thomas Thomas that in the Spring of the year 1776 a levy was made on the Militia in deponent's county on which a part was required of the several Regiments to go into actual service the companies of the Regiments were classed and each class was to furnish an able bodied man an able bodied man well equipped or in [?] a man from each class was to be taken by draft and Declarant further states that on or about the first of March in the said year 1776 he was drafted from the said company of Captain Nathaniel DeLavan & that he immediately equipped himself and was called into actual service as a Private that this Declarant was attached to Captain Henry Slawson's(2) Company in Lieutenant Colonel Samuel Drake's Regiment that he joined his company and marched with the Regiment to New York at which place the said Regiment was attached to the Continental Army that he served at Long Island and at New York until the retreat of the American Army that he was with the Army at the first Battle on Long Island (3) and retreated with his Regiment that immediately after their retreat as aforesaid this Declarant was taken sick with the Disentary [Dysentery] which then prevailed in the Army and in consequence [?????] to his father's House at North Salem to recruit that [?] during this year including the time of his sickness up to the first of December [January 1777 crossed out] when the campaign closed was seven months that he was sick in the course of this year and unable to perform duty three months and for the residue of the said time of seven months above which time he was on actual duty in an embodied corps called into service by competent authority said service was performed in the field that during the said time of seven months he was not employed in any civil pursuit.

And this declarant further states that in the year 1777 he was attached to the company of Captain Nathaniel DeLavan in the Regiment of Colonel Gilbert Drake (4) that he was a Private and called into actual service in an alarm when the Continental Army was destroyed at Danbury and when the Town was burned and Declarant further States that he served in the said Company and Regiment from early in the Spring of this year during the Summer and Autumn until Winter on the lines and below the lines in the County of West Chester at various times and was on duty for the first period or time of five months that the said service was performed in an embodied Corps called into service by competent authority and in the field that during this time he was not employed in any civil pursuit.

And this Declarant further states in the early part of the year 1778 in the Spring of that year and still being attached as a private to the company and Regiment last aforesaid now called out into actual service and was stationed with the said Company on the lines and below the lines in the County of West Chester until the first of August then next that he was in actual duty one month and a half. That on the first of August in that year Colonel Samuel Drake took command of the said Regiment which had previously been under the Command of Colonel Gilbert Drake, Ephraim Lockwood (5) took command of the Company to which Declarant was attached that Declarant was called into service that he performed actual duty on the lines and below the lines in the County aforesaid for two months after the said first day of August in the year 1778 that all the service performed by this Declarant in the year 1778 was in an embodied Corps called into service by competent authority and in the field that during this time he was not engaged in any civil pursuit.

In the year 1779 Declarant still continued attached as a private to Captain Ephraim Lockwood Company in the Regiment by Colo. Samuel Drake that he was called into actual service early in the Spring the Company was marched into the Town of North Castle, Bedford, and White Plains and was stationed on the lines and below the lines in the said County of West Chester that he was in actual Service and performed duty in the course of this year for three months and a half that all the service performed by him in this year was in an Embodied Corps called into service by competent authority and in the field that during this time he was not engaged in any civil pursuit.

And this Declarant further states that in the year 1780 a new Regiment was formed from Colonel Drake's Regiment and Colonel Thomas' Regiment in the North East part of the County of West Chester that in the Winter of the Year 1780, Lieutenant Colonel Thaddeus Crane (6) took the command of said newly formed Regiment that this Declarant still continued attached to the said Company of Captain Ephraim Lockwood as a private that the said Company was attached to Colonel Crane's Regiment that Declarant was called out with his company early in the Spring of this year was marched down from North Salem to the lines in the said County and below the lines that he was in actual service on and below the lines as aforesaid at different times and tours of duty during this year for the period of three months that such service was performed in an embodied Corps and called into service by competent authority and in the field that during this time he was not engaged in any civil pursuit—

And this declarant further saith that in the year 1781 he still continued attached as a private to the Company and Regiment last aforesaid that he was called out with the Company early in the Spring of this year, that he was in actual service during this year in the County of West Chester for the term of three months and a half, that the service performed was repelling the incursions of the Cavalry of the Enemy who were constantly passing to and from the lower Towns of the County through the center towns and was in the Northern Towns of the County descending upon the Inhabitants. The Infantry of the Enemy frequently made incursions into the Central Towns, and it became necessary to keep the Militia under arms most of the time until Winter, this Deponent performed actual duty this year for the period of time mentioned in an embodied Corps called into Service by competent authority and in the field that he was not employed in any civil pursuit during this term of service.

And this Declarant further saith that he still continued attached to the said last mentioned Company and Regiment as a private that he was enlisted into actual service in said Company early in the year 1782 that he was marched down to the lines, in the county aforesaid and was then sent on actual duty for two months that the service then performed by him was in an embodied Corps in the field which Corps was called into service by competent authority that he was not employed in any civil pursuit during this time of service.

And this Declarant further states that during the whole period of said service [?] & by him as aforesaid and at time when he was called into actual service as herein before stated he resided in the Town of North Salem in the County of West Chester. He hereby relinquishes every claim whatever to a pension or an annuity except the present and he declares that his name is not on the pension Roll of any Agency in any State. That he has no documentary evidence of his service & no other evidence except the Affidavits hereunto annexed. (Signed) Jacob Lobdell

Sworn to and Subscribed the 11th day of December 1833 before me in open court in aforesaid county. Ezra Lockwood.

We Hiram Gilliffe a Clergyman of the Protestant Episcopal Church residing in the Town of North Salem in the County of West Chester and Daniel Purdy residing in the same town hereby certify that we are well acquainted with Jacob Lobdell who hath subscribed and sworn to the above Declaration that we believe him to be seventy seven years of age that he is reputed and believed in the neighborhood where he resides to have been a soldier of the Revolution and that we concur in that opinion, we also believe him to be a man of truth and veracity. Hiram Gilliffee; Daniel Purdy.

Sworn and Subscribed before me Ezra Lockwood one of the Judges in & for Westchester County.

The following Interrogatories were prepondent by the said Judge of the said Court to the said Jacob Lobdell to wit—

1st When and in what year were your born.

Answer, I was born in the Manor of Cortland in West Chester County 22d May 1756.

2d Have you any Record of your age and if so where is it.

Answer, I have no Record of my age.

3d Where were you living when called into service, where have you lived since the Revolutionary War, and where do you now live?

Answer, I was living when called into service in Cuttandt Manor West Chester County at a place now called North Salem. I lived at the same place during the War and ever since the War of the Revolution and I now reside at the same place.

4th How were you called into service, were you drafted, did you volunteer or were you a substitute and if a substitute for whom?

Answer, In the year 1776 I was drafted and performed service as Stated in my Declaration in that year for each other times of Service set forth in his Declaration I was compelled to do Service under and by virture of the orders of my immediate Officers. I was at no time a Substitute for any person.

5th State the names of some of the Revolutionary Officers who were with the Troops when you served such Continental and Militia Regiments as you can recollect and the general circumstances of said service?

Answer, I recollect General Washington (7) I saw him on Long Island I was standing in Centry [Sentry] and the General passed by me, I do not recollect any other Regular Officers. He recollects of the Militia Officers, the following, Colonel Samuel Drake, Gilbert Drake, Col. Thomas Thomas & Thaddeus Crane Major Jesse Truesdale (8) and the other Militia Officers Stated in my Declaration. He has no recollection of any other circumstances of his service except to set forth in the Declaration other than this that he saw the British set fire to the Town of Danbury.

6th Did you ever receive a discharge from the service and if so by whom was it given and what has become of it?

Answer, I never did receive a written discharge from the service my discharge was always given by the Captain of the Company to which I was attached.

7th State the names of persons to whom you are known in your present neighbourhood and who can testify as to your character for veracity & their belief of your services as a Soldier of the Revolution?

Answer, I name Hiram Gilliffee a clergyman of the Protestant Episcopal Church residing in North Salem and David Purdy of North Salem aforesaid.

And I the said Ezra Lockwood one of the Judges of the Court of Common Pleas of the County of West Chester aforesaid do hereby declare my opinion after the investigation of the matter after putting the interrogations prescribed by the War Department that the above named deponent was a Revolutionary Solider and served as he states and I do further Certify that it appears to me that Hiram Gilliffee, that he signed the preceding certificate is a Clergyman of the Protestant Episcopal Church resident in the Town of North Salem in the County of West Chester and that Daniel Purdy who has also signed the same is a resident of the same place and is a credible person & that their statement is entitled to credit.—

And I do further certify that the said Jacob Lobdell cannot from bodily infirmity attend Court to make his Declaration. Ezra Lockwood

End Notes—S.13787—Jacob Lobdell

1. Jacob enlisted as a private in Captain Nathanial Delevan's Company in Colonel Pierre VanCortlandt's Third Regiment of Westchester County Militia. Colonel Thomas Thomas commanded the Second Regiment of Westchester County Militia. Captain Delevan was commissioned on September 20, 1775 in Colonel VanCortland'ts Regiment and was not in Colonel Thomas' Regiment. This service was probably in detachments under Colonel Thomas.
2. Captain Henry Slasson (Slawson) appointed Captain of the First Company on March 1, 1776 in the Westchester County Regiment of Minute Men. Joseph Drake was the Colonel, but by February 26, 1776, Samuel Drake is referred to as a colonel of a regiment as he had

attended the Provincial Congress to get money to pay his regiment. He was advanced £ 300 on his account. A detachment of the Westchester County Militia was ordered raised by the Provincial Congress to join Colonel Samuel Drake's Regiment at New York City. FROM: Documents Relating to the Colonial History of the State of New York, ed. Berthold Fernow, Vol. XV, State Archives, Vol. !, Weed, Parsons and Company, printers, Albany, N.Y., 1887, pp 75 and 84.

3. The Battle of Long Island, N.Y. was fought on August 27, 1776.
4. Gilbert Drake was the Lieutenant-Colonel appointed on October 19, 1775. Colonel Pierre VanCortlandt resigned because he was elected Lieutenant Governor in 1777 and Brigadier General George Clinton was elected Governor. On June 25, 1778, Samuel Drake was commissioned Colonel and John Hyatt was Lieutenant-Colonel in the Third Westchester County Militia. Gilbert Drake had resigned sometime before that event. On the same date Captain Delevan was commissioned Major of the regiment since Major Joseph Strong had also resigned.
5. Ephraim Lockwood was commissioned Captain on June 25, 1778 in Colonel Samuel Drake's Regiment.
6. On October 21, 1779 the Council of Appointment ordered that a new regiment be formed as follows: "Formed of different companies of the two regiments commanded by Colonel Thomas Thomas and Colonel Drake and sett apart as a distinct Regiment." Thaddeus Crane who was the Major of Colonel Thomas' Regiment was promoted to Lieutenant-Colonel. Major Nathaniel Delevan and Captain Lockwood were also in the new regiment.
7. General and Commander-in-Chief George Washington.
8. Jesse Truesdale served as a First Lieutenant in Captain Crane's Company in Colonel Thomas' Regiment. When Crane was promoted to Major; Truesdale was promoted to Captain and on April 12, 1782 he was commissioned Major in Colonel Thomas' Regiment.

Pension Application of Peter McArthur

W.23934 (Widow: Christian or Christiana)
State of New York
Montgomery County SS.

On this twenty first day of September 1832, personally appeared in Open Court, before the Court of Common Pleas of the County of Montgomery, now sitting Peter McArthur a resident of the town of Mayfield in the County and State aforesaid aged 82 years who being first duly sworn according to law doth on his oath make the following declaration in order to obtain the benefit of the act of Congress passed June 7, 1832. That he entered the service of the United States under the following named officers and served as herein stated. In the year 1776 sometime in the month of June he was drafted in the Militia, the company officers he does not recollect, but knows that the company belonged to Col. Hays (1) Regiment, that he went from Haverstraw Orange County, State of New York, to Peeks Kill to which place the British had come with their vessels, up the Hudson river and burnt that place that he does not recollect how long he served in the militia, but says that he was out in the militia at different times and places which he cannot now state and served about one month in all in the militia.

In the same year 1776, he this applicant says he enlisted in the New York State Troops, for the term of six months, on the first day of July of that year, at Haverstraw, aforesaid, and went from there to Tappan Bay and then from there back again to Haverstraw and then back again to Tappan Bay a second time and from there this applicant says, he marched to a place where was erected Fort Independence, that he served under Captain Derunda, Lieutenant Coe, the Ensigns name he does not recollect, belonging to Col. Nichols (2), Regiment, that he served the full time of six months, and has no recollection of the places he went to while out, and was discharged on the first day of January and has no written discharge. He has no documentary evidence of his services.

He was born in Broadalbin Pearth Shire, Scotland in the year 1750, and has no record of his age. That he resided at Haverstraw aforesaid when called into service and has resided at his present place of residence since the Revolution.

He knows of none of the names of the regular officers.

He is acquainted with the following persons residing in the neighborhood where he lives and who can testify as to his character, for truth and veracity and their belief of his services as a soldier of the revolution, to wit, Simon Hosack & Judge Haring.

He hereby relinquishes every claim whatever to a pension or annuity except the present and declares that his name is not on the Pension Roll of the agency of any state.

(Signed with his mark) Peter McArthur (3)

Sworn and subscribed the day and year aforesaid. Geo. D. Ferguson, clerk

Christiana, Peter McArthur's widow in her deposition said she was married to him on the 17th of May 1792, that he died on the 5th day of February 1841.

End Notes—W.23934—Peter McArthur

1. Ann Hawkes Hays was the Colonel of the Third Regiment of Orange County Militia.
2. Colonel Isaac Nicoll was in command of New York State Levies raised from the different Orange County Militia Regiments in 1776. There are no company muster rolls known for this regiment. Captain Jacob Deranda or Deronda, etc., was part of the regiment. The company was stationed at Peekskill and then to Fort Independence. FROM: Revolutionary War Rolls 1775-1783, Series M-246, Roll 75, folder 132, National Archives, Washington, D.C.

3. Chrisitan[a] McArthur, Peter's Widow applied for a widow's pension on January 17, 1843 at the age of 74. She was living in the Town of Mayfield. She states that Peter died on February 5, 1841. Pastor Hugh Mair of the Johnstown Presbyterian Church verifies the marriage of Peter to Christian McLaren took place on May 17th 1792. Christian McArthur died on April 11, 1853 at age 83 years. Both are buried in Section 3 of the Johnstown Colonial Cemetery.

Pension Application for Samuel McKeen or McKean

S.27,161 and S.28,806
State of New York
Otsego County SS.

On this 22d day of October 1844 came into open court Samuel McKean aged 80 years who on his solemn oath makes the following declaration in order to obtain the benefits of the provision of the act of Congress of the 7th day of June 1832.

& Applicant states that he now [is] a resident of the County and State aforesaid, that in Montgomery he was born & in that and this County he has allways resided, that he is the Identical man who is now receivingan invalid pension of the United States for wounds received during the war of the Revolution, and while in actual Service.

That in the month of May 1779 (1) his father Robert McKean was commissioned a Captain in [the] State of New York to serve as such in the levies raised for the defence of the western frontiers, that your applicant tho very young entered the service of the United States as a soldier of his father's company for nine months and served as a soldier of s'd Co. form May 1779 until the 1st day of January 1780 when he was discharged by his father. That in May 1780 (2) he was again called on & entered the service of his father's company of New York Levies and served as such until January 1781 when he was again discharged and again in April1781 he entered the service of his father's company and served in said Co. until his father was promoted to Major and he served in Capt. Marshall's Company until the 10th of July 1781. At which time and in an engagement with the Indians on the Mohawk River his father received wounds of which he died in a few days, that your applicant was also at the same time wounded in the mouth for which he is now receiving as before stated a pension. That all the service done by said Robt McKean was against the Indians in the Mohawk Valley, that owing to the fall of applicant's father in service his muster rolls was lost and as he is informed not returned to the proper office in the state, and that only the record of applicant's service in Capt. Marshall Co. Appears from the time he enlisted in May 1781 to the date of his wound in July 1781. (3) That the pay or muster rolls of Robt McKean of 1779 & 1780 were lost with him as he is informed & believes when he fell in battle, that said Robt McKean left a widow who got his arrearages of pay & as this applicant now recollects. Your applicant states that he never has made application for his pension under the act of the 7th of June 1832 not knowing he had a right to but one at a time, that he is not on any pension roll of the United States (Save & except that of an invalid as before stated), he hereby relinquishes all claim to a pension except that he is now receiving as an invalid. That he is very advanced in life & may from that cause have misstated some few matters as to dates but that he is perfectly clear in his recollection of having served from May 1779 to January of the year following & from May 1780 to the January following & from May 1781 to the date of his wound (4), in July 1781, that he is certain his father was his captain for the 1st & 2nd tour & that Capt. Marshall was his capt for the 3rd tour. That Lt. Col Harper, the year 1780 & 81, that Marinus Willett was commandant of the Regiment all the time but was a Continental officers. (Signed) Samuel McKean.

Sworn to and Subscribed the day & year aforesaid in open court. Geo. B. Wilson, Clerk

State of New York
Secretary's Office

I certify that on the 3rd day of May 1779 Robert McKean was duly appointed & Commissioned Captain of one of the companies in one of the district corps of 500 men each directed to be raised by law for the immediate defence of the State one of which corps was commanded by Lieut. Colonel Henry K. VanRensselaer and the other by Lieut. Colonel Albert Pawling—all which appears by the mintues of the Council of appointment of this state in this office.

It also appears by the said Minutes that on the 11th of May 1780 Robert McKane was appointed and commissioned a Captain in the Regiment of Levies raised for the defence of the frontiers whereof Robert Harper was Lieut Col. Commandant Arch'd Campbell Dep. Sec. of State.
Albany October 19, 1844

State of New York
Otsego County SS.

Be it known that before me Elisha Foote Esquire one of the Judges of the Court of Common Pleas in the County aforesaid Samuel McKeen personally appeared and made oath that he is the identical Samuel McKeen named in an original certificate of which the following is a true Copy, and that said certificate is now lost. "This is to certify that in pursuance of the law of the State of New York, entitled an act making provision for the officers, soldiers and seamen, who have been disabled in the service of the United States passed the 22nd day of April, 1785. We have examined Samuel McKeen of Cherry Valley in the County of Montgomery, carpenter, and find that during the late war to wit. Sometime in the spring of the year one thousand seven hundred and eighty one he enlisted as a private soldier in Captain Elihu Marshall's Company in the Regiment of New York levies in the service of the United States, commanded by Col. Marinus Willet, that on the tenth day of July in the same year, he was ordered out under the immediate command of Col. Willett to attack a party of

Indians at Turlough, in the County of Montgomery aforesaid and in the attack aforesaid he received a wound from the enemy by a musket ball in his chin which fractured the Jaw bone and came out through his left cheek, by reason of which wound he is in some measure disabled from obtaining his livelihood by labor, that on the twenty second day of June last he was twenty three years of age. Wherefore in pursuance of the law aforesaid we do further certify that upon the principles of the act of Congress of the seventeenth day of June 1783, the said Samuel McKeen is entitled to receive from the treasurer of this State a yearly pension of thirty six dollars, from the first day of January in the year one thousand seven hundred and eighty two if not before paid.

Given under our hands this twenty fifth day of July 1788. Richard Varick, Richard Stott

And the said Samuel McKeen further saith that he served as a private in Captain Elihu Marshall's Company in Col. Willett's Regiment of New York Levies in the service of the United States at the time he was disabled and that he now resides in the town of Otsego and County aforesaid and that he has resided there for the space of seven years last past and that previous hereto he resided in the town of Cherry Valley County of Otsego and State of New York. (Signed) Samuel McKeen.

Sworn and subscribed before me this 7th day of May 1824. Elisha Foote Judge.

End Notes—Samuel McKeen—S.27161 and S.28806

1. Two regiments of levies of 500 men each were authorized to be raised on March 13, 1779. Robert McKean was appointed Captain in Colonel Henry K. VanRensselaer's Regiment of New York State Levies. There are no known muster rolls for this company.
2. Captain McKean was appointed on May 11, 1780 to serve in Lieutenant-Colonel John Harper's Regiment of New York State Levies. The regiment was discharged on November 30, 1780. Again there are no known muster rolls for this company.
3. In April of 1781, Captain McKean was appointed to serve in Lieutenant-Colonel Marinus Willett's Regiment of New York State Levies. By June of 1781, Colonel Willett ordered Captain McKean to put the men of his company into Captain Elihu Marshall's Company. Samuel's name does appear on Marshall's Company payroll for 1781.
4. Samuel was wounded on July 10, 1781, at the Battle of New Dorlach (present day Sharon Springs, Schoharie County, NY). His father, Captain McKean received a mortal wound at this battle and died on the return march back to Fort Rensselaer.

Pension Application for Daniel Morrison or Morisson

W.17163 (Widow Rebecca. In 1837 at age seventy six, she applied for pension. They were married September 10, 1779 and that Daniel died on the 26th day of September 1836.)

State of New York

County of Schenectady SS.

On this thirteenth day of October in the year of our Lord one thousand eight hundred and thirty two personally appeared in open court before the Judges of the court of common Pleas in and for said County now sitting Daniel Morrison a resident of the Town of Duanesburgh in said County and State aged eighty six years, who being first duly sworn according to law, doth on his oath make the following declaration in order to obtain the benefit of the Act of Congress passed June 7th 1832.

He was born in the Parish of Perthshire Scotland in the Kingdom of Great Britain on the twenty second day of March 1746. He has no record of his age.

When he was called into the service of the United States in the army of the revolution, he was living in the town of Wallkill County of Orange in the State of New York, and since the revolutionary war he has lived in said town of Duanesburgh where he now lives.

He entered the service of the United States under the following named officers, and served as herein stated.

In the summer of the year 1776 he enlisted in Captain John Nicholson's (1) Company of the 2d New York Regiment under the command of Colonel James Clinton of his other company and Field Officers he remembers only the name of Gregg 2d Lieut (2) The term of his enlistment in this company was six months which he served out faithfully and then he received his discharge. During this engagement he marched to St. Johns Quebec and Montreal. He was with the troops under General Montgomery (3) and aided in the taking of the garrison of St. Johns & Montreal and was with General Montgomery during the siege of Quebec.

The precise time he returned from the northern campaign he cannot recollect, but when he returned he enlisted for and during the war in a company of Rangers commanded by Captain Jacob DeWitt. (4) His other officers which he recollects were John Broadhead and William Bull. While in this company he marched to Esopus, Minisink, Hackinsack & other places in New Jersey, he continued to serve in this company until it was disbanded which was about three years after his enlistment therein. He cannot remember dates.

This Declarant next inlisted in the Quarter Master's Department under Col. Hughs (5), and discharged fatigue duty for about the term of one year at King's Ferry & other places. After serving out the last described term he served pursuant to enlistment for three months in Moses Bull's Company of Rangers. He thinks this was in the year 1782. This last service was rendered at Kingston guarding Tories.

When the battle of Monmouth (6) took place he participated in it & while in Quebec, during the expedition he was in several encounters with the enemy.

The following are the names of some of the regular officers whom he knew, or who were with the troops where he served, and such continental and militia regiments or companies with which he served, or as he can recollect, viz: Captain Dubois, General Schuyler (7) & those officers whose names are herein before stated.

He never received any written discharge from the service that he recollects of and if he did it is lost.

He has no documentary evidence, and knows of no person whose testimony he can procure who can testify to his service, who is now living.

The following are the names of persons to whom he is known in his present neighborhood, and who can testify as to his character for veracity, and their belief of his services as a soldier of the revolution, to wit—the Rev'd Thomas Holliday and Daniel Morrison Junr.

He hereby relinquishes every claim whatever to a pension or annuity except the present, and declares that his name is not on the pension roll of the agency of any state. (Signed) Daniel Morrison

Subscribed and sworn to the day and year first aforesaid. John S. Vrooman Clerk

End Notes—Daniel Morrison—W.17163

1. Daniel enlisted as a private on July 12, 1775 in Captain John Nicholson's Company (Second Company) in Colonel James Clinton's Third New York Continental Regiment. A Thomas Morrison had enlisted on July 8, 1775 in the same company. FROM: Revolutionary War Rolls 1775-1783, Series M-246, Roll 69, Folder 38, National Archives, Washington, D.C.
2. The lieutenants of the company were David DuBois and James Gregg.
3. Major General Richard Montgomery.
4. On July 23, 1776 the Provincial Congress of New York authorized several companies of rangers to be raised. There were at least 10 companies. Jacob Rusten DeWitt was appointed Captain of one of these companies. All of the ranger companies were discharged on March 27, 1777. DeWitt's Company did not exist for 3 years, Captain DeWitt had been Captain of the Sixth Company (Appointed on September 29, 1775), in Colonel James Clinton's Second Regiment of Ulster County Militia. When Colonel Clinton was appointed Colonel of the Third New York, Lieutenant-Colonel James McClaughrey took command of the Second Ulster. McClaughrey was commissioned Colonel of this regiment on March 23, 1778. When Captain DeWitt left the regiment to command the Ranger Company, First Lieutenant Abraham Cuddeback assumed command of the company. Cuddeback was commissioned Captain on March 23, 1778.
5. Colonel Hugh Hughes. He was appointed on May 11, 1776 as Assistant Quartermaster General.
6. A Daniel Morrison appears to have enlisted on May 19, 1778 for 9 months in Captain James Stewart's Company (Third Company) in Colonel Lewis DuBois Fifth New York, Continental Regiment. This Daniel was discharged on June 14, 1779. The Battle of Monmouth,

New Jersey was fought on June 28, 1778. The Fifth New York was not in this battle, the regiment was still in New York.

7. Major General Philip Schuyler.

Pension Application for Richard Morrison

S.43022

Northern District of the State of New York SS.

On this first day of November 1819, before me, the subscriber, one of the Judges of the Court of Common Pleas of the County of Albany in the said district, personally appeared Richard Morrison aged sixty three years, resident in the City of Albany in the said district, who, being by me first duly sworn, according to law, doth, on his oath, make the following declaration, in order to obtain the provision made by the late act of Congress, entitled "An act to provide for certain persons engaged in the land and naval service of the United States in the revolutionary war." That he, the said Richard Morrison enlisted for the term of the continuance of the war on the first part of January in the year 1777 in Tappan Village in the state of New York in the company commanded by Captain Gregg (1) of the Regiment commanded by Colonel Gansevoort in the line of the State of New York afterwards five regiments was consolidated into two he then was in Capt. Tiebout's (2) comp. & VanSchaick's Regt. on the Continental Establishment; that he continued to serve in the said corps, or in the service of the United States, until the 8th day of June 1783, when he was discharged from service in or near New Windsor state of New York that he was in the battle of Yorktown at the taking of Lord Cornwallis (3) and that he is in reduced circumstances, and stands in need of the assistance of his country for support; and that he has no other evidence now in his power of his said services, but what has been transmitted to the war department. (Signed with his mark) Richard Morrison

Sworn to and declared before me, the day and year aforesaid. Estes Howe, Judge Albany Com. Pleas.

State of New York
County of Albany
Court of Common Pleas SS.

On this seventeenth day of June 1820 personally appeared in open court, being a court of record for the said state having an unlimited jurisdiction and proceeding according to the Course of Common Law.

Richard Morrison aged sixty five years, resident in the City of Albany in said state aforesaid, who being first duly sworn according to law, doth, on his oath, declare that he served in the Revolutionary War as follows: I Richard Morrison served in the company commanded by Capt. Graigs in the 3rd Regiment of New York Line, and continental Service that I made my declaration before Estes Howe Judge &c on the 31st of April 1818 and that I am now on the pension list at the rate of eight dollars per month that my certificate is numbered 16238.

And I solemnly swear that I was a resident citizen of the United States on the 18th day of March, 1818; and that I have not since that time, by gift, sale, or in any manner, disposed of my property, or any part thereof, with intent thereby so to diminish it, as to bring myself within the provisions of an act of Congress, entitled "An act to provide for certain person engaged in the land and naval service of the United States, in the Revolutionary war," passed on the 18th day of March, 1818; and that I have not, nor has any person in trust for me, any property or securities, contracts or debts, due to me; nor have I any income other than what is contained in the schedule hereto annexed, and by me subscribed.

That I am by occupation a [left blank] has no wife nor family nor any stated home or dwelling but lives by the charity of the citizens of Albany together with what little pittance I can earn by my daily labour, that I am quite infirm by reason of age and general debility, that I have no property whatever either real or personal except the few clothes I wear and which I purchased with my pension money. (Signed with his mark) Richard Morrison

Sworn to and declared in open court on the seventeenth day of June 1820 before H.A. Williams Depy Clk.

End Notes—S.43022—Richard Morrison

1. Richard enlisted as a private on February 14, 1777 for during the war in Captain James Gregg's Company (Sixth Company) in Colonel Peter Gansevoort's Third New York Continental Regiment.
2. Henry Tiebout was a Captain in the Third New York until 1781. On January 1, 1781, the First New York Continental Regiment and the Third were consolidated into one Regiment. Captains Gregg and Tiebout were transferred to the First New York under Colonel Goose VanSchaick. Richard was transferred to Tiebout's Company in 1781. FROM: Revolutionary War Rolls 1775-1783, Series M-246, Roll 66, Folder 15, National Archives, Washington, D.C.
3. The Yorktown, Virginia, Campaign was from September 28 to October 19, 1781 when Lord Cornwallis surrendered his British Forces. It is interesting that Richard doesn't mention the Siege of Fort Schuyler (Fort Stanwix) which lasted 21 days in August of 1777. The Third New York was in this siege. Also he doesn't mention the Sullivan-Clinton Campaign of 1779 against the Iroquois Villages in Western New York.

Pension Application for Jacob Newkirk

S.5811

Declaration of Jacob Newkirk in order to obtain the benefit of the act of Congress passed June 7th 1832.

State of New York

Greene County SS.

On this fourth day of September 1832, personally appeared in open Court before the Judges of the Court of Greene County Common Pleas now sitting Jacob Newkirk resident of the town of Catskill of said County & State aged eighty two years, who being first duly sworn according to law, doth, on his oath, make the following declaration in order to obtain the benefit of the act of Congress passed June 7th 1832.

That he entered the service of the United States under the following named officers, and served as herein stated that he was drafted or warned out and served two months under Jacob Captain Rose (1) Isaac Hallenbeck Lieutenant (2) and marched to Stoney Point in the Highlands where Colonel John Hardenbergh (3) Commanded. He served there two months was dismissed just before the fort at Stoney Point was taken by the British. The precise time of the year and year he does not recollect and that some time afterwards he served in a similar under Captain Cockrain (4) three weeks scouring the county about the enemy lines and that he was afterwards drafted or called out by Captain Jacob Rose and William Ostrander Lieutenant (5) and marched to Pyramus in the State of New Jersey and served there two months—That afterwards he served under Captain Jacob Rose for two months by substitute and that when he performed the above mentioned services he lived in the town of Shanangunk of the County of Ulster of the State aforesaid and that afterwards during the revolutionary war he moved to the town of Catskill of the then county of Albany now of the county Greene aforesaid - That he was drafted or called out by Captain—Mynderson (6) and Lieutenant Jacob Van Vechten (7) and marched to the City of Albany at the time of Burgoines (8) surrender where he stayed four weeks, and that he afterwards served under Captain Benjamin Dubois two weeks in the Neighborhood of Catskill Mountains and that he has been frequently besides called out for days and a week together on Indian alarms.

He hereby relinquishes every claim whatever to a pension or annuity except the present and declares that his name is not on the pension roll of the agency of any state. (Signed) Jacob Newkirk

Sworn to and subscribed the day & year aforesaid in open court. William V. B. Hermance, clerk

End Notes—S.5811—Jacob Newkirk

1. Captain Jacobus Rose or Roosa was in Colonel Jonathan Hasbrouck's Fourth Regiment of Ulster County Militia.
2. No record of a Lieutenant Isaac Hallenbeck has been found. There was an Ensign Isaac Hardenburgh in Captain Rose's company.
3. Johannes L. Hardenburgh was the Lieutenant-Colonel in Colonel Hasbrouck's Regiment. He was commissioned colonel of the regiment on February 27, 1779.
4. Captain Cockrain was not found in the Ulster County Militia.
5. Wilhemus Ostrander was the Ensign in Captain Cornelius Masten's Company in Colonel Hasbrouck's Regiment. Captain Masten had served as the First Lieutenant in Captain Rose's Company. When Rose died Masten was acting captain and he was commissioned as such on March 9, 1778. Ostrander was commissioned ensign on the same date as Hardenburgh was promoted to Second Lieutenant.

6. Possibly Captain John Mynderse or Mynderson of the Second Company in Colonel Abraham Wemple's Second Regiment of Albany County Militia.
7. Jacob VanVechten or Veghten was the First Lieutenant in Captain Benjamin C. DuBois' Company in Colonel Anthony VanBergen's Eleventh Regiment of Albany County Militia.
8. Lieutenant General John Burgoyne surrendered his British Army on October 17, 1777.

Pension Application for Henry Ostrander

W. 16667 (Widow: Patty)

At a Court of Common Pleas holden at the Court House in Plattsburgh, in and for the County of Clinton and State of New York, on the third day of October 1820, Present: Elisha Arnold, Caleb Nichols, Nathan Carver and Allen R. Moore. Justices of the said Court.

County of Clinton ss: on this third day of October 1820 personally appeared in open Court proceeding according to the course of the common law, and having the power of fine and imprisonment, and keeping a record of their proceedings in and for the County of Clinton, Henry Ostrander aged sixty six years resident in the town of Plattsburgh in the said County of Clinton, who being first duly sworn according to law; doth on his oath declare that he served in the revolutionary war as follows. That he enlisted in 1775 for five months in Rosecriants Company Col. Holmes N. York Regiment (1) and served out that time that in the spring of 1776 he enlisted for ten months in Rosecrints Company Dubois N. York Regiment (2) and served out that term and at the expiration of that term he again enlisted in the last mentioned company and Regiment in the N. York line for three years (3) and served out that time and was discharged at Morristown, New Jersey he was at the taking of fort Montgomery and taken prisoner then and at the battle of New town.

That his original declaration to obtain a pension under the Act of Congress of the 13th of March 1818 was made the thirtieth day of March 1818, that he has received a pension certificate Numbered 15393 and dated the sixth day of October 1819 And I do solemnly swear that I was a resident citizen of the United States on the 18th day of March 1818, and that I have not since that time by gift sale or in any manner disposed of my property or any part thereof, with intent thereby so to diminish it as to bring myself within the provisions of an act of Congress, entitled "An act to provide for certain persons engaged in the land and naval service of the United State in the revolutionary war" passed on the 13th day of march 1818 and that I have not nor has any person in trust for me any property or securities, contracts of debts, due to me, nor have I any income, other than what is contained in the schedule, hereto annexed and by me subscribed.

Real Estate. None. Personal Property Excepting my necessary Bedding and Cloathing

One old five pail kettle 3—

One tea pot 3 cups and saucers .37
Tea Kettle and 3 knives and forks 1.—
4 kitchen chairs, old 2.
1 small cow, 1 pot, I dish kettle 16.50
One fire shovel and one pair old hand iron 1.50
Total $25.97

Sworn to and declared on the third day of October 1820 before the above named Judges in Open Court. C. Platt, clerk.

I Charles Platt, Clerk of the Court of Common Pleas held in and for the County of Clinton; do certify that the foregoing oath and the schedule thereto annexed are truly copied from the record of the said Court, and I do further certify that it is the opinion of the said Court that the total amount in value of the property exhibited in the aforesaid schedule is twenty five dollars and ninety seven cents. And I further certify that the last term of this Court closed on the 11th of May last and before the promulgation of the act of Congress of the first of May 1820—in this County and that there has been no court held in said county until the present term at which the above schedule and oath could be received.

In testimony whereof, I have hereunto set my hand and affixed the seal of said Court on this third day of October 1820. Chas. Platt. Clerk of the Court for the County of Clinton.

State of New York
Clinton County SS. I Henry Ostrander of the Town of Plattsburgh in the County of Clinton & State of New York, do solemnly and sincerely swear & declare that I was a private in Captain Rosecrants Company in the Regiment commanded by Colonel Lewis Dubois in the New York line in the service of the United States of America in the war of the revolution, that I enlisted in the army of the United States, at Fishkill in the Ståte of New York in the fall of the year 1775 in the same Regiment & under the officers first mentioned above for the term of five months & was discharged the refrom at Albany some time in the Month of January 1776.—That I afterwards, in the month of February 1776, enlisted again at Fishkill for one year, in the same regiment & under the same officers, & was discharged therefrom in February 1777 at Fort Montgomery and that soon after my discharge at Fort Montgomery I again enlisted in the army of the United States at the Town of Fishkill aforesaid, for the term of three years in the Regiment & Company under the officers aforesaid and that I was taken prisoner at Fort Montgomery in October 1777 and was exchanged at the expiration of ten months & rejoined my Regiment at the White Plains in the State of New York and was discharged at Morristown in the State of New Jersey in January 1781. That I lost my discharge about thirty years since, That I am in indigent circumstances & am in need of assistance from my country for support. (Signed with his mark) Henry Ostrander

I Caleb Nichols a Judge of the Court of Common Pleas for the County & of Clinton & State of New York do certify that on the thirtieth day of March one thousand eight hundred & eighteen the above named Henry Ostrander to me known made out before me to the above statement & declaration Caleb Nichols.

State of New York
Clinton County

Be it remembered that before the Subscriber William F. Haile one of the Judges for the County Courts of said County personally appeared Patty Ostrander of Plattsburgh in said County & on her oath made the following declaration for the purpose of obtaining a pension from the United States under the act of Congress passed 4 July 1836.

She says that she is the widow of Henry Ostrander late of Plattsburgh deceased—She was married to said Henry Ostrander at Fishkill in this State in October in the year 1779 by Thomas Storm Esquire a Justice of the Peace—He the said Henry Ostrander was there & for a considerable time previous had been a private soldier in Col. Dubois Regiment in the New York line—he was in Capt. Rosekrants Company—William Alger was his Lieutenant for some time—he continued in that regiment some time after the marriage. He after the marriage went north with a party of men as a guard & took a number of the Tories out of the Country to Canada. - He continued in the army from the beginning of the Revolutionary War most of the time till peace—He was in one severe action that is when Fort Montgomery was taken. He was then taken prisoner—Soon after the Revolution & in the year 1785 Deponent & the said Henry Ostrander moved to Plattsburgh then a wilderness & where they have resided ever since & her daughter Ada was the first born white child in Plattsburgh—Her said husband drew a pension from the United States as a revolutionary soldier for several years previous to his death he died at Plattsburgh in January 1830 & she has ever since remained a widow & greatly needs a pension—She is now in the eightieth yeår of her age—She has no documentary evidence in support of her claim—previous to her marriage with said Henry Ostrander her name was Patty Nicholson. (Signed with her mark) Patty Ostrander

Sworn & subscribed to at Plattsburgh this 20th day of February 1837 before me the same having been first carefully read over to the Deponent by me, she being unable to write her name & being unable to attend court by reason of age & infirmity. The words "The said Henry Ostrander having been first enterlined. I also certify that the Deponent is a credible witness. Wm. F. Haile, a Judge of Clinton County Courts.

Reply to a letter of inquiry dated February 14, 1938.

Reference is made to your letter in which you request the Revolutionary War record of Henry Ostrander, who, was born in Dutchess County, New York, and died in Plattsburgh, New York.

The data given herein are found in the papers on file in pension claim. W. 16667, based upon service of Henry Ostrander in the Revolutionary War.

Henry Ostrander was born October 10, 1754; the place of his birth and the names of his parents are not shown. He resided in Fishkill, Dutchess County, New York, as early as 1774.

While a resident of said Fishkill (blot on a line) 1775, served five months as a private in Captain James Rosekrans' company, Colonel Holmes' New York regiment and was discharged sometime in January 1776, at Albany; he re-enlisted in the spring of 1776, and served ten months as private in Captain James Rosekrans' company, Colonel Lewis Dubois' New York regiment, then re-enlisted under these same officers, was in the battle of fort Montgomery where he was taken prisoner, was exchanged later, re-joined his regiment, was in the battle of Newtown, (4) and was discharged from service in January 1781, at Morristown, New Jersey.

Henry Ostrander was allowed pension on his application executed March 30, 1818, at which time he resided in Plattsburg, Clinton County, New York. He had lived there ever since about 1785. He died there January 25, 1830.

Henry Ostrander married in October 1779, in Fishkill, New York. Martha (called Patty) Nicholson; she was born September 18, 1757, names of her parents not shown. She was of Dutch descent.

Patty Ostrander (as her name was borne on the pension rolls) was allowed pension on her application executed February 20, 1837, at which time she resided in Plattsburgh, New York. She died January 14, 1840.

The names of children of Henry Ostrander and his wife, Martha (Patty) ware show as follow: (5)

Elizabeth Ostrander	Born April 4, 1781, died Sept. 11, 1831.
Mary Ostrander	Born July 3, 1783.
Idah Ostrander	Born September 7, 1785.
James Ostrander	Born January 6, 1788.
Sarah Ostrander	Born November 2, 1789.
Jane Ostrander	Born December 5, 1791.
Richard Ostrander	Born September 13, 1793, died Nov. 4, 1805.
Henry S. Ostrander	Born February 28, 1796.
Israel N. Ostrander	Born July 23, 1799.

Children's Marriages

Elizabeth Ostrander January 3, 1803

Mary and Robert D. Liddell July 14, 1832.

In 1837, Israel N. Ostrander, the son noted above, resided in Plattsburgh, New York. At that time soldier's widow stated that when she and her husband moved (in 1785) to Plattsburg, it was a wilderness, and that her daughter Ada (probably Idah as above) "was the first born white child of Plattsburg".

In 1820, Martha Wilson, soldier's granddaughter, lived with her grandparents in Plattsburg, New York; she was aged then about ten years. Her father was deceased, and the name of her mother was not designated.

In 1837, Permelia Storms and her husband, Primas Storms, resided in Middlebury, Addison County, Vermont. She stated that she was present at the marriage of Patty Nicholson and Henry Ostrander and that she cooked the wedding supper. She did not state any relationship to either party.

End Notes—W.16667—Henry Ostrander

1. Henry enlisted as a private on August 7, 1775 in Captain James Rosekrans (Ninth Company) in Colonel James Holmes Fourth New York Continental Regiment. FROM: Revolutionary War Rolls 1775-1783, Series M-246, Roll 70, folder 50, National Archives, Washington, D.C.
2. Colonel Lewis DuBois was appointed Colonel of an un-numbered Continental Regiment on June 26, 1776. Captain Rosekrans was not part of this regiment and so far the muster or payrolls for this regiment have not been found.
3. Henry enlisted as a private for 3 years in Captain James Rosekrans (First Company) on January 1, 1777 in Colonel Lewis DuBois Fifth New York Continental Regiment. He was taken prisoner at the taking of Fort Montgomery, N.Y. on October 6, 1777. After he was exchanged he returned to the regiment. He was discharged on January 1, 1780. FROM: Revolutionary War Rolls 1775-1783, Series M-246, Roll 72, folder 70, National Archives, Washington, D.C.
4. The Battle of Newtown was fought on August 29, 1779. This was part of the Sullivan-Clinton Campaign against the Iroquois in Western New York in 1779.
5. The pages containing the childrens' names were torn out of the family Bible and included with Patty's application.

Pension Application for Peter Ostrander

Bounty Land warrant number 7576, issued July 30, 1790
W.19946 (Widow Christina, awarded $80.00 per annum.)
State of New York
Greene County SS

On this fourth day of May 1818 before me the subscriber one of the Judges of the Court of Common Pleas in and for the County of Greene personally appeared Peter Ostrander aged 68 years, a resident of the Town of New Baltimore in the county and State aforesaid, who being by me first duly sworn according to law doth on his oath make the following Declaration in order to obtain the provision made by the late Act of Congress Entitled "An Act to provide for certain persons engaged in the Land and Navel service of the United States in the Revolutionary War". That he the said Peter Ostrander, Enlisted as a private in the Early part of the War of the Revolution, in O[?] in the State of New Jersey for during the war in the company of Infantry commanded by Captain ____ Fowler (1) attached to the Regiment commanded by Col. Van

Cortlandt in the New York line of the Army of the United States—That he continued to serve in the said Corps in the service of the United States until the termination of the said War, (2) when he was discharged from service at West Point in the State of New York which period of service above mentioned was about six years and three months—that soon after he was discharged he delivered his discharge to one Thomas Houghtaling (3) of the said Town of New Baltimore to preserve for him, that he has since called on the said Thomas Houghtaling at different time for the said discharge and has been unable to find or obtain the same and that he has reason to believe that the said discharge is lost or destroyed—and that he is in reduced circumstances and stands in need of the assistance of his Country for Support; and that he has no other evidence now in his power of his said service. (Signed with his mark) Peter Ostrander (4)

Sworn and subscribed before me the day and year aforesaid—Peter C. Adams—one of the Judges of the Court of Common Pleas in and for the County of Greene.

End Notes—W.19946—Peter Ostrander

1. Theodosius Fowler served as a First Lieutenant and then as Captain in the Fourth New York and then as Captain in the Fourth New York Continental Regiment. On January 1, 1781 the Second and Fourth New York Continental Regiments were consolidated into one regiment. The Second New York Continental Regiment was still commanded by Colonel Philip VanCortlandt. Captain Fowler was transferred to the Second New York. Peter's name does not appear on the musters roll of Captain Fowler's Company in either regiment.
2. Peter Ostrander served as a private from July 15, 1780 to October 15, 1780 in Lieutenant Colonel Frederick Weisenfel's Company in the Fourth New York Continental Regiment. Peter Ellsworth served as the Captain-Lieutenant of the Company in 1780. FROM: Revolutionary War Rolls 1775-1783, Series M-246, Roll 71, folder 55, National Archives, Washington, D.C.
3. A Thomas Houghtaling or Hooghteeling, etc., served as a Captain of the First Company in Colonel Anthony VanBergen's Eleventh Regiment of Albany County Militia which was the Coxsackie and Groote Imbacht District. A Peter Ostrander served as a private in this company.
4. In a declaration of October 5, 1852, children of Peter and Christian Houghtaling Ostrander, Elizabeth Payne, Christina Bartoe or Bartow and Peter Ostrander applied for what they believed to be owed to them as heirs of Peter and Christina. They stated Peter died at Coxsackie on September 20, 1825. Christina died at New Baltimore on February 7, 1838. She was buried in the burying ground of Andrew Houghtaling.

Pension Application for Henry Paddock

R.7854
State of New York

Oneida County SS.

On this 23d day of August 1832 personally appeared before the Subscriber a Judge of the court of Common Pleas of Oneida County Henry Paddock a resident of said county and state, aged eighty & upwards years who being first duly sworn according to law, doth on his oath make the following declaration in order to obtain the benefit of the act of Congress, passed June 7, 1832.

That he entered the service of the United States under the following named officers and served as herein stated: That he was born at now town Beekman Dutchess County, NY 10 Nov. 1751. No record of age—Resided at Lansingburgh NY when he enlisted Service. Since war has lived in Rensselaer Co., NY—Montgomery Co., NY and now at Vienna Oneida Co., NY.—On 15 January 1776 (1), Volunteered to go to Johnstown Montgomery, with five hundred sleighs loaded with volunteers to take Sir John Johnston [Sir John Johnson]—British and Indians surrendered—about 1,000 Indians as said—does not remember who had command this expedition—was engaged in this service about One Month. In Nov. 1776 went to Fort Ann under Capt. Christopher Tillman. (2) Col Stephen Schuyler's Regt—Floris Bonker Major. (3) Genl Abram TenBroeck (4)—was said to have command though not present at Fort Ann—and continued in service there two months. In July 1777 was again at Fort Ann under Capt. Henry Tinker (5) and a Captain Jacob Defreest (6) was there also—and same colonel and major as in 1776 and served then about one month. And during the rest of the year 1777 for about ten months was out constantly as a scout and minute man for almost every day—So much so that though a blacksmith by trade he never lighted his fires for the whole ten months. In 1778 went to Schoharie at CobleKill (7) at time Butler & Indians were destroying the inhabitants and served from three to five weeks. In 1779 was at Fort Hunter as a soldier again for one month—on the Schoharie Creek—this deponent stood as a minute man during the war and never to his recollection refused to go when called upon which was very often as he lived in the neighborhood where the excursions of the Indians were very frequent—and Tories very troublesome. His whole service would exceed Three Years—he has no witness to prove his services except his wife and refers to annexed affidavits of his neighbors.

He hereby relinquishes every claim whatever to a pension or annuity except the present and declares that his name is not on the pension roll of the agency of any state. (Signed with his mark) Henry Paddock.

Sworn to and subscribed the day and year aforesaid. [?] Stoddard

End Notes—R.7854—Henry Paddock

1. Major General Philip Schuyler with the Albany County Militia marched to Caughnawaga, Tryon County (now the Village of Fonda, Montgomery County) in January of 1776. He met the Tryon County Militia under the Chief Colonel Nicholas Herkimer. This means Herkimer was the Senior Colonel of the Tryon County Militia. Sir John Johnson, the son of the late Sir William Johnson, who was now living

at Johnson Hall, Johnstown was arming his tenants and threatening those who were embracing the American Cause with imprisonment or death. Sir John as a result of this assembly of nearly 1,000 man army of militia, signed a parole not to act in a harmful way to the American Government. His tenants also surrendered their arms.

2. Christopher Tillman a Captain under Colonel Stephen J. Schuyler of the Sixth Regiment of Albany County Militia.
3. Floris Bancker, Second Major of the Sixth Albany.
4. Brigadier General Abraham TenBroeck, Commanded the Albany County Militia Brigade.
5. Henry Denker (Dinker, Tinker, etc.) served as a Captain in the Sixth Albany.
6. Cobleskill was destroyed on May 30, 1778 by Captain Joseph Brant. John Butler nor Walter Butler were involved.

Pension Application for Thomas Paine

W.18720 (Huldah)
B.L.Wt.13,729-160-55 (Jany 3d 1856.)
New York & R.I.
Artillerist in the Company commanded by Captain Sawyer of the Regt. Commanded by Col. Elliott in the R.I & NY line for full term. July 20, 77 to 16 March 78, Apl 7, 78.
State of New York
Tompkins County SS.

On this third day of October 1832 personally appeared in open court before the Court of Common Pleas to wit: Andrew D. W. Bruyn, Benj'm Jennings, Nicoll Halsey, and Cyrus Powers Esquires, Judges of said Court, now sitting in & for the County of Tompkins aforesaid at Ithaca in the said County of Tompkins & State of New York, Thomas Paine a resident of the Town of Caroline in the County & State aforesaid, aged seventy three years, who being first duly sworn according to law doth on his oath make the following declaration in order to obtain the benefit of the act of Congress passed June 7, 1832.

That he entered the service of the United States under the following named officers and served as herein stated.

That in the month of June or July 1776 he was enlisted by Capt. ____ Sawyer (1) of the Rhode Island State Artillery at a place called Snonet Bridge near Taunton in the State of Massachusetts for the term of fifteen months. That soon after his said enlistment he joined his company at Fall River in the said State of Rhode Island and marched with said company to Howland's Ferry and from thence down to Fogland Ferry—from thence to Providence where he joined the Regiment commanded by Col. Elliott in which regiment her served—That he remained with said Corps in the aforesaid service at & near Providence for about five or six months where they served as a guard to the City of Providence—That they marched to Bristol and Warren—That he was in the

Battle on Rhode Island (2) in 1777 when the US troops were there & under the command of General Sullivan—

That he continued in said service in the company aforesaid till the expiration of fifteen months the said tour of his enlistment. When he was discharged at Providence R.I. by Capt. Maj. Sawyer—[sic]

That about a week after his aforesaid discharge at Providence he again there enlisted under the same officers above mentioned—He was enrolled by _____ Foster who was then a Muster-Master and who administered the oath to this Declarant—He here enlisted for one year & served during the period under the aforesaid Capt. Maj. Sawyer [sic], Capt. Gladding (3), Lieut Pierce, and Lieut Parker as a private in said company—This Declarant with his company was ordered to a place called [Eardman's?] Neck, that from thence they marched to Warren to guard Publick property—Thence he went with his company into the fort at Bristol where they lay until his time of service expired & he was discharged at Warren by Maj. Sawyer—with his aforesaid company—he was discharged from his said last mentioned service in the winter or spring of 1776—in the fall of 1777 he received a wound in his foot from the kick of a horse which disabled him from actual service for nearly two months during the said last above mentioned service and which considerably affects him still—

That in the month of April 1781 (4) he having then moved his family into Nobletown in the County of Columbia in the State of New York, there entered the service of the United States as a volunteer under of [the] same person being drafted under Capt. Newell in Col. Willet's Regiment of the New York State Militia for the term of nine months—that he served during the said term of nine months and was discharged at Fort Herkimer by Capt. Newell—That he received no written discharge—that after his said last entering the service he marched to Albany thence to Fort Hunter & thence to Johnstown & from thence to Fort Herkimer. That in the month of July (5) or August 1781 he was in an engagement with the Indians & Tories at Herkimer's House near Little Falls on the Mohawk River.

That he has no documentary evidence of his said service—that he never received to the best recollection any written discharge. That he knows of no person living whose testimony he can procure who can testify to his said services other than those whose affidavits are hereunto annexed & that he never learned to write.—

He hereby relinquishes every claim whatever to a pension or an annuity except the present & declares that his name is not on the pension Roll of the agency of any state. (Signed with his mark) Thomas Paine

Sworn & Subscribed in open court before the Judges thereof the day & year aforesaid. Saml Love, Clk

End Notes—W.18720—Thomas Paine

1. Thomas enlisted July 20, 1777 as a matross (private) in Captain Joshua Sayer's (Sayre, Sawyer, etc.) Company in Colonel Robert Elliott's Rhode Island State Artillery Regiment. He was discharged on March 16, 1778.

2. Thomas is mistaken about the year. The Battle of Quaker Hills, Rhode Island was fought on August 29, 1778. Major General John Sullivan was the American Army Commander. By the Act of 9th September 1778, it was "Resolved, that the thanks of Congress be given to Major-General Sullivan, and to the officers and troops of his command, for their fortitude and bravery displayed in the action of August 29th (Quaker Hill), in which they repulsed the British forces and maintained the field".
3. Captain-Lieutenant Nathaniel Gladding of Colonel Elliott's Regiment.
4. Again, Thomas is mistaken about the year. Captain Simeon Newell was appointed Captain in Colonel Marinus Willett's Regiment of New York State Levies in 1782. Newell was commissioned captain on July 24, 1782.
5. Thomas is referring to the last major raid into the Mohawk Valley in 1782. Captain George Singleton of the King's Royal Regiment of New York and Captain Joseph Brant attacked and burned the buildings near Forts Herkimer and Dayton on July 15, 1782. They attempted to lure the garrisons out into ambushes but it didn't work. Valentine Staring and Augustinus Hess were killed by the Indians while they attempted to run to the safety of the forts.

Pension Application for Abraham Palmateer

S.23,352 [Died Jan'y 19, 1840. Ulster Co. Captain Hasbrouck, Col. Paulding's Regt, NY Line, Private and Corporal]
State of New York
Ulster County SS.

On this Eleventh day of September in the year one thousand eight hundred and Thirty-Two, personally appeared in open court, before the Judges of the Court of common Pleas in and for the County of Ulster aforesaid, now sitting at the Court House in Kingston in said county, Abraham Palmateer of the Town of New Paltz in the County of Ulster aforesaid, aged Seventy Six years, who being first duly sworn according to law, doth on his oath make the following declaration in order to obtain the benefit of the act of Congress passed June 7th 1832—

That he entered the service of the United States under the following named officers, and served as herein stated—

In the beginning of the month of August in the year one thousand seven hundred and seventy six, he volunteered to serve his country against the British, at the town of New Paltz aforesaid for the term of five months, in a company of Militia whereof Jacob Hasbrouck Jun'r (1) was Captain, Abraham Deyo first Lieutenant, Frederick Westbrook (2) second Lieutenant and Reuben DeWitt Ensign, (3) from New Paltz deponent went immediately after his enlistment to Poughkeepsie, in the County of Dutchess, and waited one night until the Sloop from Esopus arrived with the residue of the Company on board, deponent with said company was transported on board of said Sloop to Fort

Montgomery in the County of Orange, and from thence to VerPlank's Point in the County of Westchester where we landed and marched on foot to Kingsbridge, I remained there in the service under the command of Captain Hasbrouck until the British army began to move from New York up the East river when Captain Hasbrouck with a portion of his company as ordered to White Plains. I was detached with others and put under the command of Captain Graham and Lieutenant Nathaniel Potter, we were employed in guarding the lines between Kingsbridge and Morrisania after some weeks we marched to Fort Washington on York Island, from thence crossed the Hudson River, and marched on the west side of said river to Kings ferry, where we again crossed the river and marched to Peekill [Peekskill] at which place we joined our company under Captain Hasbrouck, and marched to Fort Constitution opposite West Point, where we lay until the first of January, the expiration of our term, the whole company were honorably discharged and returned home—no written discharges were given to any of us at this time—our company belonged to Col. Levi Paulding's Regiment, General George Clinton Commanded, during this term of service I saw General Washington, Major Logan and Col. Asher—

I know Johannis Eckert, John York and Josiah Drake of New Paltz aforesaid, who are now living and belonged to Capt. Hasbrouck's Company and served the said term of five months, except the said John York who was taken sick at Kingsbridge and sent home—

In the year one thousand seven hundred and seventy seven, seventy eight and seventy nine the militia in the town of New Paltz aforesaid, was kept in constant readiness to march on short notice, in a body, on alarms given, they were also sent in classes or detachments, from which one of the number was drawn or selected, to serve the term of one month at a time, one of the class being in actual service all the time. Deponent belonged to Captain Ransom's (4) Company Nathaniel Potter was the Lieutenant, during these years & I served therein as a Corporal.—

In October one thousand seven hundred and seventy seven, Captain Ransom's Company were ordered to the north, on the approach of the British Army under Genl. Burgoine, (5) we marched to Stillwater in the County of Saratoga, Colonel Cantine commanded our Regiment, we remained there until after the Battle with the British army when we were ordered to take charge of about one hundred and fifty prisoners, which we brought to Albany and shortly thereafter we returned home, having been absent between three and four weeks—immediately after our return we were kept in actual service guarding the shores of the Hudson River, when the British ships were returning after having burnt Kingston about two weeks—at Saratoga General Gates (6) commanded the American Army, I saw General Schuyler (7) there, at Bemus Heights.—In the next year following we were again out under Captain Ransom, and Colonel Cantine, on an alarm against the Indians, we marched to a place called Freetown in the County of Albany this time we were absent three weeks.—at other times during the aforesaid years, I was out for the term of four months, at different times of one month each, out of our class,--under Captain Ransom, and Colonel Cantine, during these different times we were stationed on the frontiers in the County of Ulster aforesaid, at Shandaken, Shoean, and Lunenburgh in the Town of Rochester and Marble town.—The Indians burnt Warwarsing and committed other injuries in connection with the Tories and Refugees which rendered it necessary to keep a constant guard, on this frontier.—Deponent as Corporal, was engaged in warning the men on every occasion, our town was thinly settled and the company lived about twelve miles on the river but the length of time spent in this service deponent can not tell—Josiah Drake now living was with me in all of the above terms of service, his affidavit is hereunto annexed—

Deponent further says in answer to the questions put to him by the said Court in the county of Ulster.—He was born in the town of Poughkeepsie in the county of Dutchess sometime in the year 1756, but he cannot tell the day nor month—He has no record of his age—when called into service he lived in the town of New Paltz aforesaid and has lived there ever since except about twenty years, when he lived in the town of Middletown in the County of Delaware in said State, when he was called into service he volunteered, except when drafted for his class—In addition to the regular officers and regiments above mentioned by him, he recollects Col. Swarthout (8) and his regiment at Kingsbridge. The general circumstances of his services, he cannot state more fully than he has—

Deponent never received a written discharge, he believes the militia were not in the habit of receiving such—

Deponent is known to and well acquainted with the Reverend William Warner of the Town of Olive in said County of Ulster, and David Wooley Esqr. One of the Justices of the peace of New Paltz aforesaid who can testify to deponent's character for veracity and their belief of his services as a soldier of the revolution.—

He hereby relinquishes every claim whatever to a pension or annuity except the present and declares that his name is not on the pension roll of the agency of any state.—(Signed with his mark) Abraham Palmateer

Sworn to and Subscribed the day and year aforesaid. AD Soper, First Judge, Abrm A. Deyo, AG Hardenburgh, John Jansen, Judges.

End Notes—S.23352—Abraham Palmateer

1. Jacob Hasbrouck, Jr. was Captain of the Second Company of the Township of New Paltz. The Third Regiment of Ulster County Militia was commanded by Colonel Levi Pawling or Paulding. On February 21, 1778, John Cantine was appointed Colonel of the regiment as Pawling had been appointed 1st Judge of Common Pleas. The other company officers of the Second Company were as follows: Abraham Deyo, Jr. as First Lieutenant, Petrus Hasbrouck as Second Lieutenant and Samuel Bevier as the Ensign.

2. Frederick Westbrook was appointed Ensign on May 3, 1776 in Captain Petrus Schoonmaker's Company; First Company of the Township of Rochester in the Third Ulster.
3. Reuben DeWitt was the Second Lieutenant in Captain Andries Bevier's Company, Second Company of the Township of Rochester, Third Ulster.
4. Captain Peleg Ransom, First Lieutenant Nathaniel Potter, Second Lieutenant William Donaldson and Ensign William Ellsworth, Third Regiment of Ulster County Militia.
5. The Battles of Saratoga were fought on September 19 and October 7, 1777. General John Burgoyne surrendered his British Army on October 17, 1777.
6. Major General Horatio Gates of the American Army.
7. Major General Philip Schuyler of the American Army.
8. Colonel Jacobus Swartwout of the Second Regiment of Dutchess County Minute Men. He was appointed Brigadier General on March 3, 1780 of the Dutchess County Militia.

Pension Application for Jonathan Pettit

S.46654
Declaration. In order to obtain the benefit of the Act of Congress passed June 7th 1832.
State of New York
Madison County SS.

On this 21st day of August A.D. 1832 personally appeared before me one of the Judges of the Court of Common Pleas in and for the County of Madison, Jonathan Pettit of the town of Cazenovia County of Madison and State aforesaid, who being first duly sworn according to law doth on his oath make the following declaration in order to obtain the benefit of the act of Congress passed June 7th 1832.

I Jonathan Pettit of the Town, County and State aforesaid do hereby declare that I was born in the Town of Sharon Litchfield County and State of Connecticut on the 25th day of July 1752 as the family record has ever shown. That I am now (July 25th 1832) 80 years old. I left the town of Sharon after having served seven years at the Trade of a Tanner & currier as apprentice to Mr. James Pardy of that town and located myself in business at Fish Creek then in the county of Albany in the year 1773 being then 21 years old.

On the twentieth day of October 1775 I received the accompanying commission as Ensign in the third company of Militia of foot (of which company Henry O'Hara (1) was Captain and my brother James Pettit was Lieutenant from the Provincial Congress of New York. My Brother and myself were notified to meet at Col. Van Vechten (2) in Saratoga to receive our Commissions; which we did and they were then delivered to us by Abraham TenEyck (3) Paymaster of the Army and Col. Roseboom (4) from Albany who had in charge most of the commissions for that regiment. At the time they were delivered to us it appeared that the commissions were properly filed but on examination it was found that the commission filed [sic—filled out] with my name had in the body of it the name of my brother as Ensign and the one filed with the name of my brother had in it my name as Lieutenant. (5)

The mistake on being discovered was communicated to the above named agents at the same time & place and by their direction the commission of my brother was corrected and from that of mine. The name of my brother James was erased and my name (Jonathan) was inserted as it appears in the commission which is the same commission I received from the Provincial Congress of New York signed by Nathaniel Woodhull President thereof and Robert Benson Secretary.

The territory comprising the third company of Militia included all that part of the State North of Fish Creek and west of the Hudson River to Saratoga Lake and was at that time the strong hold of Tories.

As an instance of which I had to encounter—among the Tories I state the following. One Jonathan Jones who was a man of wealth, and carrying on a large business at Fish Creek where I resided and had in his employ a large number of men; had frequently solicited myself and others whom he supposed under his influence to flee with him to Canada. He was particularly solicitous with us after the Lexington and Concord battles.

Sometime after the affair at Lexington & before I received my commission once sent a message tome requesting me to call on him that evening. I called accordingly and found about twenty persons collected among whom were two by the name of Jessup of Albany (of Jessup's Patent Memory) three brothers of Jones and others of my acquaintance. The object of the meeting was to induce me to join the royalists in Canada to effect this every argument and entreaty was used and Jones said he was authorized to offer and engage me a commission as soon as I should arrive at the station of the Royalist troops on the northern frontier. I told them my mind was made up to stand or fall with my country and I should reject these offers. I left them about one o'clock in the morning and started for Stillwater (the place of meeting of the nearest Committee of Safety) about ten miles on the road towards Albany determined with their aid to secure the collection of Tories—the Committee were composed of Ezra Palmer & Mr. Mead of Stilwater, Capt. Norton of Saratoga Springs, Col. McRea (Brother of Jessey McRea soon after murdered) [Jane McCrea] and others whose names I do not recollect. As I was acquainted with Col. McRea I immediately informed him of the whole circumstance and requested a Military guard to arrest Jones and his associates forthwith. McRea evaded my request but promised to communicate directly with the committee and have the proper measures taken. The guard was not sent. McRae it was generally believed gave notice to the persons implicated. So that they all escaped, as he was thought not to be a friend to his country. These very Tories were afterwards the pilots of Burgoyne's Army.

Immediately after I received my commission. I was ordered by Gen. Philip Schuyler (6) to march with a detachment under my commanded to

Johnstown in Montgomery County to disarm a number of Scotch families who were Royalists and a great annoyance to that frontier. On another occasion and I believe in the spring of 1776 I was ordered by the Committee of Safety of Albany with a small detachment of men to take possession of Fort George and keep it until relieved. The Fort was held by an officer & about 30 men and according to orders I took possession and command of it until relieved by a Maj. Stephens from Connecticut. The same I believe who afterwards at the battle of the Cedars subsequent to the reduction of Montreal was taken as a hostage by the British.

From the time I received my commission such was my location, on the then frontiers and surrounded by Tories who seized every opportunity of doing injury they could; I was almost constantly engaged in actual service or in attendance on the Committee of Safety, and from my best recollection and belief, I was engaged in actual service as Ensign under my commission the full space of six months. The Captain (O'Hara) had removed to the south and the Lieut (my brother) had died soon after his being commissioned; which left me in the command of the company and was one reason of my constant employment. I removed to Albany in the month of July or August 1776 soon after I went there, a company of volunteers called exempts (7) was organized as he believed according to an act of Congress; of which company I was chosen Captain, but received no commission; the company consisted of one hundred men, mostly such as had had some civil or military commission, and by the terms of enlistment we were to stand as minute men through the war. Not long after the organization of our company we were ordered by Col. Marinus Willett (8) (late of New York) to march to Canajoharie to protect the then western frontier; which service was rendered by myself and company under the command of Col. Willet, this I believe was in August 1776. In January 1777 I was ordered by Col. Lansing of Albany again to call out my company and march to Saratoga where we rendezvoused with other militia and encamped on the south side of Fish Creek for a number of weeks. When Gen. Burgoyne (9) came down from the north and about the time of the battle of Saratoga, I was ordered to call out my company by Gen. Ten Brock (10) and march to Saratoga, accordingly we started and when part way there re'cd counter-orders to return to Albany, and take charge of the prisoners; which was done.

After the company of volunteer exempts was formed and placed under my command, it was the general military guard of the city of Albany, and this was particularly the case after the attack by the Tories and Indians on the house of Gen. Schuyler (11), on which alarm my company were all called out and after that event it was my duty to see that a military guard was kept in the city generally when not on other duty, until the close of the war. And on account of the manner in which I performed the duty [?] upon me in this respect I received from the Corporation of Albany the freedom of the city in token of their approbation and esteem. The instrument conferring which is herewith transmitted.

Besides the service specified I was called out at numerous other times all of which I cannot now particularize and which made the amount of my actual service after my removal to Albany more than one year.

But during all the time after the reception of my commission, both while living at Fish Creek and after my removal to Albany, I was bound to act at any moment under my commission; and in fact almost my whole time and labor were in one way and another devoted to the service from the time I was appointed ensign until the fall of 1778. At that time my family had suffered so many privations by my absence that I took advantage of a regulation of Congress (I believe) which authorized classing to furnish a substitute and one John Shepard of Albany and myself furnished a substitute for the remainder of the war our substitute was a foreigner whose name I do not now recollect but who was paid by us a bounty of thirty dollars and he regularly joined the army.

My sacrifices of property were very great and amongst others the following my Tannery referred to above at Fish Creek was on the very ground occupied by the two Armies at the time of Burgoyne's surrender my tanner shops, vats, etc., were all destroyed to my injury at least of one thousand dollars. After my removal to Albany I had at one time on hand a large quantity (500 boards) of lumber, piled in a lumber in the city in my absence at Canajoharie with my company under Col. Willet, they were seized by an officer of the U.S. Army and sent down the river to Poughkeepsie I believe to build barracks; they were worth at the time they were taken not less than eight hundred dollars. For all those losses I have never received a cent in renumeration, nor ever asked anything of my country. I have never before applied for a pension and never in any manner been on the Pension list or roll of any state and I hereby relinquish every claim whatever to a pension or annuity except the present.

I further state that Elisha Litchfied formerly a member of congress, John Switzer, Isaac Inger & Samuel Morey are persons living near me and can testify to my character for veracity—and their belief of my service as a soldier of the Revolution.

Since the revolutionary war I have constantly resided in this state and since the year 1821, I have lived with my son and am now supported by him. For the last ten years I have been entirely unable to labor and for the last year totally helpless from a paralytic attack.

My associates are mostly dead and proof (except what is found in my commission and the affidavit of one witness accompanying this) I am unable to procure. (Signed with his mark) Jonathan Pettit.

Sworn to and Subscribed the day and year aforesaid. Barek Beckwith, Judge of Madison Co. Com. Pleas

End Notes—S.46654—Jonathan Pettit

1. Henry O'Hara, Captain of the Third Company in Colonel John McCrea's Thirteenth Regiment of Albany County Militia (Saratoga District). Benjamin Giles (Guiles) was the First Lieutenant. Captain O'Hara in April of 1776 was appointed Captain in Colonel Cornelius D. Wynkoop's

Fourth New York Continental Regiment. On November 3, 1776 he was appointed Captain in Colonel Moses Hazen's Second Canadian Continental Regiment. He resigned on September 20, 1777. On June 22, 1778, Peter Winne was appointed Captain of the Third Company. The other officers were First Lieutenant Benjamin Giles, Second Lieutenant Isaac Doty and Ensign John Putnam.

2. Cornlius VanVeghten was the Lieutenant-Colonel of the Thirteenth Regiment of Albany County Militia.
3. Possibly Abraham TenEyck who was the Second Lieutenant in Captain John M. Beekman's Company (Fourth Company) in Colonel Jacob Lansing Jr's First Regiment of Albany County Militia. Abraham Ten Eyck was appointed Second Lieutenant and Paymaster on November 21, 1776 in Colonel Goose VanSchaick's First New York Continental Regiment.
4. Colonel Myndert Roseboom. He had originally been appointed Colonel of the Second New York Continental Regiment with Goose VanSchaick as the Lieutenant-Colonel. On his declining the appointment Lt-Col Van Schaick was appointed the Colonel and Peter Yates was appointed the Lieutenant-Colonel.
5. This kind of mistake happened more than one would think. On several of the various regimental appointments you will see the words "appointed through mistake".
6. Major General Philip Schuyler of the Continental Army.
7. Jonathan was commissioned Captain on March 6, 1779 of the Cambridge District of the Albany County Associated Exempts.
8. Marinus Willett was appointed Lieutenant-Colonel Commandant on April 27, 1781, of a regiment of New York State Levies. Jonathan is mistaken as to the year of this tour.
9. General John Burgoyne, commander of the British forces invading New York from Canada in 1777. He surrendered his army on October 17, 1777 to Major General Horatio Gates of the Continental Army.
10. Brigadier General Abraham Ten Broeck of the Albany County Militia Brigade.
11. This attempt on General Schuyler was on August 7, 1781. A guard from the First New York was stationed at the home of the general and by their defense inside the house it gave General Schuyler time to get upstairs and fire a pistol out of a window to raise the alarm. The Loyalist attackers fled with John Cockley of the First New York, and John Tubbs dispatch courier who were taken prisoners.

Pension Application for Garret Putman

W. 16687 (Widow Rebecca)

This widow received a handsome pension, $413.33 per annum. Arrears $2,273.31 plus semi-anl allowance ending 4 Mar 38, 206.66, total $2,479.97.

State of New York
County of Montgomery SS.

On this 27th day of December 1836, personally appeared before the Honorable John Hand one of the Judges of the County Courts for the County of Montgomery aforesaid, Rebecca Putman a resident of Johnstown in the said County of Montgomery and State of New York aged 72 years the 15th of March last, who, being first duly sworn according to Law, doth on her oath make the following declaration in order to obtain the benefit of the provision made by the Act of Congress passed July 4th 1836.

That she is the widow of Garret Putman who was a Captain in the Army of the Revolution and served as herein more particularly specified.

That during the period of the Revolutionary War down to the year 1781 she had no personal knowledge of the services of the said Capt. Garret Putman only from additional evidence, or as it was related to her at different times during the time of the war, and at several times since. That he, the said Garret Putman who was a Capt. in the war of the Revolution served as an officer therein several terms of 9 months at least, to say as much as 9 months in the year 1778, (1) probably the same in the Indian expedition under Gen'l Sullivan in the year 1779. (2) And a term of 9 months in the year 1780 (3) and a term of 9 months in the year 1781. (4)

That on the 8th day of July 1781 she was married to the said Capt. Garret Putman by the Rev. Mr. Throop at Fort Hunter, and that the said Capt. Garret Putman was at the time of their marriage Captain of a company stationed at fort Hunter to guard the Fort and continued in the service at different places the reminder of the said year, that her husband, the aforesaid Capt. Garret Putman died on the 12th day of April 1826; and that she has remained a widow ever since that period, as will more fully appear by reference to the proof hereto annexed and further says not. (Signed with her mark) Rebecca Putman

Sworn to and Subscribed the day and year aforesaid before me John Hand a Judge of Montgomery County Courts.

State of New York
Montgomery County SS.

On this 27th day of December 1836, personally appeared before the undersigned, a Judge of the County Court for the County aforesaid, Thomas Sammons who being duly sworn doth depose and swear that he has made a diligent search for the record of the marriage of Rebecca Putman to her late husband Garret Putman deceased and that he has been unable to find any except the following which he swears is an exact and true copy of a family record taken and by him copied from the family Bible of Abraham Garrison the Father of Rebecca Putman the present Claimant.

"Garret Putman was born the 22d day of Febuary [sic] 1752. Rebecca Garrison was born the 15th day of March 1764 and they were married in the year 1781 July 8th.

And he further swears that is well acquainted with the said Rebecca Putman and knows her to have been the wife of Garret Putman or that they have cohabited and lived together as man and wife since the above named year 1781 untill the time of her death of the said Garret Putman and since which the said Rebecca Putman the present Claimant has ever since remained his widow and he further swears that he was well acquainted with Garret Putman during the revolutionary war and well recollects of seeing him at different times in the service of his country acting as a commissioned officer and furthermore that he has every reason to believe that the services of the said Garret Putman during the war as a commissioned officer amounted to more than two years with a embodied Corps called into service by competent authority and furthermore says not. (Signed) Tho. Sammons

Sworn to and Subscribed the day and year aforesaid before me John Hand a Judge of the Montgomery County Courts.

Batavia NY Sept 22, 1846
Dear Dir—

I shall feel greatly obliged if you will answer me the following Interrogatories.

1. Has a pension ever been granted to Garret Putman a captain in the Revolutionary War?
2. Is so, when and what arrears were then due?
3. Was the money ever paid, if so how much has been paid, when paid and to whom and on what authority.

I make these enquiries in behalf of William G. Putman a son and sole legatee and devisee of Garret Putman. William G. Putman has been informed that his mother drew a large sum of money as her husband's pension but she is now dead and it can not be ascertained now how much she received it any.

Please also state whether Rebecca Putman widow of Garret Putman ever obtained a pension if so when and how much did she receive.

I am also informed that Garrett Putman never obtained his bounty land. If so can this still be obtained and on what proof? William G. Putman informed me that he can prove the Service of his father by two or three witnesses. Will this be sufficient. Is there not proof of his service in this papers on applying for a pension if so cannot this proof be referred to for the purpose of obtaining his bounty land.

If you will answer this at your earliest convenience you will confer a particular favor [to] William G. Putman.

I am with great respect your Obt Servt, Timothy Fitch.

Letter in the folder dated September 22, 1910, written in response to an inquiry.

In regard to your inquiry of last May, you are advised that while the name Garrett Putnam is not found on the Revolutionary War pension records, a further search has disclosed the following information.

Garrett Putman [typist changed the way he wrote Putman to Putnam and then back again] was born February 22, 1752, and served as a Captain in the New York Troops for nine months in 1778; nine months in 1779, and was in General Sullivan's campaign against the Indians; nine months in 1780 under Colonel John Harper; and nine months in 1781 under Colonel Marinus Willett during which time he was in the "Hall battle" near Johnstown. (5)

He married while in the service at Fort Hunter, on July 8, 1781, Rebecca Garrison born March 15, 1764, daughter of Abraham Garrison.

Soldier died April 12, 1826, and his widow Rebecca Putman was allowed pension on file No. W. 16687 on the application executed December 27, 1836, while a resident of Johnstown, Montgomery County, New York.

In 1846 it was stated that their son William C. [sic] Putman was sole legatee and devisee. No further data relative to family.

Very respectfully, [no name appears on copy] Acting Commissioner.

End Notes—W.16637—Garret Putman

1. In April of 1778 there were to be two companies of Tryon County Rangers to be raised to consist of about 60 men each. They were to be raised from the Tryon County Militia Brigade. Captain Garret Putman and Lieutenant Victor Putman and Benjamin Dickson or Dixon formed one company and the other company officers were Captain John Breadbake and Lieutenants John Adam Frederick Helmer, and John Smith. The two companies were to report to Colonel Morris Graham of the First Regiment of Dutchess County Militia. FROM: The Public Papers of George Clinton, First Governor of New York, Albany, Vol. 3, pp 251-252. So far only muster/pay rolls have been found for Captain Breadbake's Company.
2. In 1779, Brigadier General James Clinton raised an army of continental and militia troops, which formed in the Mohawk Valley, and then later joined the army of Major General John Sullivan. The combined armies marched against the Iroquois villages in western New York. Colonel John Harper of the Fifth Regiment of Tryon County Militia volunteered his services to General Clinton; Harper was appointed the captain of about 135 volunteers including Garret. Putman was then appointed as the second in command. The volunteers were not paid but drew rations. Garret was present at the Battle of Newtown, present day Elmira, NY, on August 29, 1779 but was not an active participant in the battle. Garret was in what is called today the "Groveland Ambush" on September 13, 1779. A scouting part of continental and volunteers under First Lieutenant Thomas Boyd of the First Pennsylvania Continental Regiment were ambushed. Putman and a few others escaped the ambush but the rest were either killed or captured. Garret also served as Captain in Colonel Frederick Visscher's Third Regiment

of Tryon County Militia but when he was appointed is unknown but he probably served in 1778 and 1779.

3. Garret was appointed Captain on May 11, 1780 in Lieutenant-Colonel Commandant John Harper's Regiment of Levies. The company was divided into small groups and garrisoned at different times in Forts Johnstown, Hunter, Windecker, and the Sacandaga Blockhouse. In September, Harper's Levies were sent to Fort Schuyler to replace the First New York Continental Regiment. On November 22, the Fourth New York Continental Regiment arrived at Fort Schuyler to replace Harper's Levies. On November 23, Major James M. Hughes marched from Fort Schuyler to Schenectady where they were discharged on November 30.
4. Garret was appointed captain on April 27, 1781 in Lieutenant-Colonel Commandant Marinus Willett's Regiment of New York State Levies. The company was discharged on December 31.
5. The Battle of Johnstown was fought on October 25, 1781.

Pension Application for Richard Putman

W.16686

Declaration

In order to obtain the benefit of the Section of the act of Congress of the 4th July 1836
State of New York
Montgomery County SS.

On this second day of June 1837, personally appeared before the under named a Judge of the County Courts in and for the county of Montgomery aforesaid Nelly Putman a resident of the town of Johnstown—County & State aforesaid aged Eighty Seven years past, who being first duly sworn according to law, doth on her oath make the following declaration in order to obtain the benefit of the provision made by the act of Congress passed July 4, 1836. That she is the widow of Richard Putman who was a private in the war of the Revolution—in Col. Frederick Fisher's Regiment and Captain John Davis' (1) Company from the year 1775 until in August 1777—and did duty in said war at various times and places in said State—and at the Oriscany [Oriskany] battle in said state. The said Captain John Davis was killed and her husband the said Richard Putman was appointed Ensign under the command of Captain Abraham Veeder (2) in said regiment until the close of said War—but that she this applicant has no great personal knowledge of the service of her said husband but from traditionary evidence or such as was related to her at different times during said war—and since by her said husband and others, and which she believes to be true—That (the said) the said Richard Putman served as a private in said war in the militia under said Capt. Davis at Caughnawaga in the year 1775 upwards of one week—the same year under said Capt. at different other places in said County, at least about one month in the year 1776 he was with the militia on duty under said Capt. when Sir John Johnson was disarmed & that one week in then said last mentioned year under said Capt he was at Sockendaga [Sacondaga] and in the tory settlement in service and on duty at least one month. Same year under same Capt at Stonearabia Bowmans Creek or Kill—Fort Plain and Fort Plank in service and on duty not less than one month—in the year 1777 he was out on duty in said war under said Capt. at Balstown said state at least 10 days—same year under General Herkimer on a conference with Capt. Brant to the Unadilla (3) said state, on service at least fourteen days—the same year at the Oriscany Battle under said Capt & said Genl Herkimer on duty at least one month in the fall off same year he served and done duty in said war as Ensign in the militia against General Burgoyne (4) and before the surrender of said General Burgoyne at least six weeks in the year 1778 he did duty as Ensign in said Company at Stonearabia at least ten days—Same year as Ensign (5) duty & was in service at the Sackendaga Block house at least one month in the fall of same year he did duty & service as Ensign at Fort Plain & Fort Plank at least three weeks, and she further states on her oath aforesaid that she never knew or heard of her said husband staying at home or refusing or neglecting to go on duty or service at any time when the militia of said Country was ordered out on any occasion in said war but (that) that she cannot now recollect the various times when he was called out or the various places where he went on duty & service in said war—but believes that the whole amount of time he lost in during duty tour services in said war would exceed two years—She further declares that she was married to the said Richard Putman on or about the 17th day of October 1767 (6)—that her husband the aforesaid Richard Putman died on the 14th day of April 1833 (7)—and that she has remained a widow ever since that period as will more fully appear by reference to the proof hereto annexed. (Signed with her mark) Nelly Putman

Sworn to and Subscribed on the day & year aforesaid written before me John Hand a Judge of the Montgomery County Courts.

[She was granted pension of $63.11 per annum.]

I Jacob G. Snell Town Clerk of the Town of Palatine County of Montgomery and State of New York. Do certify that upon examination of the Church Records, I find recorded the marriage of Richard Putman to Nelly VanBracklen. They were married on the 17th day of October A.D. 1767 By the Rev'd Abraham Rosencrantz. Dated April 29th 1837. Jacob P. Snell J. Clerk.

Sworn and Subscribed this 29th day of April 1837. John T. Getman Justice.

End Notes—W.16686—Richard (Derick) Putman

1. John Davis was appointed Captain of the Second Company on August 26, 1775 in Colonel Frederick Visscher's Third Regiment of Tryon County Militia.
2. Upon Captain Davis being killed at the Battle of Oriskany on August 6, 1777, First Lieutenant Abraham Veeder was appointed Captain of the company. Richard was actually appointed sergeant. Richard was appointed ensign in 1778 or 1779. Captain Veeder, First Lieutenant

Nicholas Dockstader; Second Lieutenant, Garret S. VanBracklen or VanBrocklin; and Ensign Putman were all commissioned on March 8, 1781.

3. The conference between Captain Joseph Brant and Brigadier General Nicholas Herkimer was held June 27, 1777 at Unadilla.
4. Lieutenant General John Burgoyne surrendered his army of British troops and allies on October 17, 1777.
5. Richard continued to serve in the militia after the War of Independence. In 1784 Tryon County's name was changed to Montgomery County. On October 2, 1786, Derick Putman was appointed Lieutenant in Captain Jacob Sammons Company (Fourth Company) in Lieutenant Colonel Commandant Volkert Veeder's Regiment of Montgomery County Militia in Brigadier General Frederick Visscher's (or Fisher) Brigade. FROM: Military Minutes of the Council of Appointments of the State of New York, ed. Hugh Hastings, Albany NY 1901, Vol. I, P 101.
6. Richard and Nelly had the following children: Cornelia born December 8, 1773, bapt on January 1, 1774. Caughnawaga Dutch Reformed Church Book of Baptisms page 27. Gerrit born on December 6, 1776 bapt on January 5, 1777, Caughnawaga Dutch Reformed Church Book of Baptisms page 40. Maria born September 12, 1779 bapt October 12, 1779 Caughnawaga Dutch Reformed Church Book of Baptisms book page 53. Lewis born April 27, 1783 bapt May 24, 1783 Caughnawaga Dutch Reformed Church Book of Baptisms page 66. Johannis born January 19, 1786 bapt March 6, 1786 Caughnawaga Dutch Reformed Church Book of Baptisms page 77. There may have been more children but these are the ones that were baptized by Reverend Thomas Romeyn. Caughnawaga is now called Fonda.
7. Richard and Nelly are buried in the Keck Center Cemetery, Town of Johnstown, Fulton County. The cemetery is on the New Turnpike Road. Nelly died on February 20, 1842 at the age of 100 years and 7 months. Richard is the son of Lodowick and Elizabeth Soets Putman. Lodowick and his son Aaron were killed on May 22, 1780. There is an historic marker on the corner of Route 29 and the Hales Mills Road to mark the site of the Putman Home and burial of Lodowick and Aaron.

Pension Application for Killian Ritter

W.18,815 (Widow: Hannah Bort from Greenbush in Rensselaer County.
Married July 1783. Killian died in 1835.)
B.L.Wt26019-160-55
Hannah Ritter widow of Killian Ritter, private in the war.
State of New York
County of Montgomery SS.

On the sixth day of August in the year 1832, personally came before Henry J. Diefendorf Esqr., one of the Judges of the Court of Common Pleas in and for said County of Montgomery Killian Ritter (or as is sometimes written Ridder, a resident of Canajoharie in the County of Montgomery and State of New York aged about seventy six years, who being first duly sworn according to law, doth, on his oath, make the following declaration, in order to obtain the benefit of the Act of Congress passed June 7th 1832.

That he was born in what was then called East Camp in Dutchess County about the year 1756 he cannot say positively as the records of his age were burned during the revolution in Schoharie, that he removed to Charlotte River near the present line between the County of Delaware and Schoharie in the year 1775.

That he entered the service of the United States under the following named officers and served as herein stated. That on the first of April in the year 1777 he enlisted in a company of rangers commanded by Captain Joseph Bartholomy (1) in a Regiment commanded by Col. John Harper in the New York Line for the term of nine months that in this term of service he went to the mouth of Schenevas Creek with the said Col. Harper where they surprised and took prisoners a party of Indians that during the remainder of this term of service this company was stationed in the neighborhood of Harpersfield and Charlotte River to protect the inhabitants and to watch a certain tory family by the name of Servass. He was honorably discharged on the thirst of January in the year 1778 and that his discharge is lost that he knows of no living witness by which he can prove these services.

And further that in the beginning of the year 1778 he removed to the town of Schoharie in the then county of Tryon now Schoharie where he enlisted on the first of April in the year 1778 in a company of Rangers commanded by Captain John Deitz (2) in the regiment commanded by Col. Peter (3) in the New York line, for the term of nine months, that during this term of service he was detached under the command of Col. Zebulon Butler (4) for an expedition to Oquago, that the remainder of the time he was employed principally in scouting the Country, extending to Cattskill and Batavia, that he faithfully served, until the first of January 1779 and was honorably discharged at Schoharie as stated in the affidavit of Christopher Koenig which said discharge (if it was received) is lost.

And further that in the winter of 1778-9 that the militia were classed, each class serving one month alternately, that he was detached agreeably to said classification and that he served one month he thinks in February 1779 under Captain Jacob Hager, (5) Ephriam Vrooman Lieutenant under the command of Col. Peter Vrooman, that he served at Fort Debois at Cobleskill and that he knows of no surviving witness by which he can prove this service.

That he removed soon after to Greenbush now in Rensselaer County that after said removal he turned out in case of alarms and marched as far as Schenectady, and at one time as far as Palatine now in Montgomery County that since that time has lived at Niskauna, in Albany County where he lived seven years also in Guilderland in said County; that in the year 1800 he removed to Cobleskill in Schoharie County, that he removed to the County of Montgomery in the year 1820 where he has since resided and is now poor.

He hereby relinquishes every claim to an pension or annuity except the present and declares that his name is not on the pension roll of the agency of any state. (Signed with his mark) Killian Ritter. (6)

Sworn to and subscribed the day and year aforesaid before me. Henry I. Dievendorff.

End Notes—Killian Ritter—W.18,815

1. Joseph Bartholomew was the First Lieutenant in Captain Lodowick Breakman's (Brakeman) Company in Colonel John Harper's Fifth Regiment of Tryon County Militia.
2. Johannes Dietz was a lieutenant and raised a company of Rangers raised from the Albany County Militia in 1778. The record was found showing that Andrew Ridder received the pay for his son Johannes. FROM: Revolutionary War Rolls 1775-1783, Series M 246, Roll 77, folder 167, National Archives, Washington, D.C.
3. Colonel Peter Vrooman commanded the Fifteenth Regiment of Albany County Militia. Dietz and most of the rangers came from this regiment.
4. Colonel William Butler of the Fourth Pennsylvania Continental Regiment. He commanded the expedition to Onaquaga (Acquago, Oquago, etc.). A book of interest on this expedition is Onaquaga Hub of the Border Wars, Marjory Barnum Hinman, 1975, Valley Offset Inc.
5. Captain Jacob Hager and First Lieutenant Ephraim Vrooman were in the Second Company in Colonel Vrooman's Regiment. No record of Killian serving in this company, but it could have been a detachment made up from various companies. Killian served as a private in Captain George Richtmyer's Company (Third Company) in Colonel Vrooman's Regiment.
6. It appears that Killian which some mistook on the muster rolls as William served as a private in Captain John J. Lansing's Company in Colonel Morris Graham's Regiment of New York State Levies in 1780. He may have served as a substitute for John Ridder. The July 15, 1780 muster roll has John listed but the October 14, 1780 lists William and not John. It is also possible that Killian served in the Sixth Regiment of Albany County Militia as I found Andries [Andrew] Ridder serving as a private in this regiment under Captain Jacob DeFreest or DeForest, etc.

Pension Application for Evert Rose or Roosa, Rosa

W.22,126 (Widow: Margaret)

Declaration in order to obtain the benefit of the act of Congress passed June 7th 1832.

State of New York

Tompkins County SS.

On this 17th day of July 1832 personally appeared in open court before the Judges of the Court of Oyer and Terminus now sitting Evert Rose a resident of the town of Dryden in the county of Tompkins and state of New York, aged Seventy years, who being first duly sworn according to law, doth on his oath make the following declaration in order to obtain the benefit of the act of Congress, passed June 7th 1832. That he entered the service of the United States, under the following named officers and served as herein stated. That in the summer (month nor day not recollected, of 1775 he enlisted at the town of Shongum Ulster County, State of New York under Lieut. Cornelius Masten (1) in Colonel Hardenburgh's (2) Regiment of the New York militia for the term of two months, and was employed during that season in building Forts Clinton, Montgomery—that he was discharged at Fort Clinton at the expiration of the time, the month he cannot recollect—that he resided at the time he enlisted in the said town of Shongum or Shawangunk—that he was a volunteer—that he did not serve at that time with any Continental troops or companies & know no continental officer but one Captain Stewart. (3)

That in the month of May 1776 he volunteered and entered the service as a teamster in the New York service--& that he did services as a teamster for the term of six months—that he was employed under one William Erwin who was a forage master—that this season as a teamster was performed for the army in the counties of Ulster & Orange in said state.

That in the summer of 1777 the month not recollected he enlisted as a fifer in Captain Jacobus Rose's company in the regiment commanded by Colonel McLaughlin (4) or McLaugherty for the term of three months—that at the time he entered the service he resided in the town of Shongum that he went with his company to Fort Montgomery & staid there until the fort was taken by the British. That he went from Fort Montgomery to Kingston or Esopus in Ulster County & staid there until his time expired & was discharged.

That in the spring of 1778 month not recollected, he enlisted at Shongum in Captain Wilkins (5) Company in the Regiment commanded by Colonel Hardenburgh for two months—that he volunteered in this service as a fifer—that he marched with his company to West Point where he remained until the two months expired & then he was discharged & he returned to Shongum.

That in the fall of 1778 he again enlisted at Shongum in Captain Tarpenny's (6) Company—don't recollect his Colonel's name—that he volunteered as a fifer—that he marched with his company to New Windsor below New York—that this enlistment was for three months – the he served his time out at New Windsor and was discharged.

That in the fall of 1779 he at the town of Shongum he enlisted for two months—that he does not recollect the Captain's name—that he went to the fort at Mamakating Hollow in Orange—that the fort was commanded by Lieut Hardenburgh. (7) That he remained at that fort until his time was out & he was discharged.

That in the spring or summer of 1780 month not recollected, he enlisted at Shongum he enlisted under Captain Case (8) in the regiment commanded by Colonel Johnson (9), that William Vandermark was a Lieut in the company—that he enlisted as a fifer for three months—that he did duty as a ranger in said company on the lines for the said term of three months—that he was discharged at Stoney Ridge when his time expired.

That in the summer of 1782 month not recollected he volunteered at Old Paltz in Ulster County under Capt. Deyo (10) on an alarm of the Indians & went out on a scouting party and was gone two weeks.

And this deponent further says that after the times above mentioned he volunteered on scouting parties to defend the lines, once under Capt. Johnson (11) once under Capt. Rosecrantz (12) & once under Major Hardenburgh & did duty during those times as much as three months—but the length of each time he cannot recollect—

That he has no documentary evidence--& that he knows of no person whose testimony he can procure who can testify to his same except the testimony of Jonathan Odell whose affidavit is hereunto annexed.

Here hereby relinquishes every claim whatever to a pension or annuity except the present, and declares that his name is not on the pension roll of the agency of any state. (Signed) Evert Rose

Sworn to and subscribed the day and year aforesaid. Samuel Soul, Clk

End Notes—W.22126—Evert Rose or Roosa, Rosa

1. Cornelius Masten was the First Lieutenant in Captain Jacobus Rose's Company (Southeast side of Patty River) in Colonel Jonathan Hasbrouck's Fourth Regiment of Ulster County Militia.
2. Johannes Hardenbergh, Jr. was the Lieutenant-Colonel of Colonel Hasbrouck's Regiment.
3. A James Stewart was appointed Captain of the Third Company on November 21, 1776 in Colonel Lewis DuBois Fifth New York Continental Regiment. Evert may have the wrong year for his service at Forts Clinton and Montgomery. In 1776 is when work was being done on Forts Constitution, Clinton and Montgomery. A good source on the building of these forts, besides the Public Papers of George Clinton, First Governors of New York is: The Fortification of Constitution Island 1775-1783 by LTC Charles E. Miller, Jr., Department of History, United States Military Academy, West Point, New York 1972.
4. James McClaughry was the Colonel of the Second Regiment of Ulster County Militia. This tour was done as a detachment from Colonel Hasbrouck's Regiment. Fort Montgomery was captured on October 6, 1777.
5. Jason Wilkin was appointed the first lieutenant on March 9, 1778 in Captain John Gillaspy's Company in Colonel Hasbrouck's Regiment. Jason was promoted to Captain of the company on June 29, 1780 as Gillasppy was promoted to major on the same date.
6. Captain Bordawine Tarpenny served in Colonel Hasbrouck's Regiment.

7. Second Lieutenant Isaac Hardenbergh of Captain Masten's Company in Colonel Hardenbergh's Regiment. Lieutenant Masten was promoted to captain on March 9, 1778 as Captain Rose was deceased. Lieutenant-Colonel Hardenbergh was promoted to colonel in place of Hasbrouck on February 27, 1779.
8. Stephen Case was appointed Captain on March 9, 1778 in Colonel Hasbrouck's Regiment.
9. Johannes Jansen was promoted from major to lieutenant-colonel on February 27, 1779 in Colonel Hardenbergh's Regiment. William VanDeMark was the first lieutenant in Captain Masten's Company.
10. Captain Abraham Deyo served in Colonel McClaughrey's Regiment. Again this is a detached tour of service.
11. Captain Thomas Jansen Jr. served in Colonel Hasbrouck's Regiment until March 9, 1778 when First Lieutenant Matthew Jansen was promoted to Captain in his place.
12. Probably Ensign Jacob Rosekrans of Captain Jansen's Company. It is also possible that he is the same Evert Roosa that enlisted on August 10, 1780 and discharged on November 30, 1781 in Captain John Burnet's Company in Lieutenant-Colonel Commandant Albert Pawling's Regiment of New York State Levies. A Lieutenant Johannes Jansen also served in this company. FROM: Revolutionary War Rolls, 1775-1783, Series M-246, Roll 75, folder 134, National Archives, Washington, D.C.

Pension Application for Silas Runnolds

R.9078
Revolutionary War, Indian War 1791, and War of 1812
State of Vermont
Rutland County SS

On this first day of March, 1837, personally appeared in open court, before the Honorable Probate Court of the District of Rutland in the County of Rutland aforesaid, now sitting, Silas Runnolds, a resident of Fairhaven in said County, aged 78 or 79 years, who being first duly sworn according to law, doth on his oath make the following declaration, in order to obtain the benefit of the act of Congress passed June 7, 1832.

That he entered the service of the United States under the following named officers, and served as herein stated.

That about the last of April or first of May 1775, (1) he inlisted for the term of nine months, being then at Kinderhook in the State of New York, under Captain Stoffle Miller (2) of Claverack and in Col. Willett's Regiment of New York troops was first marched under Capt. Miller to Conajohary or Fort Plain; in a few days after their arrival, less than a week, Capt. Miller returned to Albany, leaving the Company under the command of his Lieutenant, of the name of Stockwell; (3) they staid there till about the first of June, then marched to Fort Herkimer and thence to Fort Staniwx where they arrived the 4th or 5th of June;

remained there during the siege, (4) which lasted 22 days. The 15th day of the siege, Col. Willet, (5) with a Lieutenant whose name is not recollected and a private of the name of Asa Munroe, then left the fort, at night, for the purpose of passing the enemy's lines, and processing reinforcements. They did not return with the reinforcement, until the morning that the British left. General Arnold then came, with a body of 3 or 4000 American troops. After the siege, he returned to Fort Herkimer; moved from there to Fort Plain; and from there, on a scout to Fort Herkimer; where he remained about a month. After that, he was employed with his company, until cold weather the next winter; in scouting through that country; in the winter, went into garrison at Fort Plain. The term of his inlistment was out, sometime after new years of 1776; (6) just before which time, he inlisted again, at that place, for the further term of three years, under Capt. Tierce, and was presently transferred to Capt. Harrison's (7) Company—Lieuts Loup and Hans Becker of Schoharie, being his subalterns: this was at Schoharie Middle Fort—lay there perhaps 1 ½ month. Afterwards, through the season, was on scouts, from Cherry Valley, Cobleskill, Turlow (8) (a small village and block house west of Schoharie which was burnt during the war) Canajoharie, Fort Plain, Fort Herkimer, Fort Dayton and back. Col. Malcolm (9) commanded the Regiment that season.

Wintered at Schoharie. Capt. James Livingston of Livingston's Manor (10) and Lt. John Morris Faught (11) of New Windsor commanded the company that summer, and Capt. Livingston continued in the command, until toward the spring of 1777; when he was succeeded by Hans Becker (12) of Schoharie as Lt. commandant.

In this year, 1777, Col. Willett was commander of the Regiment; though Maj'r Fondy (13) was in actual command, most of the time where applicant was that season. Capt. Livingston was commander of the company though absent a good deal of the time, and left the command mostly to Lieut. Hans Becker.

In 1778, the service was similar to that of the preceding year. Lt. Stockwell (14) was commandant of the Company and Col. Willet of the Regiment. Of the many expeditions in which the applicant was this year engaged, one consisting of ten men only, commanded by a Sergeant Murphy, (15) set out from the Schoharie Middle Fort, went to Tioga Point on the head waters of the Susquehanna, and in the night crossed the river, captured a centinel on his post, got the countersign from him, then went into the enemy's camp (where there were several hundreds of English, tories, and Indians) took out six prisoners, sixteen rifles, and returned in safety to the fort, in less than a fortnight.

In 1779, before the expiration of his last term of three years, the applicant inlisted for another period of three years, under the said Lieut. Commandant, Hans Becker, in Col. Willet's Regiment. The service, throughout this last period, was similar to the former. In the summer of 1781, a hostile Indian came to the Middle Fort at Schoharie, when applicants' company then lay and gave notice, that a party of several hundred of the enemy under command of one Charles Smith, consisting of British, tories, and Indians, were about crossing the Schoharie creek, on the road to Coxsackie, for the purpose of destroying the inhabitants and laying waste the country. A party was, in consequence, dispatched under the command of Sergeant John Murphy, above mentioned, from the fort to intercept them; which was done, so successfully, that they killed a great number of the enemy—among them, their tory commander—took 5 prisoners and their guns, and returned in safety. Applicant was one of that party.

In the winter of 1782, the last expedition the applicant was engaged in, during the revolution, was Fort Herkimer, under Col. Willet, for the purpose of capturing Oswego Fort.

At the close of his last term of service, applicant lay sick at said Middle Fort in Schoharie at the house of Lt. Becker, while the rest of the troops were marched to Schenectady and there discharged, as the said applicant afterwards understood from said Lieut. Becker, who would not release applicant, until his health was reestablished, in July or August following.

And, most unfortunately for this applicant in May 1791 he inlisted for three years in Capt. Jedediah Rogers' Company of Cavalry, and marched with them into the Western Country; where, in the disastrous affair of the 4th of November, he was captured by the Miami Indians, and detained among them upwards of four years, before he was enabled to make his escape. In the summer of 1796, on the northern head waters of the Missouri he embarked on board a bark canoe; and after pursuing the course of the streams, lying by in the daytime, and travelling only in the night, after 40 days, and in an almost exhausted state (being afraid to kill game with his gun, but he should be discovered by other savages) was taken up, below New Orleans, by an English 40 gun ship (name not recollected) commanded by Capt. Venables. He escaped from the British ship at Baltimore, where she had put in, to refit, after an engagement with a French armed vessel, off the capes of Virginia; ;and on board a merchant brig, Capt. Smith, he shipped himself, secretly, and arrived in New York in January 1797. In a few days, after his arrival in New York the British vessel came in to that port; and while she lay there, this applicant gave notice to the City Authorities, and was the means thereby, of liberating about 30 American citizens, who had been impressed into the English service on board of that ship. After the river opened in the spring, applicant took passage on board a sloop to seek his family which he had left in Stephentown, in Rensselaer County, about 6 years before, and to whom he had been dead, since the battle of Miami under General St. Clair. (16)

But, the applicant had the honor and satisfaction of serving his country once more, in the War of 1812-14, one year, as a private in the 30th Infantry; during which time he conducted several parties across the lines, into Canada, and at one time assisted in capturing the British Capt. Bisbee and his whole company without the loss of a man at Odlstown in said Province. And, for the remainder of the war, he served as a volunteer on board the fleet on Lake Champlain was on board of the fleet at the battle of Plattsburgh, (17)and afterwards, in February or March 1815, was honorably dismissed, the service at Whitehall by Commodore MacDonough. (18)

And the applicant further states, that he has no documentary evidence and that he knows of no person whose testimony he can procure, excepting that of Asa Munroe of Granville in the County of Washington in the State of New York, who can testify to any part of his service.

He hereby relinquishes every claim whatever to a pension or annuity except the present and declares that his name is not on the pension roll of the agency of any state. (Signed with his mark) Silas Runnolds

Sworn to, and subscribed in open Court the day and year aforesaid, before me. Wm. Hall Judge.

End Notes—R.9078 Silas Runnolds

1. Silas is mistaken as to the years that he did his military enlistments and services.
2. There is no Stoffle (Stephen is crossed out) Miller (Muller) serving under Colonel Marinus Willett. In 1775, Willett was a Captain of the Second Company in the First New York Continental Regiment under Colonel Alexander McDougall. Some of the events that Silas refers to occurred in August 1777. Willett, at that time, was the Lieutenant-Colonel of the Third New York Continental Regiment which was commanded by Colonel Peter Gansevoort.
3. Levi Stockwell was the First Lieutenant in Captain Cornelius T. Jansen's Third Company in the Third New York. On examining the muster rolls for this regiment, Silas Runnolds (Reynolds, Rynolds, Runnels, Rannals, etc.) was not found in any of the companies.
4. The Siege of Fort Schuyler, or Fort Stanwix, which stood in the present day City of Rome, Oneida County, New York; lasted 21 days and ended when Major General Benedict Arnold marched with a relief column of about 1,000 men which reached the fort on August 23.
5. Actually Colonel Willett, Lieutenant Stockwell and Private Munroe slipped out of the fort on August 8 at 1:00 A.M.
6. Again, Silas is mistaken as to the year. The year of the enlistment was in 1782 according to the Descriptive Book No. 4, Colonel Marinus Willett's Regiment of New York State Levies, Doc. No. 11105, Special Collections and Manuscripts, New York State Library, Albany, N.Y. Silas enlisted as follows: "Enlisted May 18, 1782 by Col. Marinus Willett for 2 years 7 months 12 days. Born at Nine Partners, Dutchess County, N.Y. Age—18. Size—5 ft 7 in. Complexion—light. Hair—Brown. Eyes—Brown. Occupation—farmer. Remarks—Deserted."
   Silas' name also appears on *A Roll of Deserters from Col. Marinus Willett's New York State Regiment of Two and Three Years Troops and the Battalion commanded by Major Elias VanBunschoten.* No date for the desertion is given in either record. FROM: Revolutionary War Rolls 1775-1783, Series M-246, Roll 78, Folder 173, National Archives, Washington, D.C.

7. Captain Joseph Harrison, Lieutenants Peter Loop and Storm Becker. Silas is not listed on Harrison's PayRoll/Muster Roll of 1783. It appears that Silas did not return from desertion and that he deserted before January 1, 1783. FROM: Revolutionary War Rolls 1775-1783, Series M-246, Roll 78, Folder 173, National Archives, Washington, D.C.
8. Turlow, Terlow, Telow, etc., refers to the settlement of New Dorlach now Sharon Springs, Schoharie County, New York.
9. Colonel William Malcolm or Malcom had a regiment of New York State Levies in 1780. Silas was clearly mixing up his military service.
10. Captain Gilbert J. Livingston of Colonel William Malcolm's Regiment of New York State levies in 1780. According to the muster roll for July & August Silas had enlisted on July 27, 1780 and he was "In Fishkill Hospital". According to the September & October 1780 roll he was listed as "deserted October 15, 1780". FROM: Revolutionary War Rolls 1775-1783, Series M-246, Roll 72, Folder 73, National Archives, Washington, D.C.
11. Lieutenant John Morris McFaught or McFought, etc., served in Captain Daniel Gano's Company in Colonel Lewis DuBois' Regiment of New York State Levies in 1780. He was later appointed captain in this regiment.
12. Storm Becker was a sergeant in Captain Jacob J. Lansing's Company in Colonel Morris Graham's Regiment of New York State Levies in 1780. FROM: Revolutionary War Rolls 1775-1783, Series M-246, Roll 72, Folder 75, National Archives, Washington, D.C.
13. Jellis A. Fonda, Lieutenant and Adjutant in Colonel Graham's Regiment in 1780.
14. Again he is mistaken. Levi Stockwell was not serving under Willett. They served together only in the Third New York and Stockwell left the regiment in May of 1778. Stockwell lived in the Skenesborough District of Charlotte County which is present day Whitehall, Washington County, N.Y. Stockwell had served as a First Lieutenant in the First Regiment of Charlotte County Militia before he had joined the Third New York. In 1779 he had served as a captain in Lieutenant-Colonel Henry K. VanRensselaer's Regiment of New York State Levies. He was stationed mainly in and around Skenesborough. He again served under Lieutenant-Colonel VanRensselaer in 1780 from January to April at different times in guarding Skenesborough as the militia would not do duty or not enough of them showed up to garrison this important post. On May 11, 1780, Stockwell was appointed Captain in Lieutenant-Colonel John Harper's Regiment of New York State Levies. He was discharged on November 30, 1780 and he returned to Charlotte County. On April 12, 1782 he was commissioned as Captain in the First Charlotte.
15. He later says it is Sergeant John Murphy. Again, he appears to be mistaken in both instances of his testimony. In 1778, the Seventh

Virginia Continental Regiment which was formerly the Eleventh Virginia but better known as Morgan's Riflemen, (Colonel Daniel Morgan) under Major Thomas Posey along with the Fourth Pennsylvania Continental Regiment under Lieutenant-Colonel Commandant William Butler were sent to the Schoharie Valley. The Middle Fort was their headquarters. Timothy Murphy served in the Rifle Corps as they were referred to, as a detachment under Major James Parr of the Seventh Pennsylvania Continental Regiment which was at the Middle Fort and was in many of the expeditions to the Susquehanna River. Timothy Murphy was in the expedition in 1779 to capture Charles Smith.

16. Arthur St. Clair, Major General in the United States Army.
17. The Battle of Plattsburgh, N.Y., was fought on September 11, 1814.
18. Commodore Thomas MacDonough.

Pension Application for Gideon Salisbury or Salsbury

S.28863
Pension was granted $22.00 per annum, arrears $286.00.
Family Record of Births
Benanuel S. Salisbury was born in the year of our Lord seventeen hundred and sixty on the twenty first day of November.
Grace Salisbury was born in the thirteenth day of March in the year of our Lord seventeen hundred and sixty two.
Robert Salisbury was born on the 15th day of April A.D. 1781
Albert W. Salisbury was born on the seventeenth day of December A.D 1783.
Joseph Salisbury was born on the 22nd day of August A.D.
Mary Salisbury was born on the 4th day of November A.D. 1788.
Elizabeth Salisbury was born on the 28th day of February A.D. 1791.
Almedia Salisbury was born on the 26th day of March AD 1793.
Eleazar L. Salisbury was born on the 4th day of January AD 1798.
Warren Salisbury was born the 13th day of February 1800.
Teybella Salisbury was born on the 2nd day of October AD 1802.

Gideon Salisbury was born January 12th 1763.
Elizabeth Salisbury was born July 7th 1767
Betsy Salisbury was born July 20th 1785
Phebe Salisbury was born December 6th 1787.
Frederick F. Salisbury was born Nov. 6th 1789.
Margaret Salisbury was born May 8th 1791.
Samuel Salisbury was born May 6th 1792.
John Salisbury was born April 30th 1735.
Gideon Salisbury was born November 15th 1708.
Beno[?]will Salisbury was born Feb 15th 1802.
Alfred Salisbury was born July 15th 1804.
Samanthy Salisbury was born Aug. 6th 1807.
William J. Salisbury was born January 6th 1809.

State of New York
County of Cayuga SS.

Personally appeared before the Subscriber a Justice of the peace in & for said county Bennauel Salisbury (1) of Ledyard in said county aged eighty two years in Nov'r last past, & on being duly sworn according to law deposeth & saith that Gideon Salisbury of Potter, Ontario County New York who is applying for a pension as a soldier of the war of the Revolution is this deponents brother, & that he is better than two years younger than this deponent, that this deponent well recollects that his said brother Gideon Salisbury went out in the Militia & went with the Army to Boston, he thinks in 1777—that this deponent well recollects that his said brother the said Gideon Salisbury enlisted under Capt. Christopher Miller, this deponent thinks in 1780, that he marched with the company to the south & that this deponent well recollects of the company returning to old Shoharrie [Schoharie] & this deponent well recollects of his said brother serving under Capt. Miller four months, & that his sais brother the aforesaid Gideon Salisbury then enlisted under Capt. Joseph Harrison in the fall of the year & this deponent thinks it was in 1780—that his said brother the said Gideon Salisbury went as a soldier & acted as waiter to Capt. Harrison, that the company & this deponents brother went with them to Fort Stanwick & after a while returned & were stationed at Fort Plain on the Mohawk River, that this deponent well recollects that his said Gideon Salisbury served six months or more under Capt. Harrison, & that he then served under Capt. Wright more than one year, that this deponent being confined at home in charge of the farm & its cares, knows well of his said brother the aforesaid Gideon Salisbury being engaged in the service more than two years, over & above the three months served in the militia in 1777 or 1778—that this deponent well recollects that his said brother the aforesaid Gideon Salisbury was absent in the service of the war of the United States more than two years & that he never came home to see his parents except by permission & on furlough & that this deponent well recollects that his said brother the aforesaid Gideon Salisbury did come home on furlough, that he came home several times on furlough, & that this deponent well recollects that his aforesaid brother came home on furlough soon after the defeat of Corn Wallis & that they held a day of rejoicing, but that he returned again & the army that this deponent well recollects that his said brother received an honorable discharge. (Signed with his mark) Bennanuel Salisbury

Subscribed & sworn before me this 28day of Augt 1843. H. W. Taylor Justice of the Peace of Ledyard.

State of New York
County of Yates SS.

On this day of January in the year one thousand eight hundred and thirty five (1835) personally appeared in open court before the Judges of the court of Common Pleas of the said County of Yates now sitting, being a court of

Record—Gideon Salisbury a resident of the town of Middlesex in the said County of Yates and State of New York aged seventy three years the fourteenth day of January instant—who being first duly sworn according to same doth on his oath make the following declaration in order to obtain the benefit of the Act of Congress passed June 7, 1832.

That he has been informed by his mother and believes that he was born in the month of January in the year one thousand seven hundred & sixty two (1762) (2) at Salisbury Plains in England—that he was brought by his parents, at the age of three or four years, Emigrated to this country, and settled in Rhode Island—that when he was about eight years old he left Rhode Island with his parents who removed to Dutchess County in the State of New York fourteen miles from Poughkeepsie—that when he was about thirteen years of age he left Dutchess County with his parents who removed to Nobletown then in the county of Albany—now called Hillsdale in the County of Columbia in the State of New York, near the line of Massachusetts—where he resided until after the close of the Revolutionary War.

That he has not now in his possession any original Record of his age but that his brother Benanuel Salisbury now living in the town of Ledyard in the County of Cayuga in the State of New York, has in his possession the original record (kept by his father Gideon Salisbury, now deceased, in his family Bible) of the line of the birth of the above named applicant and of his brothers and sisters—that he has frequently seen the said family record and that by the said record he the said Gideon Salisbury was born the year 1762 as above stated.—

That he the above named applicant entered the service of the United States under the following named officers and served as herein stated—That in the year one thousand seven hundred and seventy seven (1777) at Nobletown then in Albany County now called Hillsdale in the County of Columbia—in the State of New York in the month of October about the time of Burgoyne's (3) surrender, he enlisted as a private soldier in Captain Thomas McInstry's (4) (or McKinstrys) Company of Infantry—in Colonel John McInstry's (5) Regiment (Samuel Mallory was his Lieutenant) for nine months—was sent as one of the Guard of Burgoyne's Army to Boston Massachusetts—and remained at Boston under the said Captain McInstry during the winter and spring of 1778—and then returned in said company under said captain McInstry to Albany in the State of New York, and was then discharged by the said Colonel John McInstry, by a written discharge on the last day of July in the year seventeen hundred and seventy eight (1778) After having served as such private soldier in said company for the whole of said term of nine months—which said discharge was been lost.—

That in the year one thousand seven hundred and Eighty (1780) in the month of August or September he the said Gideon Salisbury the above named applicant again Enlisted at Nobeltown aforesaid as a private Solider in Captain Joseph Harrisons Company (6) of infantry in Colonel Marinus Willetts Regiment, for one year—was immediately marched in said company to Tapan [Tappan] Bay, on the North [Hudson] River and there joined the regular American Army of twenty five thousand men, under General Washington (7)—was there put under the command of General Wayne (8), four days after he had taken Stony Point from the British—while at Tapan Bay, the said Company belonged to Colonel Morris Grahams Regiment about time Major Andre (9), was taken as a spy about this time—After remaining at Tapan Bay about three weeks, General Wayne ordered the said Regiment to March, under Colonel Willett (10), up the Mohawk River—was stationed a part of the time at old Schoharrie [Schoharie] where he was engaged in a battle (11) against the Indians in which four hundred Indians were killed—this was in the fall of the year (1780) seventeen hundred and eighty-- some seven or eight of the American Army were killed in this engagement—was stationed in said Regiment during the following winter at Fort Stanwicks (12), now called Rome in the County of Oneida and State of New York—that in the spring of the year seventeen hundred and eighty one (1781) was marched in said company to Herkimer and there built a fort called Fort Herkimer (13), and he was verbally discharged at Fort Plain by the said Captain Harrison (14) in the month of August or September in the year last aforesaid (1781)—after serving as such private solider in said company for the full term of one year—that during said year, said company was at different times under Col. Willett—Col. VanSchaick (15)—and Col. Dubois (16)—that there upon he the said Gideon Salisbury went home to Nobletown aforesaid and in the winter or spring of the following year (1782) he again enlisted as a private soldier at Nobletown aforesaid in Captain Wrights (17) Company of Infantry in Colonel Martinus [Marinus] Willetts Regiment, for the term of nine months—marched thence to Albany—thence up the Mohawk River to Old Schoharie Middle Fort—was then under Captain or Colonel Dubois (18), when the Fort was attacked by the British & Indians under Colonels Butler & Brandt (19)who were repulsed and we followed them to Oneida Lake where they got out of our reach—Afterwards at Stony Arabia (20) in the State of New York he the said applicant was in said company engaged in a Battle against the British and Indians when Captain Butler (21) of the Brittish Army (the son of the said Col. Butler) and Colonel Brown of the American Army were killed—In that Engagement there were six American Soldiers belonging to the same company with the said Gideon Salisbury to wit—Cole—Spareback, Lyon—Loomis (22) and two other were killed—and he the said Gideon Salisbury had five ball holes made through his garments in said Engagement - and have the belt of his cartridge box shot off by a Musket ball—

And that he the said Gideon Salisbury during the time of the said last enlistment at different times was under different captains to wit. Captain Wright and afterward Captain Miller (23)—that the said Captain Wright belonged to Connecticut—and the said Captain Miller resided at Claverack about five miles from Hudson, in the state of New York—and that during the said last mentioned campaign a Captain Harrison—Captain Clark & Major Rowley (24) belonged to the same regiment with said applicant.

That by reason of old age & consequent loss of memory he cannot swear positively as to the dates and times of his services above set forth but according to the best of his recollection he served as a private soldier in the war of the Revolution—in the American Army—not less than the period herein after mentioned to wit: Nine months under Captain [Joseph Harrison is crossed out] Thomas McInstry in the years 1777- 1778—One year under Captain Joseph Harrison in the years 1780-& 11781—and nine months under Captains Christopher Miller and ---Wright—Making in the whole two years and six months service as a private soldier for which he claims a pension—

That he remained in such service under the said last mentioned enlistment until the month of December in the said year seventeen hundred and eighty two (1782) when he was discharged by the said Colonel Dubois by a written discharge either at Albany or at Fort Plain but does not recollect at which place it was that he received said dlscharge—which said discharge is lost—

That he has no documentary evidence and that he knows of no person, whose testimony he can procure as to his said services—except Truman Spencer (25) and Benanuel Salisbury whose affidavits accompany this declaration and the affidavits of Archibald Armstrong which was some years ago forwarded to the war department and which he presumes now remains on file in the Pension Office.—

That there is no clergyman residing in his neighborhood whose evidence he can obtain in relation to his age and general belief in the neighborhood relative to his Revolutionary Service.

That he is personally acquainted with Chester Loomis, who is a senator in the Legislature of the State of New York—Enos P. Resmer & Hiram Torry, Merchants—and Augustus Torry a Justice of the Peace who are all his neighbors—and with R. M. Bailey of Geneva N. York who has been an agent for procuring pensions—and with Joshua Lee of Milo in said County of Yates—who is elected to Congress whose names are subscribed on a certificate which is hereunto attached. That he is also well acquainted with Truman Spencer of Benton in said County of Yates—And John Potter of Polten in said County of Yates.

That at the September term of the said court in the year one thousand eight hundred and thirty two he presented to the said court his declaration in this behalf together with such proofs as he could then procure—that the said court then passed His claim and the papers were sent by R.M. Baily Esqr of Geneva to the Pension Office and they have been returned as incomplete—and therefore he now presents a new declaration & proofs which he supposes are complete—

That his brother Benanuel Salisbury whose affidavit is hereto attached resides in Cayuga County, a distance of sixty miles from the court house in said county of Yates by the road which is most frequently traveled, that the said Benanuel Salisbury is seventy four years of age and by reason of infirmity is unable to attend the said court in the said county of Yates.

He the said Gideon Salisbury hereby relinquishes every claim whatever to a pension or annuity except the present and declares that his name is not on the pension roll of the agency of any state.

That he the said Gideon Salisbury about the year one thousand seven hundred and eighty four (1784) removed from Nobletown aforesaid to Wyoming in Pennsylvania—About three or four years. Thereafter he removed from Wyoming to the head of Seneca Lake in the State of New York—and about the year one thousand seven hundred and eighty nine removed to Big flats in the State of New York—and thence in three or four years thereafter he removed into the town of Benton then in the county of Ontario, now in the said county of Yates—where he resided until about the close of the last War, say about twenty years ago he removed to the said town of Middlesex where he has ever since resided and where he now resides. (Signed) Gideon Salisbury

Sworn and Subscribed the day and year aforesaid in open court—George Thearmus Clerk

End Notes—S.28863—Gideon Salisbury

1. Benanuel Salisbury served as a Private in Colonel Peter VanNess' Ninth Regiment of Albany Militia.
2. According to the record provided for his pension application he was born January 12, 1763. This means he was not of age to serve until 1779. Any service before that date would not count because he was under age.
3. Lieutenant General John Burgoyne surrendered his British forces on October 17, 1777. Gideon was only fourteen years of age at this time and legally he was under age to serve.
4. Thomas McKinstry served as a lieutenant in Colonel VanNess' Regiment. McKinstry served as captain in 1780 in Colonel William Malcolm's Regiment of New York State Levies.
5. John McKinstry was commissioned second major on May 28, 1778 and then as the first major on February 6, 1779 in Colonel VanNess' Regiment.
6. Gideon has almost everything in his declaration mixed up. In 1780, he enlisted as a private on July 27, in Captain Christopher Muller's Company in Colonel Morris Graham's Third Regiment of New York State Levies. The muster roll is dated September 9, 1780, camp at Albany. His term of enlistment is listed for 3 months. The company was to be discharged on October 27, 1780. FROM: Revolutionary War Rolls 1775-1783, Series M-246, Roll 72, folder 75, National Archives, Washington, D.C.
7. Commander-in-chief, General George Washington.
8. Brigadier General Anthony Wayne. General Wayne captured Stony Point on July 16, 1779 not in 1780.
9. British Major John Andre was hung for being a spy on October 2, 1780.

10. Again he is mistaken. In 1780, Lieutenant-Colonel Commandant Marinus Willett was in command of the Fifth New York Continental Regiment and they did not march to the Mohawk Valley.
11. Gideon is referring to Lieutenant-Colonel Sir John Johnson's raid into the Schoharie Valley on October 17, 1780. Captain's Muller and Jacob J. Lansing's Companies of Colonel Graham's Regiment were stationed at the Middle Fort.
12. Colonel Graham's Regiment did not march to Fort Schuyler (Fort Stanwix) and stay there for the winter. The regiment was only raised for three months and because of Sir John Johnsons' Raid it may have been kept together past that time but only to about November 1st. Fort Schuyler was garrisoned by the Fourth New York Continental Regiment from November 22, 1780 to January 1, 1781. The Second, Fourth and Fifth New York Continental Regiments were consolidated into a new Second New York. They garrisoned Fort Schuyler from January 1st to abut May 17, 1781 when the fort was no longer in condition to be used as a fort.
13. The Second New York under Colonel Philip VanCortlandt started clearing land in late June of 1781 to build a new fort but it was never completed. The Second New york was ordered to join the American Main Army and eventually arrived at YorkTown, Virginia.
14. Gideon did enlist in Captain Joseph Harrison's Company as a private in 1781 in Lieutenant-Colonel Commandant Marinus Willett's Regiment of New York State Levies. He was owed £ 9 . . 10. . 3 and it appears as if he never received it. FROM: Revolutionary War Rolls 1775-1783, Series M-246, Roll 78, folder 173, National Archives, Washington, D.C.
15. Goose VanSchaick was the Colonel of the First New York Continental Regiment. In July his regiment also marched for Yorktown, Virginia.
16. Colonel Lewis DuBois commanded a regiment of New York State Levies in 1780 and was not in active service in the Mohawk Valley in 1781.
17. Captain Job Wright's company of Willett's Regiment was stationed most of the time in 1781 in Saratoga, Stillwater or Ball'sTown.
18. Benjamin Debois was a captain in Willett's Regiment in 1781 and was stationed at the Middle Fort in Schoharie.
19. Lieutenant-Colonel John Butler and Captain Joseph Brant were with Johnson in the October 1780 raid but not in 1781.
20. The Battle of Stone Arabia happened on October 19, 1780 at 10:00 A.M. Gideon could not have been in this battle having been in the Middle Fort on the 17th.
21. Captain Walter Butler was killed October 30, 1781 at West Canada Creek not at Stone Arabia. Colonel John Brown was killed here but Gideon has it mixed up about Butler.
22. This is possibly Andrew Lummes who was a private in Captain Muller's company and Amariah Lyons a private in Captain Lansing's Company. No soldier named Sparbeck or Sparebeck, etc., was found in Graham's

Regiment and there were several Cole's but those companies were not in the Schoharie or Mohawk Valleys. Muller's and Lansing's company muster rolls were dated at Schoharie on October 14, 1780 but as they were not at Stone Arabia they probably were not killed. A Conrad Sparbeck served with Gideon in Captain Harrison's Company in 1781 but he was not killed either.

23. Captain Muller was not in this part of the Mohawk after 1780.
24. Captain Samuel Clarke and Major Aaron Rowley were in Colonel Elisha Porter's Regiment of Massachusetts Levies in 1781. They were both wounded at the battle of Johnstown on October 25, 1781.
25. Truman Spencer served as a private in 1781 in Captain Aaron Hale's Company in Colonel Willett's Regiment. In 1782 he enlisted in Captain Henry's Company and after sometime in July of 1782 he was transferred to Captain Simeon Newell's Company. Both Henry and Newell's companies were in Willett's Regiment.

Pension Application for Johannes Sammons

W.18998 (Widow: Margaret)
State of New York
Orange County SS.

On this sixth day of March eighteen hundred and thirty nine personally appeared before the undersigned a Judge of the court of common pleas in and for the said county Margaret Sammons a resident of the town of Deerpark in the County of Orange aged eighty years who being duly sworn according to law doth on her oath make the following declaration in order to obtain the benefit of the provisions made by the act of Congress passed July 4, 1836, entitled an act providing half pay and pensions for certain widows. That she the widow of Johannes or John Sammons late of the County of Orange aforesaid who was a private & Sergeant in the Militia of the State of New York and served as hereinafter stated according to the best of her recollection as she had been informed by her said husband and verily believes to be true.

That in the latter part of the month of July 1776 her said husband enlisted and volunteered with a company that was raised for the term of four months. The same company was raised in the Town of Rochester, in the County of Ulster and in the State aforesaid and rendevouz at the landing on the Hudson River near Kingston under Captain Benjamin Kortright (1), Lieut. Nath'l Pitter [Potter] esq.,(2) Frederick Westbrook and went from thence to Fort Montgomery from thence they went to Kingsbridge and remained there until New York was taken - They removed to White Plains and was there at the time of the battle (3) from thence they marched to Peekskill where the said John Sammons she believes was discharged on or about the first day of January 1777, this service was rendered in the regiment commanded by Col. Levi Pawling and under General George Clinton. (4)

She further declares that on or about the first part of January 1777 the Committee of Safety called out a number of men from the county of Ulster to be raised by volunteering or draft and that Benjamin Kortright should take charge of a company of those men as captain and that her said husband Johannes Sammons volunteered into the said company under Capt. Benjamin Kortright and went from Rochester to Fort Montgomery about the middle of January and served until the last day of March 1777 being a service of at least ten weeks when he returned home, this service was done in the Regiment then from Ulster County at Fort Montgomery under Col. Snyder (5) and Lieutenant Col. McClaughry. (6)

That in the month of August 1777 her said husband Johannes Sammons was drafted from a company of Militia then under Capt. Kortright and was placed in a company of drafted Militiaman under Captain Benjamin Kortright and in the Regiment commanded by Col. Morris Graham (7) and went to the north to meet General Burgoyne and was in the battle (8) at the taking of Burgoyne and served three months the time for which he was drafted and was discharged at the expiration of his term of service.

That her said husband Johannes Sammons in the spring of 1778 was appointed a Searjeant [Sergeant] in the company under Capt. Benjamin Kortright and that he served until the end of the war as such that she is unable to state the different times that her husband was out in service during the year of 1778, 1779 and 1780, excepting a service of nine days as a Sergeant in the company of Johannes Hardenburg (9) and in the Regiment under Co. Cantine on the western frontier in the months of November 1778 as will appear by the roll of Capt. Hardenburhg now on file in the pension office.

That sometime in 1779 or 1780 her said husband Johannes Sammons was out as a Sergeant out serving on the western frontier as a Sergeant for twenty three days as will appear from the accompanying roll kept by Capt. Kortright and lately found in his family this service was under Capt. Kortright and under Col. Cantine.

That according to the best of her recollection in her said husband Johannes Sammons entered the Levies in the Spring of 1781 and served for the term of Nine months on the western frontier as a Sergeant in a company of Levies and according to the best of her recollection in the company of Captain Henry Pawling. (10)

That in 1781 her said husband was out several times upon alarm but she is unable from old age and loss of memory unable to state the particulars. That she has no documentary evidence written of her husband's service in her possession except that which is herewith produced.

She further declares that she was married to the said the said Johannes Sammons at her father's house in the town of Rochester in the County and State aforesaid by the Rev. Derick Romeyn Pastor of the Dutch Reformed Church in the aforementioned place on the thirteenth day of March Seventeen Hundred and seventy eight and that her name before marriage was Margaretta Wynkoop that she has no record of her said marriage nor does she believe there is any in existence nor has she any other proof that she knows of except the baptism of her oldest daughter Jane or Jenneka Sammons which took place in the church at Rochester in the county and state aforesaid and that she held the said child in her own arms when she was baptized and that the aforementioned Jenneka was baptized on the 6th day of May seventeen hundred and seventy nine Just eighteen days after she was born and she further declares that the said [?] is the lawful [?] of the marriage of Johannes Sammons and Margaretta Wynkoop. That her husband Johannes Sammons died on the first day of August Eighteen hundred and thirty and that she has not since intermarried but still remains the widow of Johannes Sammons. (Signed with her mark) Margaret Sammons.

Sworn and subscribed the day and year above mentioned before me. By making her mark because she cannot see to write. Hulet Clark a Judge of Orange County Co. Common Pleas.

Letter replying to an inquiry dated May 29, 1935.

The data which follow were obtained from the papers on file in Revolutionary War pension claim W.18998, based upon the military service of Johannes or John Sammons in that war.

The date and place of birth and the names of the parents of Johannes or John Sammons are not shown.

He volunteered and served with the New York Troops, as follows: from the latter part of July 1776, as a private in a company raised in Ulster County, New York, commanded by Captain Benjamin Kortroght in Colonel Levi Pawling's Regiment, marched to New York, where he remained until after that city was captured; thence to White Plains and was in the battle at that place, and was discharged about January 1, 1777; from about January 1, 1777, ten weeks as a private in Captain Benjamin Kortroght's Company under Colonels Snyder and Pawling and was at Fort Montgomery: from August, 1777, three months in Captain Kortroght's Company, Colonel Morris Graham's New York Regiment, was in the campaign against Burgoyne and in the engagement when that officer was captured; in the spring of 1778, he was appointed sergeant in Captain Benjamin Kortroght's Company and served each year from that time until 1780 on various tours; one tour in 1779 or 1780 was for twenty-three days as sergeant under Captain Kortroght and Colonel Cantine on the western frontier; and another in November, 1778, was for nine days on the western frontier under Captain Johannes A. Hardenburgh and Col. Cantine; dates and names of officers for the other tours are not shown in 1781, he served nine months as sergeant in Captain Henry Pawling's Company, Colonel Albert Pawling's Regiment and was again on the western frontier; in 1782, he was out on a number of alarms; dates and officers' names not shown.

The soldier died August 1, 1830, in Orange County, New York.

Johannes or John Sammons married March 13, 1778, Margaret or Margaretta Wynkoop. They were married at her father's house in Rochester, New York. The date of her birth and names of her parents are not shown.

Soldier's widow, Margaret, was allowed pension on her application executed March 6, 1839, at which time she was aged eighty years and resided at Deer Park, Orange County, New York.

The only name of a child that is show is daughter Jane or Janneka, who was baptized May 6, 1779, when she was eighteen days old. The baptism was recorded on the records of the Reformed Dutch Church at Rochester, New York.

In 1839, Jane Whitehead, aged twenty-nine and a resident of Deer Park, New York, stated that she was the granddaughter of the soldier Johannes Sammons and his wife, Margaret. She did not give the names of her parents.

End Notes—W.18998—Johannes Sammons

1. Captain Benjamin Kortright was appointed Captain in 1777 and was commissioned on February 21, 1778 in Colonel Levi Pawling's Third Regiment of Ulster County Militia. The following were officers in Kortright's Company: Dirck Westbrook as the First Lieutenant, Frederick Westbrook as the Second Lieutenant and Ensign Jacob Hornbeck. FROM: Revolutionary War Rolls 1775-1783, Series M-246, Roll 75, folder 135, National Archives, Washington, D.C.
2. Nathaniel Potter served as First Lieutenant in Captain Peleg Ransom's Company in Colonel Pawling's Regiment.
3. The Battle of White Plains, New York was fought on October 28, 1776.
4. George Clinton was a Brigadier General and in April of 1777 he was elected as the first Governor of New York State.
5. Johannes Snyder was the Colonel of the First Regiment of Ulster County Militia.
6. James McClaughrey was the Lieutenant-Colonel of the Second Regiment of Ulster County Militia.
7. Morris Graham served as a Colonel in 1777 for 5 months in the militia that had been drafted from various regiments and sent to join Major General Philip Schuyler's Army on the North River or as it is known now, the Hudson River.
8. This probably refers to the Battle of Saratoga which was fought on September 19, 1777. A second battle was fought on October 7, 1777. Lieutenant General John Burgoyne surrendered his British Army and Allies on October 17, 1777.
9. John A. Hardenburgh was commissioned Captain on February 21, 1778 of the First New Paltz Company in Colonel John Cantine's Third Regiment of Ulster County Militia. Cantine was appointed colonel on the same date in place of Colonel Pawling who had been appointed First Judge of Common Pleas. FROM: Revolutionary War Rolls 1775-1783, Series M-246, Roll 72, folder 76, National Archives, Washington, D.C. The roll for this company is in this folder.
10. On searching the payrolls for Lieutenant-Colonel Commandant Albert Pawling's Regiment of New York State Levies, John's name could not be found in Captain Henry Pawling's or in any of the other companies.

FROM: Revolutionary War Rolls 1775-1783, Series M-246, Roll 75, folder 134 (Albert Pawling), National Archives, Washington, D.C.

Pension Application for Isaac Sampson

S.36280
State of Ohio
Huron County SS

On this 2d day of June 1818 before me the subscriber, one of the Associate Judges of the Court of Common Pleas of said County personally appears Isaac Sampson aged fifty six years resident of said county who being by me first duly sworn according to law doth on his oath make the following declaration in order to obtain the provision made by the late act of Congress entitled an act to provide for certain persons engaged in the land and naval service of the United States in the Revolutionary War. That the said Isaac Sampson enlisted April 1777 in the County of Orange State of New York in a company commanded by Captain James Stuart (1) of the 2 Regiment of N. York troops commanded by Col. Dubois, Gen. Clinton's (2) Brigade, that he continued to serve in this said corps in the service of the United States until the army was disbanded & that he received his discharge in June 1782 as he thinks from Col. Courtland (3) at a place called Snake Hill in the State of New York that he was in the battles at Fort Montgomery (4) or Independence in the State of New York and at the taking of the British army under Cornwallis (5) in Virginia and that he is in reduced circumstances and stand in need of the assistance of his country for support and that he has no further evidence now in his power of his said services. Sworn to and declared before me this day and year aforesaid. (Signed) Isaac Sampson

Jabez Wright, Associate Judge

And the s'd Isaac Samson [sic] further declares that he served in Capt. James Stuart Company, Col. Dubois Regiment and Gen. Clinton's Brigade as set forth in the above declaration and that the said Company Regiment and Brigade were attached to and formed a part of the New York line of the Continental establishment. I hereby certify that the said Isaac Samson is under indigent circumstances and in my opinion stands in need of the assistance of his country for support. (Signed) Isaac Sampson

Huron Ohio, July 21st 1819. Jabez Wright, Associate Judge.

End Notes—S.36280—Isaac Sampson (Samson, etc.)

1. Isaac on May 24, 1777 enlisted as a private for during war in Captain James Stewart's (Third Company) in Colonel Lewis DuBois' Fifth New York Continental Regiment.
2. Brigadier General James Clinton.
3. On January 1, 1781, the Second Fourth and Fifth New York Continental Regiments were consolidated into a new Second New York. Philip VanCortlandt remained the colonel who had been appointed as colonel of this regiment on November 21, 1776 and served as such until June 1783 when the Continental Army was disbanded. He was brevetted

Brigadier-General on September 30, 1783. Isaac was transferred to the Second New York to complete his term of enlistment. He was put in Captain Henry DuBois' Company who had also transferred from the Fifth New York. On the muster roll for Captain DuBois' Company for January to May 1781 dated June 4, 1781 at Schoharie, Isaac is listed as "on comd waiter to recruiting officer". FROM: Revolutionary War Rolls 1775-1783, M-246, Roll 67, Folder 23, National Archives, Washington, D.C.

4. The Battle of Fort Montgomery, N.Y. was fought on October 6, 1777. The Fifth New York was also part of the Sullivan-Clinton Campaign in 1779 against the Iroquois in the western part of New York.
5. The Yorktown, Va. Campaign was from September 28 to October 19, 1781.

Pension Application for Joshua Sayre

S.14403
Ensign, Artificer, Sergeant. Under Captain Hulbert, Col. Clinton.
Declaration in order to obtain the benefit of the act of Congress passed June 7, 1832.
State of New York
County of Cayuga SS.

On this first day of September AD 1832 before me Augustus F. Ferris a Judge of the Court of Common Pleas in and for the County of Cayuga personally appeared Joshua Sayre a resident of the town of Victory in the county of Cayuga and State of New York aged seventy seven years who being first duly sworn according to law doth on his oath make the following declaration in order to obtain the benefit of the act of Congress passed June 7, 1832.

That he entered the service of the United States under the following named officers and served as herein stated to wit he entered the service under Captain John Hulbert (1) afterwards (Colonel Hulbert) in whose company was Second Lieutenant William Haven and first Lieutenant John Davis in Colonel James Clinton's Regiment of the New York Troops or Militia on or about the eighth day of June 1775 under an enlistment or engagement for eight months as a volunteer or an enlisted soldier for the term of eight months that he cannot state whether he was termed a volunteer or an enlisted soldier for that term but that he signed his name to an enlistment paper that he was discharged from the service of the United States on or about the tenth day of March AD 1776—That he entered the aforesaid service at South Hampton in the County of Suffolk in the State of New York on Long Island in the State of New York. That he served a little over one month more than the engagement on account of there not being a relief sent on to the company and that in the whole of this service he served a few days over nine months—That soon after he entered this service the company of Captain Hulbert marched to Montauk Point and laid there about two months -- from there the company started for New York City and he was taken sick and left at South Hampton aforesaid and remained there sick about three weeks when he joined his company aforesaid at Fort Constitution in Dutchess County in said State where the company of Captain Hulbert then lay and remained there till January 1776 as he now thinks and from there went to Bedford to White Plains to Rye to Huntington and then to South Hampton and to the residence of Captain Hulbert in said South Hamton [sic] and was then discharged by the captain—That while he lay at Fort Constitution he was a short time put into the company of Captain Grinel while some part of Captain Hulbert's went to the north to Lake Champlain and in Captain Grinel's (2) Company he remained until Captain Hulbert's Company returned from the north when he joined his company again. General Schuyler (3) had the command of the Brigade to which Colonel Clinton's Regiment belonged—Colonel McDougle's (4) Regiment was in the same brigade as he now thinks. That he was a second Seargent [sic] in Captain Hulbert's Company.

That he entered the service of the United [States] again on or about the second day of April in the year 1776 under Captain Machin (5) in Colonel Lamb's Regiment as a volunteer or under an engagement for one year that he signed a paper that bound him to stay in this service for the term of one year that he entered the service of the United States as an artificer under the last named officers at Fort Montgomery (6) that he lived at that time at the Town of New Windsor then Ulster County now Orange County New York and was discharged from this service about the tenth day of October in the year 1777. That Captain Machin was Chief Engineer at Fort Montgomery. That Hezakiah White had the Superintendance of the Artificers at Fort Montgomery. That he was employed on the Fort at Wagons Barracks platforms, ram rods for cannon & cannon carriages and remained at this service at said Fort Montgomery til December in the year 1776, then went up the River Hudson near and a little south of the Village of New Windsor in the said County of Ulster and was set to work at the Chevaux de frize and remained there so to work till in the first of October 1777 when he was down to Fort Montgomery together with all the rest who were engaged at New Windsor when the British were coming up the Hudson River to attack Fort Montgomery and that he was taken down by water and was in the Fort was stormed by the British and was in the whole engagement at the storming of the fort and escaped after the British had got possession of said Fort Montgomery.

That a few days after the taking Fort Montgomery by the British which was on the sixth of October 1777 he was discharged on or about the tenth of same month of October.

That he was in this last service one year and six months and a few days over. That he voluntarily remained in the above service the six months after his term of one year had expired and at the request and solicitations of Captain Machin the Chief Engineer at Fort Montgomery and at New Windsor aforesaid General George Clinton (7) had the command at the said Fort Montgomery when taken as aforesaid -Colonel Lewis Dubois (8) Regiment was there in whose Regiment was Major Logan. (9)

That he entered the service of the United States again in the month of May in the year 1778 under Captain VanKuran (10) and Lieutenant Coleman (11) in whose company he (this claimant) was ensign in Colonel Cantine's (12)Regiment of Militia that he was drafted out on this service and was out one month when he was discharged. That he lived at this time he went into this service at New Windsor aforesaid at which place he entered the service under a draft and marched to a place called Nipenac on the Neversink River on the frontier against the Indians and Tories—That he received a commission of Ensign a short time before going into this last service in Militia of New York and in the spring of 1778 signed by Governor George Clinton.

That he entered the service of the United States again in the month of July as he now thinks in the year 1778 under Captain Leonard D. Nichols (13) & Samuel Arter First Lieutenant & Second Lieutenant Isaac Shultz and in same company he was ensign in Colonel Newkirk's (14) Regiment of Militia at New Windsor aforesaid at which place he then resided and marched to a place called Forrest of Dean (3) in a westerly direction from West Point went under a draft—was out less than a month and was discharged in the month of June as he now thinks AD 1778.

That he again entered the service of the United States in the month of November 1778 under Lieutenant John McNiel (15) who acted as Captain and he (this claimant) was ensign in Colonel Cantine Regiment of Militia afterwards Colonel Cantine was a General that he resided at the time of entering this service and was out about a month and over as he thinks and was discharged in December 1778 that he entered as draft and went to DeWitt's Fort which was a stone house stockade then in the County of Ulster, that he went against the Indians.

That he entered the service of the United States again in the month of October in the year 1779 as he now thinks under Captain Cuddebeck (16) but don't recollect the name of the Lieutenant & he was ensign in Colonel Newkirk's Regiment of Militia was out a month and was discharged in the month of November in the year 1779 according to his best recollection. That he was marched in this service to Gorman's Fort so called which have a stone house stockade at which place he lay while in this last service.

That besides the times above enumerated and set forth he has been in the service for short periods of time some times but a day or two at others for a week or two both before and after he received his ensigns commission and that such service has been frequent and numerous but that he cannot set forth the precise time nor the names of the officers he was under on account of the great length of time.

That he has no documentary evidence of his services that he never received any written discharge from any of the above services that he has lost his ensigns commission.

That the only persons that he knows of whose testimony he can procure who can testify to his services are Caleb Sayre of the town of Lodi in the county of Seneca and State of New York and George Humphrey of the Town of Phelps in the County of Ontario in said State.

He hereby relinquishes every claim whatever to a pension or annuity except the present and declares that his name is not on the Pension Roll of the agency of any state. (Signed) Joshua Sayre.

Augustus F. Ferris one of the Judges of Cayuga Co. Courts.

End Notes—S.14403—Joshua Sayer or Sears

1. Joshua enlisted as a sergeant on July 3, 1775 in Captain John Hulbert's Third Company in Colonel James Clinton's Third New York Continental Regiment. On the descriptive muster roll Joshua is listed as follows: Age--20, where born—Southampton, Stature—5 ft 9 in with Light Complexion & Brown Hair. On muster roll dated October 15, 1775 "Camp at Lake George" Joshua is listed as sick at S. Hampton. A James Sayre enlisted as a corporal on July 3, 1775 in the same company and is listed on the descriptive muster roll as follows: Age—21, where born—Southampton, Stature—5 ft 7 in with Light Complexion& Brown Hair. FROM: Revolutionary War Rolls 1775-1783, Series M-246, Roll 69, folder 38, National Archives, Washington, D.C.
2. John Grenell was appointed captain on June 28, 1775 of the Fifth Company in Colonel Clinton's Regiment. He was appointed captain on January 22, 1776 of an Artillery Company, Captain Grenell resigned on March 27th as congress had appointed Joseph Crane as his lieutenant which Grenell had promised to a Mr. Goddartt supposing that he had the same right to nominate his officers as had been given to Captain John Lamb.
3. Major General Philip Schuyler.
4. Alexander McDougall was appointed Colonel of the First New York Continental Regiment on June 30, 1775. He was appointed Brigadier General on August 9, 1776 and Major General on October 20, 1777.
5. Thomas Machin was appointed a Second Lieutenant in Colonel Henry Knox's Continental Regiment of Artillery. He was appointed First Lieutenant in November of 1776 in Colonel Knox's Regiment. On January 1, 1777 he was pointed Captain-Lieutenant in Colonel John Lamb's Second Regiment of Continental Artillery. He was wounded at Fort Montgomery on October 6, 1777.
6. On a list of Artificers &c employed by General Clinton at Forts Clinton and Montgomery for August 1, 1776 to December 1, 1776, Joshua is listed as a carpenter. Hezekiah White is listed as the master carpenter, list is signed by Teunis Tappan, Clerk who checked the list and Brigadier General James Clinton. Hezekiah White was also appointed Second Lieutenant on September 20, 1775 in Captain John Nicoll's Second Company in Colonel James Clinton's Second Regiment of Ulster County Militia. How long he served in this capacity is unknown but the company officers were all replaced on March 23, 1778.

7. George Clinton was also New York State's First Governor who had been elected to that office earlier in 1777.
8. Lewis DuBois was appointed Colonel of the Fifth New York Continental Regiment on November 21, 1776 with rank back to June 25, 1776.
9. Samuel Logan was appointed Major on November 21, 1776 in Colonel DuBois Regiment. He was taken prisoner at Fort Montgomery on October 6, 1777.
10. Captain Henry VanKeuren was appointed on May 2, 1776 in Colonel James McClaughrey's Second Regiment of Ulster County Militia. McClaughrey had been promoted to replace Colonel Clinton.
11. Timothy Coleman was an ensign in Captain Benjamin Veal's Company in Colonel McClaughrey's Regiment. Coleman was commissioned on March 28, 1778.
12. John Cantine was commissioned colonel on February 21, 1778 of the Third Regiment of Ulster County Militia.
13. Joshua was commissioned ensign on March 23, 1778 in Captain Leonard D. Nicoll's Company. Leonard replaced John Nicoll who had resigned. Joshua's last name is given as Sears.
14. Jacob Newkirk was the lieutenant-Colonel in Colonel McClaughrey's Regiment.
15. John McNeil was the First Lieutenant in Captain Samuel Waters' Company in Colonel Roswell Hopkins' Sixth Regiment of Dutchess County Militia. This was probably a mixed detachment of Ulster and Dutchess County Militia.
16. Abraham Cuddeback was commissioned on March 23, 1778 in Colonel McClaughrey's Regiment. The other company officers were as follows: Robert Cook as the first lieutenant, Samuel King as the second Lieutenant and the ensign was Samuel Depry or Depue.

Pension Application for Lambert Schaefer

S.6059
State of Ohio
County of Huron SS. Norwalk

On the 23 day of February A.D. 1833 personally appeared before me Timothy Baker one of the associate judges of the Court of Common Pleas within and for said County, Lambert Schaefer resident in Townsend in said county who being firstly duly sworn according to Law, doth on his oath make the following declaration in addition to his former declaration made before the Supreme Court held in said Norwalk on the 27th of July AD 1832 in order to obtain the benefit of the Act of Congress passed the 7th of June A.D 1832. The Declarant says that he was born in the Town of Coverskill [Cobleskill] in the County of Schoharie in the State of New York on the 11th of February one thousand seven hundred & fifty three. He has now no record of his age but his father kept a record of his age, who is now dead & he don't know what has become of it. When he was called into the service of the United States, he lived in said

Coverskill. That the said Revolutionary War, he lived in said Coverskill between twenty & thirty years from thence he went to Madison County State of New York where he lived as much as four years from thence he moved to Florence, from thence to Elkbridge from thence to Townsend in said county of Huron where he has ever since & now lives.

The Declarant further says that in his former said Declaration the Rev'd Joshua Phillips Clergyman and George Kellogg were his neighbors who testified as to his character for veracity & their belief of his services as a soldier of the Revolution & he now mentions Samuel Preston Esqr & William Matthewson his neighbors who can also testify respecting his character for veracity. (Signed) Lambert Schaefer

Sworn & Subscribed before me at Norwalk this 23rd day of Feby 1833. Timothy Baker. Judge of Common Pleas.

[Many of the papers in this folder are badly water damaged and not legible.]

Reply to a letter of inquiry dated August 9, 1933.

Reference is made to your request for the Revolutionary War record of Lambert Schaefer.

The data contained herein were obtained from the papers on file in pension claim, S.6059, based upon the Revolutionary War service of Lambert Schaefer.

He was born February 11, 1753 at Cobleskill, Schoharie County, New York, the names of his parents not given.

While residing at Cobleskill, New York, Lambert Schaefer enlisted in 1775 and served nine months as private in Captain Christian Brown's (1) company, Colonel Peter Vrooman's New York regiment, and was at Fort Stanwix, Fort Edward, and on Lake Champlain. He also served from in 1776 until in 1783 at various times in Captain Brown's (2) company and in other companies, in Colonel Vrooman's regiment, this service amounted to about three years.

After the Revolution, Lambert Schaefer lived in Cobleskill, New York between twenty and thirty years, then to Madison County, New York, where he lived four years, thence to Florence, to Elldridge, and Townsend, Huron County, Ohio.

The soldier, Lambert Schaefer, was allowed pension on his application executed, July 27, 1832, then a resident of Townsend, Ohio.

There are no data in this claim relative to family.

The following is from genealogical research by Herman Witthoft, Sr.

Lambert SCHAEFFER (Johann Henrich SCHAEFFER, Johannes SCHAEFFER, Maria Elizabeth) was born 11 Feb 1753 in Schoharie, Schoharie Co., NY and was christened Feb 1753 in Schoharie, Schoharie Co., NY. He died 1833 in Florence, Erie Co., OH, USA and was buried 1833 in Florence, Erie Co., OH.

MARRIAGE: Recorded: St. Paul's Lutheran Church, Schoharie, Schoharie Co., NY. Lambert Schaffer, Sara Freymeyer. Lambert apparently married second wife named Mary.

MILITARY: Served in the Revolutionary War along with his brothers John, Henry, and his half brother Jacob.
MILITARY: MILITARY RECORDS OF SCHOHARIE COUNTY VETERANS, WAR OF REVOLUTION, George H. Warner, 1891; Fifteenth Regiment, New York Levies and Militia, Lambert Shafer, did service under Miller. (3) On 27 Jul 1832, Lambert Schaefer, resident of Townsend, Huron Co., and 80 years of age, appeared in Norwalk, Huron Co., OH, before the Superior Court to apply for benefits under the act of Congress passed 7 Jun 1832. In the affidavit written at this time he stated that he entered the Continental Army in 1775 as a private for nine months into a company commanded by Captain Christian Braun or Brown, (4) in a Regiment commanded by Colonel Peter Vrooman. He first served at Fort Stanwix and from there he went to and served at Fort Edward and from thence he went to Lake Champlain. At the end of the said nine months he was honorably discharged, the discharge of which was lost. Lambert then served in the Militia of the State of New York commanded by Captain Brown and Colonel Vrooman from 1776 to the time of peace of 1783.
RESIDENCES: In his pension papers, Lambert stated that since the Revolutionary War he lived in Coverskill for between 20-30 years, from thence he went to Madison Co., NY, where he lived as much as four years. From thence he moved to Florence from thence to Eldridge and from thence to Townsend in the County of Huron, OH.

Lambert married **Sara FREEMIRE,** daughter of Johannes FREYMEYER- and Anna MATTICE- on 8 Oct 1775 in Schoharie, Schoharie Co., NY. Sara was born 17 Nov 1756 in Schoharie, Schoharie Co., NY. She died in 1821. They had the following children:
Lambert SCHAEFFER Jr.- was born 7 Jun 1776 and died about 1853.
Abraham SCHAEFFER- was born 8 Jun 1778.
Catharine SCHAEFFER- was born 31 Aug 1779 in
Elizabeth SCHAEFFER was born 19 Oct 1785 and died 22 Feb 1848.
Anna SCHAEFFER was born 8 Aug 1792
Eva SCHAEFFER- was born 24 Jan 1795
Henry SCHAEFFER-was born 19 Sep 1799

End Notes—S.6059—Lambert Schaefer or Shafer, Shaver, Schefer, etc.

1. Lambert is in error. Colonel Peter Vrooman's Fifteenth Regiment of Albany County Militia was not organized until October 20, 1775. Christian Brown was not commissioned captain until February 20, 1778. The militia were seldom in service for nine continuous months unless attached to the Continental Army on campaign. Also nothing much was happening at Fort Stanwix at this time because the fort was in disrepair. It wasn't until 1776 that the effort under various engineers and troops, was rebuilt and renamed Fort Schuyler in honor of Major General Philip Schuyler.
2. The other officers of Captain Brown's Company were Hendrick Borst as First Lieutenant, Jacob Borst as Second Lieutenant and Johannes H.

Scheffer as Ensign. On October 30, 1778, Nicholas Warner was appointed Ensign in place of Scheffer.

3. Dirck Miller was commissioned captain on February 20, 1778 in Colonel Vrooman's Regiment.
4. In "List of a Detachment of Men of Coll. Van Rensler's Regt Stationed at Fort Dupoys [or Fort DuBois] under the command Henry Borst Lieut" is found the following: Priv Lymberd Schefer August 1-Sept 4 1779. This document was found in Colonel Vroomans' papers after his death. Why VanRensselaer's name is listed is unknown because all the men on the list were from Colonel Vrooman's Regiment. FROM: Revolutionary War Rolls 1775-1783, Series M-246, Roll 77, folder 167, National Archives, Washington, D.C.

Pension Application for Frederick Schram, Scram, etc.

S.15212
$24.44 was granted to Frederick Schram
State of New York
Greene County SS.

On this fourth day of September 1832, personally appeared in open court before the Judges of the Court of Common Pleas of the County of Greene, now sitting at the Village of Catskill in the said County, Frederick Scram, a resident of the said town of Catskill, in the county of Greene and State of New York aged Eighty years who being first duly sworn, according to law, doth on his oath make the following declaration, in order to attain the benefit of the act of Congress, passed June 7, 1832, that he entered the service of the United States under the following named officers and served as herein stated—that he was born in the present town of Catskill, in the county of Greene and state of New York, on the 21st day of April 1752.

That he has no family record of his age, nor does he know that any was ever made. He has received from his parents the information of the time of his birth, which he believes to be correct. That in the month of January 1775 (1) he was drafted in the Militia to go to Johnstown, in the County of Montgomery in the State of New York that the company to which he was attached was commanded by Benjamin Dubois (2) of Catskill—the Regiment was commanded by a Major by the name of Ignatius VanOrder (3) of Catskill, that he went with the militia to Johnstown & left home on the 15th day of January and was engaged in that service about ten days.

That Sir John Johnston (4) commanded a party of Indians & Tories at Johnstown at this time, this deponent went there, and upon his surrender this deponent returned home—that the next service performed by this deponent he volunteered and went to Fort Constitution (5) in the Highlands, in the Hudson River in the State of New York—this was in the year 1775 and this deponent was at the fort. Which month was that he cannot state the month he left home, but well recollects that he returned home late in the fall of that year.

That the company to which he attached, who went to Fort Constitution, was commanded by one Williams of the city of Albany the Lieutenant of the Company was one Philip Staats (6) and Peter VanBurgen (7) was Ensign as this deponent thinks. That one Bailey commanded the Fort and this deponent knew that Capt. Jackson Lieutenant Elsworth & Lieutenant McGee (8)—that this deponent at the expiration of the said three months was permitted with the company to return home, which they did—and took passengers on Board of a Sloop that this is the year 1776. He was frequently called out as a minute man in scouting parties and arresting Tories & taking them before the Committees appointed for their trial—that he was almost constantly engaged that year in that business. That he was drafted in the militia in the year 1776 and went to Fort Edward.

That Thomas Houghtaling (9) of Coxsackie commanded the Company to which he Belonged and Wessel Salisbury (10) of Catskill was the Lieutenant. That Anthony Van Bergen of Coxsackie commanded the Regiment. That General Schuyler commanded the American troops at Fort Edward, in June this deponent arrived there—that he remained there & was in the retreat of General Schuyler (11) to Stillwater—that General Gates (12) arrived and took the command and the militia who went with this deponent were permitted to return home. That he was in the army two months at the time herein before stated.

That during the remainder of the year 1776 and until the termination of the War this deponent was in the service as a minute man and engaged in the service in scouting parties and in arresting Tories and protecting that part of the country in which he resided from the destruction of the Indians & to Tories that he was at Schoharie at the different times and in all two months in defending that place, and was in the Fort there.

This deponent further says that he has no documentary evidence of his service in the war and that he has produced the affidavits of such persons as he can attain who knows as to his services.

This deponent hereby relinquishes every claim whatever to a pension a annuity, except the present and declares that his name is not on the pension roll of the agency of any state. (Signed) Fred'k Schram

Subscribed & sworn in open court Sept 5th, 1832. William V.B. Hermance clerk

End Notes—S.15212—Frederick Schram

1. This happened in January of 1776.
2. Captain Benjamin C. Dubois in Colonel Anthony VanVergen's Eleventh Regiment of Albany County Militia.
3. First Major Ignatius VanOrder in the Eleventh Albany.
4. Sir John Johnson, son of Sir William Johnson who had died on July 11, 1774, leaving Sir John vast holdings of land and property in the Mohawk Valley. Sir John fled to Canada in May of 1776 and raised a regiment of Loyalists to fight against the patriots.
5. This service was also in 1776. Fort Constitution built on Constitution Island in the North River (Hudson River) across from West Point.

6. Second Lieutenant Philip Staats of Captain Nicholas Staats' Company in Colonel Kilian VanRensselaer's Fourth Regiment of Albany County Militia.
7. Peter VanBergen was the Ensign in Captain John A. Witbeck's Fourth Company in the Eleventh Regiment.
8. Captain William Jackson, Lieutenant Peter Elsworth and Lieutenant Peter Magee were in Colonel James Clinton's Second New York Continental Regiment of 1776.
9. Thomas Hoghtaling was Captain of the First Company in the Eleventh Albany.
10. Wessel Salisbury served as Second Lieutenant in Captain Witbeck's company.
11. Major General Philip Schuyler of the Continental Army.
12. Major General Horatio Gates of the Continental Army who replaced General Schuyler in August of 1777 as commander of the retreating American Army before General John Burgoyne's advancing British Army.

Pension Application for Henry Schram

W.9,272
Suspended Case, R No 9272
Henry Schram Rev. Soldier resided in the Town of Openheim [sic] Montgomery Co., NY in the year 1833 Agent John Nellis or Nillis resided at Palatine Bridge Montgomery Co. in 1833. His Bro. John Schram W.24914 (N.Y.) resided also at Openheim. No record of John & Henry Schram found in Bible. Dat. 23/sep/79
State of New York
Montgomery County SS.

Personally appeared before me the undersigned a Justice of the Peace of the Town of Oppenheim in the County & State aforesaid Henry Schram who being duly sworn, say in order to amend his original declaration contained in the proceedings had by him for a Pension in the Court of Common Pleas of said County on the 20th day of last September that by reason of old age & the consequent loss of his memory he cannot swear positively as to the precise length of his service, but according to the best of his recollection he served not less than the periods mentioned below in the following grades: viz:--

That he served as a private from 15th July 1777 to 17th October 1777 for three months & two days in the company whereof Jeremiah Miller (1) was Capt. One Miller (2) (whose Christian name he cannot recollect but who was a cousin of the Capt.) was Lieut. in the Regiment, whereof John VanAllen (3) was Col., Richard Esselstine Major, John Schram his father was (he thinks) Quarter Master Sergeant but on this occasion acted according to his recollection as adjutant—that he entered as a substitute said company in the place of Lambert Van Hoosen—that he was marched to Saratoga according to the best of his recollection from Claverack in the now County of Columbia that he was some time at Still-Water—that he saw Genl Schuyler (4) repeatedly—that he also saw

Genl Gates & Arnold & the whole of the American Army—that several battles were fought between the American & British under the command of Genl Burgoyne (5) before the surrender of the British Army that the militia to which he belonged were not engaged in the battles—that he & the company to which he belonged were principally stationed at or near Saratoga & Still Water that some days after the surrender of Burgoyne he returned home—that he resided where he entered said service in the Town of Claverack in the now County of Columbia State of New York--& served as such substitute & private as aforesaid for the period above mentioned—that the reason of his not giving this tour of service in his said original declaration was that he was told it was unnecessary—therefore it was not done—That said Regt & company belonged to the infantry of the revolutionary army of the militia of the State of New York—that some of the militia to which he belonged of the stoutest & strongest men were ordered & did fell and cut down some trees & they threw obstructions in the way of Genl Burgoyne—but does not recollect & thinks he was not employed in this business as he was quite young at the time of the age of about 14 years.—

That he served as a private in the company whereof James VanAllen (6) was Capt. –a Mr. Van Buren was Lieut., James Wyngard Ensign in the Regt whereof Abraham Van Alstine was Col, Philip Van Alstine Lieut. Col., Isaac Goes (7) was Major of Said Regt of infantry militia of the State of New York in the Revolutionary Army—that he served as such private in said company from Eighteenth day of September 1779 to twenty sixth day of September 1779 for ten days on a Scouting party of about fifteen men of said company in & about the Town of Clavarack—That they were either drafted or ordered out by the officers of the Regt or some one of them but cannot positively swear that they were drafted at this particular time as they were sometimes drafted & other times ordered out by the officer into service—the object was as he understood to apprehend some Tories who resisted to do duty & kept concealed—that he cannot recollect who had the command of the said party to which he belonged & in which he served during said tour of duty but believes a Sergeant whose name is forgotten commanded the party - that they were marched about & stopped at Abm Fonda & then marched to different places in & about this Town of Claverack.

That he served as a private in the said last mentioned Company & Regt to which belonged the same officers last mentioned served first day of October 1779 to fifteenth day of October 1779 for fifteen days—according to the best of his recollection a party of about thirty men of said company were drafted, he being among the number drafted—that a party of Tories disguised from the west side of the Hudson river in the Hellebarrack a mountainous & rough country covered with woods where they were concealed in the day time & in the night time, it was said, held meetings at the house of some Tory's nearest by—that he & the men to which he belonged went to break up the gang of Tories—they marched to the Hallebarrack & ranged to the woods & in the night times they watched—that the company & Regt to which he belonged during this term of service belonged to the infantry of the militia of the State of New York—that they took Peter Clough from the Tories whom they had taken prisoner—he informed them that the Tories had gone off—that he served for the period aforesaid on last mentioned tour—

That he served as a private solider in the said last mentioned company & Regt the same officers according to his recollection were attacked & belonged there to that he has before mentioned--& from the twenty sixth day of October 1779 to the fifth day of November 1779 for at least nine days—that he rendered that service on a scouting duty in the back part of the Town of Claverack in the now County of Columbia—That this scouting party consisted of about 30 men of said company ordered out (he thinks) by the officers of the company in this tour of duty—that in the Town of Claverack it was supposed that nearly half were openly or secretly disaffected to the cause of the revolution—that these held frequently meetings in the night time to concert plans to counteract the cause of those who were fighting for their country—sometime they plundered or destroyed the property of the Whigs or menaced the lives of those who were zealous in the cause of their Country—that he & those who went on said scouting party were engaged to prevent this organization of the Tories & to apprehend such of them as were active & to break them up—that he cannot recollect who commanded the party to which he belonged as sometimes a Sergeant or Corporal & Sometimes a commissioned officer of said company commanded to which he belonged and sometimes a Sergeant or Corporal & sometimes a commissioned officer of said company commanded. [sic]

That said company & Regt belonged to the infantry of the militia of the State of New York & of the revolutionary army—that a Mr. Jas. Hardick was murdered by the Tories as was said & has never been heard of since—that said party searched for his body but could not find it—that on this tour of service he served for the period last mentioned as a private.—

That he served as a private soldier in the same company & Regt & under the same officers last mentioned from the tenth day of November 1779 to Eighteenth day of November 1779 for eight days as follows—according to the best of his recollection he was drafted on this tour of service together with about 30 others of said company—that they marched to a place called Noble Town in the now County of Columbia where some Tories disguised as Indians had committed within night time depredations—that they went in pursuit of them to apprehend them—But were unable to do so—that said company & Regt belonged to the militia infantry of the State of New York of the revolutionary army & that they ranged the country & woods & one of the homes of those who were considered Tories for some time & watched nights the homes of the Tories or took suspects of being such when they returned home as near as he can recollect on said 18 day of November 1779--& served for the period last mentioned as a private, that is, from 10th Nov'r 1779 to 18 Nov. 1779.

That he served as a private soldier in the same company & Regt & under the same officers last before mentioned from March 5, 1780 to March

Eleventh 1780 for six days as follows. It was reported that a party of Tories had destroyed Some property & buildings along or near the East Side of the Hudson river & that they were disguised as Indians in the now County of Columbia & fears were apprehended & a party of about twenty men of said company together with himself volunteered according to his recollection & a Sergeant & or Corporal (whose name he has forgotten) commanded said party—that they found that some of the Whigs had been plundered & considerable property destroyed--but they after remaining some days scouring the adjacent place were unable to ferret out the Tories & apprehend them—that said Company of Regt were attached to the infantry of the militia of the State of New York of the revolutionary army. That they during this service at Toekawnie stopped some time being a place so called—that he served as last mentioned during the said period last mentioned.—

That he served as a private soldier in the same company & Regt & under same officers last mentioned from April tenth 1780 to April 15th 1780 for five days as follows—that he was ordered out by his officers or volunteered (which one he cannot recollect) that a party of said company about fifteen men under the command of a Mr. Fonda went to a Mr. Isaac Vosburg's house in the Town of Claverack & some miles beyond in the woods & remained there some days when they returned home, after a fruitless search to apprehend some Tories—That he served for the period last mentioned in the manner last mentioned as a private.—

That he served as a private in the same company Regt. aforesaid under the last named officers of the Regt of infantry of the Militia of the State of New York of the revolutionary army from April 17, 1780 to April 30th 1780 for thirteen days as follows—that the greater part of the whole of said company & all of the "Regt that could be conveniently collected the [?] were ordered into this service by some of the field officers—that they were marched in said company commanded by said Van Allen his Capt. & Major Isaac Goes accompanied them to a house in Schodick Kinderhook where there were a strong party of Tories - That a Mr. John Van Valenburgh (as he was informed) gave the information to Major Goes of the Tories beign assembled—that the said company in which he marched & belonged & the rest surrounded the house in the night time & after a skirmish of some time they took thirty Tories or thereabouts prisoners—that they took the prisoners into the Town of Kinderhook where they were tried by a committee--& punished—that he assisted in guarding the Tories until they were disposed of when he returned home—that he resides where he entered last service in the Town of Kinderhook now County of Columbia—that he served for the period last mentioned on said last mentioned tour of service.—

That he served as a private in same company & Regt. & under same officers before mentioned, that is in Capt. Van Allen's Company from May 8th 1780 to May 16th 1780 for Eight days as follows—that he was ordered out by some of his company officers—that a party of about 20 men of said company, together with others from the west side of the Hudson marched after dividing themselves into parties in various directions on the west side of the Hudson River up & down same & with the adjacent parts in order to apprehend some Tories as he understood—that the party of Tories had taken some of the Whigs as prisoners—one of them returned after escaping from the Tories & whom they met on his return—that one Vosburg a Sergeant in said company commanded the said party of men to whom he belonged—that said company & Regt to which he was attached belonged to the infantry of the militia of the said State of N. York in the revolutionary army—that he resided at the time when he entered on last mentioned tour in the Town of Kinderhook in the now County of Columbia—that he served for the period last mentioned on said last mentioned tour of service.

That he served as a private solider in said Capt. VanAllen Company under the same officers before mentioned from seventeenth May 1780 to Thirteenth day of May 1780 as follows: That according to his recollection he was drafted with others of said company on a tour of service—that on said 17 May 1780 they were marched under the command of James Wyngart their Ensign from Kinderhook where he entered said service to a small lake called Fish Lake where one of the committee man had been plundered who resided near said lake but whose name he has forgotten that the Tories were pursued into the wood by there & kept concealed—that they watched & guarded such places where they supposed most likely they would appear that he was marched in various directions in the neighborhood of said Lake—that he served on this tour from said 17th May 1780 to said 30th May 1780 for at least thirteen days before they returned home—that said company & Regt belonged to the infantry—militia of the revolutionary army of the State of New York & that he served as a private for the last mentioned period on last mentioned term of service.

That he served as a private soldier in the company & Regt last mentioned under the officers before mentioned of the militia of the State of New York, from the ninth day of June 1780 to the twentieth day of June 1780 for Eleven days as follows—That he was ordered this time by his officers into the service—that about fifteen of said company went also under the command of James Vosburg (8), Sergt, & David Hugernor also a non comm'd officer—that he was marched to a Mr. Van Slyke's in the then Town of Cooksackie in the then County of Columbia -- & thence beyond said Van Slyke' about fifty miles after Tories & searched the houses of the Tories & their barns & wherever it was supposed Tories might be concealed—that they returned home—that when he entered said service he resided in the Town of Kinderhook in the now County of Columbia ins aid State & acted as aforesaid on a scouting party—that he served as a private for last mentioned period on last mention tour of service.

That he served as a private soldier in the same company & regt last aforesaid under the same named officers from first of July 1780 to the fifteenth day of July 1780 for fifteen days as follows—that said company & Regt to the infantry & Militia of the State of N. York of the revolutionary army—that he was ordered into service this time by his commanding officers—that Ensign Wyngart accompanied the company or part thereof on this tour of service—that he resided at the time in the Town of Kinderhook—that the said Ensign & his party went on a scouting tour—that he was marched up the Hudson to where Col. Van Alstine lived & beyond said Col's house up the river to ascertain whether boats crossed the river that they made a stop at the Col's home to rest & refresh themselves—that they were after some Tories—That they marched some considerable distance beyond the home of Col. Van Alstine & marched thro' the posts in the neighborhood to Oak hill—where they remained some days & then marched from Oak Hill South westerly & so continued scouting in pursuit of the Tories who were disguised as Indians until discharged on said 15 July 1780—that some nights they stood guarding & watching all night—that he resided at the time in the Town of Kinderhook—that he served last mentioned period of service on the said tour last mentioned.

That he also served as a private from the tenth day of August 1780 for two days in said Capt. VanAllen's Company in the Regt of Abraham Van Alstine Col. Of the Militia infantry of the said state of the revolutionary Army—that his officers ordered him into this service—that Ensign Wyngart & Sergt Vosburg, officers of said company marched a part of the said company to Newton Hook where one Andrew Witbeck lived & four miles beyond Kinderhook to those places & for what purpose he cannot now recollect—that he resided at the time in the said Town of Kinderhook & served as a private during the period last mentioned on said last mentioned tour of Service.

That he served also as a private in the company & Regt aforesaid whereof VanAllen was Capt & Van Alstine Col & the other officers before mentioned also belonged to said company & Regt as aforesaid from September third 1780 to October 18, 1780 for one month & fifteen days—that he served as a substitute for Abm VanAllen, Andrew VanDerPool & others, in same company aforesaid that he & company were marched from Kinderhook to Fish Kill—that they were stationed at said place principally—that he there saw Capt. Peter Van Rensselaer, Jno. (9) Ten Broek Lieut (10) & Col. Gose VanSchaick (11) he thinks he saw also at said place & & [sic] that he served in said company commanded by his Capt. & other officers of said company & that said Capt. [blot] served this tour of duty & that the militia that went were drafted & volunteered into this service & served last mentioned period as aforesaid. That he served also as a private soldier in the Company of Jas. VanAllen Capt. & Regt of infantry whereof Abm Van Alstine was Col. in the militia of the State of New York of the revolutionary army from March fourth 1781 to March 16th 1781 for twelve days at least—that the other officers of said company & regt he believes were the same before mentioned—That he served said period of time as a private in said company & Regt as follows—that he & a party of about 15 men were ordered by their commanding officers to a place called "Anerum" from Kinderhook as a scout ranging about that place for miles in the woods after some Tories who had been seen about that place & supposed intended to destroy the property & lives of those friendly to the cause of the Country--& according to his recollection another party of said Company were sent in another direction—that his ensign Wyngart commanded the party to which he belonged—that he served for at least the period above mentioned & when he entered said service he resided in the said town of Kinderhook & served last above mentioned period of time on said last tour of service.

That he also served as a private in same company & Regt & under same officers last mentioned from April 9th 1781 to April thirteenth 1781 for at least four days as follows—that he & others were ordered into service by the commanding officers—that a non-commissioned officer of said company commanded them—that only a part of said company to wit, about 15 men were ordered into said service on a scouting party from Kinderhook where he resided there to a Mr. Close's House who was suspected of being a Tory & that there were others at his house—that they did go there & were in the neighborhood some days & he cannot say which of the non-commissioned officers commanded him & said party. That said Close' house was in the back part of said Town of Kinderhook--& that he served last mentioned period of Service in the manner last aforesaid.

That he served also as a private in same Company & Regt aforesaid under the same officers last mentioned from the tenth day of June 1781 to fifteenth day of July 1781 for 5 days--that said company belonged to the infantry & militia of said State of the revolutionary army & served said period as follows—that his commanding officers ordered him into service together with other of said company consisting of about 20 men of said company on a scout against some Tories or called so, who neglected to do duty—that after searching & watching for them for days, they returned in a circuitous route—that Sergeant Vosburg of said company commanded them—that they did not apprehend any Tories.

That he served as a private soldier in Capt. VanAllen Company aforesaid in the Regt whereof Abm VanAlstine was Col. - that the same officers before mentioned he believes still belonged to said Company & Regt.—that he entered said company as a substitute for one Henry Vosburgh who was drafted—that he served as such substitute in said company & Regt from August 22, 1781 to August 28 1781 for six days at least as a private & that he resided in the Town of Kinderhook when he entered said Service—that it was said that Major Ross at the head of a party of Indians & Tories was on the Mohawk River & that the said company & Regt & infantry or such of them as were drafted or volunteered went up the Hudson river from Kinderhook to Greenbush—that he was marched up with the rest to Green-bush—where they remained a few days & learned that Major Ross (12)was defeated—that they returned home - that Col. Abm Van Alstine with great part of his Regt were with the troops—that he was out at least six days in this tour of service & served as last aforesaid.

That he served as a private in same company & Regt aforesaid under the officers before named belonging to said Company & Regt from May 17th 1782 to May 19 1782—that he resided when he entered on this tour of service in the Town of Kinderhook in the now County of Columbia—That his Capt. James Van Allen ordered him & others on this tour of service—that about twelve men of said company marched [?] the Hudson River about three miles & then returned & marched down said river to Kinderhook landing—thence to the Kinderhook creek & so in a circuitous route home—that a non-commissioned officer of said company commanded them—that he was discharged verbally from this service on May 19 1782--& having served as aforesaid from 17 May 1782 to 19 May 1782 for at least two days as a private - that the party acted during this term of service on a scouting party--& that for the aforesaid several terms of service detailed by him as particularly as he could recollect the same he claims a pension—that he resided before mentioned Services as a private in the militia for the State of New York in the Revolutionary Army - that the aforesaid several services were rendered by him under the orders & authority of his commanding officers—that he has mentioned as particularly as he could recollect that the operators of the corps in each term of service he served—that he did other tours of service sometimes for a day, a night or half a day of which he has rendered no account & cannot set forth the same & for which he expects no pension.—[This particular copy of this deposition ends here.]

End Notes—W.9272—Henry Schram

1. Jeremiah Muller (Miller, etc.) was Captain of the First Company in Colonel Robert VanRensselaer's Eighth Regiment of Albany County Militia.
2. Joachim Muller was the Second Lieutenant in the First Company in the Eighth Albany.
3. John VanAllen was the Lieutenant-Colonel and Richard Esseltyne was the Second Major in the Eighth Albany.
4. Philip Schuyler, Horatio Gates, and Benedict Arnold were Major Generals in the Continental Army.
5. John Burgoyne, General of the invading British Army from Canada. Two major battles were fought near Stillwater; one on September 19 and one on October 7, 1777. Burgoyne surrendered his army on October 17, 1777.
6. Jacobus (Dutch for James) VanAllen, Captain in Colonel Abraham VanAlstyne's Seventh Regiment of Albany County Militia. The following were officers in said company: First Lieutenant Goose VanBuren, Second Lieutenant Peter VanAllen, and Ensign Jacob Wyngard. Jacob is short for Jacobus.
7. Lieutenant-Colonel Philip VanAlstyne and Major Isaac Goes were in the Seventh Albany.
8. Sergeant Jacobus Vosburgh and Private David Hugenin (Huganan, etc.) both of Captain VanAllen's Company
9. Captain Peter VanRensselaer had served in Colonel James Livingston's First Canadian Continental Regiment. He had resigned on December 20, 1779. He was Captain on April 27, 1781 in Lieutenant-Colonel Commandant Marinus Willett's Regiment of New York State Levies.

10. John C. TenBroeck was appointed First Lieutenant on November 21, 1776 in the First New York Continental Regiment and appointed Captain on June 29, 1781 in the First New York.
11. Goose VanSchaick was Colonel of the First New York Continental Regiment.
12. John Ross, Major of the Second Battalion of the King's Royal Regiment of New York and his second in command Captain Walter Butler with a mixed British force attacked settlements in the Mohawk Valley on October 24, 1781 and fought a Battle at Johnstown on October 25, where Major Ross was defeated by an American force under Lieutenant Colonel Marinus Willett.

Pension Application for Peter S. Schuyler

W.17778 (Widow: Catharine) Peter was granted pension of $320.00 per annum.

State of New York
City and County of Albany SS.

I, Abraham Ten Eyck Jun'r one of the Judges of the Court of Common Pleas of the County of Albany, do certify that Peter S. Schuyler of the Town of Watervliet in said County, Esquire, having in the course of the past week, been attacked with a paralytic Stroke, whereby his health is so much impaired, as to disqualify him for attending at Court to make his declaration, in order to obtain a pension for Revolutionary Services, under the act of Congress, passed June 7, 1832, and that the said Peter S. Schuyler residing in the said town of Watervliet, within the distance of one mile from my own residence in the said town to wit, at the Village of Port Schuyler, he the said Peter S. Schuyler was attended by me the said Judge, at his own residence and there in the presence of the Reverend Robert Bronk Pastor of the Reformed Protestant Dutch Church in the United Villages of Gibbonsville & Port Schuyler, and of James Van Ingen of the City of Albany, a Solicitor and Counsellor in the court of Chancery of the State aforesaid, made the following declaration to wit: that he was born in the Town, where he now resides on the 12th day of May 1758—

That he entered the Service of the United States in the militia of New York in Capt. Ostroms (1) Company and in Col. Philip P. Schuyler's Regt. in the commencement of the year 1776, and marched with the expedition against Sir John Johnson, and was present at the time he surrendered himself to General Schuyler and General Ten Broeck—

That the [he] entered the service of the United States in the militia of New York in Capt. Ostroms Company and in Col. Philip P. Schuyler's (2) Regt in the commencement of the year 1776, and marched with the expedition against Sir John Johnson, and was present at the time he surrendered himself to General Schuyler and General Ten Broeck—

That the company to which he belonged elected him their Lieutenant—Sometime in or about the month of June in the same year, he the Declarer was appointed a member of a Court martial which was ordered to assemble in the

City of Albany for the trial of Tories and disaffected persons in various parts of the County of Albany; That Col. Jacob Lansing Jr. (3) was President of the said Court martial; Jeremiah Lansing Esqr. Judge Advocate, Major Myndert Wemple (4) and Capt. John Ouderkirk (5) were member of said Court martial; all of whom, as this deponent believes are long since deceased. That in the autumn of the same year, he marched from Albany under the same officers as before, in company with the Albany City Regt. Commanded by Col. Abraham Cuyler (6) for Lake George at which Post, Col. Peter Gansevoort (7) then Commanded, with which officer this Declarer was intimately acquainted, and after having remained there with Col. Schuyler's Regt, until it was discharged, returned home—

In the following year 1777, he this Declarer was again ordered out with the Watervliet Regt. under the Command of Col. Philip P. Schuyler and the same company, officers with the addition of Jacob Weaver, as the other Lieutenant of the Company to which this Declarer belonged, and were ordered to march to Saratoga to join the army under the Command of Major General Gates, (8) which having joined at Van Schaick's Island, the regiment proceeded to Bemus's heights and served out that campaign and was present when Burgoyne (9) and his army Surrendered, and recollects the circumstances of General Arnold's (10) being wounded, and the British General Frazer (11) being killed—

That this Declarer was at the time attached to General Glover's brigade—That from a late paralytic affection, he this Declarer cannot after a lapse of more than half a Century, now recollect many of the names of the officers with whom he then served—He however still remembers Major Ebenezer Stevens (12) of the Artillery—

That this Declarer after the year 1777 was in all or nearly all the expeditions with the Company in which he was Lieutenant as aforesaid, and which was afterwards confirmed by Governor Clinton (13) and the Council of Appointment, as by reference to the annexed certificate will be seen—against the Tories, Indians and British in Schoharie and in the Valley of the Mohawk, having been stationed at different times, at two of the forts in Schoharie, at Fort Hunter, at Fort Herkimer under Governor Clinton, General Robert Van Rensselaer (14) with Col. Abraham Wemple, with Col. Bruyen (15), Col. Harper (16), Col. Peter Vrooman, Col. Ziele (17), and other field and Staff Officers not now recollected until the close of the revolutionary War, and that he has several times been ordered out before having been at home a single day after having returned from a previous tour or expedition:

This declarer doth further State that during the whole of the whole of the time before mentioned, he Served as Lieutenant in Said Company, to which he was elected by those belonging to it, until he was appointed in manner aforesaid.—

That he does not recollect at this distance period of time, the different periods of his Service, or the time of entering the same, or of his being discharged therefrom; but he doth confidently believe, & doth therefore declare, that as he has performed military duty in each year, more or less, during the Continuance of the seven years war, the whole period of his services have exceeded two years—

He hereby relinquishes every claim whatever to a pension or annuity except the present, and declares that his name is not on the pension roll of the agency of any state. (Signed) Peter S. Schuyler

Sworn to and Subscribed this 23rd day of August 1832. Abraham Ten Eyck, June, Judge County Court.

Declaration in order to obtain the benefit of the Act of Congress of 7th July 1838, entitled "an act granting half pay & Pensions to certain Widows".

State of New York

Albany County Town of Watervliet

On this tenth day of September Eighteen hundred and thirty eight at her own dwelling house in the town aforesaid personally appeared, before me Abel W. Richardson a Justice of the Peace in and for the County of Albany aforesaid Catherine Schuyler a resident of the town of WaterVliet aged seventy four years on the Seventeenth day of April last, who being first duly sworn according to law, doth on her oath, make the following declaration, in order to obtain the benefit of the provision made by the Act of Congress, passed July 7th 1838 entitled "An Act granting half pay and pensions to certain widows".

That she is the widow of Peter S. Schuyler who, as she has been informed and verily believes, was a Lieutenant in Col. Philip P. Schuyler's Regiment of New York Militia during the Revolutionary War that she has no personal knowledge of the service of her said husband; but refers respectfully to his declaration made in the month of August 1832 and to the several papers afterwards submitted in support of his claim, and upon which a certificate was on the ninth day of February 1833 granted, to her, as the widow of the said deceased, authorizing her to receive the amount which would have been due to him up to the time of his Death; a copy of which certificate was Submitted to the Commissioners of Pensions with her letter of 27th August 1838—

She further declares that she was married to the said Peter S. Schuyler on the fifth day of December Seventeen hundred and Eighty nine and that her husband died on the first day of November one thousand eight hundred and thirty two and she has since that time remained a widow. That she was not married to said deceased prior to his leaving the service but the marriage took place previous to the first of January Seventeen hundred Ninety four Viz: On the fifth day of December seventeen hundred and eighty nine as above stated—

She further declares that the paper herewith submitted containing a record of the birth of her husband and herself and of their marriage and also the birth of their children and the death of some of them was, for the purpose of being herewith transmitted, torn out of a Dutch Bible which her said husband inherited from her father in the year 1793, and which remained in his possession to the time of his death and since that time her possession and that said record as far back as her recollection extends is strictly true. (Signed) Catherine Schuyler.

Letter of inquiry dated November 10, 1938 in the pension folder.

Reference is made to your letter in which you request the Revolutionary War record of Pieter Schuyler who lived in the Mohawk Valley as late as 1785, also the parentage of Alida Schuyler who married George Herkimer on November 15, 1768.

This office has no general genealogical data on file, and Revolutionary War data furnished by this office are obtained from claims for pension and bounty land which have been made to the United States, based upon service in that war. A search of the records fails to show such claims on file on account of the Revolutionary War service of George Herkimer.

You are furnished herein the Revolutionary War record of Peter S. Schuyler, as found in claim for pension W. 17778, based on his service in that war. This is the record of the only Peter Schuyler found on file in the Revolutionary War records of this office. The name was searched under similar spellings.

Peter S. Schuyler was born May 12, 1758, at Watervliet, Albany County, New York. The names of his parents were not designated.

Peter S. Schuyler was elected, early in 1776, Lieutenant in Captain Ostrom's Company in Colonel Philip P. Schuyler's New York regiment, marched in the expedition against Sir John Johnson and was present when he surrendered to General Schuyler; he was appointed a member of a Court Martial held in Albany for the trial of Tories and others, and in the fall of 1776, was stationed near Lake George; he was in the campaign around Saratoga, was in the battle there and present when Burgoyne surrendered. He continued to serve as lieutenant at various times in same company and regiment, until the close of the war, was in several expeditions against Indians and Tories, in the Mohawk Valley, was stationed at Forts Herkimer and Hunter, length of this service as much as two years.

Peter S. Schuyler applied for pension August 23, 1832, then a resident of Watervliet, New York. The pension was allowed. He died in said Watervliet, November 1, 1832.

Peter S. Schuyler married December 3, 1789, Catherine (Caty) Cuyler. She was born April 17, 1764, place not stated, nor are the names of her parents designated.

She was allowed pension on her application executed September 10, 1838, then a resident of Watervliet, New York where she continued to live in 1850.

She died September 28, 1855.

The following data in regard to the children of Peter S. Schuyler, and wife, Catherine, are shown in the claim.

Engelica Born September 8, 1790, died September 24, 1793

Susanna Born April 17, 1793, died September 17, 1793

Engelica Born January 25, 1795, died July 16, 1796
4th daughter Born July 18, 1797, died the same day
Engelica Born October 7, 1798
John Cuyler Born December 1, 1801.
Stephen Reuben born December 5, 1804.

Sons, John Cuyler Schuyler, and Stephen Reuben Schuyler were both in 1833 living in Albany County, New York; John Cuyler Schuyler at this time referred to his father-in-law, no name given, and to his "Uncle Reuben". John Cuyler Schuyler gave his address in 1838, Watervliet, New York.

Philip S. Schuyler, brother of Peter S. Schuyler, was in 1833 of Watervliet, New York, and served in the Revolution with him.

One Jacob Cuyler was of New York in 1776; it was not stated that he was related to the widow, Catherine, nor was it shown that the Colonel Philip P. Schuyler under whom Peter. S Schuyler served during the Revolution, was a relative.

The papers on file in the claim contained no further discernible date in regard to family.

End Notes—W.17778—Peter S. Schuyler

1. Peter was appointed Ensign on October 20, 1775 in Captain Peter Schuyler's Company (Third Company) in Colonel Abraham TenBroeck's Third Regiment of Albany County Militia. On February 20, 1776 Lieutenant-Colonel Francis Nicholl was appointed Colonel of the regiment as Colonel TenBroeck had been appointed Brigadier General of the Albany County Militia. On June 22, 1778, Philip P. Schuyler was commissioned Colonel of the regiment because Nicholl had resigned. On this same date Second Lieutenant Henry Ostrom was commissioned Captain, Jacob Weaver as the First Lieutenant, Philip Hemstreet as the Second Lieutenant and Peter S. Schuyler as Ensign. On March 4, 1780 Peter was commissioned Second Lieutenant because Hemstreet had declined the commission.
2. Major General Philip Schuyler.
3. Jacob Lansing Jr. was Colonel of the First Regiment of Albany County Militia.
4. Myndert M. Wemple, Second Major in Colonel Abraham Wemple's Second Regiment of Albany County Militia.
5. Possibly he is referring to John Onderdonk who was the First Lieutenant in Captain William H. Hun's Company in the First Albany. Onderdonk was later cashiered.
6. Abram Cuyler was the Lieutenant-Colonel of the First Albany. He was commissioned Colonel on March 3, 1780 because Lansing had resigned.
7. In 1776 Peter Gansevoort was the Lieutenant-Colonel in Colonel Goose VanSchaick's New York Continental Regiment. Gansevoort was appointed Colonel of the Third New York Continental Regiment on November 21, 1776. He was appointed Brigadier General of the First

Brigade of the Albany County Militia on March 26, 1781 since Ten Broeck had resigned.

8. Major General Horatio Gates who replaced Major General Philip Schuyler as Commander of the Northern Army which was then at or near Saratoga; now the present day Village of Schuylerville, Saratoga County, NY.
9. General John Burgoyne, who, was commanding a British Army which marched down the Hudson River towards Albany, was stopped near Stillwater. On October 17, 1777 Burgoyne surrendered his army to General Gates.
10. Major General Benedict Arnold was wounded on October 7, 1777 at the Battle of Bemus Heights.
11. General Simon Fraser was probably the most liked and able general that General Burgoyne had under his command.
12. Ebenezer Stevens was appointed major May 27, 1777 of an Independent Battalion of Artillery.
13. Governor George Clinton.
14. Robert VanRensselaer was appointed Brigadier General of the Second Brigade, Albany County Militia, on June 16, 1780.
15. Lieutenant-Colonel Jacobus S. Bruyn of the Fifth New York Continental Regiment.
16. Colonel John Harper of the Fifth Regiment of Tryon County Militia. May 11, 1780, he was appointed Lieutenant-Colonel Commandant of a regiment of New York State Levies.
17. Colonel Peter Vrooman and Lieutenant-Colonel Peter W. Zielie of the Fifteenth Regiment of Albany County Militia.

Pension Application for Henry Scott

W.20049
State of Vermont
Grand Isle County
District of Grandisle

On this 29 day of August 1832 personally appeared in open court before the Hon'l the Court of Probate for the District of Grandisle, now sitting Henry Scott a resident of Isle LaMotte in the county of Grandisle and State of Vermont aged sixty nine on the 24 Nov. 1832 years, who being first duly sworn according to Law doth on his oath make the following declaration in order to obtain the benefit of the act of Congress passed June 7, 1832

1st That he entered the service of the United States under the following named officers and served as herein stated. First service tour I entered the Service in the year 1778 about the first of February in the 15 year of my age under Capt. Funday of Claverack Lieut. Decker Ensign Winecoop (1) in Claverack Albany county State of New York was my place of residence. I was marched to Albany & Billeted at a citizen's house until the River opened. The name of the citizen was called Col. Tenbrook (2) from thence to fort Miller &

afterwards to Albany on a raft of Boards of Lumber said to be for the use of Government for Barracks, I do not recollect of any other company or Troops at Albany at the time I was there except some continental troops I believe Colonel Van Schaick (3) & Col. Gansevoort's (4) Regiments or part Regiments. I entered the service by Classification the company were required to furnish a given number of men & Divided into classes equal to that number. Each of which class furnished one, either by volunteering or by engagement for additional pay as the case might require, for four months, which Term of Time I served and was dismissed at Albany by Captain Funday. I had no written discharge nor do I know of any other one in my company that had. I was paid with continental bills & allowed to return home to Claverack about the first of June of the same year.

I have no written or documentary evidence to support this claim. I was born in Rhinebeck Dutchess County and State of New York in the year 1763 as appears by a record anciently made by my parents in the Family Bible a copy of which is in my possession I know of no other record.

2d My Second Term of service was for one month I entered in Claverack as before by Classification very soon after my return home in the fore part of June 1778 under Captain Abner Hawley (5) I don't certainly Recollect the other officers but believe the Ensigns name was Vaughn (6) was taken to Cherry Valley & there remained as our head quarters, Scouting the surrounding country occasionally to the distance of 50 or 60 miles untill dismissed at the end of one month from the time of leaving home without any pay whatever from Government—I don't remember any continental troops or officers with us in this Tour of Duty I had no written discharge & no documentary Evidence of this Term of Service.

3d My next term of service was for one month I entered in the same town & in the same manner as before stated very soon after my return home from the last tour at Cherry Valley. I think in July of the year 1778. I was taken from thence through Albany & Schenectady to Canajoharie from thence to Cherry Valley & to Canajoharie alternately by each way as our officers thought fit to order. I believe my captain's name was Joshua Whitney (7) & Lieut—Elias Delong (8) in this tour of Duty & was dismissed at Cherry Valley without any pay from the Government whatever & without any written discharge. I have no documentary proof of this term of service.

4th My next Term of Service was for one month and commenced immediately on my return home I was sent back to Canajoharie was at the time of the attack on Cherry Valley (9) sent to ascertain (in company with 2 others) the Nature of the firing We found it necessary to get into the Fort which we had the good fortune to effect, closely pursued by Indians I was in the fort during two succeeding days (10) of Fighting the Indians, Colonel Alden (11) of the Continental line from the State of Massachusetts was at the time of this attack on Cherry Valley residing about ¼ of a mile (as was Lieut Col. Statia) from the fort both of them were killed before reaching the fort as were also 39 men who were washing their clothes at a brook adjacent to the fort from 38 to 50 rods distant from it by the Indians so secret was their approach the Indians killed most of the inhabitants and burned their dwellings. Were driven away by the arrival of Reinforcements of Militia. My officers were Captain Ithamar Spencer (12), Lieut. Elias Delong. I was dismissed at Canajoharie in November 1778 without pay without any written discharge or documentary Proof of this Term of Service and that at present I know of no person living whose testimony I can procure who can testify to my service in any part or all of the aforesaid terms of service. They were each for short terms and in small detachments which I consider to be the reason of my having no knowledge of the higher or superior officers either Militia or Continental under whose orders we were absolutely placed.

5th my next Term of Service was for Eight Months (13) on a regular enlistment as appears from the Documents already in the Pension office at the seat of Government commencing May of 1779.

6th My next Term of service was for Nine Months I entered the Service a Substitute was hired by one Michael Wise to take the place of his grandson whose name I do not know, nor ever did he was drafted but I served the officers under whom I served were in this tour Col. Marinus Willett (14) of N. York, Captain James McKean [Robert] who was mortally wounded in the Battle of Turlough (15) up Mohawk River. Lieut. James Kennon [Cannon] (16) Cherry Valley also Peter Loop Lieutenant Sergeants Jacob Hazeltine & Hutchins (17) he was shot at Fort Herkimer, for Plundering Col. Willetts Markee & Desertion. I was in the aforesaid battle at Turlough in which report said 300 Indians were defeated by 150 men under Col. Willett. This was a Travelling campaign I marched to Johnstown from thence to Stone Robby thence to Fort Plain from thence to Fort Herkimer, from thence my company commanded by Lt. Kennon Returned to Fort Plain from thence to Ballstown and built a Piquet Fort and called it Fort Kennon from thence to Fort Hunter on the Mohawk River & was there discharged in writing by Lieutenant Kennon which discharge was destroyed by being burnt more than twenty years ago. I have no documentary proof of this service it commanced April 1st 1780 and was discharged January 1st 1781 in this Last Term of Service. I served as a Corporal (18) one or two months can't recollect which the residue of the time a Sergeant.

7th My next Term of service was for three months I entered in the same town as before Claverack by an arrangement of the class by which I was sent. I was detached for 3 months there were 6 others in the same company who were similarly detached for 3 months the rest of the company both officers and men were for a shorter time so that at the end of six weeks, there were seven men of our company only left and we destitute of officers. I understood this State of things to have been produced by the other class undertaking (like Centinels) to relieve each other once in two weeks whereby each man in the said class would serve the said two weeks & that would make the class keep one man in for 3 months but being as before Stated left destitute of officers and in Militia Service only we returned home without any formal dismission written discharge or any documentary proof of this service or at least such is the fact so far as I know. My officers in this Term of Service were James Delong (19) Captain I cannot recollect the other officers and my duty was performed in such small detached parties as allowed me no opportunity of knowing Continental officers. We were a Frontier Guard this term of service was performed in Johnstown Canajoharie, Cherry Valley and Stone Robby all in the State of New York commencing in July or August, don't recollect which, of the year 1781 and ending about the first of October of the same year.

I was born in the town of Rhinebeck in the State of New York in the year 1763.

My birth is not recorded to my knowledge other than a copy from my fathers family record in his bible. I now reside in the Isle La Mott have resided there for thirty years or more.

I hereby relinquish every claim whatever to a pension or annuity except the present and declare that my name is not on the pension roll of the agency of any State.

Sworn and Subscribed the day and year aforesaid. (Signed) Henry Scott

In testimony whereof I have hereunto set my hand and seal of office this 29th day of August AD 1832. C. H. Burgess Register

Reply to a letter of inquiry dated February 1, 1937

Reference is made to your request for information relative to Henry Scott who served in the Revolutionary War and was from Isle LaMotte, Vermont.

The data which follow were obtained from papers on file in the pension claim W.20049, based upon the military service of Henry Scott.

He was born November 24, 1763, in Rhinebeck, New York. The names of his parents were not given.

While living in Claverack, Albany County, New York, he enlisted and served with the New York troops as follows: from about the first of February, 1778, four months as private in Captain Funday's company; from June, 1778, one month as private in Captain Abner Hawley's company; from July, 1778, one month as private in Captain Joshua Whitney's company; from November, 1778, one month as private in Captain Ithamar Spencer's company; from May 1, 1779, eight months as private in Captain Norton's company in Colonel Livingston's regiment; from April 1, 1780, nine months as corporal and sergeant in Captain James McKean's Company in Colonel Marinus Willett's regiment; from July or August, 1781, until the first of October, 1781, as private in Captain James DeLong's company. He was in the battles of Cherry Valley, Newtown and Turlock.

He applied for pension April 30, 1829, at which time he stated that he lived at Vineyard, Grand Isle County, Vermont. The claim was allowed.

In 1832 he was living at Isle LaMotte, Grand Isle County, Vermont and stated that he had lived there thirty years or more.

Henry Scott died March 27, 1834.

This soldier married January 2, 1783, Christiana, her maiden name not given, who was born October 15, 1760.

She was allowed pension on her application executed September 19, 1838, at which time she was living in Isle LaMotte, Vermont.

Henry and Christiana Scott had the following children:

John	Born March 12, 1784	
Mary	July 2, 1785	
Attee	September 19, 1786	Died April 3, 1825
Peggy	April 1, 1788	
Betina or Belinda	August 19, 1789	
Hery or Henry	October 12, 1790	
Christiana	February 11, 1792	
Simeon	May 15, 1794	
Hannah	July 17, 1794	
Cornelius	April 28, 1797	
Daniel	July 8, 1799	
Sullivan	February 9, 1802	Died June 18, 1817
A son	February 18, 1805	Died March 4, 1805

John's wife, Patty, died October 5, 1818.

In 1838 one Simeon R. or N. Scott of Isle LaMotte, Vermont, stated that he was the administrator of the estate of Henry Scott but it was not shown that he was identical with the soldier's son, Simeon Scott.

End Notes—Henry Scott—W.20049

1. These officers were not from Claverack but from the Tenth Regiment of Albany County Militia commanded by Colonel Peter R. Livingston. The officers are Captain John A. Fonda of the Fifth Company, First Lieutenant John L. Decker of the Fourth Company and Petrus Wyncoop who was the QuarterMaster.
2. Possibly Lieutenant Colonel Dirck TenBroeck of the First Regiment of Albany County Militia.
3. The First New York Continental Regiment under the command of Colonel Goose VanSchaick.
4. The Third New York Continental Regiment under the command of Colonel Peter Gansevoort.
5. Captain Abner Hawley in the Ninth Regiment of Albany County Militia (also known as the Second Claverack Battalion) under the command of Colonel Peter Van Ness.
6. Ensign Edward Vaughan of Captain John McKinstry's Company in the Ninth Regiment.
7. First Lieutenant Joshua Whitney was promoted to Captain on February 6, 1779 as McKinstry had been promoted to Major.
8. Elias Delong was a Second Lieutenant in 1775 in Captain Philip Bartel's Company (First Company) in the Ninth Regiment. But on May 28, 1778 Benjamin Allen was commissioned the Second Lieutenant in

Bartel's Company. On the same date Francis Delong was commissioned the Ensign. On February 6, 1779, First Lieutenant Cornelius Hogeboom was commissioned Captain because Bartel had resigned. Allen became the First Lieutenant and Francis Delong the Second Lieutenant.

9. Cherry Valley was attacked on November 11, 1778.
10. Fort Alden.
11. Colonel Ichabod Alden of the Sixth Massachusetts Continental Regiment was killed but Lieutenant-Colonel William Stacy was taken prisoner.
12. Henry was mistaken about Captain Ithmar Spencer, because Abner Hawlley had been commissioned Captain in place of Spencer on May 28, 1778.
13. He enlisted as a private for eight months on May 1, 1779 in Captain Theodosius Fowler's Company in the Fourth New York Continental Regiment commanded by Colonel Frederick Weisenfels. Henry was discharged on January 1, 1780. FROM: Revolutionary War Rolls 1775-1783, M-246, Roll 71, Folder 61, National Archives, Washington, DC.
14. This service was in 1781. Henry was in Captain Robert McKean's Company for only a short time. The recruits were put in Captain Elihu Marshall's Company of Lieutenant Colonel Commandant Colonel Marinus Willett's Regiment of New York State Levies.
15. The Battle of New Dorlach (present day Sharon Springs) was fought on July 10, 1781. Captain McKean was mortally wounded and died on the return march back to Fort Rensselaer.
16. Lieutenants James Cannon and Peter Loop of Captain Marshall's Company.
17. Henry was referring to Sergeant Jacob Esseltyne and Private George Hodgeson of Marshall's Company. They were not arrested or executed. Esseltyne applied for a pension based on his services and Hodgeson received his pay of his services in 1785. The roll was sworn to on October 28, 1785.
18. Henry was listed on Marshall's payroll as Corporal. He was owed £ 22..15..8½ which was delivered to Bartle Hendricks in 1785. FROM: Revolutionary War Rolls 1775-1783, Series M-246, Roll 78; folder 173, National Archives, Washington DC.
19. James Delong appears to have only been an Ensign in Captain Joseph Heath's Company in the Ninth Albany.

Invalid Application for Henry Seeber or Seber

S.27,469

Henry Seber, a private in Captain VanYarren's Company of Col. Cox's Regiment was disabled in the Battle of Oriskany due to injury to both thighs.

State of New York
County of Herkimer SS.

Bet it known that before me a Justice of the Peace in and for the County aforesaid duly authorized by law to administer oaths personally appeared Suffrenus Seeber a resident of the town of Warren in the county and State aforesaid who being duly sworn according to Law, States that he is a son of Henry Seeber deceased who was also a resident in said County & State & who was a Revolutionary Soldier & pensioner and that he this deponent believes the United States are still indebted under existing laws for pension that was due under the applications heretofore made & that he is directly interested, as a claimant in the pension for which application was heretofore made as aforesaid & constitutes and appoints George C. Ames D.C. my true and lawful attorney with irrevocable power to examine into, investigate and establish the claims for said pension and do all acts necessary thereto.

Witness whereof I have hereinto set my hand & seal this 17th day of February 1858. (Signed) Suffrenus Seeber. Witness Joseph R. Reed

Signed, sealed, acknowledged and sworn to before me this 17 day of February 1858—Leonard Edwards, Justice of the Peace.

County of Herkimer SS.

On this 20the day of April 1824 before me John Dygert Esqr one of the Justices of the Peace of the County aforesaid personally appeared Henry Seeber who on his oath declares he is the same person who formerly belonged to the company of Capt. Reynier Van Yarren (1) [Ryner VanEveren] in the Regiment commanded by Col'n Cox in the service of the United States that his name was placed on the pension roll of the State of new York but has never received a formal certificate and now wishes to obtain one. (Signed) Henry Seeber

Sworn and subscribed to before me the day and year aforesaid. John Dygert Just. Peace.

Letter to reply for information.

Reference is made to your request for information in regard to the Revolutionary War pension claim of Henry Seber.

The data which follow were obtained from papers on file in pension claim, S.27469, based upon the disability of Henry Seeber, which disability was incurred during his military service.

Henry Seeber enlisted in 1777 and served as private in Captain Ryner VanEveren's company in Colonel Cox's New York regiment. He was wounded in the thighs at the battle of Oriskany. (2) The place of his enlistment and length of his service are not given.

On account of the disability resulting from the wounds mentioned above, he was pensioned from November 25, 1786, at which time he was forty years of age and was living in Johnstown, Montgomery County, New York.

In 1828 he was living in German Flats, Herkimer County, New York.

He died prior to December 29, 1853.

His son, Suffrenes, was living in Warren, Herkimer County, New York in 1858. The papers in this claim contain no further data relative to the soldier's family.

Reply to a letter asking for information on Henry Seeber.

Some weeks ago I wrote asking for the record of three Seebers in the Revolution, but have received no reply—Perhaps, this is too early to expect a reply, but a reply to a former inquiry came in three days—I asked for three Seebers, but I am now interested in only one of those three, and I shall appreciate the courtesy if I am hear from your office as to this—Henry Seeber: born 1741 in Germany (according to my record) fought at Oriskany under Gen. Herkimer—was wounded and crippled—lived to the age of 104 years—died 1845—name on Oriskany Monument.

We the Subscribers Abraham Ten Broeck and Peter Gansevoort Jun. do certify that upon an examination in pursuance of the Law, entitled an Act making provision for Officers, Soldiers and Servicemen, who have been disabled in the Service of the United States", Passed the 22d of April 1786. We do find that Henry Seber residing in Johnstown, Montgomery Co. State of New York aged forty years late a Private in Capt. Rynier VanEveret's Comp'y in the Regiment of Militia Commanded by Colo'l Cox and Claiming relief under the Act of Congress recited in the said Law as such valid in fact and that he became disabled in the service of the United States in Consequence of a Wound in this Thigh at the Battle of Oriska in the Month of August 1777 and do further certify that upon the Principle of the said Act of Congress the said Henry Seber is entitled to the Pay of Four Dollars per Month.

Given under our hands in the City of Albany, on the twenty fifth Day of November in the year of our Lord one thousand seven hundred and eighty six. Abm.Ten Broeck, Peter Gansevoort Junr.

I certify the above certificate to be a true copy of the original lodged in the State Auditor Office. Peter Curtenius

State of New York
Herkimer County SS.

We the Subscribers Practicing Physicians of the Town of Herkimer and County aforesaid being duly appointed by Sanders Lansing Esquire, one of the Judges of the County of German Flatts in and for the County of Herkimer; examine Henry Seber who is now enrolled on the Pension Roll of the New York Agency at the degree of three fourths disabled. We hereby certify that after a careful examination in the case of the aforesaid Henry Seber, we are of opinion that his disability still continues viz in consequence of two gunshot wounds in the right thigh, one near the hip joint the other a little below and one in the left thigh—and further that the degree of disability under which he now labours is total, being one fourth more than the original degree of disability for which he was placed on the pension list Roll. C.W. Smith. Lester Green

Sworn and Subscribed this seventh day of March 1828 before me. Sanders Lansing, a Judge of Herkimer County Courts in the State of New York.

End Notes—S.2749—Henry Seeber

1. Rynler VanEvera or Yeveren, Everat, etc., was Captain of the Seventh Company under Colonel Ebenezer Cox, of the First Regiment of Tryon County Militia.
2. The Battle of Oriskany was fought on August 6, 1777.

Pension Application for Moses Seers

S.43113

Private New York Line. Capt. Smith, Cortlandt's Regt.

State of New York SS.

To the Hon. Richard Riker

Recorder of the City of New York, and one of the Judges of the Court of Common Pleas, called the Mayor's Court of the City of New York, which is a Court of Record of the State of New York.

The Declaration under Oath of Moses Seers formerly a private soldier-engaged in the Service of the United States during the Revolutionary War, now a Citizen of the United States and resident of the City and County of New York, respectfully sheweth, That the said Moses Seers—sometime in the month of January 1781 Inlisted in Colo. Courtlandt's Regt, Cap'n Israel Smith's Company, Genl James Clinton's (1) Brigade, and was discharged in the month June 1783 having served the full period of his enlistment which was to the end of the war.

And the declaration further sheweth, that the said Moses Seers is now a citizen of the United States, resides in the city of New York, and is, by reason of his reduced circumstances in life, in need of assistance from his country for support.

Therefore the said Moses Seers conceives himself entitled to the benefit of the Act of the Congress of the United States, entitled, "an Act to provide for certain persons engaged in the Land and Naval Service of the United States in the Revolutionary War," approved 18th March, 1818, and requests your honor will examine into the truth of the matter aforesaid, certify and transmit the testimony in the case, and the proceedings had thereon, to the Honorable the Secretary of the Department of War, to the end that such relief may be had in the premises, as is by law, in such case made and provided. And in support of the fact above set forth, the said Moses Seers refers to Benjamin Rome, who served in the same Regt and Company

City and County of New York SS. Moses Seers of the City and County of New York, being duly sworn, saith, that the matters by him set forth in the foregoing Declaration, are in all respects just and true. (Signed with his mark) Moses Seers.

Sworn before me this second day of April 1818. R. Riker.

New York Mayor's Court.

In the Court of Common Pleas, called the Mayor's Court of the City of New York, held at the City Hall, in and for the said City, before the Judges of the same Court, of June term, in the year of our Lord one thousand eight hundred and twenty.

Present the Honorable Peter Augustus Jay Esquire.

City of New York, SS. Be it remembered, that on the twenty eighth day of June in the year of our Lord one thousand eight hundred and twenty, personally appeared in the Court of Common Pleas, called the Mayor's Court of the city of New York, in open court, the said court being a court of record for the city and county of New York, according to the charter of the said city and the laws of the state of New York, Moses Seers aged sixty three years, resident in the City of New York in the State of New York, United States of America who being first duly sworn according to law, doth on his oath declare, that he served in the revolutionary war as follows: that is to say, he enlisted as a private in the Continental Army for during the war in a company of Infantry in the Continental Army for during the war in a company of Infantry commanded by Captain Harry Dubois (2) in the second New York Regiment commanded by Colonel VanCalloundt at Pompton in the State of New Jersey about the middle of January 1782, having entered at Pompton the Regiment proceeded to VerPlank's Point from thence to West Point where the Regiment lay about two months, from thence the Regiment went to a place called Snake Hill where they wintered in huts, in the spring they went to White Plains from thence to Snake Hill again when in June 1783 the Regiment was disbanded and where deponent received his honorable discharge having served his country the whole of the period from the time of his enlistment to the end of the war being for seventeen months.

Deponent was transferred he thinks in the summer of 1782 into Israel Smith's (3) company, Third New York Regiment(4) in which he was when he was discharged, and received his honorable discharge which has been lost some how or other—deponent has received a pension since the second day of April 1818 and that his original declaration is dated the second day of April one thousand eight hundred and eighteen and that his pension certificate is No. 957. (Signed with his mark) Moses Seers.

And I do solemnly swear that I was a resident citizen of the United States on the 18th day of March 1818, and that I have not since that time, by gift, sale, or in any manner, disposed of my property, or any part thereof, with intent thereby so to diminish it as to bring myself within the provisions of an act of Congress, entitled, "An act to provide for certain persons engaged in the land and naval service of the United States, in the Revolutionary war," passed on the 18th day of March, one thousand eight hundred and eighteen; and that I have not, nor has any person in trust for me, any property or securities, contracts or debts, due to me; nor have I any income other than what is contained in the schedule hereto annexed, and by me subscribed, to wit:

Real Estate—None.

Personal Estate. None (necessary clothing excepted)

Declarant has no wife, no family residing with him—no children—Declarant is a mason by trade, but cannot work at his trade in consequence of being lame and very much afflicted with the Rheumatism. He has no occupation at present he has six children, Ann Minikhouse, aged thirty one, is supported by her husband, Phobe Minikhouse, aged twenty eight years, she is supported by her husband, Hester Millan aged twenty five years, she is also supported by her husband, Betsey Seers unmarried aged twenty three years, who is in Canada, she also supports herself, Moses Seers is an apprentice aged 19 years he is supported by his master. Mary Ann Seers aged 12 years she at present lives with her sister none of deponents children are able to contribute any thing towards deponents support, he is afflicted with the Rheumatism & is not attended by the doctor in consequence of broken ribs—he Is In such indigent circumstances as to be unable to support himself without the assistance of his country except by private or public charity—he at present stays at the alms house where he has been eight months. (Signed with his mark) Moses Seers.

Sworn this 28th June 1820 in open court. Benj Ferris Clk.

End Notes—S.43113—Moses Seers (Sears, Sayers, etc.)

1. Brigadier General James Clinton.
2. Moses enlisted as a private for during war on January 23, 1782, in Captain Henry DuBois' Company in Colonel Philip VanCortlandt's Second New York Continental Regiment. FROM: Revolutionary War Rolls 1775-1783, Series M-246, Roll 67, folder 23, National Archives, Washington, D.C.
3. Israel Smith was the Captain of the fifth company in Colonel VanCortlandt's Regiment. Moses is on Captain Smith's 1783 Muster Rolls. FROM: Revolutionary War Rolls 1775-1783, Series M-246, Roll 69, folder 32, National Archives, Washington, D.C.
4. Moses is in error as the Third New York Continental Regiment was consolidated with the First New York Continental Regiment on January 1, 1781. After this date the Third New York ceased to exist.

Pension Application for Andrew Sherwood

W.19021 (Widow: Judith)
B.L.Wt. 7853-100-1798
B.L.Wt. 249-60-55

Schedule

State of New York
Tompkins County SS.

On this twenty eighth day of September 1820 personally appeared in open court, being a court of record by the law of said state, for the said County of Tompkins Andrew Sherwood aged seventy four years resident in the town of Dryden in the said County of Tompkins who being first duly sworn according to law doth on his oath declare that he served in the revolutionary war as follows: That he enlisted in 1777 in Capt. Thomas Machin's (1) Company in Col. John

Lambs regiment of Artillery during the War on the Continental Establishment. That he served till the Close of the War, about six years. That he was in the Battle at Fort Montgomery (2), at the taking of Cornwallis at Yorktown (3), and in various skirmishes in the revolutionary war. The date of his original application was the 27th April 1818 and his pension certificate is numbered 11182. And I do solemnly swear that I was a resident citizen of the United States on the 18th day of March 1818 and that I have not since that time by gift sale or in any manner disposed of my property or any part thereof with intent thereby so to diminish it as to bring myself within the provisions of an act of Congress entitled "An act to provide for Certain persons engaged in the land & naval service of the United States in the revolutionary War" passed on the 18th day of March 1818 and that I have not nor has any person in trust for me any property or securities in trust or debt due to me nor have I any income other than what is contained in the Schedule hereto annexed, and by me subscribed.

Real estate I have none. I have 3 yearling hogs, 1 scythe, 1 old axe, 1 pail, 1 pot, 1 pail disk kettle, 1 Teakettle , 1 five pail kettle, 1 old table good for nothing, 1 pr shovel & tongs 1 tramel, 3 tea cups & saucers, old & broken, ½ sett old knives & forks, 4 old chairs poor, the [?] of fifty acres of land improved but how long he may improve it. (Signed) Andrew Sherwood.

And the said Andrew Sherwood farther swears that he is by occupation a farmer, that he has a wife living with him named Judith aged fifty two being his second wife, is healthy and able to work, that the said Andrew has been [un]able for about five years to perform manual labor in consequence of debility & old age. That he has two children living with him, Stephen aged fifteen years, and Nancy aged thirteen years, both healthy who together assist in maintaining the said Andrew & his wife. That he shared the hardships & deprivations of the revolutionary war, often received tokens of respect from Washington the father of his country and always performed his duty with alacrity & with fidelity to his country, and is now left in his old age destitute of any support except that derived from his wife & children. (Signed) Andrew Sherwood

Sworn to & Declared at the 29 day of September 1820 before me in open court. Augustine Crary one of the Judges of Tompkins Court of Comm Pleas.

Letter of reply for a request for information, Dated July 28, 1938

Reference is made to your letter in which you request the Revolutionary War record of Andrew Sherwood of Dryden, Tompkins County, New York.

The data furnished herein were obtained from papers on file in claim for pension, W.19021, based on the military service of Andrew Sherwood in the Revolutionary War.

Andrew Sherwood was born in the month of February, 1746, place not stated, nor were the names of his parents given.

While a resident of New Windsor, Orange County, New York, Andrew Sherwood enlisted in 1777, served as private and first sergeant in Captain Thomas Machin's company in Colonel John Lamb's Regiment of Artillery; he was in the battles of Fort Montgomery, Monmouth (4), Yorktown, and several skirmishes, and was discharged at the close of the war.

He was allowed pension on his application executed April 27, 1818, at which time he was a resident of Dryden, Tompkins County, New York.

He died August 29, 1831, In Independence, Allegany County, New York.

Andrew Sherwood married December 8, 1784, in Cornwall, Orange County, New York, Miss Judah or Judith Ryckman or Richman. She was his second wife; name of the first wife not stated, nor are there any details in regard to her.

The widow, Judah Sherwood, was allowed pension on her application executed February 4, 1840 at which time she was seventy-seven years of age and a resident of Independence, New York.

The names of the children of Andrew Sherwood and his wife, Judah or Judith:

Joseph born September 2, 1785
William born February 13, 1788, deceased in 1844
David born October 29, 1791
Sarah born February 19, 1794
Samuel born July 12, 1796
Hannah born August 3, 1800
Stephen born March 16, 1803
Nancy born September 2, 1806

It was not stated that there were any children by the first wife.

The widow, Judah Sherwood, was living in 1844 in Independence, New York, with her son, Joseph Sherwood, and in 1856, she was living in Liberty Township, McKean County, Pennsylvania. She died August 31, 1861.

William Sherwood, brother of the soldier, Andrew Sherwood, was eighty-one years of age in 1840, and living in Potter, Yates County, New York. William M. Strobridge stated in 1844 in Allegany County, New York that he was the grandson by marriage of the soldier and the widow, Judah Sherwood.

End Notes—W.19021—Andrew Sherwood

1. Thomas was appointed Captain-Lieutenant on January 1, 1777 in Captain Thomas Theodore Bliss' Company in Colonel John lamb's Second Regiment of Continental Artillery. Andrew's name was not found on the company muster or in any of the other companies of this regiment in 1777. Machin was promoted to captain on August 21, 1780 in Colonel Lamb's Regiment. Andrew is listed as enlisting on January 17, 1781 in Captain Machin's company for during war and his rank is listed as sergeant. On the April 1781 muster roll Sergeant Sherwood is listed as "Recruiting at Albany". FROM: Revolutionary

War Muster Rolls 1775-1788, Series M-246, Roll 118, folder 39, National Archives, Washington, D.C.
2. The Battle of Fort Montgomery, NY, was fought on October 6, 1777. Captain-Lieutenant Machin was wounded in this battle.
3. The Yorktown, Virginia, Campaign was from September 28 to October 19, 1781.
4. The Battle of Monmouth, NY was fought on June 28, 1778. Captain Bliss was taken prisoner during this battle.

Pension Application for John Sherwood

S.42282
Continental (Mass.)
Sergeant—line of Vermont May 77 till March 78
Green Mt. Boys
New York

To the Honorable James Smott First Judge of the Court of Common Pleas, of the County of Dutchess which is a Court of Record of the State of New York

The Declaration under oath of John Sherwood formerly a sergeant engaged in the Service of the United States, during the Revolutionary War, and now a Citizen of the United States, and resident of the Town of Stanford, Dutchess County & State of New York Respectfully Showeth, that the said John Sherwood in the month of May in the year one thousand seven hundred and seventy seven at Poughkeepsie—Dutchess County enlisted in a company in the American service commanded by Captain Thomas Dewitt (1) in the third regiment of the New York line commanded by Colonel Peter Gansevoort for during the war of the revolution, that he served in the said company as an orderly sergeant under his said enlistment until some time in the month of December following when he was taken sick and lay three months in the hospital where he was sent home by his officers on furlough being unfit for duty, that some time in the spring following being still sick and unable to join his regiment he wrote to this captain stating his situation and by the fall thereafter received a letter from his captain stating that he was discharged from service and need not return to his company—which letter he has lost.

And this Delcaration further representeth that the said John Sherwood is now a Citizen of the United States and residing in Stanford aforesaid, and by reason of his reduced circumstances in life, in need of assistance from his country for support; and that he has never received any pension from the government of the United States.

Therefore he conceives himself entitled to the benefit of the Act of the Congress of the United States, entitled, "An Act to provide for certain persons engaged in the Land and Naval Service of the United States, in the Revolutionary War," approved, March 17, 1818, and requests that Honor will examine into the truth of the matters aforesaid, certify and transmit the testimony in this case and the proceedings had thereon to the Honorable the

Secretary of the Department of War, to the end that such relief may be had in the premises, as is by law in such case provided. And in support of the facts above set forth, he refers to the affidavit of himself and of Isaac Hunting hereafter set forth.

Dated the 22nd day of April 1818. (Signed) John Sherwood.

County of Dutchess. SS. John Sherwood being duly sworn says, that the matters by him set forth in the foregoing Declaration, are in all respects just and true.

Sworn the 22nd day of April 1818 before me. James Smott

At a Court of Common Pleas held at the Court House in the Village of Poughkeepsie in and for the County of Dutchess in the State of New York on Monday the twenty sixth day of June in the year one thousand eight hundred & twenty.

Present the Honorable James Smott First Judge.

Daniel C. Ver Planck, Abraham D. VanWyck, Thomas Sweet. Esquires & Judges.

State of New York
Dutchess County SS.

Be it remembered that on the twenty sixth day of June in the year one thousand eight hundred & twenty, personally appeared in the Court of Common Pleas, in open court, the said court being a court of record for the County of Dutchess, in the State of New York, John Sherwood, aged about sixty eight years, resident in the town of Stanford in the said County of Dutchess, who being first duly sworn according to law, doth on his oath declare, that he served in the revolutionary war as follows,

On the ninth day of May in the year one thousand seven hundred & seventy five, he entered the service as a common soldier, having volunteered for that purpose under the command of Col. Ethan Allen, (2) and the next morning, was at the capture of Ticonderoga Fort. From this time, this deponent remained with the army & went through the Canada Expedition until the main army retreated out of Canada.

The first year that this deponent was in the service, he belonged to the regiment, called the Green Mountain boys, commanded by Col. Seth Warner, (3) after the capture of Allen.

Sometime in the month of May one thousand seven hundred & seventy six, this deponent enlisted for the term of nine months, under Captain John Sloan (4) in a Boston regiment, commanded by Col. Patterson, & remained in that regiment until the period of his enlistment expired.

On the thirteenth day of May, one thousand seven hundred & seventy seven, this deponent enlisted as an Orderly Sergeant, during the war, under the command of Captain Thomas DeWitt in the Third Battalion or Regiment of New York forces, commanded by Col. Peter Gansevoort & remained in the service until sometime in the year one thousand seven hundred & seventy eight, when from ill health this deponent obtained leave, by furlough from said

Col. Gansevoort, to return home; & in the latter part of the summer one thousand seven hundred & seventy eight, this deponent's ill health continuing so that he was unable to return to duty, he, this deponent, wrote to his said Captain, the said Thomas DeWitt, informing of his situation, & in December then next this deponent received a letter from his said Captain, that he this deponent was discharged from the service, & need not again return, which letter this deponent has since lost.

And this deponent further says that his original declaration is dated, according to the recollection & belief of this deponent, the twenty second day of April one thousand eight hundred & eighteen & that his pension certificate is No. 2901.

And I do solemnly swear that I was a resident citizen of the United States on the 18th day of March 1818 & that I have not since that time by gift, sale, or in any manner disposed of any property or any part thereof with intent thereby so to diminish it as to bring myself within the provisions of an act of Congress entitled, "An Act to provide for certain persons engaged in the land & naval service of the United States in the revolutionary war" passed on the 18th day of March 1818 & that I have not , nor has any person in trust for me, any property, or securities, contracts of debts due to me, nor have I any income, other than what is contained in the schedule hereunto annexed & by me subscribed, to wit:

Real Estate—I have none & never had any.

Debts. I have none.

Personal Property (necessary clothing & bedding excepted) to wit:

1 small swine, 8 Dunghill fowls, 1 old table, 1 Loom (old), 1 cupboard (old), 1 Stand, 9 Chairs (old) 6 knives & forks, 6 Earthen plates, 1 pewter platter, 4 small earthen bowls, 1 small chest, 1 meat cask, 2 meal casks, 1 iron pot, 2 Iron Kettles (small), 1 iron tea kettle, 1 old iron shovel & tongs, ½ Doz tea cups & saucers, 1 small looking glass, 1 pr. Bellows, 1 pair Andirons, 1 ax, 1 hoe, 1 large spinning wheel, 1 small spinning wheel, 1 earthen tea pot, 2 iron candlesticks, 1 wash tub, 1 corn basket, 1 water pail, 4 glass quart bottles, 2 small stone jugs, 1 stone pot, 1 small pickle tub, 1 old gridiron, 2 Doz pewter spoons.

This deponent further says that before the revolutionary war he was but a farmer & never had any trade or other employment, either before, or since the war, that since the sickness that compelled this deponent to leave the army, he has never been an able bodied man; & it has been with great difficulty that this deponent has been able to labour sufficient for his support & that of his family which he has brought up; & that from his age & increased infirmities, he is not hardly able to work at all. That the family of this deponent consists of the deponent & his wife aged about sixty years who is also considered infirm. (Signed John Sherwood)

Sworn and Subscribed this 26 day of June 1820 in open court. W Henry Bulkey, Depy Clerk

Reply to a letter of inquiry dated July 13, 1932.

Reference is made to your letter in which you request information in regard to John Sherwood, a soldier of the War of the Revolution.

The data contained herein were obtained from the papers on file in pension claim, S.42282, based upon the military service of John Sherwood, during the Revolutionary War.

He enlisted May 9, 1775 and served one year as a private in Colonels Ethan Allen's and Seth Warner's regiment of Green Mountain Boys, was at the capture of Ticonderoga and the expedition to Canada. He enlisted sometime in May, 1776 and served nine months as a private in Captain Sloan's company in Colonel Paterson's Massachusetts regiment. He enlisted in Poughkeepsie, New York, May 13, 1777 and was an orderly sergeant in Captain Thomas DeWitt's company in Colonel Peter Gansevoort's New York regiment, he was taken sick sent to the hospital in December, 1777, stayed three months and went home on furlough, and was discharged in December, 1778, having never been able to return to the army.

He was allowed pension on his application executed April 22, 1818, then a resident of Stanford, Dutchess County, New York.

In 1820 he was sixty-eight years of age, and stated that his wife, whose name he did not give, was about sixty years old, and at this time referred to a "family which he has brought up".

The soldier, John Sherwood, died November 29, 1841 in Poughkeepsie, New York, leaving no widow but the following children survived him—Stephen A. Sherwood a resident of Albany, New York and Jasper Sherwood a resident of Cooperstown, Otsego, County, New York.

There are no further data relative to his family.

End Notes—S.42282—John Sherwood

1. John was appointed orderly sergeant on May 14, 1777 in Captain Thomas DeWitt's Company (Second Company) in Colonel Peter Gansevoort's Third New York Continental Regiment. He was discharged on account of ill health in November of 1778. FROM: "Return of Sick in the Garrison of Fort Schuyler, March 1st, 1778". John is listed as follows: Names: Sergt Sherwood. Companies: Cap. DeWitt. Diseases: Convulsive Asthma. Where sick: Hospital. The return was signed by Lieutenant-Colonel Marinus Willett, Commanding Officer and H(unloke) Woodruff, Surgeon. The return of the sick is from the Collections of the New York Historical Society, pp 430-431.
2. Colonel Ethan Allen captured Fort Ticonderoga, N.Y., on May 10, 1775.
3. Seth Warner was the Lieutenant-Colonel of the Green Mountain Boys, and was appointed July 27, 1775. Colonel Allen was taken prisoner on September 25, 1775 in his failed attack on Montreal. The regiment was re-organized and Warner was commissioned Colonel on July 5, 1776.
4. A Captain Samuel Sloan in Colonel John Paterson's Fifteenth Continental Regiment. It is interesting that John doesn't mention any

of the battles he was in or the Siege of Fort Schuyler (or Fort Stanwix) in August of 1777.

Pension Application for Thomas Sherwood

S.15637
Connecticut & New York (Continental)
State of Connecticut, County of Fairfield SS
Ridgefield—

On this third day of Aug't 1832 personally appeared in open court before the Court of Probate in the District of Danbury in the said County and State, the same being a court of record, now sitting at Ridgefield, a resident, Thomas Sherwood a resident of the said viz the said applicant Town of Ridgefield aged seventy nine years, who being first sworn according to Law, doth on his oath make the following declaration in order to obtain the benefit of the Act of Congress passed June 7th 1832.

That he entered the service of the United States under the following named officers and served as herein stated. Viz—

That about the first of January 1776 he enlisted into the service of the United States for two months in a company under the command of Captain Ebenezer Jones in Connecticut State Troops—that he enlisted as a private soldier and served in the City of New York for the full period of the enlistment and was verbally discharged by said Captain Jones the said company among others was ordered to New York for the defense of the same, under the apprehensions of a speedy attack of the British as they [were] about leaving the Harbor of Boston.

And this declarant further states, that in the month of April 1776, he enlisted as a private soldier in a company under the command of Captain Cornelius Steinrod, (1) (for one year) in Colonel McDougal's Regiment at this time of the New York State Troops—That said Corps was mustered for service in the City of New York, on or about the first day of May 1776 and encamped in the "Bowery" about five weeks, when I made an exchange with one Gilbert Williams belong to a company under the command of Captain Leavenworth (2)- and in Colonel Webb's Regiment, and was transferred from the company of Captain Steinrod to that of Captain Leavenworth and proceeded soon to Harlem in said State of New York—where he remained until the day previous to the Surrender of New York to the British—

Thence marched to the White Plains, halting for a few days at the "Walnuts" so called—where we remained about a month, thence to Crampond, thence crossed the Hudson River and marched to Morristown thence under the command of General Lee (3), to Basking Ridge, where said Lee was taken prisoner by a party of the enemy—Thence in a forced march of two or three days we arrived, cold and fatigued at the Delaware River and crossed over to Easton in the State of Pennsylvania—

Thence marched to a place called Newtown passing through the Moravian Settlement at Bethlehem—passed there within about a mile of the

Delaware River where the detachment encamped for a few days with provision put up and canteens filled, holding ourselves in readiness for a march at a moment's notice—were called into the field and formed into a hollow square and heard read, the orders which were "death to leave the ranks" and a Prayer offered to the Throne of Grace by the Chaplain, Reverend Mr. Gano (4) then marched to the Delaware River and immediately crossed over, exhausted and fatigued, and nearly frozen having been out in a severe storm of Hail and rain, the Regiment to which this detachment belonged, being new with the main army under General Washington (5) marched in the direction of Trenton (6) in New Jersey, and having arrived within about four miles of the town.

The Army halted and on resuming their march separated one division under Gen. Washington taking the left and the other division with whom was the detachment taking the right—the said divisions to united at said Trenton, the said division on the right having marched within about a mile of the Town were ordered to "halt" being now near daylight in the morning—heard said division remained in a State of uncertainty until the Artillery passed, then formed into Platoons and advanced rapidly upon the town and then arrived about the moment that a body of Hessian soldiers had surrendered to the division under Gen. Washington. When said Hessian prisoners were secured the division which this declarant belonged marched back to the encampment on the west side of the Delaware river and about one mile from the same, having suffered incredible hardships from the cold, and the fatigues of the march, being without shoes or clothing or food and literally marching on paths with blood—this being as this declarant believes on the morning of the 26 December 1776—the troops remained encamped at this place for about three days when the encampment broke up and the troops returned to Trenton and this declarant remained at said Trenton until the first day of January 1777, and the period of his enlistment having expired viz, nine months. He was honorably discharged (verbally) and returned home.-- Said Colonel Wemple's Regiment was Connecticut State troops.

And this declarant further states that in the month of April 1777 when a party of the enemy landed at Campo and marched to Danbury (7) and there destroyed the stores, he was in the service as a volunteer followed the British from Danbury and at Ridgefield (8) he with a few others were standing near General Wooster (9), under cover of a [?] and was unexpectedly nearly surrounded by the enemy and hastily ordered by Gen'l Wooster to "retreat as they were surrounded, and almost at the same moment, he, Gen'l Wooster rec'd a mortal wound—and this declarant narrowly escaped having been repeatedly hit by the British bullets—the above tour occupying one week—

And further that in the month of July 1779 this declarant volunteered as a private soldier to go to Norwalk in said county for the defence of that place, performed the service in a company of Militia under Captain Gray, was on duty in said Norwalk when it was burned (10) by the enemy, and continued in said service one week.

And this declarant further states that in the month of January 1779 while the army of General Putnam (11) consisting of "Poor" Parsons and Huntington's Brigade (12) was encamped at Redding in said County of Fairfield he was employed as a superintendent of teams and served in that capacity for three months and was discharged on the last of March 1779—

And this declarant states that prior to the last term of service viz, in October 1777 he was at Crumpond in the State of New York, and that he went as a volunteer in a company of Militia, under the command of Lieutenant Hawley in Colonel Cook's (13) Regiment, to the defence of Fort Montgomery (14) on the Hudson River and was on duty on the east bank of the River when said Fort was taken by the British under Gen'l Clinton (15) , that soon after said troops marched to Fishkill and encamped for a short period, when they marched down the River to the place of their former encampment opposite the fort, and finding all the Barracks destroyed, they were dismissed, and this declarant returned home, having served in this term half a month.

And further, that in the year 1779 (in the fall) he was in the service of the United States for two months in a company of drafted Militia under the command of Captain Daniel Godfrey.—Said company being stationed for a part of the above period at [?]farms in the county of Fairfield and the remainder employed in guarding the coast from Stratford to Fairfield and that he served in said company as a Private and was honorably discharged.—

And this declarant further states, that in the year 1781 (as he believes) knows it was the same that the French Fleet arrived in America, he performed two tours of service in a company of drafted Militia as a private soldier and the company to which he belonged, was stationed at Horseneck Watching the movements of the enemy, that while there a person was taken up on suspicion of being a Spy, and this declarant with two or three others was sent to guard said suspected person, and deliver him safely to the head quarters of the American Army then lying in the vicinity of West Point—That they faithfully performed said duty and returned to Horseneck and this declarant was soon after discharged—having served in the two drafts one month and a half—He states that he cannot at this late period recollect the names of the officers of his company or Regiment and knows of no person now living by whom he can prove such service and has no documentary evidence in relation thereto—

Her further states that in the same year viz 1781, he was drafted and served half a month in the town of Fairfield, in a Serjeants guard (Militia) but does not recollect the name of the Sergeant nor does he know of any person living by whom he can prove such service. Neither has he any documentary evidence relating to it.

That he was born in the Town of Fairfield aforesaid, on the 24 May 1753—has no record of his age, but depends on the information received from his parents.—That he lived in Redding and Ridgefield in said county at the same period when he entered service as aforesaid, that subsequent to the war of the

Revolution he has resided in the Town of Ridgefield aforesaid and still resides in the same place—That has no written or documentary evidence of his services, other than that transmitted herewith. That he is acquainted with Levi Mondor and Jesse Reading and others who can testify as to his character for veracity and their belief of his services as a soldier of the Revolution—

He hereby relinquishes every claim whatever to a pension or annuity except the present and declares that his name if not on the pension roll of the agency of any State—

Sworn to and subscribed the day and year aforesaid. (Signed) Thomas Sherwood.

Attest, Edward Leizler, Clerk

Letter of reply requesting information, dated January 17, 1938.

The data which follow are shown in the papers on file in pension claim, S.15637, based upon service of Thomas Sherwood in the Revolutionary War.

Thomas Sherwood was born May 24, 1753, in Fairfield County, Connecticut; the names of his parents are not shown. He resided in the towns of Redding and Ridgefield, both in Fairfield County, Connecticut, during the period of the Revolutionary War.

Thomas Sherwood enlisted in January 1776, and served two months as a private in Captain Ebenezer Jones' Connecticut Company, engaged in the defense of New York City. He enlisted between the first and middle of April 1776, and served five weeks as a private in Captain Cornelius Steinrod's company, Colonel McDougal's regiment of New York troops, camped in the "Bowery" in New York City, then joined Captain Leavenworth's company, Colonel Charles Webb's Connecticut regiment, was with the troops at White Plains, marched through New Jersey, crossed the Delaware River with the main army under General Washington, suffered the incredible hardships of the winter, and was discharged January 1, 1777. He volunteered in April 1777, when Danbury was burned, and was so close to General Wooster when he was mortally wounded at Ridgefield, that he was hit by British bullets, length of this service one ; in the fall of 1777, he served one half a month under Lieutenant Hawley and Colonel Cook in the Connecticut troops at Fort Montgomery, From January 1, 1779, he served three months as superintendent of teams, Generals Parsons and Huntington's Brigades; he volunteered in July 1779, and served one week in Captain Gray's company, in the defense of Norwalk; he enlisted in the fall of 1779, and served two months as a private in Captain Daniel Godfrey's Connecticut company. In 1781, he served several tours as private in the Connecticut troops, amounting to all to about two months, engaged in Horseneck and Fairfield, Connecticut, officers' names not given.

After the Revolutionary War, Thomas Sherwood resided in Ridgefield, Connecticut.

Thomas Sherwood was allowed pension on his application executed August 3, 1832, at which time he resided in Ridgefield, Connecticut. He died November 25, 1838.

No reference was made to wife or children of the above noted soldier.

Zalton Sherwood was a resident of Ridgefield, Connecticut, in 1832, aged then sixty years; no relationship between him and Thomas Sherwood was stated.

End Notes—S.15637—Thomas Sherwood

1. Cornelius Steinrod (Steenrod etc.) was appointed Captain on April 27, 1776 in Colonel Alexander McDougal's First New York Continental Regiment. There are no known muster roll for this company, but there is a payment receipt with several names along with signatures or "his mark" for November of 1776 of men who received payment. Sherwood's name is not on this list. FROM: Revolutionary War Rolls 1775-1783, Series M-246, Roll 65, folder 2, National Archives, Washington D.C.
2. Eli Leavenworth was appointed captain on January 31, 1776 in Colonel Charles Webb's Nineteenth Continental (Infantry) Regiment.
3. Major General Charles Lee was taken prisoner at Basking Ridge, N.J., on December 13, 1776. He was exchanged on May 6, 1778.
4. Reverend John Gano, Chaplain of Colonel Webb's Regiment. He was appointed on January 1, 1776. Reverend Gano remained with the regiment until he was appointed Chaplain on November 21, 1776 in Colonel Lewis Dubois' Fifth New York Continental Regiment.
5. General and Commander-in-Chief General George Washington.
6. The Battle of Trenton, N.J. was fought on December 26, 1776. Sherwood's description of the hardships in this expedition and in particular "being without shoes or clothing or food and literally marching on paths with blood" is accurate. It should be noted that detachments of the First and Third New York Line (which were continental regiments) were in this battle.
7. Danbury, Connecticut was raided and burned on April 25, to April 27, 1777.
8. The Battle of Ridgefield, Connecticut was on April 27, 1777.
9. Brigadier General David Wooster died of his wounds on May 2, 1777.
10. Norwalk, Connecticut was burned on July 12, 1779.
11. Israel Putnam was appointed Major General on June 19, 1775.
12. Brigadier General Samuel H. Parsons (appointed on August 9, 1776) and Major General Jedediah Huntington (appointed on May 12, 1777).
13. Possibly Colonel Thaddeus Cook of the Connecticut Militia.
14. Fort Montgomery, N.Y. was captured on October 6, 1777.
15. Brigadier General James Clinton.

Pension Application for William Sherwood

R.9504
State of New York
Yates County SS.

On this twenty eighth day of September in the year eighteen hundred and thirty-two personally appeared in open Court before the Judges of the Court of Common Pleas of the County of Yates, aforesaid now sitting William Sherwood a resident of the town of Italy in the County of Yates aforesaid aged seventy three years, who being first duly sworn according to law doth on his oath make the following declaration in order to obtain the benefit of the Act of congress passed June 7th 1832.

That he entered the service of the United States under the following named officers and served as herein stated.

In the latter part of the year 1775 and according to the best of his recollection in the month of November, he enlisted to serve as a soldier for the term of five months, in a company of New York State Militia commanded by Capt. Samuel Raymond and Lieuts Langdon and Reynolds in Col. Isaac Nichols' Regiment of Militia (1) State troops. He was enrolled and mustered in the said company at Cornwall in the County of Orange and State of New York and was forthwith marched to the Hudson River to a place since known as Fort Constitution where he was stationed and served as a soldier of the said company and regiment six months, being one month more than his term of enlistment as aforesaid. He was then discharged.

In the Autumn of the next year (1776) but in what month he cannot determine he again entered as a soldier at Cornwall aforesaid, to serve for the term of nine months in a company of state troops of the State of New York under Capt. John Wisner (2) and Lieuts Strong and Little (3), in Col. Dubois' Regiment (4) immediately marched to Fort Montgomery and thence soon after to Haverstraw Bay where he was stationed and served in the said Company and Regiment about three months. Within a few weeks after being so stationed at Haverstraw, a detachment of British troops was landed from the British shipping then lying in Haverstraw Bay, about six miles from the encampment of the Regiment to which he belonged.

Immediately after such discharge he returned home to Cornwall aforesaid, and there learned that his father Daniel Sherwood had been drafted as a soldier and was then in actual service of the United States at Clarkstown in the State of New York in a company of militia under Capt. Van Duzer (5) and Lieut Smith (6). The said deponent immediately proceeded to Clarkstown aforesaid and took the place of his said father, Daniel Sherwood in the said company and served as his substitute three or four weeks then the said company was dismissed.

A few months after, and as the deponent now has the impression, in the month of January of the year 1778 he again enlisted as a soldier to service for the term of nine months in a company of volunteers under Capt. Tallman (7). The said Company was attached to a Regiment commanded by Col. Hays and was stationed at Clarkstown aforesaid four or five months. The Regiment then marched to Haverstraw. A detachment of the troops at that place marched under the command of the said Col. Hays to Hackensack in New Jersey deponent being of the number. He continued to serve in the said company and regiment till the expiration of his said term of enlistment when he received an honorable discharge.

He further said that subsequently at various times during the War of the Revolution, he was called into actual service as a soldier for a few days at a time on short expeditions, and on sudden alarms, and that on every occasion the promptly obeyed such calls.

That when Fort Montgomery (8) was attacked by a British force, he was serving in the said Fort as a soldier of the garrison under Gov. George Clinton, and that he the said deponent was in the engagement which then took place.

Deponent saith that he served as above stated.

Under Capt. Raymond—six months.

Under Capt. Wisner—nine months.

Under Capt. VanDuzer—one month.

Under Capt. Tallman—nine months.

On several other occasions - say three months.

The said deponent further saith

1st. That he was born at Cornwall in the County of Orange and State of New York on the day of [blank] in the year 1759.

2nd. That he has no record of his age.

3rd. That he lived at Cornwall aforesaid when called into service as above stated; he continued to reside at that place twenty five years after such service. He then removed to the town of Gorham in the County of Ontario in the same state where we resided then years from whence he removed to the town of Middlesex in the County of Yates in the same state where he has since resided except that recently he has removed a distance of about four miles, from his former residence in Middlesex aforesaid and into the adjoining town of Italy where he now resides.

4th. That he enlisted or volunteered when in service as herein before stated except that he served one month as a substitute for his father Daniel Sherwood.

5th. He recollects to have seen the following regular officers at different times, with troops where he served. Viz. Gen. Washington, Gen. LaFayette, Gen. Wayne, Gen. Putnam, Gov. George Clinton, Col. Stevens of the Artillery, and Capt. Matchin.

6th. He does not recollect to have received but one written discharge. That which he does remember to have received as signed by Col. Hays. He lost the same as he believes before the close of the war nor has he any knowledge of having seen it since.

7th. Deponent saith that he is known to Gilbert Ireland and Elisha Kelly—who reside in the town of Middlesex aforesaid and in the vicinity of his residence, and who as he believes can testify as to his character for veracity and their belief of his services as a soldier of the Revolution.

He knows of no person now living who has personal knowledge of his said services as a soldier except his brother Andrew Sherwood who if yet living resides in the County of Tompkins and State of New York but who is entirely blind, and so infirm and superannuated as to be unable to transact any business.

He hereby relinquishes every claim whatever to a pension or annuity except the present and declares that his name is not on the Pension Roll of the agency of any state. (Signed) Wm. Sherwood.

Subscribed and Sworn the day and year aforesaid. Thomas J. Nevins, Deputy Clerk.

End Notes—R.9504—William Sherwood

1. Captain Samuel Raymond, First Lieutenant David Reynolds, Second Lieutenant Richard Langdon or Landon, etc., and Ensign Jeremiah Fowler from the Cornwell Precinct were part of Colonel Isaac Nicoll's Regiment of Orange County Minute Men. The company officers were commissioned on November 9, 1775.
2. John Wisner was appointed Captain on March 6, 1776 of the Florida and Warwick's Company in Colonel Nicoll's Regiment of Minute Men. The other company officers were as follows: Abraham Dolson as First Lieutenant, Nathan Sayre as Second Lieutenant and Asa Wisner as Ensign.
3. It appears Henry is referring to Second Lieutenant James Little and Ensign Nathan Strong of Captain Thomas Moffat's Company, the Blooming Grove Company, in Colonel Nicoll's Regiment.
4. They were not part of Colonel Lewis DuBois' New York Continental Regiment which was un-numbered, but he may have been in command of Fort Montgomery.
5. Captain Christopher VanDuzer of the Third Company in Colonel Jesse Woodhull's First Regiment of Orange County Militia which was also known as the East Orange or Cornwall Regiment.
6. Obadiah Smith was the Second Lieutenant in Captain Van Duzer's Company.
7. Probably First Lieutenant Teunis Tallman of Captain Arie Smith's Company in Colonel Ann Hawkes Hays' Third Regiment of Orange County Militia or otherwise known as the Haverstraw Precinct Regiment.
8. The Battle of Fort Montgomery, N.Y. was fought on October 6, 1777. George Clinton was the Governor of New York and General of the Militia.

Pension Application for Jacob Shew

S.22985

Pension granted $85.33 (increase from $83.00) per annum, commencing March 4, 1831. Certificate of pension issued 31 March 1851.

Broadalbin NY

June 4th 1849

Sir,

Sometime in the month of April last (say near the middle), I wrote to you respecting the "error" in my venerable fathers, (Jacob Shew's) certificate of pension, and haven not as yet heard from you on the subject.

The Act of 20th May 1836, as construed by B. F. Butler, appears to be direct to the point, and applicable in this case, &c, &c., as more particularly described and set forth in said communication in April last, and having waited, what we suppose to be a reasonable time for a reply, we hereby inform you that an appeal to the Secretary of War, or the Home department has been formally made out, and forwarded through the mails accordingly.

Respectfully &c. John I. Shew

Hon. J. L. Edwards Comr. of Pensions.

N. B. if the communication, above spoken of has been lost through the mails, and that you have not as yet received it, please advise me of the fact.

State of New York
County of Jefferson SS.

On this 16th day of November 1848, personally appeared before me, Jerome Whitaker, a Justice of the Peace, in and for said County of Jefferson, Godfrey Shew, aged seventy seven years, who being first duly sworn according to law, doth, on his oath, depose and say that, he is brother of Jacob Shew, who was a pensioner of the United States under the Act of Congress of 15th May 1828, and has been suspended, and is now an applicant for a pension under the act of Congress of June 7th 1832, as this deponent has been informed and verily believes to be true.

That on the 3rd day of June 1778, the said Jacob Shew was taken prisoner in presence of this deponent, by a party of Indians, and returned from captivity on the 17th March 1779, being St. Patrick's day.

That in the Spring season of the year 1780, the said Jacob Shew enlisted for a term of nine months in a company commanded by Capt. Garret Putman in Col. Harpers regiment, the said Jacob Shew having been previously enrolled in a Company of Militia, commanded by Capt. John Little, in Col. Fisher's regiment. That the said Jacob Shew continued in the service until the expiration of the said nine month, and then returned home.

That in the Spring season of the year 1781, the said Jacob Shew again enlisted for nine months, in Capt. Garret Putman's Company, in Col. Willet's regiment, and served therein until the expiration of the said nine months and was then discharged or dismissed from the service, and returned home.

That again, in the Spring season of the year 1782 the said Jacob Shew again enlisted for a term of nine months in a company commanded by Capt. Abner French, in Col. Willet's regiment, and again continued in the service until the expiration of said nine months, and then again returned home. And further this deponent saith not. (Signed with his mark and it is a squiggly mark!) Godfrey Shew

Sworn to and subscribed on the day and year first above written, before me. Jerome Whitaker, Justice of the Peace.

I, Jerome Whitaker the above named Justice of the Peace, do hereby certify that I am well acquainted with Godfrey Shew above named, and that he uniformly sustains an irreproachable character, and that the facts set forth by him in the foregoing affidavit are entitled to credit,--and that by reason of a trembling hand he cannot write his name. Jerome Whitaker, Justice of the Peace.

State of New York
County of Fulton SS

On this fourth day of July one thousand eight hundred and forty-eight, personally appeared in open court before the Honr. John Wells Judge in and for said County of Fulton in the Village of Johnstown. Jacob Shew, a resident of the town of Broadalbin, in the said County of Fulton and State of new York, aged eighty five years on the fifteenth day of April last, who being first duly sworn according to Law, doth on his oath make the following declaration in order to obtain the benefit of the provision made by the Act of Congress passed June 7th 1832: That he was born in the town of Johnstown (on the 15th day of April 1763.) then the County of Tryon (since Montgomery) now Fulton County in the State of New York. That some eight years previous to the commencement of the Revolutionary War, Godfrey Shew (this applicants father)n with his family removed from Johnstown to a place called Sacondaga at that time which place is now called the Fish house in the town of Northampton, on the west branch of the Hudson's river about eighteen miles from Johnstown.

That he entered the service of the United States under the following named officers; and served as herein stated.

That on the 2nd day of June 1778, a man by the name of Solomon Woodworth, (1) a resident of Mayfield, assuming himself to be a Sergeant in Colonel Fishers regiment of Militia, while out as a spy, or on a Scout, discovered a house plundered of its contents, within about two miles of the residence of Godfrey Shew.

The said Solomon Woodworth repaired immediately to the residence of the said Godfrey Shew, and informed him and family of what he had discovered and that he by his authority as a non-commissioned officer, ordered all who were able to bear arms in defence of their country to turn out in militia service immediately, expecting the enemy to attack them the approaching night, the night was spent by a regular order of keeping garrison (by the said Solomon Woodworth, Godfrey Shew & his sons to wit: Stephen Shew, John Shew, Godfrey Shew Jr. & this applicant), according to the rules and regulations of armies in time of war. On the morning following June 3rd, (2) all the above named persons turned out, on scouts in one direction, one party some considerable distance ahead of the other for the purpose of ascertaining where the enemy might be. A party of Indians and Tories, about one hundred in number lay in ambush, and the foremost party was taken prisoners. They immediately repaired to the residence of said Godfrey Shew, and then took the other party who had returned to the house at the approach of the enemy.—The said party had previously taken prisoners whose names were John Putman, Christopher Morris, Robert Martin, Harmanus Salisbury, John Reece & David Harris. The names of those taken at the residence of the said Godfrey Shew, and those last described as being taken while the party lay in ambush, were said Godfrey Shew, Solomon Woodworth, John Shew, Stephen Shew and this applicant. After some consultation, the party plundered the house & barns of their contents, and after destroying all the buildings by fire &c. set out for Canada down the west branch of the Hudson or Sacondaga river by the way of Lakes George & Champlain. Arriving at an Indian village called Caughnawaga, about nine miles above Montreal, crossed the river, and went down to Montreal, and part of our number was given up as prisoners of war, and the others taken with the Indians to their northern settlements. Solomon Woodworth made his escape the first night after being taken. The names of those persons given up as prisoners of war were Robert Martin, David Harris, Godfrey Shew, Stephen Shew, and this applicant. The summer season was spent in close confinement on a ship at Montreal, and Quebec, from thence to Halifax, and there exchanged and about the first of December was sent to Boston and there set at liberty. After thus being set at liberty and arriving at Sudbury, about twenty miles from Boston, this applicant was taken sick with the small pox, and by order of Asahel Wheeler then Chairman of the Select men of Sudbury, medical aid was procured, and all assistance, requisite, was provided until in the early part of March following when, on the 17th being what is commonly called St. Patrick's day, this applicant returned to Johnstown where his mother & her younger children had designed to go, at the time of their separation when taken prisoner, in company with others as above stated.

The summer season passed away (to wit 1779.) without any particular engagement in regular service, until the fall season, when the applicant went out as a substitute about four weeks for Michael Gollinger, (3) who was an exempt in Capt. Giles Fonda's (4) Company. Col. Fisher's regiment, for the purpose of keeping garrison in Minden, going out on scouts, &c, &c.

1780. Enlisted in Capt. Garret Putman's (5) Company at Johnstown in the Spring season of the year, Col. Harpers regt for nine months. Soon after having enlisted, was ordered to go to Fort Plain, for the purpose of keeping garrison, going on scouts &c. until about the first of August when by a special order from said Capt. Putman was ordered to go to Johnstown & join a company commanded by Capt. John Little, (6) for the express purpose of exploring the frontier settlements, woods, mountains, rivers &c. &c. until some time in the fall season of the same year, when he was ordered by said Capt. Little to return to said Capt. Putman's company, which was then stationed at Fort Plain.

1781. (7) Again enlisted in Capt. Garret Putman's Company for nine months, under Col. Willett, in the Spring season of the year; was mustered, or enrolled, and joined said Capt. Putman's Company at Fort Hunter. Soon after went to Fort Plain to guard the Fort, go out on Scouts &c, &c. And on the arrival of several boats, (up the Mohawk river, bound for Fort Stanwix,) loaded with provisions for the Army, went on shore to look out for enemy some distance ahead of the boats; the object of which was to guard the boats, so that they might arrive in safety at Fort Stanwix. Soon after returned to Fort Plain, with the boats in company with said Capt. Putman, and several others, members of his company. That again in the summer season of the same year, was ordered by Capt. Putman to go to Fort Stanwix, in company with several others, soldiers, (this applicant being then a Corporal,) for the express purpose of guarding the Fort, when in about ten days after arriving at Fort Stanwix, said Fort was evacuated, and all its contents removed to Schenectada, in boats down the Mohawk river.

1782. In the Spring season of the year, enlisted in a company commanded by Capt. Abner French, (8) Col. Willet for nine months at Johnstown. From thence to Fort House, then in Palatine, to guard the fort, go on scouts, &c, &c, and spent said nine months by guarding the different Forts along the Mohawk river as far up as Herkimer, and also at, and about Johnstown. The service thus rendered was in the capacity of a Corporal.

The sequel will exhibit more particularly the several engagements and battles in which he was engaged, and descriptive answers to the several interrogatories prescribed by the War Department, but prior to entering into those particulars, a more definite description must be given about the manner of entering the service in Col. Hazen's regiment, commanded by Col. Antle, for which a pension or pay had been allowed under the act of 1828. That some time in the fall season of the year 1782, while serving as above stated in Capt. French's company in Col. Willet's regt. there was a regt. of the Continental line, came up the Mohawk river as far as Caughnawaga, commanded by Lt. Col. Antle, (9) of which Hazen was the Colonel commandant, and as they were strangers to the surrounding country; this applicant was detached from Capt. French's company and by mutual consent of the officers placed under the command of Colonel Antle for the express purpose of assisting his regt in sending out scouting parties, that they might serve to advantage in exploring the frontier settlements.—That Col. Antle with his regt. remained in and about Johnstown, until after the close of the year 1782, and as far into the year '83 as the time when the news was fast circulating that peace was declared, which was some time in the winter or spring season. That this applicant remained in said regt. until after the time had expired for which he enlisted in Capt. French's Company, and that about the time when Col. Antle was about to leave Johnstown with his regiment, this applicant received a discharge from Col. Antles regt, signed either by himself or Capt. Lloyd, (10) and was immediately enrolled in Capt. Little's Company of Militia because Capt. French's company had served out the time for which they had engaged, and were all discharged from the service, and returned to their respective places of abode:--Therefore, whatever is found on file in the claim under the Act of 1828, or any communication having been sent to the Pension Office, since that time which might differ from the above statement was not designed to fraud, or deceive the department, or government of the United States, but was sincerely believed that said Act of 1828, both in letter and spirit embraced such a claim.

That in the year 1781, summer season, while going the second time to Fort Stanwix, as previously described, the party was fired at by a small party of Indians who fell in their way, and after a few shots were exchanged, the enemy fled, with their wounded and one man on our side was also wounded.

That soon after the evacuation of Fort Stanwix (11) Col. Willet gave authority to Lt. Solomon Woodworth (12) to select out of his regiment or from the militia a company of men to be at his command for the purpose of ranging the frontier settlements, to make discoveries &c. &c. A company of forty men being soon selected, they set out in a northeasterly direction, and after traversing the woods a distance of some ten miles, a party of Indians and Tories lay in ambush said to be eighty in number, and that in less than a minute after the firing commenced, twenty-five men were killed and lay dead on the field of battle. A few men made their escape after the firing ceased, at the time of taking the remainder prisoners, by being swifter on foot than the Indians; this applicant having been one of that number, after having been through the midst of the firing when bullets flew in every direction around him. After the burial of the dead the next day, and the fatigue of the battle had passed away, this applicant returned to the company from which he had been taken.

Again in the fall season of the same year a battle was waged near Johnstown between a party of Indians and Tories, about four hundred in number and Colonel Willet with his regt. and many others. This applicant being out with a scouting party the same day, consisting of twelve in number viz: Capt. Little, John Eikler, John Brothers, Peter Yost, Henry Shew, this applicant & others whose names are forgotten; on hearing the firing, turned their course towards Johnstown and came in as a reinforcement before the battle was over. This is what is commonly called the Hall battle. (13)

Having thus served through a war of suffering and hardships & privations to establish a Republican form of government &c, &c, he now hereby claims a pension for services rendered, as set forth in the foregoing declaration, and particularly requests that for services rendered in the capacity of a Corporal shall be first computer, and the remainder of the time filled up with that of a private soldier, and that of having been a prisoner of war.

He hereby relinquishes every claim whatever to a pension or annuity except the present, and declares that his name is not on the pension roll of the agency of any state, but that he had been pensioned under the Act of 1828, and has been suspended.

Interrogatiories.

Question I. Where & in what year were you born?

Answer. On the 15th April 1763 at Johnstown.

II. Have you any record of your age?

Ans. My father recorded it in his bible and it was destroyed by fire June 3rd, 1778, the day we were taken prisoners. My sons Godfrey recorded it in a Bible some forty years ago, and has it now in his possession in Jefferson Co.

III. Where were you living when called into service?

Ans. Sacondaga. After that, resided in Johnstown at the several times of going into the service as more particularly described in the foregoing application.

IV. Where have you lived since the Revolutionary War and where do you now live?

Ans. Johnstown, Montgomery Co. NY

Northampton, Montgomery Co. NY

Leray, Jefferson County and now in Broadalbin, Fulton Co. NY.

V. How were you called into service?

Ans. First, by being ordered into, by Solomon Woodworth a noncommissioned officer. Second, a substitute for Michael Gollinger. Third, by and agreement with a class, termed enlisted, at Johnstown for 7 months at three different periods to wit, 1780, '81, & '82, as set forth in the foregoing declaration.

VI. State the names of some of the regular officers who were with the troops where you served; such continental regiments as you can recollect &c.

Ans. Col. Frederick Fisher, Lt. Col. Veeder (14), Col. Gansevoort (15), Lt. Col. Willet, Col. Harper, Lt. Col. Antle, Major VanBenscouten (16), Fink (17), Eisenlord (18), Capt. Lloyd, Lt Martin, Capt. Sacket (19), Capt. Little, Capt. Fonda, Capt. Bennett (20), Capt. Van Slyck (21), Vrooman (22), Tierce (23).

VII. Did you ever receive a discharge.

I think I had some kind of a discharge from Lt. Col. Antle or Capt. Lloyd, if so, it has been mislaid or lost. (Signed) Jacob Shew

Sworn to and subscribed this 4th day of July A.D. 1848. A. S. Wait, Clerk

Letter of inquiry dated March 4, 1939 in the pension folder.

The data which follow were obtained from papers on file in claim for pension, S.22985, based upon the service of Jacob Shew in the Revolutionary War.

Jacob Shew was born April 15, 1763 in Johnstown, New York. He was the son of Godfrey Shew, name of his mother not stated. Godfrey Shew moved his family from Johnstown, to Sacondaga, New York.

While living in Sacondaga, New York, June 2, 1778, Jacob Shew, with his father Godfrey Shew (24), and brothers, Stephen, John, and Godfrey, Junior, were ordered out by Sergeant Solomon Woodworth of Colonel Fisher's New York Regiment, on an alarm in pursuit of Indians; they were captured by Indians, their home was burned and their mother was driven back to Johnstown. Godfrey Shew and his sons, Stephen and Jacob Shew were carried to Canada and held on a prison ship at Montreal, at Quebec, and at Halifax, about December, 31, Jacob Shew was sent to Boston, and there exchanged, on reaching Sudbury, he had small pox, and did not reach Johnstown until March 17, 1779, where his mother was still living.

Jacob Shew volunteered in the fall of 1779, served four weeks in Captain Giles Fonda's company, Colonel Fisher's regiment; he enlisted in the spring of 1780, served nine months in Captains Garret Putnam's and John Little's companies, part of the time in Colonel Harper's regiment; he enlisted in the spring of 1781, served nine months as corporal in Captain Garret Putnam's company, Colonel Willet's regiment; he enlisted in the spring of 1782, served as corporal in Captains Abner French's and P. Tearse's companies, Colonel Marinus Willet's regiment, was transferred to Colonel Hazen's regiment, and served therein until the close of the war. He was out in frequent alarms, and much of his duty was in guarding the forts along the Mohawk River.

The soldier, Jacob Shew (25), was allowed pension on his application executed August 22, 1828, at which time he was living in Northampton, Montgomery County, New York. He was later in life allowed pension under the Act of June 7, 1832. He was living in 1848 in Broadalbin, New York. He died January 23, 1853.

The soldier's sons, Godfrey Shew was living in 1848 in Jefferson County, New York, soldiers' son, John I. Shew, was living in 1849 in Broadalbin, New York.

Godfrey Shew, brother of the soldier, was seventy-seven years old in 1848.

Reference was made to one Henry Shew, but no relationship to the family is given.

End Notes—S.229854—Jacob Shew

1. Solomon Woodworth was at this time a Sergeant in Captain Samuel Rees' or Reese, Reece, etc., Company in Colonel Frederick Visscher's or Fisher's Third Regiment of Tryon County Militia.
2. The commander of the raiding party was Lieutenant John Ross of the 34th Regiment. Ross is the same man who raided the Mohawk Valley in October of 1781 as a Major of the Second Battalion of the King's Royal Regiment of New York.
3. Michael Gallinger served as a private in Captain Jellis Fonda's Company of Exempts in Colonel Visscher's Regiment. The muster roll was misfiled in Colonel Abraham Wemple's Second Regiment of Albany County Militia. There was a Captain Jellis J. Fonda in that regiment but they are two different officers. FROM: Revolutionary War Rolls 1775-1783, Series M-246, Roll 77, Folder 170, National Archives, Washington, D.C.
4. Giles Fonda and Jellis Fonda are one and the same. His first name is often misspelled and or mispronounced. In the Dutch and German languages the J is pronounced as a Y but in English it is usually is written as Giles.

5. Captain Garret Putman was appointed on May 11, 1780 in Lieutenant-Colonel Commandant John Harper's Regiment of New York State Levies. The regiment was discharged on November 30, 1780.
6. John Little was a captain in Colonel Visscher's Regiment. He received his commission on March 8, 1781.
7. On April 27, 1781, Garret Putman was appointed Captain in Lieutenant-Colonel Commandant Marinus Willett's Regiment of New York State Levies.
8. Abner French was commissioned on July 24, 1781 as Captain in Colonel Commandant Willett's Regiment. Willett was appointed colonel on April 10, 1782.
9. Jacob is mistaken as to the year 1782 when Lieutenant-Colonel Edward Antill of Colonel Moses Hazen's Second Canadian Continental Regiment came up the Mohawk River. The Second Canadian actually arrived in late spring at Caughnawaga and left in early July 1781 for West Point. Captain French lived at or near Warrens Bush which is present day Town of Florida, Montgomery County, New York, and was in the area in 1781 but was not in active service in 1781.
10. Richard Lloyd was a Captain in Colonel Hazen's Regiment. Jacob's name does not appear on any of their muster rolls. FROM: Revolutionary War Rolls 1775-1783, Series M-246, Rolls 131 and 132, National Archives, Washington, D.C.
11. It was Colonel Philip VanCortlandt's Second New York Continental Regiment which was at Fort Schuyler or Fort Stanwix from January 1, 1781 to June of the same year. A serious fire at the fort destroyed the barracks and severe flooding in May had put the fort in such a state that the Second New York could not repair the fort, and after a council of officers it was decided to abandon the fort and by mid-June all of the military stores had been removed to Fort Herkimer.
12. Woodworth and Richard Randolph Wilson were serving as Lieutenants in Captain Thomas Skinner's Company in 1781 in Lieutenant-Colonel Willett's Regiment. They were both in the Ranger Company and both of them were killed in the ambush on September 7, 1781.
13. John Eikler, John Brothers, Peter Yost, and Henry Shew all served in Captain Little's Company in Colonel Visscher's Regiment. Captain Little was wounded and Corporal Eikler was killed in the Battle of Johnstown on October 25, 1781.
14. Lieutenant-Colonel Volkert Veeder of Colonel Visscher's Regiment.
15. Peter Gansevoort, Colonel of the Third New York Continental Regiment.
16. Elias VanBenscouten served as a Major in Colonel Willett's Regiment.
17. Andrew Finck or Fink served as a Major in Willett's Regiment in 1781 and 1782.

18. John Eisenlord served as a Major in the Fourth Regiment of Tryon County Militia commanded by Colonel Peter Bellinger. Eisenlord was killed at the Battle of Oriskany on August 6, 1777.
19. Samuel Sacket was a Captain in the Fourth New York Continental Regiment. This company was stationed at Fort Johnstown from November of 1778 to about May of 1779.
20. Amos Bennett was commissioned as the Second Lieutenant in Captain Joseph Yeomans' Company in Colonel Visscher's Regiment on March 8, 1781.
21. Major Hermanus VanSlyke of Colonel Jacob Klock's Second Regiment of Tryon County Militia. He was killed at the Battle of Oriskany on August 6, 1777.
22. Captain Walter Vrooman was in Colonel Harper's Regiment in 1780.
23. Peter B. Tierce was a captain in Colonel Willett's Regiment in 1782 and 1783.
24. Godfrey and Stephen Shew both served in Captain Fonda's Company in Colonel Visscher's Regiment. Godfrey Shew Jr. was too young to serve.
25. Jacob married Hannah Putman on March 10, 1787. Hannah died on October 5, 1847. Jacob died January 23, 1853. They are buried in the Evan Mills cemetery, Town of LeRoy, Jefferson County, N.Y.

Pension Application for John Shulp

S.28877
Private, Captain Faulkner, Col. Paulding
State of New York
Orange County SS

On this fourth day of September 1832, personally appeared in open court before the Judges of the court of common pleas in and for said County of Orange now sitting John Shulp a resident of the town of Montgomery in said county of Orange and state aforesaid aged seventy two years who being first duly sworn according to law doth on his oath make the following declaration in order to obtain the benefit of the act of Congress passed June 7, 1832.

That he entered the service of the United States under the following named officers and served as herein stated. That at the time he entered the service he resided in said town and county and shortly before Fort Montgomery on the North River was taken by the English in the year 1777 as he believes he was ordered out by Captain Mattheas Felter (1) of said town and County to go to said Fort Montgomery that he went and served in the company commanded by Captain William Faulkner (2) till after said Fort was taken—that he was there at the time it was taken (3) and that said Capt Faulkner was wounded.

That he then returned home and in a few days was ordered out again and served at Newburgh and New Windsor in said County of Orange under Henricus Smith (4) a Lieutenant in said company commanded by Captain Felter and was engaged in guarding those places against the English who had after the taking of Fort Montgomery from up the North River to Kingston.

That in these two several tours of service he was out and in service about one month.

That in the year 1779 as he thinks he went out in the eight months service and served under said Captain William Faulkner in the Regiment commanded by Col. Paulding (5) & Maj. VanBenschoten (6)—that he first went with the company to Warwasink in the county of Ulster in said state on the frontiers—then to Hunk in said county and from thence to [Luskanora?] to join some troops who were there on an expedition to go further west (7)—that when he came there the troops had marched on and left word by a paper posted upon a tree that the troops with which he served might come on a return as they pleased—that they returned to Warwasink and from thence marched to Haverstraw in the State of New Jersey when he was discharged from service at the end of the eight months by Col. Paulding.

That in the summer of 1780 he served three months under Captain Drake (8) in the said Regiment commanded by Col. Paulding and Maj VanBenschoten—that he was taken by Cap Cris (9) over to Fishkill in the County of Dutchess and then delivered over to said Cap. Drake and after staying there a few days went with said Cap. Drakes Company to West Point—after staying there eight or ten days marched to Albany and laid there about eight days—from thence marched to Schenectady and remained there a few days—from thence marched to Fort Ranseller (10) near a place called Stone Robby and remained there for some time—and from there marched with a part of said Regiment to Fort Stanwix (11) and after remaining there a short time returned to Stone Robby and was there dismissed the service at the end of said three months by said Col. Paulding.

That the said discharges are lost and that he has no written evidence of his service except as herein after evidenced—and that the periods of his services are stated under certain years yet he is not certain of their accuracy and states them according to the best of his recollection.

That said Cap William Faulkner died within one year and that shortly before his death he called upon him to learn if he recollected his services in his company during the revolution—that said Cap Faulkner informed the applicant that he did remember the same and produced an original pay roll of the company in which the applicant served and that his name was written in said roll.

He hereby relinquishes every claim whatever to a pension or annuity except the present and declares that his name is not on the pensin roll of the agency of any state that he was born in the town of Montgomery in said county of Orange and ahs always resided there—has no record of his age and does not recollect the names of any of the regular officers and that Henry Crest, Christian Roat, of Montgomery can testify in his favour. (Signed with his mark) John Shulp

Sworn & Subscribed the day & year aforesaid. Asa Dunmore, Clerk

End Notes—S.23877—John Shulp

1. Mathias Felter or Felton was the Captain of the Fourth Company, Hanover Precinct, in Colonel James McClaughrey's Regiment.
2. William Faulkner was the Captain of the Fifth Company, west side of Wallkill, in Colonel McClaughrey's Regiment.
3. Fort Montgomery was attacked and captured on October 6, 1777.
4. Henry Smith was the first lieutenant in Captain Felter's Company.
5. In April of 1779, Albert Pawling was appointed Lieutenant-Colonel Commandant of one of two regiments of levies to be raised in New York. Captain Faulkner was appointed in April to serve in the regiment. His lieutenants were Levi DeWitt and Thomas Ostrander. The October 1779 Pay Roll of Captain Faulkner's Company does contain John's name as serving as a private at a rate of pay of 6 1/3 dollars per month.
6. Elias VanBenschoten was appointed Major to Pawling's Regiment on April 22, 1779.
7. They were supposed to join Major General John Sullivan's Army to attack the Iroquois Village in the western part of New York State in 1779.
8. Joshua Drake was appointed July 1, 1780 as a Captain in Colonel William Malcolm's Regiment of New York Levies. Major VanBenschoten was appointed to serve in Malcolm's Regiment. On Captain Drake's Muster Roll of the July & August 1780, John is listed as enlisting on July 25, 1780 as a private for 3 months. On the Muster Roll, September & October 1780, John is listed as deserting on Oct 16th. FROM: Revolutionary War Rolls 1775-1783, Series M-246, Roll 72, folder 75, National Archives, Washington, D.C.
9. Possibly Ensign William Crist of Captain Felter's Company.
10. Colonel Malcolm arrived in late August at Fort Rensselaer in the Mohawk Valley.
11. On September 25, Captains Drake, Jonathan Lawrence and Lieutenants Cornelius Ackerson or Eckerson, and Peter TenBroeck transferred to Lieutenant-Colonel Commandant John Harper's Regiment of New York State Levies. On September 26, Colonel Malcolm with his regiment and Harper's Regiment marched for Fort Schuyler or Fort Stanwix, to relieve the First New York Continental Regiment which had garrisoned that post since late November of 1778. Colonel Malcolm left Harper's Regiment at the fort under the command of Major James M. Hughes who had transferred from Colonel Lewis DuBois' Regiment of New York Levies to Harper's Regiment. Colonel Malcolm marched with his regiment towards the Highlands as word had been received of Major General Benedict Arnold's treason and defection to the enemy.

Pension Application for Henry Sitts

S.42297
State of New York
Montgomery County

On the Fourteenth day of December 1830 appeared before the Court of Common Pleas of the County of Montgomery in said State being a court of Record for said county being made for in express terms by the Statute creating it, Henry Sitts resident in said county and Seventy Six years and upwards who being who being first duly sworn according to law does on his oath make the following declaration in order to obtain the provision made by the act of Congress of the 18th of March 1818. And of the first of May 1820. That in the month of March or April 1776 he enlisted in the State of New York in the Company Commanded by Captain Getman (1) in the Regiment Commanded by Col. Gansevort (2) in the New York Line of Continental troops on the Continental establishment, that he continued to serve in Said Corps until the month of August 1777, when he was honorably discharged at what is now Palatine in the County of Montgomery in the State of New York.

That he hereby relinquishes every claim whatsoever to a pension except the present, that his name has not been placed on the pension list, that in the month of September 1818 this deponent made a declaration in order to obtain the benefits of the Law of the 18th of March 1818 which is hereto annexed. Marked (A) and at that time procured the affidavit on John Bockus which is hereto annexed. Marked (B) but at that time this deponent had a little personal property and was able to labour and this deponent supposed that the amount of the property he then had and his ability to labour might prevent his obtaining a pension under said act and he did not then go on with it. The expending and loss of the property which he then had and his increasing years and infirmities and inability to labour, now renders a pension absolutely necessary for the support of this deponent.

And in pursuance of the act of the first of May 1820, I do solemnly swear that I was a resident citizen of the United States on the 18th day of March 1818 and that I have not since that time by gift, sale or in any manner disposed of my property or any part thereof with intent thereby so to diminish it as to bring myself within the provisions of an act of Congress Entitled "an act to provide for certain persons engaged in the land and naval service of the United States in the Revolutionary War passed on the 18th day of March 1818 and that I have not nor has any person in trust for me any property or securities contracts or debts due to me nor have I any income other than what is contained in the schedule hereto annexed and by me subscribed. That since the eighteenth day of March 1818 the following changes have been made in my property viz.

Description of property owned on 18th March 1818	Names of Persons to whom disposed of	Time of Sale	Amt of Money or description of property rec'd in

			return
One Cow	Adam Kesler	1822 March	$13.00 on a debt I owed him
One other Cow	George Sitts	1822 March	Paid in board I am not agreed on
A quantity of household furniture consisting of kettles and dishes, bedding, clothing which I then owned. I have since given and distributed among my nine girls upon my wife's death in June 1823. The whole net worth more than $60 or $70.			

I have no other property on the 18th of March 1818 nor have I owned or had any since. Sworn and declared the 14th day of December 1830, in open court. Real estate None, Personal Estate none whatever, except my clothing. Henry Sitts (signed) A.J. Comrie Clerk

I owe John Warner of Minden, Montgomery County Merchant for goods, about fourteen dollars. I owe also Moris Graves of Springfield Otsego County a NY Physician for doctor's bills about $5.50. The occupation of the declarant Henry Sitts is that of a farmer but owing to his old age, he is unable to pursue it and never expects to be. He has no family, has fourteen children alive on whom he is entirely dependant for support. Henry Sitts.

Sworn in open court the 14th of December 1830. A. J. Comrie, Clerk

End Notes—S.42297—Henry Sitts or Suts, Sutes, Suts, Sit, Seats, etc.

1. Henry's name is not on the muster or payroll of Captain Christian Getman's Second Company of Tryon County Rangers, only a Johannes Sutes appears on the rolls. This company was formed in August of 1776 and it was discharged on March 27, 1777. FROM: Revolutionary War Rolls 1775-1783, Series M-246, Roll 74, folder 103, National Archives, Washington, D.C.
2. Peter Gansevoort in 1776 was serving under Colonel Goose VanScahick in an un-numbered New York Continental Regiment. Gansevoort for most of this time at Fort George near Lake George. On November 21, 1776, Gansevoort was appointed Colonel of the Third New York Continental Regiment. This regiment didn't come to the Mohawk Valley until March of 1777.
3. In one of his other applications he said he had served in the militia. A Hendrick Sits is listed as a private serving in Captain John Hess'

Company and in the Captain Peter Wagner, Jr. Company in Colonel Jacob Klock's Second Regiment of Tryon County Militia. He also says the fought in the Battle of Stone Arabia on October 19, 1780 and the Battle of Johnstown on October 25, 1781. He also stated his father was Peter and that he (Henry) was born on August 29, 1754.

Pension Application for William Slutt or Sloat or Sloot

W.19370 (Widow: Susannah)
B.L.Wt.13199-160-55
State of New York
Ulster County SS.

On this seventeenth day of April one thousand eight hundred & eighteen before me the subscriber one of the Judges of the Court of Common Pleas in & for the County of Ulster in the State of New York personally appeared William Slutt aged Fifty Six years resident in the town of Shawangunk in said County of Ulster who being by me first duly sworn according to Law doth on his Oath make the following declaration in order to obtain the provision made by the late Act of Congress Entitled "An Act of provide for certain persons engaged in the Land and Naval service of the United States in the Revolutionary War", that he the said William Slutt enlisted at Fort Montgomery in the State of New York in the company commanded by Thomas Lee in the 5th New York Regiment commanded by Col. Dubois (1) in the beginning of the year 1777, that he continued to serve in said regiment in the same corps until the fifth day of February 1780. When he was discharged from service at "Hut near Morris Town in the State of New Jersey at which time he received the Original Discharge from John Johnston, (2) Captain commandant to this Deposition annexed—that he was in the Battle of Fort Montgomery (where he was taken prisoner & remained such prisoner for about thirteen months) at the taking of Onondaga (3) and with the detachment commanded by General Sullivan (4) sent against the Indians and that he is in reduced circumstances & stands in need of the assistance of his country for Support. (Signed) William Slutt.

Sworn & declared before the day & year aforesaid. James Kain, Judge

State of New York
Orange County SS.

On the seventh day of Augt 1838 personally appeared before me the undersigned one of the Judges of the Court of Common Pleas in and for the said county Susannah Sloot but called Slutt or Slote a resident of Montgomery in said County and State aged seventy one years who being duly sworn according to law doth on her oath make the following declaration in order to obtain the benefit of the provision made by the act of Congress passed July 7th 1838 entitled "An act granting half pay and pension to certain Widows" That she is the widow of William Sloot who was a private in the war of the Revolution & a pensioner under the act of Congress passed 18th of March 1818.

She further declares that she was married to the said William Sloot on the first day of Nov'r in the year seventeen hundred and eighty four.

That her husband the upon said William Sloot died on the first day of January 1823. That she was not married to him prior to his leaving the service but the marriage took place previous to first of January Seventeen Hundred and ninety four viz at the time above stated. (Signed with her mark) Susannah Sloot

Sworn to and subscribed on the day and year above written before me. H.W. Elliott Judge of Orange Com. Pleas.

End Notes—W.19370—William Slutt

1. William enlisted as a private on April 9, 1777 in Captain Thomas Lee's Company (Eighth Company) in Colonel Lewis DuBois Fifth New York Continental Regiment for three years. Also an Abraham Slutt enlisted on the same date and a Marvil Slutt had enlisted on January 1, 1777. Captain Lee resigned on May 19, 1778 and Samuel English the Second Lieutenant commanded the company until late 1780. The First Lieutenant Henry Pawling who had been taken prisoner at Fort Montgomery on October 6, 1777 and William was also taken prisoner. William returned from captivity on August 12, 1778. William and Abraham were discharged at Morristown, New Jersey on December 9, 1780. Marvil Slutt was discharged on January 1, 1780. No relationship on the muster rolls is given between Marvel, Abraham, and William. FROM: Revolutionary War Rolls 1775-1783, Series M-249, Roll 72, folder 68, National Archives, Washington, D.C.
2. John Johnson was appointed captain on November 21, 1776 in Colonel DuBois Regiment. When the Fifth New York was consolidated with the Second New York on January 1, 1781, Captain Johnson was discharged.
3. The Onondaga Village on Oneida Lake was destroyed on April 20, 1779. Colonel Goose VanSchaick of the First New York Continental Regiment commanded the American forces.
4. The Sullivan-Clinton Expedition against the Iroquois of Western New York was in 1779. The Fifth New York had been stationed in the Schoharie and Mohawk Valleys from November 1778 until about mid June 1779.

Pension Application for Cornelius Smith

S.22996

Invalid, Cornelius Smith, priv., Rev. War. Act June 7th 32. Index:--Vol. 2, Page 380?

A payroll of Capt. Jellis Fonda's Co. of Associate Exempts of Col. Frederic[k] Fisher's Regt NY Militia from Aug 10 to 15, 1777, an abstract of pay rolls of Capt. Jellis Fonda's Co. of Associate Exempts from 1777 to 1781. A paper dated 1777, entitled Frederick Wemple's (1) statement or account of militia service.

A list of Capt. Jellis Fonda's men from June 6 to 13, 1777.

The above papers have been removed from this claim to be forwarded to the war Dept. AW. Sent to War Dept. Jan 16, 1913. [Stamped: Oct 8, 1910]

Cornelius Smith of Montgomery Co. in the State of N. York who was a Private in the company commanded by Captain Fonda of the Regt commanded by Col. Fisher in the N. York Line for 6 months. Inscribed on the Roll of Albany at the rate of 20 Dollars ---- Cents per annum, to commence on the 4th day of March 1831.

Certificate of pension issued the 16th day of July 1838 and sent to Thos. Sammons, Present

Arrears to the 4th of March '38 140.00; Semi-anl. Allowance ending 4 Sep. '38 10.00. $150.00 (Revolutionary Claim Act June 7, 1832. Recorded by D. Bruen Clerk, Book E. Vol. 4 Page 67.

Montgomery County
State of New York SS.

On this 13th Day of June 1838 personally appeared in open Court before the Hon. Abam Morel, the First Judge of the Montgomery County Court and Samuel Gilbert, John Hand, David F. Sacia & Stephen Yates, Judges of said Court now sitting Cornelius Smith (2) Town of Mohawk, County of Montgomery, State of New York aged 94 years the 19th day of August last past old style, who being duly sworn according to law doth on his oath make the following declaration in order to obtain the benefit of the act of Congress passed July 7th 1832. That he entered the service under the following named officers and served as hereafter stated. That he was a private in the War of the Revolution and served in Capt. Jellis Fonda's Company of Associated Exempts in Colonel Frederick Fisher's Regiment and served in the above company till the close of the war, that old age and infirmity prevents him from giving a more particular statement of Identifying the service or the duration of each tour of service that he has seen an abstract of part of the Pay Rolls of Capt. Jellis Fonda's Company when the said company was credited for 3 months and 8 days service and also to separate pay rolls of Capt. Jellis Fonda Company not included in the abstract the one allowing 6 days the other 7 days service in 1777 in the above abstract the service commenced in the year 1778 and ended in the year 1782 and furthermore that he saw an old Statement or record of Hendrick Wemple who was a private in the above said Company and who was always considered a man of veracity and truth and that after examining the statement or record of the above Hendrick Wemple which record specifies 10 separate tours and designates the places where the duty was performed he fully believes the above statement or record of the said Wemple to be true which several tours amount to 32 days and in which several tours he well recollect serving and that the above duty was performed in the then County of Tryon State of New York and also that he was one year a member of the Tryon County Committee and that he done a considerable teaming for the garrison and troops stationed in

Tryon County. And furthermore he does not know of a single officer or private now living who served in Capt. Jellis Fonda's Company of Associated exempts excepting himself & therefore must rely upon Documentary evidence such as the abstract of Capt. Jellis Fonda, the Pay Rolls of the said Fonda and the statement or record of Mr. Hendric Wemple (3) as herein before stated making it all together 6 months and 23 days. He hereby relinquishes every claim whatever to a pension or annuity except the present and declares that his name is not on the pension roll of the United States or any state whatever and the documents and reference to papers are hereunto attached. (Signed) Cornelius Smith

Sworn in open court the day and year above written. A. J. Comrie Clerk

I, the Rev. Abraham Van Horne of the Town of Mohawk in the County of Montgomery lately the Clergyman of the Congregation of Caughnawaga in said town, and still residing in the same Town do hereby certify that I am well acquainted with Cornelius Smith who has subscribed and sworn to the above declaration. That I believe him to have been ninety four years of age in August last. That he has been a member of my church in good standing for thirty six years past. That he is respected and believed in the neighborhood where he resides to have been a soldier of the Revolution, and that I concur in that opinion. (Signed) Abraham Van Horne N.D.M.

Sworn in open court 14th June 1838. A. J. Comrie Clerk

End Notes—Cornelius Smith—S.22996

1. According to Cornelius' declaration it is Hendrick Wemple that had made a statement.
2. Cornelius is listed in several of Captain Fonda's Company muster and pay rolls serving at different times as a private or corporal. The Company of Exempts was in Colonel Frederick Visscher's (Fisher's) Third Regiment of Tryon County Militia. FROM: Revolutionary War Rolls 1775-1783, Series M-246, Roll 74, folder 100, National Archives, Washington DC. Some of the rolls are misfiled in Colonel Abraham Wemple's Regiment, Roll 77, folder 170. There was a Captain Jellis J. Fonda that served in the regiment.
3. Hendrick Wemple served as a sergeant in Captain Fonda's Company in Colonel Visscher's Regiment.

Pension Application for John Edward Smith

W.1503 (Widow: Mary Jersey, made her application on September 6, 1848 at Clarkstown, Rockland County, New york and gave the following information. She married John Edward Smith July 6th AD 1797, by the Rev'd John N. Boyd, Presbyterian minister. John was born April 25, 1760, Mary was born April 3, 1774.) Children: Abraham Snider Smith born Dec 6, 1798; Jacob Halstead Smith born Nov. 28, 1802; Phebe Smith born January 30, 1805; Anna Smith born April 19, 1807; Peter Smith born February 21, 1800. John died January 13, 1848.)

State of New York
Rockland County SS.

On this twenty eighth day of November—in the year A.D. 1832, personally appeared in open court, before the Judges of the Court of Common Please [Pleas] now sitting John Ed. Smith, a resident of the town of Clarkstown, in the county of Rockland and State of New York aged seventy two years, the twenty fifth day of April 1832, who being first duly sworn according to law, doth on his oath make the following declaration, in order to obtain the benefit of the act of Congress, passed June 7, 1832. The he entered the service of the United States under the folloing [following] named officers and served as herin [herein] stated. That in the Month of March 1777, he then residing in the town of Clarkstown aforesaid, enlisted for nine months in a company commanded by Capt. John Stagg (1), who was an agent in the Continental line and ordered to enlist men to break stone for the magizene [magazine] built at West Point, and they was stationed at Capt. Jacob Onderdonks (2), where he served his term of enlistment, a breaking stone for that purpose, then in the spring of the year 1778 he entered the service in a company commanded by Capt. Jacob Onderdonk, in a Regiment commanded by Col'n A. Hawkes Hay, and served in that company every fourth week until the spring of the year 1779, that then he entered the service in a company commanded by Capt. Aury Smith (3), in the aforesaid regiment, which was mostly commanded by Gilbert Cooper (4), the Lieutenant Col'n and served therein every fourth week until the close of the Revolutionary War, or at least to the latter part of the year 1782. That during the time he served under Capts Onderdonk and Smith he was chiefly employed a guarding along the West Shore of the Hudson River, but at times a scouting through the now County of Rockland and the County of Bergen in the state of New Jersey to protect the inhabitants from the inroads of the enimy [enemy] who was in the constant habit of marching through the countys aforesaid, taking everything of value that came in their way, that positively to state the time he was out on duty under Capt's Onderdonk (5) and Smith he cannot but is confident it exceeds one year, the he has no documentary evidence of any of his services, as he did not receive any written discharge, that from his infancy he has resided in the now town of Clarkstown, and all the positive proof he can offer is some of the men that served with him. He hereby relinquishes every claim whatever to a pension or annuity except the present, and declares that his name is not on the Pension Roll of the agency of any state sworn to and subscribed, the day and year aforesaid. (Signed) John Ed. Smith. In open court. David Pye, Clerk

End Notes—W.1503—John Edward Smith

1. So far a record of this Captain John Stagg has not been found. The only John Stagg found was a Second Lieutenant in Colonel William Malcolm's Additional Continental Regiment. Lieutenant Stagg was

appointed on March 4, 1777 and Malcolm's Regiment was in the Highlands during 1777 which leads to the possibility that it was this Lieutenant Stagg that John was referring to.

2. Jacob Onderdonck was a Captain in Colonel Ann Hawkes Hay's Third Regiment (Haverstraw Precinct) of Orange County Militia.
3. Arie Smith also was a Captain in Colonel Hays' Regiment.
4. On May 28, 1778, "Resolved on application to his Excellency the Governor for consolidating the two Regiments lately commanded by Colonel A. Hawkes Hays and Colonel Lent, in Orange County". Colonel Hays now commanded the consolidated regiments and Gilbert Cooper was the Lieutenant-Colonel.
5. On February 19, 1834, John amended his earlier application and added that in July of 1776 he enlisted in Captain Jacob Onderdonck's Company in Colonel Isaac Nicoll's Regiment of Levies for five months. The company for the most part was stationed at or near Peekskill for most of this term. First Lieutenant Resolvert VanHouten made out a deposition on February 17, 1834 confirming John's five months service. Lieutenant VanHouten also served under Captain Onderdonck in Colonel Hays Regiment. There are only regimental returns for Colonel Nicoll's Regiment which list only the officers and the strengths of their companies. FROM: Revolutionary War Rolls 1775-1783, Series M-246, Roll 75, Roll 132, National Archives, Washington, D.C.

Pension Application for Levi Smith

W.2261 (Widow: Elizabeth) Levi was born Mar 20, 1764 at Derby Conn. Died at New Milford, Litchfield Co., Conn. June 7, 1842 or June 18, 1841.
B.L.Wt.31322-160-55
Declaration: In order to obtain the benefits of the 2d Section of the Act of 3d February 1853.
State of Connecticut
Litchfield County SS.

On this 11th day of April 1853 before me Judge of the Probate Court for the District of New Milford, personally appeared Elizabeth Smith a resident of New Milford in the County of Litchfield, State of Connecticut aged eight two 82 years, who first being duly sworn according to law, doth on her oath, make the following declaration in order to obtain the benefits of the provision made by the Act of Congress passed on the 3d February, 1853, granting pensions to widows of persons who served during the Revolutionary War.

That she is the Widow of Levi Smith who was a private in the Army of the Revolution and a pensioner of the United States on the roll of the Connecticut agency under the Act of June 7, 1832 at Eighty dollars per annum his pension certificate was issued at the War Department 20 May 1833.

She further declares that she was married to the said Levi Smith on the ninth day of July—one thousand eight hundred and twenty six and that her husband the aforesaid Levi Smith died on the 27th day of June 1842. That she was not married to him prior to the 2d day of January 1800, but at the time above stated. She further declares that she is now a Widow. (Signed with her mark) Elizabeth Smith.

Sworn to and subscribed on the day and year above written before me. Frederick Chittendon, Judge of the Probate for the District of New Milford in the County of Litchfield & State of Connecticut.

State of Connecticut
County of Litchfield
Probate, District of New Milford SS.

On this 4th day of August AD 1832, personally appeared in open Court, before the Court of Probate for said district now sitting at New Milford in s'd District & County, Levi Smith a resident of said town of New Milford aged Sixty Eight years who being first duly sworn according to law, doth on his oath, make the following declaration; in order to obtain the benefit of the provision of the Act of Congress passed June 7th 1832.

That he entered the service of the United States under the following named officers & served as herein stated.

That in the winter of 1780 - 1 he enlisted in the Company commanded by Capt. Job Wright (1) of the New York forces at Spencer in the State of New York and in April 1781 he marched to Saratoga where he joined the Regt commanded by Col. Willet and remained there till August of the same year and then marched from there to Albany where he was first mustered in Augt 1781. He remained there about two weeks and then returned to Saratoga where he remained till November of the same year when the company to which he belonged was ordered to Ballstown for winter quarters where he remained till the month of May 1782 and then marched to Johnstown & there joined the regiment again, at which place he remained till the month of September of the same year when he & a part of the Regiment went to Fort Timmerman on the Mohawk River to keep garrison where he remained till about the 1st of October of the same year and then joined the Regiment again at Fort Plain where he remained through the next winter & summer till the month of Sept'r 1783 (2) and then marched to Fort Herkimer on the Mohawk River where he remained a few days only and then went to Fort Stanwix on the Mohawk and then assisted in building a stone house & block house at which place he remained till the last of November of the same year, and then marched to Schenectady where he continued till the 6th day of January 1784 (3) and was there & then regularly & honorably discharged which discharge was signed by Col. Willet, but which he has unfortunately lost—General Stark (4) commanded at Saratoga while the declarant was there—His Lieutenant's name was Jesse Hubbel (5) who was afterwards, while the declarant was in the service, appointed adjutant, his Ensign's name was Bingham—His orderly Sergeant was Seth Rowley.

He was born at Derby in Connecticut March 20th 1764. At about the age of 8 years (as he is informed) he removed to Spencertown in the State of New York at which place he resided when he entered the service. After he left the service he returned to Spencertown where he remained till December of the same year 1784 when he returned to Derby since which time he has resided in Derby Oxford, Southbury & New Milford in this state at which latter place he now resides and has resided for about twenty two years past.

He has no documentary evidence of his services—He annexes hereto some testimony to prove his services taken to substantiate his claim for a pension on a former occasion. (6) He knows of no other witnesses name than Lake Champlain whose testimony he can prove and is not certain that they are living.

He hereby relinquishes every claim whatever to a pension or annuity except the present, and declares that his names is not on the pension roll of the agency of any state. (Signed with his mark) Levi Smith. (7)

Sworn & subscribed the day & year aforesaid. Nathaniel Perry Judge of the Court of Probate

End Notes—W.2261—Levi Smith

1. The regiment did not exist until April 27, 1781 when Lieutenant-Colonel Commandant Marinus Willett and the other officers were appointed to raise a regiment of Levies. Levi probably enlisted in May. On August 12, 1781, he was mustered in as a 3 years man in Captain Job Wright's Company. According to the Descriptive Book No. 4 of Willett's Regiment, Document No. 11105, Special Collections and Manuscripts, New York State Library, Albany, N.Y., the following is given. Enlisted August 12, 1781 at Spencertown, Albany County, New York for 3 years by Lieutenant Pliney Moor, Born at Darbytown, New Haven County, Connecticut. Age 17, size 5 ft 7 in, complexion Dark, Hair Dark, Eyes Dark, Occupation Laborer.
2. In 1783, Levi served in Captain Joseph Harrison's Company for 10 months and was then transferred to Captain Jonathan Pearce's (or Percy, Pearse, etc.), Company. Both companies were in Willett's Regiment. FROM: Revolutionary War Rolls 1775-1783, Series M-246, Roll 78, folder 173, National Archives, Washington, D.C.
3. According to the book "An extract from the Register of the New York State Battalion", Levi was discharged January 6, 1784. It was signed by Captain Commandant Peter B. Tearce, Attest P. Moor, Adjut. These are the two officers that signed Levi's discharge as Willett had retired from the service on November 1, 1783. FROM: Revolutionary War Rolls 1775-1783, Series M-246, Roll 78, folder 173, National Archives, Washington, D.C.
4. Brigadier General John Stark. On August of 1781, he was in command of the Northern Department.
5. Lieutenants Jesse Hubble, Rial Bingham and Sergeant Seth Rowley all served in Willett's Regiment.
6. In Levi's pension application is testimony by Lieutenant Moor.
7. Elizabeth Smith, widow of Levi applied and received a widow's pension. The following was part of her application. Levi Smith of New Milford

was married to Elisabeth Hoy of Newtown on the 9th of July 1826 by me William Mitchell Pastor of the Congregational Church. Town Clerk's Office, Newtown April 12/53. Recorded by Town Clerk on July 11, 1826. Caleb Baldwin. Attest Monroe Judson, Town Clerk. (1853)

Pension Application for Moses Smith

S.40447

Pennsylvania SS.

Be it remembered that on this 30th day of April AD eighteen hundred and eighteen before me the subscriber Jos. Hemphill President of the District Court of the City & County of Phi'a, personally appeared Moses Smith aged fifty nine years now resident in the City of Philadelphia in the State aforesaid, who being by me duly sworn according to law, doth make the following declaration on oath in order to obtain the provisions made by the late act of Congress, entitled "an act to provide for certain persons engaged in the Land & Naval Service of the United States in the Revolutionary War", that the said Moses Smith did in the spring of seventeen hundred and seventy six in the Township of Walkill County of Orange and State of N. York enlist in to Capt. Crages (1) Company of foot for one year, was mustered at Fort Constitution and joined Colonal [sic] VanSeoyks [VanSchaick] Regiment (2) served the year in said Regiment, and then enlisted in Capt. Smiths (3) Company for during the war, joined the second N. York Regiment commanded by Colonal VanCoartland [sic] (4) on the Continental establishment, that he served in said regiment to the end of the war, and that he was discharged in the spring of seventeen hundred & eighty three with the main army at Snake Hill in Orange County & State aforesaid, that he drew his land in the State of N. York and his Continental bounty land from the United States, that he was in the battles of Long Island, giving up of N.York & White Plains & at the capture of Cornwallis (5) and many small or skirmishes during the war, was slith [slightly] wounded in the face & leg, that he never received any pension & humbly releases to the United States all claims thereto, that he is a native born resident citizen of the U't States, and that he by old age and reduced circumstances in life is in need of assistance from his country for support and that he knows of no other testimony here in the City he can give of his services but a reference to his enlistments, discharge, and drafts of the land he drew for his services, recorded in the war office. Sworn to & declared before me the day and year aforesaid. 30th April 1818, Jos. Hemphill.

End Notes—S.40447—Moses Smith

1. Captain James Gregg in Colonel Isaac Nicoll's Regiment of Levies in 1776. Colonel Nicoll had been in command of the Orange County Minute Men. Colonel Nicoll also commanded at times at Fort Constitution on Constitution Island which can be seen from West Point. There are only ruins left of the fort and the island is privately owned. There haven't been any muster rolls found for this regiment. FROM:

Revolutionary War Rolls 1775-1783, Series M-246, Roll 75, folder 132, National Archives, Washington, D.C.

2. Goose VanSchaick in 1776 was Colonel of an un-numbered Continental Regiment raised to reinforce the American Army in Canada. The army retreated from Canada by May and VanSchaick's Regiment garrisoned forts in the Lake George and Fort Edward area. Also they were at Johnstown in Tryon County for a short period.
3. Moses enlisted as a private for "during war" on December 23, 1776 in Captain Israel Smith's Company, Seventh Company, in Colonel Henry B. Livingston's Fourth New York Continental Regiment. He deserted on July 22, 1778. He is listed as rejoining the regiment on October 18, 1779. FROM: Revolutionary War Rolls 1775-1783, Series M-246, Roll 71, folder 57, National Archives, Washington, D.C.
4. On January 1, 1781, the Second New York and Fourth New York Continental Regiments were consolidated into one regiment. The Second New York remained under the command of Colonel Philip VanCortlandt. Captain Smith was transferred to the Second New York and so was Moses. He continued his service until he was discharged in June of 1783. FROM: Revolutionary War Rolls 1775-1783, Series M-246, Roll 69, folder 32, National Archives, Washington, D.C.
5. The Battle of Long Island was on August 27, 1776, the Battle of White Plains was fought on October 28, 1776 and the Yorktown, Virginia Campaign was from September 28 to October 19, 1781.

Pension Application for Obadiah Smith

S.40458
The State of Ohio
Clermont County SS.

On this 8th day of June 1820, personally appeared in open court being the Court of Common Pleas within and for said county and also being a court of record, which have the power of fine and imprisonment, Obadiah Smith aged sixty one years, resident in the said County, who first being duly sworn, according to law, doth on his oath declare, that he served in the revolutionary War, as follows to wit.

In the reg't commanded by Col. H. B. Livingston (1) in the company commanded by Capt'n Jonathan Titus in the New York line & that he was notified of his being inscribed on the pension list roll, of the Ohio agency, at eight dollars per month, commencing on the 19th day of May 1818 by a pension certificate No. 7824, bearing date 18th March 1819 & I do solemnly swear, that I was a resident citizen of the United States, on the 18th day of March 1818 & that I have not since that time by gift, sale or in any manner disposed of my property or any part thereof, with intent, thereby so to diminish it as to bring myself within the provisions of an act of Congress entitled, "An act to provide for certain persons engaged in the land and naval service of the United States in the revolutionary war", passed on the 18th day of March 1818 & that I have not nor has any person in trust of me any property or securities contracts or debts due to me, nor have I any income other than what is contained in the schedule hereunto annexed, & by me subscribed to wit, four half acre lots, two cows, one sow & pigs, one desk, two small tables, 1 pot, 1 teakettle, 1 bake oven, one frying pan, & one small looking glass, 2 candlesticks, seven old chairs & do. Smal, one side saddle, one old mans saddle & saddle bags, 1 half set tea cups & saucers, 1 half dozen plates, 3 old buckets, 1 shovel, 1 old axe, 1 old churn, 2 old spinning wheels, and he is a shoemaker by trade, but of very weak and debilitated constitution & unable to do but very little work, he has only three in the family besides himself, Peninah his wife aged. . .years, very sickly, Caroline his daughter aged 10 years, Harriet is daughter aged two years, all of which depend on him for support. (Signed) Oba'd Smith.

Sworn to and declared on the 8th day of June 1820 before the said court.

The State of Ohio
Clermont County SS.

Be it remember[ed] that on the 19th day of May one thousand eight hundred and eighteen personally came before me John Morris a Judge of the Court of Common Pleas within and for said County Obadiah Smith aged fifty nine years and being duly sworn on the Holy Evangelist deposeth and saith that he is a resident in the County of Clermont aforesaid, that he enlisted as a private soldier in the year 1777 in the month of February at Duches [Dutchess] County in the State of New York in the Company commanded by Capt. Jonathan Titus in the fourth Regiment commanded by Coll Livingston in the New York Line on Continental Establishment that he was in several skirmishes when the British troops burned the Village of Peekskill (2) and destroyed the stores at that place that he remained in the American Army & at that & other places & at the White plains until about the 1st of June in the same year. This deponent with others of the army marched to Fishkill to the barracks to be inoculated with the small pox after recovering from that and a severe fit of sickness so far as to travel he embarked on board a vessel I went to Albany in the month of August (3) in the same year from thence to half Moon Point thence to Skenectada and German Flats returned to Skenectada sick and was shut up in the hospital the Regt proceeded (and left this deponent) to join the Army under the command of Genl Gates who captured the British Army under Genl. Burgoyne after this deponent had somewhat recovered he was ordered to Albany remained at that place til the hospital was crowded with the wounded of the army he was then removed in the month of October the same year to Skenectada where this deponent was—discharged from the hospital with orders to join in his Regt this deponent afterwards did join his regiment at Fishkill as aforesaid at that place owing to a bad state of health he obtained a furlow (4) from the army until fit for duty, that this declarant went to Wethersfield in the State of Connecticut and there remained in a bad state of health which appeared to the Colonel of the Reg't from the certificates of Physicians, in consequence of which he obtained the enclosed Certificate from Colonel Courtlandt (5) and that this deponent never received any other discharge, the De'r further saith that he did remain in and about Wethersfield in readiness if able to obey orders till the conclusion of the war and that he did not receive any further "Bounty or Wages" and that he served in the war of the Revolution for the term of nine months and longer and he never obtained or claimed any pension heretofore allowed by the Laws of the United States and that he hereby relinquishes all pensions heretofore allowed that he has no other evidence in his power to offer and further this deponent the said Obadiah Smith declares on his oath aforesaid that from his reduced circumstances he needs the assistance of his country for support. (Signed) Obad'h Smith

I certify that the said Obadiah Smith took and subscribed before me the foregoing and above both on the 14th day of May 1818 and that it appears to my satisfaction that he served in the Revolutionary War against the Common Enemy for nine months and longer. John Morris.

End Notes—S.40458—Obadiah Smith

1. Obadiah enlisted on March 1, 1777 for during war as a private in Captain Jonathan Titus' Company (Eighth Company) in Colonel Henry B. Livingston's Fourth New York Continental Regiment.
2. Peekskill, New York was attacked by the British on March 22, 1777.
3. Colonel Livingston's Regiment along with Colonel Philip VanCortlandt's Second New York Continental Regiment were sent to reinforce Major General Benedict Arnold's relief column at German Flatts. Arnold then left the German Flatts and marched to relieve the garrison of the besieged Fort Schuyler which was Fort Stanwix. The General Arnold relief column returned to the American Army under Major General Horatio Gates at Stillwater. They fought in the Battles of Saratoga on September 19, 1777 and October 7, 1777. Lieutenant General John Burgoyne surrendered his British Army on October 17, 1777.
4. On Captain Titus' Muster Rolls, Obadiah is listed as sick on several of them but he is listed as a deserter and not furloughed. He is listed as deserting on April 5, 1778. Captain Titus' Muster Rolls are in folder 59, Roll 71, Series Microfilm 246, Revolutionary War Rolls 1775-1783, National Archives, Washington, D.C.
5. This is fortunate for Obadiah that Colonel VanCortlandt accepted the doctor's certificates and issued him the following certificate: *The bearer hereof Obadiah Smith a soldier of Captain Jonathan Titus Company late fourth New York Regiment having been absent four years and most part that to me unfit for service as is the case at present as appears by several certificates from a Number of Physicians and other persons residing in Connecticut [?] therefore in consequence of the above certificates [torn & worn] hereby permit the said Obadiah Smith to remain unmolested in and about Wethersfield until called for by the commanding officer of the Second N. York Regt (to whom he belongs) upon condition that he be of no expence to the publick nor*

receive any further bounty nor wages for any services as a soldier but in the regiment he belongs too until he shall be Legally Discharged the Service.—Given under my hand the 30 day of April 1782. P. Courtlandt Colo 2 NYR Comm'g N York Brigade
To all concerned.

Pension Application for Amos Sorels or Sorils

R.9937

Amos Sorrils a soldier application of Durand Sorrels a Colored man for a pension under act of June 7th 1832. Joseph Ellis ageant Bloomingburgh Sillivan County NY. The within is support the aplication of Durand Sorrels son of Amos Sorrels to a pension whose papers are on file in your office. [entire paragraph typed as written.]

State of New York
Delaware County SS.

Be it known personally appeared before me, a Justice of the Peace in and for said county, David Honeywill a resident of said county aged 63 years, who being duly sworn by me according to law, states that he was personally acquainted with Amos Sorels, deceased, a late resident of said county, for several years previous to his death in 1838, and that he the said Sorels bore a good character, and was generally reported and believed to have been a soldier and to have served as such for some time during the war of the revolution, all of which he believes to be true. (signed) David Honeywell.

Sworn to and subscribed before me this 7th day of April 1851. Platt Townsend, Justice of the Peace.

At a Surrogate's Court, held at the office of the Surrogate in Delhi in the county of Delaware in the State of New York, the same being a Court of Record, on the 7th day of July in the year 1850, personally came before me, Durang Sorils, a man of color a resident of said county of Delaware aged 33 years, who being first duly sworn according to law in who being first duly sworn according to law in open court makes the following declaration to wit—That he is one of the children of Amos Sorils a man of color, deceased, a late resident of said county, and that he makes this declaration in order to obtain the pension which was due his said father the said Amos Sorils at the time of his death under the act of Congress passed on the 7th day of June 1832—and that his father served in the war of the Revolution as follows—he entered the service in the early part of the war and served under different officers and at one time was in Vansco (1) regiment, and that during some portion of the time he was in the army General Washington (2) commanded the regiment to which he belonged, and that the said Amos Sorils served in the war from the commencement until near the close of the same—and that his father the said Amos Sorils with the view of making application for his pension left his home and went into the western part of the State of New York in the year 1835 or '36 in search of persons who served with him in said war in order to get their testimony to prove his services as a soldier during said war, and that his said father returned to his home in the county of Delaware in the State of New York and that he heard his said father say after his return that all the persons who served with him in said war had died and that he knew of no one of them then living who had served with him during said war by whom he could prove his services—and this declarant further states that his father Amos Sorils died on or about the 18th day of February in the year 1838, and that he left no widow—at the time of his death, but left the following named children, to wit—Lavinia Sorils and Durang Sorils, this declarant, both residents of the County of Delaware in said State and that they are both of lawful age, and they are now the only so living children of said Amos Sorils, deceased. This declarant further states that his said father served as above stated, as he has heard from his said father, and from other persons, that he believes the same to be true—and that this declarant himself knows of no person or persons now living by whom he can prove the services of his said father and that he calls upon the Commissioner of Pensions to give him all the aid and assistance that he consistaully [consistently?] can under the rules of his department by searching the records in the War Department and in furnishing the necessary proof to support his claim for said pension, and giving this declarant all other information he may require to make out his claim for said pension. (Signed) Durang W. Sorils

Subscribed & sworn this 8th day of July 1850. [?] Surrogate

End Notes—R.9937—Amos Sorels

1. Possibly referring to Colonel Goose VanSchaick of the First New York Continental Regiment. Unfortunately Amos Sorel's name does not appear on the company Muster Rolls.
2. Commander-in-Chief General Washington.

Pension Application for Nathan Staples or Steeples

W.13937 (Widow: Ruth)

I Nathan Staples of Glocester in the County of Providence & State of Rhode Island on solemn do declare and say that in the month of April 1775 I enlisted as a private soldier, Capt. John Nicholson's company (1) & Col. Paulding's (2) regiment in the continental army of the United States in the New York line. In which service I continued nine months, afterwards in the month of May 1776 I enlisted as a private soldier in Capt. William Forkinder's (3) company in Colo. Hortenback's (4) regiment in the same army and line, in which service I continued ten months—afterwards in 1777—I enlisted in the same capacity in Capt. James Humphrey's (5) company & Colo James McClautherly's regiment & in the same army & line in which service I continued nine months—being the time for which I enlisted, afterwards in the month of May 1778—I enlisted in the same capacity in Capt. William Walker's (6) company & Col. Peter Renur's (7) regiment in the service in army & line in which service I continued one year then next following being the time for which I enlisted. Afterwards I enlisted in the same capacity in Capt. Henry Brewster's

(8) company & in the same regiment last mentioned, in army & line in which service I continued [?] months—I further declare that I was regular discharged after all the times of my enlistment but my discharges are now lost—I further declare that I am now in reduced circumstances & stand in need of the assistance of my country for support. (Signed) Natham Staples. Rhode Island District.

Be it remember that on this seventh day of April 1818 came before me the Nathan Staples and made solemn oath to the truth of the declaration by him above subscribed in witness whereof I have hereto set my hand & have caused the seal of the District Court to be hereto affixed. David Howell, District Judge.

Letter dated November 10, 1927, written in response for information.

In response to your request of the ninth instant, I have the honor to advise you from the papers in the Revolutionary War pension claim, W.13937, it appears that Nathan Staples was born in Smithfield, Providence County, Rhode Island, date not stated.

While residing at New Windsor, Orange County, New York, he enlisted and served as a private with the New York Troops, as follows—

From April 1775, nine months in Captain John Nicholson's Company, Colonel Paulding's Regiment; from May 1776 about ten months in Captain Faulkner's Company; in 1777 about nine months in Captains William Tellford's (9) and James Humphrey's Companies, Colonel McClaughrey's Regiment; from in May 1778, one year in Captain Walker's Company, Colonel Pierre Regnier's Reg. from in May 1779, five months in Captain William Tellford's Company; and in 1782 five months in Captain Henry Brewster's Company, Colonel Weissenfiel's Regiment. It is stated that he was in several battles, one in which he was wounded, no names of battles given.

He died in March 1820 at Glocester, Providence County, Rhode Island.

He married in February 1780 at Smithfield, Rhode Island, Ruth, daughter of Nathaniel Horton. She was born in Scituate, Rhode Island, but at the time of her marriage was living at said Smithfield. The date of her birth not given.

She was allowed pension on her application executed March 28, 1838, while a resident of Scituate, Rhode Island, aged seventy-eight years.

They had eight children, Mary the oldest, who died when she was twelve years of age is the only name stated.

End Notes—W.13937—Nathan Staples

1. Nathan is listed as Steeples in Captain John Nicholson's Company Muster Roll in Colonel James Clinton's Third New York Continental Regiment, Nathan is listed on the Muster Roll dated *"Camp at Ticonderoga 28th September 1775"* as enlisting on July 5th as a private. FROM: Revolutionary War Rolls 1775-1783, Series M-246, Roll 69, folder 38, National Archives, Washington, D.C.

2. Nathan maybe is referring to Colonel Levi Pawling of the Third Regiment of Ulster County Militia but Colonel Pawling was not part of this regiment.
3. Captain William Faulkner of the Fifth Company in Colonel James McClaughrey's Second Regiment of Ulster County Militia.
4. Lieutenant Colonel Jacob Hornbeck of Colonel Pawling's Regiment.
5. James Umphrey or Humphrey, was the Captain of the Eighth Company (New Windsor Company) in Colonel McClaughrey's Regiment.
6. Nathan is listed as Staples in Captain Benjamin Walker's (Sixth Company) in Colonel Henry B. Livingston's Fourth New York continental Regiment on May 5, 1778 as a private and he was discharged on February 5, 1779. FROM: Revolutionary War Rolls 1775-1780, Series M-246 Roll 71, National Archives, Washington, D.C.
7. Pierre Regnier de Roussi was appointed Lieutenant-Colonel on November 21, 1776 in the Fourth New York Continental Regiment. Transferred to the Second New York Continental Regiment on June 28, 1779.
8. Captain Henry Brewster in Lieutenant-Colonel Commandant Frederick Weissenfels' Regiment of New York State Levies in 1782.
9. Captain William Telford or Tilford in Colonel McClaughrey's Regiment.

Pension Application for Adam Staring (Starin, Storing, Stanning, etc.)

W.19,106 (Widow: Nelly)
State of New York
Montgomery County SS

On this 14th day of April A.D. 1837, personally appeared before the Hon. David F. Sacia, one of the Judges of the Court of Common Pleas in and for said County, Nelly Staring a resident of the Town of Oppenheim in the said County, aged 77 years last 1836 May who being first duly sworn according to law doth on her oath make the following declaration in order to obtain the benefit of the act of Congress passed 4 July 1836, that she is the widow of Adam Staring who was a soldier of the revolution & served as such & believes part of the time as a Sergeant--& remembers that he was enlisted under Capt. Garret Putman (1) in said war & served under him some time at Fort Hunter & other places but the particular time or place she cannot recollect but it was after she was married to said Adam—she also remembers that her said late husband served under Capt. Gardinier (2) at different times & that her said husband she always understood served under Capt. Gardinier at the Oriskany battle (3)--& that he was on a tour of duty to Johnstown or Sacondaga as she at the time & ever since understood-- & she also says that her late husband according to her recollection, in the said war was enlisted as a boatman under she thinks Capt. DeGraff (4) & that she heard him say that he had served at Newburgh--& also that he enlisted in ferrying Washington's Army across some river the name of which she has forgotten & also a large number of cattle & that her husband told her he had seen Washington at the time he assisted in ferrying his army across the river—that her said husband she thinks must have served chiefly in said was as a private & part of the time as a Sergeant as she understood & believes—but she has no record of her husband's service & cannot on account of her age & infirmity & length of time give the names & time he served nor the different places nor his officers otherwise than before stated--& she relies on the testimony hereto annexed of those who served with her said late husband in the war of the revolution for the services he rendered in said tour—She further declares that according to the best of her recollection & belief she was married to the said Adam Staring in the fall of the year 1777 & thinks in the month of November of said year the particular day she cannot state--& further says that the date of her marriage aforesaid was put in a Bible of her said husband as she thinks that it was together with the dwelling of her said husband, in said war destroyed & burnt by the Indians & Tories--& knows of no record of the marriage & believes there is none, but the Rev. Thomas Romyne married her—that her maiden name was Quackenboss—that her said late husband the aforesaid Adam Staring died on the sixth day of June 1812 (5) & that the time of his death was recorded or noted in the bible of her son with whom she resides & is the same as before stated--& that she has remained a widow ever since that period as will more fully appear by reference to the proof hereto annexed--& the services of her said husband in the said war will more fully appear by reference to the proof hereto annexed—that her said husband when he rendered said services resided in the Town of Charlestown in the said County of Montgomery—that she has no documentary evidence of his service--& cannot from her infirmity attend court without [?]able injury to her heath--& further says not—that she does not write her name. (Signed with her mark) Nelly Staring. (6)

Sworn to & Subscribed on the day & year above written before me. D.F. Sacia, Judge of Montgomery County Courts.

End Notes—W.19106—Adam Staring

1. Garret Putman served as a captain of a company of rangers for Tryon County in 1778. There is no known muster roll for this company. Adam may have belonged to this company but as he was in the bateau service in this year it is doubtful. Captain Putman also served as a Captain in Colonel Frederick Visscher's Third Regiment of Tryon County, Lieutenant Colonel Commandant John Harper's Regiment of Levies in 1780 and Lieutenant-Colonel Commandant Marinus Willett's Regiment of Ne York State Levies in 1781. Adam's name does not appear on any of those muster rolls. Captain Putman was assigned garrison duty at Fort Hunter frequently during his service and Adam may just have served under him on detachment service.
2. Captain Jacob Gardinier of the First Company in Colonel Visscher's Regiment. Adam's name also appears on Captain John Visscher's Fourth Company and Captain Abraham Veeder's Second Company both in Colonel Visscher's Regiment. His service in these two companies

were probably in detachment service as his residence was in the company beat of Captain Gardinier.

3. The Battle of Oriskany was fought on August 6, 1777.
4. Captain Simon DeGraff's Company of Bateaumen for 1778. Adam enlisted as a private on April 23, 1778. The company was raised for service until December 31, 1778. FROM: Revolutionary War Rolls 1775-1783, Series M-246, Roll 122, Folder 78 (Quartermaster General's Department), National Archives, Washington, D.C.
5. Adam's will is dated June 4, 1812 and it was probated on June 16, 1814. The children of Adam and Nelly that are listed in the will as follows: Frederick, Phillip, John, Harry, Betsey Fishback (wife of Jacob), Elly Fishback (wife of John), Peggy (Margaret) and Caty. Margaret, John, and Philip were still alive in 1837.
6. Nelly was still living in 1841 as she filed another petition on March 31, 1841 while a resident of the Town of St. Johnsville, Montgomery County. In this petition she claims her daughter Margaret who had been on friendly terms had given her the pension certificate for safe keeping but now because of a misunderstanding Margaret claims that it is lost. Nelly claims that her daughter is illegally detaining this certificate. That she (Nelly) is to receive $43.33 per annum by virtue of said certificate granted to her on account of services rendered to the United States during the War of the Revolution that her said late husband served. She again states that Adam served in Captain Garret Putman's Company of Infantry and in the regiment she thinks whereof Marinus Willett was Colonel. Again Adam's name does not appear on Captain Putman's payroll for 1781. FROM: Revolutionary War Rolls 1775-1783, Series M-246, Roll 78, folder 173, (Willett's), National Archives, Washington, D.C.

Pension Application for Cornelius Swartwout

W.29605 (Widow: Sarah. Married March 30, 1780. Cornelius Swartwout died 22 Sept. 1831. Sergeant in the company commanded by Captain Robert Wood, Pawling was Colonel.)

State of New York
Albany County SS.

On this 30th day of April in the year one thousand eight hundred, and thirty nine, personally appeared before the subscriber, one of the Judges of the County Court of the County of Albany, (being Court of Record) Sarah Swartwout, of Westerlo, in said County aged eighty two years, who being first duly sworn, according to law, doth, on his oath make the following declaration in order to obtain the benefit of the provision made by the Act of Congress passed July 4, 1836.

That she is the widow of Cornelius Swartwout, who was a private and musician, and served as such in the Army of the United States, or Militia of the State of New York, in the War of the Revolution in Capt. Swartwout's (1)

Company, in Col. VanBenschotten's (2) Regiment & under other officers, as will more fully appear by her affidavit and that of Josiah Hinkley, hereto annexed.

She further declares that she was married to the said Cornelius Swartwout on the thirtieth day of March in the year one thousand seven hundred and eighty; that her husband the aforesaid Cornelius Swartwout, died on the twenty second day of September in the year one thousand eight hundred and thirty one; and that she has remained a widow ever since that period, as will more fully appear by reference to the proof hereto annexed.

And she further states, that the record of her marriage hereto annexed is the only record of that fact of which she has any knowledge. That it was written on a leaf of the family Bible many years ago, in the life time of her said Husband, and she believes it to be in the hand writing of her said husband.

Her name previous to her marriage was Sarah TerBush—That she is unable to write her name from old age & bodily infirmity. (Signed with her mark) Sarah Swartwout.

Sworn to & subscribed, on the day & year first above written before me. John Niles, A Judge of Albany County Courts.

Family Record

Births:

Cornelius Swartwout was Boarn [born] in the year of our Lord 1757 July 12th.

Sarah TerBush was Boarn in the year of our Lord 1757 March 30th. [Born in Fishkill, Dutchess County.]

Our First Born was a son named Johannis Swartwout was born Sept. 15th in the year of our Lord 1780 and was Baptized by Reverend Mr. Fraligh.

1782 May 24th Second son was Board named Henry Swartwout and was Baptized by the Reverend Dr. Livingston.

1783 Sept. 15th our first Dauter was Board [June 3?] Nelly Swartwout and was Baptized by the Reverend Docter Livingston.

1785 May 31th our third son was born named Myndert Swartwout and was baptized by the Reverend Mr. Rizendike.

1787 March 25th our forth son was born named Abraham Swartwout and was Baptized by the Reverend Mr. Rizendike.

1788 December 20th our fifth son [was born] named Gorge Wasinton [Washington] Swartwout and was Baptized by Reverend Mr. Rizendkie.

1790 October 19th our Sixth son [was born] named Jacobus Swartwout and was Baptized by Reverend Mr. Gray.

1792 October 17th our seventh son was born named Nathan Swartwout and was Baptized by the Reverend Mr. Fraligh.

Record of Marriage; Cornelius Swartwout and Sarah TerBush joined in Bond of Matrimony in the Year of Lord 1780 March 30th by the Revered Mr. Fragighs.

Letter dated April 15, 1932, written in reply to a request for information.

You are furnished herein the record of Cornelius Swartwout as found in pension claim W.29605, based upon his service in the Revolutionary War.

Cornelius Swartwout was born July 12, 1757, and was sometimes referred to as Cornelius C. Swartwout. The place of his birth and names of parents were not given.

The soldier married in March 1780, Sarah TerBush who was born March 30, 1757, in Fishkill, Dutchess County New York. They were married in Poughkeepsie, Dutchess County, that state, where they were both then living. The names of Sarah's parents are not shown. About 1801, they moved to that part of the Town of Rensselaer which was later Westerlo in Albany County, New York. He died there September 22, 1831.

Sarah Swartwout, soldier's widow, applied April 30, 1839, for pension due on account of the service of her husband. She was then living in Westerlo, Albany County, New York. It was stated that Cornelius Swartwout, while a resident of Fishkill, New York, enlisted in 1776 and served at various times until the close of the war, amounting to four years, as fifer and sergeant in the New York troops, a part of the time under Captain Swartwout, his uncle, and Robert Wood, (3) and Colonels Elias VanBunshoten, Swartwout (relationship to soldier not designated) and Pawling. Here claim was allowed. Sarah Swartwout died May 23, 1842.

The following names of children of Cornelius Swartwout and his wife, Sarah, are shown in the claim: (4)

Jonannis (first child) Swartwout, born September 15, 1780.

Henry Swartwout, born May 24, 1782.

Nelly (their first dau.) Swartwout born September 15, 1783.

Mynderd (3rd son) Swartwout born May 31, 1785.

Abraham Swartwout, born March 25, 1787.

George Washington Swartwout born December 20, 1788, in 1839, his mother living with him in Westerlo, NY.

Jacobus (James) Swartwout born October 19, 1790

Nathan Swartwout, born October 17, 1792.

Simon Swartwout date of birth not shown.

Sarah Miller, date of birth not shown.

In 1851, Henry Swartwout, administrator of Sarah Swartwout's estate, reported the following surviving children, only: John, Abraham, George, James, Simon Swartwout and Sarah Miller.

End Notes—W.29605—Cornelius Swartwout

1. Captain Bernardus Swartwout of Colonel Tobias Stoutenbergh's Fourth Regiment of Dutchess County Militia.
2. He may be referring to Elias VanBenschoten or Bunschoten, Benschouten, etc., but he was only a captain at the beginning of the war and finally was commissioned a major in 1779 in the levies not in the militia.
3. Cornelius enlisted as a private on May 5, 1779 in Captain Robert Wood's Company in Lieutenant-Colonel Commandant Albert Pawling's

Regiment of New York State Levies. On October 1, 1779, Cornelius was appointed Sergeant in Captain Wood's Company. He was discharged on January 1, 1780. FROM: Revolutionary War Rolls 1775-1783, Series M-246, Roll 75, Folder 134, National Archives, Washington, D.C. Elias VanBenschoten was appointed a major in this regiment.

Pension Application for Spencer Taylor

W.3620 (Widow: Sally)
B.L.Wt.6411-160-55
Declaration.
State of New York
County of Albany SS.

On this fourth day of April A.D. 1855 before me John J. Cole, a commissioner of deeds in and for the county and state aforesaid, personally appeared Sally Taylor aged 84 years, a resident of Watervliet in the State of New York, who being duly solemnly affirmed according to law, doth, on her affirmation make the following declaration in order to obtain the Bounty Land to which she is entitled under the Act of Congress approved March 3d, 1855.

That she is the widow of Spencer Taylor who was a private in the Revolutionary War, that on account of the services of her husband, the aforesaid Spencer Taylor in said war, she now receives a pension at the rate of eighty dollars per annum, under the act of 29th July 1848 as will more fully appear by reference to the evidence now on file in the Pension Office at Washington.

She further declares that she is now a widow; that she has never before applied for nor received any Bounty Land under this or any other Act of Congress. Claimant's Signature, Sally Taylor

State of Connecticut SS.
County & Town of Litchfield. This 6th day of April A.D. 1818.

I James Gould a Judge of the Superior Court for said State, do hereby certify that on the day above mentioned personally appeared before me Spencer Taylor now residing in & belonging to Warren in said County & made declaration under oath that he belonged to & served as a soldier in the American Army in the War of the Revolution & on the Continental establishment that he enlisted into said Army in the spring of the year A.D. 1782 for the term of three years—that he enlisted at Farmington in the State of Connecticut under Capt. Simon Newell (1) of Col. Willett's Regiment of the New York line—That soon after he enlisted he joined his Regiment at Albany & continued faithfully to serve in said Army until the war terminated, that after the termination of the War he continued to serve the United States in laboring on the Block House at Fort Stanwix (2) & on the roads from Fort Stanwix to German Flats in said State of New York under said Col. Willett (3) till about the expiration of said three years when he was honorably discharged at Schenectady by said Col. Willett, which discharge he has lost.

That by reason of his reduced circumstances in life he is very poor & in need of assistance from his country for support.

I also certify that from the foregoing declaration & from other testimony before me I am satisfied that said Spencer Taylor served in the Revolutionary War as aforesaid against the common enemy. (Signed with his mark) Spencer Taylor

Sworn April 6, 1818 before me James Gould a Judge of the Supr. Court. Sworn before me at Litchfield this 6th day of April 1818.

End Notes—W.3620—Spencer Taylor

1. Captain Simeon Newell of Colonel Marinus Willett's Regiment of New York State Levies. According to Captain Newell's payroll for 1782, Spencer served 12 months as a private received £ 26. .50 of his pay of £80. .0 and the balance due was £ 53. . 30 FROM: Revolutionary War Rolls 1775-1783, Series M-246, Roll 78, folder 173, National Archives, Washington, D.C.
   The following information was extracted from Colonel Willett's Descriptive Book No. 4, Doc. No. 11105, Special Collections and Manuscripts, New York State Library, Albany, NY. "Born Connecticut, resided at enlistment at Colehead, New London County, Conn. Enlisted by Captain Newell on June 1, 1782 for 2 years. Age 16, Size 5 ft 1 in, Complexion Brown, Hair Brown, Eyes Light, Occupation Farmer.
2. Fort Schuyler, which was Fort Stanwix, was abandoned in May of 1781 because the fort was in a ruinous state from a severe flood and a fire which had burned part of the fort. In 1783 a blockhouse was built to garrison a small number of men to protect the area.
3. Spencer was discharged December 31, 1782 by Major Elias VanBenschoten because Colonel Willett had retired from the service on November 1, 1783.

Pension Application for William Terrell

S.42467
State of New York
Montgomery County SS

On this 12th day of June 1821 personally appeared in open court being a Court of Record for the said County of Montgomery, called the Court of Common Pleas, proceeding according to the principles of Common Law, having the power of fine and imprisonment, William Terrell aged 67 (Sixty seven) years resident in Palatine in said County and State, who being first duly sworn according to Law, doth on his oath declare that he served in the Revolutionary Was as follows—Enlisted in the month of July 1775 (1) and served till the 1st day of January following in Captain Joseph McCracken's company in the 2d New York Regiment on the Continental establishment commanded by Colonel

Gooshen VanSchaick. In the month of January 1776 (2) he reinlisted for one year and served till the 1st January 1777 when he was honorably discharged. And I do solemnly swear that I was a resident Citizen of the United States on the 18th day of March 1818. And that I have not since that time, by gift, sale or in any manner disposed of my property, or any part thereof, with intent thereby, so to diminish it, as to bring myself within the provisions of an Act of Congress entitled "An Act to provide for certain persons engaged in the land and naval service in the land and naval service in the revolutionary War", passed on the 18th day of March 1818, and that I have not, nor has any person in trust for me, any property, or securities, contracts of debts due to me, nor have I any income, other than what is contained in the schedule hereto annexed and by me subscribed. (Signed) William Terrell

Sworn to and declared in open court on the 12th day of June 1821. Peter H. Bostwick, Clerk of the County of Montgomery.

Real property I have none either in possession, reversion remainder or expectancy.

Personal property, 1 old Cherry Table, 1 old Cupboard, 1 Tin Teapot, 2 old Tin Pails, 2 old iron spoons, 1 old pewter platter, one small looking glass, 1 old foot stove, 1 old [phuse?], 1 Bible, one psalm book, 1 old axe, 1 hoe, 1 drawing knife, 1 inch auger, 2 small chizzles, 1 spike Gimblet, 2 old sheep, 2 lambs, 1 pig, I was brought up to the farming business but have not been able to labor for three years by reason of a lame foot, proceeding from a fever which I took at Lake George when in the service of the United States. I have a wife named Jane living with me aged seventy one years who is very feeble and unable to work, whom I must support that I have no other means of support than what I receive from the pension of the United States which I received up to the 4th March 1820, I further saith not. The number of the original certificate from the war office of the United States is [15236?] & dated the 1st October 1819, and the date of the original application was on the 16th day of May 1818. (Signed William Terrell. Filed June term 12th June 1821.

State of New York
Montgomery County SS

William Terrell of the town of Palatine in the County and State aforesaid on the sixteenth day of May, in the year of our Lord 1818 before me James Hildreth one of the Judges of the Court of Common Pleas of said County personally appeared and being duly sworn saith that he was aged sixty four years on the twenty second day of February now last past, that he resides in the town aforesaid and on his oath makes the following declaration in order to obtain the provision made by the late act of Congress entitled "An Act to provide for certain persons engaged in the land and naval service in the land and naval service in the revolutionary War", he the said William enlisted in the town of Salem County of Charlotte now County of Washington in the state aforesaid in the month of July in the year of our lord 1775 in the company commanded by Captain Joseph McCracken in the Regiment commanded by Colonel Goose VanSchaick of the Infantry in the army of the United States in the line of the State aforesaid and enlisted to serve until the month of January then next, that he continued to serve in said Corps or in the service of the United States until in the month of January in the year 1776 in the capacity of drummer when he the said William at Salem aforesaid in the same month of January 1776 reenlisted in the same company and regiment for the term of one year, that he continued to serve in the said Corps or in the service of the United States in the capacity as Corporal until the first day of January in the year 1777 when at Salem aforesaid he was discharged from service, that he was in the battle of Montreal (3) and aided in taken[taking] it and was in the various skirmishes with the enemy whilst the British Fort of St. Johns (4) was besieged & which terminated in the surrender and capture of that Fortress to & lay down the arms of the United States in the year 1775 and that he is in reduced circumstances and stands in need of the assistance of his country for support & that this deponents discharge is worn out and lost & this deponent was honorably discharged the service. (Signed) William Terrell

Sworn and Subscribed before me the day and year aforesaid the day and year first mentioned. James Hildreth

Reply to a letter of inquiry dated December 13, 1898.

Replying to your recent communication you are advised that William Terrell, made an application for pension on May 16th, 1818, at which time he was 64 years of age and residing at Palatine, NY and his pension was allowed for one year's actual service as a private in the New York troops, Revolutionary War. He enlisted at Salem, New York and served under Capt. McCracken and Col. VanSchaick.

End Notes—S.42467—William Terrell

1. There are no known muster rolls for this company. On June 28, 1775 the following officers were appointed for the Seventh Company in Colonel Goose VanSchaick's Second New York Continental Regiment: Captain Joseph McCracken, First Lieutenant Martin Moses, and Second Lieutenant John Barns.
2. Joseph McCracken was appointed Captain on February 16, 1776 in Colonel VanSchaick's Continental Regiment (unnumbered in 1776). Again there are no known muster rolls for this company.
3. There were two Battles of Montreal. These were September 25 and November 12, 1775.
4. The Siege of St. Johns was from September 18 to November 3, 1775.

Pension Application for Matthew Trotter

W.19471 (Widow: Margaret. Married 27 May 1787, husband died Dec. 9, 1830)
Lieutenant, NY Levies under Col. Willett
State of New York
County of Albany SS.

On this 9th day of October in the year one thousand eight hundred and thirty nine, personally appeared before the Justices Court of the City of Albany, (being a court of record) Margaret Trotter, a resident of the City of Albany, aged sixty two years, who being first duly sworn according to law, doth on her oath make the following declaration in order to obtain the benefit of the provision made by the act of Congress passed July 7, 1838, entitled "An act granting half pay and pensions to certain widows—"

That she is the widow of Matthew Trotter, who was a Lieutenant (1) and Quarter Master (2) in the service of the United States during the revolutionary war, & served such Lieutenant in the New York Levies in the Company commanded by Capt. TenEyck (3) & as Quarter Master in Col. Willett's Regiment as will more fully appear by the proof hereto annexed.

She further declares that she was married to the said Matthew Trotter, on the twenty seventh day of May in the year one thousand seven hundred and eighty seven—That her husband the aforesaid Matthew Trotter died on the 9th day of December in the year one thousand eight hundred & (30) thirty.

That she was not married to him prior to his leaving the service, but the marriage took place previous to the first of January seventeen hundred & ninety four—viz—at the time above stated.

She further declares that her name previous to her marriage was Margaret Wendell. (Signed with her mark) Margaret Trotter.

Sworn to & subscribed on the day & year above written in open court. Witness to the seal of said court and the signature of the clerk thereof. J. G. Wasson, Clk John H. Trotter, Witness.

Dutchess County SS.

To whom it may concern, I Elias VanBenschoten (4) depose and say that in the year 1782 when I joined Col. M. Willett's Regt, that soon after Lieut. Matt'w Trotter was appointed Qur. Master to the three years troops raised on the Bounty of unappropriated lands, and also to an extra duty as Qur. Master to the garrison to take charge of the public stores as there was no garrison Qur Master at any of the garrisons on the Mohawk river. In consequence of the extra duties assigned Lieut. Trotter, there were no recruiting instructions granted him, and as there was no mode pointed out in what manner Qur Masters were to be introduced, and it was absolutely necessary for a Qur Master to be appointed to take charge of the stores of three years troops, and it always has been practiced that the staff officers have been chosen by the Field Officers of their respective troops, that said Trotter has been continued under my command in like rank and aforesaid duties until the whole of the troops were discharged.

N. B. If Lieut Trotter has not been returned to the Honorable Council of appointment as an officer in my care it is an omission in the return. (Signed) E. V. Benschoten commt of N. Your Three years troops.

End Notes—W.19471—Matthew Trotter

1. Matthew served as a Lieutenant in 1781 in Captain Abraham Livingston's Company in Lieutenant-Colonel Commandant Marinus Willett's Regiment of New York State Levies. He was paid in 1785 £ 57. .4. . 0 the balance due to him for his 1781 services.
2. Matthew served as Lieutenant and Quartermaster from April 7, 1782 to December 31, 1782. He served 8 months and 24 days. His pay for each month £ 15. . 17. . 4 for a total of £ 139. . 12. . 6. Matthew served as a Lieutenant in 1783 in Captain Jellis A. Fonda's Company in Colonel Willett's Regiment. He served 10 months retiring from the service on November 1, 1783. He was paid £ 26. .60 per month and his total amount was £ 266. . 60. He had been paid £ 106. . 60. And balance due was £ 160. . FROM: Revolutionary War Rolls 1775-1783, Series M-246, Roll 78, folder 173 (Willett's Regt), National Archives, Washington, D.C.
3. Abraham TenEyck served as a Lieutenant and PayMaster in Willett's Regiment.

Pension Application for Abraham VanAtten or VanEtten

R.10,863
State of New York
County of Schenectady SS.

On this seventeenth day of October in the year of our Lord one thousand eight hundred and thirty two personally appeared in open court before the Judges of the Court of Common Pleas in and for said County now sitting Abraham VanEtten a resident of the town of Glenville in said county & state, aged sixty-eight years who being first duly sworn according to law, doth on his oath make the following declaration in order to obtain the benefit of the act of Congress passed June 7th 1832.

He was born in the town of Rhinebeck in the County of Dutchess in the state aforesaid on the eighteenth day of October, 1764. He has no record of his age except that made by his father which is now in the possession of the claimant.

When he was called into the service of the United States in the army of the revolution, he was living in the town of Fishkill, County of Dutchess in said state, and since the revolutionary war he has lived in Albany County & in Montgomery in said state. He now lives in the town of Glenville aforesaid.

He entered the service of the United States under the following named officers and served as herein stated.

In the summer of the year 1779 when he was only 15 years of age, he went out as a scout on several occasions under command of Major Benschoten (1) to places in the neighbourhood where he lived.

When he arrived at the age of sixteen he was enrolled in the company of Militia in his beat viz, the company commanded by Captain Tunis Benschoten in the Regiment whereof Alias Benschoten was Colonel. The other company and field officers whom he recollects, were John Everson Lieutenant.

He continued to serve in said company until the end of said war, and the service he was engaged in during said period was, as a scout as aforesaid, and in patrolling and reconnoitering parties the particular time he served thus he cannot possibly specify as alarms were very frequent, and his tours were sometimes not longer than two or three days each—If he should be required to state how long in the whole he was actually from his residence in these expeditions he can state conscientiously that they exceeded six months.

The following are the names of some of the regular officers whom he knew, or who were with the troops where he served, and such continental and militia regiments or companies with which he served, or as he can recollect, viz: Colonel Dubois (2) & others whose names are herein before given.

He never received any written discharge from the service.

He has no documentary evidence, and knows of no person whose testimony he can procure who can testify to his service.

The following are the names of persons to whom he is known in his present neighborhood, and who can testify as to his character for veracity, and their belief of his services as a soldier of the revolution to wit: Matthias Barhydt & John Van Eps, Henry G. [?]

He hereby relinquishes every claim whatever, to a pension or annuity except the present, and declares that his name is not on the pension roll of the agency of any state. (Signed) Abraham VanAtten.

Subscribed and sworn to the day and year first aforesaid. John S. Vrooman, Clerk

End Notes—R.10863—Abraham Van Atten

1. Elias VanBenschoten was appointed Major on April 22, 1779 in Lieutenant-Colonel Albert Pawling's Regiment of New York State Levies. Abraham was too young to have enlisted and on searching the known muster rolls for this regiment his name was not found nor was Lieutenant John Everson. So far no record has been found on Abraham for service in the Dutchess County Militia.
2. Lewis DuBois was Colonel of the Fifth New York Continental Regiment until he resigned on December 22, 1779. On July 1, 1780, he was appointed Colonel of a regiment of New York State Levies. Major VanBenSchoten was also appointed on the same date to this regiment. A check of this regiment's known Muster Rolls did not list Abraham or Lieutenant Everson.

Pension Application for Isaac VanNatter or Vanattor or Vannnattor

R.10,878

Declaration in Order to Obtain The Benefit of The Act of Congress, Passed June 7, 1832.

State of New York

County of Herkimer SS.

On this twelfth day of October 1832, personally appeared in open court before the Judges of the court of Common Pleas of said County now sitting,

Isaac Vannattor a resident of Salisbury in the County of Herkimer and State of New York, aged 75 years, who being first duly sworn according to law, doth, on his oath, make the following declaration, in order to obtain the benefit of the act of Congress passed June 7, 1832.

That he entered the service of the United States under the following named officers, and served as herein stated.

That he was drafted as a militia man in the County of Dutchess and State of New York his place of residence, to old Fort Constitution now West Point, this applicant thinks under Colonel Livingston (1) or Col. Radcliff (2) and in the company of Captain Kipp (3) & Elias Benschouten (4) where he served two months principally in erecting fortifications, laying walls &c. That he was dismissed at the expiration of two months and returned home.

That in the month of December 1776 he was again called into service as a drafted militia man for six months in the company of Henry Humphrey (5) in the Regiment of Colonel Grahams and was marched first to the Nine Partners or Cold Spring where Colonel Graham resided, from thence they were marched to Pine Bridge where they arrived on new year's day. From thence to North Castle where they lay some time and drew arms out of the North Castle meeting house. From thence to the vicinity of Kingsbridge, that whilst there he was in the skirmish and assault upon Fort Independence (6) on Friday in which the Americans failed, that the enemy on Sunday following made a sally upon the American forces and were repulsed and driven back that he was in service this time six months and was then dismissed.

That in the spring of 1777, but what precise month this applicant cannot state he was again drafted and marched to West Point under Captain Peter Westfall (7), and was engaged for three months in digging and preparing a magazine to keep powder in and to secure it from bomb shells &c, the expiration of three months he was again dismissed and returned to Staatsberg, his place of residence in Dutchess County. That he was again drafted about the summer 1777 and marched from Staatsberg aforesaid to Albany from there they were marched to Half Moon Point, and from there to Stillwater where this applicant was in service and remained during the battle of Stillwater and until about one week after the surrender of Burgoyne (8) when the militia were all dismissed. That after they started on this tour a waggon and horses were pressed into service and this applicant was appointed by Captain Abraham S. Kip who commanded the company in which this applicant was drafted to drive said waggon whilst they were on the march. That he served in this tour two months and a half and more. Was drafted for three months, That in the summer or forepart of the fall of 1778 he was again drafted and marched under Captain John Steenburgh (9) from his resident to Fish Kill in Dutchess County and State of New York where they remained two months guarding the Hudson River and were then dismissed. His Lieutenant in this service was Jacob Shultz.(10) His Colonel he thinks was William Radcliff or Radley.

That in the month of August 1779 Stephans Frelich of Staatsburg aforesaid with whom this applicant was living at the time was drafted for six

{6} months and this applicant took his place as a substitute and was marched in the company of Captain Hermans (11) of Rhinebeck in Dutchess County in the Regiment of Colonel William Radley or Radcliff of Rhinebeck aforesaid to Esopus in Ulster County, from thence to a place called the Mannbackus towards the Pennsylvania line and in the County of Ulster and State of New York, from thence to Warwarsing in the same county from thence down the Delaware River a long distance to an Indian settlement or town on the west side of said river but the name of which this applicant cannot recollect, that it was a large settlement the Indians in pursuit of whom they had marched had fled leaving their squaws and children there. They passed through a place called Minisink in the County of Orange and State of New York where the Indians had a few weeks before committed depredations burning a number of buildings and a fort. That it was to check these depredations of the Indians under Colonel Brandt or "Brand" (12) as he was called that they were marched down to the Indian Town aforesaid. That they were on this expedition going and returning more than five of the six months for which they were drafted.

This applicant has no documentary evidence and that he knows of no person, whose testimony he can procure who can testify to his service.

1. That he was born at Staatsberg in the County of Dutchess and State of New York in the month of February 1757, as he calculates by his age.—
2. That he has no record of his age.
3. That he resided in Staatsberg aforesaid when he was called into service and continued to reside there during the war. That he then removed to the Nine Partners in Dutchess County aforesaid, where he resided twenty five years, that he then removed to Johnstown in the County of Montgomery and state of New York and resided there eight years, from thence he removed to Salisbury in the County of Herkimer where he has ever since resided.
4. That he was called into service by being drafted at each tour of service above specified, with the exception of the last service against the Indians as above stated, and in that tour of duty he went as a substitute for Stephanns Frelick with whom he was then living.
5. That he cannot recollect what General when they were marched down to KingsBridge and Fort Independence but Colonel Graham was the Colonel, Van Rensselaer's (13) Regiment and Colonel Livingston's Regiment were in the battle of Stillwater and General Schuyler was there, and that he recollects no other officers or troops in the regular service that served with the regiment to which he was attached. That he was at West Point at two different tours of service and was whilst there engaged in erecting fortifications and bomb proofs &c. That he was once marched to FishKill and stationed there to watch the movements of the enemy

on the Hudson River. That he was marched to and present at the Battle of Stillwater. That he was marched in another tour to Kingsbridge and Fort Independence which the Americans attempted to storm but did not succeed. And he was also marched far down the Delaware River in pursuit of the Indians.

6. That he never received a written discharge excepting when dismissed after the surrender of General Burgoyne and that the written discharge he then received has since been lost and he cannot find it. That he served as a private soldier in each tour.
7. That he refers the Court to David Potter & Francis Van Nattor of Salsburg.

Persons residing in the present neighborhood who are well acquainted with this applicant and who can testify as to his character for truth and veracity and as to their belief of his having served in the Revolution.

And this applicant in fact says that he was in actual service in camp, in garrison or Fort on the march or as a scout during the several tours above specified eighteen months and one half.

He hereby relinquishes every claim whatever to a pension or annuity except the present, and declares that his name is not on the pension roll of the agency of any state. (Signed with his mark) Isaac Van Natter.

Sworn to and subscribed the day and year aforesaid. Julius C. Nelson, Clerk.

End Notes—R.10878—Isaac VanNatter

1. Without Colonel Livingston's Christian name it is not possible to know which one he is speaking about. There is no Colonel Livingston in the First Regiment of Dutchess County Militia, Petrus TenBroeck was the colonel.
2. William Radcliff was appointed Captain of the Second Company of the Rhinebeck Precinct of the First Regiment of Dutchess County Militia on October 19, 1775. Radcliff was commissioned First Major on March 18, 1778 in the First Dutchess. Radcliff appears to serve in that capacity until the end of the war.
3. Abraham T. Kipp was appointed First Lieutenant in Captain Radcliff's Company on October 19, 1775 in the First Dutchess. Kipp was commissioned captain on March 18, 1778 in the same regiment.
4. It was Ignus Benschoten who was commissioned as the Second Lieutenant on March 18, 1778 in Captain Kipp's Company.
5. This enlistment was a draft of the Dutchess County Militia Regiments as Captain Henry Humphrey was in the Sixth Regiment of Dutchess County Militia. Lieutenant Colonel Morris Graham was of the First Dutchess.
6. The Battle of Kingsbridge was fought on Friday, January 17, 1777.
7. Peter Westfall was appointed First Lieutenant on October 19, 1775 in Captain Simon Westfall's Company (First Company of the

Rhinebeck Precinct (there were a total of five companies for this precinct) in the First Dutchess. Peter was commissioned Captain on March 11, 1776 of the same company and regiment.

8. The first Battle of Saratoga was fought on September 19, 1777. General John Burgoyne surrendered his British Army on October 17, 1777.
9. There appears to be no John Steenbergh as Captain in the First Dutchess. However, there was a Captain John VanSteenburgh of the Seventh Company in Colonel Morris Graham's Regiment of Dutchess County (Men raised from the different Dutchess County Militia Regiments). This detachment list is dated September 10, 1776 at Kingsbridge, N.Y.
10. Jacob Shultz was commissioned Ensign on June 25, 1778 in Captain Kipp's Company.
11. Andrew Hermanse (Hermance) was commissioned captain on March 18, 1778 in the First Dutchess.
12. Isaac is referring to Captain Joseph Brant.
13. Without Christian names it is not known which VanRensselaer or Livingston Isaac is referring to as there were several.

Pension Application for Samuel VanNetter or VanEtter, VanAtta, Van Atter, Van Etten.

W.18193 (Widow: Elizabeth)
State of New York
Lewis County SS.

On this 20th day of April in the year of our Lord 1837 personally appeared before the subscriber a Justice of the Peace in and for the said County Jacob VanAtta of Watson in said County who being duly sworn according to law doth depose and say that Elizabeth VanAtta of Watson aforesaid is his mother. That his father Samuel VanAtta (or as his father spelled his name Van Etten) died in the year 1815 and that his said mother has remained a widow ever since his death. That his father wrote his name "VanEtten" or Van Netter" but his children have usually written their names "VanAtta", and the name is then usually so written. That his said mother's mind has been so much impaired by reason of old age that she has not been able for a number of months to converse coherently upon any subject & wholly incompetent to make a Declaration to obtain the benefit of the pensions of the Act of Congress passed July 4, 1837.

That his mother's maiden name was Elizabeth Becker (1) that his said father resided during the Revolutionary War and for sometime after in the Town of Palatine, Montgomery County, New York. That his said father had in his possession since deponents recollection a commission as a Lieutenant in the New York Militia & which has been lost since his father's death.

That this deponent has no record of the ages of his said parents or of their marriage. But that his father if living would be, according to the best information deponent can attain, upwards of one hundred years of age & that his mother's age is upwards of ninety years.

That this deponent has not been able to procure any evidence of his father's services except the affidavit of Jacob Shultz. But that this deponent has been informed that John Reed late of the town of Lowville Lewis County now deceased and Peter Suts late of this county drew pension under the act of 1832 for services under his said father and further this deponent saith not.

(Signed) Jacob Vantta

Sworn & Subscribed before me the day & year above written.

L. Knox, Justice of the Peace.

State of New York
Lewis County SS.

On this 20th day of April in the year of our Lord 1837 personally appeared before the subscriber a Judge of the Court of Common Pleas in and for said County Jacob Shultz of Watson in said County and aged Seventy Seven years who being duly sworn doth depose and say that during the Revolutionary war he resided in the Town of Palatine in the County of Montgomery and State of New York and that he was well acquainted with Samuel VanAtta during the time of the Revolution and that he was during the said war and for sometime previous well acquainted with Elizabeth VanAtta the then wife of the said Samuel VanAtta, late a resident of the Town of Watson in the County of Lewis and State of New York. That the said Elizabeth and the said Samuel lived together as husband and wife before the Revolutionary War and this deponent verily believes they were lawfully married. That he saw the said Elizabeth frequently during the Revolutionary War and that she had three or four children which were born before and during the war. And this deponent further says that from the year 1777 to the year 1802 [sic] he this deponent served as a private under the said Samuel VanAtta as a Lieutenant in the company of New York Militia commanded by Captain Henry Miller (2) & Captain Fox. That he this deponent was allowed a pension under the act of 1832 for upwards of one years service under the said Lieutenant VanAtta and this deponent knowing to said VanAtta having served all the time that this deponent claimed in his the deponents Declaration on file at the War Department in the Regiment commanded by Colonel Klock in the Militia aforesaid. But that said VanAtta was in the service of the United States from 1777 to [sic] much more then this deponent , but that this deponent cannot specify the periods & length of service which said VanAtta rendered except when this deponent served under him nor can he specify the period & length of service in each instance when this deponent served under & with said VanAtta with precision but that the same or specified in his declaration on which deponents pension was granted & in his supplement affidavit or particularly as this deponent can recollect the same and this deponent further states that John Reed late of this county deceased and Peter Suts (3) late of this County drew pension under the Act of 1832 for services rendered under said VanAtta as a Lieutenant as this deponent has been informed & believes.

And this deponent further deposes that he served under Lieutenant VanAtta in the Regiment Commanded by Colonel Klock in The New York Militia in the Company Commanded by Captain Miller & Captain Fox not less than the periods mentioned below. In 1777 fifteen days in 1778 one month in September & October in 1779 one month in July and August in 1780 one month & eight days. The above Service was rendered under Captain Fox in the regiment aforesaid he also served with and when Said VanAtta in 1781 three months and fifteen days in August , Sept. & October also in November & Dec. of same year one and a half months in 1782 three and a half months in Summer & fall two months. The service was under Captain Henry Miller in the Regt aforesaid and this deponent further says that said VanAtta (4) served at least one year in addition with above service.

That said VanAtta lived at the time of entering into the service at Palatine Montgomery County New York at the time of entering the service aforesaid and that he served as a volunteer that said VanAtta died upwards of twenty years ago & that since his death said Elizabeth has remained a widow.

Sworn & Subscribed before me this 20th day of April 1837 & I certify that I am personally acquainted with the deponent & that he is a reliable witness. Amasa Dodge, A Judge of Lewis Coun. Cts.

End Notes—W.18193—Samuel VanNetter

1. Samuel and Elizabeth Bekker or Becker were married on October 1, 1769. FROM: Book of Marriages of the Stone Arabia Dutch Reformed Church, page 187. Elizabeth died May 17, 1837.
2. Samuel was appointed Ensign on August 26. 1775 in Captain Christopher W. Fox's Company which was the third company, in Colonel Jacob Klock's Second Regiment of Tryon County Militia. He was appointed second lieutenant on March 4, 1780 in place of Henry Miller who had been promoted to first lieutenant. On September 29, 1780, Captain Fox was promoted to major. Miller was then promoted to captain and Samuel was promoted to the first lieutenant.
3. Jacob Shultz, John Reed and Peter Suts had served as privates in Captain Miller's company.
4. A few pensioners claim that a Lieutenant VanEtta was one of the first militiamen to cross the Mohawk River to the south side and informed the gathering troops of the defeat of Colonel John Brown on October 19, 1780 at the Battle of Stone Arabia.

Pension Application for Frederick VanPetten or Van Patten

S.28926

State of New York

County of Schenectady SS.

On this twelfth day of October in the year of our Lord one thousand eight hundred and thirty two personally appeared in open court before the Judges of the Court of Common Pleas in and for said county, now sitting Frederick Van Patten a resident of the town of Glenville in said county & state, aged nearly seventy two years, who being first duly sworn according to law, doth on his oath make the following declaration in order to obtain the benefit of the act of congress passed June 7th 1832.

He was born in the town of Westina within the township of Schenectady in the County of Albany, now County of Schenectady in the state (then colony) of New York on the eleventh day of November 1760. He has no record of his age except that.

When he was called into the service of the United States in the army of the revolution, he was living in said town of Westina and since the revolutionary war he has lived in the same place now town of Glenville in the County of Schenectady in said state & he now lives in the town of Glenville aforesaid.

He entered the service of the United States under the following named officers and served as herein stated.

In the month of November 1776 he was enrolled in Captain John VanPatten's (1) company in the Regiment of Colonel Abraham Wemple. The names of his other company & field officers whom he recollects were Tunis Swart, Lieutenant & Philip Vedder Lieutenant.

The inhabitants of Tryon & Albany Counties being threatened with incursions from the enemy at every point, the militia were called out on numerous occasions, and received scarcely any aid from the regular troops to defend their frontiers. He the claimant was out with scouts of the militia & Indians to sundry places, the particular periods of which engagements it is impossible for him to specify.

At the Westina fort he mounted guard almost every day when not out on distant expeditions. He served for the term of three weeks on an alarm to Johnstown—for the term of one month he performed garrison duty at Stone Arabia—he was on duty at the upper fort in Schoharie for a term exceeding one month—After Cobleskill (2) had been destroyed by the enemy, he marched with a detachment to Cobleskill aforesaid in pursuit of the enemy—and after aiding in burying the dead there, returned to said fort in Schoharie & remained on duty at said fort the term of one week. He has marched to [Fort] Hunter several times—was on duty at Sacondaga one week. While at the last named place he was sergeant of the guard under Major Myndert Wemple. When Caughnawaga was burnt in 1780 (3), he marched with a detachment of militia from Westina aforesaid to German Flatts, and was out in this tour more than one week.

In the year 1778, he was drafted & marched to Saratoga & served with the troops at that post and in guarding the artificers under Colonel Christopher Yates (4) for two months. In the fall of the year 1781, he was called out & marched to Johnstown when & where he was taken sick & returned home.

Judging from the short periods of time he remained at home, the whole period which he served in the garrison & in the field during the revolutionary was not less than eighteen months.

It did not fall to his lot to engage in any battles or skirmishes during said war.

The following are the names of some of the regular officers whom he knew, or who were with the troops where he served, and such continental and militia regiments or companies with which he served, or as he can recollect, viz: General Schuyler (5), Colonels Gaansevoort, Ten Broeck, Willett, VanDyck & others.

He never received any written discharge from the service.

He has no documentary evidence, and knows of no person whose testimony he can procure who can testify to his service.

The following are the names of person to whom he is known in his present neighborhood, and who can testify to his character for veracity, and their belief of his services as a soldier of the revolution, to wit. John Sanders and John VanEps.

He hereby relinquishes every claim whatever, to a pension or annuity except the present, and declares that his name is not on the pension roll of the agency of any State. (Signed) Frederick VanPetten

Subscribed and sworn to the day and year first aforesaid. John S. Vrooman, Clerk

Letter dated December 6, 1932, written in reply to a request for information.

Reference is made to your letter in which you request the record of Frederick VanPatten, whose name appears on the printed list of pensioners of 1840, as a resident of Glenville, Schenectady County, New York, age 79 years.

The data furnished herein are obtained from the papers on file in Revolutionary War pension claim, S.28926, based upon the service of Frederick Van Patten, as his signature appears, in that war.

Frederick Van Petten was born November 11, 1760 in the town of Westina, Schenectady Township, Albany County, New York, which town was later within the bounds of Glenville, Schenectady County, New York.

While residing in his native town, he enlisted sometime in November, 1776, and served two months as private in Captain John VanPatten's (no relationship to the soldier stated) Company, Colonel Abraham Wemple's New York Regiment; he enlisted early in March 1777,and served ten months as private in Captain Myndert A. (or R.) Wemple's (6) Company part of the time in the bateau service transporting supplies between Schenectady and Fort Stanwix. After this he served on tours during the succeeding years of the war until 1782 under Captains John VanPatten and Roseboom, Colonels Abraham Wemple, and Christopher Yates, specific dates and length of these services not given; he was on alarms at Cobleskill, Saratoga, Caughnawaga, Schoharie, Stone Arabia and at Johnstown.

He was allowed pension on his application executed October 12, 1832, at which time he resided in Glenville, Schenectady County, New York.

In 1832, Adam VanPatten, the soldier's brother, was living in the town of Rotterdam, in Schenectady County, and in 1837, his residence was Glenville, that same county, New York. The soldier's sister, Rebecca Bradford, was living in said Glenville, New York, in 1837, and gave her age as sixty-nine years.

It is not stated that the soldier, Frederick VanPetten was ever married.

End Notes—S.28926—Frederick VanPetten

1. John VanPatten was appointed Captain of the Third Company in Colonel Abraham Wemple's Second Regiment of Albany County Militia on October 20, 1775. The other company officers were as follows: First Lieutenant Cornelius Mabey or Mabee, Maybe, Mabie; Second Lieutenant Simon F. VanPatten; Ensign Daniel Toll. Captain Van Patten was commissioned on June 20, 1778. The other company officers commissioned were as follows: First Lieutenant Teunis Swart; Second Lieutenant Philip Vedder; Ensign Daniel Toll.
2. Cobleskill was destroyed May 30, 1778 by Captain Joseph Brant.
3. Caughnawaga was destroyed on May 22, 1780 by Sir John Johnson.
4. Yates of Schenectady served in the Quartermaster's Department.
5. Major General Philip Schuyler, Colonel Gansevoort of the Third New York Continental Regiment, Brigadier General Abraham TenBroeck, Lieutenant Colonel Marinus Willett (served in several regiments at different periods) and Lieutenant Colonel Cornelius VanDyck of the First New York Continental Regiment.
6. Myndert M. Wemple was commissioned Second Major on June 20, 1778 in the Second Albany. Myndert A. Wemple was commissioned First Lieutenant in Captain John Myndertese's (or Mynderson's) Company in the Second Albany on February 25, 1780.

Pension Application for John D. VanPatten

W.18187 (Widow Wyntie)
B.L.Wt. 9430-160-55

John died 24 Oct. 1835, private in Company of Captain Van Duzen, Col. Wemple's Regt. NY Line for 9 mos. & 14 days. Wyntie applied for bounty land under the 1855 act and stated she was 99 years of age. Isaac Groot in a later deposition stated in his deposition he was present at the marriage of John and Wyntie in 1772 and that they were residents in the town of Niskayuna and married by the Reverend Barent Vrooman, minister of the Reformed Dutch Church of Schenectada.

State of New York
County of Montgomery SS.

On this nineteenth day of September in the year of our Lord 1832, personally appeared in open court before the Judges of the court of common pleas in and for said county now sitting John D. VanPatten a resident of the town of Glen in said county, aged seventy nine years, who being first duly sworn according to law, doth on his oath make the following declaration, in order to obtain the benefit of the act of Congress passed 7th June 1832.

He was born in the then town of Norman's kill in the county of Albany in said State, now town of Rotterdam in the County of Schenectady on the fourth day of January 1753—His age is recorded in the register of baptisms kept by the reformed protestant Dutch Church in the City of Schenectady. . . . . .When he entered the service of the United States, he lived in said town of Norman's kill at the close of the year 1776 he removed with his family to, and has since the revolutionary war lived in Guilderland in said County of Albany, and now resides in the town of Glen aforesaid. . . . . .He entered the service of the United States under the following named officers and served as herein stated.

He was called into service in the spring of the year one thousand seven hundred and seventy five in the company of militia whereof Abraham Oothout (1) was the captain. His first Lieutenant was John Roseboom second Lieutenant Nicholas Barheydt, Ensign Cornelius L. VanSantvoort, in the regiment of militia commanded by Colonel Abraham Wemple & Myndert Wemple & Abraham Swits Majors. (2) He served in said company for the term of two years, then having removed to Guilderland as aforesaid he enlisted for the term of nine months in Captain Jacob VanDusen's (3) company in the New York line, and served in said company at Ticonderoga and Skeenesborough under the command of Major Hay or Hale, and was employed at those fortresses with artificers in building boats and cannon carriages for the use of the American Army and in erecting fortifications.

He was at Ticonderoga in service as aforesaid when that fortress was invested by Burgoyne and was thereupon evacuated by the American Army.— after he had completed his term of service in said company of Captain Jacob VanDusen, he enlisted in the company of militia that came within his beat, to wit—the company commanded by Captain John Groot (4), of which company George Waggoner (5) & Derick Hamestreet were Lieutenants, the names of the colonel of the regiment and of the other field officers he does not recollect.

He continued to serve in said company of Captain John Groot until the end of the revolutionary war.—He was marched through Schoharie, Canajoharie, Stone Arabia, Fort Hunter, Caughnawaga, Saratoga, Fort Edward, Ticonderoga, Albany and Fort Stanwix, was at the destruction of Schoharie (6) and Cobleskill, (7) and he was at the surrender of Burgoyne (8), and has performed garrison duty at all of the above mentioned places except Albany and Cobleskill at what particular periods and how long each time, he performed military duty at each of the above places he cannot possibly recollect; but he knows that in addition to the nine months service as above specified he was on actual duty as a scout, in garrison and in the field and in guarding different posts and passes at least for the term of one year. . . . He recollects Colonel Dubois (9) of the State Levies, General VanRensselaer (10) and General Gansevoort (11), Colonel Cornelius VanDyck (12), Philip Schuyler(13) & does not recollect any others.

He has no documentary evidence but can produce the testimony of Cornelius VanDyck, Simon A. Groot and John DeGraff who can testify to his services. . . . He never received any written discharge from the service.

The following are the names of persons to whom he is known in his present neighbourhood, and who can testify as to his character for veracity & their belief of his services as a soldier of the revolution, viz. Teunis Ostrander & Henry Davis.

He hereby relinquishes every claim whatever to a pension or annuity except the present and declares that his name is not on the pension roll of the agency of any state. (Signed with his mark) John D. VanPatten

Subscribed & sworn the day & year aforesaid in open court. Geo. D. Ferguson, Clerk

State of New York
County of Schenectady SS.

Simon A. Groot of the City of Schenectady in said County being duly sworn and examined doth depose and say that he is well acquainted with John D. VanPatten referred to in the preceding deposition of John DeGraff and Cornelius VanDyck—that said John D. VanPatten served with this Deponent in the company of Captain Jacob VanDusen, which company with several others were under the Command of Major Hale of the New York line at Ticonderoga & Skeensborough & were employed at those posts during the year one thousand seven hundred and seventy seven in erecting fortifications, and building boats & other vessels for the American Army—that said John D. VanPatten served with this Deponent as aforesaid for the term of about seven months to wit, until the month of July, in the year aforesaid when said fort of Ticonderoga was evacuated by the American troops—how much longer said John D. VanPatten served, and in what other companies, this deponent cannot say. But although he has no personal knowledge of the other military services of said John D. VanPatten yet he has no doubt but that he served for the different terms in his declaration set forth, said John D. VanPatten having always been reputed and believed to have been a true and faithful soldier during the whole war of the revolution and further this deponent saith not. (Signed) Simon A. Groot.

Subscribed & Sworn this 30th August 1832, before me John Worden, Justice of the Peace

State of New York SS.

On this thirty first day of January 1837 personally appeared before Samuel W. Johnson one of the Judges of the Court of Common Pleas in and for the County of Schenectada in said state Wyntie VanPatten a resident of the town of Glen in the County of Montgomery in said State of New York, aged Eighty years, who being first duly sworn according to law, doth on her oath, make the following declaration, in order to obtain the benefit of the provision made by the act of Congress, passed July 4, 1836; that she is the widow of John D. VanPatten who was a soldier in the army of the revolution and received a pension under the act of 7 June 1832, of eighty dollars per annum.

She further declares that she was married to the said John D. VanPatten on the fifth day of June in the year seventeen hundred and seventy two; that her husband the aforesaid John. D. Van Patten, died on the twenty fourth day of October 1835 and that she has remained a widow ever since that period, as will more fully appear by reference to the proof hereunto annexed. (Signed with her mark) Wyntie VanPatten.

Sworn to and subscribed on the day and year above written before me said Judge. S. W. Jones

Schenectada, Nov 27, 1839.
J. L. Edwards Esq, Commissioner of Pensions. War Department, Washington DC.
Sir.

The application of Wyntie VanPatten widow of John D. VanPatten has been sleeping in your office more than two years. Mr. VanPatten during his life time received a full pension; but when his widow applied it was said that his claim had been admitted on insufficient evidence. His services were rendered partly in the militia & partly in the Quarter Master's Department—If reference be had to the militia service alone, I think it very probable that at the most not more than 8 or 9 months services can be established. But Mr. VanPatten served in the Company of Captain VanDusen as will be seen by reference to his original papers on file under the act of 7th June 1832. I beg leave to call attention to this point; which must have been overlooked in deciding upon her claim. This was the same service for which many pensioners have received certificates; e.g. Wm. Van Benthuysen, Simon A. Groot &c and I only ask that the same justice be extended to Mrs. VanPatten which others receive.

I am very respectfully your obt. Serv't. G. F. Yates

End Notes—John D. VanPatten—W.18187

1. Captain Abraham Oothout (Oathout, etc.) with company officers as stated were all commissioned on June 20, 1778 in Colonel Abraham Wemple's Second Regiment of Albany County Militia.
2. Abraham Swits was the First Major and Myndert M. Wemple was the Second Major. Both were commissioned on June 20, 1778 in Colonel Wemple's Regiment.
3. So far no muster roll for Captain VanDeusen's Company has been found. Colonel Undney Hays served in the Quartermaster's Department. This company would not be considered part of the New York line which were Continental Soldiers.
4. Captain John Groot (Groat, etc.) was in Colonel Philip P. Schuyler's Third Regiment of Albany County Militia. Captain Groot and the following officers were commissioned on June 22, 1778: First Lieutenant—Barent Myndersen; Second Lieutenant—Levy VanAaken; Ensign—Dirck Hemstreet.
5. Actually John Groot had served as the First Lieutenant and George Wagener as Second Lieutenant in Captain Jacob Van Aernam's Company in the Third Albany. When Groot was commissioned

Captain, Wagener was commissioned the First Lieutenant in Captain VanAernam's Company.

6. The Schoharie Valley was destroyed on October 17, 1780 by Sir John Johnson. Detachments of the Third Albany were in the Lower and or Middle Forts.
7. Cobleskill was destroyed on May 30, 1778 by Captain Joseph Brant.
8. General John Burgoyne surrendered his British Army on October 17, 1777 at Saratoga (present day Schuylerville, NY).
9. Lewis DuBois had been the Colonel of the Fifth New York Continental Regiment until he resigned on December 22, 1779. Colonel DuBois was then appointed Colonel of a regiment of New York State Levies on July 1, 1780.
10. Robert VanRensselaer was appointed Colonel in 1775 of the Eighth Regiment of Albany County Militia. He received his commission on February 25, 1778 as colonel. He was appointed Brigadier General on June 16, 1780 of the Second Brigade of Albany County Militia.
11. Peter Gansevoort was appointed Colonel of the Third New York Continental Regiment on November 21, 1776. When the First and Third New York Regiments were consolidated on January 1, 1781, Colonel Gansevoort was deranged (discharged). Gansevoort was appointed Brigadier General on March 26, 1781 of the First Brigade of Albany County Militia. Brigadier General Abraham TenBroeck had resigned because of infirmity.
12. Lieutenant-Colonel Cornelius VanDyck was appointed on November 21, 1776 to serve in the First New York Continental Regiment under Colonel Goose VanSchaick. He served in this regiment until the end of the war.
13. Philip Schuyler was appointed Major General in the Continental Army on June 19, 1775. He resigned on April 19, 1779.

Bounty Land Claim for Goose Van Scaaiek or VanSchaick

B.L. Wt. 2245-500-Col. Issued Sept 15, 1790 to Mary Van Scaaick executrix. Also recroded as B.L. Wt. 2146-500-Col. Issued Sept. 15, 1790 to Mary VanSchaaiek Executrix. No Papers

8-7-28

Hon. Commr-Bureau of Pensions.

Dear Sir:--

Col. Goose Van Shaick of 1st & Second NY Line (1) etc. the Rev. War—Have you his service record? Particulary ante 1779. He was wounded at Fort Ticonderoga, July 16 or about, 1777 (2) in the Burgoyne Campaign, I seek data that will verify the above (see Heitman), and the use of 1st NY Line—stemming Burgoyne's advance to Albany. T.E. Cassidy, Box 420, New Rochelle, NY.

Still another letter of inquiry brings more information on the colonel.

227 Wilbraliam Road,Springfield Mass. Sept. 10th 1926
Gentlemen-

Please look among the records in your office for the name of Coln. Goosen VanSchaick who served in the War of the Revolution from the State of New York—did not know but that his wife might have a pension.—

His daughter Elizabeth who married Lybrant Quackenbush had one & I have the papers. Am trying to connect records of Coln. Goosen VanSchaick's birth, marriage (to Maycke Van Den Bergh) (3) & death of each.

Any information will be very gladly received. Yours Sincerely (Mrs.) Clara W. Atwater.

Reply to the letter of inquiry.

I have to advise you that from the records of this Bureau, it appears that Warrant 2245 for five hundred acres (4) of Bounty Land was allowed on September 15, 1790, to Mary Van Scaaick or VanSchaaick, executrix on account of the services of Colonel Goose VanSaaick or Van Schaaick of the New York Line, War of the Revolution. It does not appear that pension was claimed on account of his services.

There are no further data on file as to this claim, either service, or family, owing to the destruction of papers when the War Office was burned in 1800.

The relationship of the executrix is not stated.

[In the margin, handwritten: Colonels only entitled to 500 acres. Both warrants issued same date. I used highest no. as I have always thought it was a correction of some error in first Warrant.

End Notes—B.L.Wt.2245-500-Col. Goose VanSchaick

1. Goose VanSchaick was appointed Colonel of the Second New York Continental Regiment on June 28, 1775. On February 15, 1776 he was appointed Colonel of a New York Continental Regiment which was un-numbered and was sent to reinforce the Continental Army still in Canada. On November 21, 1776, Goose was appointed Colonel of the First New York Continental Regiment. He served until the end of the War in 1783. He was appointed a Brigadier General (brevet) on October 10, 1783.
2. Colonel VanSchaick was not wounded at this time as many later books state such as Francis B. Heitman's Historical Register of Officers of the Continental Army During the War of the Revolution, on page 557. Goose was actually wounded on July 6, 1758 near Fort Ticonderoga while serving as a Lieutenant in a regiment of New York Provincials. He was with the advance party of Lord Howe who was killed during the fight with the French. Goose was struck on the left cheek by a French musket. This wound turned cancerous and may have contributed to his death on July 4, 1789.
3. Goose married Mary TenBroeck
4. Goose actually was granted a total of 3,600 acres for his services during the War of Independence.

For Further Reading:

History of the First New York Regiment 1775-1783, by Ted W. Egly, Jr., Peter E. Randall Publisher, 1981 and Goose VanSchaick of Albany 1736-1789, Ted W. Egly, Jr. 1992.

Pension Application for Bartholomew VanValkenburgh or VanVolkenburgh

R.10,899
State of New York
Montgomery County SS.

On this 19th day of September 1832 personally appeared in open court at the Court House in Johnstown in said county now sitting Bartholomew VanValkenburgh aged seventy two years who being first duly sworn according to law doth on his oath make the following declaration in order to obtain the benefit of the Act of Congress passed June 7th 1832. That he was born in Kinderhook, Columbia County State aforesaid that he was about 19 years of age when he first entered the service of his country, that his first captain was Isaac VanValkenburgh, (1) that the chief business of the company was in scouring the country, watching the Tories & keeping off what were then called the cow boys. That he served off & on in such capacity about one year—when a detachment from said county consisting of about eight hundred men were ordered up the Mohawk River under the command of Genl Henry VanRensselaer [It was General Robert VanRensselaer], Col. Abraham VanAlstine, Major Harman VanBuren (2) & John Lansing, who I have understood has since been chancellor of this state, was quartermaster, that we marched up said River & got near Stonearabia, where we met the Tories & Indians & had a Battle (3), I well remember it for Col. Brown was killed on the field. [Oct 1780] That he then went with the army across the river to Fort Plain, that while the said Lansing (4) was out on a scouting party & was chased & got his horse swamped, that he came in the Fort about day break & asked the men who dared to try to get his horse, this deponent said "I am one" that three others also volunteered, two I remember Jacob Staats & Peter VanSlyck (5), that they went & found his horse & brought him to the camp, that because I was the first who said I would go, Genl VanRensselaer gave me a discharge, That I then went home but was soon again ordered out & most of our business then was for some time in watching the Tories & marching to different parts of the county, that one time we was sent by Col. VanAlstine & Major VanBuren to surprise & take some Tories that we fired & killed one & then we took seventeen of them & took them to camp, Peter Hugener was one I remember that we took—That we again went up the Hudson River under Genl VanRensselaer staid a while at Albany, we was then ordered to Saratoga, and I was one of those who saw that glorious day when Burgoine (6) surrendered to the American arms, [Oct 1777] Arnold the traitor was there, so was Gates, and Morgan (7) the old Rifle Man, after that I went home & served the rest of the war under Bartholomew Jacob

VanVolkenburgh (8), that he saved [served] under him the remainder of the war on scouting parties, watching the Tories & catching the Cow Boys. That altogether he saved [served] more than four years the precise time however he cannot state. He hereby relinquishes every claim whatever to a pension or annuity except the present & declares that his name is not on the pension roll of the agency of any state. (Signed with his mark) Bartholomew VanVolkenburgh

Subscribed & Sworn in open court this 19th September 1832. Geo. D. Ferguson, Clerk

End Notes—Bartholomew VanValkenburgh—R10899

1. Most likely he enlisted he enlisted in 1776 when he turned 16 years of age in Captain Lambert Borghardt's Company (First Company) in Colonel Andries Witbeck's Seventh Regiment of Albany County Militia. On April 2, 1778, First Lieutenant Isaac P. VanValkenburgh was commissioned Captain of the First Company in place of Borghardt. On the same date Abraham VanAlstyne was commissioned Colonel of the Seventh Regiment in place of Witbeck.
2. Harmon VanBuren was appointed major on September 5, 1776 and he received his commission on October 30, 1778 in the Seventh Albany.
3. Bartholomew was referring to the Battle of Klocksfield which was fought in the afternoon of October 19, 1780. Colonel Brown was killed in the morning of October 19, 1780 at Stone Arabia. Brigadier General Robert VanRensselaer with the Albany County Militia were closer to Fort Hunter when this battle took place.
4. The only John J. Lansing in 1780 to serve as a Quarter Master served in the Twelfth Regiment of Albany County Militia. But it does not appear that this regiment was with General VanRensselaer. Their district would have taken in what was then Ball's Town. Ballstown was attacked and a good part of it was burned on October 17, 1780. Many of the militia including its Lieutenant-Colonel James Gordon were taken prisoners in this raid.
5. Staats and VanSlyck served as privates in Captain VanValkenburgh's Company.
6. General John Burgoyne surrendered his British forces on October 17, 1777 to Major General Horatio Gates of the Continental Army.
7. Major General Benedict Arnold and Colonel Daniel Morgan in 1777.
8. Bartholomew J. VanValkenburgh served as a Lieutenant in the First Continental New York Regiment under Colonel Goose VanSchaick. He did not serve in the Seventh Albany.

Pension Application for Bernard VanValkenburg

S.11637

State of New York, County of Columbia SS.

On this day to wit the 31st day of August 1832 personally appeared in open court before the Justices of the Justices Court of the City of Hudson in said county now in session Bernard VanValkenburgh of the Town of Chatham in said County and State aforesaid aged seventy-seven years who being first duly sworn according to law doth on his oath make the following Declaration in order to obtain the benefit of the Act of Congress passed June 7, 1832.

That he entered the service of the United States under the following named officers and served as herein stated.

In the fall of 1776 does not recollect the month thinks the month of November this applicant with the regiment then commonly called the Kinderhook Regiment was called out or Drafted to go up the Mohawk river to repel the aggressions of the Indians in the then Tryon County 60 or 70 miles from Albany. On this expedition this applicant served under the following officers and was bound to duty six weeks—the officers were Andrew Whitbeck—Colonel—Harman VanBuren Major—Lambert Burgert Capt.—Isaac VanValkenburgh first Lieutenant -John Van Alstyne 2d Lieutenant -Andress Whitbeck Jnr ensign—(1)

The following spring was drafted to go to Lake George to protect a large quantity of provision proceeded as far as Albany—was ordered to return and was kept on duty in and near the village of Kinderhook for the purpose of carrying into effect the orders and requisitions of a committee appointed to examine persons suspected of Toryism—take oaths of allegiance &c—Served three months on this expedition.

This applicant further states that he was left on duty as a minute man with the rest of his company who would volunteer during the summer and fall of 1777 except the time of service as above stated for the purpose of scouring the country for tories for the space of two months at different times and served under the command of John VanAlstyne Lieutenant—William and John Scott were serjeants during these scouting expeditions which extended through the county principally.

During the time of service as stated in the 2d description Abram VanAlstyne was Colonel and Isaac VanValkenburgh Capt John VanAlstyne first Lieutenant. (2)

A few weaks [sic] previous to the taking of Burgoyne (3) this applicant with several others of this company volunteered to take provisions to the troops there engaged in the bloody conflict at Saratoga was absent three weeks and returned home after the surrender of that army.

This applicant further sets forth that he has no documentary evidence nor does he know of any person (except those whose certificates is hereto annexed) whose testimony he can procure who can testify to his service.

He hereby relinquishes every claim whatever to a pension or annuity except the present and declares that his name is not on the pension roll of the agency of any state.

Answers to the Interrogatories &c

1. This applicant was born in the Town of Kinderhook (Then) County of Albany and State of New York in the year 1755.
2. He has no record of his age.

3. When called into service, lived in the Town of Kinderhook aforesaid—has lived there ever since except the last ten years during which time he has resided in the adjoining town of Chatham.
4. This applicant was drafted to go the expedition up the Mohawk river—Drafted to go to Lake George - Volunteered to go on Scouting parties—volunteered to go to Saratoga.
5. The names of the officers who were with the troops where he served were those before mentioned, according to his best recollection. The Regiments this application remembers were those of militia—to wit Kinderhook, Canaan, and Claverack. Does not recollect the names of the officers of the two latter.
6. Never received a written discharge from service.
7. The names of persons to whom I am known in my present neighborhood and who can testify as to my character for veracity and their belief of my services as a soldier of the Revolution are Martin VanDeusen, Peter Groot, and James VanValkenburgh. (Signed with his mark) Bernard VanValkenburgh.

Sworn to and subscribed the day and year aforesaid. Hiram Wilbur, Clerk.

End Notes—Bernard VanValkenburg—S11637

1. The officers for the Seventh Regiment of Albany County Militia were appointed in 1775 as follows:
   Colonel Andries Witbeck
   Lieutenant-Colonel Barent VanDerPool
   First Major Lawrence Goes
   Second Major Cornelius VanSchaick
   Adjutant Isaac VanDerPool
   QuarterMaster John D.Goes
   On September 5, 1776 Harman VanBuren was appointed Major and was commissioned on October 30, 1778.
   The officers of the First Company were:
   Captain Lambert Borghart
   First Lieutenant Isaac P. VanValkenburgh
   Second Lieutenant Johannes J. VanAlstyne
   Ensign Nicholas Kittle, Jr.
   Andries Whitbeck, Jr. was not found as serving as an Ensign in this company. He was listed as serving as a private.
2. On April 2, 1778 the following officers were commissioned for the Seventh Albany:
   Abraham VanAlstyne as Colonel
   Philip VanAlstyne as Lieutenant-Colonel
   Isaac Goes as Major
   The officers for the First Company on the same date are as follows:
   Captain Isaac P. VanValkenburgh

First Lieutenant Johannes J. VanAlstyne
Second Lieutenant William Vosburgh
Ensign John VanHousen

3. General John Burgoyne invaded New York via Lake Champlain—Lake George to Saratoga in 1777. The Americans were under Major General Philip Schuyler until August. Major General Horatio Gates took command of the North American Army in August.

Pension Application for Christian VanValkenburg or Valkenburgh

W.15810 (Widow: Catharine)
State of New York
City of Hudson SS.

On this 28th day of July AD 1837 personally appeared before the Justices Court of the City of Hudson & the Justices thereof Catharine Valkenburgh of the town of Clermont in the County of Columbia & State aforesaid aged Eighty four years, who being first duly sworn according to law doth on her oath make the following declaration in order to obtain the benefits of the provision made by the act of Congress passed July 4th 1836.

That she is the widow of Christian Valkenburgh who was a Lieutenant & Quartermaster (& the same individual named in the annexed Commissions) in the Regiment of Militia commanded by Lieut. Col. Henry Livingston & of which Peter R. Livingston (1) was Colonel when her said husband was Lieutenant in the company of Capt. Philip Smith. (2)

That she was married to said Christian in the year of 1777 in the month of May she thinks. Her said husband held a commission of some kind before her marriage & was out in service at the north before said marriage, in said regiment she thinks six weeks & after her marriage her said husband was out & absent in the service several times—She recollects he left soon after marriage & was gone till about the time of her confinement with her first child—he came home at that time & before she was well he left her again & was absent some time. This service was also at the north. He was also in service with General Putnam (3) at one time but how long she can't say & in the year 1780 & 1781 he was absent in service at the north twice while he was quartermaster (4), but how long she can't say—she further says that by reason of old age & infirmity, she cannot state any of his service with any great particularity than as above. That her said husband died in the year 1813 or 14 & she has remained a widow ever since. (Signed with her mark) Catharine Valkenburgh

Sworn to & subscribed the day & year above written in presence of Andrew Hover & in open court -- P. Dean Carrique

State of New York
Columbia County SS.

Barent Sipperly being duly sworn says that he resides in Germantown in said County & is now seventy nine (79) years of age, that during the

Revolutionary War this deponent belonged to Capt. Tealer Rockefeller (5) company in Col. Peter R. Livingston's Regiment - That he was well acquainted with Christian Valkenburgh the husband of Catharine Valkenburgh—that said Christian belonged to Captain Smith company in said Regiment--& was a Lieutenant in said Company & afterwards quartermaster of said Regiment—That said Christian was out in service with this deponent in the spring of 1776 & marched as far as Greenbush were they stayed two weeks & were discharged—This he thinks was in June & said Christian he thinks was Sergeant or First Lieutenant—again in the latter part of 1776 & fore part of 1777 said Christian was in service with this deponent at Fishkill for two months—said Christian was a Lieutenant in the company of Capt Cline or Kline (6), But he does not recollect the colonel's name—They were drafted for this service--& he thinks it was the latter half of November all of December & half of January following—

Again in the summer & fall of 1777 said Christian was in service at the north with this deponent for three months or more—They went to Fort Edward in July, the said Christian being Lieutenant in said Smiths Company—They were on the retreat before Burgoyne & were at the battle of Saratoga (7) & discharged soon after the surrender of Burgoyne (8). They were out in actual service at this full three months—Again said Christian was out in service with this deponent at Schenectady Ballstown & Saratoga about six weeks in the fall of 1780 or 81. The Indians & Tories had burnt several buildings at Baltown (9) & this expedition was on that account—said Christian Valkenburgh was on this service quartermaster of the Regiment—and this deponent thinks said Christian Valkenburgh performed much other service, which he cannot now specify—and this deponent further says that said Christian was married to Catharine Minkler in the fall of 1775 by the Revd Mr. Cock & this deponent was at the wedding & saw them married—That said Catharine is now the widow of said Christian who died in 1812. (Signed with his mark) Barent Sipperly

In presence of Jonas Dinegar.

Words "& saw them married" written on erasure & sworn before me this June 26th 1838. J. W. Fairfield Comsr [commissioner] of Deeds.

End Notes—Christian VanValkenburgh - W15810

1. Peter R. Livingston was Colonel of the Tenth Regiment of Albany County Militia. Henry Livingston was the Lieutenant-Colonel in the same regiment.
2. Philip Smith was the Captain of the Eighth Company in the Tenth Albany.
3. Major General Israel Putnam of the Continental Army.
4. Christian was commissioned as the Second Lieutenant in Captain Smith's Company on; May 28, 1778. He was commissioned the Quarter Master of the Tenth Albany on September 28, 1780. Petrus Wynkoop who had been the Quartermaster had moved.
5. Teil Rockefeller was the Captain of the Tenth Company in the Tenth Albany.

6. Conradt Klyne was the Captain of the Fourth Company in the Tenth Albany.
7. The Second Battle of Saratoga was fought on October 7, 1777. This is the battle that Brigadier General Abraham TenBroeck's Brigade of Albany County Militia fought in under Major General Benedict Arnold.
8. General John Burgoyne surrendered his British forces on October 17, 1777.
9. Balls Town (present day Ballston Spa, Saratoga County) was destroyed on October 17, 1780 by British troops and their Indian Allies under Captain John Munro of the King's royal Regiment of New York.

Pension Application for Francis VanValkenburgh

W.19,571 (Wife: Sylvia or Sylva)
Copy of Family Record
Nobletown, Columbia County New York.

Francis VanValkinburgh born December 25th 1755 inlisted in the American Army in the Revolution in Second New York Regiment under Col. Philip Countlon, Capt. William Pell Discharged June 7th 1783.

Sylva Coval born the 18 day of October 1765-78.

Francis VanValkinburgh and Sylva Coval was married September the 11th 1784 marriage took place before Elden Smith Published three times in Nobletown in Columbia County. Zachuis Vanvalkinburgh was born May 9th 1785. Michael Vanvalkinburgh was born January the 28 1791. Elizabeth Vanvalkinburgh was born June the 9th 1793. Hannah Vanvalkinburgh was born Feb. 24th 1796. Sylva Vanvalkinburgh was born May 11th 1798. Isaac Vanvalkinburgh was born April 14, 1801. Amy Vanvalkenburgh born Feb 6th 1803. Polly Vanvalkinburgh born January 19th 1806. Francis Vanvalkenburgh deceased March 19th 1813.

Sylva Vanvalkinburgh says or near as she can recollect Francis Vanvalkinburgh inlisted the second year of the war thinks he was during the war does not recollect all the battles or engagements he was in was at Stillwater at the taking of Bogoine was discharged June the 7th 1783. I kept his discharge till several years after the war delivered to a man to see about his bounty land her husbd died and she did not gait the discharge again says his capt that he served under name was William Pell and Colonel Phillip Countlon. Philip VanCortlandt is not able to attend court in person. Jany 25, 1844.

Declaration

In order to obtain the benefit of the act of Congress of the 7th July 1838, entitled "An act granting half pay and pensions to certain widows.
State of New York
County of Erie SS.

On this fifteenth day of July AD 1844 personally appeared before the subscriber a Judge of the court in and for said County, Sylva VanValkenburgh a resident of Holland in the said county aged Seventy eight years who being first duly sworn according to law, doth on her oath make the following declaration in order to obtain the benefit of the provision made by the Act of Congress, passed July 7, 1838, entitled "An act granting half pay and pensions to certain widows." That she is the widow of Francis VanValkenburgh who as a soldier in the war of the revolution; that her said husband the aforesaid Francis VanValkenburgh served in the war of the revolution as a soldier of the New York line; that he served under Capt. William Pell, Col. Philip VanCortland (1) or Courtland, that he enlisted for during the war, that he was in the battle of taking Burgoine, Saratoga, (2) that he continued in the service till the 7th June 1783 (3), when he was honorably discharged, that this deponent had often seen the discharge that her said husband drew a lot of bounty land in the County of Onondaga, as this deponent believes, and near Skaneatles Lake; that her said husband was called by the Dutch, Francis Fralick, Zochum VanValkenburgh, but his real name was, as above stated; she further declares that she was married to the said Francis VanValkenburgh on the 11th day of September 1784, Seventeen Hundred and Eighty four, that her husband the aforesaid, Francis VanValkenburgh died on the 19th day of march 1813, eighteen hundred and thirteen; that she was not married to him prior to his leaving the service, but the marriage took place previous to the first of January Seventeen hundred and ninety four, viz, at the time above stated. (Signed with her mark) Sylva Van Valkenburgh.

Subscribed and sworn to on the day and year above written below. Bela H. Colegrove, a Judge of Erie County.

End Notes—Francis VanValkenburgh—W.19571

1. Francis enlisted as a private for "during war" on January 10, 1779 in Captain Peter VanRensselaer's Company in Colonel James Livingston's First Canadian Continental Regiment. FROM: Revolutionary War Rolls 1775-1783, Series M-246, Roll 133, Folder 223, National Archives, Washington, D.C.

   On January 1, 1781, the New York Continental Regiments were consolidated from 5 into 2.

   The several Additional Continental Regiments and the two Canadian Continental Regiments were also consolidated. Men who enlisted from New York were put into Colonel Philip VanCortlandt's Second Continental Regiment. We was assigned to Captain Samuel T. Pell's Company and served in this company until he was discharged.

   On some of the muster rolls in the First Canadian and the Second New York he is sometimes listed as Van Wahlenburgh, VanWalkenburgh, etc. FROM: Revolutionary War Rolls 1775-1783, Series M-246, Roll 68, Folder 29 (Pell's Company 2 NY), National Archives, Washington, D.C.
2. It appears that Francis was serving in one of the Albany County Militia Regiments during the Saratoga Campaign of 1777. So far Francis had not shown up on muster rolls but they are far from complete. I did find a Francis VanValkenburg enlisted on Mary 5, 1778 in Captain

Jonathan Pearsee's Company for nine months in Colonel Henry B. Livingston's Fourth New York Continental Regiment. He was discharged on February 5, 1779. It appears to be another Francis as the pensioner Francis enlisted on January 10, 1779 into a Continental Regiment but it is possible that he had been recruited and served out the first enlistment and then joined the First Canadian. FROM: Revolutionary War Rolls 1775-1780, Series M-246, Roll 71, Folder 55, National Archives, Washington, D.C.

3. The Second New York was in the Yorktown Virginia Campaign from September 28 to October 19, 1781.

Pension Application for William VanValkenburgh

S.11597
State of New York
Columbia County SS.

On this third day of September in the year of our Lord 1832 personally appeared in open court before the Justices of the Justices Court of the City of Hudson now sitting William VanValkenburgh a resident of the Town of Stuyvesant in the County aforesaid who being first duly sworn according to Law doth on his oath make the following declaration in order to obtain the benefit of the act of Congress passed June 7th 1832. That he was born in the Town of Kinderhook now Stuyvesant in the County & State aforesaid in the year 1760.

That he was first called into the New York State Malitia in the Revolutionary War about the first of October 1776—his officers were Capt. Phillip VanAlstine (1), First Lieutenant Peter Hugenan, Second Lieut. Gocia VanBuren (2) march from the town of Kinderhook aforesaid to GreenBush opposite Albany and was there drilled for the term of three weeks and was Discharged about the last of October Term of service three weeks.

Enlisted again under Capt. Phillip VanAlstine Lieut Peter Hugenan under the command of Colonel Andrus Widbeck Started in the month of May 1777 it was in the time of Planting Corn marched to Albany Remained there three weeks then to Half Moon Point then to Schenectady & then to Johnstown, north of Albany and was Dismissed in the month of July after a service of two months this term of service is proven by the annex'd affidavit Abraham Clark sworn before John J. VanAllen Jun Esqr. Two Months.

Was again called out under Capt. James VanAllen (3), Peter Hugenan Lieutenant James Wengard Ensign in the month of August on a scouting party against the Torys & Robbers in this Tour Abraham VanNess was killed by the Robbers was absent on this service one week.

Again this applicant Enlisted about the last of February 1778 at the Town of Kinderhook in the county aforesaid under Capt. Abraham Fonda (4) Lieutenant Pitcher (5) John Decker Robinson (6) Second Lieutenant Thomas Beacraft, Sergt under the command of John Beekman (7) Colonel encamped at Albany and remained there until he was discharg'd in the month of May being daily drilled by my officers. This term of service was Two & ½ months.

Again enlisted in the month of May 1778 in the Town of Kinderhook in the County aforesaid under Capt. James VanAllen Lieut Peter Hugenan Ensign James Wyngard as a company of Vigilance to Guard that section of the Country from the Torys & Robbers he enlisted for three months stood guard two nights in each week & frequently - oftener was discharged in the month of August 1778 served in this tour if only allowed two nights in each week one month—Thinks he should be allowed the whole 3 months as the Duty was arduous—leaves it to the decision of the Department has no living witness to prove this service.

Again enlisted in the month of September about the 15th under Capt. Jas VanAllen first Lieutenant John VanAlstine (8) Second Lieutenant Gocia VanBuren & Ensign James Wingard in a Regiment commanded by Colonel Waterman (9) Marched from the Town of Kinderhook to FishKill on the North River and remained there until the time of his enlistment expired when he was discharge being the middle of December 1778. Time of service Three months.

The above Term of service is also proven by the annex'd affidavit of Abraham Clark.

Was again in the month of October about the first again enlisted under Capt. Isaac VanValkenburgh Lieutenant Gocia VanBuren & Ensign James Wingard and marched from the Town of KinderHook to Bemises Heights and remained there nearly three weeks and was Discharged about 25th Oct 1779.

And to the interrogatories prescribed by the War Department he answers he was born in the Town of KinderHook in the County of Columbia & State of New York on the 7th of Sept. 1760.

Has no record of his age it has been lost for many years.

Lived in the Town of KinderHook when called into the service and has lived there ever since and still lives there although that part of it where he resides has been changed to Stuyvesant.

Always enlisted voluntarily in the service.

There were some Continental soldiers at Albany while this applicant was stationed there does not recollect the names of any except a Capt. David VanNess (10) who is since Dead has had many a glass of grog of said VanNess.

The General Circumstances of his service are fully embodyed in this application.

Never rec'd a written discharge. He would refer the Department for Character to Lucas Hoes Esqr, James VanDerpoel Esqr, District Judge Hose.

And this applicant hereby further states that John J. Sharp and Abraham Clark whose affidavits are hereunto annexed are the only living witness that he can find and that although he made repeated efforts to bring them into Court it was without effect and was therefore under the necessity of having their affidavits taken out of Court that he has no documentary evidence.

He hereby relinquishes every claim whatever to a pension or annuity except the present and declares that his name is not on the pension roll of the agency thereof—(Signed with his mark) William VanValkenburgh

Sworn & subscribed the day & year first above mentioned. Hiram Wilbur, Clerk

End Notes—William VanValkenburgh - S11597

1. Captain Philip VanAlstyne's Company (Third Company) of Colonel Andries Witbeck's Seventh Regiment of Albany County Militia. The other officers were First Lieutenant John J. Goes, Second Lieutenant Peter Hugunine and Ensign Andries VanDerPoll.
2. Goose VanBuren was not commissioned until April 2, 1778 as a First Lieutenant in Captain Jacobus (James) VanAlen's Company in the Seventh Albany.
3. Captain VanAlstyne had been promoted to Lieutenant-Colonel and he was commissioned as such on April 2, 1778 and Jacobus VanAlen was then appointed Captain and he was also commissioned on April 2, 1778. The other officers commissioned on the same date were First Lieutenant Goose VanBuren, Second Lieutenant Peter VanAlen and Jacob Wyngard as Ensign. Goes and VanDerPoll were replaced as they were "disaffected" (Loyalists). Hugunine no longer served as Second Lieutenant.
4. Abraham Fonda was a captain in Colonel Robert VanRensselaer's Eighth Regiment of Albany County Militia.
5. Jonathan Pitcher served as the First Lieutenant in Captain Araham Hawley's Company in Colonel Peter VanNess' Ninth Regiment of Albany County Militia.
6. John Decker Robinson is unknown.
7. John H. Beekman was the Lieutenant-Colonel of the Fourth Regiment of Albany County Militia. This service was a mixed detachment of the Albany County Militia.
8. First Lieutenant John J. VanAlstyne in Captain Isaac P. VanValkenburgh's Company (First Company) in the Seventh Regiment.
9. Lieutenant-Colonel Asa Waterman of the Seventeenth Regiment of Albany County Militia.
10. Captain David VanNess had served in the First New York Continental Regiment under Colonel Goose VanSchaick.

Pension Application for Cornelius Vedder

R.10946

Declaration in order to obtain the benefit of the Act of Congress passed June 7, 1832.

State of New York

County of Wyoming SS.

On this Nineteenth day of October in the year of our Lord one thousand eight hundred and forty one personally appeared in open court before the Court of Common Pleas of the County of Wyoming aforesaid now sitting Cornelius Vedder (1) a resident of the Town of Attica in the County of Wyoming and State of New York aged eighty one years who being first duly sworn according to law doth on his oath make the following declaration in order to obtain the benefit of the Act of Congress passed June 7, 1832—That he entered the service of the United States under the following named officers and served as herein stated.—

That in the forepart of May in the year 1776 he entered the service as a volunteer at Albany in the State of New York for the term of one year.—he did not join or unite with any company or Regiment but volunteered under Aaron Van Doozer (2) at Albany aforesaid and the next day after he so volunteered at Albany he was put into the magazine room or laberatory to making cartridges in Albany aforesaid under the said Aaron VanDoozer and David Fundy who superintended the making of cartridges—he drew his rations out of the store owned by Jeremiah Wendell and John Fisher was quartermaster. He worked at making cartridges in Albany aforesaid for the term of one year which was the forepart of May 1777 and was then discharged but received no written discharge. He was discharged by the said Aaron Van Doozer—

Then the next day after he was so discharged he volunteered again under the said Aaron Van Doozen but for no particular period and continued on making cartridges at Albany aforesaid for the term of five months longer from the first of May 1777 till the forepart of October 1777—That he served in the last period the full term of five months and was then in the fore part of October 1777 discharged by the said Aaron Van Doozer but received no written discharge—That he served in the whole just one year and five months as above stated at Albany aforesaid in making cartridges for the United States—

That he was born in Albany aforesaid on the thirteenth day of March in the year 1760—

That when he was called into service he lived in Albany aforesaid—That since the Revolutionary War he has lived in Brunswick New York, Canajoharie, Decatur, Schoharie County, Cato New York and that he now lives in Attica aforesaid.

That he was called into service as a volunteer—Colonel Van Schaick's (3) Regiment was stationed in Albany when he was in the service—He was acquainted with the said Colonel and Abraham Teneyck (4) his paymaster—He also knows Colonel Willett (5) and Colonel Gansvoort (6)—That he never received a written discharge—That he has no documentary evidence of his service and that he does not know of any person - who is living by whom he can prove his service—The names of the persons in my neighborhood to whom I am known are Conrad N. Spencer, Josiah Smith, Ephraim Whaley and Salmon Wheat who can testify as to my character for veracity and their belief of my services as a soldier of the Revolution—That his name was called every day and generally by the said Aaron Van Doozer and when he was absent, the said David Fundy called the roll and this declarant answered to his name every day—That a guard was kept around the building night and day and his name was on the roll of the said Aaron VanDoozer—That he belonged to no regiment (7) as he ever knew for he was never embodied in any regiment to his knowledge as his whole business was in making cartridges as aforesaid.

He hereby relinquishes every claim whatever to a pension or annuity except the present and declares that his name is not on the pension roll of the agency of any state. On reflection he thinks he can prove part of his services by living witnesses. (Signed with his mark) Cornelius Vedder

Sworn to and subscribed the day and year aforesaid in open court. N. Wolcott, Clerk.

End Notes—R.10946—Cornelius Vedder

1. There are two different Cornelius' in this application. Cornelius Vedder applied for the pension and Harriet Zielly the widow of Cornelius Veeder applied for her late husband's bounty land.
2. This service is in the Quartermaster's Department and was considered as a civilian working for the government and not military duty. This is probably why his application was rejected.
3. In May of 1776, Goose VanSchaick was the Colonel of an un-numbered Continental Regiment. On November 21, 1776, VanSchaick was appointed Colonel of the First New York Continental Regiment.
4. Abraham TenEyck was appointed Second Lieutenant and Pay Master on November 21, 1776, in the First New York.
5. Marinus Willett was appointed Lieutenant-Colonel of the Third New York Continental Regiment on November 21, 1776.
6. Peter Gansevoort was appointed Colonel of the Third New York on November 21, 1776.
7. A Cornelius Vedder served also in the Second Regiment of Albany County Militia commanded by Colonel Abraham Wemple. It is not known if it is the same man at this time.

Bounty Land Application for Cornelius Veeder

B.L.Wt.43513-160-55

Declaration of a Revolutionary Widow who claims a Land Warrant under act of March 3, 1855.

State of New York

Montgomery County

On this 13 day of September A.D. one thousand eight hundred and fifty five personally appeared before me a [blank] within and for the [blank] County and State aforesaid, Harriet Veeder aged 84 years, a resient of the Town of Glen Montgomery County in the State of New York, who being duly sworn according to law, declares that she is the widow of Cornelius Veeder deceased, who was a private [in] Col. Frederick Fisher's (1) Regiment in the District then of Caughnawaga Company commanded by Captain Veeder (2) Lieut. Garret VanBranklen, Ensign Richard Putnam in the War of the Revolution then the County of Tryon & served fourteen days.

She further states that she was married to the said Cornelius Veeder in Caughnawaga District on the eighteenth day of October A.D. 1789 by one Revd Thomas Romeyn a Dutch Reformed Priest and that her name before her said marriage was Harriet Zielley [Zielley] and said husband died at Glen

Montgomery County on the ninth day of November A.D. 1848, and that she is now a widow that her husband the foresaid Cornelius Vedder was born September 14th A.D. 1764.

She makes this declaration for the purpose of obtaining the bounty land to which she may be entitled under the act approved March 3, 1855, and she hereby requests the Commissioner of Pensions to forward her warrant to [?] VanHorne Fonda Montgomery Co., and appoint him my attorney to receive the same for me. (Signed with her mark) Harriet Veeder

We Francis B. Vedder and James Winne residents of Glen Montgomery Co., in the State of New York, upon our oaths declare the foregoing declaration was signed and acknowledged by Harriet Veeder in our presence, and that we believe from the appearance of the applicant that she is the identical person she represents herself to be. Francis B. Vedder, James Winne.

The forgoing declaration and affidavit were sworn to and subscribed before me on the day and year above written and I certify that I know the affiants to be credible persons, that the claimant is the person she represents herself to be and that I have no interest in this claim. John Everson Justice of the Peace in and for said County of Montgomery aforesaid.

State of New York
Montgomery County

Personally appeared before me Francis B. Vedder of the Town of Glen in the County of State aforesaid aged fifty four years being first duly sworn according to Law deposeth & saith that he knew Cornelius Veeder in his life time also his wife Harriet who is still living that he this deponant had known Cornelius Veeder over forty years that he has examined the Family Bible which contains the Births Marriages & Deaths of Cornelius & Harriet Veeder's Family & children & is now in the possession of the widow Harriet Veeder, Cornelius Veeder's widow in which I find recorded the name of Cornelius Veeder under the Head of Births Cornelius Veeder Sept. 14th A.D. 1764, Harriet Zielly July 18, 1779. Marriages Cornelius Veeder to Harriet Zielly by the Rev'd Thomas Romeyn 18th October A.D. 1789. It appears by the record that they were married as above stated. Cornelius Veeder departed his life November 9th A.D. 1848 all of which I find on the Record in the Family Bible of Cornelius Veeder Deceased. Francis B. Vedder.

Subscribed & sworn to before me this 13th day of September 1855. John E. Versen, Justice of the Peace.

End Notes—Cornelius Veeder--B.L.Wt.43513—160-55

1. The Third Regiment of Tryon County Militia was commanded by Colonel Frederick Visscher raised from the Mohawk District. The District of Caughnawaga did exist until 1784.
2. Captain Abraham Veeder, First Lieutenant Nicholas Dockstader, Second Lieutenant Garret S. VanBrocklin and Richard Putman were commissioned on March 8, 1781, in Colonel Visscher's Regiment.

Pension Application for Frederick Vedder

S.21547
State of New York
County of Schenectady SS.

In this thirtieth day of April in the year of our Lord one thousand eight hundred and thirty four personally appeared in Open Court before the Judges of the Court of Common Pleas in and for said County now sitting Frederick Vedder a resident of the Town of Duanesburgh in the County of Schenectady and state aforesaid aged seventy three years and upwards who being first duty sworn according to law doth on his oath make the following declaration in order to obtain the benefit of the act of Congress passed June 7, 1832.

That he was born in the place now called Glenville in the said County on the 28th day of April in the year 1761, a certified copy of the record of his baptism is hereto annexed.—

He has always resided in the County of Schenectady except three years during which time he resided in Broadalbin in the County of Montgomery and except the period engaged in the Revolutionary War. That he resided at the place called Rotterdam when he entered the service of the United [States] in the War of the Revolution.

That in the year 1779 he was enrolled in the Militia of the State of New York in company whereof Colonel Wemple (1) was Colonel and Captain Outhout (2) was Captain and Cornelius Z. Van Zantvoord was Ensign and this deponent was first or orderly serjeant.

And this deponent further says that in the month of September in the year 1779, he this deponent in the company aforesaid was ordered out in actual duty as a serjeant in said company to go to Stone Arabia and that this deponent together with the company aforesaid was marched from Schenectady to Stone Arabia and continued to do actual duty there for the space of three weeks when he was discharged he had no discharge in writing.

And this deponent further says that in the year 1779 in the month of October he this deponent was again called out with the company aforesaid and was marched to Caughnawaga that he did military duty at this time faithfully as a serjeant in said company for the term of three weeks when he was discharged he had no discharge in writing.

And this deponent further says that on the 22d day of May in the year 1780, he was ordered to warn the men of the said company to go to Caughnawaga at the time the family of the Fishers (3) were murdered by the enemy that he this deponent together with said company marched to Caughnawaga and continued on duty this period for the term of three weeks when he was again discharged and this deponent further says that he was out with said company on another expedition in the same year 1780 to Fort Hunter for two weeks when he was discharged. That he never had any written discharge.

That in the same year the time when Canajoharie (4) was destroyed he was at that place to repel the enemy on an expedition for two weeks when he was discharged at the expiration thereof.—

And this deponent further says that he was again in the year 1780 called out on duty in the said company and was marched to Fort Clyde that the expedition lasted for two weeks.

This deponent further says that in the month of October in the year 1780, he was again called out on an expedition to go to Ballston (5) that he was out on this excursion eight days and this deponent further says that he verily believes that he was out in actual duty in the year 1780 as much as five months.

And this deponent further says that in the year 1781, he this deponent together with Captain Outhout's Company aforesaid was stationed at a place called Claus Vielies Pass or the Rifts about four miles west of the City of Schenectady. That he remained there from the first of August until the first of November making three months when he was discharged and this deponent further says that in the same year year [sic] 1781, in the summer of that year he was on an expedition to the BeaverDam so called in pursuit of Tories with a part of his company that this expedition employed this deponent three days.

And this deponent further says that he was on an expedition from Schenectady to Currysbush (6) this lasted only two days.

And this deponent further says that the foregoing services were performed by him as Orderly Serjeant in the said company of Captain Outhout in the Regiment of Col. Wemple and that he can not detail more minutely than he has done the particulars of his services in the war of the Revolution.

The following are the names of some of the regular officers whom he knew, or who were with the troops where he served, and such continental and militia, regiments or companies with which he served, or as he can recollect, viz: Co. Wemple, Major Wemple (7), Captain Fonda (8), Cornelius Z. VanZantford Ensign, Capt. Walter Swits (9), Captain Banker.

He never received any written discharge from the service.

He has no documentary evidence, and knows of no person whose testimony he can procure who can testify to his service.

The following are the names of persons to whom he is known in his present neighborhood and who can testify as to his character for veracity, and their belief of his services as a soldier of the revolution, to wit, Simon J VanAntwerp, Bartholomew, Schmerhorn and Cornelius Z. Van Zantfoord.

He hereby relinquishes every claim whatever, to a pension or annuity except the present, and declares that his name is not on the pension roll of the agency of any state. (Signed) Frederick Vedder

Subscribed and sworn to the day and year first aforesaid. John S. Vrooman, Clerk

Reply to a letter of inquiry dated April 10, 1936.

Reference is made to your letter in which you request the Revolutionary War record of Frederick Vedder, a pensioner, in 1834.

The record of Frederick Vedder is given herein as shown in the papers on file in his claim for pension, S. 21547, based upon his service in that war.

Frederick Vedder was born April 28, 1761 in a town later called Glenville, in Schenectady County, New York. He was the son of Arent Vedder and Catrina VanPetten, and was baptized May 3, 1761 in the Protestant Reformed Dutch Church in Schenectady, New York.

While a resident of a town later called Rotterdam, in said Schenectady County, he enlisted in September 1779, served on various tours as late as November 1781, amounting in all to about six months and fourteen days, as sergeant in Captain Outhout's company, Colonel Wemple's New York regiment; during his service, he was engaged against the enemy in the vicinity of Stone Arabia, Fort Hunter and Fort Clyde.

He was allowed pension on his application executed April 30, 1834, at which time he resided in Duanesburg, Schenectady County, New York. He stated then that he had resided in that county always, with the exception of three years when he resided in Broadalbin, Montgomery County, New York.

Frederick Vedder made no reference to wife or children.

End Notes—S.21547—Frederick Vedder

1. Abraham Wemple was appointed Colonel of the Second Regiment of Albany County Militia (Schenectady District) on October 20, 1775.
2. On June 28, 1778 the following company officers were commissioned in Colonel Wemple's Regiment: Abraham Oothout—Captain. John Roseboom—First Lieutenant. Nicholas Barheyt—Second Lieutenant. Cornelius Van Santfort—Ensign.
3. Frederick is referring to Colonel Frederick Visscher who had been tomahawked and scalped but survived, his mother also had been tomahawked and survived but his brother's Captain John Visscher and Private Harmanus Visscher were killed in this raid led by Sir John Johnson.
4. Captain Joseph Brant destroyed what is now the Village of Fort Plain and the Town of Minden, Montgomery County, New York on August 2, 1780.
5. BallsTown now the Town of Ballstown, part of the Village of Ballston Spa, Saratoga County, N. Y. was destroyed on October 17, 1780, by Captain John Munro.
6. Curry's Bush or Curries Bush is in present day Town of Princetown. This settlement is in present day Schenectady County, NY. This settlement is often confused with Currrytown Tryon County (now Montgomery County), NY.
7. Second Major Myndert M. Wemple in the Second Albany.
8. Captain Jellis J. Fonda of the First Company in the Second Albany.
9. He is probably referring to First Major Abraham Swits of the Second Albany.

Pension Application for Peter V. Veeder

W.19,574

In the matter of Jane Veeder widow of Peter V. Veeder, dec'd.

Albany Mar 13th 1847.

Sir,

I am favored with your communication of the 1st inst. in the above matter in which you state that "the alleged service of claimants in which you state that "the alleged service of Claimants husband in 1778 under Capt. Jellis Fonda is discredited by the Rolls of that company in your office. The name on these rolls is Peter S. Veeder & not Peter V. Veeder" and that "this service cannot of course be computed in the adjustment of Mrs. Veeder's claim."

I do not know that I can give a satisfactory explanation of this discrepancy, but I will attempt to explain the matter as I understand it.

The baptismal name of the claimant was "Peter Veeder (or Veader)—His father's name was "Vrooman Veeder" & hence particularly in the latter part of his life; he used "V" as a middle letter in his name. Several years ago when for the first time I saw the document (to which I have referred in my previous letters in this case) giving the names of the 20 men drawn out of or from Capt. Jellis Fonda's (1) Company to serve 9 months, I noticed that there were several names on that list not borne on the Militia Rolls of Capt. Jellis Fonda + —(e.g. Ephraim Bradt, John Visscher, John & Jacob Glen, Solomon Terillliger & others while Abm. (J.) Yates, John Clute, John Cassity & others are there). I have just examined Fonda's Rolls of 1781 which is all I have, his militia rolls for 1777 &c I deposited in your office about the time I presented Capt. Jellis Fonda's claim for a pension.

Several intelligent gentlemen of the revolution who had served in the regiment of militia to which Capt. Fonda belonged (to wit of Col. Abm. Wemple) represented to me (and I have stated the fact before to your department that two minute companies were organized in the Schenectada District, which at a minute's warning when any number of effective men were required to be raised on an emergency, supplied the requisition. These minute companies were made up of volunteers from the different companies of militia of Col. Wemple's Regiment & they were commanded, the one by Captain Jellis Fonda aforesaid & the other by Capt. John Mynderse, who were both also Captains of Companies of militia in said Regiment. The law of the state before quoted by virtue (2) of which 9 months men were raised to guard the frontiers of this state in 1778, was passed 1st Apl of that year and it would seem from the Document & alluded to that three months after (in July) there were some needed to make up the quota of Levies required & these 20 men were selected from said minute company of Fonda to served till 1 Jany 1779. These Minute Companies gave up their organization under the new arrangements which were adopted in the subsequent years of the war. Hence the name of my claimant is not borne at all on the Militia Rolls of Capt. Fonda for he belonged to this Minute Company, and the Militia Company in which he was enrolled, was that of Capt. Van Patten

(3), and in that company of Militia the Comptrollers Rolls (advanced in this case) place him in subsequent year of the war.

+ Note: There were 2 captains of the militia named Jellis Fonda, one from the Caughnawaga & the other from the Schenectada District.

I will not undertake to say that the name of "Peter S. Veeder" on the Roll in your office is intended for the claimant, the S. being a clerical error; but in considering this matter the fact should be borne in mind, that the same militia man was sometimes or in one expedition, set down in the returns made, under one Captain or Commandant, & at another under a different one.

But be all the things as they may, it is certain that the name of Peter V. Veeder is recorded as one of the 20 from the Schenectada District & Col. Abm. Wemple's Regiment (in a document certified by said Col. Wemple) for the 9 months service in 1778 on the N. York frontiers, pursuant to a law of the state in such case made & provided.

It is to be observed however that as the Draft in question was not made till July, no more than 6 months of the nine, can be claimed in the present case.

I am very respectfully your mo. Obt servt. G.F. Yates.

To Col. J. S. Edwards, Comm. of Pensions.

State of New York SS.

On this 29th day of April 1840, personally appeared before the Judges of the Court of Common Pleas in and for the County of Schenectada now sitting.—

Jane Veeder a resident of the town of Rotterdam in the County of Schenectada in said State aged seventy four years, who being duly sworn according to law, doth on her oath make the following declaration in order to obtain the benefit of the provision made by the act of Congress passed 7th July 1838, entitled "an act granting half pay and pensions to certain widows." That she is the widow of Peter V. Veeder who was a private & sergeant in the war of the revolution but of the particulars of his services she can give no account from her personal knowledge, as she did not become acquainted with him till after the close of said war. She remembers to have heard him relate, that among other tours he accompanied to Schoharie & other places and one engagement for several months also at Stone Arabia & at the taking of Burgoyne—That her maiden name was Van Eps—That she was married by the Rev'd Thomas Romeyn of the Dutch Church of Schenectada, and that he served under Captain's Jellis Fonda & Emanuel DeGraff (4)—That she was married to said Peter V. Veeder on the twenty eighth day of July one thousand seven hundred & eighty nine (1789) that her husband the aforesaid Peter V. Veeder died on the ninth day of October 1814. That she was not married to him prior to his leaving the service, but that her marriage took place previous to the first day of January one thousand seven hundred and ninety four, viz, at the time above stated—and further she saith not. (Signed) Jane Veeder.

Subscribed and sworn to the day and year first above written in open court before me. Arch'd Campbell, Clerk

End Notes—Peter V. Veeder—W.19574

1. Jellis J. Fonda was the Captain of the First Company in Colonel Abraham Wemple's Second Regiment of Albany County Militia.
2. John Mynderse (Myndertse, Mynderson, etc.) was the Captain of the Second Company in the Second Albany.
3. John VanPatten was the Captain of the Third Company in the Second Albany.
4. For Peter to have served in Captain Emanuel DeGraff's Company (Seventh Company) in Colonel Frederick Visscher's Third Regiment of Tryon County Militia, he would have to move from Albany County to Tryon County. It appears that Peter never moved from the Schenectady area during the War of Independence.

Pension Application for Adolph Wallerath (Walrath, Walradt)

W.18275 (Anna) Pension granted to Adolph $46.08 per annum. Anna received 10.44 per annum. Adolph died 15 June 1837, Jefferson County

State of New York

Montgomery County SS

On this Nineteenth day of September personally appeared in open Court before the Court of Common Pleas in and for the County of Montgomery, Adolph Walradt a resident of the town of Oppenheim in the county of Montgomery & State of New York aforesaid, formerly the County of Tryon aged seventy-one years last April and who being first duly sworn according to Law doth on his oath make the following declaration in order to obtain the benefit of the act passed by Congress June 7th 1832. That he entered the service of the United States under the following officers here mentioned and served as hereafter stated. (VYL) That he was enrolled in the year 1777 in a company of Militia commanded by Captain John Breadbeck. (1) And in the Regiment Commanded by Col. Jacob Klock & Lieut Col. Peter Waggoner. (2)

That this applicant declares, that emedietly [immediately] after he arrived to the age of Sixteen in compliance with the orders of his superior Officers as also in conformity to the Resolution passed the 7th day of May 1775. That it was Resolved by the old Congress That the Militia of New York be armed and Trained and in constant readiness to Act at a Moment's Warning.

That this Claiment conformable to the foregoing hath always kept himself well armed and acquipt [equipped] and always in readiness and actually did turn out on all, each and Every Emergency when called upon in Guarding against the incursions of the Common Enemy and in support of his Common Cause—And that this Applicant declares it to be impractible for him to describe all the dates relative to his duties and Services performed during and to the close of the War.

That this Claiment declares that in the summer 1779 he was forced with a number of other of the Militia with Waggons & Horses, drawing Batous [bateau] to Lake Otsego, distance of about 20 miles to Lake Otsego from the Mohawk River, Gen'l Sulivan's Expedition (3) to the west among the Indians for about three weeks.

This Claimant further declares that he hath been prepared several times to go to the Little Falls Now Herkimer County & drawing boats over fording places vizt when whole company of Boatmen with their boats in Co. went up the Mohawk river to Fort Stanwix and Fort Dayton with supplies to the Garrison Pressed to take Provisions with teams to Fort Stanwix—Also gone to war with the militia under the Command of Col. Klock twice to now Herkimer County Then Tryon County once to Town of German Flats, and west to Town of Herkimer where murder & prisoners taken & General Conflagration caused by the cruel Incendieries from Canada as to the No. of days he does not recollect—he was gone from home, drafted to Fort Blank with others there stationed for he believes two weeks—frequently and often stationed at Fort Paris for service and often times, for at least 3 years, calculating and averaging a two months annually watching and Guarding against the incursions of the Enemy.

That this applicant further declares that he has been in that Memorable Battle then under the Emidient Command of Col. Brown (4) Generally called Browns battle, in town of Palatine when Col. Brown was Slain in Battle and about 45 killed on the retreat of Col. Browns men & Militia—

And again on the same day in pursuit of Sir John Johnson at a distance of about Eight Miles up along the Mohawk river in Battle on Failings and Klocks flats when Tories, Indians, with their Commander took flight where he the claimant kept on the ground to the last, this general Conflagration took place on the 19th day of Oct 1780. (5)

This applicant further declares That on the 25th day of Oct 1781, marching out with his Capt. John Zielly & Company to Johnstown Battle, there joining Under the Emedient Command of Col. Willett. (6) Which became a Serious Conflict against Maj'r Ross (7) and his Incendiery band from Canada, but Col. Willett sustained the field of Battle, and the Enemy retreating into the Woods. That this applicant the next day again went under the Command of Col. Willett in pursuing the Enemy, Vizt, Major Ross with his Incendieries at the distance of about 50 Miles to the West Canada Creek when a number of the Enemy were taken prisoners, and killed, before their arrival at the Creek and Capt. Tory Butler (8) shot across the Creek by one of our Indians both battles was attended with a number of lifes lost & prisoners taken on the British side and Considerable number lost by the Americans.

That this claimant further declares that he has performed duty and services from the year 1777 occasionally and he would say continually to the close of the war, that he kept himself always in readiness to watch out against the common enemy whenever any occurrence or Emergency did acquire his aid—that he feels satisfied that he has omitted many a tour which he cannot describe or recollect. (Signed with his mark) Adolph Wallerath.

Sworn and subscribed the day and year aforesaid. Geo. D .Ferguson

We, Isaac S. Ketcham a Clergyman residing in the Town of Palatine and County of Montgomery and Joseph Waggoner residing in the Town of Minden and County of Montgomery aforesaid, hereby Certify that we are well acquainted with Adolph Wallerath who has subscribed and Sworn to the above declaration that we believe him to be aged Seventy one years last April, that he is reputed and believed in the Neighborhood where he resides, to have been a soldier of the Revolution and that we concur in that opinion. Isaac S. Ketcham; Joseph Waggoner.

Sworn and Subscribed the day and year aforesaid.

Following is a deposition on May 3, 1839. Abraham G. Rosencrantz, Son of George Rosencrantz and grandson of Reverend Abraham Rosencrantz. In his deposition he explains that his grandfather was the minister of the Reformed protestant Church of German Flatts & Herkimer. That on the 26th day of December 1781, that Adolph Walrath was married to Anna Fink, widow.

Letter in the Pension Folder, dated August 17, 1931, written in response to an inquiry.

You are advised that it appears from the papers in the Revolutionary War pension claim W. 18275, that Adolph Walrath, Wallerath or Walradt, was born April 4, 1761, place not stated.

While a resident of Palatine, Tryon County, New York, he served at various times from 1777 until sometime in 1782, entire length of service not shown, as private with the New York troops under Captains John Bradbig, Miller (9), Adam Lipe (10) and John Zilley, and Colonels Jacob Klock, Wagoner, Clyde, Brown and Marinus Willett. He was with General Sullivan during his Indian expedition and was in the battle of Palatine (also known as Stone Arabia) and the battles of Johnstown and West Canada Creek.

He was allowed pension on his application executed September 19, 1832, at which time he was living in Oppenheim, Montgomery County, New York.

He died June 15, 1837.

This soldier married December 26, 1781, Anna, the widow of Christian Fink who was killed at the battle of Oriskany. (11)

On account of the Revolutionary War service of Adolph Walrath, his widow, Anna, was allowed pension on her application executed May 24, 1839, at which time she was eighty-four years of age and was living in Pamelia, Jefferson County, New York.

There are no data relative to children.

End Notes—W.18275—Adolph Wallerath

1. John Breadbake was the Captain of the Fifth Company in Colonel Jacob Klock's Second Regiment of Tryon County Militia.
2. Peter Waggoner was appointed the Lieutenant-Colonel on August 26, 1775 in Colonel Klock's Regiment.
3. Brigadier General James Clinton gathered troops and supplies in the Mohawk Valley and later joined Major General John Sullivan's Army. Together they destroyed several Iroquois Villages in western New York in 1779.
4. John Brown was the Colonel of a Regiment of Massachusetts

Levies in 1780 to reinforce the troops in the Mohawk and Schoharie Valleys. Colonel John Brown and his force of Massachusetts and New York Levies and Tryon County Militia were defeated in the Battle of Stone Arabia on October 19, 1780 which was fought in the morning. A battle was fought in the afternoon on the same day called the Battle of Klocksfield. The American troops in the second battle were under Brigadier General Robert VanRensselaer.

5. John Zeely or Zielie was the First Lieutenant in Captain Breadbake's Company. When Captain Breadbake was in the Ranger service, Zeely commanded the company acting as Captain. Lieutenant Zeely was taken prisoner in the Battle of Johnstown.
6. Lieutenant-Colonel Commandant Marinus Willett of the New York State Levies.
7. Major John Ross of the Second Battalion of the King's Royal Regiment of New York.
8. Captain Walter Butler was killed at West Canada Creek on October 30, 1781.
9. Captain Henry Miller served in Colonel Klock's Regiment.
10. Captain Adam Leipe served in Colonel Samuel Campbell's First Regiment of Tryon County Militia. Samuel Clyde was the Lieutenant-Colonel of this regiment. This service is probably for a different Adolph.
11. The Battle of Oriskany was fought on August 6, 1777.

Pension Application for Adam Walter

R.11099 (Widow: Elizabeth or Mariah)
State of New York
Onondaga County SS.

On this 11 day of Sept'er 1832 personally appeared in open court before Daniel Mosely Vice Chancellor at a Court of Chancery for the State of New York, now sitting at Onondaga, Adam Walter a resident of the town of Manilus County of Onondaga, and State of New York, aged seventy nine years, who being first duly sworn according to law, doth on his oath make the following declaration in order to obtain the benefit of the Act of Congress, passed June 7, 1832.

That he entered the Service of the United States under the following named officers and served as herein stated. That he entered as a volunteer, in the early part of the month of April 1777, in Captain Loucks (1) Company, Col. Clocks Regiment, of the New York Militia, and was during that summer stationed at Fort Herkimer, Fort Dayton and other places on the Mohawk River and was employed in Scouting parties against the British Indians, and Tories. In the month of August (2), or September of that year was in the Battle near Oriskany Creek under General Herkimer (3); who was killed by a wound in that Battle, after wards was sent to Stillwater near the Hudson River, went about that time with a part of the company to which he belonged to Albany having Charge of Some Tories taken on the Mohawk River after that joined the Army at Stillwater was with the company under Captain Loucks (4) on their march between Saratoga and Schenectady in the month of October when General Burgoyne (5) was taken was discharged in the early part of the winter having served for nine months as near as he can recollect.

In the early part of the month of April 1779, 1779 [sic] again volunteered under Captain John Cosselman (6), in Col. Clock's Regiment of the New York Militia for nine months, and was stationed as before, at Stone Arabia, Fort Herkimer and other places along the valley of the Mohawk was in the Battle at Stone Arabia (7) in the month of August. Thinks the Americans were commanded by Col. Brown (8), who was killed there, that the British Indians & Tories were commanded by Col. Butler (9) & Major Ross, knew Col. Henry Van Rensselaer (10), who was in that service. The same day there was a Battle near Col. Clock's House (11), was discharged when winter set in, lived at the time of his entering into the service at Stone Arabia, Montgomery County. The next year and every year until the close of the war this applicant lived in Stone Arabia and was subject to frequent, calls into the service, and went very frequently on Scouting parties, some times for two or three days, and at others for a week or more being subject to Continual dangers from the Tories & Indians who were constantly around them, and that during the years 1780, & 1781, this applicant was in the service of the United States for the defence of the inhabitants on the Mohawk River, both winter & summer for more than three months in each year, although not regularly enlisted for any fixed tour of time in those years, yet he always volunteered when soldiers, were wanted for any scouting parties, or other purposes of defence. That this applicant was born on the 15th day of April [May written about the word April] 1753 in Frederick County in the State of Maryland has no record of his age, was living when called into the service at Stone Arabia Montgomery County State of New York continued, to live at that place, until 1802 when he moved to Manlius County of Onondaga State New York where, he now lives always went voluntarily into the service. Does not recollect ever having, a written discharge, has no documentary evidence or proof of his services except what is hereunto annexed. That the names of the persons with whom he is acquainted, and who will testify to his character for veracity and their belief, in his services as a Soldier of the Revolutionary war Allen Breed & George Rancier.

He hereby relinquishes every claim whatever to a pension or annuity except the present and declares that his name is not on the pension roll of the agency of any State. (Signed with his mark) Adam Walter

Sworn and Subscribed the day and year aforesaid D. Mosely. Circuit Judge Vice Chancellor.

In pursuance of a law passed the 27th of April 1784, entitled "An act for the settlement of the pay of the Levies and Militia, for their service in the late War, and for other purposes therein mentioned," the following certificates have been issued, bearing interest at five per cent per annum, viz:

17th Augt 1779—Adam Walter Priv. £ 4. 0. 0
31st Decr Do---Do—Do £0. 19. 6[?]
31st Dec Do---Do—Do £0. 14. 2
1st Sept 1780 Adam Walter Do £4. 17. 9 1/2
31st Decr 1782 Adam Walter Do £1. 12. 0

State of New York, Comptroller's Office, Albany Mar. 28th 1844.
I hereby certify the above true extracts from book no. 1 & 4 now remaining in this office, and that the service for which the certificates above named were issued, were performed under the following officers viz:

First—under Capt. Henry Miller(12) in Col. Jacob Klock Regt.
Second under Capt. Do [ditto] in Do Regt.
Third under Capt. John Cayser in Col. Peter Waggoner Regt. (13)
Fourth under Capt. Henry Miller in Col. Jacob Klock Regt.
Fifth under Capt. Do in Col. Peter Waggoner Regt. Signed Philip Phelps, Dep. Comptroller

State of New York
Madison County SS.

Mary Watts being duly sworn deposes and says that she is the sister to Adam Walter deceased and I was present and saw said Adam Walter married to Elisabeth Hurtick on the eighth day of August in the year of our Lord on thousand seven hundred and ninety. (14) That she was acquainted with said Elisabeth Hurtick previous to her marriage and has been acquainted with her ever since such marriage. That said Elisabeth Hurtick was married to said Adam Walter in the presence of deponent on the day aforesaid by a Mr. Peak (15) at Stone Arabia in said state of New York. Deponent further says that she was present at the funeral of said Adam Walter and from what was said by the family at the time and from the best information and belief of deponent said Adam Walter died on the thirteenth day of March in the year of our Lord one thousand eight hundred and thirty four, from a stoppage of the blood in the main artery, deponent further says that she is still acquainted with said Elisabeth and that to the best of deponents knowledge and belief said Elisabeth has not intermarried since the death of said Adam Walter and is still the widow of said Adam deponent further says that she has frequently heard said Adam in his life time say that he was in the nine months service in the Revolutionary service, and that was common[ly] report[ed] that he was in such service. And further she says not. (Signed with her mark) Mary Watts.

Sworn and Subscribed before me the 12th day of October 1838. [Jarius?] French Com. of Deeds

Adam Walter was granted pension of $60.00 per annum commencing 4th March 1834. He died March 13, 1834.

End Notes—R.11099—Adam Walter

1. Adam enlisted in Captain Christopher W. Fox's Company, which was the Third Company, as a private in Colonel Jacob Klock's Second Regiment of Tryon County Militia. The following were officers of Captain Fox's Company: First Lieutenant—Peter Loucks. Second Lieutenant—Henry Miller. Ensign—Samuel Van Etten or VanNatter, etc. FROM: Revolutionary War Rolls 1775-1783, Series M-246, Roll 75, folder 121, National Archives, Washington, D.C.
2. The Battle of Oriskany was fought on August 6, 1777.
3. Brigadier General Nicholas Herkimer of the Tryon County Militia Brigade.
4. Adam is again referring to First Lieutenant Peter Loucks who was in command of the company at this time because Captain Fox had been wounded at the Battle of Oriskany.
5. Lieutenant General John Burgoyne surrendered his British Army and Allies on October 17, 1777.
6. Adam has the wrong year for this service, it should be 1780. Adam enlisted as a private on July 5, 1780 on "A Pay roll of Captain John Kasselmans Company of Rangers raised out of Colo Jacob Klock's Regiment of Tryon County Militia for the defence of the Frontier of said County in the year 1780". FROM: Revolutionary War Rolls 1775-1783, Series M-246, Roll 75, folder 121, National Archives, Washington, D.C.
7. The Battle of Stone Arabia was fought in the morning of October 19, 1780.
8. Colonel John Brown commanded the American troops at Stone Arabia.
9. The British forces were under Lieutenant-Colonel Sir John Johnson not Lieutenant-Colonel John Butler. Major Ross was not at this battle.
10. Probably Lieutenant-Colonel Henry J. VanRensselaer of the Eighth Regiment of Albany County Militia.
11. The Battle of Klocksfield was fought in the afternoon of October 19, 1780.
12. Henry Miller was commissioned captain on September 29, 1780 because Captain Fox was promoted to major.
13. Captain John Keyser, or Cayser, Kyser, Kaiser, etc., in Colonel Klock's Regiment. Peter Waggoner, or Wagner, etc., was the lieutenant-colonel in Klock's Regiment.
14. According to the Stone Arabia Dutch Reformed Church Book of Marriages page 195, Adam Walter married Elizabeth Hurtig on August 8, 1790.
15. Reverend D.C. Pick, or Peck, Peek, Peak, etc.

Pension Application for George Walter

S.10040
State of New York
Montgomery County SS.

On this Nineteenth day of June in the year 1835 personally appeared before the Court of Common Pleas of said county now sitting George Walter of Johnstown in the County of Montgomery and State of New York aged seventy nine years who being first duly sworn according to law doth on his oath make the following declaration in order to obtain the benefit of the act of Congress passed June 7th 1832—That he entered the service of the United States under the following named officers and served as herein stated.

That he entered the service of the United States at Palatine in said County and State where he then lived at the commencement of the revolutionary War in the year 1775 as a militia man under the command of Captain Andrew Dillenback (1) in the Regiment of Militia commanded by Colonel Jacob Klock and Lieutenant Col. Peter Waggoner (2) and that he continued in said service at various periods doing the various duties until the month of August in the year 1777 when his said Captain was slain in the Oriskana Battle (3) and was then succeeded by Captain Suffrenus Cook (4) and in which battle this deponent was engaged and was twice severely wounded for which he now receives an invalid pension that according to the best of this applicants recollection he commenced service in the spring of the year 1775 and served occasionally till the fall of that year and that he is certain he served at least a month during that year that he was eight days at Mounts in Jersey field on a scouting party and that he went from Stone Arabia where he then lived which in going and returning made in the whole eleven days service—that he was during that year ten days at Fort Plain keeping guard and was engaged several other times in that year in other services amounting in the whole to at least a month.

That in the year 1776 he was at Caughnawaga and marched to Johnstown and was at the taking of Sir John Johnson and was then engaged at least two days in that service and was engaged during that summer in going out upon several alarms the time he was engaged in each tour he turned out and how long he was out on each tour he finds it impossible to state with precision—but he thinks at least twenty times and therefore charges for twenty days service in those tours.

That in the year 1777 in the Spring he went to Unadilla (5) under his said officers and under the command of General Herkimer (6) in pursuit of Brant and his Indians and was engaged in that expedition twenty one days and after returning to Stone Arabia he again was engaged in service which led to the Oriskany battle on the 6th of August that he believes he was under arms at least fifteen days and engaged previous to that battle that after the wounds which he received in that battle (and which were very severe) he was confined and unable to do actual service during the remaining part of that campaign, the wounds he received in that battle having disabled him—that the whole time he was engaged during that season including the time that he was laid up from the wounds he received amounts to six months.

That in the year 1778 he went under Colonel Waggoner in June or July but under what Captain he does not now recollect in pursuit of the enemy to Springfield at the time that it was burnt by Brant and his Indians and Tories—

he recollects distinctly of having seen horse meat roasted on a fire which [served] them for food—This term of service as charged at least six days—He continued in occupational service during the summer according to the emergency of the times and in November he thinks went under the same officers to the defence of Cherry Valley (7) at the time the same was burnt by Brant and Butler (8) and their incendiary troops and when the general massacre so well known in history took place there he was out then at least six days, upon this tour and was engaged during that year frequently in small excursions for a day as the advance or retreat of the Indians and Tories rendered it necessary which for certainty he is constrained to limit to ten days.

That in the years 1779 & 1780 he was engaged in Boat service (9) for which he is informed he cannot be allowed under the act of June 7, 1832 as military service and will not therefore specify the service.

That in the year 1781, he enlisted in the month of March for nine months in a company of Levies and that he actually served the said nine months under the command of Captain Lawrence Gross (10), Lieut Jacob Sammons and 2nd Lieut Peter Vrooman (11) and that himself as well as the company to which he belonged were under the command of Col. Willett that this applicant was during that period engaged in three battles first the Turlough Battle (12) in July—the second battle was commonly called Landman's Battle (13) occurred soon after the first and the third battle was the Johnstown Battle (14) which was fought in the month of October and after the battle he pursued the enemy to the West Canada Creek (15) where Butler was killed and that he served out the full nine months that he enlisted and until his company were disbanded—and he received no discharge further than was disbanding.

That he has no documentary evidence to prove his claim and that although he is positive as such from the nature of the services he was engaged was from his general recollections of that service that he has been engaged full two years in such military service never the less when he wishes to tax his memory for particular services and therefore tours he finds that by reason of the great length of time as well as the infirnment of age he is unable to be more definite than he has been [?] in and that he could not have recollected the particular services herein stated were they not connected with prominent events which were collimated to make an indelible impression on the mind of every one who participated in them—That he has no record of his age--that since the Revolutionary War he has lived in Johnstown in said County. That he was born in the year 1756 in State of North Carolina. And the claimant further states that the reason why he has not presented this his claim before now is that he made enquiry upon the subject but that he was informed that he could not obtain a claim under the act of 1832 without surrendering his invalid pension and he never knew the [?] to be true until he was so informed this summer upon inquiry by Charles McVean Esqr and this Deponent immediately upon such information commenced preparations for presenting this his claim to the department and the said claimant hereby relinquishes every claim to a pension or annuity except the present (and except his said pension as an invalid) and declares that his name is not on the pension roll of any agency of any state—only on that of the State of New York for his said invalid pension that the clergyman to whose church he belongs has lately left his church and this town and gone away into parts unknown to this applicant and he has as yet found no personal acquaintance with his successor who is a stranger in these parts & that this claimant is well acquainted with Aaron Haring Esqr who has lately been for many years past first judge of said county and for 25 years past a Justice of the Peace residing in said town and that he has known Joseph Packard for more than 20 years a merchant in said town both of whom have known him during that time and in whose neighborhood he has resided during the whole of that time and who can testify as to his character for veracity and their belief of his services as a soldier of the revolution. (Signed with his mark) George Walter.

Subscribed and sworn the day and year aforesaid in open court. Geo. D. Ferguson, Clerk.

Increase of Pension

It is hereby certified that George Walter formerly a private of Captain Andrew Dillenbach's company in the Infantry Regiment of Colonel Jacob Klock's New York State who it appears by the accompanying certificate was placed on the pension roll at the rate of two dollars & fifty cents per month, on account, as he sates, of having received two musket balls the one in his left hip and the other in his neck while in the line of duty, and in the said service, on or about the twentieth day of August in the year 1776 [The Battle of Oriskany occurred August 6, 1777] at a place called the Oriskany in the state or territory of New York, is not only still disabled in consequence of the said injury, but, in my opinion is entitled to more than he already receives as a pensioner, being disabled to a degree amounting to three-fourths, from obtaining his subsistence by manual labor. James W. Miller M.D.; Saml Maxwell M.D.

Subscribed & sworn to this 3rd day of April in the year 1825, before me Aaron Haring, First Judge of Montgomery County Common Pleas New York State.

End Notes—George Walter—S.10040

1. Andrew Dillenbach (Dillenbeck, Dillenbagh, etc.) was appointed the First Lieutenant in Captain John Keyser Jr's company (Fourth company) on August 26, 1775, in Colonel Jacob Klock's Second Regiment of Tryon County Militia. Captain Keyser in 1775 was appointed Second Lieutenant in Captain Christopher P. Yates' company in Colonel Goose VanSchaick's Second New York Continental Regiment. Dillenbach commanded the company in Keyser's absence. Keyser died in Canada in November of 1775. Dillenbach was in 1776 appointed Captain of the Fourth Company.
2. Peter Waggoner (Wagner) was the Lieutenant-Colonel in the Second Tryon.
3. The Battle of Oriskany was fought on August 6, 1777.

4. Severinus Klock was the First Lieutenant in Captain Dillenbach's Company. Klock was commissioned on June 25, 1778. Klock was appointed Captain sometime in 1778 and was commissioned as Captain on March 4, 1780.
5. On June 27, 1776 at Unadilla General Herkimer and Joseph Brant held a conference. Herkimer attempted to persuade Brant and his warriors to remain neutral in the war between England and America.
6. Nicholas Herkimer was appointed Brigadier General of the Tryon County Militia on September 5, 1776.
7. Cherry Valley was destroyed on November 11, 1778.
8. Walter Butler was a Captain in Butler's Rangers which was commanded by his father Colonel John Butler.
9. Captain Samuel Gray's Company of Bateaumen.
10. George enlisted as a private on May 22, 1781 in Captain Lawrence Gros' Company in Lieutenant-Colonel Marinus Willett's Regiment of New York State Levies. FROM: Revolutionary War Rolls 1775-1783, Series M-246, Roll 78, Folder 173, National Archives, Washington, D.C.
11. The Lieutenants in Captain Gros' Company were Jacob Sammons and Simon J. Vrooman.
12. The Battle of New Dorlach (Terlow, Turlough, etc.), was fought on July 10, 1781.
13. The Battle of Lampman's was fought on July 29, 1781.
14. The Battle of Johnstown was fought on October 25, 1781.
15. The Skirmish at West Canada Creek was fought on October 30, 1781.

Pension Application for John Wasson or Wanson, Wauson

W.18236 (Widow: Betshannah)
State of New York
Chenango County SS.

On this 14th day of February 1845, personally came before me a Judge of Chenango County, Betshannah Wasson, a resident of Norwich, in said county and state, aged, seventy eight years and upwards, and being duly sworn according to law, makes this declaration to obtain the benefit of the Act of Congress of July 7, 1838, and the acts amending or extending the same, viz.

Her maiden name was Betshannah Gibson, a daughter of John Gibson of Schenectady; she was born on 19th of May 1766, and was married to John T. Wasson at Schenectady on the 14th of February 1792, by George Wasson, Esq. a Justice of the Peace of that vicinity. Her banns of marriage had been published in the Reformed Dutch Church of Schenectady and it was her intention to have the minister of that church marry her, but from his inability to attend the ceremony was solemnized by Mr. Wasson as above. Her husband died at Norwich aforesaid on the 25th day of January 1839.

She refers the Department for proof of her husband's services, to his papers on file. She would sooner have made this declaration, but did not until recently know of the law for her benefit. Her husband's pension under the law of June 7, 1832 was $30 per annum. Her age and infirmities render it impracticable for her to attend Court to make her declaration. She has never intermarried since her husband's death. (Signed) Betshannah Wasson

Subscribed and sworn to this 14th day of February 1845 and I certify that I am satisfied that from her age and severity of the weather, she cannot attend Court to make this declaration.

Chenango County SS.

Sophia Ransford of Norwich in said county being duly sworn says she is 40 years of age and upwards and is a daughter of the above deponent with whom she has always resided. That her father died on the 25th day of January 1839, leaving her mother a widow and that she has continued his widow ever since and has never intermarried since his death. Sophia Ransford

Subscribed and sworn to this 14th day of February 1845—and I certify that the above Sophia Ransford is a woman of entire credibility—and I am satisfied that the above Betshannah Wasson is the true widow of the written named John T. Wasson (1) the Revolutionary Pensioner.-- Philo Robinson, Judge of Chenango County Courts.

State of New York
Chenango County SS.
AMENDED DECLARATION

On this 28th day of May 1833, personally appeared before me the undersigned, a Justice of the peace of the town of Norwich in said County John Wasson who being duly sworn according to law deposes and says—that he served as he as stated in his declaration as a private in the New York Line—in the New Levies under Captain Gross, and Col. Willet for the full period of nine months, and for that time he claims a pension—he further states that during the said period of nine months for which he served and claims a pension he was not engaged in any civil occupation or pursuit but was engaged exclusively in the army which he believed and does now was called out by the authority of this state. (Signed) John Wasson

Subscribed & sworn this 28th May 1833 before me, James Thompson, Justice of the Peace.

State of New York
County of Chenango SS.

On this [?] day of October A.D. 1832 personally appeared in open Court before the Court of Common Pleas of said county now sitting.

Present. John Tracy, Nathan Taylor, Levi Biglow Hezekiah Read, Charles York, Judges

John Wasson a resident of the town of Norwich in the County of Chenango and State of New York aged sixty eight years and upwards who being first duly sworn according to law doth on his oath make the following declaration in order to obtain the benefit of the act of Congress passed June 7, 1842.

That he entered the service of the United States under the following named officers and served as herein stated.

In 1781, on the last day of March he enlisted at Schenectady, Schenectady County State of New York for nine months (each company in Town were divided into classes and each class had to furnish a man he enlisted as a man for one of the classes) into what was called the New Levies in a company commanded by Lawrence Gros (1) of Canajoharie Montgomery County (then Tryon County) State of New York Captain, one Simmons (3) first Lieutenant, Simon Froman (4), Second Lieutenant one Hutton (5) of Albany third Lieutenant the regiment to which his company was attached and belonged was under the command of Marinus Willet Colonel one Troop [Throop] (6) Major Jellis A. Fundy (7), Adjutant, Seth Rowley (8), Sergeant Major, knows not who was the general and the regiment was never reviewed by a General at the time he enlisted he passed muster, at Schenectady was mustered by Jellis A Fundy that he was employed by the class as mentioned before and enlisted to the said Jellis A. Fundy, received from the class at the time of enlistment fifty dollars as a bounty—in four or five days after time of enlistment went with that part of the company which was raised at Schenectady to Helderbergh Albany County and there was also a company of Continental soldiers of Colonel Cortland's (9) regiment and about fifty Oneida Indians under the command of an Indian called Colonel Lewy (10) who marched down with his company they went to attack Brandt whom report said was at that place, but not finding him after scouring the woods, returned to Schenectady the next day and then remained in Schenectady about a week and then went up the Mohawk river in boats with his company or as many of them as was then raised to Fort Stanwix (now Rome) which was then occupied by a company of Continental soldier of Colonel Cortlandt's regiment went up for the purpose of carrying provisions to the company at the Fort remained at the Fort one day and then returned back down the Mohawk to Fort Plain where his company joined his regiment and was there stationed that being the rendezvous of his regiment remained a part of the summer at that place some part at the Fort Dayton & a part of the time at Fort Herkimer but does not recollect the precise time he was at each as he was not at anytime in either place over two or three weeks at one time and also in the time was sent out on scouting parties, and sometime in October was engaged in a skirmish with the British tories and Indians, said to be under the command of Major Ross (11) which skirmish was about a mile north of Johnstown Village in Montgomery County (then Tryon County) and which skirmish lasted most of the afternoon and about dusk those under the command of Major Ross retired leaving the ground in possession of the Americans about four hundred and fifty under the personal command of Colonel Marinus Willet first commenced the skirmish or battle but before it was finished they were joined by the rest of the regiment and some militia and it was said at the time there were about nine hundred of the enemy – on the next morning the most of the regiment under the command of Colonel Willet marched for West Canada Creek Herkermer [Herkimer] County (then in Tryon County) for the purpose of intercepting the enemy but when they reached the place they had all crossed the creek and the main body had marched on leaving one company under the command of Captain Butler (12) as it was said, as a rear guard and to prevent the Americans from crossing the creek, had a skirmish with this company which was a short one Captain Butler being killed in short time and they retreated and a few were taken prisoners and after crossing the creek followed the enemy about five miles and then camped for night and then next morning marched back to Fort Plain and remained there a few days and then was one that went down to Albany to escort the prisoners captured at the skirmish at West Canada Creek remained at Albany only one night and then returned to Fort Plain and there remained until the expiration of the nine months for which he enlisted and then received a written discharge from his Captain which is hereunto annexed. Was engaged in no battles or skirmishes except the afore mentioned. Sergeant Orderly, Peter Young (13), Canajoharie, 2d Sergeant Reuben Brainer of New Cannan also called Chatam in Columbia County NY, Corporal Joseph Crawford of Schenectady, Moses VanCamp a Sergeant of Canajoharie, Ephraim Ketchum Sergeant of New Caanan, Henry Flanders, Jacob Flanders, Henry House, Henry Tick, Peter Fox all of Canajoharie privates all served in the company to which he belonged.

And he further states that he has no documentary evidence of his services except his written discharge hereunto attached, and knows of no person whose testimony he can procure who can testify to his services except Seth Rowley of Norwich whose affidavit is hereunto annexed.

In answer to the interrogatories required to be put by the War department to applicants for pensions he answers as follows viz.

1st Was born in the town of Schenectady, Schenectady County New York on the eighth day of June 1764.

2nd Has a record if his age in a family bible which he has which was copied from the record of his father which was destroyed in moving.

3rd He resided at the time he enlisted at Schenectady and resided there after his service until the year 1793 and thence moved to the town of Norwich Chenango County New York and remained a year and then moved to Guilford Chenango County and remained there until 1805 and then removed back to Norwich and there resides now and has ever since resided.

4th He enlisted voluntarily into the service as stated in his declaration for the class which was obliged to furnish a soldier.

5th his discharge was written one and is hereunto annexed.

6th He knew Captain Elsworth (14), Captain McKeen (15), Captain White and Captain Phelps (16) who were Captains in the same regiment but knew no other regimental officers besides those mentioned in his declaration. The general circumstances of his services are stated as fully in the body of his declaration as he can recollect them.

7th He give the name of Perez Randall late Clerk Jarvis K. Pike Clerk, Samuel Pike, Justice of the Peace, James Thompson, Justice of the Peace, Cyrus Wheeler Merchant, Benjamin Chapmen Merchant, David E. Bedford, Merchant, Truman Enos, Tanner, all of Norwich Chenango County his present residence as men to whom he is known and can testify to his character for veracity and their belief of his services as a soldier of the Revolution.

He hereby relinquishes every claim whatever to a pension or annuity except the present and declares that his name is not on the pension roll of the agency of any state. (Signed) John Wasson

Sworn to and subscribed the day and year aforesaid, J.K. Pike CLK

End Notes—W.18236—John Wasson

1. Sophia Ransford in another affidavit says her father signed his name as John or as John T. Wasson. he used the T as a middle initial at times when he lived in Schenectady because he had a cousin named John Wasson.
2. John enlisted as a private in Captain Lawrence Gros' Company on April 23, 1781, in Lieutenant-Colonel Commandant Marinus Willett's Regiment of New York State Levies. FROM: Revolutionary War Rolls 1775-1783, Series M-246, Roll 78, folder 173, National Archives, Washington, D.C.
3. First Lieutenant Jacob Sammons of Gros' Company.
4. Second Lieutenant Simon J. Vrooman of Gros' Company.
5. Lieutenant Timothy Hutton of Gros' Company.
6. Josiah Throop was appointed Major on April 28, 1781 in Willett's Regiment.
7. Jellis A. Fonda served as a Lieutenant and Adjutant in Willett's Regiment in 1781 and most of 1782. In November of 1782, he was appointed Captain of Captain Abner French's Company since French had retired from the service.
8. Seth Rowley was a sergeant in Captain Stephen White's Company in Willett's Regiment. The Sergeant Major in 1781 was Jesse Wilson and not Rowley.
9. Colonel Philip VanCortlandt of the Second New York Continental Regiment.
10. Colonel Lewis Atayataroughta or Atayataghrohghta.
11. Major John Ross of the Second Battalion of the Kings' Royal Regiment of New York commanded the British forces and Willett commanded the American forces at the Battle of Johnstown which was fought on October 25, 1781.
12. Walter Butler was a Captain in Lieutenant-Colonel John Butler's Rangers and second in command under Major Ross. Butler was killed in the skirmish at West Canada Creek on October 30, 1781.
13. Peter Young served as the Orderly Sergeant of Capt. Gros' company, Reuben Brainer was the Second Sergeant, Joseph Crawford was a Corporal, Moses VanCamp was a Sergeant, Ephraim Ketcham was a

private and is listed as deserting on July 24, 1781. Henry Flanders, Jacob Flanders, Henry House, Henry Deck, and Peter Fox were privates.

14. Peter Elsworth was appointed Captain in Willett's Regiment on April 27, 1781. Elsworth was killed in an ambush on July 6, 1781.
15. Robert McKean was a Captain in Willett's Regiment and was mortally wounded on July 10, 1781 in the Battle of New Dorlach which is present day Sharon Springs, Schoharie County.
16. Phelps is Captain Anthony Whelp. The name is also called Welp or Phelps. He was also appointed on April 27, 1781 in Willett's Regiment.

Pension Application for David Weaver

R.11,238 (Widow: Catharine)
New York & War of 1812

At a Court of Chancery held for the State of New York at the town of Poughkeepsie in the County of Dutchess on the third day of December One thousand eight hundred and thirty eight. Present Charles H. Ruggles Vice Chancellor of the Second Circuit.

Dutchess County SS:

Catharine Weaver the widow of David Weaver, deceased comes now here into court and being duly sworn according to law doth on her oath make the following declaration in order to obtain the provision made by the Act of Congress passed July 7, 1838, entitled An Act granting half pay and pensions to certain widows. That she is the widow of said Weaver, who enlisted in the Revolutionary Army as a fifer in Colonel Albert Pauldings Regiment in the New York troops, and in Captain Pearsa's (1) Company; that she does not know the exact time when he enlisted but believes it was near the close of the war to the best of her recollection and thinks it was for nine months, and that he served out his time. She has no knowledge of his having been in battle or engagement; that he lived in Poughkeepsie, Dutchess County when he enlisted. That she has no documentary testimony proving the service of her said husband in the Revolutionary War. And said deponent further says that her maiden name was Catharine Wiltsie and that she was married to her husband the said David Weaver at the town of Poughkeepsie in the County of Dutchess on the thirtieth day of August one thousand seven hundred and eighty three by the Reverend John. H. Livingston then the Pastor of the Reformed Dutch Church in the said town of Poughkeepsie, and that a [minute?] of such marriage was made in the records of the said church as this deponent is informed and believes and as will appear from the certificate and affidavit of Alexander M. Mann the present pastor of the said church hereto annexed. And this deponent further says that she has been informed and believes and charges that her husband the said David Weaver departed this life at Sackett's Harbour (2) in the State of New York, while in the service of the United States as a soldier, for this deponent says that her husband the said David Weaver in the winter or spring of the year one thousand eight hundred and nine enlisted as a fifer, at

Poughkeepsie aforesaid under Lieutenant Killean VanRensselaer in the service of the United States in the regular army for the term of five years, that said David Weaver left Poughkeepsie under and after such enlistment, and deponent has never seen him since but has always understood and believes that he died as aforesaid at Sackett's Harbour in 1813, and this deponent is informed and believes that the memorandum or registry of his death is among the files of the War department in Washington on this deponent after the close of the late war received, as widow, the back pay due to the said David Weaver at the time of his death, this such back pay was received through the agency for this deponent of Doctor William Thomas. That a son of this deponent who is now deceased was also a soldier in the Army of the United States during the last war, and on his return home to Poughkeepsie after the close of the war, reported and stated to this deponent that his father the said David Weaver died at Sackett's Harbor aforesaid in the year 1813, that he there saw him dead, and assisted and was present at his burial. And this deponent produces a support of her claim aforesaid, the affidavit of Mathew Tompkins, Alexander M. Mann and William Thomas which is hereto annexed. (Signed with her mark) Catharine Weaver

Sworn the 3rd day of December 1838 in open Court. Alex. Forbes, Clerk

State of New York
Dutchess County SS

Before me Silas C. Haight a justice of the peace in and for Dutchess County appeared William Thomas late Hospital Surgeon in the Army who deposeth and says that he knew David Weaver formerly of Poughkeepsie and that said Weaver enlisted as a private in a company raised and enlisted by Killean VanRensellear then Lieutenant in the army that he, said Thomas was requested to examine said Weaver by said Lt. VanRensellear to ascertain that he was sound, and that said Thomas did so examine him that in 1813 he, said Thomas then a Surgeon's mate in the Hospital knew said Weaver at Sacket's Harbor and that he was then sickly and from this circumstance he has no doubt of his death that said David Weaver had a son named John Weaver who was a soldier in the army during the late war and that said John Weaver died about one year since in this village and this deponent has repeatedly heard said John Weaver say that his father died at Sacket's Harbor in 1813 and that he helped to bury him and further more this deponent knew said John Weaver to have been a soldier in the United States Army and that he saw said Weaver while a soldier and doing duty at the Harbor about August 1813 that said David Weaver was a fifer and was about fifty years old. And furthermore said deponent is well acquainted with Catharine Weaver and he knows her to be the widow of said David Weaver late of the army and he knows that she has not again been married and that he has know[n] her for more than thirty years and this deponent has lived in Poughkeepsie since 1816 to his knowledge at which time he quit the army. (Signed) William Thomas

Subscribed & Sworn to before me this 28th day of November 1838. Silas E. Haight Justice of the Peace in & for Dutchess County.

End Notes—R.11238—David Weaver

1. David served as a private in Captain Jonathan Pearse's or Pearce, Piercy, etc., Company in Colonel Albert Pawling's Regiment of New York State Levies in 1781.
2. Sackett's Harbor is in present day Jefferson County, N.Y. Hundreds of men died of diseases such as small pox and were buried in the military cemetery. Sackett's Harbor Battlefield State Historic Site is located in the Village of Sackett's Harbor, New York.

Pension Application for Edward Weaver

S.43280
State of New York
Supreme Court
City of Albany

On this tenth day of August 1820 personally appeared in open court, (being a court of record in and for the said State according to the solemn adjudications of the said Supreme Court of this state, and being a court which proceeds according to the course of common law, with a jurisdiction unlimited in point of amount keeping a record of its proceedings and possessing the power of fine and imprisonment Edward Weaver late an Ensign aged seventy four years, resident in the Town of Westerlo in said County who, being duly sworn according to law, doth on his oath declare, that he served in the revolutionary war as follows: in the company commanded by Captain Hutchins in Col. Dubois' Regiment (10 of Infantry, on the Continental Establishment in the New York line for the term & in the manner specified in his original declaration on file in the Pension office at Washington City—dated the second day of April 1818—his certificate is numbered 2.774—and was issued on the 23 of September 1818—and he has recd his pension at the rate of twenty dollars per month, up to the fourth of March last.

And I do solemnly swear that I was a resident citizen of the United States on the 18th day of march 1818; and that I have not, since that time, by gift, sale, or in any manner, disposed of my property, or any part thereof, with intent thereby so to diminish it, as to bring myself within the provisions of an act of Congress, entitled "An act to provide for certain persons engaged in the land and naval service of the United States in the revolutionary war," passed on the 18th of March 1818; and that I have not, nor has any person in trust for me, any property or securities, contracts, or debts, due to me; nor have I any income other than what is contained in the schedule hereto annexed, and by me subscribed, that I have a Wife aged sixty four years that I am by occupation, a cooper & by reason of old age & a broken shoulder, I am unable to subsist with out assistance from my country for support, that the following is a Schedule of my real & personal estate—viz, Real Estate, None, Personal Estate viz—one cow, fifteen dollars, one hog, eight dollars, one ax one dollar—

one shovel thirty seven cents—eight cups and saucers, Tea Pot—Sugar cup & milk pot, one dollar, six knives & forks one dollar—ten plates, two dishes, one dollar fifty cents, six bowls, thirty seven Cents, two candlesticks & snuffers fifty cents—five chairs & one table two dollars, shovel & tongs one dollar seventy five cents—six barrels & two Pails, one dollar fifty cents. (Signed with his mark) Edward Weaver

Sworn to and declared in open court this 10th day of August 1820. R. Bloodgood Clk

Letter in the folder replying to an inquiry for information.

I advise you from the papers in the Revolutionary War pension claim, S.43280, it appears that Edward weaver enlisted November 21, 1776, served as Ensign in Captain Thomas Hutchins' (2) Company, Colonel Lewis DuBois New York Regiment, and was discharged December 16, 1777.

He was allowed pension on his application executed April 2, 1818, at which time he was a resident of Westerlo, Albany County, New York.

In 1820 he was aged seventy-four years and resided in Westerlo, New York. He then referred to his wife, aged sixty-four years but did not give her name.

He died January 29, 1828.

End Notes—S.42280—Edward Weaver

1. Edward was appointed ensign on November 21, 1776 in Captain Amos Hutchings' (Hutchens, etc.) Company (Second Company) in Colonel Lewis DuBois' Fifth New York Continental Regiment. He was discharged on December 16, 1777. He is listed as sick absent in September and had been recruiting for the regiment until then. FROM: Revolutionary War Rolls 1775-1783, Series M-246, Roll 72, folder 66, National Archives, Washington, D.C.
2. This is an error because the Captain's first name is Amos.

Pension Application for Josiah Weaver

R.11243

New York & Vermont

At a Court of Common Pleas holden at the Court house in the Village of Elmira in and for the County of Tioga in the State of New York Commencing on the fourth day of September 1832—Present Hon. Grant B. Baldwin first Judge...John R. Drake, Darius Bentley, Joseph L. Darling & Elijah Shoemaker Esquires Judges.—

State of New York

Tioga County SS.

On this 4th day of September 1832, personally appeared in open court before the Judges aforesaid being a court of record because made so by the Laws and constitution of the State, having by Law a Clerk and Seal now sitting Josiah Weaver a resident of the Town of Elmira in the County of Tioga and State of New York aged eighty four years, the sixteenth day of June last who being first duly sworn according to law doth on his oath make the following declaration in order to obtain the benefit of the Act of Congress passed June 7th 1832; that he entered the service of the United States under the following named officers and served as herein stated.

That about the first of June in the year 1777 the militia in the Town of Clarrendon County of Rutland and State of Vermont and also in that County generally were called upon to furnish two companies for the service of the United States in the common cause of liberty and this declarant volunteered for three months in the company commanded by Capt. Seely and under the command of Col. Mead (1) who then resided in Rutland aforesaid—That he this declarant together with the said company were marched to Bennington in the said State of Vermont and he was in the Battle on the 16th of August of that year under Gen. Stark (2) in which engagement he received a bullet wound in his left hand which crippled three of his fingers so that they have remained crooked up and useless to the present day—he finished this campaign of three months and was dismissed—sometime in the fall of the same year '77 he took his small family a wife and two children and removed on to the North River in the County of Dutchess in the State of New York at a place in the neighborhood of what was called the Nine Partners. On his arrival at this place he found that the enemy had the command of the river and a call was made upon the militia to guard the bank of the river at every assailable point from the said Nine Partners down to Fishkill a distance of about twenty miles—This declarant volunteered for that purpose he thinks in the latter part of October '77 in the company of Captain Israel Veal under Col. Vanderbergh (3) in which company he served upwards of two years receiving regular pay and rations—another company was in the same service at the same time under Captain Reynolds (4) and under the same Col. the nature of this service was to guard the bank of the River so as to prevent the enemy from the shipping in the River from landing and pillaging the property of the inhabitants along the shore and its vicinity; and also to prevent any intercourse of the tories with them with which this region was very much infested. In this service he continued without any special engagement as to the length of time till the beginning of the winter or the month of December in the year 1779 when he was dismissed—He then removed with his family to Half Moon Point in the now county of Saratoga but then county of Albany and about ten miles above the City of Albany at which place he continued to live upwards of thirty years but instead of getting beyond the seat of war he found he was getting more and more into it—at this place he immediately volunteered in the company of Capt. Joshua Taylor (5) and under Col. VanSchoonhover for one year which he completed about the first of January in the year 1781 when he was dismissed from any further service—during this last year's service he was stationed most of the time at Half Moon aforesaid on guard and sentry except in the summer of 1780 he performed an expedition under Capt. Taylor to Lake George where he staid about one week and returned—That he has no documentary evidence of his said services and that he knows of no person whose testimony he can procure who can testify to his said service.—

And in answer to the several interrogatories put to him by the Court he says that he was born in the Town of Warwick in the State of Rhode Island on the 16th day of June in the year 1748; that he had a record of his age which he took from his parents record and placed it in his family Bible when he was young; but about five years since it got burnt with his dwelling house and he has now no record by his memory which he believes is correct, and is as above stated—that when he first entered the service of the United States he lived in the town of Clarrendon, County of Rutland and State of Vermont; that at the close of the Revoluitonary war he lived in the town of Half Moon, in the County of Saratoga and State of New York and lived there for the space of about thirty years, then lived about fourteen years in the Town of Dryden, County of Tompkins and state last mentioned and for the last five years or since his house was burnt he has had no permanent place of resident and that he now lives in the Town of Elmira aforesaid—that he went into the service at the several times above stated as a volunteer—that which in the service aforesaid he was acquainted with Gov. George Clinton (6)—he was along in the expedition to Lake George already mentioned—he was also acquainted with Gen. James Clinton—but his recollection of any other Troops or Regiments than those already mentioned is very indistinct—that he never received any paper discharge from the service—That he would refer to the Hon. Thomas Maxwell, Elijah Jones and the first Judge of this Court all of Elmira aforesaid as persons who are acquainted with his reputation for the good standing of truth and veracity and for their belief in the truth of the foregoing declaration.

That he hereby relinquishes every claim whatever to a pension or annuity except the present and declares that his name is not on the pension roll of the agency of any state. (Signed with his mark) Josiah Weaver

Sworn to & subscribed the day & year aforesaid. Green M. Tuthill, Clk

Letter dated June 24, 1929, written in reply to an inquiry about the solider.

I advise you from the papers in the Revolutionary War pension claim, R.11243, it appears that Josiah Weaver was born June 16, 1748, at Warwick, Rhode Island.

While residing at Clarendon, Rutland County, Vermont, he enlisted in June 1777, and served three months as a private in Captain Seely's Company Colonel Mead's Vermont Regiment and was in the battle of Bennington, where wounded in his left hand.

He stated that in the fall of 1777, he moved with his wife and two children (their names not given) to North River, Dutchess County, New York, and from in October, 1777, served two years under Captain Israel Veal and Colonel Vanderberg with the New York Troops, guarding the banks of the river to prevent the enemy from landing; in 1779, moved to Half Moon Point, Albany County, New York, and served one year under Captain Joshua Taylor and Colonel VanSchoonhover and was on guard duty at Half Moon.

He applied for pension September 4, 1832, while residing at Elmyra, Tioga County, New York.

The claim was rejected on the ground that the soldier failed to render six months actual service in an embodied corps, the three year service constituted patrol duty which was not embraced in the Act of 1832 under which he applied.

There are no further data as to family.

End Notes—R.1124--Josiah Weaver

1. Probably Colonel James Mead of the Vermont Militia.
2. Brigadier-General John Stark of the New Hampshire Militia. He was appointed Brigadier-General in the Continental Army on October 4, 1777.
3. Israel Vail was appointed Captain on March 10, 1778 in Colonel James VanDeburgh's (also appointed on March 10, 1778) Fifth Regiment of Dutchess County militia.
4. Joseph Reynolds was the Captain of the Third Company (commissioned October 17, 1775) in Colonel VanDebrugh's Regiment (Colonel William Humphrey's in 1775).
5. Joshua Taylor is Commissioned the First Lieutenant on March 4, 1780, in Captain Elias Steenburgh's Company in Colonel Jacobus VanSchoonhoven's Twelfth Regiment of Albany County Militia (Half Moon and Ballston Districts).
6. George Clinton, Governor of New York State, and Brigadier General James Clinton of the Continental Army were brothers.

Pension Application for Nicholas Weaver

W.15860 (Widow: Elizabeth)
State of New York
County of Montgomery SS.

Cornelius Veeder of the town of Glen in said county, aged eighty years and upwards, being duly sworn saith, that he served during the war of the Revolution in the Militia of the then County of Tryon now Montgomery, but he never applied (nor does he intend so to do) for a pension. He this deponent lived during the war of the revolution in the town of Caughnawaga in the military beat or jurisdiction under command of Colonel Frederick Fisher. That during said war he became well acquainted with Nicholas Weaver who lived in the same town of Caughnawaga & belonged to the same beat of Colonel Frederick Fisher (1) and this deponent never knew or heard of any other Nicholas Weaver than the one above referred to and he is well satisfied and assured that there was no other person of that name living in said beat and town. That he said deponent & the said Nicholas Weaver continued after said war to reside in said town, the said Nicholas Weaver until he died, & he this Deponent until about thirty five years ago when he removed to the aforesaid town of Glen.

This deponent further saith, that said Nicholas Weaver served during said war in the Militia company in said Regiment commanded by Captain Abraham Veeder the said Abraham Veeder being his (this deponent's) father's brother. This deponent further saith that said Nicholas Weaver belonged during said war to the Company of Batteaumen commanded by Captain Leffler (2) & he believes in the year 1777 and this Deponent further saith that he recollects that said Nicholas Weaver was reported at the time thereof to have belonged to the company of State Levies commanded by Captain Garret Putman (3) under Colonel Willett. This deponent further saith that he has heard read to him an order for the pay of said Weaver in the said Company of Captain Putman for four months services in the year 1781, also the receipt indorsed on said order signed by Volkert Veeder Colonel—said Receipt being for £9..19..1, (4) and said order being dated at Caughnawaga aforesaid, April 11, 1786 & witnessed by Simon Veeder & M.W. Quackenbush. This deponent is apprised that said order was given by said Nicholas Weaver the identical person he this deponent has above described that he then resided in Caughnawaga aforesaid the place at which said order was dated—That said Simon Veeder was an uncle of this deponent & is now deceased, Myndert W. Quackenbush, was a neighbor & acquaintance of this Deponent & the said Colonel Veeder (5) to whom said order was given was this Deponent's Father, & that said Quackenbush & Volkert Veeder are deceased. (Signed) Cornelius Veeder

Subscribed & Sworn this 25th day of October 1843 before me. Abm. A. VanHorne, Justice of the Peace.

This is to certify that Michl Mayers had been employed with thirteen men him included for to go to Skinectady with four boats to bring up provisions for this Garrison, he and the Men being Six Days from this past, wherefore they are entitled to the Wages as Batteau Men from the public as witness my Hand this 2d of April 1779. Peter Bellinger Colo.

FROM: Herkimer Family Portfolio, Doc. No. SC 11965, No. 14, Dept of Manuscripts and Special Collections, New York State Library, Albany, New York.

End Notes—W.15860—Nicholas Weaver

1. Nicholas Weaver served as a private in Captain Abraham Veeder's Company (Second Company) in Colonel Frederick Visscher's Third Regiment of Tryon County Militia, also known as the Mohawk District Regiment.
2. There is one known muster roll for Captain Leffler's Company of Bateaumen for 1778 but Weaver's name is not on it. Captain Leffler had been serving as Ensign and was appointed on January 7, 1777, in Captain Giles Woolcott's Company which was the Eighth Company in Colonel Seth Warner's Regiment, designated as an Additional Continental Regiment. Ensign Leffler was with the regiment until he resigned on August 4, 1777. FROM: Revolutionary War Rolls 1775-1783, Series M-246, Roll 134, folder 230, Warner's Regiment, National Archives, Washington, D.C. The Batteauman Companies are on Roll 122, folder 78, Quartermaster General's Department.

3. Nicholas served as a private in Captain Garret Putman's Company in Lieutenant-Colonel Commandant Marinus Willett's Regiment of New York State Levies in 1781.
4. This is the same amount recorded in Captain Putman's Company payroll. FROM: Revolutionary War Rolls 1775-1776, Series M-246, Roll 78, folder 173, National Archives, Washington D.C.
5. Myndert W. Quackenbush was commissioned on March 8, 1781 First Lieutenant in Captain John Wemple's Company in Colonel Visscher's Regiment. Simon Veeder was commissioned Quartermaster on March 8, 1781 in Colonel Visscher's Regiment. Volkert Veeder was appointed Lieutenant-Colonel in 1776 and he was commissioned on June 25, 1778 in Colonel Visscher's Regiment.

Pension Application for Richard Weaver

S.11726
State of Vermont
Rutland County SS.

On this 14th day of July A.D. 1832 personally appeared in open Court before the Judge of the Probate Court of Rutland now sitting, Richard Weaver a resident of the County of Rutland and State of Vermont, aged 81 years, who being first duly sworn according to law, doth on his oath make the following declaration, in order to obtain the benefit of the act of Congress, passed June 7, 1832.

That he entered the service of the United States under the following named officers, and served as herein stated. In 1775 he lived at a place called [Sacajo?] near Poughkeepsie, New York, & in May or June of that year he enlisted for five months in Capt. DeBois' (1) Company, Col. Schuyler's (2) Regt & marched to Albany thence to Lake George thence to St. Johns under Genl. Montgomery (3) & assisted in taking St. Johns (4) after which he was sent back to Albany as a part of the guard with prisoners & was discharged at Albany in December having served about seven months—he received no written discharge. In April 1776 he enlisted at Dover, New York for nine months & was appointed sergeant & was put on the recruiting service in Dutchess County & about [?] May the company being filled up & mustered marched to Poughkeepsie, thence took water & went to the City of New York where he joined the Regt of Col. Ritsman's (5) Regt, Genl M.Dougal's (6) Brigade & remained there until after Long Island was taken when he retreated to Harlaem Heights & after the battle thence retreated across Kingsbridge to White Plains—thence to Peekskill—thence through New Jersey to Pennsylvania & was discharged in Bucks County in January 1777—he was in the battles of White Plains, Harlaem & Trenton (7). He immediately returned to [Sacajo?] N. York, where he was hired by a class to go into service for six weeks & served in Capt. Vail's Company, Col. Van Rensellaer's Regt (8) & marched to White Plains and was dismissed at White Plains after serving six weeks. In April 1777 he came to Vermont, & on the news of Burgoyne's approach he volunteered & served in

Capt. Cook's Company & was chosen Ensign & marched to Ticonderoga, and when the British troops came down he retreated to Castleton & was there when the battle of Hubbardton (9) was fought, thence retreated near Rutland to Pownal and dispersed, having served about six weeks as Ensign. He afterwards volunteered and was on the way to Bennington (10), but did not arrive in time to be in the battle. He afterwards served about four weeks in Capt. Sawyer's (11) Company at Shelburn in guarding the frontier. He knew Genl. Washington, Putnam, Lord Sterling, Sullivan, Starks, St. Clair (12)& many others - He has no documentary evidence, & he knows of no person whose testimony he can procure who can testify to his services. He was born at East Greenwich R. Island, the 18 May 1751 O.S.—but knows of no record of his age—Since the revolution he has lived in Vermont until about 29 years ago he moved to Tioga Point where he lived a year or two—thence to Queensbury & last spring removed to Clarendon where he now lives with his daughter—he never received a written discharge—he is known to Eden Peck, Hatter Green & many other inhabitants of Clarendon.

He hereby relinquishes every claim whatever to a pension or annuity except the present, and declares that his name is not on the pension roll of the agency of any state. (Signed with his mark) Richard Weaver

Sworn to and subscribed the day and year aforesaid. [?]

Letter replying to a request for information dated March 2, 1926.

In response to your letter of the twenty-fourth instant, you are herewith furnished the history of the only soldier of the Revolution named Richard Weaver, found on the records of this Bureau.

From the papers in the Revolutionary War pension claim, S.11726, it appears that Richard Weaver was born May 18, 1751, (old style) at East Greenwich, Rhode Island.

While living near Poughkeepsie, New York, he enlisted in May, or June 1775, served seven months as a private in Captain Dubois' Company, Colonel Schuyler's New York Regiment and was at the Siege of Saint Johns.

He enlisted in April 1776, served nine months as a Sergeant in Captain Nathaniel Pearce and Captain David Baldwin's Companies, Colonel Ritzema's New York Regiment, and was at the battles of Harlem, White Plains and Trenton.

He enlisted immediately after and served six weeks in Captain Vail's Company, Colonel VanRensselaer's New York Regiment.

In April 1777 he went to Vermont, and there enlisted and served six weeks as Ensign of Captain Cook's Vermont Company and was at the battle of Hubbardton, and he afterwards served four weeks in Captain Sawyer's Company of Vermont Troops, dates not stated.

In 1824 he was living in Queensbury, Warren County, New York and had a wife aged sixty years, her name is not stated.

He was allowed pension on his application executed July 14, 1832, at which time he was residing in Clarendon, Rutland County, Vermont, with a daughter, whose name is not given.

He died at Clarendon, Vermont, June 4, 1842, leaving no widow, but the following children survived him: Joseph, Richard, Benjamin, Peter, William, Mrs. Betsy Baxter and Mrs. Sally McCoy.

End Notes—S.11726—Richard Weaver

1. Richard enlisted as a private on July 6, 1775 in Captain Lewis DuBois' company in Colonel James Clinton's Third New York Continental Regiment. On the muster roll dated September 28, 1776 recorded in the camp at Ticonderoga, Richard is listed as "Deserted September 16". FROM: Revolutionary War Rolls 1775-1783, Series M-246, Roll 69, Folder 38, National Arachives, Washington D.C.
2. There was no one by the last name of Schuyler who was a Colonel in the Third New York. It is possible he was referring to Major-General Philip Schuyler, the overall commander of the New York troops.
3. Brigadier General Richard Montgomery, was appointed on June 22, 1775. December 9, 1775 he was appointed major general.
4. General Montgomery started the siege of Fort St. John on September 18, 1775 two days after Richard deserted. The fort surrendered on November 3, 1775. There is no proof that Richard returned from desertion. There appears to be no muster roll after September 28, 1775 but as late as this date he is still listed as deserted.
5. Rudolphus Ritzema was appointed Colonel of the Third New York Continental Regiment on March 28, 1776.
6. Alexander McDougall was appointed Colonel of the First New York Continental Regiment on June 30, 1775. He was appointed brigadier general August 9, 1775 and major general on October 20, 1777.
7. The Battle of Harlem Heights was fought on October 16, 1776, the Battle of White Plains on October 28, 1776 (both in New York), and the Battle of Trenton, New Jersey was fought on December 26, 1776.
8. There were two Colonel VanRensselaers. Kilian of the Fourth Regiment of Albany County Militia and Robert of the Eighth Regiment of Albany County Militia. There does not appear to be a Captain Vail (Veal, Viele, Ville, Etc.) serving in either regiment. The Captain Vail's—Benjamin, Isaiah and Israel all served in the Second Regiment of Ulster County Militia under Colonel James McClaughrey.
9. The Battle of Hubbardton was fought on July 7, 1777. This was the only battle fought in Vermont during the War of Independence. The Hubbardton Battlefield is a Vermont State Historic Site.
10. The Battle of Bennington (Walloomsac, NY) was fought on August 16, 1777.
11. Either Thomas or Joseph Sawyer, Captains in the Vermont Militia.
12. Generals George Washington, Israel Putnam, William Alexander (Lord Stirling), John Sullivan, John Stark, and Arthur St. Clair.

13. Captain Nathan Pearce of Ritzema's Regiment was dismissed from the service by General McDougall. Lieutenant David Baldwin was then appointed captain in his place. *A weekly return of ye 3rd Regiment of New York Forces Commanded by Colonel Ritzema. Septr 20th 1776.* FROM: Revolutionary War Rolls 1775-1783, Series M-246, Roll 69, Folder 39, National Archives, Washington, D.C.

Pension Application for John Wiley

Donated by Kenneth Lifshitz

S.44223

State of New York SS.

To the Hon. Richard Riker, Recorder of the City of New York and one of the Judges of the Court of Common Pleas, called the Mayor's Court of the City of New York, which is a Court of Record of the State of New York.

The Declaration under Oath of John Wiley—formerly an officer engaged in the Service of the United States during the Revolutionary War, now a Citizen of the United States and resident of the City and County of New York, respectfully sheweth,

That the said John Wiley Sometime in the year 1776, to wit, on the 24 Feby 1776 (1) joined the American Army & accepted & acted as Captain of the first Regiment of New York Forces (2) in the Continental service as appears by his commission for John Hancock President of Congress—That he acted under the said Commission for upwards of Ten Months & accepted an appointment under the New arrangement & volunteered on different occasions in the Revolutionary Army against the common Enemy. And the declaration further sheweth, that the said John Wylie is now a citizen of the United States, resides in the city of New York and is, by reason of his reduced circumstances in life, in need of assistance from his country for support & is now near seventy years of age.

Therefore the said John Wiley conceives himself entitled to the benefit of the Act of Congress of the United States, entitled, "An Act to provide for certain persons engaged in the Land and Naval Service of the United States in the Revolutionary War," approved 18th March 1818, and requests your Honor will examine into the truth of the matter aforesaid, certify and transmit the testimony in the case, and the proceedings had thereon, to the Honorable the Secretary of the Department of War, to the end that such relief may be had in the premises, as is by law in such case made and provided. And in support of the facts above set forth, the said, John Wyley refers to the deposition of the Col. Richard Platt, (3) Colonel. (Signed) John Wiley.

City and County of New York SS. John Wiley of the City and County of New York being duly sworn, saith, that the matter by him set forth in the foregoing Declaration, are in all respects just and true.

Sworn before me this first day of April 1818, John Wiley

R. Riker, Recorder of the City of New York

City and County of New York SS Richard Platt of the City of New York being sworn, saith that he is well acquainted with John Wiley above named that he & the deponent served together in the army of the revolution against the common enemy & that the facts by him stated are true as he verily believes.
(Signed Richd Platt
Sworn before me this first day of April 1818. R. Ricker, Recorder.

New York Mayor's Court.

In the Court of Common Pleas, called the Mayor's Court of the City of New York, held at the City Hall, in and for the said City, before the Judges of the same Court of August term, in the year of our Lord one thousand eight hundred and twenty.

Present the Honorable Peter A. Jay, Recorder of the City of New York SS. Be it Remembered, that on the second day of September in the year of our Lord one thousand eight hundred and twenty, personally appeared in the Court of Common Pleas, called the Mayor's Court of the city of New York, in open court, the said court being a court of record for the city and county of New York, according to the charter of the said city and the laws of the state of New York, according to the charter of the said city and the laws of the state of New, John Wiley, aged Seventy Two years, resident in the City of New York, in the State of New York, United States of America who being first duly sworn according to law, doth on his oath declare, that he served in the revolutionary war as follows: he received a Captains Commission on the 24th day of February in the year 1776 in the Continental establishment in New York signed by John Hancock in the first New York Regiment of Infantry, commonly called hairy Caps, commanded by Colonel Alexander McDougal, in the line of the State of New York and was in the battle of Haerlaem [Harlem] Heights and covered the retreat of the American Army on Long Island when the regiment had some skirmishing the same regiment also covered the retreat of the American Army from New York. Deponent continued in the command of his company in the same regiment for ten months & until December 1776 when his regiment was broken up—Declarant then accepted an appointment as Captain in the first regiment of New York State Artillery commanded by Colonel Lamb (4) but was unable from circumstances to take up his commission—In the beginning of 1777 he served as brigade Major for General McDougal during the sickness or absence of Colonel Platt. In 1778 he acted in the capacity of volunteer as Brigade Major under colonel Henry Sherbourne who commanded the Brigade and was in the battle of Rhode Island after the French fleet left Rhode Island. In 1780 he was appointed Brigade Major by Col. Dayton who commanded a Brigade and was in the battles of Connecticut farms & Springfield still as a Volunteer—and after this headed the Militia as a Volunteer on the New Jersey line against the Common Enemy—In 1780 he was appointed by Governor and General George Clinton a Commissary of Purchases for the troops credited to the State of New York served as a Commissary about six months lost most of he property by the depreciation of the Continental money & all his houses distillery & stables & furniture was burned in the Great fire at New York to which he returned poor and penniless and that his original declaration is dated the first day of April one thousand eight hundred and eighteen and that his pension certificate is No. 2030. (Signed) John Wiley

And I do solemnly swear that I was a resident citizen of the United States on the 18th day of March 1818, and that I have not since that time, by gift, sale, or in any manner, disposed of my property, or any part thereof, with intent thereby so to diminish it as to bring myself within the provisions of an act of Congress, entitled, "An act to provide for certain persons engaged in the land and naval service of the United States, in the Revolutionary war," passed on the 18th day of March, one thousand eight hundred and eighteen and that I have not, nor has any person in trust for me, any property or securities, contracts or debts, due to me; nor have I any income other than what is contained in the schedule hereto annexed, land by me subscribed, to wit:

Real Estate—None

Personal Estate/necessary clothing excepted having noted, none as follows.—

1 Watch given to declarant by his brother which he has worn upwards of 56 years and which cost exclusive of the case which is a silver one $5-$7.00

A family picture 149 years old $10.00

$17.00

Declarant has an account against Samuel Lopez of the City of New York amounting to 7.00

The whole amount of his estate is $24.00

Declarant at present has no occupation, he was formerly a distiller but through unforeseen misfortunes, he has been so much reduced in his circumstances, as to be unable to carry on that business, he has no trade, and is unable to support himself without his pension.

Declarant has no family residing with him, he has theretofore been aided by his son upon whom he is dependant with whom he lives, whose name is Charles Wiley whose age is 39 and who is able to support himself.

Declarant saith that after the War, he went into business and was assisted by his friends, but became unfortunate in business inconsequence of misplaced credit and in consequence of the misfortunes which prudence could neither foresee nor retrieve lost his all and has been left deeply involved in debts which he is unable to pay—He saith that he is in such indigent circumstances as to be unable to support himself without the assistance of his country, that is today without the aid of the General Government except by private or public charity.

(Signed) John Wiley

Sworn in open court the 2d day of Sept 1820. Benj. Ferris Clk.

Letter in Pension Application Folder.

May 22, 1913

Hon. William H. Wiley
432 Fourth Avenue
New York city
My dear Mr. Wiley:

In response to your letter dated the 14th and received the 15th instant, I have the honor to advise you that John Wiley, Sur. File No. 44,223, Rev. War was allowed a pension of $20 per month from April 1, 1818 on account of the following services in the Revolutionary War.

He stated that he was commissioned February 24, 1776 (5), Captain of the sixth company in Colonel Alexander McDougall's regiment, 1st New York Infantry commonly called "Hairy Caps", was in the battle of Harlem Heights, and covered the American retreat from Long Island and New York, and served until December 1776, when the regiment was broken up; he then accepted an appointment as Captain in Colonel Lamb's regiment of 1st New York State Artillery, but was unable from circumstances to take up his commission; that in the beginning of 1777, he served as Brigade-Major for General McDougall during the absence of Colonel Platt; volunteered in 1778, as Brigade-Major under Colonel Henry Sherbourne and was in the battle of Rhode Island; in 1780, was appointed Brigade-Major by Colonel Dayton and was in the battle of Connecticut Farms and Springfield and after that he voluntarily headed the New Jersey Militia against the common enemy; in 1780, he was appointed Commissary of Purchases by Governor and General George Clinton of New York, and served about six months.

There are no further particulars of his services.

In 1820 he stated that he was seventy-two years of age and a resident of New York City, and that he had no family residing with him except his son Charles Wiley who was thirty-nine years of age. In 1847 it was stated that soldier died January 29, 1829 and that is daughters Rebecca Ballard and Phoebe L. Osborne survived him.

In 1855, John Wiley of New York City, aged forty-six years, claimed to be one of the heirs of the soldier, but did not state their relationship.

Very respectfully,

J. L. Davenport, Commissioner

End Notes by Kenneth Lifshitz

John Wiley is an interesting and colorful character. He was displaced from a fairly well to do existence in New York with the arrival of the British, relocating to Elizabeth New Jersey. In 1776 he was offered and declined a Captain's commission in John Lamb's Artillery regiment (See Chapter "The Declension of Wiley" in "Donderberg's Pumpkin Vine,-Kenneth Lifshitz") citing straightened public circumstances due his personal losses in the great New York fire. This may have been an exaggeration as that same month he declined the commission he travelled to Boston and became part owner of a privateer cargo out of Rhode Island. He eventually became the purchasing commissary for the State of New York and was instrumental in supplying the troops in the Mohawk Schoharie Valley area near Albany. He used his connections in the commissary and quartermaster departments to set up what appears to be a black market iron trade running from New Jersey to the French Fleet's purchasing agents in Rhode Island, transporting raw iron and other goods through the commissary network. (See "LETTER OF CAPTAIN JOHN WILEY OF THE REVOLUTIONARY ARMY." *The Historical Magazine, and Notes and Queries Concerning the Antiquities, Hi...*Mar 1869; 5, 3; pg. 199.)

Despite his refusal of the commission in his regiment, he would remain fast friends with John Lamb and would personally help barricade Lamb's residence on Cherry Street defending it from a drunken pro-federalist mob some years after the close of the war. His wife Phebe (Halsted) was a notable beauty who excited the admiration of Lamb and many others before her untimely demise at age 38 (presumably from Yellow Fever contracted while visiting Lamb's son-in-law, Charles Tillinghast). His son would go on to form what would become the publishing empire, John Wiley & Sons. Aside from the letter published in Historical Magazine, several of his correspondence are held in the New York Historical Society including his letters to Lamb (see John Lamb collection).

End Notes—John Wiley—S.44223

1. John is listed as a First Lieutenant in Colonel John Lasher's First Battalion of the New York Independents. On January 31, 1776 a memorandum was delivered by Colonel Lasher to the Provincial Congress "of such officers in his Regt as are willing to go into the Continental Service." Documents Relating to the Colonial History of the State of New York, ed. Berthold Fernow, Vol. XV, State Archives, Vol. I, Albany, NY, Weed, Parsons and Company Printers, 1887, pp 50-52.
2. In 1775 and 1776 Alexander McDougal was the Colonel of the First New York Continental Regiment. On August 9, 1776, McDougal was promoted to Brigadier General and to Major General on October 20, 1777.
3. Platt was Second Lieutenant in Captain Frederick Weissenfel's Company (First Company) in the First New York Continental Regiment. Brigade Major August 12, 1776 and Aide-de-Camp to General McDougal. Revolutionary War Rolls 1775-1783, Series M-246, Roll 65, Folder 1(McDougal's 1775), National Archives, Washington DC.
4. Colonel John Lamb Commanded the Second Continental Regiment of Artillery.
5. There is a muster roll and billeting roll for Captain Wiley's Company for Colonel McDougal's Regiment in 1776, Revolutionary War Rolls 1775-1783, Series M-246, Roll 65, Folder 2, National Archives, Washington DC.

Pension Application for Jacob Willsey or Wilsie or Woolsey

W.28001 (Abigail Riker) This woman's last husband was also a pensioner. See case of Gerardus Riker, New Jersey and New York S.11293. Abigail Riker,

Formerly Widow of Jacob Woolsey was awarded a pension of $120.00 per annum

State of New York

City and County of New York SS.

On this twenty fifth day of August 1837 before me Richard Riker Recorder of the City of New York and one of the Judges of the Court of Common Pleas personally appeared Abigail Riker a resident of the State of New York and of the City and County of New York aged ninety four years who first being duly sworn, according to law, doth on her oath make the following declaration, in order to obtain the benefit of the provision made by the act of Congress passed July 4th 1836 and the act of explanatory of said act passed March 3rd 1837—That she married to Jacob Woolsey, who was a non-commissioned officer in the Revolutionary Army, and who served in the Second Regiment of New York Artillery, Commanded by Colonel Lamb (1), and of which Regiment Stevens (2) was Lieutenant Colonel, Doughty (3) and Boman (4) were Majors and in a company attached to the said Regiment of which Nistle (5) was Captain Fenno (6) was Lieutenant or afterwards Captain, George Leacraft (7) was 1st Lieutenant, Campbell (8) 2nd Lieutenant, that said Woolsey entered the service on or about the commencement of the war, and left the same on or about the 9th of June 1783 on Furlough being sick. The said Joseph Woolsey [sic] was at the Battle of White Plains (9) in the year 1776 and of Yorktown, Virginia in 1781 under Genl Knox (10) at Whiteplains Col. Lamb commanded the Regiment & Mott the company at Yorktown (11)—Col. Stevens commanded the Regiment & Lieut. Fenno the Company, Captain Machin (12) acting as engineer, both under command of Genl Knox, the said Joseph [sic] Woolsey at the time of his entering into his service resided in the town of Tappan in Rockland County in the State of New York and he volunteered his services, entered for the war and as deponent believes received a bounty, and served during the war faithfully—The Regiment during the war was marched from New Windsor in the State of New York to Yorktown Virginia, from Yorktown to Burlington in New Jersey and there had winter quarters, from there to West Point; and deponent saith that the said Joseph [sic] Woolsey (13) never received any pension, and that deponent has no documentary evidence in support of her claim. She further declares that she was married to the said Joseph [sic] Woolsey in the spring of the year 1761 that her husband the aforesaid Joseph [sic] Woolsey died on the 31st day of May 1784 of Measles at his residence in Rockland County aforesaid, and that she was a widow on the 4th of July 1836 And that she was afterwards married to Gerardus Riker (who was also a soldier in the Revolutionary Army) who died on the 4th of October 1833. That she was a widow on the 4th of July 1836 and she remains a widow—as will more particularly appear by reference to the proof hereto annexed—and Deponant further saith that she has no certificate of her marriage to the said Joseph [sic] Woolsey and the Clergyman who married them, and those present at the marriage are all deceased, all which is to the best of the deponants knowledge recollection and belief—and that Deponent has no property except her clothing. (Signed with her mark) Abigail Riker

Subscribed and Sworn to the day and year first above written, before me; the said Abigail Riker being unable from bodily infirmity to attend in court. R. Riker, Recorder of the City of New York and one of the Judges of the Court of Common Pleas of the said City & County.

New York Nov. 3, 1838
Sir,

The pension certificate of the widow I take came duly to hand, In relation to that of Abigail Riker, you will receive a Document signed by William B. Aitken, sworn to before our Recorder making most beggarly excuse for the man errors committed by him, in drawing up the papers, and which was the means of leading others in error also. In one of the Documents forwarded made by Elizabeth Riker, daughter of said Abigail Riker you will perceive that she discovered the mistake made by Aitken, and mentioned it to him, which he promised to rectify, but which he neglected. In a conversation had with Mrs. Abigail Riker with my father last spring, in relation to the services of her husband, she was consistent in every respect, and also where she was named as well as the name of the clergyman, the place where her children were born, viz at Tappan, that is four of the number which document is at the Department. Your obt servt, Casper C. Childs 80 Nesey Street.
J.S. Edwards Esq, Com of Pensions

State of New York
City and County of New York SS.

I Robert H. Morris, Recorder of the City of New York and one of the Judges of the Court of Common Pleas, in and for the City and County of New York, do hereby certify that on the twenty-ninth day of October 1838, before me appeared Elizabeth Riker, who says that Abigail Wilsie and Jacob Wilsie were her father and mother and that he mother is a religious woman and has always borne a good character and has no doubt whatever that she has stated facts in her affidavit, that her mother had eight children by her father, that she has often heard her mother and acquaintances speak of his services during the Revolution, and also of his having served in the Regiment commanded by Colonel Lamb, that he died at Tappan, with the disease called the measles, in the following year after the war, and I further state that our right name is Wilsie, although some part of the family have been called Woolsey, and she further stated that when the first Document was forwarded to the Department, drawn up by William B. Aitken, she then discovered the many errors made, he promised to rectify them, which he never attended to, and gave his reason for not doing so, which is most inglorious and she further states she was six [probably meant sixty] years of age in February last—and she further says that after the death of her father her mother married the father of deponents husband. (Signed with her mark) Elizabeth Riker.

Rbt H. Morris, Recorder of the City of New York & Judge of the Court of Com. Pleas. Therein.

State of New York
City & County of New York SS.

I Robert H. Morris Recorder of the City of New York and one of the Judges of the Court of Common Pleas in and for the City and County of New York do hereby certify that on the twenty ninth day of October 1838, before me appeared, Gerardus Riker, who says that he is the son of Elizabeth Ricker, and grandson of Abigail Wilsie, and he has in possession a remnant of an old deed with the endorsement of John Wilsie, on the back, and in the body the name of John Wilsie, is also mentioned (this deed was given for a piece of land to my father, in Bergen County N.J) said John Wilsie was the eldest son of Jacob and Abigail Wilsie the name of the deed is spelled Willsey nevertheless, it is the same, and in all the transactions, the name has been Wilsie or Willsey, and not Woolsey, as has been incorrectly stated. That he further states, that his grandmother was the mother of eight children, by Wilsie and that from her good character, and the many proofs that he has had, that no doubt rests on his mind, that she may be the lawful wife of Jacob Wilsie, deceased and he further states that his grandmother, was taken unwell some time previous to her application for said pension and at her request he placed in the Family Register, her birth day and the date of her marriage, without thinking it would ever be asked for any other purpose, than it was intended for at the time, a memorandum. (Signed) Gerardus Riker
Rbt. H. Morris, Recorder of the City of New York & Judge of the Court of Com. Pleas. Therein.
Town of Greenburg, Westchester Co.
State of New York, July 24th 1838.

Ann Brown of said village aged eighty seven years and upwards, says that she will state on her oath, all the facts within her knowledge, relative to her half sister Abigail Fosha (maiden name) that she was married to Jacob Wilsie, a soldier of the Revolution on the 7th day of September 1761, agreeable to her statement under oath. I was very young at the time she was married, and recollecting her return to her father's house after the marriage, that soon after Mr. Willsie started on a journey and that during his absence I slept with his wife until he return, that she had eight children by said Wilsie, all of whom, I was well acquainted with namely - John Willsie, Peter Willsie, James Willsie, Samuel Willsie, Jacob Willsie, Elizabeth Willsie, Isaac Willsie, Henry Willsie. My mother had two husbands viz, first Peter Fosha, and the second her father Benjamin Laforgy. My maiden name was Ann Laforgy. I was married the early part of the Revolution at White Plains Westchester Col. NY Upon diligent enquiry I find that the records of these early marriages were destroyed, when the British were in possession at White Plains, during the Revolutionary War.

I further state that my sister became religious soon after the death of her first husband, , which happened soon after the Revolutionary war, that she has lived an exemplary life, and that I consider her character without a stain, and that she afterwards married a Mr. Riker, a respectable old gentleman of the City of New York, long since dead. (Signed with her mark) Ann Brown. In presence of J. A. Constant, E. Childs

Sworn before me one of the Judges of the County Courts in & for the County of Westchester State of New York, this twenty fourth day of July in the year of our Lord one thousand eight hundred & thirty eight. Joseph A. Constant

End Notes—W.28001—Jacob Wilsey

1. Jacob Willsie enlisted on July 22, 1777 as a matross (private) for 3 years in Captain Gershom Mott's Company in Colonel John Lamb's Second Continental Artillery Regiment. On the March and April 1779 Muster Roll of Captain Mott's Company Jacob is listed as having enlisted for war. On the December 1779 Muster Roll Jacob is listed as one of the Gunner's for Captain Mott's Company. On the February 1782 Muster Roll for Captain Mott's Company, Jacob is listed as a corporal. FROM: Revolutionary War Rolls 1775-1783, Series M-246, Roll 119, Folder 46, National Archives, Washington, D.C.
2. Ebenezer Stevens wasn't appointed Lieutenant-Colonel in Colonel Lamb's Regiment until November 24, 1778. Stevens was originally appointed Lt.-Col. in the Third Continental Artillery Regiment on April 30, 1778. Eleazer Oswald was the Lieutenant-Colonel of Colonel Lamb's Regiment having been appointed on January 1, 1777. He resigned on June 28, 1778.
3. John Doughty was appointed Captain in Colonel Lamb's Regiment on January 1, 1777. He may have acted as a major but he was never commissioned as such in Colonel Lamb's Regiment.
4. Sebastian Bauman was appointed captain on January 1, 1777 in Colonel Lamb's Regiment. He was appointed major of the regiment on September 12, 1778.
5. Peter Nestle was appointed second lieutenant on January 1, 1777 in Colonel Lamb's Regiment. He was appointed First Lieutenant on February 1, 1779. He was appointed Captain Lieutenant on September 20, 1781. When the regiment disbanded on June 17, 1783, Peter retired from the service.
6. Ephraim Fenno was appointed Captain-Lieutenant on January 1, 1777 in Colonel Lamb's Regiment. He was taken prisoner at Fort Clinton on October 6, 1777.
7. George Leacraft (Laycraft, Leaycraft, etc.) was appointed Second Lieutenant on January 1, 1777 in Colonel Lamb's Regiment. He was appointed First Lieutenant on August 21, 1780.
8. John Campbell was appointed Second Lieutenant on June 29, 1781 in Colonel Lamb's Regiment.
9. The Battle of White Plains, New York was fought on October 28, 1776. This was before Jacob's enlistment in Colonel Lamb's Regiment of Artillery.

10. Brigadier General and Chief of Artillery Henry Knox. He was appointed to this position on December 28, 1776. He was appointed Major General on March 22, 1782, to rank from November 15, 1781.
11. The Yorktown Virginia Campaign was from September 28 to October 19, 1781.
12. Thomas Machin was appointed Captain-Lieutenant on January 1, 1777 in Colonel Lamb's Regiment. He was wounded at Fort Montgomery on October 6, 1777. He was appointed Captain on August 21, 1780.
13. For some reason Henry Riker, Recorder continually writes in the pension application Joseph Woolsey. Abigail cannot read or write and therefore is most likely unaware of the mistake. In later depositions by her children it is made clear about there being several mistakes in the previous deposition made by their mother.

Pension Application for Daniel Woodworth

S.32612
State of Indiana
Green County SS.

Green County Probate Court Nov. [1?] 1839.

Be it remembered that on this the 12th day of November in the year of our lord one thousand eight hundred and thirty nine personally appeared in open court before the Hon. Willis D. Lester Probate Judge of the county of Green Aforesaid Daniel Woodworth a resident Citizen of the County of Green aforesaid aged eighty seven years on the 14 day of January last past and who being duly sworn doth on oath declare that in order to avail himself of the benefits of the Act of Congress of the 7th of June 1832.

That he was born in the County of Ulster in the State of New York on the 14th day of January 1752, in which County he continued until he entered the Army in the Service of the United States as hereinafter stated. To wit, that on the first day of June in the year 1777 he volunteered for the term of seven months in the company commanded by Captain Nicholas Johnson (1) in Ridgement commanded by Col. Van Horne, and Major Benjamin Scooter. That his Lieutenants were Houze Johnson (brother of Captain Johnson) and Mr. Allsworth, the (Christian name of the 2d Lieutenant Allsworth not now remembered) That his Ensign was Robert Mould (2), and his Orderly Sergeant was of the name of Jacob R. Rose.(3)

That during this 7 months engagement the nature of his was to protect and defend the frontiers from the predatory incursions of Indians and Tories, and that he was posted the whole time at Mamma Catting Fort except (when they were ordered out in pursuit of the Indians) that during this 7 months whilst they were stationed at Mamma Catting fort the Indians and Tories destroyed a whole dutch settlement and fort on Van Tines Kill distance about 15 or 20 miles from Mamma Catting, that in two or three weeks after the destruction of the inhabitants of VanTine Kill, that the Indians and Tories again returned, into the neighbourhood, and also destroyed another whole dutch settlement on the mouth of the Navissing Creek about 10 miles from Mamma Catting. That upon the destruction of this last settlement that the whole Regiment to which this declarant was attached left Mamma Catting fort and pursued the Indians and in three days marching we overtook the Indians, at the big bend of the Delaware river being about 700 in number where we had a general engagement with them, and defeated them killing about 600 of them and the rest making their escape by swimming the river after the battle with the Indians we again returned to Mamma Catting where this declarant continued until his term of service had fully expired which was on the first day of January 1778.

That he was then discharged & received his discharge in writing which discharge was signed and handed to him by Col. Van Horne or by Maj. Benjamin Scooter, he will not say positively which of them signed said discharge, that after he was, thus discharged he returned home, where he remained from the first of January 1778 up to the 10th or 12th of April 1778, when he again volunteered for three months under the same officers and was also forted at the same fort.

That during this last three months engagement that he was in no battle nor in any very active service but was all the time in the fort except on some few occasions when with some others would be sent to some neighbouring forts to carry some messages from this fort to other forts relative to the movements of the Indians & c.—he also states that he fully served out his full tour of three months herein last mentioned & was discharged on the 12th of July 1778 & received his discharge in writing & that the same was signed and handed to him by Col. Van Horne, after which he again returned home where he remained until the first of Oct 1778.

This declarant further states that on the first day of Oct 1778 he gain volunteered in the company commanded by Capt. Drake (4) in the Regiment commanded by Col. Van Horne, for the term of three months that the other subaltern officers attached to said company were strangers to this declarant--that as soon as he had volunteered on this last tour, that s'd Capt. Drake & Company was composed of 100 volunteers besides the officers, that the day this declarant joined said company that they were ordered from Mamma Catting fort where he joined them to a place called the Bazin on the Lake a distance of about 150 or 200 miles from Mamma Catting for the purpose of destroying the crafts at that place belonging to Indians and Tories. That as Capt. Drake & his company came to the Bazin the place of their destination that the Indians about 6-700 in number had just landed and that a general battle then commenced between our company & the Indians, that the Indians the very first fire killed Capt. Drake & nearly all the officers that in said engagement—all our company were killed except five that is this declarant and four other privates who after the battle was over by the darkness of the evening (night fall coming on before the battle was ended) were enabled to make their escape & who had arrived safe back again at MammaCatting after this declarant had returned from this last battle with the Indians, he with the other four privates with him were attached to another Captain's Company—the name of whom this declarant does not now remember—but that he was still stationed at Mamma Catting, under the Command of the s'd Capt. Until he had fully served out this said term of three months, and was discharged by his Capt.

On the first of January 1779—without having received any written discharge—but having been discharged by word of mouth—after which he returned home, and remained at home until the first day April 1779 when he again entered as a Volunteer for the term of Six months in the Ranging service of the U.S. in the company commanded by John Newkirk (5) in the Regiments commanded by Col. Philips (6) who lived near Goshen. That his Lieutenants in said company were Alldridge Rose and Mr. Hornbrook (7) (the first name of the said Hornbrook not now remembered) that the nature of his service during this 6 months tour was that of Indian Spy and was continually engaged in Travelling from Fort to Fort and giving information to the several Forts of the Movements of the Indians—That during said 6 months as a spy he had made several trips to Cashafton on the Delaware which had been previously destroyed by the Indians, and which was a great place of resort for the Indians at that period.

That during this last 6 months tour he was not in any battle but that he often saw larger Companies of Indians of whose movements he always immediately gave intelligence to the nearest fort. That he fully served out his said tour of six months and was then discharged on the 1st day of Oct 1779, that he was discharged by Capt. Newkirk without ever having received a written discharge after which on the same day he enlisted for during the war in the regular service of the U.S. at Mamma Catting in the company commanded by Captain Allsworth who was my Lieutenant in the 7 months tour herein first stated, that after this declarant had enlisted as herein stated that he was mustered into the service of the US of regulars at Mamma Catting on the first day of July 1779 (8)—That he was never marched into the service of U.S. as a regular in his last tour of duty out of the said County of Ulster, and that the reason of his not having been marched out of said County was because that peace had been concluded or the war was then considered as at an end, and his Captain Mr. Allsworth (9) discharged him, stating at the same that their services were no longer necessary.

That he and the other recruits enlisted by the s'd Allsworth had never served any regiment and were still permitted to remain at home until discharged by him as herein stated by meeting him once a week for the purpose of training—That he continued in the service as a regular as herein stated from the time of his enlistment to the last day of Oct 1779 making four months from the time of his enlistment till he was discharged. That he never received any discharge in writing from this last term of service that the said Captain Allsworth discharged all his recruits on the same day by the word of mouth without any written discharges after which he returned home. (Signed with his mark) Daniel Woodworth.

End Notes—S.32612—Daniel Woodworth

1. Captain Nicholas Johnson; Col. VanHorne; Lieutenants, Houze Johnson and Allsworth; Major Benjamin Scooter, are unknown at this time. It is hard to know if he is mistaken about the names or that his memory is faulty as to the periods of service. It is possible that these officers were officers before the war since Daniel turned 16 in 1768 and would have been required to serve in the militia from that time on.
2. Daniel served in Captain William Cross' Company in Colonel Jonathan Hasbrouck's Fourth Regiment of Ulster County Militia. Robert Mould was the Ensign of this company. It is possible when he said Johnson he meant Jansen. In the Fourth Ulster there was a Captain Thomas Jansen Jr., and his First Lieutenant was Matthews Jansen. "Houze" could be for Hews which could be a nickname for Matthews. He also claims that the length of service was for seven months which is probably for his Levie service in 1781.
3. Jacob Roosa (Rose, Rosa, etc.) served as a sergeant in the Levie service with Daniel in 1781.
4. "Captain Drake" does not appear on the rolls of the Fourth Ulster; there are several Captain Drakes in the Westchester County Militia. The only Captain Drake found in the Ulster County Militia is Uriah Drake who was appointed Captain of the Newburgh Company of Associated Exempts in the Ulster County Militia, June 25, 1778.
5. John Newkirk was commissioned captain on March 23, 1778 in Colonel James McClaughrey's Second Regiment of Ulster County Militia. The First Lieutenant was Mathew Neely.
6. Moses Philips was commissioned Major on March 23, 1778 in the Second Ulster County Militia.
7. Allridge Rose and Mr. Hornbrook were not in the Second Ulster. Allridge Rose could possibly be Aldert Roosa who served as a Lieutenant in the Levies and Mr. Hornbrook was possibly Ensign Jacob Hornbeck who served in Colonel John Cantine's Third Regiment of Ulster County Militia.
8. Again Daniel has events mixed up. If he supposedly served for the same time period under Captain Newkirk in 1779 he couldn't have served under Captain Allsworth in 1779. Also there was no sign of peace on the horizon at this time.
9. Again this Allsworth, Aylesworth or Elsworth is unknown. A Peter Elsworth had served as a Captain-Lieutenant in Colonel Philip VanCortlandt's Second New York Continental Regiment until January 1, 1781. He was appointed captain on April 27, 1781 in Lieutenant-Colonel Commandant Marinus Willett's Regiment of New York Sate Levies. Captain Elsworth was killed in an ambush on July 6, 1781.

Pension Application for John Wormwood

W.24797 (Widow: Hannah Rawley)
State of New York

Schoharie County SS.

On this 28th day of August 1843, personally appeared before the undersigned a Judge of the County of Common Pleas of the said County of Schoharie Hannah Rawley a resident of Cobleskill in the County of Schoharie aforesaid aged seventy five years who being first duly sworn according to law doth on her oath make the following declaration in order to obtain the benefit of the provisions made by the act of congress passed July 7th 1838 and the acts and resolutions according the same including the act passed August 23d, 1842 granting half pay and provisions to certain widows. That she was married to John Wormwood who was a private in the war of the revolution. That she the declarant is unable to specify the particulars of the services of her said husband from her own personal knowledge as she was not married to him until after the war of the Revolution But that she has frequently and credibly been informed that he did serve on various occasions. That he enlisted into Captain Christian Getman's (1) Company of Rangers of the County of Tryon on the 23d day of August 1776 and served therein until the 27th day of March 1777 as will appear reference being had to Captain Getman's Muster Roll and the resolutions of the committee of safety and convention of New York now on file at the war department of the United States. And further that he served as set forth by records found in the comptrollers office of this state reference being had to the certificate of the comptroller herewith accompanying her said husband relates his services and has heard others relate that he served as a batteauman but she cannot name his Capt. But she would refer to the rolls of Capt. Samuel Gray (2) and the Capt. John Lefler (3) which she has been informed are on file at the war department for his services therein. And that he also served under Captain Andrew Dillenback (4) in Col. Jacob Klock's Regiment of the New York Militia Commanded by Gen. Nicholas Herkimer and was engaged in the Oriscany [Oriskany] Battle under said officers in August 1777 and was present when Capt. Dillenbach was killed in said Battle by the enemy.

All of which she has reason to believe will show clear proof of the services of her said husband. And therefore presents her claim to a pension for his said services. She further declares that her maiden name was Hannah Kane. That she was married to the said John Wormwood on the 9th day of April seventeen hundred and eighty seven. That her husband the said John Wormwood died on the 17th day of December seventeen hundred and ninety nine. And this declarant would further state that the said John Wormwood's name was sometimes wrote John Warmouth. And this declarant would further state that she was afterwards married to Thomas Rawley who died on the 25th day of March eighteen hundred and fourteen and that she is now his widow as will now fully appear by reference to the proof hereto annexed. (Signed with her mark) Hannah Rawley

Subscribed and sworn before me this 28th day of August 1843 and I certify that the declarant Hannah Rawley is unable to attend court by reason of old age and bodily infirmity and also that she is she's a creditable witness. John Westover, Judge of Schoharie County Courts.

Reply to a letter of inquiry dated April 3, 1939, written in response to an inquiry.

Reference is made to your letter in which you request information in regard to the husband of Hannah Rawleigh; she received a pension from the United States and died in 1853, but you do not know the name of her husband.

The data which follow are found in the papers on file in pension claim, W.24797, based upon service of John Wormwood or Warmouth in the Revolutionary War; his widow, Hannah, was doubtless the pensioner to whom you refer.

John Wormwood or Wormouth enlisted August 23, 1776, and served as private in Captain Christian Getman's company of rangers in the New York troops until March 27, 1777; he served as private in the Battle of Oriskany and was present when Captain Andrew Dillenback was killed, also, rendered boat service under Captains Samuel Gray and John Lefler. During the years 1778, 1780, 1781 and 1782, he served at various times, amounting in all to nearly one year, as a private in the New York troops under Captain John Bedhig, Rudolph Kock, Thomas Skinner (5) and Peter B. Tearse (6), and Colonels Jacob Klock, Peter Waggoner and Marinus Willett.

The soldier married April 9, 1787, Hannah Kane. Their names were borne on the records of the Reformed Dutch Church of Stone Arabia, town of Palatine.—Johannes Warmuth and Johanna Kahn.

John Wormouth (Wormwood) died December 17, 1799. Sometime later, his widow, Hannah, married Thomas Rawley or Rawleigh, who died March 25, 1814. The date and place of birth of said Thomas are not shown, nor the date and place of their marriage.

Hannah Rawley (as her name was borne on the pension rolls) was allowed pension on account of service of her former husband, John Wormouth, in the Revolutionary War on her application executed August 28, 1843, at which time she resided in Cobleskill, Schoharie County, New York. She was aged then seventy-five years; the date and place of her birth and the names of her parents were not given. It was not stated that Thomas Rawley rendered service in the Revolutionary War. In 1848, said Hannah resided in Deerfield, Oneida County, New York.

In 1844, Nancy Empie, the daughter of the soldier, John Wormouth and his wife, Hannah, made affidavit in behalf of her mother in Fulton County, New York; her brother, John Wormouth (as he signed his name) was in Fulton County, New York, at that time. Both of them referred to brothers and stated that the names Wormouth and Wormwood were interchangeable.

In 1844, Daniel Rawley, the son of Thomas Rawley and his wife, Hannah, was a resident of Cobleskill, New York. He signed his name Rawley. There are no further data in regard to any other children with the surname Rawley.

End Notes—John Wormwood - W.24797

1. On July 23, 1776 New York's Provincial Congress authorized 3 companies of Rangesr to be raised for the defense of Tryon County

Christian Getman was appointed Captain of one of the companies. John enlisted on August 23, 1776 and the company was discharged by the Provincial Congress on March 27, 1777. FROM: Revolutionary War Rolls 1775-1783, Series M-246, Roll 74, Folder 103, National Archives, Washington, D.C.

2. Captain Samuel Gray Commanded a company of Batteaumen in 1779 and 1780. FROM: Revolutionary War Rolls 1775-1783, Series M-246, Roll 122, Folder 77, National Archives, Washington, DC.Captain John Leffler commanded a company of Batteaumen in 1778. John's name does not appear on the muster roll. FROM: Revolutionary War Rolls, 1775-1783, M-246, Roll 122, Folder 78, National Archives, Washington, D.C.
3. Captain Andrew Dillenbach (Dillenback, Dillenbagh, etc.) of the Fourth Company in Colonel Jacob Klock's Second Regiment of Tryon County Militia.
4. John enlisted in 1781 in Captain Thomas Skinner's Company in Colonel Marinus Willett's Regiment of New York State Levies. He was owed £6..18..8 and it was delivered to William Willson. FROM: Revolutionary War Rolls 1775-1783, Series M-246, Roll 78, Folder 173, National Archives, Washington, DC.
5. According to the Colonel Marinus Willett's Descriptive Book No. 4, Special Collections and Manuscripts, New York State Library, Albany, NY. Doc. No. 11105, John enlisted as follows: August 10, 1782, in Captain Peter B. Tearce's Company in Colonel Willett's Regiment. Born at Stone Arabia, Tryon Co., New York, enlisted by John Taylor for 2 years 4 months, 22 days, age 22, size 5 ft, complexion dark, hair dark, eyes black, occupation weaver, Remarks—scar on left eye. In 1783, Tearce commanded the Light Infantry Company and John was still in the company. Tearce's payroll states John served 12 months. He had been paid £26..0..60 and was owed £53..0..30. FROM: Revolutionary War Rolls 1775-1783, Series M-246, Roll 78, Folder 173, National Archives, Washington, D.C.

Pension Application for George Youger or Youker or Jukker, Uker, Yuger, Yuker, Jucker, Yougher

S.29,566

Pension was granted $30.77 per annum.

State of New York

Montgomery County SS.

On the 20th day of September 1832 personally appeared in open court before Abraham Morell, Samuel A. Gilbert, Henry J. Dievendorf and John Hand, Judges of the Court of Common Pleas now Sitting George Youker a resident of the town of Oppenheim in the county of Montgomery and State of New York aged 75 years and seven months who being first duly sworn according to law doth on his oath make the following declaration in order to obtain the benefit of the Act of Congress passed June 7th 1832—That he entered the Service of the United States under the following named officers and served as herein stated viz That in the Spring of the year 1776 he this applicant then lived in the now town of Oppenheim in the County of Montgomery and State of New York and was enrolled in a Company of Militia under the command of Captain Christian House, in Co. Jacob Klock's Regiment (1) and marched to Fort Stanwix (2) and was there stationed doing duty in the garrison until exchanged how long this term of service was the applicant does not now recollect when discharged he returned with the company to the town of Oppenheim and was still in Captain Houses Company and with the militia continued to defend the country from the depredations of the Indians and Tories who were continually making depredations on the defenceless inhabitants, that he continued there to serve until July 1777 (3) when he marched to Unadilla along with Gen. Herkimer and Col. Cox (4) that after making a treaty with the Indians they returned and did the duty as heretofore, except we went with the company to guard Boats from the German Flats to Fort Stanwix the expedition at this time was under the command of General VanRensselaer. (5) That he was marched to Cherry Valley (6) under Col. Klock to assist the Militia in that quarter against the Indians who had burnt that place and were still committing their depredations on the inhabitants in those parts, that he continued in said Klock's Company until the 1st day of April 1782 when he enlisted into the company of Captain Abner French (7) for the term of nine months and was stationed at Fort Plain and Fort Herkimer doing duty in the garrison and going on Scouts untill the 1st day of January 1783 when he was discharged and returned to his place of residence in the now town of Oppenheim—That he knows of no other or more testimony relative to his service than that contained in the affidavits hereunto annexed—He hereby relinquishes every claim whatever to a pension or annuity except present and declares that his name is not on the roll of any agency of any State.

To the questions directed to be proposed he answers that he was born in Canajoharie on the 16th day of February 1757. He knows of no record of his age except by the tradition of his mother and the age of some persons who were of his age who are still living. He lived in the now town of Oppenheim when he entered the service. After and since the revolutionary war he has always lived where he now resides in the said town of Oppenheim he was called into the service by being or ordered out with the Company in the first instance and afterwards by enlisting voluntarily into the company of Captain French as above stated—He served along with General Herkimer, Gen. Van Rensselaer, Col. Cox, Col. Willet, Col. Klock and the officers on the Stations along the Mohawk River and in Tryon County and the regiments and those Stations. That the names of officers with militia company whith whom he served were Christian House Captain, John Zimmerman (8) Lieut,. Henry Zimmerman, (9) Ensign, in the nine months service Abner French, Captain Shaver (10), Lieut., and David McMasters (11) ensign. (Signed with his mark) George Youker (12)

Sworn and Subscribed this 20th Septr 1832.

Letter of inquiry dated November 26, 1933

I have to advise you that from the papers in the Revolutionary War pension claim, S.29566, it appears that George Youker or Youger was born in Canajoharie New York, February 16, 1757.

While residing in Oppenheim, Montgomery County, New York, he enlisted in the spring of 1775 and served at various times as a corporal in Captain Christian House's company, Colonel Jacob Klock's New Klock's New York Regiment, until April 1, 1782; he then enlisted and served nine months as a private in Captain Abner French's Company, Colonel Fischer's New York Regiment, and was discharged January 1, 1783.

He was allowed pension on his application executed September 20, 1832, while living in Oppenheim, New York. There is no data on file as to his family.

End Notes—S.29566—George Youker

1. George served as a private in Captain Christian House's Company (Seventh Company) in Colonel Jacob Klock's Second Regiment of Tryon County Militia.
2. Fort Schuyler or Fort Stanwix stood in the present day City of Rome, Oneida County, New York.
3. This conference between Captain Joseph Brant and Brigadier General Nicholas Herkimer at Unadilla took place on June 27, 1777.
4. Ebenezer Cox was the Colonel of the First Regiment of Tryon County Militia.
5. This happened in July of 1780, Robert Van Rensselaer was appointed June 16, 1780 as Brigadier General of the Second Brigade of the Albany County Militia.
6. Cherry Valley was destroyed on November 11, 1778 by Captains Walter Butler and Joseph Brant.
7. George served as a private in Captain Abner French's Company in Colonel Marinus Willett's Regiment of New York State Levies in 1782. In November, Captain French retired from the service and Lieutenant Jellis A. Fonda was appointed Captain in his place.
8. John Zimmerman was appointed the First Lieutenant in Captain House's Company on August 26, 1775.
9. Henry Zimmerman was commissioned as Ensign in Captain House's Company on June 25, 1778.
10. John C. Shafer (Shaver) served as a Lieutenant in Captain James Cannon's Company in Colonel Willett's Regiment.
11. David McMaster was Captain of the Sixth Company in Colonel Frederick Visscher's (or Fisher) Third Regiment of Tryon County Militia. He was commissioned on June 25, 1778.
12. Pay receipts for George show in the records as follows: Date of Receipt Roll is November 4, 1784.

    Na 1774 £ 0..0..10
    1609 14..3 ¼

1447 19.. 6 2/3
Witnessed by Gott Fiedler.
Another roll for services in Captain Christian House's Company from February 1, 1779 to September 1, 1780 is as follows:
2122 £ 1..8..5 1/3
2163 1..3..1 1/3
Paid on October 27, 1784. FROM: Revolutionary War Rolls 1775-1783, Series M-246, Roll 75, folder 212, National Archives, Washington, D.C.

Pension Application for Alexander Young

S.45,480
Continental (NY)

To the Honorable James Emott, First Judge of the Court of Common Pleas, of the County of Dutchess which is a Court of Record of the State of New York.

The Declaration under oath of Alexander Young, formerly a soldier engaged in the Service of the United States, during the Revolutionary War, and now a Citizen of the United States, and resident of the town of Clinton in Dutchess County and State of New York, Respectfully Showeth, that the said Alexander Young, on or about the month of April in the year one thousand seven hundred and seventy seven enlisted in a company of Artillery in the American service commanded by Captain Andrew Moody (1) in a regiment commanded by Colonel Lamb for the term of three years—that he served as a private soldier in the said company of Artillery under the said enlistment the full term of his said enlistment and until he was discharged at West Point on or about the month of April in the year one thousand seven hundred and eighty—that his discharge is lost but when or where he does not recollect.

And this Declaration further representeth that the said Alexander Young is now a Citizen of the United States, and residing in Clinton aforesaid, and by reason of his reduced circumstances in life, in need of assistance from his country for support, and that he has never received any pension from the government of the United States.

Therefore he conceives himself entitled to the benefit of the Act of the Congress of the United States, entitled, "An Act to provide for certain persons engaged in the Land and Naval Service of the United States, in the Revolutionary War," approved, March 18, 1818, and requests that your Honor will examine into the truths of the matters aforesaid, certify and transmit the testimony in this case, and the proceedings had thereon to the Honorable the Secretary of the Department of War, to the end that such relief may be had in the premises, as is by law in such case provided. And in support of the facts above set forth, he refers to the affidavit of himself and of James Baremore hereafter set forth.

Dated, the 22nd day of April 1818. (Signed with his mark) Alexander Young.

County of Dutchess vs. Alexander Young being duly sworn says, that the matters by him set forth in the foregoing Declaration, as in all respects just and true. Sworn the 29th day of April 1818 before me, James Emott.

I Alexander Young of the town of Genoa in the County of Cayuga and State of New York, formerly of the County of Dutchess in the State aforesaid, do hereby solemnly swear, that on the 18th day of March 1818, I was in the possession of and owned the following named property in the town of Clinton in the aforesaid county of Dutchess, viz.

Two acres of land on which a dwelling house and a together with the necessary apparatus for the same, 10 kitchen chairs, 2 cherry tables & 2 spinning wheels, 2 feather beds and bedding for the same, 6 bowls, 1 church, 1 wash tub & 2 pitch forks, 1 Rake, 1 brass kettle, 1 pot, 1 dish kettle & tea kettle, 1 frying pan, 1 spider, 1 shovel & 1 pr. Tongs, 1 pair [?] and [?] 6 knives, & 6 forks, 2 chests, & 2 cows, 5 meat bags, & 10 fowls, 1 swine, one looking looking glass & one Corn hoe.

My wife has been afflicted with ulcers and in a debilitated state of health for the term of eighteen years, during the principal part of which time she has been under the Physician's care at a very heavy expense: during which affliction I was under the necessity of selling a part of the above named property viz, the 10 fowls and sow & four of the meat bags, to assist in defraying the said expenses.

Being deeply involved in debt, and unable to give my Creditors satisfaction, my remaining property (except what is enumerated in my schedule) was sold by virtue of execution at Sheriff's sale which did but in part satisfy my debts, the following is now due.

The reason I did not exhibit a schedule of my property to the war office prior to the [18th?] of March 1823, was That while in possession of my property as before named I did not suppose myself entitled according to the law of the United States and its construction by the Attorney General: But when stripped of my remaining substance, I became destitute of a home & was compelled to seek another place of residence and being destitute of a Dollar to help myself with, I was compelled to defer my application for a continuation of my pension which I was as fortunate as to find a friend who was willing to aid me in my [?] to make the attempt. (Signed with his mark) Alexander Young

In presence of Henry Hillerd [or Miller], Jno. W. Hulbert.

Sworn to by Alex. Young this 21st day of Sept. 1824 in open court. Geo. B. Throop, Clerk

Letter in reply to a request for information; dated June 7, 1829.

I advise you from the papers in the Revolutionary War pension claim, S.45480, it appears that Alexander Young enlisted in the State of New York, in April, 1777, and was a private in Captain Andrew Moodie's Company, Colonel John Lamb's Regiment of Artillery, was taken prisoner in October (2) following, held one year and then returned to his company at White Plains, and served until April, 1780.

He was allowed pension on his application executed April 23, 1818, at which time he was living in Clinton, Dutchess County, New York.

In 1824, he was living in Genoa, Cayuga County, New York, and stated that he was sixty-seven years of age and referred to his wife, her name and age not given.

There are no further family data.

The above noted Alexander Young is the only soldier of that name found on the Revolutionary War records of this bureau, who served with the New York Troops or was pensioned while residing in that state.

End Notes—S.45480—Alexander Young

1. Alexander enlisted as a matross (private) on April 22, 1777 for 3 years in Captain Andrew Moody's Company in Colonel John Lamb's Second Continental Artillery Regiment.
2. Alexander was taken prisoner on October 6, 1777 at Fort Montgomery, N.Y. On the Muster Roll he is listed as returned from captivity on August 18, 1778. On December 24, 1778 he is listed on furlough by Major Boman (Major Sebastion Bauman) 36 days. He was discharged on April 23, 1780. FROM: Revolutionary War Rolls 1775-1783, Series M-246, Roll 119, folder 45, National Archives, Washington, D.C.

Pension Application for Barney (or Barent) Young

W.22,715 (Widow: Elizabeth)
State of New York
Herkimer county SS.

On the 8th day of June 1843--Personally appeared in open court, before the Judges of the Court of Common Pleas in & for said County now sitting, Elizabeth Young, a resident of the town of German Flatts in said County, aged seventy six years and upwards, and who being first duly sworn according to law, doth on her oath make the following declaration in order to obtain the benefits of the provision made by the act of Congress passed 7th July 1838, and the joint resolution passed 16 August 1842—

That she is the widow of Barney Young who served in manner & for the terms detailed in his papers in the matter of his application for a pension under the Act of Congress passed 7th June 1832, and that he received a yearly stipend of $27 /100. She further declareth & saith, that she was married to said Barney Young on the fourteenth day of June—in the year of our Lord one thousand seven and eighty-five—by the Pastor of the Reformed Dutch Church of Albany in the church over which said Pastor presided—that she said Declarant then lived in Albany aforesaid—Thence she moved with her husband to German Flatts aforesaid--& continued to reside there until the present time. That she had by her husband the said Barney Young twelve children, ten of whom are now living & the oldest John being now fifty seven years of age. That said Barney Young departed this life on the ninth day of June 1842, leaving this declarant his widow him surviving, and that since his death she has remained single and unmarried, and is still his widow. (Signed with her mark) Elizabeth Young.

Subscribed & sworn the day and year first aforesaid in open Court as aforesaid. Witness E. A. Munson, Clerk of said Court at Herkimer with said County and set the seal of said County. E. A. Munson Clerk

Letter replying to a request for information, dated June 6, 1836.

You are furnished herein the record of Barney Young as found in pension claim, W.22715, based upon his service in the Revolutionary War.

The date and place of birth and names of the parents of Barney, also known as Barent Young are not shown.

Barney Young enlisted at Albany, New York, in the year that Colonel Brown (1) was killed at Stone Arabia, served as private in Captain Peter B. Tearse's and Fonda's Company, Colonel Willett's New York regiment, stationed at Fort Plain, Stone Arabia and Fort Herkimer engaged in scouting, and was discharged after having served a tour of nine months. He enlisted April 30, 1782, served as private in Captain Peter B. Tearse's (2) Company, Colonel Marinus Willett's New York regiment, and was discharged the first of January, following, then returned to the home of his sister in Albany, her name not stated. Other sisters were referred to but no names designated.

Pension was allowed on account of the service of Barney Young on an application executed February 5, 1839, at which time he was a resident of German Flats, Herkimer County, New York. He died June 9, 1842.

Barney Young married June 14, 1785, in Albany, New York, Elizabeth or Betsey Rankins or Rykins who was born in March, 1763. After their marriage they resided about two years in said Albany then moved to Herkimer County, New York, where they continued to reside with the exception of a few years spent in Montgomery County, New York.

Elizabeth Young, soldier's widow, was allowed pension on her application executed June 8, 1843, at which time she was a resident of German Flats, Herkimer County, New York, where she was still living in 1845. In 1848, she was a resident of Danube, Herkimer County, New York.

Barney Young and his wife, Elizabeth, had twelve children, ten of whom were still living in 1843. The only name of children designated were those of John Young, the oldest, who was born April 24, 1786, and baptized May 13, 1786, in the Dutch Reformed Church of Albany, New York, and in 1839 was living in German Flats, New York, and Michael Young, born December 4, 1789.

A copy of the church register of baptisms of the Dutch Reformed Church of Albany showed the name John and Delia Young with no explanation of their relationship to the family of Barney and Elizabeth Young.

End Notes—W.22715—Barney Young

1. This is incorrect. Colonel John Brown was killed on October 19, 1780 in the Battle of Stone Arabia. It is stated later that he enlisted in 1782 which would be the correct year as Lieutenant-Colonel Commandant

Marinus Willett's Regiment of New York State Levies didn't exist until April 28, 1781.

2. Peter B. Tearce was a Captain in Willett's Levies in 1782 and 1783. Barney's name is not listed on the 1783 payroll for this company. FROM: Revolutionary War Rolls 1775-1783, Series M-246, Roll 78, folder 173, National Archives, Washington, D.C. Barney's is also referring to Jellis A. Fonda who had served as a Lieutenant and Adjutant in Willett's Regiment in 1781 and 1782. He was promoted to Captain in November of 1782 in place of Captain Abner French who had retired from the service. He does not appear on Captain Fonda's payroll for 1783.

Pension Application for Gotfrield Young or Godfrey Youngs

S.26974
Revy, File No. 26,974. Index:--Vol. 2, Page 496
Herkimer County Invalids, death shown as July 31, 1830.

State of New York
Herkimer County SS.

Godfrey Youngs of the Town of Minden in the County of Montgomery being duly sworn deposeth and saith that he is the identical person mentioned and described in the original application hereto annexed executed by Abraham TenBrook & Philip Schuyler entered by Thomas Pratt Clerk bearing date on the 22d day of Septr in the year one thousand seven hundred and eighty six. (Signed with his mark) Godfrey Youngs

Subscribed and sworn on this 21st day of July A.D. 1824, before me, Henry Brown First Judge of the Herk. County Court.

We The Subscriber Abraham TenBroeck and Philip Schuyler Do Certify that upon an Examination, in pursuance of the Law; entitled an act making Provision for Officers, Soldiers and Seamen who have been disabled in the service of the United States, passed the 22d April 1786, We Do find that that [sic] Godfrey Young residing in the State of New York aged about thirty four years late a Corporal in Capt. Copemen's (1) Company in the Regt. of Militia Commanded by Colonel Clyde (2) and Claiming Relief under the Act of Congress recited in the said law, as an Invalid in Fact and that he became disabled in the service of the United States in Consequence of a Wound in the lower part of his Belly on the Sixth Day of August 1777 (3) and So further Certify that from the principle of the said Act of Congress the said Godfrey Young is entitled to the pay of five Dollars per month given under our hands, in the City of Albany on the twenty second Day of September in the year of our Lord one thousand seven hundred and Eighty Six. Abm. Ten Broeck, Ph. Schuyler

I certify the foregoing to be a true Copy from the Original Certificate as recorded in the State Auditors Office. Tho's Pratt, Clerk

Danube July 29th 1824.
Dr. Sirs

Inclosed I Return Godfrey Youngs affidavit, he has been qualified by a Judge of this County, Herkimer and Certified by the County Clerk the Same as Pickard & Murphy, he is in hopes it will be found to be correct & satisfactory to the Department.—

Conrad Frans an old Revolutionary Soldier applied under the act of 1818 and was placed on the pension list, and has since been suspended and he supposes through the influence of some person or person to him unknown, more out of injury to him then for the publick good.

I am well acquainted with Mr. Frans and believe he was a true faithful and valuable soldier during the war, and was in most of the important battles, and received several wounds it is true he has or had a piece of Land & Bargained it away with his son in law in 1807, who has a large family & he himself a poor fool, which leaves the old man a very scanty support, he thinks it is very hard that his pension is Stopt, while others draw that did nothing in the war compared to what he underwent & performed, but says if nothing can be allowed him, that he would be glad to have his Discharge sent back to him it was sent on with his application in 1818 he prises his Dicharge very highley because it is Signed by Washington, a name he venerates above all others on Earth—

I hope I may be Excused for writing this as I have no other motive in it but to gratify a worthy old Soldier. Your Humble Servant, De. Van Horne
TO: The Hon. J.C. Calhoon, Esq. Sec'ty of War—

End Notes—Gotfried Young—S.26974

1. Captain Abraham Copeman (Sixth Company), in the First Regiment of Tryon County Militia commanded by Colonel Ebenezer Cox.
2. Samuel Clyde was appointed the Lieutenant-Colonel of the First Tryon on June 25, 1778.
3. The Battle of Oriskany was fought on August 6, 1777.

Pension Application for Richard Young

S.11,923
Montgomery County

On this 20the day of September 1832, personally appeared in Open Court before Aaron Staring, Abraham Mosier, Samuel A. Gilbert, Henry I. [J?] Dieffendorf and John Hand, Judges of the Court of Common Pleas now sitting Richard Young a resident of the town of Ephratah, County of Montgomery and State of New York aged 78 years and 10 months who being first duly sworn according to law, doth on his oath make the following declaration in order to obtain the benefit of the act of Congress passed 7th June 1832—That he entered the service of the United States under the following named officers and served as herein stated—That at the commencement of the Revolutionary War this applicant viz Richard Young resided in the town of Minden in Montgomery County, State of New York and was enrolled in the Militia Company of Captain

Robert Crouse (1) in Col. William Seavers (2) Regiment and General Nicholas Herkimer's Brigade. That in the latter part of May or the beginning of June 1776 he marched with the said company by order of General Herkimer from Fort Herkimer to Fort Stanwix to intercept a number of boats loaded with supplies for the use of the Indians. That the said boats were taken at Fort Stanwix and Wood Creek and sent to Schenectady, that he this applicant did not return immediately but at the solicitation of Major Clapsaddle (3) entered the commissarys department and served in that department untill redordered to join his company which he did after serving as above two or three weeks and marched with the said company back to Fort Herkimer and on his arrival there he immediately enlisted into a company of Rangers commanded by Capt. John Winn (4), and attached to Col. Seavers regiment. This was a company raised and organized by order of the Committee of Safety of Tryon County. The officers of this Company were John Winn Captain, Lawrence Gross 1st Lieut, and Peter Scramlin (5) 2nd Lieut.—That he served in this company from June 1776 untill July 1777—That while in the company he was in constant service ranging the country by what was then termed Scouting parties from Lake Otsego (now Cooperstown) where the company was stationed to the Susquehanna river and the interior about the lakes in that quarter until some time in Jany 1777 when this applicant was drafted from said Winns company and attached to Captain Christian Getman's (6) Company and ordered to Ticonderoga (7) that he marched with said Getman from Albany where he joined said Getman's Company to Fort George and from there to Ticonderoga, that while there the rangers were commanded by Col afterwards General Wayne (8), and were by his orders employed making fortifications and keeping garrison at the fort, that they returned to the Mohawk river in the forepart of April and again joined the company of Capt. Winn and continued with the same until June or July as above stated when the company was divided, that the applicant then sought to repose himself from the fatigues of the war and engaged himself as [can't read a whole line] That Sir John Johnson with his murderous hoards of Indians and Tories were on their march from Canada to make an attack on Fort Stanwix when the Militia of Tryon County was ordered in to check his progress and this applicant again took the field against the common enemy and marched with the company of Capt. John Bradbeck (9) to Oriskany and fought in that sanguinary conflict on the 6th day of August 1777 (10), under General Herkimer and rendered assistance to that brave officer after he had received a mortal wound in the Battle. That the Americans were overpowered and in their retreat suffered severely and were not suffered the privilege of burying their dead, such was the inhumanity of the enemy with whom they had to contend. That after the return of the Company the Applicant was drafted as a guard to convey a number of Tories who had been taken prisoner in Schoharie County from Fort Plain on the Mohawk River to Esopus and on our arrival there they were delivered into the Custody of General George Clinton. That when the applicant returned from Esopus which was in October 1777 he again did the duty of a soldier in Capt. Bradbeck's company of Militia and through the fall and winter was constantly in service engaged on scouting parties which was at that time considered as the most effectual manner to keep the Indians in check. That about the first of April 1778, he enlisted into the bateau service under Capt. John Lefler (11) and was engaged on the Hudson River from that time until the close of the navigation that he was verbally discharged at Albany on the 1st day of Jany 1779—that he then returned to his home at that time at Stone Arabia where he remained during the winter and whole of the year following doing such Militia Service as was required by Captain Sylvanius Cook (12) in whose company applicant was at this time enrolled. That in the month of June 1780 entered again into the company of Captain Bradbeck(13) for three months as a volunteer was stationed at Fort Herkimer and did duty in the garrison, at the expiration of which service he joined under General VanRensselaer at Fort Paris as clerk and waiter and marched with him to Fort Stanwix returned with him to Fort Herkimer & Fort Plain, where he again joined the company of Bradbeck and continued to serve in said company in garrison, and guarding the country untill he [?] in 1783 was at the Battle at Lampmans (14) field in the company of Capt. Cook. He knows of no more or other testimony relative to his services than the affidavits hereunto annexed. That he hereby relinquishes every [claim] whatsoever to a pension or annuity except the present and declares his name is not on the roll of any agency of any state—

To the questions to be propounded he answers—

That he was born at Minden 24th October 1753—That he had a record of his age but it is now not to be found—That he lived in Canajoharie when he entered the service—He lived after the revolutionary war five years at Manheim in the County of Herkimer and one year in Minden and since then in the town of Ephratah where he now resides—That he served with Gen. Van Rensselaer, Gen. Wayne, Col. Baldwin, Col. Cox, Col. Willet, Coll. Malcomb (15) and the officers in the stations as well as the regiment in those stations. (Signed) Richard Young

Subscribed and sworn to this 20th day of September 1832. Geo. D. Ferguson, Clerk

End Notes—Richard Young—S.11923

1. Captain Robert Crouse was appointed in 1776 in Colonel Nicholas Herkimer's First Regiment of Tryon County Militia. Herkimer wasn't promoted to Brigadier General until September 5, 1776.
2. William Seeber was a Major in the First Tryon. When Herkimer was promoted to Brigadier General, Lieutenant-Colonel Ebenezer Cox was promoted to Colonel and Seeber was promoted to Lieutenant-Colonel.
3. Major Augustinus Clapsaddle of Colonel Peter Bellinger's Fourth Regiment of Tryon County Militia.
4. John Winn was the captain of one of three companies of Rangers for Tryon County. Richard enlisted as a private on August 12, 1776. The company was discharged on March 27, 1777. FROM: Revolutionary War Rolls 1775-1783, Series M-246, Roll 78, Folder 175, National Archives, Washington, D.C.

5. Lawrence Gross and Peter Schrambling were officers under Captain Winn.
6. Christian Getman also was a Captain of one of the Ranger Companies.
7. A detachment of the Tryon County Militia and Rangers were sent to Fort Ticonderoga, NY, to help build a floating bridge across Lake Champlain to connect with Mount Independence, Vermont. Colonel Cox commanded this detachment.
8. Anthony Wayne was appointed Colonel of the Fourth Pennsylvania Continental Regiment on January 3, 1776. He was promoted to Brigadier General of the Continental Army on February 21, 1777.
9. Richard by this time must have moved to the north side of the Mohawk River and joined Captain John Breadbake's Company (Fifth Company) in Colonel Jacob Klock's Second Regiment of Tryon County Militia.
10. The Battle of Oriskany was fought on August 6, 1777. Captain Breadbake was wounded, Colonel Cox and Captain Crouse were killed, Lieutenant Colonel Seeber and General Herkimer died later from their wounds and/or leg amputations.
11. Richard enlisted as a private in Captain John Leffler's Company of Bateaumen on June 4, 1778. FROM: Revolutionary War Rolls. 1775-1783, Series M-246, Roll 122, Folder 78, National Archives, Washington, D.C.
12. Richard is referring to Captain Severinus Klock's company in Colonel Klock's Regiment. The captain is often referred to as Cook and/or Koch but Severinus Klock was commissioned. There was a Captain Rudolph Koch in Colonel Klock's Regiment which may add to the confusion. When the men went out in detachments they could be under an officer other than their usual company commander which after several decades after their military service they might not remember as clearly and accurately as one would like.
13. On July 1, 1780, Colonel Lewis DuBois was authorized to raise a regiment of New York State Levies. Captain John Breadbake was commissioned on July 1, 1780 and immediately started to recruit for his company. Richard according to the muster roll did not enlist until September 12, 1780 as a private in Captain Breadbake's Company. He was discharged on October 24 and had served 1 month and 13 days. FROM: Revolutionary War Rolls, 1775-1783, Series M-246, Roll 72, Folder 96, National Archives, Washington, D.C.
14. The skirmish at Lampman's took place on July 29, 1781.
15. Brigadier General Robert VanRensselaer, Colonel Jedutham Baldwin of Artillery Artificers from 3 September 1776 to 29 March 1781, Marinus Willett served in several regiments but on April 27, 1781 was appointed Lieutenant-Colonel of a regiment of New York State Levies, and William Malcom (Malcolm), served as a colonel of a regiment of New York State Levies in 1780.

Peter Sailly
(1754-1826)
A Pioneer of the Champlain Valley
with Extracts from His Diary and Letters
By George S. Bixby
New York State Library.
Albany, The University of the State of New York.
February 1, 1919
Excerpts from the diary. Pages 58-71.

Diary of Peter Sailly on a Journey in America in the Year 1784.

1784, May 11.—I arrived at Philadelphia.

May 14.—Left Philadelphia to examine the iron works near Newark; accompanied by the proprietor.

May 17.—I left Newark to visit Mr. Faesch, the proprietor of the iron works at his house. Left there on the 18th for New York, where I arrived the same day.

May 19.—I embarked on the Hudson River for Albany, by the way of Poughkeepsie, with the intention of exploring the interior of the country.

May 20.—We arrived within view of West Point; a large fort, where the Americans had their principal forces during the late war. The tide and the wind being adverse, we were obliged to anchor. I profited by the delay to examine this locality, celebrated both from its position, which renders it almost impregnable and from the treason of General Arnold. To reach the first fort on the south, I ascended, with great labor, a mountain and some very large rocks. I found the mountain covered with walnut trees, and fragrant with roses, aromatic herbs and wild vines in blossom. I had scarcely reached the summit, and was within fifty paces of the fort, when the captain made the signal to leave, which obliged me to descend the mountain in haste and not without danger. In ascending, as we passed around the forts and redoubts I counted ten *terre-pleins* upon the heights, where the sides are nearly impracticable. The Hudson River, a magnificent stream, runs through a deep channel between two chains of high mountains. The mountains are not cultivated and can not be.

May 20.—I landed at Poughkeepsie, where I expected to find Mr. Dezong, a gentleman I had seen in New York, and who intended to be my traveling companion.

May 21.—This day at Poughkeepsie, a small and pleasant village, but the environs of which are not very pleasing, with the exception of the country seat of Mr. Livingston, which is upon the borders of the river, in a most charming location. I forgot to notice, that I passed in sight of two villages between West Point and Poughkeepsie, called New Windsor and Newburgh; but they did not equal the smallest villages in France.

May 22.—I left Poughkeepsie for Albany in company with Mr. Dezong on horseback. (1) The country between these two places is fine and well cultivated. We passed three small villages. The roads were very good.

(1) In the time-worn and yellowed original journal of William Gilliland, one of the most romantic and spirited of all the early pioneers in Camerica, is an entry under the year 1784 as follows: "Monsr. Sailly from France, Frederick Augustus de Zeng at Poughkeepsie."

May 23.—Arrived at Albany which is 84 miles from Poughkeepsie and 168 miles, or 56 French leagues from New York. Here the valley enlarges and presents a charming appearance. Albany, situate upon the North or Hudson River, is a flourishing village, very advantageously located, particularly for a fur trade with the Indians.

May 24.—This day at Albany, where I had several letter of introduction to deliver.

May 25.—Left Albany for Schenectady, by the way of the falls of the Mohawk. These falls are sixty feet high, and present a most magnificent appearance. Schenectady is eighteen miles from Albany. It is a pleasant village with fine houses upon the banks of the Mohawk River. It numbers about 450 inhabitants. The country is beautiful along the Mohawk from a point six miles above the falls to Schenectady.

May 26.—Left Schenectady for Johnstown, about twenty-four miles distant, and five miles from the Mohawk River. The country between these two villages is indifferently good. The borders of the Mohawk are contracted by the surrounding hills. Johnstown contains sixteen dwellings, a church, court house and jail. The house of General Johnson is one-fourth of a mile from the village. All his property has been confiscated by the state; against which he took part in the late war. The commissioners were at Johnstown to take legal proceedings concerning his property, consisting in this section, of about fifty thousand acres of land and forests. The soil is good about this place. Johnstown is situated upon a small stream which turns several mills, and upon which forges could be built. There are but few fish in the river and game is not abundant.

May 27.—Sunday. We took a walk seven or eight miles in the woods, north of the village. We saw fine oaks and pines from three and one half to four feet in diameter and sugar maples two and one half feet.

May 28.—I went about twelve miles from Johnstown, to the house of Madam, the widow Paris, whose husband was killed by the English at the commencement of the late war. (2)

(2) Note made by Peter Sailly Palmer: Probably Col. Isaac Paris who was a firm and zealous patriot. As chairman of the Tryon County Committee of safety he had rendered himself obnoxious to the Tories residing in the Mohawk Valley. He was murdered by some of St. Leger's Indians about the time of the Battle of the Oriskany in 1777.

He was their terror. This brave man was Colonel of Militia, originally from L'Orient, France, I believe. He has a brother in Philadelphia with whom I am acquainted; and had also many friends in Nates. His widow has a mill in good condition, but it lacks water. She manufactures potash. Near her residence we passed through as section of country called "Stone Arabia." It is one of the finest sections I have seen in America. The cultivated land is about eight miles in length by two miles in width and lies upon an elevated plain along the immense forests which border upon the Mohawk. The soil is fertile and the inhabitants will be prosperous if they do not again undergo the evils of war, from which they have suffered by the loss of houses and cattle, stolen and burned by the Indians. They have since then built a small fort into which they can retreat in case of any new incursion, if peace does not render the tardy precaution unnecessary.

May 29.—Colonel Melcher, Captain Dezong and myself left Johnstown with the intention of visiting Fort Stanwix and the Indians of Lake Oneida. We purpose to sleep at German Flats, a section celebrated in North America for its beauty and the richness of its soil. The valley here expands and forms a beautiful plain, which the Mohawk River divides in the center. A fine stream called Canada Creek, traverses a portion of the German Flats and joins its waters with the Mohawk. The inhabitants have suffered more from the late war than in other sections, as their neighbors, the Indians, have treated them with greater severity, having burned their houses, stolen their cattle and brought other misfortunes upon them. It would seem that Nature itself were in league with the enemy to desolate the country, for the land, naturally fertile, has been unproductive the present year. The most beautiful country in the world now presents only the poor cabins of a impoverished population who are nearly without food and upon the verge of starvation. The German Flats are about forty miles from Johnstown.

May 31.—We continued our route toward Fort Stanwix. Our progress being retarded by several events of little interest, we were obliged to sleep in a small Indian village, composed of four or five cabins, and containing between twenty-five and thirty inhabitants. These Indians dwell upon the borders of the Orisque, a branch of the Mohawk. We were received with a cordiality we have not found in any other part of American, and which is not always found in France. They gave us salmon, which they catch in Oneida Lake, twenty-four miles higher up, where the main body of the tribe resides. This little tribe, which forms the main part of the Onontagues, one of the Six Nations of Iroquois, numbers about two hundred families. They were the friends of the United States in the late war. The savages gave up to us their beds, which are made of a blanket spread upon a bedstead eighteen inches high. The couch is of the bark of trees. These Indians show nothing of the savage except in dress. Many of them conversed in English with my companions, with as much spirit and ease as we could ourselves assume. I found them much more polite than the peasants of France, who are the most civilized and polished of that class in Europe. We saw several fine and very tall men; one young man of twenty-two years, who was tall and well proportioned, with a most martial figure and address. Few men in Europe are by nature as noble in appearance (and distingues de la nature). The females are inferior; rendered so by labor, harsh treatment and their unbecoming dress.

Upon the borders of the Orisque General Herkimer gained a battle over the English and their Indian allies, commanded by M. de St. Leger, a man of French parentage but born in Ireland. This engagement took place in the woods, while General Herkimer was on his way to relieve Fort Schuyler, then besieged by the English. About four miles before reaching the Indian Village we saw Fort Schuyler, which is no more than a rampart of earth, now overgrown with thorns and bushes.

July 1.—Prepared to continue our journey, but the horse of Mr. Dezong becoming lame we returned to sleep at German Flats. Col. Melcher continued on. The whole country on both sides of the Mohawk is very fine. The lands are excellent. About five miles above German Flats are immense forests of primitive growth. The ground is covered with old and decayed trees which render the roads difficult. The mosquitoes are extremely troublesome. This section must sometimes become the most beautiful and richest in America. It contains a fertile soil, rich meadows and a great number of lakes and rivers filled with fish.

July 3.—We started to visit Lake Schuyler and several other small lakes in its vicinity. We passed through a forest twenty-four miles in length from German Flats over a road blocked up, at every step, by fallen trees. At the lake we found the land to be of very inferior quality, if we except the bottom lands, but these latter are exposed to annual inundations during the rainy season. Lake Schuyler is six miles long, in some places two miles wide and in others less than one mile. We passed over it in a canoe, as far as its outlet, which forms part of the Susquehanna River, sixteen miles below. We caught many fine fish in the lake with lines, with which we were provided. On our arrival we let loose our horses on the banks of the lake, but the next day, Sunday, mine could not be found. I think it was stolen by some hunters who were near the lake. The lake is full of fish and two streams of considerable size enter into it, but the land is so level near the lake that it is not possible to construct mills. A small piece of elevated land which we saw at the head of the lake, where there is an old house inhabited and several acres fit for cultivation, presents a favorable place for building a mill. There is not much current, yet, by making a dam to retain the waters about two hundred and fifty paces higher up, a mill could be turned twelve hours during twenty-four and the dam would cause no further expense.

On Monday the fifth we started on our return to German Flats, without obtaining any information about my horse. We visited an ancient Indian village wile descending the Mohawk. This is a fine section and the lands are of better quality. Mills and forges can be built upon a large stream which traverses the country and empties into the Mohawk. We continued our route for Johnstown, where were the commissioners of the State, who propose to make a road to an iron ore mine upon a mountain near the borders of the Mohawk. Certain points upon this river present advantageous sites for forges. There is but little commerce upon the Mohawk. The inhabitants are poor since the war. It is nevertheless a desirable location as this part of America will soon be thickly peoples. The rich lands will attract settlers. A merchant here can only sell in exchange for grain and peltries. With both of these he can do well in New York. Wheat can not be sold as it is received. It must be made into flour. New York then receives it for her own consumption and for shipment to the Islands (West Indies). It is of great importance to a merchant on the Mohawk that he own a mill, some land, a house and a little stock. With these he can carry on a very good business.

July 7.—I returned to Fort Henry, twenty-four miles from Johnstown, upon the Mohawk, to purchase some excellent lands, I could not agree with the proprietors as to the terms.

July 10.—Arrived at Albany.

July 11.—Sunday. I saw Mr. Gilliland who owns lands upon Lake Champlain. As the price and terms of payment were satisfactory, and the lands were represented to be very good, I determined to look at them. Mr. Guilliland could not leave until Thursday the 15th, and the same night we slept at Saratoga; a locality celebrated in America from the surrender of General Burgoyne with an army of seven thousand men to the American General Gates. We saw the encampments of the two generals and the ground where the two battles were fought between them. Saratoga is twenty-four miles from Albany and comprises a great extent of territory, but little cultivated. General Schuyler has a large farm upon the borders of the North River. A small and rapid stream empties near his house upon which he has built several mills. There are a number of mills along the borders of the North River. The land in this section is of poor quality.

July 16.—This evening we arrived at Fort Edward where we slept. It is fifty miles from Albany. I visited the fort built upon the borders of the Hudson River. The ruins of the rampart and ditch only remain. The rampart is built of wood and is quite high. The inclosure of the fort is not extensive. I saw beyond the fort a graveyard where were buried the officers and soldiers who died of wounds received in the attack upon Ticonderoga, on Lake Champlain, in 1758, then occupied by the French and forming a part of Canada. At the present day it is within the limits of the State of New York, with the whole of Lake Champlain; the boundaries of the two provinces having been changed at the time the English too possession of Canada. Fort Edward is situated in a fine plain, but th eland is poor, as is that which we passed as far north as Fort George, where we arrived on the 17th at noon, distant fourteen miles from Fort Edward. Fort George is built upon the borders of Lake St. Sacrament, called by the English Lake George. There we sent back our wagon, and prepared to embark as soon as the wind was favorable. We visited Fort George, which is yet in good repair. It is built of stone and is of difficult approach. The English captured it from the Americans during the late war. The garrison capitulated and should have been conducted to Fort Edward, but in violation of their promises, and to the eternal disgrace of the English, they posted their troops upon the passage the poor Americans were to take and massacred them all. (3) There is on the borders of Lake George an old fort of earth, built by the English and called William Henry. It was taken by the French under General Montcalm.

(3) Note interpolated by Peter Sailly Palmer. Mr. Sailly has confounded the massacre of the English garrison of Fort William Henry by the Indians under Montcalm in 1757, with the abandonment of Fort George, twenty years afterwards. The latter was a bloodless affair, as the American troops evacuated the fort before the English had reached the upper end of the lake.

July 18, Sunday—I went to the lake and caught two fish, called by the English "Black fish", which were of fine size and very good. In the afternoon I visited Fort William Henry, but could only see the remains of the old ramparts of earth. They were covered with wild cherry trees. The cherries, now ripe, are small and red and more tart than the wild cherries of France. There were here a great number of small birds of different kinds. I discovered for the first time that some of them resembled in every particular the little thrush of France. A little above the fort is a level place where we yet see the remains of an entrenched camp. There is in the center a graveyard where are buried about one thousand officers and soldier, victims of a large battle which was fought there. The graves are covered with strawberries and wild roses, which are here very abundant, notwithstanding the poor quality of the soil.

July 19.—Monday We left in a canoe at three o'clock. Our progress was delayed by a head wind. We slept in a cabin upon the borders of the lake, about twenty-five miles from Fort George and seven from the lower end of the lake, which is thirty-one and three-fourths miles long. On each side of the lake are high mountains covered with rocks on which were some pines, some cedars and thickets of thorns. The soil is sterile. The water of the lake is very clear, and the lake is well filled with fish. We ate of them during our whole voyage.

July 20.—We landed and took a wagon which brought us to Ticonderoga on Lake Champlain which we visited. It is one of the most famous places in America. It is situated upon an elevated plain with double ramparts of very high and strong walls of stone. It was built by the French, who called it Fort Carillon. We saw the retrenchments of the French and English armies in the vicinity. This frontier place was always the theater of war. The English were beaten in an attack upon the French camp of General Montcalm. Fort Independence is directly opposite. The Americans in the late war built a bridge across the lake which separates Mount Independence from Ticonderoga. We saw its remains. We also saw the ruins of several batteries, which the French erected to guard the entrance of the lake. During the wars there were flotillas on Lake Champlain composed of vessels, some of which carried twenty-four guns.

The same day at night we embarked aboard a vessel for Crown Point, a fort built by the French fifteen miles below and which they called Fort

Frederic. Head winds obliged us to case anchor and we passed the night on board. The next day (the 21st) the wind continuing unfavorable we returned to Ticonderoga, which gave me an opportunity to examine the environs and the batteries which were built upon the borders of the lake. There are a great many redoubts in the neighborhood. The French were not parsimonious in fortifying this section. The nature of the ground was also favorable. We can yet see the ruins of the houses of the French inhabitants. These ruins are now better than the poor cabins, which the Americans poorer still, have built here.

July 22.—I arose at two o'clock in the morning and finding the wind favorable, I called the captain of the sloop and we set sail at three o'clock. We arrived at Crown Point at eight in the morning. This fort, built by the English, is fifteen miles from Ticonderoga. It is very strong from its position and is larger than Fort Ticonderoga, but it is not in repair. The ramparts are of earth and wood. I inspected all the vicinity about the fort. Crown Point is situated upon a point of land at the commencement of the lake and near to Fort St. Frederic, which has fallen into ruins. The rocks are of the color of slate and well adapted to make into lime.

We left Crown Point about noon of the same day and visited an iron ore bed of very rich quality, which Mr. Gilliland has upon Lake Champlain about five miles north of Crown Point. I took with me several pieces of the ore. There is a small stream of water near the bed where they can build a furnace. The fall of water is very great. The wind being contrary we were obliged to return and we slept within two miles of Crown Point, on the east side of the lake.

The next day, the 23d, the wind continuing to blow we returned to Crown Point where I revisited the fort and the environs. The English built three large rangers of barracks within their fort, which can conveniently lodge two thousand men.

July 24.—The wind being favorable we embarked and continued our journey, visiting the lands of Mr. Gilliland on our route. The districts of Willsborough, Jamesborough and Cumberland Head contain fertile what land of easy culture. (4)

(4) Note interpolated under this date by Peter Sailly Palmer: Willsborough lay on both sides of the Boquet River and Janesborough at the mouth of the Salmon River. Mr. Gilliland's claim Cumberland Head was based upon the purchase of the claim of Lieutenant Abram Lowe to 2000 acres of land. At the time of Mr. Sailly's visit Mr. Gilliland was urging this claim before the commissioners of the state land office; it was rejected. The claim of Mr. Gilliland to other large tracts of land on Lake Champlain and to the ore bed near Crown Point was not recognized by the State.

In general I have never in my life seen anything which approaches in beauty the borders of Lake Champlain, although they are uninhabited. On the east side of the east side of the lake there is a very fine plain, ten leagues in width. The lake is as many miles wide at some places and sometimes a great deal less. We can see for fifteen leagues along the length of the lake. If this section is ever inhabited, it will be the finest in the world. The best lands are sold from fifteen to eighteen francs per acre. I would not hesitate of purchase if I was not afraid that in the first war with the English the inhabitants of Lake Champlain would be their first victims. They have forts upon the borders of the lake at Point Au Fer and again at Isle Aux Noix. The Americans, on the contrary, have not a redoubt in serviceable condition, nor a soldier to protect the inhabitants on their frontier. Indeed, the savages or English could bur or ravage forty or fifty leagues of country before even a poor army could be collected to oppose them. We arrived at Isle Aux Noix on the morning of the 25th, much fatigued, after passing a stormy and wet night.

Isle Aux Noix is five leagues from St. Johns, the extremity of the lake. There are four forts on the island, although it does not contain more than three hundred and sixty acres. Three of the forts are not garrisoned. The land here is fertile and the lake well filled with fish. The fever attacked me the day of my arrival. I allowed Mr. Gilliland to return and, finding a good opportunity to visit Montreal, I decided to go there. From the night of the 25th to the night of the 27th the fever did not leave me, although it was not very violent. I attribute this fever to the great fatigue I have undergone for the last six weeks. A head wind delayed our departure for Montreal which is thirteen leagues from Isle Aux Noix.

July 27.—We left Isle Aux Noix for St. Johns at six o'clock in the evening in a small canoe. We landed at St. Johns at half past eleven o'clock at night. I was so much annoyed by the fever I would have laid down had the size of the vessel permitted. The slightest movement would cause the miserable overloaded pirogue to roll from side to side. At length, on landing I had the misfortune to fall into the water, shoulders deep. This aggravated the fever, which tormented me cruelly all of the night. St. Johns is a fort at the entrance of Lake Champlain, occupied by the English. Here navigation terminates as the river is rapid for five or six leagues below. The river empties into the St. Lawrence thirteen leagues below Montreal. Here the mail, baggage &c are carried into the government storehouse where they are examined to prevent the importation of foreign merchandise into Canada. St. Johns is a place of considerable size. The land is of middling quality.

July 28.—We took a small carriage with two places, here called a calash, and went to La Prairie, upon the banks of the River St. Lawrence, opposite Montreal, and seven leagues from St. Johns. The country between these places is very flat and is well inhabited. The wheat, which is sown throughout Canada in the spring, is very fine but yet green. The whole country is cultivated. We saw no woods. The approach to Montreal is very fine, affording a view of the beautiful valley through which the St. Lawrence runs. Several mountains are seen in the distance, upon those summits, covered with beautiful groves, the eyes of the weary traveler can repose with delight. At length, a short distance from La Prairie de la Madeleine we saw Montreal, stretching along the bank of the river, at the foot of a mountain. Here again a most beautiful picture is produced by the borders of the River St. Lawrence, covered with houses as far as the eye can reach. The villages, the fine churches, the cultivated fields, the surrounding country, the most level I have ever seen, the city itself with its steeples and towers scattered here and there, and the pastures covered with cattle, present a most charming *coup d'oeil.* The view is magnificent.

At La Prairie del la Madeleine we embarked in a bateau for Montreal. The river here is at least one league and a half in width. We passed over the rapids. At this point the river ceases to be navigable for the largest vessels, until we reach fifteen or twenty leagues higher up, when it again assumes its magnificent size. We arrived at Montreal in the evening of the 28th, where we remained the 29th, and on the 30th left for Sorel, with the intention of visiting the lands of Mr. Ross, upon the River Ya Maska. We arrived at Sorel on the 30th at ten o'clock at night. It is fifteen leagues from Montreal. It is a depot for artillery. The soldiers have barracks here. Sorel is only a village. It has a church. All the inhabitants here were originally French, as they were in all the Canadas. The village is situate on the bank of the St. Lawrence, at the outlet of a considerable stream here called the Sorel, higher up the Chambly river, still higher up the St. Johns, and at length the Outlet of Lake Champlain, which flows into the River St. Lawrence.

The country between Montreal and Sorel is very good, very level and more thickly inhabited than any other part of Canada that I have seen. After crossing the St. Lawrence at Montreal, we passed the seignory of Longueuil, where there is a priest and a church. Two leagues below is Boucherville, a small village pleasantly situated upon the borders of the river. Two leagues below is Varennes, a considerable village, where they have just built a very pretty church, more adorned than those in the small villages of France. The altar attracts attention from the delicacy of the work and the variety of its decorations. Farther on is Verchere, another large seignory thickly settled. After these succeed Contrecoeur and St. Ours. All of these large seignories are upon the east bank of the St. Lawrence river, as far down as Sorel. These are only the largest villages. Besides these are the houses of the farmers all along the river, three arpents distance from each other. This is because the seignors in Canada grant their lands in lots three arpents in front by thirty arpents in depth, which makes a farm sufficiently large and causes all their lands to be peopled. It appears as if there was a continuous village along the margin of the river. The opposite bank of the river presents the same appearance, and it is the same as far as Quebec.

August 2, Sunday.—This day at Sorel.

August 3.—We left the next day in a wagon for the river Ya Maska, four leagues distant from the Sorel river. We arrived at Maska in good time, notwithstanding the bad roads. There we took a canoe, in which we ascended the river to the seignory of Mr. Ross, which is yet uninhabited. It is two leagues from the church as Maska. The borders of this river present throughout a charming appearance; a fine level country, fertile and thickly peopled and a beautiful river. We reached the seignory of Mr. Ross, which is three leagues in width on the river and three leagues in depth. The trees are very fine and of good quality; a great many maples (a sugar tree), some oak and pine and some elm. The land is excellent. The only inconvenience is the great number of mosquitoes.

August 4. Tuesday.—We slept at Maska after having examined a great part of the seignory extending along the little river Chibonet, upon which a mill has been built, now in ruins. On Wednesday I returned to Sorel, and the same day left in a canoe and ascended the river as far as Chambly, fourteen leagues distant. This river, which empties from Lake Champlain, is a little larger than the Ya Maska. It waters a fine country, level, fertile and thickly settled as far as the borders of the River St. Lawrence. The two banks of this river present two lines of houses. We have passed fourteen leagues up and have found, since we left Sorel, the seignories of St. Ours, St. Denis, St. Antoine, St. Charles, Bel-Oeil and Chambly. In each there is a church and a priest. The churches are about two and a half leagues distant from each other.

We arrived at Chambly on Thursday. There is a large fort here and a garrison. Here commence the rapids which obstruct the navigation as far as St. Johns. Some mills have been built upon the rapids. The same day we left Chambly for St. Johns in a calash. We saw several small dams which the Indians had made in the rapids, where the water was shallow, to catch eels, which are to be had at this season. They barricade the river and leave at certain places small holes where they place willow nets. The eels descending the rapid current are forced into the nets. The eels descending the rapid current are forced into the nets, from whence they can not escape. These fish bring a good deal to the Indians, who sell them.

August 7, Friday—We arrived at St. Johns, which I had no opportunity to examine the first time I was here. The forts are extensive. The English have hat this place, which is the entrance into the lake, several vessels of war of 18, 10 and 24 guns. The same day we slept at Isle Aux Noix.

August 8th and 9th we remained here and left on the 10th. We slept in the woods in a miserable house that had been abandoned. It was about seven leagues from Isle Aux Noix.

August 11.—We continued our route notwithstanding the wind and slept on an uninhabited island.

August 12.—We continued our route notwithstanding the wind which was against us, and this day made about twenty-five miles. We stopped at the river Boquet, which we ascended about two miles, in a canoe, to the place where Mr. Gilliland had a mill. We caught four salmon. The next day we dined at Crown Point and slept at Ticonderoga.

August 14.—Left Ticonderoga and reached Lake George before noon.

August 16.—Arrived at Albany, where I found my horse, but in a very bad condition.

August 18.—Left Albany for New York by water.

August 20.—Arrived at Poughkeepsie.

August 21.—I saw upon the borders of the North River, about two miles from Newburgh, a mine of coal which they have commenced to work. I took several specimens. (5)

(5) Referring to slate rock formation in Orange County, the third annual Geological Report of New York, age 113 (Doctor Horton) says: In very many places in the county this rock is loaded with carbon, so much so as to deceive the inexperienced eye into the belief that it is coal . . . Mining for coal in a small way has been undertaken in several places.

August 22.—We passed West Point. The wind having been contrary from the commencement, we are borne slowly along by the stream. (6)

(6) Here the journal terminates abruptly.

Letter from Mr. "St. John" to Zephaniah Platt at Plattsburg, introducing Peter Sailly.
New York June 14, 1785.
Dear Sir:

This letter will be delivered to you by Mr. Sailly a French Gent'm to whom I can freely give that name, his is Going to settle in & deserves all your Esteem & Friendship & he wants to Purchase Land. He has brought over with him his wife & a good one she is & some children. Do pray let me beg of Judge Platt to show this Good Man every kindness & Good Counsel he may stand in need of you will thereby gain one Good Neighbor and do an action worthy of a good American.

Battle of Oriskany

Records of the narrative of Dr. Moses Younglove.
Giving an account of the Battle of Oriskany and of His Experience After Being Taken Prisoner. Written by His Brother Samuel Younglove.
From: The Johnstown Daily Republican, Nov. 21, 1896.

About the time Gen. Burgoyne was making preparations in Canada to attack New York, orders were given to Col. St. Ledger to ascend the St. Lawrence and cross Lake Ontario, to pass Oswego garrison, ascend the Seneca river, cross Oneida lake and go up Wood creek and attack and take Fort Stanwix at the head of the Mohawk river, then commanded by Col. Leonard Gansevoort, and descend that river and join Gen. Burgoyne at or near Albany.

St. Leger proceeded agreeably to orders and besieged Fort Stanwix about the first of August, 1777. Gen. Herkimer, commanding the militia of Tryon, now Herkimer county, New York, was called on to march with his brigade to relieve Fort Stanwix. Moses being surgeon to the brigade, joined them on the 6th of August, 1777. Gen. Herkimer paraded his men near Fort Dayton and made a speech to them, exciting them to valor and patriotism, and after examining their arms he marched them two deep, they being 760 in number, occasioned too great a distance between the front and rear for a sudden attack, he marched with front flank and rear guards.

St. Ledger being informed of their approach, sent Sir John Johnson with his regiment of Tories and Indians to ambush them. Gen. Herkimer marched on without molestation to a place called Orisco, now called Oriskany, six miles from the Fort and upon a beautiful clear day about 11 o'clock in the morning, the flank guard on the left hand in the van, commanded by Col. Cox, was fired on.

Moses was riding with the general and supposing it to be a false alarm, dismounted and tied his horse to a tree leaving his saddlebag and medicine on his horse. Col. Cox and his men stood the charge until the most of them were killed. The remainder of the guard fled to the main body; the general ordered them to retreat to an eminence not far distant, expecting to gain the advantage of the area. Moses had not time to remount his horse. He and Capt. Cox were the first on the ground that were ordered to make a stand. The men kept running by and Capt. Cox ordered them to stop and form or he would shoot the first man that passed and he did shoot and kill one dead in the road. Then all that were in front of the place stopped and formed in a circle round the top of the hill, about 160 in number.

At that time a major, badly frightened, came running, calling out in low Dutch, "Run, boys, run, you are all dead," and all that were in the rear of the major fled. There were many fallen trees on the ground.

The general sat on his horse in the circle formed by the men round the top of the hill, urging them to fight to the last, as they could not expect mercy either by yielding or retreating. The enemy with the greatest resolution attempted to break the circle and penetrate the centre but were held by Spartan valor.

Not one man flinched from his post although the enemy were in number 6 to 1. Those who could formed behind fallen trees and kept the circle from being broken, leveled their guns with the most unerring and deadly aim. Though the enemy were to strong that they would sometimes break in upon them, but those who did were all put to death in a few minutes. Not one of them escaped who made the attempt. Moses says that he saw them more than once take the tomahawk from the hand of the Indians and dash out their brains with their own weapon. Not a sign of fear could be discovered in any, but they were all determined to keep the ground or period in the attempt.

The brave general received a mortal wound and was seated on a log. Moses was called on to attend him and dress his wounds. In that situation the general all the while exhorted his men to be valiant, telling them what an amount of fame they would raise. The general being unable to command, the two colonels were sent for and when found were snugly packed away under the roots of a fallen tree.

The major who had fled in the fright had taken the greater part of the men with him, so that the command dropped to Capts. Fox and Breadbeg, two valiant officers. Capt. Fox observed some men at a great distance, whom he thought to be of his party. He requested Moses to go and bring them to the main body. In compliance with his request he went and when near them he discovered they were Hessians belonging to the enemy. As he turned form them they fired at him and had nearly surrounded him. He had to bear off to the left from them, and in so doing fell in with a party of Indians, that were scalping and cutting the throats of the wounded, and he saw an Indian sucking the blood from the throat of a white man and he passed a white man and an Indian both so badly wounded that they could not stand and were fighting with their knives as they lay on the ground. The Indians surrounded Moses and came at him with great fury. He handed his rifle to a stout elderly looking warrior. Another Indian attempted to pull the watch from his fob, but in attempting to do so only broke the chain. Moses then gave his watch to the Indian to whom he had given his rifle and then that Indian protected him from the tomahawks of the others. They now had several prisoners and took them to the foot of a hill near a stream of water where Sir John Johnson was with some other officers. They placed Moses on a log where several Tories were seated.

The Indians had twelve chiefs and many warriors killed on that day, which filed them with rage, they came running and began to dash out the brains of those sitting on the log. Moses rose and begged his life or Sir John Johnson, who drove the Indians off. He then wiped the blood and brains from his face that flew from the heads of the Tories whilst the Indians had been tomahawking them. Moses and the other prisoners were divested of all their clothing except their shirts and drawers and taken to the British army and placed under a strong guard near the fort. The battle with Herkimer lasted until four o'clock in the evening, at which time the enemy fled leaving, many slain on the ground. Herkimer's men were left in possession of the battle ground although something more than one-half the men were killed wounded or prisoners.

They were still able to take off their general and all the wounded. The general soon after died of his wounds. St. Ledger now invested the fort more closely extending his battalions to within 150 yards of the fort, and by written and verbal messages kept urging the surrender of the fort, stating that Herkimer's party were entirely cut off and that Burgoyne was gaining advantage daily and that the people were everywhere submitting to him. Col. Gansevoort, the commander of the fort, replied that as he was intrusted with the care of that garrison he would defend it to the last extremity without regard to consequences.

Col. Willett and Capt. Stockton left the fort in the night and passed safely through the Indians at the risk of life and torture, intending to proceed to gen. Gates' headquarters nearly 100 miles distant, to solicit relief, but Gen. Gates had anticipated the state of affairs and had started Gen. Arnold with his brigade. Col. Willett met Arnold half way on the route to Fort Stanwix. On the march Arnold had captured Honyost Schuyler and his brother. They were

Tories that had been with the British army and had been sent to spy out the strength of Gen. Gates' army. They had been much with the Indians and could speak their language well. They owned a large amount of property and by our laws both life and property were forfeited.

Arnold promised them both, if one of them would go forward in haste and alarm the British and Indians in such manner as to cause them to leave the fort immediately. Arnold kept one of these as a hostage for the true performance of the other, who undertook the job and went with great speed. He arrived at night and gave an Indian yell which drew the Indians around him. He expatiated on the number of Arnold's men and of their near approach, which frightened the Indians. Col. St. Ledger endeavored to pacify them and induce them to stop, and could not and was commanded to leave the fort abruptly. The officers engaged the Indians to take their baggage, but they secreted and kept the most of it.

The next morning when the men from the Fort examined the deserted camp they found a drunken Indians in the camp. They tied a knot in his long hair and ran a stick through it and drew him face downward into the fort. St. Ledger put his prisoners all on board his boats and descended Wood Creek to Oneida Lake, when he passed an island on which lived a Frenchman named John David. Shortly after peace, when I was in that part of the country, the same Frenchman still lived there and was known as John the Divine and the island by the name of Patmos.

St. Ledger continued his retreat until he arrived at Oswego garrison, where he tarried several days to attend to the sick and wounded, of which there were a great many. There had also been many of the Indians killed and wounded, which fired them with revenge at the prisoners. They were allowed to go into the guardhouse and take out any of the prisoners and treat them as they chose. When they would take one of the guardhouse the British would go and give them a barrel of rum and they would go on to an island, and bend a small tree and split it open, and put the arms of the prisoner through the split, and let the tree fly up and in that way roast and eat the prisoners.

Moses said when in the guardhouse he could hear the last shrieks of those unhappy victims strewn around with marks of the carving knife on them. Amongst the prisoners was a highly respectable man by the name of Parris, who had been a member of congress. The Indians took him from the guardhouse and tortured him to death in sight of the prisoners. He being a great man every one of them had to have a blow at him with the tomahawk.

Moses endeavored in vain to describe his feelings while hearing him beg for mercy and hearing the Indians mock his dying groans. All of this was done in sight of British officers. Moses attempted to expostulate with St. Ledger on the barbarous manner in which the prisoners were treated, but he would exclaim, "Damn the rebels; they deserve no better treatment." Moses was every moment expecting his turn of torture to come, and it was not long before an Indian came into the guardhouse and fixed his eyes upon him, when Moses sprang to a bar of iron which was in the room and got between the

Indian and the door and made at him with the intention of killing him; but he escaped through the window and no Indian after that came into the guardhouse. Moses having been divested of most all of his clothing except shirt and drawers, suffered much from the cool nights and from the scorching heat of the August sun and from flies and mosquitoes.

After a short stay at the fort they all went on board their boats and started for Canada. While on the lake Moses saw several boats loaded with Indians with Hessian uniforms. He supposed they had killed the Hessians, sold their scalps to the British and dressed in their clothing. In battle the Indians had one side of their head shaven bare and the other side painted red. Moses with the other prisoners was in a few days landed in Canada at or near where Kingston now stands. The British officers used great exertions to get the prisoners to enlist, but Moses in a great measure prevent it by telling them if they conducted themselves soberly and wisely he would get them released on parole.

The prisoners were soon sent down the St. Lawrence to Quebec in the naked condition they were, in only shirt and drawers. They there received a scanty supply of clothing and were confined in irons in Quebec jail. Moses petitioned Governor Carleton almost daily to let the prisoners return home on parole, and it was not long until the governor consented to send them home.

They were put on board a ship with their irons on to be sent down the St. Lawrence to New York. After they got on board one of the prisoners enlisted. He was a young Irishman and fond of liquor. On deck they got him drinking and playing pranks. He swore that he could play any prank that any of them could. Thereupon one of them went up and stood upon his head, pitched over and fell about ten feet, struck a rope and hung a moment, broke his hold and fell and struck another rope and hung on a little and at last struck safe on deck. He looked up and dared them to do it. This was the only one of the prisoners that enlisted.

Moses and Major Blavin had their legs ironed together. Major Blavin died soon after the left Quebec, being yet ironed to Moses. They descended in good weather, but when they came to the gulf they experienced a severe storm that drove them off nearly to the West Indias. When they got to New York the officers showed a spite they held against Moses for preventing the prisoners from enlisting. They brought him on deck and placed him between the prisoners from enlisting. They brought him on deck and placed him between four bayonets. The captain then came on deck and gave him a severe caning. Moses had written Major Blavin's will while ironed to him; just before his death. The first thing he did when liberated was to visit his widow and deliver to her the last message of her dying husband. He next went to see his father's family, and I well remember the meeting we all had with him.

This was late in December, 1777. My father then asked him to sit down and relate the whole circumstances. He replied that he could do it with pleasure, for troubles past were present joys. I sat by and heard the whole of the above narrative nearly word for word as I have related above. Samuel Younglove.

The foregoing is taken from a manuscript in the possession of James I. Younglove of this city. Dr. Moses Younglove was one of the six brothers who took part in the revolution. The other five brothers served as follows:

Isaiah Younglove, Jr., was sergeant major in Colonel Dayton's regiment called the Jersey Grays. When in command of a scouting party at Fort Oswego he was taken prisoner by the Indians, after being wounded. He was taken to Canada. He was paroled, and being the first prisoner to return from Canada, gave much valuable information to General Schuyler.

Colonel John Younglove was in the 16th or Cambridge regiment. He took a prominent part in the battle of Bennington being one of the council of war with General Stark.

Dr. David Younglove was surgeon in the 1st Tryon County Regiment. He was wounded in the Battle of Bennington, for which he received a pension.

Joseph Younglove was adjutant and quartermaster in Colonel Lewis VanWoert's regiment.

Samuel Younglove was in Captain Allen's company of the Green Mountain Boys. He was in the Battle of Bennington when 14 years old. He took part in the Hall battle in Johnstown and was one of Governor Clinton's Life Guards when in pursuit of Sir John Johnson on his retreat. He assisted in the capture of the notorious spy and Tory, Jose Bettes.

The Battle of Johnstown

Daily Press, Sept. 17, 1892.

Interesting and Hitherto Unpublished Facts Concerning the Revolutionary Battle Fought at Johnstown as Related by One of the Participants to a Venerable Citizen of this Place.

Mr. Henry R. Snyder, having presented a cannon ball to the Johnstown Historical society, and being requested by the president and other members to give the history of the missile, has prepared the following account which he knows to be correct in every detail.

"I was born in the town of Johnstown, in a house which stood near where Lewis Veghte now lives, on the 22d day of June 1807. After residing there a year of two, we removed to the Albany and Schenectady turnpike, where my father was the proprietor of the principal state house on that much traveled thoroughfare. We remained there until I was about five years of age, when we returned to Johnstown and my father erected the house upon the "Snyder Farm," which my mother inherited from her father, Edmund Aken, he having purchased the Hall and 740 acres of land of Sir William Johnson's estate.

My father, Abram Snyder, was born in the town of Hoosac, and remembered well seeing the men in that vicinity rush to the battle of Bennington. Having grown up in those perilous times, and being at an age when deep impressions are made upon the mind, he developed a love for the history of what period which never left him. Although not a native of this place, when he removed here he set about learning all he could of the events that transpired in this vicinity during the colonial and revolutionary times, and as the facilities offered were the best that could possibly be afforded, he succeeded in acquiring an authentic knowledge of them.

There was living just north of Gloversville at that time, the celebrated patriot and revolutionary soldier, Lieut. William Wallace, the Grandfather of Mrs. Peter T. Yost of this village, concerning whom when he died on the 25th day of February, 1837, the late Judge Wells, who had known him from boyhood, wrote:

DIED: in this village, February 25th 1837 William Wallace, in the 92nd year of his age.

Mr. Wallace was born in this town, and resided here during the whole period of his long and eventual life, having passed through nearly a whole century. He arrived at manhood before the commencement of the revolution; and when the breasts of the patriots of that day were burning with indignation and zeal against tyranny and oppression, Mr. Wallace joined the Spartan band and devoted himself to the defence of his country during the whole of that perilous struggle, and fought and bled for the liberty which we now enjoy. He was engaged in the battle of Johnstown, fought on the Hall farm near this village, where he rendered very valuable services to the brave Col. Willett, the commander of the American forces in that engagement. He was promoted for his bravery to a lieutenancy in the Revolutionary Army, and was attached to the regiment commanded by the late Col. James Livingston. His country remembered with gratitude his important services, and granted him a liberal pension for his support in his declining years. At his birth this country was very thinly inhabited, while all west of it was but a vast wilderness; but he lived to see it covered with a dense population, and to blossom as the rose. Generations arose and departed during his existence, while nearly all with whom he commenced the journey of the life have long since numbered with the dead. He has at length, been gathered unto his father.

How sleep the brave who sink to rest.
By all their country's wishes blest.

Father's interest and enthusiasm in studying the history of this place, to which, no doubt, the added romance of living upon and owning the piece of ground that was the scene of a short but sanguinary and decisive battle of the war, led him to put forth every effort in his search for facts, and he left no stone unturned in his investigations.

Becoming acquainted with Lieut. Wallace and knowing that he had been an actor in the stirring events of those days, he invited him to pay us a visit, which he did. I was 13 years old at that time and well do I remember how, as we sat about the roaring old fireplace, the old veterans, eye kindled and his towering frame again took on something of the strength of his vigorous manhood as he recounted the heroic deeds and hair breadth escapes of the worthies of those days. A man of powerful frame and great strength of character, whose physical and mental abilities were only commensurate with his bravery and intense patriotism, he threw such a vividness into his stories that my boyish mind was denuded of all ideas of fear, and the matter of meeting a red coat, or facing in Indian's tomahawk, did not seem so dangerous as before. Boy-like, I was fascinated with his stories of various deeds, and most of them are still as fresh in my memory, although seventy years have passed away, as if I had heard them but yesterday, and especially is this true concerning the cannon ball which I have presented to the Society, and the battle field upon which it was found.

You are all so familiar with the location of my father's farm that I do not deem it necessary to describe it any more than I am compelled to in relating the history of thc occurrence that happened there, the details of which I learned from Lieut. Wallace. His description of the battle was very vivid and real.

News had reached this vicinity that the British and Tories with the usual contingent of Indians, had started on a raid through this section, and were coming, I think, from the south. Col. Willett, the commander of the Continental troops, collected his forces and set out for the Hall, knowing that that would be their objective point, and determined to defend it and defeat the invaders if possible.

The two armies met on a hill just east of the orchard back of the house, where Mr. Nicholas Veghte now lives, and about eighty rods west from the Hall, and there the battle, concerning which much that is erroneous has been written, was fought. Who began the attack I do not remember, but the British showed the first signs of weakness.

The onset of the Americans was so severe that their enemies where compelled to retreat toward the village, leaving their cannon, a three pound field piece, behind. They rallied, however, and made another advance, before which the Americans retreated, still retaining possession of the gun, but the Red Coats, overtaking them, recaptured the piece and held it until the close of the fight. The battle continued until late in the afternoon, and the Americans, being worsted in the struggle, were compelled to leave the field, and the King's troops continued on their journey toward the north.

Lieut. Wallace said that the woods, which were then the primeval forest, were very dense, and it was impossible for them to take their cannon with them, yet what disposition they made of it was never positively known. Perhaps it may be surmised later. The Lieutenant entered largely into a description of the details of the battle, but the general impression alone remains with me, and, as I desire to state only those things of which I am positive, I refrain from giving anything except what I have already recounted.

One incident, however, a personal encounter between the lieutenant and a British soldier, I am able to remember very clearly, According to the English custom Sir William had dug ditches which ran ;north and south through the farm, and upon the ridges of earth which were thrown out, planted thick hedges, and these afforded a ready means of defence as breastworks. During one of the retreats which the Americans made, Lieut. Wallace ran to the north end of one of those hedges, having his flint lock musket cocked and in his right hand. As he approached the east side of the ditch, a British soldier arose from it and drew his musket up, ready to fire. 'I was quick as he', said the lieutenant in telling me the story, 'and I brought my gun to position also. There was but one report, for we fired simultaneously. The British soldier fell; I felt a dreadful sting on my right hand and on looking at it, found that the space between my thumb and the index finger had been badly lacerated, and the hammer of my gun shot off while I held it to my shoulder.'

My boyish heart was frozen with horror at the thought of taking human life, and I said, 'Did it not make you feel badly to kill a man?'

'Why so, sonny, was the reply, 'he drew up first, and you see how near he came to killing me. I did it in self defence.'

After telling me these things as I have related them, the old soldier said, 'Come with me sonny, and I will show you the battlefield,' and taking me out to the ground which I have described, he showed me where the conflict occurred, and pointed out the spot where the British soldier met death at his hands.

About two years after this father brought the cannon ball into the house, one day, and said that he had plowed it up on one of the fields, and I, myself, in hoeing, have found many a bullet, flint and iron ramrod, besides and iron used in spiking cannon, upon the same ground, so that there can be no doubt but that this identical ball was actually used in the light which occurred that day, and that the place which Lieut. Wallace pointed out to me as the battlefield was the spot where the forces met.

I have long desired to place my knowledge of these facts to some form where they could be preserved, and the opportunity now offered fills me with delight, not because I wish to appear before the people in any way, but because I cherish the memory of the noble men of those days, and desire to perpetuate the knowledge of their heroism and unswerving patriotism.

In a recent conversation with Mr. Peter T. Yost concerning the battle, in which I related the facts as given above, he told me that when he was a boy his uncle, John Yost, who then resided on the farm afterwards owned by his son, the late William Yost of West Main street, told him that on the day of the battle he was at work in a tan yard belonging to his father, located near the present site of Schriyer's mill, and that the spent balls from the fight rattled on the hides where he was. He heard the firing and told Mr. Yost that the battle was fought upon the Snyder farm towards the Matthew's place.

The Battle of Johnstown

From The Johnstown Daily Republican of October 25, 1899.
The 118th Anniversary of That Memorable Conflict.
Was Fought Near Johnson Hall

The Last Battle Fought In Tryon County and
Really the Last One In the Entire Record of the Revolution –
Colonel Willett's Forces Victorious over Their Old Enemies.

Today—Wednesday, October 25th 1899—marked the one hundred and eighteenth anniversary of the battle of Johnstown which as the readers of the Republican know, was fought October 25th 1871, [sic—should be 1781—misprint] on the level plot of ground opposite Johnson Hall. Here the troops commanded by Colonel Willett met and defeated the British, eventually driving them into the woods, it being the last battle fought in Tryon County and practically the last conflict in the entire record of the revolution. A description of the battle which took place on that day will, doubtless, be interesting reading to many, and the Republican reprints the following, taken from Stone's life of Joseph Brant:

"It had been seen from the commencement of the contest, that the Johnsons and those loyalists from Tryon County most intimate in their alliance with them, appeared to be stimulated by some peculiar and ever-active principle of hostility against the former seat of the baronet, and the district of country by which it was environed. Another expedition against Johnstown was, therefore, secretly planned in the summer of 1781, and planned with such silent celerity, that on the 24th of October 'the Philistines' were actually 'upon' the settlements before their approach was suspected. The expedition was organized at Buck's Island. In the river St. Lawrence, a few miles below the foot of Lake Ontario, and consisted of four companies of, the second battalion of Sir John Johnson's regiment of royal Greens, Colonel Butler's Rangers, under the direction of Major Butler, his son, and two hundred Indians—numbering in all about 1,000 men—under the command of Major Ross. Proceeding from Buck's Island to Oswego, and thence through the Oneida lake, they struck off through south-eastern forests from that point, and traversed the woods with such secrecy as to break in upon Warrensbush, near the junction of the Schoharie-kill with the Mohawk river, as suddenly as though they had sprung up from the earth like the warriors from the dragon's teeth of Cadmus, full grown, and all in arms, in a single night. This was on the 24th of October, Warrensbush was about twenty miles east from Fort Rensselaer ,the headquarters of Colonel Willett; so that Ross and Butler had ample time for the work of havoc and devastation on the south side of the river, and to cross over to the north side, before the former could rally his forces and dispute their farther progress. Not a moment was lost by Colonel Willett, on hearing the news, in making such dispositions to repel, the unexpected invaders, as within his limited means. With such forces as were in the garrison, together with additional recruits from the militia as could be collected in the neighborhood, Willett marched for Fort Hunter on the same evening—simultaneously dispatching orders for the militia and levies in contiguous posts and settlements to follow and join him with all possible expedition. By marching all night, the colonel reached Fort Hunter early in the following morning, where he learned that the enemy were already in the occupation of Johnstown. The depth of the river was such that floats were necessary in crossing it, and although Willett had but four hundred and sixteen men all told—only half the enemy's number, exclusive of the Indians—yet it was afternoon before the crossing was effected. Ross and Butler had crossed the river some distance below Tripe's Hill, the preceding day, and moved thence directly upon Johnstown—killing and taking the people prisoners, and destroying buildings and cattle, and whatsoever came in their way. Soon after ascending the hill just mentioned the enemy came upon a small scouting party commanded by Lieutenant Saulkill, who was on horseback. He was fired upon by the enemy's advance, and fell dead to the ground. His men sought safety in flight, and succeeded. This was early in the morning of the 25th. The advance of the enemy being slow, they did not arrive at the village of Johnstown until past 12 o'clock at noon. Even then, the main body of their forces, avoiding the town, marched round to the west, halting upon the grounds of the baronial hall. The enemy's baggage wagons, however, passed through the village, and their conductors were fired upon from the old jail—then serving the purpose of a fortress. One man only was wounded by this consumption of ammunition.

"Having effected the passage of the river, Colonel Willett pushed on in pursuit with all possible expedition. But deeming it unwise, where the disparity of their respective forces was so great, to hazard an attack in front with his whole forces, the position of the enemy was no sooner ascertained with certainty than Major Rowley, of Massachusetts, was detached with a small body of the Tryon county militia and about sixty levies from his own state, for the purpose, by a circuitous march, outflanking the enemy, and falling upon his rear—thus attacking in front and rear at the same time. These and other necessary depositions having been adjusted, Willett advanced upon the enemy at the head of his column. Entering an open field adjoining to that occupied by the enemy, Willett displayed his right into line, and pressed Major Ross so closely as to compel him to retire into the fringe of a neighboring wood. Here a skirmishing was kept up while the remainder of the Americans were advancing briskly in two columns, to hear a part. The battle became spirited and general: and although the only field piece belonging to the Americans was taken it was speedily re-taken, and for a time, the action proceeded with a promise of victory. But just at the crisis, the militia of Willett was seized with one of those causeless and unaccountable panics, which on most occasions render that description of troops worse than useless in battle, and without any cause, the whole of the right wing turned and fled. The field piece was abandoned and the ammunition wagon was blown up. The former, of course, fell into the hands of the enemy. Colonel Willett did his utmost to rally his men, but to no purpose. They ran in the utmost confusion to the stone church in that village. Here having induced them to make a halt, the colonel commenced bringing them into such order as best he might. But the defeat would still have been complete, had it not been for the precautionary disposition previously made of Major Rowley. Most fortunately as it happened, that officer emerged from the woods, and arrived upon the field, just in time to fall upon the enemy's rear in the very moment of their exposition at their easy victory. Rowley pressed the attack with great vigor and intrepidity, while the enemy was engaged in making prisoners of the stragglers, and the Indians were scalping those who fell into their hands. The fight was now continued with equal obstinacy and irregularity for a considerable time. Major Rowley was early wounded with a shot through the leg, and carried from the field; and the enemy were engaged indifferent bodies, sometimes in small bodies, separated nearly a mile from each other. In some of these contests the advantage was on the side of the enemy, and in others the Americans were the temporary victors. The battle continued after this fashion until nearly sunset, when, finding such to be the fact, and that Rowley's detachment was holding the enemy at bay, Willett was enabled to collect a respectable force, with which he returned to the field, and again mingled in the fight. The battle was severely contested until dark, when the enemy, pressed upon all sides, retreated in discomfiture to the woods,--nor stopped short of a mountain top, six miles distant.

"Among the officers who signalized themselves in this occasion, in addition to the leaders. Willett and Rowley, was the brave Captain Gardinier, who fought with such desperation at the battle of Oriskany, and was so severely wounded in the death-struggle with one of the McDonalds. After the enemy had retired, Colonel Willett procured lights, and caused the wounded of the enemy, as well as his own, to be collected, and their wounds carefully dressed. The loss of the Americans was about forty. The enemy lost about the same number killed, and some fifty prisoners. The Tryon county militia under Major Rowley, behaved nobly."

"Pursuing on the enemy's trail, the Americans came up with his main body in a place called Jerseyfield on the north side of the Canada Creek. A running fight ensued, but the enemy made a very feeble resistance—exhibiting symptoms of terror, and attempting to retreat at a dog-trot by Indian files. Late in the afternoon, as they crossed the creek to the west or south-western side, Butler attempted to rally his forces and make a stand. A brisk engagement ensued, the parties being on opposite sides of the creek: during which about twenty men fell. Among them was their bold and enterprising but cruel leader, Walter N. Butler. He was brought down by the rifle of an Oneida Indians, who, happening to recognize him as he was looking at the battle from behind a tree, took deliberate aim, and shot him through his hat and the upper part of his head. Butler fell, and his troops fled in the utmost confusion. The warrior, who made the successful shot, sprang first across the creek in the general rush, and running directly up to Butler, discovered that he was not dead, but sorely wounded. He was in a sitting posture near the tree, and writhing in great agony. The Indian advanced, while Butler looked him full in the face, shot again through the eye, and immediately took his scalp. The Oneida no sooner saw the bleeding trophy, than they set up the scalp-yell, and stripping the body, left if lying upon the face, and pressed forward in pursuit was followed closely up: but darkness and fatigue compelled the colonel to relinquish it till morning. The enemy, however, continued their flight throughout the night. And truly never were men reduced to a condition more deplorable. The weather was cold, and they had yet a dreary and pathless wilderness of eighty miles to traverse, without food, and even without blankets, having been compelled to cast them away to facilitate their escape. But, scattered and broken as they were, and having the start of one night, it was judged inexpedient to given longer pursuit: especially as Willett's own troops were supplied with provisions for but two days more. The victory was, moreover, already complete. The Colonel therefore, wheeled about and led his little army back in triumph to Fort Dayton. The loss of the Americans in the pursuit was only one man. That of the enemy was never known. In the language of Colonel's Willett's official dispatches, 'the fields of Johnstown, the brooks and rivers and hills and mountains, the deep and gloomy marshes through which they had to pass, these only could tell; and, perhaps the officers who dispatched them on the expedition.'

"In repassing the battle-ground, the body of Butler was discovered as it had been left; and there, without sepulcher, it was suffered to remain.

"so perished Walter N. Butler, one of the greatest scourges, as he was one of the most fearless men, of his native country. No other event of the whole war created so much joy in the Mohawk Valley as the news of his decease. He is represented to have been of a morose temperament, possessing strong passions, and of a vindictive disposition. He was disliked, as has already more than one appeared, by Joseph Brant, who included him among those he considered greater savages than the savages themselves. It is quite probably, however, that Walter Butler may have possessed other and better qualities, his friends being judges, than have been awarded him by his enemies.

Quit Rents

by AJ Berry

Why did the British fight so hard to keep America? The government really didn't generate much revenue from trade with her colony. The British merchants made a profit off their sales and so did the Americans. Even if the colonies had their own government this was not likely to halt the trade back and forth. This nagged me for many years. What was in it for Britain? What was all the fighting really about? It had to be money because that was always the real reason behind most wars. Exactly how did the crown gain financially? Sure England tried the tea tax, but there had to be some way England made money in the previous 100 years. They didn't just colonize out of the goodness of their hearts or simply for power. There had to be financial gain from someplace, and a lot of it.

Enter--Quit Rents; how the British crown really made money from her colonies. Here was the answer, at last.

And what was a quit rent? Many of the old documents use the term quit rent and it seemed to be something the older writers understood, but I did not. Here is what I found out about Quit Rents.

The definition of QUIT RENT:

> **--Quit rent is/was a medieval term used to designate the portion of the agricultural product planted, raised, and harvested by the sharecropping tenant-peasant serf that was withheld by the feudal landlord. Both taxes AND profit are the present-day expressions of quit rent.**
>
> **--According to Black's Law Dictionary "A rent paid by the tenant of a freehold, by which he goes quit or free,--that is, discharged from any other rent." The "quit rent" paid in colonial times went to the Governor of a colony [as the representative of the Crown, or the Crown's Designee] for the use of the land.**

Before launching into the subject of quit rents, it is important to note the Mohawk Valley was for the most part, settled peacefully. White and red men lived side by side and there were very few instances of violence, with the exception a few raids until the Revolutionary War. Land was always the big issue, red men had it and white men wanted it. There had to be money in the land, money for the British government.

<u>In the early view, simply put, the English crown viewed all land as theirs, and the occupants paid rent on it. Quit Rent.</u>

Our system of taxation grew out of the quit rents of the early days of the colony. Even after independence, the term quit rent was used for many years and the nation used the English pounds.

I was surprised to discover some very early assessment records in the New York State Archives.

> **The early state Assessment Roll of real and personal Estates in the Town of Palatine in the County of Montgomery made this eighteenth Day of October in the Year of our Lord One Thousand seven hundred and ninety nine, according to the Directions of the Statute entitled "An Act for the Assessments and Collection of Taxes."**

There has been a lot of disagreement as to the exact nature of the title held by the American Indians for the soil on which they lived. European governments, upon the discovery of America, branded the American Indians as nomads. They laid down the proposition of international law that the European Government had an absolute right to the land on the American continents, which either they or their representative citizens should discover. Proprietorship by right of discovery was asserted, with utter disregard to the true rights of the American Indians.

Often in the history books you read, "I discover this land in the name of the King of England....." Usually the person discovering the land had no idea how much his discovery encompassed, he simply declared it as being owned by the crown.

The American Indians had a very loose arrangement for land usage; they hunted and fished and then when necessary, moved to a new place. The white man saw it differently, he wanted absolute possession of land, as much of it as possible, to cultivate, fence in and to build house and barns on.

Under the colonial government it was customary that the Indian title, should be surrendered before land grants were issued to the parties wishing to purchase. A deed from the Indians was usually procured by holding a council with them, and this being accomplished, the Surveyor General was directed to make the survey and in his report furnish a map and field notes of the premises.

The draft of a patent was then prepared by the Attorney General, and, if approved by the Governor of the colony and his council it was granted and recorded. Under an established ordinance, only one thousand acres could be granted to one person, but this regulation was frequently overlooked by associating, as patentees, a large number of persons who were only nominally parties to the purchase. Land speculators were plentiful in those early times and there was corruption among the officials.

In addition, the officials who charged the remunerative fees obtained by the performance of their duty, were often participants in the purchase. In a few instances land grants were issued from the Crown of England instead of through the colonial government. In some of the grants for patents under the colonial government, the conditions required the payment of the annual quit-rent, which at that time constituted an important source of revenue, and which subsequently became due to the State. The payments for quit-rent were sometimes specified to be made in money, but oftener in grain or other produce such as furs.

In a word, TAXATION.

In an effort to contain foreign interference, the Federal Government prohibited the Indian tribes in the United States from making or entering into treaties with political powers other than the Federal Government.

"Necessity is paramount to law."

Source Material:

English Crown Grants by S. L. Mershon, p. 90, 1918

A History of Herkimer County

BY NATHANIEL S. BENTON. ALBANY: J. MUNSELL, 78 STATE STREET 1856.

Audited Accounts for William Norton, Samuel Hill and Lt. William Wilson.

By James F. Morrison

Many times a pensioner in his application states a service or "a tour" and his name is not found on a muster roll or pay roll for the regiment. Such is the case of William Norton who requested he be paid because he was omitted from a payroll. Unfortunately the company he belonged to is not mentioned.

State of New York D to William Norton Dr, 1781 Dec'r 31. For my Pay as a private in Col. Willett's Regt of Levies from 22d April 1781 to this day which was omitted being inserted in the Pay Rolls of that Reg't through Mistake as certified by Col. Willet is 8 mo. & 9 days a 53/4 [per] month. 22. .2. . 8

Audited 10th May 1785.

Audited Accounts, Vol. A, Page 234, Manuscript and Special Collections, New York State Library Albany, N.Y.

A William Norton served as a private in Captain Jacob DeFreest's Company (Sixth Company) in Colonel Stephen J. Schuyler's Sixth Regiment of Albany County Militia. A William Norton served as a private in Captain Peter. B. Tearce's Company in Colonel Willett's Regiment in 1782.

Pay Roll for Capt. Peter Wagner's (1) Coy (Company) Col. Jacob Klock's Regt of Militia for service at sundry times from 1st April 1780 to 26th October 1782 consisting of one Capt. Two Lieutenants one Ensign Four Serjeants Three Corporals' One Drummer & Sixty Nine Privates amounting Drummer & Sixty Nine Privates amounting to 360. .1. . 9 Audited 25th May 1785.

1. A date of appointment to Captain is unknown but he was serving as a captain by April 1, 1780 in Colonel Jacob Klock's Second Regiment of Tryon County Militia. Peter, son of Lieutenant-Colonel Peter Wagner was appointed Second Lieutenant in Captain William Fox Jr's Company (First Company) on August 26, 1775. On June 25, 1778, First Lieutenant John Hess was commissioned Captain of the First Company and Peter was commissioned the First Lieutenant. Most likely Captain Wagner was appointed on March 4, 1780 when other appointments were made in Colonel Klock's Regiment.
   FROM: Audited Accounts, Volume A., Page 242, Manuscripts and Special Collections, New York State Library, Albany, N.Y.

State of New York D to Samuel Hill for 9 months service as a Private in Col. Willett's Regt of Levies, being ommitted in Col. Willet's Pay Roll as (per) Col. Willett's Certificate @ 53/4 (per) month.

Audited 21st July 1786.

A Samuel Hill served as a private in Captain Jacob DeFreest's Company (Sixth Company) in Colonel Stephen Schuyler's Sixth Regiment of Albany County Militia.

Hill's service in Colonel Willett's Regiment was in 1781. Unfortunately he did not give the company that he had served in.
From: Audited Accounts Vol. A., Page 37, Manuscript and Special Collections, New York State Library, Albany, N.Y.

State of New York to William Wilson D. To my Pay as a Lieut. in Col. Marinus Willet's Regt of Levies from 7th April to 7th Augt 1782 omitted through mistake in the Muster & Pay Rolls heretofore rendered 4 months @ 26/3 Dollars (per) Month. 42. . 13. . 4

Audited 27th June 1785.
FROM: Audited Accounts, Vol. A. Page 249, Manuscripts and Special Collections, New York State Library, Albany, NY.

Abstract of PayRoll of a detachment of Capt. Isaac Foreest's (1) Company of Col. Jacob Lansing's Regt of Albany County Militia order'd out on Public Service at Stone Arabia (2) from 26th October 1779 to 6th Novem'r 1779 both day included Consisting in One Captain, One Lieutenant, One Ensign, Four Serjeants, Two Corporals & Twenty Six Privates amounting in the whole of the sum of 50. . 12. . 2 Audited 11th May 1786.
FROM Audited Accounts Vol. B. page 25, Manuscripts and Special Collections, New York State Library, Albany, NY.

1. Isaac DeFreest was appointed First Lieutenant on October 20, 1775 in Captain John M. Beeckman's Company (Fort Company) in Colonel Jacob Lansing's First Regiment of Albany County Militia. Sometime after this there was a change but so far it is unknown when. The First Lieutenant Abraham TenEyck was aopointed Second Lieutenant on November 21, 1776 in Colonel Goose VanSchaick's First New York Continental Regiment. It is known that Isaac I. Fonda, Ensign on October 20, 1779 in Captain DeForrest's Comp., Vice (in place of) Jacob H. Wendal, declined. On March 3, 1780, Gerrit Groesbeck is commissioned Captain of the Company heretofore commanded by Isaac DeForrest, who declined.
2. In 1779 several detachments from the Albany County Militia Regiments were sent to garrison forts in the Mohawk Valley as most of the Continental troops had gone with Brigadier General James Clinton to join Major General John Sullivan in an expedition against the Iroquois Villages in Western New York.

Schohary June 11, 1779
Sir

You will remain at Fort Duboise (1) with the party under your command and take necessary scouts until a further order form me. The Continental troops (2) stationed here are mostly marched to Schenectady and the rest will soon, I expect. I have some of our militia now on scout and an obliged to order more of them in the forts. As soon as the militia from Albany arrive here I will have those of my regiment now at Cobus Kill, under your command belonging to Schohary all releaved. I remain Sir Your humble servant Peter Vrooman Col. (3)

To Capt. Richtmeyer. P.S. If there is any danger of an appearance of the enemy it will be very soon as the troops are now on their marching therefore keep a good lookout and be on your guard.
[On the reverse side of the letter.]
On Publick Service
To Capt. George Richtmeyer (4)
Fort Duboise

The Mohawk Valley Historic Association, June, Sixth Annual Meeting, August 6, 1925, Old Stone Fort Museum, Schoharie, New York, Schenectady, 1926.

1. Fort DuBois was a block house built by the Fifth New York Continental Regiment during the winter of 1778-1779 at Cobleskill. Lewis DuBois was the Colonel of the Fifth New York and the block house was named in his honor.
2. The Continental troops that wintered in the Schoharie and Mohawk Valleys during the winter of 1778-1779 were gathering at different stations in preparation to march to Canajoharie to join the army of Brigadier General James Clinton. From there they would march to Lake Otsego and by bateaus eventually meet Major General John Sullivan's Army. Once they merged together they marched against the Iroquois Villages in Western New York.
3. Peter Vrooman Colonel of the Fifteenth Regiment of Albany County Militia. This regiment was raised from the United Districts of Schoharie and Duanesburgh.
4. George Richtmeyer (Rechtmyer, Rightmyer, etc.) was appointed Captain on October 20, 1775 of the Third Company in Colonel Vrooman's Regiment.

NormansKill February 28, 1785

Sir Please to pay to Alexander McLeod or his order all the pay and subsistence money Due me for my services money Due me for my services During the late War in Colonel Vrooman's Regiment of Militia and this order with a receipt shall be a voucher for the same. By me John Valck
To Colonel Vrooman at Schoharry

Received of Coll Peter Vrooman for John Valck five pounds sixteen shillings four pence 1/3 in certificates for service in the Late War in the militia as witnessed my hand Schoharry. August 4th 1785. Alexander McLeod.
FROM: Albany County Militia, Box 9, Special Collections, New York State Library, Albany, N.Y.

John served as a private in Captain Jacob Hager's Company (Second Company)

A John Falk is also listed as serving as a private in Captain Christian Stubrach's Company. Both companies were part of the Colonel Peter Vrooman's Fifteenth Regiment of Albany County Militia.

Roll of the Officers Appointed in the Levies for the Defence of the Frontier of the State &c. &c. &c. vizt.

Henry K. Van Renselaer, Lieut-Colonel Command't Albert Pawling.

Commission'd	Elias VanBenscoten Major.
Captains	
Do	Levi Stockwell
Do	Robert Wood
Do	Robert McKean
	John Wood
	Matthew Jansen
	Joshua Whitney
	William Faulkner
	Ebenezer Smith Platt
	Jonathan Lawrence
Lieutenants	Levi DeWitt
Do	Wouter J. Vrooman
	John Smith
Do	John McBridge
	Peter Rosa
Resign'd	Jonah Hallet
	Patrick Cronan
Do	Dirck Westbrouck –resigned
	Abraham Westfall
Resign'd do	Dunahm, late Lieut in Coll. VanSchaick's Regt.
Lieuts	Henry Pawling
Do	William Erskin
Do	Thomas Oostrander
Do	Thos Boggs
Do	Elsworth-Adjutant
Q'r Master	Jonathan Hardenbergh
Surgeon	John Smedes

Memo. Coll. Van Rensselaer recommends Nanningh VanDerHeyden, to be a First Lieut. in the Regt of Levies.
(Note by Geo. W. Clinton) "This must be '78 or rather '79. (1)
FROM: Public Papers of George Clinton, ed. Hugh Hastings, Wynkoop, Hallenbeck, Crawford Co., Albany, Vol. I, pp 568-569, 1899.

(1) The year for these two regiments was 1779 but were put by the editor of the Clinton Papers in the year 1777 (Vol 1) The levies were to be 1,000 to be raised under Act 33 which was passed March 13, 1779. The Council of Appointment, in their session of May 3, 1779, decided to divide the men into two distinct regiments but did not make clear what regiments the company officers belonged to. FROM: Documents Relating to the Colonial History of the State of New York, ed.. Berthold Fernow, Vol. XV, State Archives, Vol. I, Weed, Parsons, and Company, Printers, Albany, 1887, page 256. Revolutionary War Rolls, 1775-1783, Series M-246, Roll 75, Pawling's Levies, folder 126, National Archives, Washington, D.C. The Captains that were to be part of Pawling's Regiment were: Robert Wood, William Faulkner, Ebenezer Smith Platt and Jonathan Lawrence. Platt and Lawrence both declined. Robert Hunter replaced Platt and Josiah Hallet replaced Lawrence, Hunter, and Hallet were commissioned on October 20, 1779. John Hardenburgh who had been appointed a lieutenant and the Quartermaster for Pawling's regiment also declined the appointments and Edward Conner was appointed lieutenant and Quartermaster in his place.

State of New York
To his Excellency Governor Clinton D for so much paid to the Seneca Chief by the Commissioners of Indian Affairs at Albany as (per) Concurrent Resolution of the Legislature passed 2 April 1787 £ 81. . 10. . 9
To cash advanced to Lewis Dean an Indian and his two sons for service in the Militia as (per) con current Resolution of the Legislature dated 15 March 1787 £45/£ 126. . 10. . 9
Audited 21 August 1787
Audited Accounts, Vol B, page 118, Manuscripts and Special Collections, New York State Library, Albany, N.Y.

State of New York to Jacobus Myers (per) D 1787 April 12 to casting the Monument of Genl Montgomery to St. Pauls Church £ 1. . 0. . 0 Audited 26th July 1788.
Audited Accounts, Vol B, Page 159, Manuscripts and Special Collections, New York State Library, Albany, N.Y.

Abstract of a Detachment of Col. VanAlstyn's (1) Regt of Albany Militia in the Service of the United States to Fort Harkimer from 15th Augt 1779 to 7th September following inclusive Consisting of One Lieut Two Serjeants & six Privates amounting to 28. . 14. . 8

Audited 9th May 1785.

1. Colonel Abraham Van Alstyne's Seventh Regiment of Albany County Militia

Audited Accounts, Vol A, page 232, Manuscripts and Special Collections, New York State Library, Albany, N.Y.

Fourth Battalion of Tryon County Militia

Company Officers

Captain Frederick Getman (Kitman) commissioned June 25, 1778
First Lieutenant John Ruff (Roof)
Second Lieutenant Jacob Meyer Commissioned June 25, 1778
Ensign John Meyer Commissioned June 25, 1778

Sergeants

Ittig (Edick) Christian; Stale, George

Corporals

Phyfer (Piper), Jacob; Shoemaker, Thomas (PAR9525)

Privates

Bonny, Ichabod
Clapsattle, Andrew
Clapsattle, William
Cokin, Dome (Thomas)
Dygert, Peter
Frank, Henry
Getman, Conrad (PA19497)
Getman, Jr. Frederick
Getman, Peter (PAW16257)
Herkimer, John
Hyser [Hiser], Martin
Ittig, Conrad (PAW1776)
Ittig, George (PAS12854)
Ittig, Jacob C. (PAW26155)
Lapious, Jacob (PS15284)
Lighthall, George
Lighhall, Nicholas
Lins (Lints, Lentz, Lenz), Jacob
Myer, Joseph
Piper, Andrew (PA26893)
Shoemaker, Han Jost
Smith, William
Weaver, George

Tryon County Militia—Box 14, Special Collections and Manuscripts, New York State Library, Albany, N.Y.

There were two muster rolls for this company in the box. The first covered June and July 1779 and April and May of 1780. The second was dated October 21, 1780 at Fort Herkimer.

The same muster rolls were transcribed in October 1896 in the R. & P. Office, War Dept, 454712, Revolutionary War Rolls 1775-1784, Series M-246, Roll 72, folder 78, National Archives, Washington, D.C.

The following were taken prisoners during the War of Independence:

Taken prisoners on June 21, 1782 at Ellis and Phyn's Grist Mill at Little Falls:

Captain Frederick Getman—Released November 14, 1782.

Sergeant Christian Ittig—Released December 14, 1782.

Corporal Thomas Shoemaker—Released December 14, 1782.

Private Andrew Piper—Released December 14, 1782.

Audited Accounts, Vol. B. page 265, Special Collections and Manuscripts, New York State Library, Albany, N.Y.

John Lintz was killed on October 6, 1780.

FROM: Audited Accounts, Vol. B, page 255, Special Collections and Manuscripts, New York State Library, Albany, N.Y.

Unveiling of the Sammons Monument, August 26, 1899

Mohawk Valley Democrat

Fonda, N. Y. August 31, 1899.

Address of William L. Stone

What song the Sirens sang, or what name Achilles assumed when he hid himself among women, though puzzling questions are not beyond conjecture. What time the persons of these ossuaries entered the famous nations of the dead, and slept with princes and counselors might admit a wide solution. But who are the proprietors of these bones, or what bodies these ashes made up were a question not to be resolved by man, nor easily, perhaps, by spirits."

Thus discoursed Sir Thomas Browne--who has been called "The laureate of the King of Terrors"--in his sublime and fearful essay upon "Urn Burial" which he was led to write by the discovery of the celebrated urns in a field of "Old Walhsingham" two hundred and 50 years ago. Fortunately for this day and this occasion, no such mystery hangs over the graves of those whose clustering memories we are here this day to recall. This spot nevertheless, as Mr. Starin had said is consecrated ground. We may here figuratively at least, tread upon the ashes of kings.

I have said that we were treading upon the ashes of kings. It is true that the royal title was unknown to those who, in the words of Gray, "Now among the rude forefathers of the hamlet sleep." But in their patriotic rank, their order of descent from the early settlers of the Mohawk Valley, they were in truth sovereigns. Patriotic kinds they indeed were: kings who reveled not in voluptuousness, nor wasted their time among the delights of the Harem, nor yet degraded their manhood by plying the distaff like Sardanapolis; nor yet were they of those who sought immorality by rearing cities and palaces and solemn temples like those of Thebes and Babylon and Tyre. They affected not the graves of giants, nor yet sought to mark the age of their glory by the stupendous pyramid of the costly mausoleum. They were not of the common order of men, but of a race self reliant and whose powers and characteristics were of mingled moral grandeur and primitive simplicity, and who like the Gnomes and Fates of Grecian Mythology, seemed born amid the convulsions of terrible border warfare in cloud and in storm. It is to this patriotic race that we owe the present celebration. Help me then with reverent hands to lift the veil which has too long shrouded these patriots from the ken of the present generation.

The Starin and Sammons families (closely related by marriage) were, from their first settlement in the Mohawk Valley in 1705 inseparably connected with every movement having for its object the public weal. They were ever to be found on the side of the right, and in whatever constitutes good citizenship, and this--too--at a period when such conduct meant more than can be conceived of at the present day, when mere professions is too apt to take the place of action. Hence, they are found among the most prominent participants both in Queen Anne's and the old French and Indian Wars. In this connection and as illustrating the above remark, may be mentioned as one among many of a similar character, the following incident in the life of the great grandfather of John H. Starin, vix: Philip Frederick Adam Starin. He was by trade a machinist, and for many years, was the sole reliance of the settlers for the repair of their agricultural implements and their rifles.

One day as he was at work at his forge three Indians came in and peremptorily commanded him to drop at once the work upon which he was then engaged and attend to some job for them. Upon his not immediately complying with their demand one of the Indians plunged a knife into his abdomen, letting out a portion of his bowels. Notwithstanding, however, this terrible wound, he pulled out from the fire a red hot iron bar he was mending at the time, and with one blow laid the savage dead at his feet, whereupon the other two Indians fled in the direst consternation. Starin recovered from this wound, and lived many years after wards.

Mr. Starin -- the great-grandson of Philip--has (among many other precious family relics) a wrought iron sconce for holding candles, the same plan as the new-fashioned piano lamp which was designed and manufactured by him. It is a very ingenious piece of work and demonstrates that the design of the present piano or banquet lamp is by no means of modern origin.

Then there was Nicholas Starin who died at German Flatts in 1802, having attained the patriarchal age of 95. During his life time he passed successively through Queen Anne's war, 1702-1713; the French war, 1754-63; and the Revolutionary war, dying almost on the threshold of the war of 1812. In some of these wars, moreover, he took an active part, fighting at the age of 65 side by side with his nephew Heinrich and Nicholas, at the battle of Oriskany. His business was that of an Indian trader, and he often made journeys among the Indian settlements far beyond the frontiers. During these trips he endured hardships of the severest kind, which at the present day would be deemed simply incredible, for at that time the northwestern part of that which is now New York State was a primeval wilderness, whose silence was unbroken save by the hooting of the owl or the scream of the panther; and whose solitude was undisturbed except by savage beasts or still more savage tribes; with here and there a trading post or fort.

He was, also, a warm personal friend of Sir William Johnson whom he often accompanied on his fishing trips tot he fish house on the Sacandaga, and was frequently his companion on his many journeys from Fort Johnson to Schenectady and back. Regarding on of these trips the following story is still told in the Mohawk Valley at the expense of the Baronet. There were numerous little swamps along the road, and Sir William once upon a time returning to Fort Johnson accompanied by Nicholas passed a marsh in which he heard, as he believed, the voice of a new animal. Turning to Starin he enquired: "What animal are those making such a strange noise?" His companion replied with a grin that they were bull frogs. Whereupon the Baronet spurred up his horse, not a little chagrined to think that he had but first learned, as his Irish countrymen would say "what a toad or a frog was."

And here if time and your patience permitted I could also dwell upon the marvelous escapes from the Indians of his nephew Judge Heinich Starin, the hero of the celebrated "Yankee Pass." Especially on one of the many similar occasions the fear of the faggot and it accompanying torture furnishing, a stimulus to his flight, he was forced to take refuge in a tree, so close were his pursuers upon him. The tree was a hemlock, the thick foliage of which effectually concealed his person. The Indians came in numbers past his hiding place, but although their dogs had lost the scent they suspected, not the place of his concealment. After they had passed, Starin descended from his perch, and took to the channel of a brook close by, continuing his course in its bed until he should reach a path which led from Oneida to Old Fort Schuyler, a mud fort built on the present site of Utica, during the old French war. Starin discovering a canoe lodged in the willows growing on the edge of the bank, took possession of it, and by a rigorous use of its paddle finally succeeded in reaching his home. In fact a narrative of these hairbreadth escapes would alone easily fill a small volume. The curious reader, however, will find all of his adventures succinctly given in my father's life of Brant, and in Judge Tracy's address.

Again when the Seven Years war broke out, and the scene of conflict was transferred from the battlefields of the Old World to those of the New, the Starins and Sammons took an active part in all of the skirmishes on the northern frontier, and some of both families were present, under Sir William Johnson when that General defeated Baron Dieskau at the battle of Lake George in 1755. Coming down to the Revolutionary War, the same warm zeal, mingled with similar patriotic impulses, is found in the two families. And now, as illustrative of these preliminary remarks, let me first summes(?) before you the forms of John Starin and Jane his wife, whose mortal remains lie within our vision across the valley.

John Starin, the grandfather of John H. Starin, was an Indian interpreter, a confidential friend of General Washington; fought throughout the war for American Independence; and was one of the forty members of the Starin family who served in the Continental army directly under Washington himself. After the war he kept an Inn in the present village of Fultonville, which was a kind of halting place for bands of western Indians, who were on--their way east to visit their great father at Philadelphia, and often at night the hall of the Inn would be so thickly filled with sleeping red men that "Mine host" could hardly pick his way among them. There was also a permanent encampment of Mohawks just beyond the Inn, while directly in its front there were several eel wiers that the Indians had built in the river, one of which is still plainly to be seen.

Jane Starin, his wife, whose maiden name was Wemple, shared with her husband all the vicissitudes and perils of a border warfare and often by her advice and encouragement, when times looked dark, aided him in matters of grave moment. She was a very neat old lady, and her grandchildren still recall the short gown (spun and woven by herself) that she wore, and its pockets fastened by a string around her waist, and worn underneath the gown, which had to be pulled up whenever she wished to reach its contents. She always carried in it some tidbit for "the boys." She had long survived the frightful perils and numerous atrocities which she had been compelled to witness, and being a keen observer with a remarkable retentive memory, she had in store a thousand legends of that stirring period. Often, on a winter's night, while the flames when roaring up the huge chimney, and the firelight merrily played among the flitches of the bacon handing from the smoked rafters overhead, she would--as she was knitting--for she was never idle--recount to her grandchildren fathered around her many adventures in a newly settled country, and the sufferings endured by herself and kindred when forced to fly on the approach of the savage hordes of Sir John Johnson and Col. St. Leger.

At the breaking out of the Revolutionary War the Wemples at once ranged themselves on the side of the Colonists, becoming the staunchest and most ardent Whigs in the Valley of the Mohawk. They were, together with Henreich Staring, of whom I have previously spoken, in the bloody fight at Oriskany, and as a consequence of their zeal were among those marked out by Sir John Johnson and Captain Walter Butler for the tomahawk and the firebrand. Indeed, while writing this I have before me an old manuscript (handed down to me by my father) yellow with age and almost crumbling to pieces, on which--written more than a century ago-- are inscribed in its now fading ink the names of those who suffered for their patriotism during the raid of St. Leger and among those names are those of the Starin and Wemple families.

I see again rising before me the form of Sampson Sammons to who belongs the high honor of having had fired at him in 1775, by Johnson's Rangers, the first shot in the American Revolution west of the Hudson. The occasion was as follows: A Tory sheriff had on some trifling pretext arrested a

Whig by the name of John Fonda and committed him to prison. His friends under the conduct of Sampson Sammons whet to the jail at night, and released him by force. From the prison they proceeded the lodgings of the sheriff and demanded his surrender. While the sheriff looked out from the second story window and inquired "Is that you Sammons?" Yes, was the prompt reply, upon which White discharged a pistol at the sturdy Whig. This, as we have stated was the first shot in the American Revolution west of the Hudson. Sampson Sammons served with great credit throughout the war, and distinguished himself especially at the battle of Klock's Field. He was moreover an active member of the Committee of Safety for Tryon County--a county which at this time included all of the present state of New York, west of Albany.

When the Revolution began he was appointed to take charge of the confiscated property in Tryon county, and in that capacity he resided for a time at Johnson Hall. Nor was the part played by his son, Jacob Sammons in these troublous times of less moment. At a public meeting of the Whigs called to erect a liberty pole, the most hateful object at that time in the eyes of the loyalists, and to sympathize with those slain at the battle of Lexington, Sampson Sammons and his two sons Jacob and Frederick were present. Before, however, they had accomplished their purpose of raising the emblem of the rebellion, the proceedings were interrupted by the arrival of Sir John Johnson, accompanied by his brothers-in-law, Cols. Claus and Guy Johnson together with Col. John Butler and a large number of their retained, armed with swords and pistols. Guy Johnson mounted a high stoops and harangued the people at length and with great vehemence. He dwelt upon the strength and power of the King and subsequent folly of revolting against the authority of the crown. A single ship, he said, would be sufficient to capture all the navy which could be set afloat by the Colonies, while on the frontiers, the Indians were all under his majesty's control. He was very virulent in his language toward the disaffected, causing their blood to boil with indignation. But they were unarmed and for the most part unprepared, if not indisposed, to proceed to any act of violence.

The orator at length became so abusive that Jacob Sammons, no longer able to restrain himself interrupted Johnson's tirade by pronouncing him a liar and a villain. Guy Johnson thereupon seized Sammons by the throat and called him a damned villain in return. A scuffle ensued between them, during which Sammons was struck down with a loaded whip. On recovering from the momentary stupor of the blow, he sprang to his feet, threw off his coat and prepared to fight. Two pistols were at once presented to his breast, but not discharged and on recovering from his stupor he perceived that this Whig friends with the exception of the Fondas, Veeders and Vischers had all decamped. Sir John Johnson also retreated with his Loyalists, and Jacob Sammons returned to his father's house bearing upon his body, as I have said, the first scars of the revolutionary contest in the country of Tryon. Jacob afterwards became a lieutenant in the New York lines, and rendered much valuable assistance to Col. Marinus Willet, the hero of Oriskany, in his forays against the Indians, who in the pay of the British constantly menaced the northern border. His son Jacob, Jr., was in the war of 1812, under Genl Wool and did much hard fighting.

And yet again there appears the form of THOMAS SAMMONS, Major Thomas Sammons, like his father Sampson, and his brother, Jacob and Frederick also took part in the perils of the war. He was apparently a favorite of Sir John Johnson, for when himself and his brothers Jacob and Frederick, also took part in the pero;s perils of the war. He was apparently a favorite of Sir John Johnson, for when himself and his brothers Jacob and Frederick had begun their march as prisoners into Canada, he chanced to see Sir John who was witnessing their departure from the roadside, he immediately feigning to have a lame foot appealed to Johnson to be liberated, fortifying his appeal by saying: "I was your friend in the Committee of Safey, and exerted myself to save your person from injury, and how am I requited." Your Indians have murdered and scalped old Mr. Fonda at the age of eighty years, a man, who I have heard your father say, was like a father to him when he settled at Johnstown and Kingsborough. You cannot succeed, Sir John in such a warfare, and you will never enjoy your property more.

A most true prophecy, since all of Sir John's vast estates in the Mohawk Valley were afterwards confiscated, and he himself died a poor man at Montreal in the early part of this century. Whether Sir John was moved by this reminiscence or not he replied in jovial mood, "Well, Thomas you are no good anyway, go home." Thus was Thomas saved from the terrible sufferings which, as we shall see was the lot of his brothers. Douw Fonda, here referred to, moved from Schenectady to Caughnawaga in 1757, and built a large stone house on the banks of the Mohawk. In this raid of Sir John Johnson, not only was his house burned, but he was killed as he was going to his spring for water, by a one-armed Indian. He left three sons, Douw, Jelles and Adam. The latter was a famous captain in the Tryon County Militia Regiment, commanded by General Herkimer. He died in 1808.

Thomas Sammons, who lived to be a very old man, and who related to may father in person most of the anecdotes I have presented in this address, was likewise a warm personal friend of Gov.George Clinton, that distinguished man constantly relying upon him whenever rigorous measures and sagacious councils were required. He was also a member of the Council of appointment and represented the Montgomery county district to congress from 1809 to 1811, while fourteen of his descendants bore arms in the union army during the late civil war.

FREDERICK SAMMONS, like his brothers, Thomas and Jacob, also did yeomen service for the cause of freedom. He served under Gen. Gates at the battle of Saratoga, and bore himself throughout that campaign as a brave and gallant soldier. He was--moreover--at the side of Gen. Arnold when that officer was wounded at the "Brunswick Redoubt." In 1780, he with his brother Jacob, was carried a prisoner into Canada whence after experiencing the most romantic adventures and suffering; untold privations and cruelties from his captors, he finally escaped in a canoe, which becoming entangled in a submerged treetop was upset. Regaining the shore of the St. Lawrence he plunged directly into the unbroken forest, extending from the St. Lawrence to the Sacandaga, and after a journey of twelve days of excessive hardship emerged from the woods within six miles of the point for which, without chart or compass, Sammons had laid his course. His provisions lasted but a few days, but his only subsequent food consisted of roots and herbs and a rattlesnake which he had killed. The whole journey was made almost in a state of nudity, he being destitute of pantaloons. Having worn out his shoes, the last few days he was compelled to travel barefooted, and long before his journey was completed his feet were dreadfully lacerated and swollen. On his arrival at Schenectady, the inhabitants were alarmed at his wild and savage appearance, half naked, with unkempt beard and matted hair. The people at length gathered around him with strange curiosity; but on his being recognized, the welcome fugitive was forthwith supplied with food and raiment and sent on his way to his family at Johnstown, who received him as one almost literally risen from the dead.

Then there was VALENTINE STARIN, who followed the business of farming until the breaking out of the Revolution, when, like so many others of the Starin family he enlisted as a private in the second Ulster County Regiment, Col. Bellinger commanding. His death was particularly sad. Upon the 17th of July, 1782, a party of six hundred Indians and Tories entered the town of German Flatts and destroyed nearly the entire settlement, tomahawking all of the inhabitants who had not the good fortune to escape to the fort or blockhouse. Among the latter was Valentine Starin, who was captured and tortured to death, within the hearing of the garrison of the fort, who were too feeble to attempt his rescue.

Next we see MYNDERT STARIN the father of our Mr. Starin, who distinguished himself in the contest of 1812, when that war was declared against Great Britain. Although seriously ill at that time of the draft, he refused exemption on that ground and enlisted and served bravely during that contest. He was at the battle of Plattsburg, as a Captain of Infantry and took part also during the vicissitudes of the campaign on the Niagara Frontier. At the close of that contest he received an honorable discharge, Major General Scott, then in ocmmand complimented him highlin in "general orders" on his good and efficient service. He was also the first regular mail carrier West of Albany, and like his son Mr. John H. Starin, at an early age engaged in the passenger and transportation line, owning several row boats built expressly to carry some twenty passengers each from Utica to Schenectady. These boats which were tastefully fitted up and curtained were in use on the Mohawk River from 1810 to 1815. They were called "River packets" and three of them were named respectively, the "Myndert Starin", "Jacob Lasher" and "Rob Roy:. Upon the completion of the Erie Canal, in which project he was of much assistance to his personel friends Gov. DeWitt Clinton, its originator, and to my father, Col. William L. Stone, Gov. Clinton's right hand man in the project, he became one of the most prominent men in the Mohawk Valley. He also took great interest in church matters and some of the old residents even of today, doubtless among my hearers, kindly remember Myndert Starin leading the singing in the old Caughnawaga Stone church in the German and Dutch languages in the morning, and in English in the evening.

And finally; I see before me, one, that many of my audience must still remember in affectionate remembrance, viz:

Col. Simeon Sammons, son of Thos., who, during the late Civil War, equipped; put in marching order, and conducted to Harpers Ferry his regiment, the 115th N. Y. vol. of eleven hundred men in the amazing time of twenty-nine days. When Col. Sammons reached Washington and was asked the usual question, "What he had come for?" Instead of expressing as many did a desire for easy quarters near the Capitol, he answered in his bluff manner, "To fight, by God," and as evidence of the sincerity of this purpose, and that these were not mere empty words, he brought home after the war, two bullets in his body. Again at the springing of a mine in front of Petersburgh, Va., he leaped over the parapet, and though his foot was shattered by a minnie-ball, he caught up the standard from the hands of one who had fallen, and planted it in triumph over the works of the enemy.

MAJOR STEPHEN SAMMONS of the 153rd regiment, was a younger brother of Col. Simeon Sammons. He was a lawyer by profession, and had been an editor in New York. He went through the campaigns of the Civil War with great honor, and died in Fonda soon after his brother, the Colonel.

From these brief sketches it will be seen that it is a mistake to suppose that either Lexington or Bunker Hill was the first school in which the Colonists were taught their ability to struggle with veteran soldiers. It was in the Mohawk Valley that this lesson was fast learned, and it is very doubtful if the Colonists would have dared to take the stand they did had it not been for the lessons of the old French war, in which as we have seen, the Starin family were the leaders. In the Mohawk valley provincial prowess signalized its selfrelying capabilities; and Putnam and Stark, the Starins and the Sammonses came into the old French war, as to a military academy to acquire the art of warfare which they all exercised at Bunker Hill. George Washington himself, as a military man, was nurtured for himself and America and the world amid the forests of the Alleghenies, and in view of the rifles and tomahawks of these French and Indian fighters led by the Starin and Sammons families.

"Lake George,", "Saratoga" and the "Mohawk Valley" are contiguous not merely in territory, but in historic associations. As these conflicts in the Mohawk Valley were certainly, in a measure at least, a source of our present national life, so should the name of those who took such a prominent part deserve to be commemorated not only in story and in song, but in enduring granite and bronze; One, in fact is but the correlative of the other, *sana mens in corpore Sano* is as true of the body politic as of the body physical, and if our existence as a united nation is to be preserved, it will be by keeping intact the mental and physical energies of the people.

"Soldiers," said Napoleon, on the eve of one of his greatest battles, and in one of those bulletins with which he was wont to electrify all Europe, "Soldier," from yonder pyramids forty centuries are looking down on you. But during thc American Revolution, far *nobler* and *grander* heights, the Providence of God was looking down upon that little band of patriots in the Mohawk Valley, molding and shaping their deliberations; so that their influence upon American civilization should endure not for this world only, but throughout the Ages.

Address of Hon. John H. Starin. My Friends--To those of you who know me best, and I cherish(?) the belief that there are some of you who know me well, it is needless to say that in the erection of this memorial I was actnated (?) by no motives of self-glorification nor of self-aggrandizement. My one desire, in its construction has been to perpetuate not only thc memory of noble ancestors, but in lasting and enduring form to keep alive the memory of heroic deeds.

We stand here upon consecrated ground. Looking backward through the dim vistas of the past, it is easy for even the most commonplace and prosaic mind to picture the struggles the trials, the sufferings,and at last the triumphs of the men who fought and bled in the fight to establish the American Republic.

The applause of admiring multitudes was not theirs.

They struggled isolated and alone. No hope of personal reward was in their hearts. They fought, they bled, they died for a principle. For that, and for that alone.

The history of the world furnishes no grander example of disinterested, unselfish and devoted patriotism. And so, my friends, I say we stand upon ground sacred and consecrated because it contains the dust of such men as I describe. And though we are here to honor especially the family of Sammons who were participants in the war of Queen Anne, the old French war, the Indian wars, the Revolutionary war, the war of 1812, and the Great Rebellion, we do not honor them only as individuals or as a family, but we honor and revere in them the grand type of American yeomanry, which they represent.

It is in this view, and with these motives that I have caused to be erected the memorial which we are dedicating today.

I am not one of those who believe in the degeneracy of our time, on the contrary I hold that the world grows better as the years go on, every trial, every danger which may come to this beloved land of ours will call to the front new men, strong, high hearted and fresh for the right. It was so in the war with Spain just closed. It will be so for all time. From my point of view it were as well to try to stop the tides of the sea, as to retard or impede the progress of the American Republic, and with this faith strong within me, I dedicate this monument of granite and of bronze to the memory of the heroes who have gone, steadfast in the faith that when my country calls there will be loud and quick response from countless heroes yet to come.

Remarks of W. Frothingham. Mr. Frothingham humorously said that his speech would be like the old saying "a short horse, soon curried." In other

Visscher's words he intended to be brief. He opened by an allusion to the marshal of the day, General O'Bierne, who had won his rank by the hardest fighting, having served under General Kearney in the terrible slaughter at Chancellerville where he was severely wounded and lay three days on the battlefield, also fought at Malvern and other bloody fields. The speaker also alluded to the great pleasure which the General must feel in meeting so many of the Grand Army, fellow soldiers with himself in that terrific struggle for the preservation of the Union. Mr. F. then referred to the resemblance which the General bore to Colonel Sammons which others had noticed as well as himself and which rendered the General doubly welcome. He then spoke of the felicity of Commodore Starin's address and added that the Commodore was a man of deeds rather than words as shown by what he has done for the public both in Fultonville and Fonda and his free excursions in New York. Next the speaker alluded to the representatives of the old Revolutionary families, the Fondas and the Vischers, heroes of Oriskany whose descendants were present. He also referred appropriately to the orator of the day, William L. Stone, son of an eminent New York editor, and himself an editor and an historian and the author of the Life of Sir William Johnson the pioneer and patriot of a former age. Mr. F. also said that the importance of that occasion was increased by the fact that never again would that spot witness such a gathering of the heroism intelligence and beneficence of the Mohawk Valley. He was glad to see so many ladies present and then alluded specially to one of the number who had done so much for the public weal and had so faithfully cooperated with her husband in his beneficent work and he closed by calling for three cheers for Mrs. John H. Starin which were given with unbound enthusiasm.

Colonel Visscher's Third Regiment of Tryon County Militia
Captain Garret Putman's Company
Company Officers

Captain Garret Putman		P.A. No. W.16687
Lieutenant Henry Vrooman		
Ensign Garret Newkirk		
Ensign George Stine or Stein		P.A. No. S.11471
	Sergeants	
Aaron Borus		
Jacob Frank		
Joseph Staring		
Gilbert VanDeusen		
	Corporals	
John Conyne [Conine, Canine]		
Jacob Files [Philes]		
John Hansen		

John VanHorne		
	Privates	
George Acker [Ecker, Eacher, Ekker]		
John Acker		
Aron Cormwell [Crommel, Cromil, etc.]		
Andrew Frank		
Nicholas Gardinier		
Victor Hansen		
Richard Hose		
John Lewis		
John McDonald		
John Marshall		
Philip Martin		
Conrad Moore		
George Moore		
Francis Prime		
Henry Prime		
John Prime		
Lewis Prime		
Francis Putman		
George Putman		
Henry Putman		
Victor Putman		
Victor Putman, Jr.		
John Quackenboss [Quack, Quackenbush]		
Nicholas Quackenboss		
Dewalt Schrembling [Shremling, Scrambling]		
Rudolph Shoemaker		
John Staring		
William VanBrute		
Abraham Van Deusen		
Albert Van DeWarkin [VanderWerker, etc.]		
John Van Derwerkin		
John VanNaps [VanNeps]		

Lieutenant-Colonel Commandant John Harper's Second Regiment of New York State Levies--1780
Captain Garret Putman's Company

	Company Officers	
Captain Garret Putman		P.A. No. W.16687
Lieutenant Isaac Paris		

Lieutenant Solomon Woodworth		
	Sergeants	
John Dunham		
John Servis		P.A. No. S.22971
Henry Shew		P.A. S.29948
	Corporals	
John Eikler [Eckler, Eighler]		
Robert Martin		
Daniel VanDeBurgh		
	Privates	
Annias Archey [Onies, Orsher, Archer, Earcher]		
Frederick Baum [Boom] P.A. No. W.15833		
Christian Bellinger		P.A. No. S.29277
William Berry		P.A. S.10636. Taken Prisoner October 23, 1780.
Incris Billins		
Thomas Caine [Cane, Kane, Kaine]		
Jacob Carcker [Karker]		
John Christman		
Philip Clements		
Samuel Coplin		
Adam Davy		
Philip Deharsh		P.A. No. S.22730
John Demuth		
Robert Dickson [Dixon, Dickinson]		P.A. No. R.13762
Sevenus Dygert [Dagert, Deygert, Tygert]		
George Ecker [Acker, Eacker]		
Leonard Eckler		P.A. No. W.25333. Taken prisoner October 23, 1780
John Ellis		
Godrey Fidler		
Conrad Folmer		
Henry Frank		P.A. S.39544
Tunis Gardinier		
Peter House		P.A. No. 15236. Taken prisoner October 23, 1780.
Peter Hoyer [Hyer, Huyer, Hayer]		

John Hyser [Hiser]		
James Keech [Kaach]		P.A. No. R.5805.
Henry Kelly		
William Kisner		P.A. No. S.13642.
William Kline [Cline, Clyne, Kline]		
Frederick Lepper [Lepper, Leperd]		P.A. No. W. 20447.
Jacobus Miller		
George Nestel		
Jacob Newkirk		P.A. No. W.19912. Taken prisoner October 23, 1780.
Jacobus Philips [Phillipse, Phillipsey]		P.A. No. S.11238.
Jacob Rickert [Rikert, Rickard]		Taken prisoner October 23, 1780.
Paul Roliver		
John Shall		
Adam Shaver [Schafer, Shafer]		
James Sherwood [Sharwood, Shairwood]		
Jacob Shew [Shoe, Shaw, Shue]		P.A. W.22985
Christopher Shoemaker		
John Shoemaker		
James Simons		
George Staring		Taken prisoner October 21, 1780 and released on May 21, 1783.
Moses VanCamp		
John Vandebogart		
John VanHorn		
Rynier VanSickler		
George VanSlyke [VanSlyck, VanSlike]		

Lieutenant-Colonel Commandant Marinus Willett's Regiment of New York State Levies -- 1781

	Company Officers	
Captain Garret Putman		P.A. No. W.16687
Lieutenant John Fonda		
Lieutenant Garret Newkirk		
Sergeant Major Jesse Wilson		
Quartermaster Sergeant William Sowles [Sools, Soles, Soules]		Taken prisoner on July 9. 1781 and escaped on or about

		July 10.
	Sergeants	
William Laird [Lord, Lard]		
Thomas Lord		
Daniel Orendorff [Urendorff]		
Lambert Swayer [Sayer]		
	Corporals	
James Miller		
George Price		
Comfort Shaw		
Jacob Shew [Shoe, Show, Shue]		P.A. No. S.22985
	Privates	
Philip Becker [listed as Barker]		P.A. No. W.18849
John Cain [Caine, Kaine, Cane, Kane]		P.A. W.18849
Thomas Campbell [Cammel, Campell, Camble, Cambell]		
John Crosset [Crossard, Crosate]		Killed October 25, 1781
Uriah Deline [Ryer]		
John Delway [Dellaway]		
Samuel Dingman		
Daniel Dodge [Daudge]		Killed September 7, 1781
Christian Drisselman [Trisselman]		
John Dusler [Duesler, Tusler]		P.A. No. W.16244
John Ellis		
Moyers Fowler		
Andrew Frank		
Henry Guiles [Giles]		
William Hall		
Harmon Harson [Hanson or Harrison]		
Peter Harson [Hanson or Harrison]		
Samuel Hobbs [Hubbs]		P.A. No. S.13497
Henry Kelly		
George Kitts		
John Locharty [Laughaday]		Wounded October 25, 1781.
John Malone [Maloon]		
John Mason		P.A. No. W.18479, Wounded October 25, 1781.

George Mour [Moore, Mower, Mouer]		P.A. No. S.27210
Peter Mower [Moore, Mouer, Mouer]		P.A. No. W.2683
Lodowick Moyer [Mayer, Meyeer, Myer]		P.A. No. S.11115
Frederick Olman [Ulman, Ullman, Oilman]		P.A. No. S.14743, Taken prisoner October 24, 1781.
Jacob Orr [Ohr, Ore, now it is Alter]		P.A. No. S.14059
Onies Orser [Annias Archer, Archey, Earcher]		Killed September 7, 1781.
John Payer [Boyer, Buyer, Boyca]		P.A. No. W.522
John Philips [Philipse, Philipsey]		P.A. No.S.11238
John Prime		
Benjamin Puley [Bully]		P.A. No. W.709
Henry Rightmyer		P.A. No. S.14312, wounded October 25, 1781.
Henry Rikert		
William Scarborough [Crowley, Crawley—stepfather Jeremiah Crowley]		Killed October 25, 1781
William Shute		
Jacob Tanner [Tawner, Tenner]		P.A. No. S11513. Taken prisoner October 24, 1781.
William Tryon		
Joseph Tuttle [Tortle]		
John Vanderwerker		Killed September 7, 1781.
David VanSickler		P.A. No. W.19566
John Wart [Wals]		
Nicholas Weaver [Wheever,Wever, Weber]		P.A. No. W.15860